T0301446

Financial Decisions and Markets

Financial Decisions and Markets:
A Course in Asset Pricing

John Y. Campbell

Princeton University Press
Princeton and Oxford

Published by Princeton University Press, 41 William Street,
Princeton, New Jersey 08540
In the United Kingdom: Princeton University Press,
6 Oxford Street, Woodstock, Oxfordshire OX20 1TR

press.princeton.edu

Library of Congress Cataloging-in-Publication Data

Names: Campbell, John Y., author.
Title: Financial decisions and markets : a course in asset pricing / John Y. Campbell.
Description: Princeton : Princeton University Press, [2018] | Includes bibliographical references and index.
Identifiers: LCCN 2017013268 | ISBN 9780691160801 (hardback : alk. paper)
Subjects: LCSH: Securities—Prices—Mathematical models. | Capital assets pricing model. | Investments—
        Decision-making.
Classification: LCC HG4636 .C36 2018 | DDC 332.63/2—dc23 LC record available at
        https://lccn.loc.gov/2017013268

British Library Cataloging-in-Publication Data is available

This book has been composed in ITC New Baskerville

Printed on acid-free paper. ∞

Printed in the United States of America

10 9 8 7 6 5 4 3 2

To Graham, Malcolm, Naomi, and Sophia

Contents

Figures

Tables

Preface

This book is based on the second-year PhD course, "Asset Pricing," that I have taught at Harvard for almost 25 years, and at Princeton for a decade before that. The subtitle of the book, *A Course in Asset Pricing*, is intended to convey not only the subject area, but also the approach: academic rather than practitioner-oriented, integrated rather than encyclopedic, and reflecting my personal views on what is most important to teach PhD students about the field.

The book follows the outline of my course fairly closely. Part I, on static models, begins with a brief summary of key results and issues in the theory of choice under uncertainty (Chapter 1), and follows this with an application to static portfolio choice (Chapter 2), including both the decision how much risk to take and the problem of combining risky assets efficiently. Armed with this understanding, Chapter 3 presents basic static equilibrium asset pricing models: the Capital Asset Pricing Model (CAPM) and multifactor extensions. Chapter 4 presents similar ideas using the modern paradigm of the stochastic discount factor (SDF).

The models of Part I take the second (and higher) moments of asset returns as given and use them to determine expected returns. Part II, on intertemporal models, starts in Chapter 5 by discussing how expected returns influence prices. This enables one to derive the implications of models of time-varying expected returns for the behavior of realized returns. This chapter also covers the large empirical literature on the prediction of aggregate stock returns, using predictor variables suggested by financial theory including cross-sectional asset pricing models. Chapter 6 introduces the main puzzles that motivate the literature on consumption-based asset pricing: the equity premium puzzle (that the equity premium is high on average), the riskfree rate puzzle (that the riskfree interest rate is relatively stable over time at a low level), and the equity volatility puzzle (that stock returns are much more volatile than consumption growth). The chapter discusses various theoretical responses to these puzzles, covering topics such as rare macroeconomic disasters, Epstein-Zin utility, stochastic volatility in consumption, habit formation, and durable goods. Chapter 7 asks how firms alter their investment decisions in response to asset prices, and how consumption and asset prices are jointly determined in general equilibrium with production. Chapter 8 surveys the literature on fixed-income securities, which has its own terminology and historically developed somewhat independently from the literature on equity pricing. This chapter explores affine pricing models, which restrict the time-series behavior of the SDF in a way that makes it easy to price bonds of any maturity. The chapter also discusses the literature on interest rates and exchange rates. Chapter 9 uses concepts from the fixed-income literature to explore topics in intertemporal portfolio choice and asset pricing.

Part III covers topics for which the heterogeneity of the investor population is critical. Chapter 10 summarizes the literature on household finance: the use of financial markets by ordinary households to solve their financial problems. The chapter discusses the effect of labor income on portfolio choice, the evidence that some households make investment mistakes such as failing to participate in risky asset markets or failing to diversify their risks, and the potential impact of such mistakes on asset prices. Chapter 11 explores asset pricing models in which frictions prevent perfect risksharing, or in which investors choose not to share risks because they have different beliefs that lead them to speculate against one another. Chapter 12 concludes the book by discussing models of asymmetric information and liquidity, and the field of market microstructure.

The order of these topics is one that I have found to work well in the course. The choice of topics reflects four views that I hold strongly.

First, one cannot understand asset prices only from a macroeconomic or general-equilibrium point of view. One also has to understand the decisions that individual market participants make, taking prices as given in partial equilibrium. This is particularly important in models with heterogeneous investors, which are increasingly central to the field. For this reason, I do not orient the whole book around the SDF in the manner of Cochrane (2005). Instead, I start with a micro perspective in Chapters 2 and 3, and return to this perspective in Chapters 9 and 10. The title of the book, *Financial Decisions and Markets*, reflects this orientation.

Second, financial markets both set prices and allocate resources. The latter is the ultimate function of the markets, and the justification for the costs of operating them. Hence, I discuss resource allocation in Chapters 10 and 11.

Third, not all financial market participants are fully rational and financially literate. At the same time, some market participants are. In the book, I take the perspective of rational investors while recognizing the possible presence of irrational investors. Thus the book is neither a behavioral finance book, nor an ideologically antibehavioral work. Chapters 10 and 11 make the point that even if irrational agents have only modest effects on asset prices, they may change the allocation that corresponds to those prices, with important effects on social welfare.

Fourth, financial economics has normative implications. Portfolio choice models, for example, can be used to guide the decisions of investors, and equilibrium asset pricing models with heterogeneous investors pose many interesting problems in applied welfare economics. Chapter 2 and Chapters 9–12 discuss some of these implications although there is not space in the book to develop them fully.

The choice of topics also reflects an important constraint: I want the book to contain material that can be taught, by an ambitious professor to smart and hardworking students, in a single semester. While the chapters do present additional material, the core content of the book obeys this constraint. For this reason I do not discuss any continuous-time models, because I do not have the time (in the course) or space (in the book) to explain the stochastic calculus methods that are required to use these models. This in turn precludes any treatment of option pricing, which cannot meaningfully be discussed without continuous-time modeling. For the same reason I give minimal attention to securities such as corporate bonds that have strong optionality. I do however spend time developing a discrete-time approximate framework that is an alternative to continuous-time modeling for the study of intertemporal portfolio choice and asset pricing.

In explaining these topics, I follow certain core principles.

Modern finance is an empirical field. Models are essential for qualitative understanding, but asset pricing models are quantitative, with parameters that can be calibrated or estimated. Much of the debate in the academic literature concerns parameter values, not qualitative properties of models or even their functional forms. For this reason I stress the interplay of empirical and theoretical research. In Chapter 3 on the CAPM and multifactor models, for example, I summarize the anomalies that have motivated researchers to move beyond the CAPM. In Chapter 6 I present the equity premium, riskfree rate, and equity volatility puzzles that have inspired the rich variety of consumption-based asset pricing models discussed in the chapter. The book contains numerous tables and figures, some reproduced from published research.

The important models to teach PhD students are simple enough to be solved in closed form. The solutions relate endogenous to exogenous variables in an explicit manner, and show how parameter values influence the properties of the endogenous variables. Many recent asset pricing models are complex "black boxes" that can only be solved numerically. While I summarize some recent numerical research, the book also devotes serious attention to older, simpler models that have become workhorses of the literature. In Chapter 12, for example, I present the Glosten and Milgrom (1985) and Kyle (1985) models as a way to build intuition about market microstructure.

To simplify analysis, the models in this book often treat endogenous variables such as unexpected asset returns and consumption as if they were exogenous. This is standard practice in asset pricing, and it is legitimate so long as the models under consideration are based on investors' first-order conditions that hold whether the variables in the model are exogenous or chosen by investors. This asset pricing perspective contrasts with the current emphasis in applied microeconomics on the use of exogenous random shocks to identify causal effects.

A common challenge in solving asset pricing models is that the models are nonlinear. Very often this is so because some effects in the model are additive, while others are multiplicative; hence the model is linear neither in levels nor in logs. Portfolio construction, for example, combines asset returns linearly while compounding of returns over time operates multiplicatively. Similarly, consumption subtracts from wealth but reinvestment returns multiply it. This book emphasizes approximations that are accurate when risks are small, when time intervals are short, or when the consumption-wealth ratio is close to constant, that allow models to be written in linear or loglinear form and then solved explicitly. Such approximations must be used with care, but they deliver insights that are hard to obtain in any other fashion.

PhD students need to learn to ask and answer questions about models. In my course I frequently pause to ask questions, both to show students how they can do this in their own studies, and to induce students to propose answers to the group. It is a challenge to replicate this process in a textbook. I do this by posing questions in the text, which I answer on separate pages at the end of each chapter. The book also includes numerous analytical and a few numerical problems, and provides answer sets in a separate solution manual.

Throughout the book, I have tried to use intuitive, readable notation while staying as close as possible to common usage in the literature. Given the range of topics covered, this inevitably requires using some letters to denote different variables in different chapters or, occasionally, in different sections of the same chapter. Letters such as x and λ are particularly flexible and are used as wild cards with different meanings in many parts of the book.

It may be helpful to relate *Financial Decisions and Markets* to my earlier work, and to competitors. My first book (Campbell, Lo, and MacKinlay, CLM 1997) covers much of the same material (specifically Chapters 3–8 of this book), but by now has become dated. In addition, CLM emphasizes econometric methods more, and finance theory less, than the current book. I draw upon CLM Chapter 7 in Chapter 5 of this book, and CLM Chapters 10 and 11 in Chapter 8 of this book. My second book (Campbell and Viceira, CV 2002) is more similar in style to the present book, but has a much narrower focus on intertemporal portfolio choice. I draw upon CV to a limited extent in Chapter 2, and significantly in Chapters 9 and 10. I also draw upon surveys that I have written over the past 15 years, particularly Campbell (2000) on asset pricing and the SDF; Campbell (2014) on the contributions of the 2013 Nobel laureates, Eugene Fama, Lars Peter Hansen, and Robert Shiller; Campbell (2008) on return predictability in Chapter 5; Campbell (2003) on consumption-based models in Chapter 6; and my presidential address to the American Finance Association (Campbell, 2006) and my Ely Lecture to the American Economic Association (Campbell, 2016) on household finance in Chapter 10.

Precursors to this book, which share its empirical emphasis, include distinguished textbooks by Cochrane (2005), Singleton (2006), and Bali, Engle, and Murray (2016), and trade books by Ilmanen (2011) and Siegel (1994). There are many other textbooks with a strong theoretical orientation, including Back (2010), Duffie (2001), Gollier (2001), Huang and Litzenberger (1998), Ingersoll (1987), Munk (2013), Pennacchi (2007), and Skiadas (2009). These books are highly recommended for their rigorous treatment of asset pricing theory, but pay relatively little attention to empirical phenomena.

Writing *Financial Decisions and Markets* has occupied much of the last five years, and I am deeply grateful for the loving support of my wife, Susanna Peyton, throughout the process. She watched our children mature faster than the manuscript, but gave me confidence that it too would step out into the world in due time.

During the later stages of preparation, Argyris Tsiaras became a particularly important collaborator on this book. He proofread the manuscript with extraordinary care, coordinated comments from students, and contributed large amounts of material and exposition particularly for Chapters 4 and 12. He is also the coauthor of the problem solution manual (Campbell and Tsiaras, 2017).

Several colleagues spent significant time reading and commenting on the first draft of the manuscript. I am particularly grateful to Eduardo Dávila, Emmanuel Farhi, Xavier Gabaix, Ben Hébert, David Hirshleifer, Owen Lamont, Matteo Maggiori, Tarun Ramadorai, and Jessica Wachter for their written comments and thoughtful responses to questions.

The material in this book has been influenced by professional interactions throughout my career, and I owe too many debts to be able to do them justice here. However, I must thank my dissertation advisors at Yale, the late Steve Ross and Jim Tobin, and above all Bob Shiller with whom I went on to write numerous papers; colleagues and coauthors at Princeton including Ben Bernanke, Angus Deaton, Sandy Grossman, and Pete Kyle; my other coauthors including John Ammer, Cristian Badarinza, David Barr, Jason Beeler, Laurent Calvet, George Chacko, Yeung Lewis Chan, Richard Clarida, João Cocco, John Cochrane, Ken Froot, Stefano Giglio, Francisco Gomes, Yasushi Hamao, Ludger Hentschel, Jens Hilscher, Howell Jackson, Hyeng Keun Koo, Martin Lettau, Andrew Lo, Sydney Ludvigson, Craig MacKinlay, Brigitte Madrian, Pascal Maenhout, Burt Malkiel, Greg Mankiw, Jianping Mei, Yves Nosbusch, Parag Pathak, Pierre Perron,

Christopher Polk, Tarun Ramadorai, Benjamin Ranish, Kim Schoenholtz, Allie Schwartz, Karine Serfaty-deMedeiros, Paolo Sodini, Adi Sunderam, Jan Szilagyi, Glen Taksler, Sam Thompson, Peter Tufano, Bob Turley, Luis Viceira, Tuomo Vuolteenaho, Jiang Wang, Joshua White, Yexiao Xu, and Motohiro Yogo; colleagues in the Harvard economics department including Robert Barro, Emmanuel Farhi, Xavier Gabaix, Matteo Maggiori, Greg Mankiw, Neil Shephard, Andrei Shleifer, Jeremy Stein, Jim Stock, and Tomasz Strzalecki; my research colleagues at Arrowstreet Capital, LP led by Peter Rathjens and Tuomo Vuolteenaho; my research assistant during the summer of 2013, Emily Wu, who produced many of the tables and figures in the book; Gianluca Rinaldi, who carefully proofread the problems and solutions; and the many talented students who have helped me teach the PhD course over the years, including Eric Budish, Eduardo Dávila, Stefano Giglio, Sam Hanson, Jens Hilscher, Dirk Jenter, Vassil Konstantinov, Borja Larrain, Eben Lazarus, Ian Martin, Tim McQuade, Stephen Shore, Argyris Tsiaras, Luis Viceira, Joshua White, and Yao Zeng. Merely listing these names should convey the extraordinary quality of the students I have been privileged to teach. They have made a tremendous contribution to this book.

Financial Decisions and Markets

Part I

Static Portfolio Choice
and Asset Pricing

1

Choice under Uncertainty

ASSET PRICING THEORY aims to describe the equilibrium in financial markets, where economic agents interact to trade claims to uncertain future payoffs. Both adjectives, "uncertain" and "future," are important—as suggested by the title of Christian Gollier's book *The Economics of Risk and Time* (2001)—but in this chapter we review the basic theory of choice under uncertainty, ignoring time by assuming that all uncertainty is resolved at a single future date. The chapter draws on both Gollier (2001) and Ingersoll (1987).

Section 1.1 begins by briefly reviewing the axiomatic foundations of expected utility theory. Section 1.2 applies expected utility theory to the measurement of risk aversion and the comparison of risk aversion across agents. Section 1.3 discusses the hyperbolic absolute risk averse (HARA) class of utility functions, which are widely used because they are so tractable in applications. Section 1.4 discusses critiques of expected utility theory, including the Allais (1953) paradox and the Rabin (2000) critique. Section 1.5 shows how to compare the riskiness of different distributions.

1.1 Expected Utility

Standard microeconomics represents preferences using ordinal utility functions. An ordinal utility function $\Upsilon(.)$ tells you that an agent is indifferent between x and y if $\Upsilon(x) = \Upsilon(y)$ and prefers x to y if $\Upsilon(x) > \Upsilon(y)$. Any strictly increasing function of $\Upsilon(.)$ will have the same properties, so the preferences expressed by $\Upsilon(.)$ are the same as those expressed by $\Theta(\Upsilon(.))$ for any strictly increasing Θ. In other words, ordinal utility is invariant to monotonically increasing transformations. It defines indifference curves, but there is no way to label the curves so that they have meaningful values.

A cardinal utility function $\Psi(.)$ is invariant to positive affine (increasing linear) transformations but not to nonlinear transformations. The preferences expressed by $\Psi(.)$ are the same as those expressed by $a + b\Psi(.)$ for any $b > 0$. In other words, cardinal utility has no natural units, but given a choice of units, the rate at which cardinal utility increases is meaningful.

Asset pricing theory relies heavily on von Neumann-Morgenstern utility theory, which says that choice over lotteries, satisfying certain axioms, implies maximization of the expectation of a cardinal utility function, defined over outcomes.

1.1.1 Sketch of von Neumann-Morgenstern Theory

The content of von Neumann-Morgenstern utility theory is easiest to understand in a discrete-state example. Define states $s = 1 \dots S$, each of which is associated with an outcome x_s in a set X. Probabilities p_s of the different outcomes then define lotteries. When $S = 3$, we can draw probabilities in two dimensions (since $p_3 = 1 - p_1 - p_2$). We get the so-called Machina triangle (Machina 1982), illustrated in Figure 1.1.

We define a compound lottery as one that determines which primitive lottery we are given. For example, a compound lottery L might give us lottery L^a with probability α and lottery L^b with probability $(1 - \alpha)$. Then L has the same probabilities over the outcomes as $\alpha L^a + (1 - \alpha) L^b$.

We define a preference ordering $\succeq$ over lotteries. A person is indifferent between lotteries L^a and L^b, $L^a \sim L^b$, if and only if $L^a \succeq L^b$ and $L^b \succeq L^a$.

Next we apply two axioms of choice over lotteries.

Continuity axiom: For all L^a, L^b, L^c s.t. $L^a \succeq L^b \succeq L^c$, there exists a scalar $\alpha \in [0, 1]$ s.t.

$$L^b \sim \alpha L^a + (1 - \alpha) L^c \tag{1.1}$$

This axiom says that if three lotteries are (weakly) ranked in order of preference, it is always possible to find a compound lottery that mixes the highest-ranked and lowest-ranked lotteries in such a way that the economic agent is indifferent between this compound lottery and the middle-ranked lottery. The axiom implies the existence of a preference functional defined over lotteries, that is, an ordinal utility function for lotteries that enables us to draw indifference curves on the Machina triangle.

Independence axiom:

$$L^a \succeq L^b \Rightarrow \alpha L^a + (1 - \alpha) L^c \succeq \alpha L^b + (1 - \alpha) L^c \tag{1.2}$$

for all possible lotteries L^c.

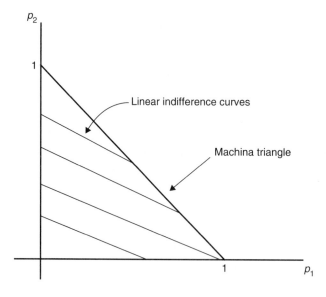

Figure 1.1.   *Machina Triangle*

This axiom says that if two lotteries are ranked in order of preference, then the same rank order applies to two compound lotteries, each of which combines one of the original two lotteries with an arbitrary third lottery, using the same mixing weights in each case.

The independence axiom implies that the preference functional is linear in probabilities. In the Machina triangle, the indifference curves are straight lines, as illustrated in Figure 1.1. This means that a given increase in one probability, say p_1, requires the same change in another probability, say p_3, to leave the agent indifferent regardless of the initial levels of p_1 and p_3.

Then we can define a scalar u_s for each outcome x_s s.t.

$$L^a \succeq L^b \Rightarrow \sum_{s=1}^{S} p_s^a u_s \geq \sum_{s=1}^{S} p_s^b u_s. \tag{1.3}$$

The scalars u_s define the slopes of the linear indifference curves in the Machina triangle. Since probabilities sum to one and a constant can be added to all u_s without changing preferences, two scalars can be normalized (say the lowest to zero and the highest to one).

Equation (1.3) shows that a lottery is valued by the probability-weighted average of the scalars u_s associated with each outcome x_s. Call these scalars "utilities." A probability-weighted average of utilities u_s in each state s is the mathematical expectation of the random variable "utility" that takes the value u_s in state s. Hence, we have implicitly defined a cardinal utility function $u(x_s)$, defined over outcomes, such that the agent prefers the lottery that delivers a higher expectation of this function. The free normalization of lowest and highest utility corresponds to the two arbitrary parameters a and b that define the units in which cardinal utility is measured.

This construction can be generalized to handle continuous states. Strictly speaking, the resulting utility function must be bounded above and below, but this requirement is routinely ignored in modern applications of utility theory.

1.2 Risk Aversion

We now assume the existence of a cardinal utility function and ask what it means to say that the agent whose preferences are represented by that utility function is risk averse. We also discuss the quantitative measurement of risk aversion.

To bring out the main ideas as simply as possible, we assume that the argument of the utility function is wealth. This is equivalent to working with a single consumption good in a static two-period model where all wealth is liquidated and consumed in the second period, after uncertainty is resolved. Later in the book we discuss richer models in which consumption takes place in many periods, and also some models with multiple consumption goods.

For simplicity we also work with weak inequalities and weak preference orderings throughout. The extension to strict inequalities and strong preference orderings is straightforward.

1.2.1 Jensen's Inequality and Risk Aversion

An important mathematical result, Jensen's Inequality, can be used to link the concept of risk aversion to the concavity of the utility function. We start by defining concavity for a function f.

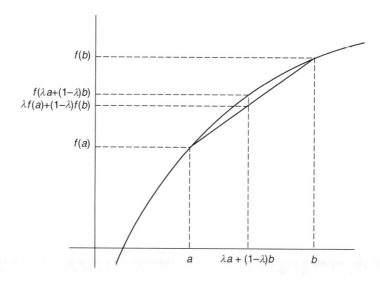

Figure 1.2.   *Concave Function*

Definition. f is *concave* if and only if, for all $\lambda \in [0, 1]$ and values a, b,

$$\lambda f(a) + (1 - \lambda)f(b) \leq f(\lambda a + (1 - \lambda)b). \tag{1.4}$$

If f is twice differentiable, then concavity implies that $f'' \leq 0$. Figure 1.2 illustrates a concave function.

Note that because the inequality is weak in the above definition, a linear function is concave. Strict concavity uses a strong inequality and excludes linear functions, but we proceed with the weak concept of concavity.

Now consider a random variable $\tilde{z}$. *Jensen's Inequality* states that

$$\mathrm{E}f(\tilde{z}) \leq f(\mathrm{E}\tilde{z}) \tag{1.5}$$

for all possible $\tilde{z}$ if and only if f is concave.

This result, due to the Danish mathematician and telephone engineer Johan Jensen, is so useful in finance that the field might almost be caricatured as "the economics of Jensen's Inequality." As a first application, we can use it to establish the equivalence of risk aversion and concavity of the utility function.

Definition. An agent is *risk averse* if she (weakly) dislikes all zero-mean risk at all levels of wealth. That is, for all initial wealth levels W_0 and risk $\tilde{x}$ with $\mathrm{E}\tilde{x} = 0$,

$$\mathrm{E}u(W_0 + \tilde{x}) \leq u(W_0). \tag{1.6}$$

To show that risk aversion is equivalent to concavity of the utility function, we simply rewrite the definition of risk aversion as

$$\mathrm{E}u(\tilde{z}) \leq u(\mathrm{E}\tilde{z}), \tag{1.7}$$

where $\tilde{z} = W_0 + \tilde{x}$, and apply Jensen's Inequality.

Since risk aversion is concavity, and concavity restricts the sign of the second derivative of the utility function (assuming that derivative exists), it is natural to construct a quantitative measure of risk aversion using the second derivative u'', scaled to avoid dependence on the units of measurement for utility. The *coefficient of absolute risk aversion* $A(W_0)$ is defined by

$$A(W_0) = \frac{-u''(W_0)}{u'(W_0)}. \tag{1.8}$$

As the notation makes clear, in general this is a function of the initial level of wealth.

1.2.2 Comparing Risk Aversion

Let two agents with utility functions u_1 and u_2 have the same initial wealth. An agent rejects a lottery if taking it lowers expected utility, that is, if the expected utility of initial wealth plus the lottery payout is lower than the utility of initial wealth. Continuing with our use of weak inequalities, we will also say that the agent rejects the lottery if it gives her the same expected utility as the utility of initial wealth.

Definition. u_1 is *more risk-averse* than u_2 if u_1 rejects all lotteries that u_2 rejects, regardless of the common initial wealth level.

Many utility functions cannot be ranked in this way. It is quite possible for agents to disagree about lotteries at a given initial wealth level (with the first agent accepting some that the second agent rejects and vice versa). It is also quite possible for the initial wealth level to matter, so that the first agent rejects all lotteries that the second agent rejects at a low level of initial wealth, but the second agent rejects all lotteries that the first agent rejects at a higher level of initial wealth.

What else is true if u_1 is more risk-averse than u_2? To answer this question, we first define a function

$$\phi(x) = u_1(u_2^{-1}(x)). \tag{1.9}$$

This function has three important properties:

(a) $u_1(z) = \phi(u_2(z))$, so $\phi(.)$ turns u_2 into u_1.
(b) $u_1'(z) = \phi'(u_2(z)) u_2'(z)$, so $\phi' = u_1'/u_2' > 0$.
(c) $u_1''(z) = \phi'(u_2(z)) u_2''(z) + \phi''(u_2(z)) u_2'(z)^2$, so

$$\phi'' = \frac{u_1'' - \phi' u_2''}{u_2'^2} = \frac{u_1'}{u_2'^2}(A_2 - A_1). \tag{1.10}$$

The second of these properties is obtained by differentiating the first, and the third by differentiating the second. This trick (repeated differentiation to obtain restrictions on derivatives) often comes in handy in this field.

The third property is important because it shows that concavity of the function $\phi(x)$, $\phi'' \le 0$, is equivalent to higher absolute risk aversion for agent 1, $A_1 \ge A_2$.

Now consider a risk $\tilde{x}$ that is rejected by u_2, that is, a risk s.t. $\mathrm{E}u_2(W_0 + \tilde{x}) \le u_2(W_0)$. If u_1 is more risk-averse than u_2, we must also have $\mathrm{E}u_1(W_0 + \tilde{x}) \le u_1(W_0)$. Using the function $\phi(.)$,

$$\mathrm{E}u_1(W_0 + \tilde{x}) = \mathrm{E}\phi(u_2(W_0 + \tilde{x})), \tag{1.11}$$

while

$$u_1(W_0) = \phi(u_2(W_0)) \geq \phi(Eu_2(W_0 + \widetilde{x})) \quad (1.12)$$

since $\phi' > 0$. So for u_1 to be more risk-averse than u_2, we need

$$E\phi(u_2(W_0 + \widetilde{x})) \leq \phi(Eu_2(W_0 + \widetilde{x})) \quad (1.13)$$

for all $\widetilde{x}$. By Jensen's Inequality, this is equivalent to the concavity of the function $\phi(x)$, $\phi'' \leq 0$.

Putting these results together, we have shown that if one agent is more risk-averse than another, then the more risk-averse utility function is a concave transformation of the less risk-averse utility function and has a higher coefficient of absolute risk aversion at all levels of initial wealth. We have also shown the converse of these statements.

These concepts can be related to the amounts of wealth that agents are prepared to pay to avoid a zero-mean risk.

Definition. The *risk premium* π (W_0, u, $\widetilde{x}$) is the greatest amount an agent with initial wealth W_0 and utility function u is willing to pay to avoid a risk $\widetilde{x}$, assumed to have zero mean. Suppressing the arguments for notational simplicity, π is found by solving

$$Eu(W_0 + \widetilde{x}) = u(W_0 - \pi). \quad (1.14)$$

Defining $z = W_0 - \pi$ and $\widetilde{y} = \pi + \widetilde{x}$, this can be rewritten as

$$Eu(z + \widetilde{y}) = u(z). \quad (1.15)$$

Now define π_2 as the risk premium for agent 2, and define z_2 and $\widetilde{y}_2$ accordingly. We have

$$Eu_2(z_2 + \widetilde{y}_2) = u_2(z_2). \quad (1.16)$$

If u_1 is more risk-averse than u_2, then

$$Eu_1(z_2 + \widetilde{y}_2) \leq u_1(z_2), \quad (1.17)$$

which implies $\pi_1 \geq \pi_2$. The same argument applies in reverse, so $\pi_1 \geq \pi_2$ implies that u_1 is more risk-averse than u_2.

We can extend the above analysis to consider a risk that may have a nonzero mean μ. It pays $\mu + \widetilde{x}$ where $\widetilde{x}$ has zero mean.

Definition. The *certainty equivalent* C^e satisfies

$$Eu(W_0 + \mu + \widetilde{x}) = u(W_0 + C^e). \quad (1.18)$$

This implies that

$$C^e(W_0, u, \mu + \widetilde{x}) = \mu - \pi(W_0 + \mu, u, \widetilde{x}). \quad (1.19)$$

Thus if u_1 is more risk-averse than u_2, then $C_1^e \leq C_2^e$. Again, the reverse implication also holds.

In summary, the following statements are equivalent:

- u_1 is more risk-averse than u_2.
- u_1 is a concave transformation of u_2 at all initial wealth levels.
- $A_1 \geq A_2$ at all initial wealth levels.
- $\pi_1 \geq \pi_2$ at all initial wealth levels.
- $C_1^e \leq C_2^e$ at all initial wealth levels.

It is also possible to use the above ideas to ask how risk aversion for a single agent changes with the agent's level of wealth. It is natural to think that a richer person will care less about a given absolute risk than a poorer person, and will pay less to avoid it; in other words, that the risk premium for any risk should decline with initial wealth W_0. One can show that the following conditions are equivalent:

- π is decreasing in W_0.
- $A(W_0)$ is decreasing in W_0.
- $-u'$ is a concave transformation of u, so $-u'''/u'' \geq -u''/u'$ everywhere. The ratio $-u'''/u'' = P$ has been called *absolute prudence* by Kimball (1990), who relates it to the theory of precautionary saving.

Decreasing absolute risk aversion (DARA) is intuitively appealing. Certainly we should be uncomfortable with increasing absolute risk aversion.

1.2.3 The Arrow-Pratt Approximation

In the previous section, we defined the risk premium and certainty equivalent implicitly, as the solutions to equations (1.14) and (1.18). A famous analysis due to Arrow (1971) and Pratt (1964) shows that when risk is small, it is possible to derive approximate closed-form solutions to these equations.

Consider a zero-mean risk $\tilde{y} = k\tilde{x}$, where k is a scale factor. Write the risk premium as a function of k, $g(k) = \pi(W_0, u, k\tilde{x})$. From the definition of the risk premium, we have

$$\mathrm{E}u(W_0 + k\tilde{x}) = u(W_0 - g(k)). \tag{1.20}$$

Note that $g(0) = 0$, because you would pay nothing to avoid a risk with zero variability.

We now use the trick of repeated differentiation, in this case with respect to k, that was introduced in the previous subsection. Differentiating (1.20), we have

$$\mathrm{E}[\tilde{x}u'(W_0 + k\tilde{x})] = -g'(k)u'(W_0 - g(k)). \tag{1.21}$$

At $k = 0$, the left-hand side of (1.21) becomes $\mathrm{E}[\tilde{x}u'(W_0)] = \mathrm{E}[\tilde{x}]u'(W_0)$, where we can bring $u'(W_0)$ outside the expectations operator because it is deterministic. Since $\mathrm{E}[\tilde{x}] = 0$, the left-hand side of (1.21) is zero when $k = 0$, so the right-hand side must also be zero, which implies that $g'(0) = 0$.

We now differentiate with respect to k a second time to get

$$\mathrm{E}\tilde{x}^2 u''(w_o + k\tilde{x}) = g'(k)^2 u''(W_0 - g(k)) - g''(k)u'(W_0 - g(k)), \tag{1.22}$$

which implies that

$$g''(0) = \frac{-u''(W_0)}{u'(W_0)}\mathrm{E}\tilde{x}^2 = A(W_0)\mathrm{E}\tilde{x}^2. \tag{1.23}$$

Now take a Taylor approximation of $g(k)$ around the point of zero variability, $k = 0$:

$$g(k) \approx g(0) + kg'(0) + \frac{1}{2}k^2 g''(0). \tag{1.24}$$

Substituting in the previously obtained values for the derivatives, we get

$$\pi \approx \frac{1}{2}A(W_0)k^2 \mathrm{E}[\tilde{x}^2] = \frac{1}{2}A(W_0)\mathrm{E}[\tilde{y}^2]. \tag{1.25}$$

The risk premium is proportional to the *square* of the risk. This property of differentiable utility is known as *second-order risk aversion*. It implies that people are approximately risk-neutral with respect to a single small risk (and more generally to small risks that are independent of other risks they face). The coefficient of proportionality is one-half the coefficient of absolute risk aversion, so we have a quantitative prediction linking the risk premium to the scale of risk and the level of risk aversion. This result is the basis for much modern quantitative research.

A similar analysis can be performed for the certainty equivalent. The result is that

$$C^e \approx k\mu - \frac{1}{2}A(W_0)k^2 \mathrm{E}[\tilde{x}^2]. \tag{1.26}$$

This shows that the mean has a dominant effect on the certainty equivalent for small risks.

In finance, risks are often multiplicative rather than additive. That is, as the level of wealth invested increases, the absolute scale of the risk increases in proportion. The above theory can easily be modified to handle this case. Define a multiplicative risk by $\widetilde{W} = W_0(1 + k\tilde{x}) = W_0(1 + \tilde{y})$. Define $\hat{\pi}$ as the share of one's wealth one would pay to avoid this risk:

$$\hat{\pi} = \frac{\pi(W_0, u, W_0 k\tilde{x})}{W_0}. \tag{1.27}$$

Then

$$\hat{\pi} \approx \frac{1}{2}W_0 A(W_0)k^2 \mathrm{E}\tilde{x}^2 = \frac{1}{2}R(W_0)\mathrm{E}\tilde{y}^2, \tag{1.28}$$

where $R(W_0) = W_0 A(W_0)$ is the *coefficient of relative risk aversion*.

1.3 Tractable Utility Functions

Almost all applied theory and empirical work in finance uses some member of the class of utility functions known as linear risk tolerance (LRT) or hyperbolic absolute risk aversion (HARA). Continuing to use wealth as the argument of the utility function, the HARA class of utility functions can be written as

$$u(W) = a + b\left(\eta + \frac{W}{\gamma}\right)^{1-\gamma}, \tag{1.29}$$

defined for levels of wealth W such that $\eta + W/\gamma > 0$. The parameter a and the magnitude of the parameter b do not affect choices but can be set freely to deliver convenient representations of utility in special cases.

For these utility functions, risk tolerance—the reciprocal of absolute risk aversion—is given by

$$T(W) = \frac{1}{A(W)} = \eta + \frac{W}{\gamma}, \tag{1.30}$$

which is linear in W. Absolute risk aversion itself is then hyperbolic in W:

$$A(W) = \left(\eta + \frac{W}{\gamma}\right)^{-1}. \tag{1.31}$$

Relative risk aversion is, of course,

$$R(W) = W\left(\eta + \frac{W}{\gamma}\right)^{-1}. \tag{1.32}$$

There are several important special cases of HARA utility.

Quadratic utility has $\gamma = -1$. This implies that risk tolerance declines in wealth from (1.30), and absolute risk aversion increases in wealth from (1.31). In addition, the quadratic utility function has a "bliss point" at which $u' = 0$. These are important disadvantages, although quadratic utility is tractable in models with additive risk and has even been used in macroeconomic models with growth, where trending preference parameters are used to keep the bliss point well above levels of wealth or consumption observed in the data.

Exponential or constant absolute risk averse (CARA) utility is the limit as $\gamma \to -\infty$. To obtain constant absolute risk aversion A, we need

$$-u''(W) = Au'(W) \tag{1.33}$$

for all $W > 0$. Solving this differential equation, we get

$$u(W) = \frac{-\exp(-AW)}{A}, \tag{1.34}$$

where $A = 1/\eta$. This utility function does not have a bliss point, but it is bounded above; utility approaches zero as wealth increases. Exponential utility is tractable with normally distributed risks because then utility is lognormally distributed. In addition, as we will see in the next chapter, it implies that wealth has no effect on the demand for risky assets, which makes it relatively easy to calculate an equilibrium because one does not have to keep track of the wealth distribution.

Power or constant relative risk averse (CRRA) utility has $\eta = 0$ and $\gamma > 0$. Absolute risk aversion is declining in wealth — a desirable property — while relative risk aversion $R(W) = \gamma$, a constant. For $\gamma \neq 1$, a and b in equation (1.29) can be chosen to write utility as

$$u(W) = \frac{W^{1-\gamma} - 1}{1 - \gamma}. \tag{1.35}$$

For $\gamma = 1$, we use L'Hôpital's rule to take the limit of equation (1.35) as γ approaches one. The result is

$$u(W) = \log(W). \tag{1.36}$$

Power utility is appealing because it implies stationary risk premia and interest rates even in the presence of long-run economic growth. Also it is tractable in the presence of multiplicative lognormally distributed risks. For these reasons it is a workhorse model in the asset pricing and macroeconomics literatures and will be used intensively in this book. The special case of log utility has even more convenient properties, but relative risk aversion as low as one is hard to reconcile with the substantial risk premia observed in financial markets as we discuss in Chapter 6.

Subsistence level. A negative η represents a subsistence level, a minimum level of consumption that is required for utility to be defined. Litzenberger and Rubinstein (1976) argued for a model with log utility of wealth above the subsistence level, which they called the Generalized Log Utility Model. The proposal did not gain traction, perhaps in part because economic growth renders any fixed subsistence level irrelevant in the long run.[1] Models of habit formation, discussed in Chapter 6, have time-varying subsistence levels that can grow with the economy.

1.4 Critiques of Expected Utility Theory

1.4.1 Allais Paradox

This famous paradox, due to Allais (1953), challenges the von Neumann-Morgenstern framework. Consider a set of lotteries, each of which involves drawing one ball from an urn containing 100 balls, labeled 0–99. Table 1.1 shows the monetary prizes that will be awarded for drawing each ball, in four different lotteries L^a, L^b, M^a, and M^b.

Lottery L^a offers \$50 with certainty, while lottery L^b offers an 89% chance of \$50, a 10% chance of \$250, and a 1% chance of receiving nothing. Many people, confronted with this choice, prefer L^a to L^b even though the expected winnings are higher for lottery L^b. Lottery M^a offers an 11% chance of winning \$50 and an 89% chance of receiving nothing, while lottery M^b offers a 10% chance of winning \$250 and a 90% chance of receiving nothing. Many people, confronted with this choice, prefer M^b to M^a.

The challenge to utility theory is that choosing L^a over L^b, while also choosing M^b over M^a, violates the independence axiom. As the structure of the table makes clear, the only difference between L^a and L^b is in the balls labeled 0–10; the balls labeled 11–99 are identical in these two lotteries. This is also true for the pair M^a and M^b. According to the independence axiom, the rewards for drawing balls 11–99 should then be irrelevant

Table 1.1.   *Allais Paradox*

	0	1–10	11–99
L^a	50	50	50
L^b	0	250	50
M^a	50	50	0
M^b	0	250	0

[1] The model's gloomy acronym may also have hurt its prospects. Possibly only Deaton and Muellbauer (1980) were less fortunate in this respect.

to the choices between L^a and L^b, and M^b and M^a. But if this is the case, then the two choices are the same because if one considers only balls 0–10, L^a has the same rewards as M^a, and L^b has the same rewards as M^b.

There is a longstanding debate over the significance of this paradox. Either people are easily misled (but can be educated) or the independence axiom needs to be abandoned. Relaxing this axiom must be done carefully to avoid creating further paradoxes (Chew 1983, Dekel 1986, Gul 1991).[2] Recent models of dynamic decision making, notably the Epstein and Zin (1989, 1991) preferences discussed in section 6.4, also relax the independence axiom in an intertemporal context, taking care to do so in a way that preserves time consistent decision making.

1.4.2 Rabin Critique

Matthew Rabin (2000) has criticized utility theory on the ground that it cannot explain observed aversion to small gambles without implying ridiculous aversion to large gambles. This follows from the fact that differentiable utility has second-order risk aversion.

To understand Rabin's critique, consider a gamble that wins \$11 with probability 1/2 and loses \$10 with probability 1/2. With diminishing marginal utility, the utility of the win is at least $11u'(W_0 + 11)$. The utility cost of the loss is at most $10u'(W_0 - 10)$. Thus if a person turns down this gamble, we must have $10u'(W_0 - 10) > 11u'(W_0 + 11)$, which implies

$$\frac{u'(W_0 + 11)}{u'(W_0 - 10)} < \frac{10}{11}.$$

Now suppose the person turns down the same gamble at an initial wealth level of $W_0 + 21$. Then

$$\frac{u'(W_0 + 21 + 11)}{u'(W_0 + 21 - 10)} = \frac{u'(W_0 + 32)}{u'(W_0 + 11)} < \frac{10}{11}.$$

Combining these two inequalities,

$$\frac{u'(W_0 + 32)}{u'(W_0 - 10)} < \left(\frac{10}{11}\right)^2 = \frac{100}{121}.$$

If this iteration can be repeated, it implies extremely small marginal utility at high wealth levels, which would induce people to turn down apparently extremely attractive gambles.

Table 1.2 is an extract from Rabin (2000), Table I. The original caption reads "If averse to 50-50 lose \$100/gain g bets for all wealth levels, will turn down 50-50 lose L/gain G bets; G's entered in table." Values g are entered in the column headings, and values L are entered in the row labels, while the cells of the table report G. In other words, as one moves to the right, each column corresponds to an agent who is turning down more and

---

[2]For example, suppose that $L^a \succ L^b$ and $L^a \succ L^c$ but contrary to the independence axiom $L^d = 0.5L^b + 0.5L^c \succ L^a$. Then you would pay to switch from L^a to L^d, but once the uncertainty in the compound lottery L^d is resolved, you would pay again to switch back to L^a. This is sometimes called the "Dutch book" problem. It can be avoided by imposing Chew's (1983) property of "betweenness," that a convex combination of two lotteries (L^b and L^c in the example above) cannot be preferred to the more preferred of the two, and the less preferred of the two cannot be preferred to the convex combination.

Table 1.2.   *Extract from Rabin (2000), Table I*

L/g	$101	$105	$110	$125
$400	400	420	550	1,250
$1,000	1,010	1,570	∞	∞
$4,000	5,750	∞	∞	∞
$10,000	∞	∞	∞	∞

Table 1.3.   *Extract from Rabin (2000), Table II*

L/g	$101	$105	$110	$125
$400	400	420	550	1,250
$1,000	1,010	1,570	718,190	160 billion
$4,000	5,750	635,670	60.5 million	9.4 trillion
$10,000	27,780	5.5 million	160 billion	5.4 sextillion

more favorable small gambles. As one moves down the table, each row corresponds to a larger possible loss, and the table entries show the winnings that are required to induce the agent to take the bet. An entry of ∞ implies that the agent will turn down the bet for any finite upside, no matter how large.

A first obvious question is how is it possible for an agent to be unresponsive to arbitrarily large winnings, refusing to risk a finite loss. To promote careful thought, this question is posed as an informal problem and is answered at the end of the chapter. As a clue, Table 1.3 is an extract from Rabin (2000), Table II. The only difference between this and the previous table is that the numbers here are conditional on a specific initial wealth level ($290,000), and the aversion to 50-50 lose $100/gain g bets is known to hold only for wealth levels up to $300,000.

1.4.3 First-Order Risk Aversion and Prospect Theory

Rabin's critique shows that the standard theory of expected utility cannot explain risk aversion with respect to small gambles over a significant range of wealth levels. At any one level of wealth, one can increase aversion to small gambles within the standard theory by relaxing the assumption that utility is twice differentiable, allowing a kink in the utility function that invalidates the standard formula for the risk premium given in (1.25). Such a kink makes risk aversion locally infinite and implies that the risk premium for a small gamble is proportional to its standard deviation rather than its variance; this is called "first-order" risk aversion by contrast with the "second-order" risk aversion implied by twice differentiable utility (Segal and Spivak 1990). However, this approach only increases aversion to small gambles at a single point, and Rabin's argument (which does not assume twice differentiability of the utility function) still applies if an agent is averse to small gambles over a range of wealth levels.

In response to this, economists and psychologists have explored models with reference points, in which utility results from gains or losses relative to a reference point that is often set equal to current wealth. This has the effect of moving the kink in the utility function so that it is always relevant and induces first-order risk aversion at arbitrary levels of initial wealth.

The most famous example is Kahneman and Tversky's (1979) prospect theory, which has not only a kink at the reference point but also two other features designed to fit experimental evidence on risk attitudes: a preference function that is concave in the domain of gains and convex (risk-seeking) in the domain of losses, and subjective probabilities that are larger than objective probabilities when those probabilities are small. A standard parameterization of the prospect-theory preference function is

$$u(x) = x^\beta \text{ for } x \geq 0,$$

$$u(x) = -\lambda |x|^\beta \text{ for } x \leq 0, \tag{1.37}$$

where $x = W - W_{REF}$, the difference between wealth and the reference level of wealth. We assume $0 < \beta < 1$ to get concavity for gains and convexity for losses, and $\lambda > 1$ to deliver a kink at the reference point. Gul's (1991) disappointment averse preferences also have a kink at a reference point set equal to the endogenous certainty equivalent of a gamble (Backus, Routledge, and Zin 2004).

Barberis, Huang, and Thaler (2006) point out that even these preferences cannot generate substantial aversion to small delayed gambles. During the time between the decision to take a gamble and the resolution of uncertainty, the agent will be exposed to other risks and will merge these with the gamble under consideration. If the gamble is uncorrelated with the other risks, it is diversifying. In effect the agent will have second-order risk aversion with respect to delayed gambles. To deal with this problem, Barberis et al. argue that people treat gambles in isolation, that is, they use "narrow framing."

In this book, we will continue to work primarily with standard utility functions despite their inability to explain aversion to small risks. This reflects my belief that the theory is useful for asset pricing problems, consistent with Rabin's acknowledgement that it "may well be a useful model of the taste for very-large-scale insurance" (Rabin 2000). One might make an analogy with physics, where the force of gravity is dominant at cosmological scales even though it becomes negligible at subatomic scales where other forces are far more important.

Finally, it is worth noting that expected utility theory can be enriched to generate differences in aversion to medium-scale and large-scale risks. Notably, Chetty and Szeidl (2007) show that "consumption commitments" (fixed costs to adjust a portion of consumption) raise risk aversion over medium-sized gambles, relative to risk aversion over large gambles where extreme outcomes would justify paying the cost to adjust all consumption.

1.5 Comparing Risks

Earlier in this chapter we discussed the comparison of utility functions, concentrating on cases where two utility functions can be ranked in their risk aversion, with one turning down all lotteries that the other one turns down, regardless of the distribution of the risks. Now we perform a symmetric analysis, comparing the riskiness of two different distributions without making any assumptions on utility functions other than concavity.

1.5.1 Comparing Risks with the Same Mean

In this subsection we consider two distributions that have the same mean. Informally, there are three natural ways to define the notion that one of these distributions is riskier than the other:

(1) All increasing and concave utility functions dislike the riskier distribution relative to the safer distribution.
(2) The riskier distribution has more weight in the tails than the safer distribution.
(3) The riskier distribution can be obtained from the safer distribution by adding noise to it.

The classic analysis of Rothschild and Stiglitz (1970) shows that these are all equivalent. Consider random variables $\tilde{X}$ and $\tilde{Y}$, which have the same expectation.

(1) $\tilde{X}$ is weakly less risky than $\tilde{Y}$ if no individual with an increasing concave utility function prefers $\tilde{Y}$ to $\tilde{X}$:

$$E[u(X)] \geq E[u(Y)] \tag{1.38}$$

for all increasing concave u (.). $\tilde{X}$ is less risky than $\tilde{Y}$ (without qualification) if it is weakly less risky than $\tilde{Y}$ and there is some increasing concave $u(.)$ which strictly prefers $\tilde{X}$ to $\tilde{Y}$.

Note that this is a partial ordering. It is not the case that for any $\tilde{X}$ and $\tilde{Y}$, either $\tilde{X}$ is weakly less risky than $\tilde{Y}$ or $\tilde{Y}$ is weakly less risky than $\tilde{X}$. We can get a complete ordering if we restrict attention to a smaller class of utility functions than the concave, such as the quadratic.

(2) $\tilde{X}$ is less risky than $\tilde{Y}$ if the density function of $\tilde{Y}$ can be obtained from that of $\tilde{X}$ by applying a *mean-preserving spread* (MPS). An MPS $s(x)$ is defined by

$$s(x) = \begin{pmatrix} \alpha \text{ for } c < x < c+t \\ -\alpha \text{ for } c' < x < c' + t \\ -\beta \text{ for } d < x < d+t \\ \beta \text{ for } d' < x < d' + t \\ 0 \text{ elsewhere} \end{pmatrix}, \tag{1.39}$$

where $\alpha, \beta, t > 0$; $c + t < c' < c' + t < d < d + t < d'$; and $\alpha(c' - c) = \beta(d' - d)$; that is, "the more mass you move, the less far you can move it." This is illustrated in Figure 1.3.

An MPS is something you add to a density function $f(x)$. If $g(x) = f(x) + s(x)$, then (i) $g(x)$ is also a density function, and (ii) it has the same mean as $f(x)$.

(i) is obvious because $\int s(x)\, dx =$ area under $s(x) = 0$.
(ii) follows from the fact that the "mean" of $s(x)$, $\int x s(x)\, dx = 0$, which follows from $\alpha(c' - c) = \beta(d' - d)$. The algebra is

$$\int x s(x)\, dx = \int_c^{c+t} x\alpha\, dx + \int_{c'}^{c'+t} x(-\alpha)\, dx + \int_d^{d+t} x(-\beta)\, dx + \int_{d'}^{d'+t} x\beta\, dx$$

$$= \alpha \left[\frac{x^2}{2}\right]_c^{c+t} - \alpha \left[\frac{x^2}{2}\right]_{c'}^{c'+t} - \beta \left[\frac{x^2}{2}\right]_d^{d+t} + \beta \left[\frac{x^2}{2}\right]_{d'}^{d'+t}$$

$$= t\left[\beta(d' - d) - \alpha(c' - c)\right] = 0. \tag{1.40}$$

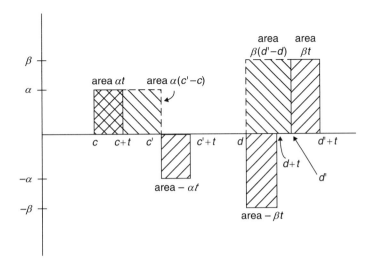

Figure 1.3.   *Mean-Preserving Spread*

In what sense is an MPS a spread? It is obvious that if the mean of $f(x)$ is between $c' + t$ and d, then $g(x)$ has more weight in the tails. This is not so obvious when the mean of $f(x)$ is far to the left or the right in Figure 1.3. Nevertheless, we can show that $\widetilde{Y}$ with density g is riskier than $\widetilde{X}$ with density f in the sense of (1) above. In this sense the term "spread" is appropriate.

We calculate the expected utility difference between $\widetilde{X}$ and $\widetilde{Y}$ as

$$E[u(\widetilde{X})] - E[u(\widetilde{Y})]$$

$$= \int u(z)[f(z) - g(z)]\,dz = -\int u(z)s(z)\,dz \tag{1.41}$$

$$= -\alpha \int_c^{c+t} u(z)\,dz + \alpha \int_{c'}^{c'+t} u(z)\,dz + \beta \int_d^{d+t} u(z)\,dz - \beta \int_{d'}^{d'+t} u(z)\,dz$$

$$= -\alpha \int_c^{c+t} \left[u(z) - u(z + c' - c) - \frac{\beta}{\alpha}\{u(z + d - c) - u(z + d' - c)\} \right] dz.$$

The definition of an MPS implies that $\beta/\alpha = (c' - c)/(d' - d)$. In addition, $u(z + h) - u(z) = u'(z^*)h$ for some z^* between z and $z + h$.

Thus

$$u(z) - u(z + c' - c) = -(c' - c)u'(z_1^*) \tag{1.42}$$

for some z_1^* between z and $z + c' - c$, and

$$u(z + d - c) - u(z + d' - c) = -(d' - d)u'(z_2^*) \tag{1.43}$$

for some z_2^* between $z + d - c$ and $z + d' - c$. Substituting into (1.41), we get

$$E[u(\widetilde{X})] - E[u(\widetilde{Y})] = \alpha(c' - c) \int_c^{c+t} \left[u'(z_1^*) - u'(z_2^*) \right] dz > 0, \tag{1.44}$$

where the inequality follows because $z_1^* < z_2^*$ so $u'(z_1^*) > u'(z_2^*)$.

(3) A formal definition of "added noise" is that $\widetilde{X}$ is less risky than $\widetilde{Y}$ if $\widetilde{Y}$ has the same distribution as $\widetilde{X} + \widetilde{\varepsilon}$, where $E[\widetilde{\varepsilon}|X] = 0$ for all values of X. We say that $\widetilde{\varepsilon}$ is a "fair game" with respect to X.

The fair game condition is stronger than zero covariance, $\text{Cov}(\widetilde{\varepsilon}, \widetilde{X}) = 0$. It is weaker than independence, $\text{Cov}(f(\widetilde{\varepsilon}), g(\widetilde{X})) = 0$ for all functions f and g. It is equivalent to $\text{Cov}(\widetilde{\varepsilon}, g(\widetilde{X})) = 0$ for all functions g. To develop your understanding of this point, Problem 1.1 at the end of this chapter asks you to construct examples of random variables $\widetilde{X}$ and $\widetilde{\varepsilon}$ that have zero covariance but do not satisfy the fair game condition, or that satisfy the fair game condition but are not independent.

It is straightforward to show that added noise is sufficient for a concave utility function to dislike the resulting distribution, that is, (3) implies (1):

$$E[U(\widetilde{X} + \widetilde{\varepsilon})|X] \leq U(E[\widetilde{X} + \widetilde{\varepsilon}|X]) = U(X)$$

$$\Rightarrow E[U(\widetilde{X} + \widetilde{\varepsilon})] \leq E[U(\widetilde{X})]$$

$$\Rightarrow E[U(\widetilde{Y})] \leq E[U(\widetilde{X})], \tag{1.45}$$

because $\widetilde{Y}$ and $\widetilde{X} + \widetilde{\varepsilon}$ have the same distribution.

More generally, Rothschild and Stiglitz show that conditions (1), (2), and (3) are all equivalent. This is a powerful result because one or the other condition may be most useful in a particular application.

None of these conditions are equivalent to $\widetilde{Y}$ having greater variance than $\widetilde{X}$. It is obvious from (3) that if $\widetilde{Y}$ is riskier than $\widetilde{X}$ then $\widetilde{Y}$ has greater variance than $\widetilde{X}$. The problem is that the reverse is not true in general. Greater variance is necessary but not sufficient for increased risk. $\widetilde{Y}$ could have greater variance than $\widetilde{X}$ but still be preferred by some concave utility functions if it has more desirable higher-moment properties. This possibility can only be eliminated if we confine attention to a limited class of distributions such as the normal distribution.

1.5.2 Comparing Risks with Different Means

The Rothschild-Stiglitz conditions apply only to distributions that have the same mean. However, they extend straightforwardly to the case where a riskier distribution, in the Rothschild-Stiglitz sense, is shifted downward and therefore has a lower mean. Some brief definitions illustrate this point.

Definition. $\widetilde{X}$ *(first-order) dominates* $\widetilde{Y}$ if $\widetilde{Y} = \widetilde{X} + \widetilde{\xi}$, where $\widetilde{\xi} \leq 0$. In this case every outcome for $\widetilde{X}$ is at least as great as the corresponding outcome for $\widetilde{Y}$.

Definition. $\widetilde{X}$ *first-order stochastically dominates* $\widetilde{Y}$ if $\widetilde{Y}$ has the distribution of $\widetilde{X} + \widetilde{\xi}$, where $\widetilde{\xi} \leq 0$. Equivalently, if $F(.)$ is the cdf of $\widetilde{X}$ and $G(.)$ is the cdf of $\widetilde{Y}$, then $\widetilde{X}$ first-order stochastically dominates $\widetilde{Y}$ if $F(z) \leq G(z)$ for every z. In this case every quantile of the $\widetilde{X}$ distribution is at least as great as the corresponding quantile of the $\widetilde{Y}$ distribution, but a particular outcome for $\widetilde{Y}$ may exceed the corresponding outcome for $\widetilde{X}$. First-order stochastic dominance implies that every increasing utility function will prefer the distribution $\widetilde{X}$.

Definition. $\widetilde{X}$ *second-order stochastically dominates* $\widetilde{Y}$ if $\widetilde{Y}$ has the distribution of $\widetilde{X} + \widetilde{\xi} + \widetilde{\varepsilon}$, where $\widetilde{\xi} \leq 0$ and $E[\widetilde{\varepsilon}|X + \xi] = 0$. Second-order stochastic dominance (SOSD) implies that every increasing, concave utility function will prefer the distribution $\widetilde{X}$. Increased risk is the special case of SOSD where $\widetilde{\xi} = 0$.

SOSD, based on the consistent preference of all risk-averse decision makers for one gamble over another, offers an uncontroversial comparison of risks. Unfortunately this also limits its applicability: SOSD is only a partial order of gambles; that is, many pairs of gambles cannot be ranked using SOSD. Specifically, when a riskier distribution, in the Rothschild-Stiglitz sense, is shifted upward—implying that it has a higher mean—then one cannot assert that any concave utility function will prefer the safer alternative. The choice will depend on the scale of the risk and the form of the utility function. This tradeoff is the subject of portfolio choice theory, which we explore in the next chapter.

It is possible to create a complete order, delivering a ranking of any two gambles, if one confines attention to a more specific set of decision makers (defined by their utility functions and wealth levels). A complete order can be used to create a riskiness index, that is, a summary statistic mapping a gamble to a real number that depends only on the attributes of the gamble itself. For example, Aumann and Serrano (2008) propose a riskiness index based on the preferences of agents with CARA utility, for whom wealth does not affect their attitudes toward gambles. The Aumann-Serrano index is the risk tolerance (the reciprocal of risk aversion) that makes a CARA agent indifferent to a gamble. Problem 1.2 invites you to explore this and another riskiness index proposed by Foster and Hart (2009). While riskiness indices lack the generality of SOSD and depend on the preferences considered, they can nonetheless be useful for descriptive and regulatory purposes.

1.5.3 The Principle of Diversification

We conclude this chapter by showing how the Rothschild-Stiglitz analysis can be used to prove the optimality of perfect diversification in a simple portfolio choice problem with identical risky assets.

Consider n lotteries with payoffs $\widetilde{x}_1, \widetilde{x}_2, \ldots, \widetilde{x}_n$ that are independent and identically distributed (iid). You are asked to choose weights $a_1, a_2, \ldots, a_n$ subject to the constraint that $\sum_i a_i = 1$. It seems obvious that the best choice is a fully diversified, equally weighted portfolio with weights $a_i = 1/n$ for all i. The payoff is then

$$\widetilde{z} = \frac{1}{n} \sum_{i=1}^{n} \widetilde{x}_i. \tag{1.46}$$

The Rothschild-Stiglitz analysis makes it very easy to prove that this is optimal. Just note that the payoff on any other strategy is

$$\sum_i a_i \widetilde{x}_i = \widetilde{z} + \sum_i \left(a_i - \frac{1}{n} \right) \widetilde{x}_i = \widetilde{z} + \widetilde{\varepsilon}, \tag{1.47}$$

and

$$\mathrm{E}[\widetilde{\varepsilon}|z] = \sum_i \left(a_i - \frac{1}{n} \right) \mathrm{E}[\widetilde{x}_i|z] = k \sum_i \left(a_i - \frac{1}{n} \right) = 0. \tag{1.48}$$

Thus, any other strategy has the payoff of the equally weighted portfolio, plus added noise (Rothschild-Stiglitz condition (3)). It follows that any concave utility function will prefer the equally weighted portfolio (Rothschild-Stiglitz condition (1)).

1.6 Solution and Further Problems

An informal problem posed in this chapter was how it is possible for an agent to turn down a 50-50 gamble with a fixed loss, regardless of the size of the potential winnings, as claimed in Rabin (2000), Table I. The answer is that if utility is bounded above, then the utility gain from a win converges to a finite limit even as the size of the win becomes arbitrarily large. Rabin's assumption in Table I—that an agent with expected utility turns down a given small gamble at all initial wealth levels—requires that absolute risk aversion is nondecreasing (because with decreasing absolute risk aversion, at some high enough level of wealth the agent will accept the small gamble). But the utility function with constant absolute risk aversion, the exponential utility function, is bounded above, and the same is true of all utility functions with increasing absolute risk aversion such as the quadratic utility function. This discussion suggests that Table II may be a more relevant critique of expected utility than Table I. Table II makes a weaker assumption about the range of wealth over which an agent turns down a given small gamble and is thus consistent with decreasing absolute risk aversion.

Problem 1.1 Fair Games

State whether each of the following statements is true or false. Provide a proof if the statement is true or a counterexample if the statement is false.

(a) If $\widetilde{X}$ is a fair game with respect to $\widetilde{Y}$, and $\widetilde{Y}$ is a fair game with respect to $\widetilde{X}$, then $\widetilde{X}$ and $\widetilde{Y}$ are independent.

(b) If $\widetilde{X}$ and $\widetilde{Y}$ have zero means and zero covariance, then $\widetilde{X}$ is a fair game with respect to $\widetilde{Y}$ and $\widetilde{Y}$ is a fair game with respect to $\widetilde{X}$.

(c) For jointly normally distributed random variables, zero covariance implies independence.

Problem 1.2 Riskiness Indices

This exercise explores the properties of two recently proposed riskiness indices: the Aumann and Serrano (AS 2008) index and the Foster and Hart (FH 2009) index.

A decision maker is characterized by an initial wealth level W_0 and von Neumann-Morgenstern utility function u over wealth with $u' > 0$ and $u'' < 0$. A gamble is represented by a real-valued random variable g representing the possible changes in wealth if the gamble is accepted by the decision maker. An investor (W_0, u) rejects a gamble g if $E[u(W_0 + g)] \leq u(W_0)$ and accepts g if $E[u(W_0 + g)] > u(W_0)$. We only consider gambles with $E[g] > 0$ and $\Pr(g < 0) > 0$. For simplicity, we assume that gambles take finitely many values. Let $L_g \equiv \max(-g)$ and $M_g \equiv \max g$ denote the maximal loss and maximal gain of g, respectively.

For any gamble g, the AS riskiness index $R^{AS}(g)$ is given by the unique positive solution to the equation

$$E\left[\exp\left(-\frac{1}{R^{AS}(g)}g\right)\right] = 1. \tag{1.49}$$

For any gamble g, the FH riskiness $R^{FH}(g)$ index is given by the unique positive solution to the equation

$$\mathrm{E}\left[\log\left(1+\frac{1}{R^{FH}(g)}g\right)\right]=0. \qquad (1.50)$$

(a) Show that the AS riskiness index equals the level of risk tolerance that makes a CARA investor indifferent between accepting and rejecting the gamble. That is, an investor with CARA utility $u(w)=-\exp(-Aw)$ will accept (reject) g if $A<1/R^{AS}(g)$ (if $A\geq 1/R^{AS}(g)$).

(b) Show that the FH riskiness index equals the level of wealth that would make a log utility investor indifferent between accepting and rejecting the gamble. That is, a log investor with wealth $W_0>R^{FH}(g)$ ($W_0\leq R^{FH}(g)$) will accept (reject) g.

(c) Consider binary gambles with a loss of L_g with probability p_L and a gain M_g with probability $1-p_L$. Calculate the values of the two indices for the binary gamble with $L_g=\$100$, $M_g=\$105$, and $p_L=1/2$ (Rabin 2000). Repeat for the binary gamble with $L_g=\$100$, $M_g=\$10,100$, and $p_L=1/2$. (The calculation is analytical for FH but numerical for AS.)

(d) Consider binary gambles with infinite gain, that is, M_g arbitrarily large. Derive explicit formulas for the two indices as a function of L_g and p_L at the limit $M_g\to+\infty$. Explain the intuition behind these formulas. Why do the indices assign nonzero riskiness to gambles with infinite expectation? What happens as $p_L\to 0$?

(e) The Sharpe ratio, defined as the ratio of the mean of a gamble to its standard deviation, $SR(g)\equiv\mathrm{E}[g]/\sqrt{\mathrm{Var}(g)}$,[3] is a widely used measure of risk-adjusted portfolio returns. We can interpret its reciprocal as a riskiness index.

   (i) Show by example that the (inverse) Sharpe ratio violates first-order stochastic dominance (and hence second-order stochastic dominance). That is, if gamble h first-order stochastically dominates gamble g, then it is not always true that $SR(h)\geq SR(g)$.

  (ii) AS (2008) propose a generalized version of the Sharpe ratio $GSR(g)\equiv\mathrm{E}[g]/R^{AS}(g)$, a measure of "riskiness-adjusted" expected returns. Argue that GSR respects second-order stochastic dominance (and hence first-order stochastic dominance).

 (iii) Show that $GSR(g)$ is ordinally equivalent to $SR(g)$ when g is a normally distributed gamble.

     Hint: use the probability density function of the normal distribution to show that $R^{AS}(g)=\mathrm{Var}(g)/(2\mathrm{E}[g])$.

---

[3]The definition of the Sharpe ratio in terms of asset returns is given in equation (2.37) of the next chapter.

2

Static Portfolio Choice

IN THIS CHAPTER we apply the theory of rational decision making under uncertainty, embodied in the expected utility theory developed in the previous chapter, to the financial problem of choosing a portfolio. In section 2.1 we consider the choice between a safe asset and a single risky asset, showing how several alternative modeling frameworks lead to the same formula for the amount of risk that an investor should take. We consider first a risk with a small reward, using the Arrow-Pratt analytical method presented in Chapter 1; then a normally distributed risk faced by an investor with constant absolute risk aversion; and finally a lognormally distributed risk faced by an investor with constant relative risk aversion. We also discuss the special properties of the growth-optimal portfolio chosen by an investor with log utility.

In section 2.2 we consider the problem of combining risky assets, starting with only two assets and then moving to the general N-asset case, using the classic mean-variance analysis of Markowitz (1952). We discuss the properties of the global minimum-variance portfolio of risky assets and present the mutual fund theorem of Tobin (1958). Putting the two sections together, we have a theory of optimal portfolio choice. We conclude with a discussion of the difficulties of implementing this theory in practice, which motivates the static equilibrium models to be explored in the next chapter.

Throughout the chapter we continue to work in a two-period setting in which portfolios are chosen in an initial period, after which all uncertainty is resolved and all wealth is consumed in a second period. The fascinating issues raised by time-varying investment opportunities in a dynamic model are not addressed until Part II of the book.

2.1 Choosing Risk Exposure

2.1.1 The Principle of Participation

We begin by considering a choice between one safe and one risky asset, making only weak assumptions on preferences and the distribution of returns on the risky asset. An investor with initial wealth W can invest in a safe asset with return R_f or a risky asset with return $R_f + \widetilde{x}$. Importantly $\widetilde{x}$, the excess return on the risky asset over the safe asset, need not have a zero mean.

After investing for one period the investor's wealth is

$$W(1 + R_f) + \theta\widetilde{x} = W_0 + \theta\widetilde{x}, \qquad (2.1)$$

where θ is the dollar amount (not the share of wealth) invested in the risky asset. The notation W_0 helps to make it clear that this is the wealth level in the next period if the investor holds none of the risky asset.

The investor's optimization problem is

$$\max_\theta V(\theta) = \mathrm{E}u(W_0 + \theta\widetilde{x}). \tag{2.2}$$

The first-order condition for this problem is

$$V'(\theta^*) = \mathrm{E}\widetilde{x}u'(W_0 + \theta^*\widetilde{x}) = 0, \tag{2.3}$$

where θ^* is the optimal amount invested in the risky asset, and the second-order condition is

$$V''(\theta^*) = \mathrm{E}\widetilde{x}^2 u''(W_0 + \theta^*\widetilde{x}) < 0, \tag{2.4}$$

which must hold for a risk-averse investor with twice differentiable concave utility.

Without solving the problem explicitly, we can evaluate the first derivative of utility at zero investment in the risky asset:

$$V'(0) = \mathrm{E}\widetilde{x}u'(W_0), \tag{2.5}$$

which has the same sign as $\mathrm{E}\widetilde{x}$. This tells us that—unsurprisingly—there should be no investment in a risky asset with a zero expected excess return, but the investment in the risky asset should be positive if it has a positive expected excess return, regardless of the level of risk aversion.

This "principle of participation" tells us that nonparticipation in risky asset markets with positive risk premia cannot be justified by risk aversion alone. To rationalize nonparticipation we need to add some other ingredient to the model, such as fixed costs of participation or a kink in the utility function that makes it nondifferentiable, as discussed in section 1.4.3.

2.1.2 A Small Reward for Risk

The principle of participation tells us the sign of the optimal investment in a risky asset, but we would like to derive an explicit expression for the magnitude. As a first approach, we use the Arrow-Pratt methodology discussed in section 1.2.3, and consider a risk with a small reward:

$$\widetilde{x} = k\mu + \widetilde{y}, \tag{2.6}$$

where k, positive but close to zero, scales the mean μ and $\widetilde{y}$ is the zero-mean component of the risk. Note that $\widetilde{y}$ here has a fixed scale, so the notation here is distinct from that in section 1.2.3.

The first-order condition (2.3) now becomes

$$\mathrm{E}(k\mu + \widetilde{y})\,u'(W_0 + \theta^*(k)(k\mu + \widetilde{y})) = 0. \tag{2.7}$$

Differentiating with respect to k,

$$\mu\mathrm{E}u'(\widetilde{W}) + \theta^*(k)\mu\mathrm{E}(k\mu + \widetilde{y})\,u''(\widetilde{W}) + \theta^{*\prime}(k)\mathrm{E}(k\mu + \widetilde{y})^2 u''(\widetilde{W}) = 0. \tag{2.8}$$

Evaluating this expression at $k = 0$, and using the fact that $\theta^*(0) = 0$,

$$\theta^{*\prime}(0) = \frac{\mu}{\mathrm{E}\widetilde{y}^2}\frac{1}{A(W_0)}. \tag{2.9}$$

Then a Taylor expansion for the investment in the risky asset gives

$$\theta^*(k) \approx \theta^*(0) + k\theta^{*\prime}(0) = \frac{\mathrm{E}\widetilde{x}}{\mathrm{E}(\widetilde{x} - \mathrm{E}\widetilde{x})^2}\frac{1}{A(W_0)}. \tag{2.10}$$

In words, the optimal dollar investment is the mean-variance ratio for the risky excess return, divided by absolute risk aversion.

We can divide θ by wealth to find the share of wealth invested in the risky asset. Call this α. We find

$$\alpha^*(k) = \frac{\theta^*(k)}{W_0} \approx \frac{\mathrm{E}\widetilde{x}}{\mathrm{E}(\widetilde{x} - \mathrm{E}\widetilde{x})^2}\frac{1}{R(W_0)}. \tag{2.11}$$

The optimal share of wealth to invest is the mean-variance ratio for the risky excess return, divided by relative risk aversion.

2.1.3 The CARA-Normal Case

The above formula for dollars invested in the risky asset is exact when risk is normally distributed (Gaussian), $\widetilde{x} \sim N(\mu, \sigma^2)$, and utility is CARA (exponential), with risk aversion A. In this case the general problem (2.2) becomes

$$\max_\theta V(\theta) = \mathrm{E}[-\exp(-A(W_0 + \theta\widetilde{x}))], \tag{2.12}$$

or equivalently

$$\min \mathrm{E}[\exp(-A(W_0 + \theta\widetilde{x}))]. \tag{2.13}$$

The term in square brackets in (2.13) is lognormally distributed—that is, its log is normally distributed—if $\widetilde{x}$ is normally distributed. Then we can apply the following extremely useful result, which any student of asset pricing should memorize.

For any lognormal random variable $\widetilde{z}$,

$$\log \mathrm{E}(\widetilde{z}) = \mathrm{E}\log(\widetilde{z}) + \frac{1}{2}\mathrm{Var}\log(\widetilde{z}). \tag{2.14}$$

In words, "the log of the mean is the mean of the log plus one-half the variance of the log." This result says that the wedge between the log of the mean and the mean of the log, which we know to be positive from Jensen's Inequality, is exactly one-half the variance of the log in the case where the log is normally distributed.[1]

Applying this result, the portfolio choice problem (2.13) is equivalent to

$$\min \log \mathrm{E}[\exp(-A(W_0 + \theta\widetilde{x}))] = -A(W_0 + \theta\mu) + \frac{1}{2}A^2\theta^2\sigma^2, \tag{2.15}$$

---

[1]This and many other properties of the lognormal distribution are summarized in Johnson, Kotz, and Balakrishnan (1994, Chapter 14).

which in turn is equivalent to

$$\max A(W_0 + \theta\mu) - \frac{1}{2}A^2\theta^2\sigma^2. \tag{2.16}$$

The solution is

$$\theta^* = \frac{\mu}{A\sigma^2}, \tag{2.17}$$

independent of the initial level of wealth. This is exactly the same formula as (2.10), with a constant absolute risk aversion parameter A, but it does not require that the mean excess return μ is small relative to the risk σ^2, so it can be applied to problems with attractive risks and correspondingly large allocations to risky assets. Similarly, the formula for the optimal risky share, (2.11), holds here with relative risk aversion $R(W) = AW$ proportional to wealth.

The CARA-normal framework is widely used because it has numerous tractable features. Specifically:

Multiple assets can easily be analyzed. Equation (2.16) shows that the investor trades off the mean return on the portfolio against the variance of return, and thus the apparatus of mean-variance analysis, developed later in this chapter, can be used to solve portfolio choice problems with multiple assets.

Additive background risk, arising from random income or nontradable assets, can be added to the model. Background risk does not affect the demand for tradable risky assets if it is uncorrelated with their returns, and background risk that is correlated with returns generates simple hedging demands for assets as discussed in section 10.1.1 of Chapter 10.

Equilibrium with heterogeneous agents is easy to calculate because wealth does not affect the demand for risky assets. Thus, equilibrium conditions that equate the demand and supply of risky assets can be solved without keeping track of the wealth distribution in the economy. Related to this, it is straightforward to calculate the volume of trade in a CARA-normal model.

On the other hand, the CARA-normal framework also has several serious difficulties:

Wealth irrelevance for risky investment. Wealth does not affect the amount invested in a risky asset. The solution for dollars invested in the risky asset, (2.17), makes no reference to the investor's wealth. To caricature this result, it implies that Bill Gates and a graduate student should invest the same amount in stocks, and Bill Gates should keep all his extra wealth in Treasury bills. This is precisely the property that makes CARA-normal equilibrium models so tractable, but it is obviously counterfactual.

Bounded utility and unbounded returns. CARA utility is bounded above, which implies that arbitrarily large gains will not necessarily offset finite losses as discussed in sections 1.4.2 and 1.6. At the same time, in CARA-normal models there is no lower bound on asset returns (contrary to the principle of limited liability), so wealth and consumption can go negative, although parameters can be chosen to make the probability that this occurs extremely small.

Trending risk premia. Growth in the economy, with constant multiplicative risks (volatilities of rates of return) implies growth in the absolute dollar risk that must be absorbed by investors. If investors have constant absolute risk aversion, economic growth does not increase their willingness to absorb absolute risk, so in equilibrium risk premia must grow with the economy. There is no historical evidence for such an upward trend in risk premia.

Arbitrary time interval. The assumption of normality cannot hold over more than one time interval. Consider a two-period model where returns in each period are normally distributed, and assume for simplicity that returns have the same normal distribution in each period. Then the two-period gross return is the product of two identically distributed normal random variables and does not itself have a normal distribution. The problem of course is that sums of normal random variables, not products, are themselves normal; but the compounding of returns over time is multiplication, not addition.

2.1.4 The CRRA-Lognormal Case

The last difficulty suggests a different set of assumptions, which we now explore in detail. If returns are identically distributed with finite variance in every period, and if we compound them over time, the distribution of returns will converge to a lognormal distribution. This follows from the central limit theorem and the fact that the log of compounded returns is the sum of the logs of returns in each period. The log compounded return converges to a normal distribution, implying that the compounded return itself is lognormal. This property makes it appealing to assume that returns are lognormal in a discrete-time model with iid returns, because returns will then be lognormal over multiple periods as well.

The Objective Function in Wealth
Assume that an investor's wealth is lognormally distributed, and the investor has power utility with relative risk aversion γ. The investor's problem can be written as

$$\max \left[\mathrm{E}_t \frac{W_{t+1}^{1-\gamma}}{1-\gamma} \right], \tag{2.18}$$

where for now we omit the choice variables and simply state the object that is to be maximized.[2]

Maximizing this expectation is equivalent to maximizing the log of the expectation. If $\gamma < 1$, then the scale factor $1/(1-\gamma) > 0$, and it can be omitted since it does not affect the solution. If $\gamma > 1$, then $1/(1-\gamma) < 0$, and we turn the problem into a minimization problem, which turns out to have the same solution. Proceeding with the $\gamma < 1$ case, if next-period wealth is lognormal, we can again use the formula for the log of the mean of a lognormal random variable, (2.14), to rewrite the problem as

$$\max\left[\log\left(\mathrm{E}_t W_{t+1}^{1-\gamma}\right)\right] = \max\left[(1-\gamma)\mathrm{E}_t w_{t+1} + \frac{1}{2}(1-\gamma)^2\sigma_{wt}^2\right], \tag{2.19}$$

where $w_t = \log(W_t)$ and σ_{wt}^2 is the conditional variance of log wealth.

The Objective Function in Portfolio Return
The budget constraint is

$$w_{t+1} = r_{p,t+1} + w_t, \tag{2.20}$$

---

[2]The power utility function as written in equation (1.35) subtracted $1/(1-\gamma)$, but this does not affect choice and can therefore be omitted from the objective function here.

where $r_{p,t+1} = \log(1 + R_{p,t+1})$ is the log return on the portfolio. So we can restate the problem as

$$\max\left[\mathrm{E}_t r_{p,t+1} + \frac{1}{2}(1 - \gamma)\sigma_{pt}^2 \right], \qquad (2.21)$$

where σ_{pt}^2 is the conditional variance of the log portfolio return.

At first sight this expression appears odd, because it says that for a given mean log portfolio return, the investor prefers higher variance of log return if the coefficient of relative risk aversion $\gamma < 1$—even though an investor with low risk aversion is still averse to risk. To understand this result, apply the useful formula (2.14) one more time to see that

$$\mathrm{E}_t r_{p,t+1} + \sigma_{pt}^2/2 = \log \mathrm{E}_t(1 + R_{p,t+1}). \qquad (2.22)$$

Thus we can rewrite the portfolio return objective (2.21) as

$$\max\left[\log \mathrm{E}_t(1 + R_{p,t+1}) - \frac{\gamma}{2}\sigma_{pt}^2 \right]. \qquad (2.23)$$

This shows that the investor does trade off mean against variance in the portfolio return and dislikes variance for all positive coefficients of relative risk aversion. The relevant mean return is the mean simple return, or arithmetic mean return, and the investor trades the log of this mean linearly against the variance of the log return.

Log Portfolio Return and Log Asset Returns

Now we need to relate the log portfolio return to the log returns on underlying assets. The simple return on the portfolio is a linear combination of the simple returns on the risky and riskless assets. The log return on the portfolio is the log of this linear combination, but this is not the same as a linear combination of logs. This is an example of the challenging interaction of additive and multiplicative effects that so often complicates the analysis of asset pricing models.

Over short time intervals, however, we can use a Taylor approximation of the nonlinear function relating log individual-asset returns to log portfolio returns. Writing α_t for the portfolio share in the risky asset, which has log return r_{t+1}, and writing $r_{f,t+1}$ for the log return on the riskless asset, we have

$$r_{p,t+1} - r_{f,t+1} = \log(1 + \alpha_t(\exp(r_{t+1} - r_{f,t+1}) - 1))$$

$$\approx \alpha_t(r_{t+1} - r_{f,t+1}) + \frac{1}{2}\alpha_t(1 - \alpha_t)\sigma_t^2, \qquad (2.24)$$

where the approximate equality comes from a second-order Taylor approximation of the function $f(x) = \log(1 + \alpha(\exp(x) - 1))$ around $x = 0$, using the fact that for short time intervals and lognormally distributed returns, $(r_{t+1} - r_{f,t+1})^2 \approx \sigma_t^2$.[3]

To understand equation (2.24), note first that the difference between the log portfolio return and a linear combination of log individual-asset returns is given by

---

[3]With lognormal returns, the squared excess return scaled by a multiple of the period duration Δ, $(r_{t+1} - r_{f,t+1})^2/(\sigma_t^2\Delta)$, has a noncentral χ_1^2 distribution. Hence, the mean squared excess return $\mathrm{E}[(r_{t+1} - r_{f,t+1})^2] = \Delta\sigma_t^2\mathrm{E}\chi_1^2$, and the variance of the squared excess return $\mathrm{Var}[(r_{t+1} - r_{f,t+1})^2] = \Delta^2\sigma_t^4\mathrm{Var}(\chi_1^2)$, which becomes negligible relative to the mean as the period duration Δ shrinks toward zero.

$\alpha_t(1 - \alpha_t)\sigma_t^2/2$, which is zero if $\alpha_t = 0$ or 1. When $0 < \alpha_t < 1$, the portfolio is a weighted average of the individual assets, and the term $\alpha_t(1 - \alpha_t)\sigma_t^2/2$ is positive because (using Jensen's Inequality yet again) the log of an average is greater than an average of logs.

Another way to understand (2.24) is to rewrite the equation as

$$r_{p,t+1} - r_{f,t+1} + \frac{\sigma_{pt}^2}{2} \approx \alpha_t \left(r_{t+1} - r_{f,t+1} + \frac{\sigma_t^2}{2} \right), \qquad (2.25)$$

using the fact that $\sigma_{pt}^2 = \alpha_t^2 \sigma_t^2$. Taking the conditional expectation of (2.25), and again using the formula for the mean of a lognormal random variable, we have that

$$\log \mathrm{E}_t \left[\frac{1 + R_{p,t+1}}{1 + R_{f,t+1}} \right] \approx \alpha_t \log \mathrm{E}_t \left[\frac{1 + R_{t+1}}{1 + R_{f,t+1}} \right]. \qquad (2.26)$$

At conventional investment horizons of a year or less, expected net simple returns are typically sufficiently small that the first-order approximation of $\log(1 + \mathrm{E}_t R_{t+1})$ around $\mathrm{E}_t R_{t+1} = 0$, $\log(1 + \mathrm{E}_t R_{t+1}) \approx \mathrm{E}_t R_{t+1}$, is very accurate. Thus the left-hand side of equation (2.26) is well approximated by $\mathrm{E}_t(R_{p,t+1} - R_{f,t+1})$ and the right-hand side by $\alpha_t \mathrm{E}_t(R_{t+1} - R_{f,t+1})$, so (2.26) recovers the fact that the mean simple excess return on the portfolio is linear in the mean simple excess return on the risky asset.

The approximation (2.24) is extremely useful and will be frequently applied in this book. It becomes more accurate as the time interval shrinks, and is exact in continuous time when asset prices follow diffusions, which have continuous paths (then it follows from Itô's Lemma). Thus (2.24) gives discrete-time asset pricing models some of the tractability of continuous-time models.

However, note that (2.24) rules out bankruptcy, even with a short position ($\alpha_t < 0$) or leverage ($\alpha_t > 1$). Bankruptcy is indeed impossible in continuous time with continuous price paths, because then the portfolio can be continuously rebalanced. In practice, this approximation should be used cautiously over discrete intervals or when prices can jump, particularly if short positions or leverage are involved.

Solving the Approximate Problem

If we are willing to use the above approximation, it becomes straightforward to solve the portfolio choice problem. With two assets, the mean excess portfolio return is $\mathrm{E}_t r_{p,t+1} - r_{f,t+1} = \alpha_t(\mathrm{E}_t r_{t+1} - r_{f,t+1}) + \frac{1}{2}\alpha_t(1 - \alpha_t)\sigma_t^2$, while the variance of the portfolio return is $\alpha_t^2 \sigma_t^2$. Substituting into the objective function, we get

$$\max \alpha_t(\mathrm{E}_t r_{t+1} - r_{f,t+1}) + \frac{1}{2}\alpha_t(1 - \alpha_t)\sigma_t^2 + \frac{1}{2}(1 - \gamma)\alpha_t^2 \sigma_t^2. \qquad (2.27)$$

The solution is

$$\alpha_t = \frac{\mathrm{E}_t r_{t+1} - r_{f,t+1} + \sigma_t^2/2}{\gamma \sigma_t^2} \approx \frac{\mathrm{E}_t R_{t+1} - R_{f,t+1}}{\gamma \sigma_t^2}, \qquad (2.28)$$

which again has the same form as the Arrow-Pratt solution for a risk with a small reward and the solution for an investor with constant absolute risk aversion facing a normally distributed risk. In this case, however, relative risk aversion rather than absolute risk aversion is a fixed parameter independent of wealth, and the risk is assumed to be lognormally distributed.[4]

Problems 2.1 and 2.2 at the end of this chapter invite you to explore optimal risk taking in greater detail. Problem 2.1 asks what happens when risk has a discrete two-point distribution, and Problem 2.2 undertakes welfare analysis of the portfolio choice problem with power utility.

2.1.5 The Growth-Optimal Portfolio

When $\gamma = 1$, the investor has log utility and chooses the *growth-optimal portfolio* with the maximum expected log return as shown by equation (2.21). When $\gamma > 1$, the investor seeks a safer portfolio by penalizing the variance of log returns; when $\gamma < 1$, the investor actually seeks a riskier portfolio because a higher variance, with the same mean log return, corresponds to a higher mean simple return. The case $\gamma = 1$ is the boundary where these two opposing considerations cancel.

The growth-optimal portfolio has the property that as the investment horizon increases, it outperforms any other portfolio with increasing probability. To see this, note that the difference between the log return on the growth-optimal portfolio and the log return on any other portfolio is normally distributed with a positive mean. Call this difference the excess log return on the growth-optimal portfolio. Under the assumption that returns are iid over time, as the horizon increases, the mean and variance of the excess log return both grow in proportion to the horizon. This implies that the ratio of mean to standard deviation, the Sharpe ratio of the excess log return, grows with the square root of the horizon. The ratio of mean to standard deviation for a normally distributed random variable determines the probability that the random variable is positive, so the probability that the excess log return is positive increases with the investment horizon.

Markowitz (1976) used this fact to argue that long-term investors should invest as if they have log utility (or at least, should avoid investing more aggressively than the growth-optimal portfolio), but Samuelson (1969) pointed out that this does not follow from rational maximization of expected utility, since utility functions must be taken as primitives and cannot be derived from external considerations.[5]

Although the growth-optimal portfolio is only optimal for an investor with log utility, it has properties that give it an important role in the theory of the stochastic discount factor discussed in Chapter 4. We discuss these properties in section 4.1.4.

2.2 Combining Risky Assets

We now consider the problem of combining multiple risky assets, using the classic mean-variance analysis of Markowitz (1952) that judges portfolios by their first two moments of returns. While higher moments can also matter to investors, mean-variance analysis

---

[4]The equality between the log risk premium adjusted for Jensen's Inequality and the simple risk premium is exact only in the continuous-time limit, just like the approximation (2.24). Relatedly, the fact that the variance of log returns appears in the denominator of (2.28), while the variance of simple returns appears in the Arrow-Pratt and CARA-normal formulas is not an essential difference, because for lognormal returns $\text{Var}_t(R_{t+1}) \approx \text{Var}_t(r_{t+1})$ when returns are measured over short periods of time.

[5]Samuelson (1979) went so far as to write an article on this topic that concludes: "No need to say more. I have made my point. And, but for the last, have done so in words of but one syllable." The article is a tour de force but is almost incomprehensible because of the difficulty of expressing oneself clearly with such a limited vocabulary. The article also contains a few errors (two-syllable words).

delivers much of the important intuition about portfolio construction with risky assets, in particular, the importance of diversification.[6]

In a static two-period model, mean-variance analysis can be justified either if investors have quadratic utility or if returns have distributions for which the first two moments are sufficient statistics. Quadratic utility is appealing in that it requires no assumptions on return distributions, but unappealing because it implies increasing absolute risk aversion as discussed in section 1.3. Return distributions that allow the use of mean-variance analysis include the normal distribution, the multivariate t distribution, or the lognormal distribution (using the approximation that holds for a short period duration as discussed in section 2.1.4 so that portfolio returns and individual asset returns can both be lognormal). It is also possible to add an arbitrarily distributed common risk to all asset returns since such a common risk will not affect portfolio choice.

As discussed in section 2.1, we may combine assumptions on return distributions with assumptions on investor preferences (combining normal distributions with CARA preferences or lognormal distributions with CRRA preferences) to get tractable closed-form portfolio rules. But given the assumptions on returns, these assumptions on preferences are not needed to justify mean-variance analysis.

We shall assume that short sales are permitted. Short-sales restrictions introduce additional constraints that destroy the analytical simplicity of the basic mean-variance analysis. We first consider the problem of combining two risky assets, then discuss the special case where one of the two assets is riskless (returning briefly to the framework of the previous section), then generalize to N risky assets, and finally consider the problem with one safe asset and N risky assets.

2.2.1 Two Risky Assets

With two risky assets, what combinations of mean and variance (or equivalently standard deviation) can you get? The return on a portfolio containing two risky assets with returns R_1 and R_2 is

$$R_p = w_1 R_1 + w_2 R_2 = w_1 R_1 + (1 - w_1) R_2, \tag{2.29}$$

since portfolio weights must sum to one. The mean return is also linear in portfolio weights,

$$\overline{R}_p = w_1 \overline{R}_1 + (1 - w_1) \overline{R}_2, \tag{2.30}$$

but the variance of return is quadratic:

$$
\begin{aligned}
\sigma_p^2 &= \text{Var}(w_1 R_1 + (1 - w_1) R_2) \\
&= w_1^2 \text{Var}(R_1) + (1 - w_1)^2 \text{Var}(R_2) + 2 w_1 (1 - w_1) \text{Cov}(R_1, R_2) \\
&= w_1^2 \sigma_1^2 + (1 - w_1)^2 \sigma_2^2 + 2 w_1 (1 - w_1) \sigma_{12}.
\end{aligned}
\tag{2.31}
$$

The quadratic relation between w_1 (or equivalently $\overline{R}_p$) and σ_p^2 implies that a plot of mean against variance is a parabola; a plot of mean against standard deviation (the square root of variance) is a hyperbola.

---

[6]Kraus and Litzenberger (1976) extended mean-variance analysis to allow for investor preferences over portfolio skewness, the third moment of portfolio return. We defer consideration of higher moments until sections 4.3.3 and 6.3.

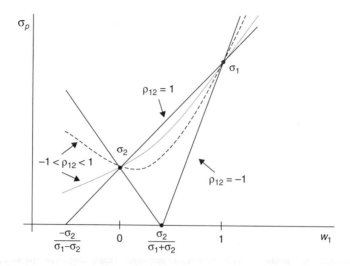

Figure 2.1. *Portfolio Standard Deviation as a Function of Portfolio Weight w_1*

Since $\sigma_{12} = \sigma_1 \sigma_2 \rho_{12} \leq \sigma_1 \sigma_2$, where ρ_{12} is the correlation between R_1 and R_2,

$$\sigma_p^2 \leq (w_1 \sigma_1 + (1 - w_1) \sigma_2)^2 \tag{2.32}$$

or equivalently $\sigma_p \leq w_1 \sigma_1 + (1 - w_1) \sigma_2$, whenever $0 \leq w_1 \leq 1$. This illustrates the power of diversification to reduce portfolio risk. The geometry is shown in Figure 2.1, which plots portfolio standard deviation against the weight w_1 for a range of possible correlations ρ_{12}.

We can calculate the derivative of variance with respect to the portfolio weight in asset 1:

$$\frac{d\sigma_p^2}{dw_1} = 2w_1 \sigma_1^2 - 2(1 - w_1) \sigma_2^2 + 2(1 - 2w_1) \sigma_{12}$$

$$= 2w_1 \left[\sigma_1^2 + \sigma_2^2 - 2\sigma_{12} \right] - 2 \left[\sigma_2^2 - \sigma_{12} \right]. \tag{2.33}$$

This derivative is increasing in w_1, showing that the risk penalty for increasing an asset's portfolio weight is increasing in that weight.

We can find the *global minimum-variance (GMV) portfolio* with the smallest possible variance by setting the derivative (2.33) to zero. The implied portfolio weights are

$$w_{G1} = \frac{\sigma_2^2 - \sigma_{12}}{\sigma_1^2 + \sigma_2^2 - 2\sigma_{12}}, \quad w_{G2} = \frac{\sigma_1^2 - \sigma_{12}}{\sigma_1^2 + \sigma_2^2 - 2\sigma_{12}}. \tag{2.34}$$

These weights simplify nicely in special cases. When the two assets are uncorrelated, $\sigma_{12} = 0$, then the global minimum-variance weights hold each asset in proportion to the variance share of the other asset in total variance:

$$w_{G1} = \frac{\sigma_2^2}{\sigma_1^2 + \sigma_2^2}, \quad w_{G2} = \frac{\sigma_1^2}{\sigma_1^2 + \sigma_2^2}. \tag{2.35}$$

When the two assets have equal variance, $\sigma_1^2 = \sigma_2^2$, then the global minimum-variance weights are equal at $1/2$ for each asset, regardless of their covariance. In this case the covariance of the assets only affects the variance of the GMV portfolio and not its weights on the two assets.

2.2.2 One Risky and One Safe Asset

The above results simplify if one asset, say the second, is riskless. If we set $\sigma_2^2 = 0$ and write $R_2 = R_f$, the riskless interest rate, we can rewrite the mean portfolio return (2.30) as $\overline{R}_p - R_f = w_1(\overline{R}_1 - R_f)$, and the variance of portfolio return (2.31) as $\sigma_p^2 = w_1^2 \sigma_1^2$, which implies $w_1 = \sigma_p/\sigma_1$. Combining these two expressions,

$$\overline{R}_p - R_f = \sigma_p \left(\frac{\overline{R}_1 - R_f}{\sigma_1} \right). \tag{2.36}$$

This defines a straight line, called the *capital allocation line (CAL)*, on a mean-standard deviation diagram. The slope

$$S_1 = \left(\frac{\overline{R}_1 - R_f}{\sigma_1} \right) \tag{2.37}$$

is called the *Sharpe ratio* or *reward-risk ratio* of the risky asset. Any portfolio that combines a single risky asset with the riskless asset has the same Sharpe ratio as the risky asset itself.

The standard rule of myopic portfolio choice, derived in section 2.1 using several alternative sets of assumptions and approximations, is

$$w_1 = \frac{\overline{R}_1 - R_f}{\gamma \sigma_1^2} = \frac{S_1}{\gamma \sigma_1}, \tag{2.38}$$

where γ is the coefficient of relative risk aversion (that need not necessarily be a constant independent of wealth). The optimal share in the risky asset is the risk premium divided by relative risk aversion times variance, or equivalently the Sharpe ratio of the risky asset divided by relative risk aversion times standard deviation.

Since $w_1 = \sigma_p/\sigma_1$, we can rewrite this as

$$\sigma_p = \frac{S_1}{\gamma}. \tag{2.39}$$

The optimal risk in the portfolio is the Sharpe ratio divided by the coefficient of relative risk aversion.

The assumption throughout this discussion that the second asset is riskless is of course an arbitrary normalization. A riskless asset can be constructed from two risky assets whenever the two assets have perfect positive or negative correlation, as can be verified by setting $\sigma_{12} = \sigma_1 \sigma_2$ or $\sigma_{12} = -\sigma_1 \sigma_2$ and solving for the global minimum-variance portfolio with weights given by (2.34). This fact is illustrated in Figure 2.1.

2.2.3 N Risky Assets

When there are only two risky assets, the mean return on a portfolio pins down a unique set of portfolio weights. This is no longer true when we have N risky assets. Now we can consider the problem of finding portfolios that have minimum variance for a given mean return. These are called minimum-variance portfolios and we say they lie on the *minimum-variance frontier.*

To handle this problem requires vector notation and matrix calculus. We assume that no riskless asset exists. Define $\overline{R}$ as the vector of mean returns on the risky assets, Σ as the variance-covariance matrix of returns, w as the vector of portfolio weights, and ι as a vector of ones. We can write the problem as

$$\min_{w} \frac{1}{2} w' \Sigma w \quad \text{s.t.} \quad \overline{R}' w = \overline{R}_p, \qquad \iota' w = 1. \tag{2.40}$$

The coefficient of $1/2$ in the objective function appears merely for notational convenience and does not change the form of the solution.

We set up the Lagrangian

$$\mathcal{L}(w, \lambda_1, \lambda_2) = \frac{1}{2} w' \Sigma w + \lambda_1 (\overline{R}_p - \overline{R}' w) + \lambda_2 (1 - \iota' w), \tag{2.41}$$

where λ_1 and λ_2 are the Lagrange multipliers on the two constraints. The first-order conditions are

$$\frac{\partial \mathcal{L}}{\partial w} = \Sigma w - \lambda_1 \overline{R} - \lambda_2 \iota = 0. \tag{2.42}$$

Premultiplying (2.42) by Σ^{-1}, we get:

$$w = \lambda_1 \Sigma^{-1} \overline{R} + \lambda_2 \Sigma^{-1} \iota. \tag{2.43}$$

An immediate question is how we know Σ is invertible, so that Σ^{-1} exists. You are invited to respond to this question, which is answered at the end of this chapter.

The Lagrange multipliers λ_1 and λ_2 can be found by using the two constraints

$$\overline{R}_p = \overline{R}' w = \lambda_1 \overline{R}' \Sigma^{-1} \overline{R} + \lambda_2 \overline{R}' \Sigma^{-1} \iota = \lambda_1 A + \lambda_2 B \tag{2.44}$$

$$1 = \iota' w = \lambda_1 \iota' \Sigma^{-1} \overline{R} + \lambda_2 \iota' \Sigma^{-1} \iota = \lambda_1 B + \lambda_2 C, \tag{2.45}$$

where $A \equiv \overline{R}' \Sigma^{-1} \overline{R}$, $B \equiv \overline{R}' \Sigma^{-1} \iota = \iota' \Sigma^{-1} \overline{R}$, and $C \equiv \iota' \Sigma^{-1} \iota$. Note that A and C are mathematically guaranteed to be positive; B is not, but for economic reasons we normally expect it to be positive as explained in section 2.2.4.

Solving these equations, we get

$$\lambda_1 = \frac{C\overline{R}_p - B}{D}, \quad \lambda_2 = \frac{A - B\overline{R}_p}{D}, \tag{2.46}$$

where $D \equiv AC - B^2$.

The minimized portfolio variance is

$$\sigma_p^2 = w' \Sigma w = w' \Sigma \left(\lambda_1 \Sigma^{-1} \overline{R} + \lambda_2 \Sigma^{-1} \iota \right)$$

$$= \lambda_1 w' \overline{R} + \lambda_2 w' \iota = \lambda_1 \overline{R}_p + \lambda_2$$

$$= \frac{A - 2B\overline{R}_p + C\overline{R}_p^2}{D}. \tag{2.47}$$

Thus $d\sigma_p^2 / d\overline{R}_p = 2\lambda_1$, or equivalently $d((1/2)\sigma_p^2)/d\overline{R}_p = \lambda_1$. λ_1 measures the cost of a higher mean return target to the investor's objective (one-half variance). This cost is increasing in $\overline{R}_p$, so increases in the return target have an increasing marginal impact on the risk of the portfolio.

2.2.4 The Global Minimum-Variance Portfolio

Next we solve for the global minimum-variance portfolio. The first constraint (on the mean) is dropped from the problem; this is equivalent to setting $\lambda_1 = 0$. Using a subscript G to denote the portfolio, we get

$$w_G = \lambda_2 \Sigma^{-1} \iota, \tag{2.48}$$

and the remaining constraint, that the portfolio weights sum to one, implies that

$$1 = \iota' w_G = \lambda_2 \iota' \Sigma^{-1} \iota. \tag{2.49}$$

So $\lambda_2 = 1/(\iota' \Sigma^{-1} \iota) = 1/C$, and

$$w_G = \frac{\Sigma^{-1} \iota}{\iota' \Sigma^{-1} \iota}. \tag{2.50}$$

In the 2×2 case,

$$w_{G1} = \frac{\text{sum of top row of } \Sigma^{-1}}{\text{sum of all elements of } \Sigma^{-1}}, \tag{2.51}$$

$$w_{G2} = \frac{\text{sum of bottom row of } \Sigma^{-1}}{\text{sum of all elements of } \Sigma^{-1}}, \tag{2.52}$$

and we can use the standard formula for the inverse of a 2×2 matrix,

$$\Sigma^{-1} = \frac{1}{\sigma_1^2 \sigma_2^2 - \sigma_{12}^2} \begin{pmatrix} \sigma_2^2 & -\sigma_{12} \\ -\sigma_{12} & \sigma_1^2 \end{pmatrix}, \tag{2.53}$$

to show that the portfolio weights of the global minimum-variance portfolio are the same that we got before in (2.34).

The mean return on the global minimum-variance portfolio is

$$w_G' \overline{R} = \left(\frac{\iota' \Sigma^{-1} \overline{R}}{\iota' \Sigma^{-1} \iota} \right) = \frac{B}{C}. \tag{2.54}$$

We expect the mean return on the global minimum-variance portfolio to be positive, and thus we expect B to be positive, but this is an assertion about economically plausible parameters, not a mathematical truth.

In the general model with an arbitrary mean return constraint, we can verify that when $\overline{R}_p > B/C$—so the required expected portfolio return exceeds that of the global minimum-variance portfolio—then the Lagrange multiplier for the mean constraint is positive: $\lambda_1 > 0$. The set of minimum-variance portfolios that satisfy this condition is called the *mean-variance efficient set*. When $\overline{R}_p < B/C$, then the Lagrange multiplier $\lambda_1 < 0$, implying that a higher mean return is consistent with a lower variance. No agent who likes mean and dislikes variance would hold such a portfolio, which is minimum-variance given its mean but not maximum-mean given its variance. Figure 2.2 illustrates the mean-variance efficient set as a solid line, and the set of portfolios that are minimum-variance but not mean-variance efficient as a dotted line. Problem 2.3 asks you to perform further analysis of the geometry of the mean-variance efficient set.

The variance of the return on the global minimum-variance portfolio is

$$ w'_G \Sigma w_G = \frac{\iota' \Sigma^{-1} \Sigma \Sigma^{-1} \iota}{(\iota' \Sigma^{-1} \iota)^2} = \frac{1}{(\iota' \Sigma^{-1} \iota)}. \tag{2.55}$$

This simplifies in the case where all assets are symmetrical, having the same variance and the same correlation ρ with each other. Then the global minimum-variance portfolio is equally weighted, $w_G = \iota/N$, and

$$ w'_G \Sigma w_G = \frac{\iota' \Sigma \iota}{N^2} = \rho \sigma^2 + \frac{(1-\rho)\sigma^2}{N}. \tag{2.56}$$

To understand this formula, note first that in the symmetrical case, the variance of the global minimum-variance portfolio is just the equally weighted average of all the elements

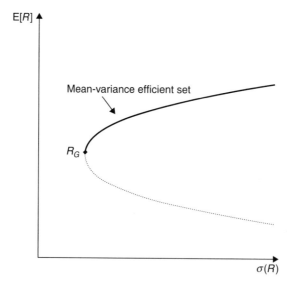

Figure 2.2.   *The Global Minimum-Variance Portfolio and the Mean-Variance Efficient Set*

of Σ. This matrix has N^2 elements, which are σ^2 on the diagonal and $\rho\sigma^2$ off the diagonal. Writing the diagonal terms as $\sigma^2 = \rho\sigma^2 + (1-\rho)\sigma^2$, there are N^2 instances of $\rho\sigma^2$ that average to $\rho\sigma^2$ and N instances of $(1-\rho)\sigma^2$ that average to $(1-\rho)\sigma^2/N$.

The variance of the equally weighted portfolio cannot be negative, and this restricts the set of admissible values for ρ. With only two assets, ρ can vary between -1 and $+1$, but as the number of assets increases the negative values of ρ become increasingly constrained until with an infinite number of assets, ρ itself must be nonnegative. Intuitively, as the number of assets increases it becomes more and more difficult to find ways for them all to be negatively correlated with one another. This is an example of the general principle that variance-covariance matrices must always be positive semidefinite.

When ρ is positive, we can think of $\rho\sigma^2$ as undiversifiable risk that must be borne by any portfolio, while $(1-\rho)\sigma^2/N$ is diversifiable risk that is inversely proportional to the number of stocks and vanishes in the limit as N grows. In a market with an arbitrarily large number of identical stocks, $\rho\sigma^2$ is the variance of the market index.

Figure 2.3, following Campbell et al. (CLMX 2001), presents an empirical analysis inspired by this decomposition. The figure reports the cross-sectional average monthly correlation between any two stocks, calculated over rolling five-year windows and randomly selecting 500 stocks every five years with continuous trading data. This is a simplified version of the procedure of CLMX, updated to include data from 1997 through 2012 that were not part of their sample.

The figure shows a strong decline in the average cross-sectional correlation from the late 1970s until the mid-1990s, with some reversal since then that is particularly pronounced during the last five years. CLMX observed the decline but not the more recent increase. The volatility of the market return does not show the same low-frequency variations, which is possible because changes in ρ and σ^2 can offset each other to keep the

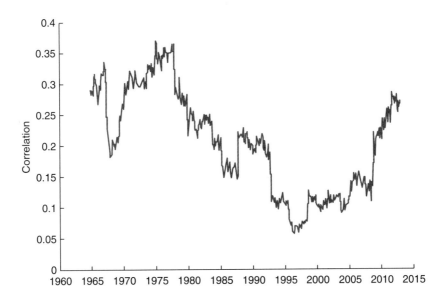

Figure 2.3.   *Average Correlations of Individual Stock Returns Over Time*

product $\rho\sigma^2$, the volatility of a highly diversified portfolio, roughly constant (or varying in a different higher-frequency manner).

Portfolios that are not perfectly diversified contain idiosyncratic risk, beyond the undiversifiable risk of the market index, of $(1 - \rho)\sigma^2/N$. Declining ρ and increasing σ^2 increase this excess risk for any N; equivalently, they increase the number of stocks N that must be held to keep this excess risk at a given level. The opposite happens when ρ increases and σ^2 decreases, as in more recent years. CLMX illustrated this point by plotting the average excess standard deviation of an N-stock portfolio above an equally weighted index. They calculated this by randomly selecting N-stock portfolios, but in the symmetric example this would be

$$\sqrt{\rho\sigma^2 + \frac{(1-\rho)\sigma^2}{N}} - \sqrt{\rho\sigma^2}.$$

Figure 2.4 shows an update of this calculation, for sample periods 1960–1975, 1976–1985, 1986–1995, 1996–2005, and 2006–2012. The lowest curve is for the earliest 15-year sample period. The highest two curves are for the two samples from 1986 to 2005. The curve for 2006–2012 lies below those curves but above the curve for 1976–1985. Thus recent developments have lowered the diversification curve but not back to the level of the late 1970s and early 1980s, let alone the level that prevailed in the 1960s and early 1970s. The lesson of the figure is that conventional rules of thumb about portfolio construction, such as the notion that a portfolio of 25 stocks is adequately diversified, may need to be revised as market conditions change. Even in the most recent data, more than 50 stocks are needed to achieve the same low level of idiosyncratic risk that 25 stocks would have delivered in the 1960s and early 1970s.

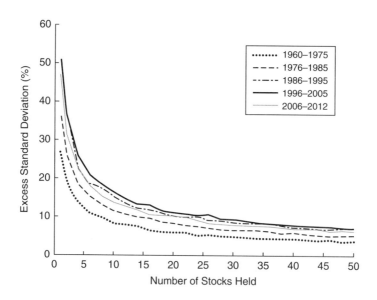

Figure 2.4. *Excess Standard Deviation as a Function of Number of Stocks Held*

2.2.5 The Mutual Fund Theorem

Returning to our analysis of the main portfolio choice problem (2.40), the mutual fund theorem of Tobin (1958) says that all minimum-variance portfolios can be obtained by mixing just two minimum-variance portfolios in different proportions. Thus if all investors hold minimum-variance portfolios, all investors hold combinations of just two underlying portfolios or "mutual funds."

To show this, rewrite the equation for portfolio weights, (2.43), as

$$w = \lambda_1 \Sigma^{-1}\overline{R} + \lambda_2 \Sigma^{-1}\iota$$

$$= \lambda_1 \iota' \Sigma^{-1}\overline{R} \left(\frac{\Sigma^{-1}\overline{R}}{\iota' \Sigma^{-1}\overline{R}} \right) + \lambda_2 \iota' \Sigma^{-1}\iota \left(\frac{\Sigma^{-1}\iota}{\iota' \Sigma^{-1}\iota} \right)$$

$$= \lambda_1 B \left(\frac{\Sigma^{-1}\overline{R}}{\iota' \Sigma^{-1}\overline{R}} \right) + \lambda_2 C w_G, \tag{2.57}$$

and note that $\lambda_1 B + \lambda_2 C = 1$ from (2.45). Thus, for any mean return target $\overline{R}_p$, the optimal portfolio is a combination of two mutual funds, the second of which is the global minimum-variance portfolio, and the first of which invests more heavily in assets with high mean returns. The mean return target determines the weights on these two funds but not their composition.

The precise formulation in (2.57) is to some extent arbitrary. Once we know that the whole minimum-variance frontier can be constructed from two mutual funds, we can choose any two minimum-variance portfolios on the frontier and represent all other minimum-variance portfolios as combinations of these two funds. However, it is natural to choose the global minimum-variance portfolio as one of the funds, and then the other fund must have weights that are sensitive to mean returns on individual assets.

The mutual fund theorem follows naturally from the assumption of mean-variance analysis that investors are trading off two attributes of portfolios, mean return and variance of return. Nonetheless, investment practitioners initially found it counterintuitive and indeed offensive.[7] In academic finance, this was the first of many analyses to reduce the dimension of the portfolio choice problem from N individual assets to a smaller number of portfolios or mutual funds. We discuss more such analyses in the next chapter.

2.2.6 One Riskless Asset and N Risky Assets

The mutual fund theorem becomes even starker in the case where a riskless asset exists along with N risky assets. To handle this case, we write the riskless asset return as R_f. We rewrite the problem (2.40) as one of choosing weights w in the risky assets, where the portfolio is completed by lending or borrowing at the riskless rate R_f. Thus we no longer require $\iota'w = 1$. Dropping this constraint, we can write the problem as

$$\min_{w} \frac{1}{2} w' \Sigma w \quad \text{s.t.} \quad \overline{R}_p - R_f = (\overline{R} - R_f \iota)' w. \tag{2.58}$$

[7]Peter Bernstein, in his history of modern financial economics, *Capital Ideas* (1991), describes the pre-mutual-fund-theorem approach of investment practitioners as "the interior decorator fallacy." Practitioners felt that, like interior decorators, they should customize portfolios to accommodate clients' preferences and were insulted by the notion that their work could be reduced to two dimensions.

As before, we set up the Lagrangian

$$\mathcal{L}(w_1, w_2, \lambda_1) = \frac{1}{2}(w' \Sigma w) + \lambda_1 [\overline{R}_p - R_f - (\overline{R} - R_f \iota)' w], \qquad (2.59)$$

and get first-order conditions

$$\frac{\partial \mathcal{L}}{\partial w} = \Sigma w - \lambda_1 (\overline{R} - R_f \iota) = 0, \qquad (2.60)$$

so

$$w = \lambda_1 \Sigma^{-1} (\overline{R} - R_f \iota). \qquad (2.61)$$

The constraint in the problem tells us that

$$\overline{R}_p - R_f = (\overline{R} - R_f \iota)' w = \lambda_1 (\overline{R} - R_f \iota)' \Sigma^{-1} (\overline{R} - R_f \iota) = \lambda_1 E, \qquad (2.62)$$

where $E \equiv (\overline{R} - R_f \iota)' \Sigma^{-1} (\overline{R} - R_f \iota)$. Thus we can solve for the Lagrange multiplier as a function of E:

$$\lambda_1 = \frac{R_p - R_f}{E}. \qquad (2.63)$$

The minimized portfolio variance depends on the Lagrange multiplier and on E:

$$\sigma_p^2 = w' \Sigma w = \lambda_1^2 (\overline{R} - R_f \iota)' \Sigma^{-1} \Sigma \Sigma^{-1} (\overline{R} - R_f \iota) = \lambda_1^2 E. \qquad (2.64)$$

If we now substitute out the Lagrange multiplier, we find that $\sigma_p^2 = (\overline{R}_p - R_f)^2 / E$, or

$$| \overline{R}_p - R_f | = \sqrt{E} \sigma_p. \qquad (2.65)$$

This gives a V-shaped line on a plot of mean against standard deviation. The upper branch of the V is a tangency line from the riskless asset return on the vertical axis to the mean-variance efficient set obtainable if one can only hold the risky assets and not the riskless asset. This upper branch is also known as the Capital Allocation Line (CAL).

There is a unique portfolio that is on the CAL but that contains only risky assets, and therefore is also on the mean-variance efficient set that can be constructed from risky assets. This portfolio is known as the tangency portfolio. The slope of the CAL, $\sqrt{E}$, is the Sharpe ratio of the tangency portfolio. The tangency portfolio has the highest Sharpe ratio of any risky asset or portfolio of risky assets. Figure 2.5 illustrates this geometry.

In the presence of a riskless asset, Tobin's mutual fund theorem simplifies because one of the two mutual funds is the riskless asset and the other, the tangency portfolio, contains only risky assets. Then the mutual fund theorem says that all investors, regardless of their risk aversion, should hold risky assets in the same proportion. Conservative investors should dilute their risky asset portfolio by holding more of the riskless asset ("cash"), while aggressive investors may even borrow cash to increase their returns; but both groups should hold long positions in the risky portfolio and neither group should alter its composition.[8]

---

[8]In other words, all investors choose to be on the upper branch of the V in Figure 2.5 rather than the lower branch that is obtained by shorting the tangency portfolio. This explains why the upper branch rather than the lower branch of the V is tangent to the minimum-variance set obtainable from risky assets alone. If this were not the case, all investors would wish to short risky assets, which would be inconsistent with an equilibrium with a positive supply of risky assets.

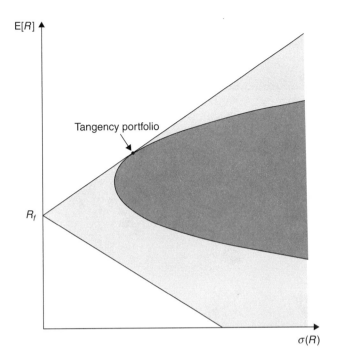

Figure 2.5.   *Investment Opportunity Set with and without a Riskless Asset*

This proposition contradicts conventional investment advice, a point emphasized by Canner, Mankiw, and Weil (CMW 1997) who call it the "asset allocation puzzle." Table 2.1, taken from CMW, illustrates the puzzle.

The table reports the portfolio allocations recommended by four financial advisors to hypothetical "conservative" investors with high risk aversion, "moderate" investors with intermediate risk aversion, and "aggressive" investors with low risk aversion. Three assets are included in the analysis: cash, bonds, and stocks. If we interpret cash (equivalently, money market mutual funds or Treasury bills) as a safe asset, and bonds and stocks as two alternative risky assets, then the mutual fund theorem implies that the ratio of bonds to stocks should be constant across recommended portfolios, while the ratio of cash to the sum of bonds and stocks should move in the same direction as risk aversion. The far-right column of the table shows that, instead, the ratio of bonds to stocks moves with risk aversion: highest for conservative investors and lowest for aggressive investors.

CMW explore various possible solutions to this puzzle. For example, they consider the effect of treating cash as a risky asset, since short-term fixed-income securities promise safe nominal returns but offer real returns that are exposed to short-term inflation shocks. They find, however, that over a short period like a quarter, the effect of inflation shocks is negligible and does not generate important variation in the bond-stock ratio.

Another possibility is that investors may not be able to borrow to fund risky asset portfolios. Once a borrowing constraint binds, an investor who wishes to increase risk must do so by altering the composition of the risky portfolio toward risky assets (presumably stocks). As an informal exercise, you are asked to evaluate the assumptions that would be needed to justify any of the financial advisors' recommendations along these lines.

Table 2.1.   *Asset Allocations Recommended by Financial Advisors, from Canner, Mankiw, and Weil (1997)*

Advisor and investor type	Percent of portfolio			Ratio of bonds to stocks
	Cash	Bonds	Stocks	
A. Fidelity				
Conservative	50	30	20	1.50
Moderate	20	40	40	1.00
Aggressive	5	30	65	0.46
B. Merrill Lynch				
Conservative	20	35	45	0.78
Moderate	5	40	55	0.73
Aggressive	5	20	75	0.27
C. Jane Bryant Quinn				
Conservative	50	30	20	1.50
Moderate	10	40	50	0.80
Aggressive	0	0	100	0.00
D. *The New York Times*				
Conservative	20	40	40	1.00
Moderate	10	30	60	0.50
Aggressive	0	20	80	0.25

Finally, it may be that the financial advisors are recommending portfolios that would be optimal for long-term investors but not for the two-period short-term investors who have been discussed in this chapter. Long-term bonds are risky assets for a short-term investor but may be almost riskless for a long-term investor, while cash is safe for a short-term investor but must be rolled over at uncertain future interest rates and hence may be risky for a long-term investor. We discuss this resolution of the asset allocation puzzle in Chapter 9.

2.2.7 Practical Difficulties

We finish this chapter with a cautionary note on the application of mean-variance analysis. We have presented formulas for optimal portfolio choice that take as given the vector of means of all asset returns, and the variance-covariance matrix of those returns. Modern implementations of this analysis use mean-variance optimization software to find optimal portfolios numerically, taking into account additional constraints such as short-sales constraints or limits on the maximum positions in individual assets. However, both the formulas in this chapter and mean-variance optimizers rely on estimates of the means and variance-covariance matrix of returns. This creates numerous difficulties.

Estimates of means are imprecise over short periods, but means may not be constant over long periods of time. This is of particular concern when the assets under analysis are individual stocks, whose equilibrium returns (as determined by the nature of a company's business, the attitudes of investors to the risks of that business, and so forth) are likely to drift over time. Two standard approaches to deal with this problem are to estimate functions that map characteristics of assets to their returns—since the characteristics of companies are likely to be more stably related to expected returns than are the names of those companies—or, in a similar spirit, to form portfolios of stocks with similar characteristics and then estimate the historical average returns on these portfolios rather than on individual stocks.

Even if one has estimated mean returns, there remains the problem of estimating the variance-covariance matrix. With N assets, this matrix has $N(N + 1)/2$ parameters. So with 2,000 stocks, for example, over two million variances and covariances have to be estimated. The obvious approach of calculating the sample variance-covariance matrix in historical data breaks down if N is greater than or equal to T, the number of return observations in the historical sample. In this case the sample variance-covariance matrix is always singular because some combination of $N \geq T$ assets can be found that delivers the same return in each of T historical periods. A mean-variance optimizer working with such a matrix will perceive an arbitrage opportunity (to be discussed in Chapter 4) if the mean return on the riskless combination of risky assets differs from the return on the safe asset or if there are multiple riskless combinations of risky assets with different mean returns.

There is abundant evidence that variances and covariances change over time, and this, together with the short history of some assets of interest, limits the potential to estimate second moments using a long historical sample. An alternative approach, which has been explored intensively by financial econometricians over the past 15 years, is to increase the number of historical observations by measuring returns at high frequency.

Even with large T, however, the data often spuriously suggest that some combinations of N risky assets are almost riskless. This can lead a mean-variance optimizer to pick a highly leveraged portfolio that performs poorly out of sample. DeMiguel, Garlappi, and Uppal (2009) compare the out-of-sample performance of mean-variance optimal portfolios estimated from historical data using several alternative methods, and find that in many circumstances, an equal-weighted portfolio (a naively diversified portfolio) has better performance than an estimated mean-variance optimal portfolio out of sample. Discouragingly, even portfolio construction methods that are intended to reduce reliance on historical variances and covariances, by imposing priors on the variance-covariance matrix, perform relatively poorly.[9]

In response to these difficulties, a large literature has sought to simplify the portfolio choice problem. The next chapter explores this literature.

2.3 Solutions and Further Problems

In the chapter, we posed the informal problem of how we know that with N risky assets and no riskless asset, the variance-covariance matrix is invertible so that Σ^{-1} exists. The answer is that if this were not the case, if Σ were singular, then the risky assets could be combined to create a riskless asset, contrary to the assumption that no riskless asset exists. The singularity of Σ is the multiasset equivalent of perfect correlation between two assets.

---

[9]Recent responses to this article include Kritzman, Page, and Turkington (2010), who argue that the use of longer historical samples helps mean-variance analysis, and Kirby and Ostdiek (2012), who point out that the DeMiguel, Garlappi, and Uppal procedure often leads a mean-variance optimizer to pick an extremely high expected return. When the expected return is fixed exogenously at reasonable levels, mean-variance optimization delivers better results. See also Jorion (1986) and Ledoit and Wolf (2003) on shrinkage methods for covariance matrix estimation.

We also asked whether the asset allocation puzzle of Canner, Mankiw, and Weil (1997) illustrated in Figure 2.1, can be resolved by the presence of binding borrowing constraints on the investors who are being advised. An obvious objection to this solution is that borrowing binding constraints imply zero cash holdings. While two of the financial advisors in Figure 2.1 (Jane Bryant Quinn and *The New York Times*) recommend zero cash for aggressive investors, none of them recommend zero cash for conservative or moderate investors. The observed variation in the bond-stock ratio between conservative and moderate investors therefore remains a puzzle. However, Merrill Lynch recommends a 5% cash allocation for both moderate and aggressive investors. If this is interpreted as a liquidity reserve, to be held for reasons not captured by mean-variance analysis, then Merrill Lynch's portfolios could be interpreted as borrowing-constrained for both moderate and aggressive investors, in which case their recommended bond-stock ratios might be consistent with mean-variance analysis.

Problem 2.1 Kelly Rule

In racetrack betting, a \$1 bet placed at odds of 5:1 pays \$6 if you win, and \$0 if you lose. The odds ratio in this example is 5. A gambler who believes that he has inside information has an "edge" equal to the expected profit per \$1 bet. For example, if the gambler believes the 5:1 bet will pay off with probability 1/2, the expected payout on a \$1 bet is \$3, the expected profit is \$2, and the edge is 2.

The "Kelly rule" is a famous formula that tells gamblers what fraction of their money to bet on each race. The formula is

$$k = \frac{\text{edge}}{\text{odds}},\tag{2.66}$$

or 2/5 in the example above.

(a) Is it possible for a gambler using the Kelly rule to go bankrupt? Explain.

(b) Find a utility function for which the Kelly rule is an optimal gambling strategy. (Do not use any formula that assumes small risks, as the Kelly rule may involve large gambles, or that assumes a normal or lognormal distribution for the risk, as the racetrack bet has a discrete distribution.)

(c) Show that if the gambler has no edge—that is, if the bet is fair—the odds ratio equals the variance of the payoff to a \$1 bet.

(d) Relate your analysis to the formulas for optimal portfolio choice developed in this chapter.

(e) It has sometimes been argued that the Kelly rule is optimal for all gamblers. Do you agree?

Problem 2.2 Welfare Analysis with Power Utility

Consider an investor who chooses a portfolio to maximize his expected utility of wealth next period, where the utility function is power (CRRA) with coefficient of relative risk aversion γ. Assume that there are two assets, a riskless asset with log return r_f and a risky asset with log return r. Assume that the log risky return is normal with variance σ^2 and that the optimal portfolio places a weight α on the risky asset. Use the approximation to the log portfolio return (2.24) to analyze this model. Also use the formulation of the Sharpe ratio in terms of moments of log returns, as discussed in section 2.1.4. That is, write the Sharpe ratio as $S = (\mathrm{E}[r] - r_f + \sigma^2/2)/\sigma$.

(a) Derive an expression for the value function (the investor's maximized utility) as a function of initial wealth, the riskless interest rate, the coefficient of relative risk aversion, and the Sharpe ratio of the risky asset.

(b) Suppose that the time period is one year. The log riskless interest rate is 2%, the log of the expected simple return on the risky asset is 10%, and the standard deviation of the log risky asset return is 40%. The investor initially chooses to hold 25% of his portfolio in the risky asset. What must his risk aversion be?

(c) Now suppose that the standard deviation of the log risky asset return declines to 20%, but the riskless interest rate and the expected simple return on the risky asset do not change. (This could result from improved diversification of underlying idiosyncratic risky opportunities that are packaged into a single fund that is marketed to the investor.) If the investor's portfolio weight in the risky asset does not change, show that the effect on the value function is equivalent to an increase in the riskless interest rate of a percentage points. What is a? If the investor adjusts his portfolio weight in the risky asset to its new optimal level, show that the effect on the value function is equivalent to an increase in the riskless interest rate of b percentage points. What is b? Is b larger or smaller than a? Explain.

(d) When risky assets become safer (because of improved diversification or for other reasons), do conservative (relatively risk-averse) or aggressive (relatively risk-tolerant) investors gain the most? How does your answer depend on the ability of investors to adjust their holdings of risky assets? Explain.

Problem 2.3 Geometry of the Minimum-Variance Frontier

Consider a set of N risky assets and, for parts (a)–(c), no riskless asset.

(a) Prove that for any minimum-variance portfolio p, except the global minimum-variance portfolio, the expected return on a minimum-variance portfolio z that is uncorrelated with p can be found as follows. On a mean-standard deviation diagram, draw a tangency line to the minimum-variance frontier at the point p. The point where this tangency line reaches the vertical axis of the diagram gives the expected return on the zero-beta portfolio z. (This expected return is known as the zero-beta rate for portfolio p.) This construction is illustrated in the left panel of Figure 2.6.

(b) Prove that every portfolio has the same covariance with the global minimum-variance portfolio. Give the economic intuition for this result. Explain why this is consistent with the exclusion of the global minimum-variance portfolio in part (a).

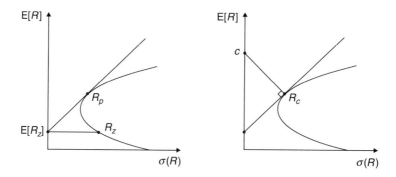

Figure 2.6. *Geometry of the Minimum-Variance Frontier*

(c) Consider a linear regression of a constant $c \in \mathbb{R}$ on the N risky returns that is restricted so that the regression coefficients sum to one:[10]

$$c = R'w_c + \varepsilon \qquad \text{s.t. } \iota'w_c = 1. \qquad (2.67)$$

Show that w_c corresponds to the weights of the minimum-variance portfolio R^c depicted in the right panel of Figure 2.6. That is, R^c is the portfolio whose depiction in a mean-standard deviation graph is closest to point $(0, c)$. It follows that as one varies the constant c in equation (2.67) the regression weights trace out the portfolios in the minimum-variance frontier. Interpret this result intuitively.

(d) Now suppose that there exists a riskfree asset in addition to the N risky assets. Argue graphically that the weights of the tangency portfolio can be obtained as $w_c/\iota'w_c$, where w_c is the vector of coefficients in an (unrestricted) linear regression of an arbitrary nonzero constant c on the N excess risky asset returns, $c = (R - R_f\iota)'w_c + \varepsilon$.

[10]That is, $w_c = \text{argmin}_{w\in\mathbb{R}^N:\iota'w=1} E[(c - R'w)^2]$. Note that the regression has no intercept so $E[\varepsilon]$ need not equal zero. In a finite sample with T observations, w_c can be estimated via the restricted least squares regression $c\iota_T = Xw_c + u$ with the linear restriction $\iota'_N w_c = 1$, where $X = [R'_1, \ldots, R'_T]'$.

Static Equilibrium Asset Pricing

THE PRACTICAL DIFFICULTIES with mean-variance analysis, summarized at the end of the previous chapter, have motivated a search for shortcut methods to find optimal portfolios. One classic approach is to use an equilibrium argument to identify the mean-variance efficient portfolio of risky assets. This is the Capital Asset Pricing Model, or CAPM. An alternative approach is to assume a factor structure in the variance-covariance matrix of risky returns, effectively reducing the dimension of the portfolio choice problem from N to K, where K is the number of factors. This is the Arbitrage Pricing Theory, or APT.

Both these theories have many other uses besides portfolio choice. They impose testable restrictions on asset returns and lie at the heart of the field of asset pricing, motivating and structuring much of the research discussed later in this book. They also have implications for capital budgeting (the choice of a discount rate to use in evaluating investment projects) and performance evaluation for active asset managers, topics that are outside the scope of the book.

Section 3.1 derives the CAPM and discusses its implications for asset pricing and portfolio choice. Section 3.2 introduces multifactor models. Section 3.3 covers econometric issues that arise in testing these models, summarizes some of the basic evidence, and reviews alternative responses to this evidence.

3.1 The Capital Asset Pricing Model (CAPM)

The classic derivation of the CAPM makes assumptions needed to ensure that all investors perceive the same investment opportunity set, illustrated in Figure 2.5, and pick a mean-variance efficient portfolio from that set. Specifically, the model assumes that all investors are price-takers who evaluate portfolios using the means and variances of single-period returns; that investors have common beliefs about the means, variances, and covariances of returns; that there are no nontraded assets, taxes, or transactions costs; and, in the basic version of the model due to Sharpe (1964) and Lintner (1965), that investors can borrow or lend at a given riskfree interest rate.

Under these assumptions, all investors hold a mean-variance efficient portfolio and agree on which portfolios are mean-variance efficient. But with a riskless asset, the mutual fund theorem implies that all mean-variance efficient portfolios combine the riskless asset with a fixed portfolio of risky assets, the tangency portfolio. Hence, all investors hold risky assets in the same proportions to one another.

In equilibrium, the demand for assets must equal the supply of assets. This requires that the portfolio weights of the mean-variance efficient risky portfolio are those of the *market portfolio* or *value-weighted index* that contains all risky assets in proportion to their market value. Thus, *the market portfolio is mean-variance efficient.*

The implication for portfolio choice is that as long as a mean-variance investor accepts the assessments of other investors about the joint distribution of returns, he need not actually perform mean-variance analysis. The investor can "free-ride" on the analyses of other investors reflected in asset prices and use the market portfolio (in practice, a broad index fund) as the optimal mutual fund of risky assets. The optimal capital allocation line (CAL) is just the *capital market line (CML)* connecting the riskfree asset to the market portfolio.

What if we relax the assumption that investors can borrow and lend at a given riskless interest rate? Given the other assumptions of the CAPM, it remains true that all investors choose combinations of two mutual funds. The market portfolio must be a combination of these mutual funds and must therefore still be mean-variance efficient.

The statement that the market portfolio is mean-variance efficient is the defining content of the CAPM. The brief verbal derivation above shows that this statement requires no formal analysis beyond that of the previous chapter. However, it has implications for asset returns that do require further work to obtain.

3.1.1 Asset Pricing Implications of the Sharpe-Lintner CAPM

The mean-variance efficiency of a portfolio implies that mean returns on individual assets must be related in a particular way to the covariances of individual asset returns with that portfolio.

An increase in the weight of asset i in portfolio p, w_i, financed by a decrease in the weight on the riskless asset, affects the mean and variance of the return on portfolio p as follows:

$$\frac{d\overline{R}_p}{dw_i} = \overline{R}_i - R_f, \tag{3.1}$$

$$\frac{d\text{Var}(R_p)}{dw_i} = 2\text{Cov}(R_i, R_p). \tag{3.2}$$

To understand equation (3.2), write out the individual-asset variances and covariances in $\text{Var}(R_p)$ and note that the terms involving w_i are

$$2w_i w_1 \text{Cov}(R_i, R_1) + \cdots + w_i^2 \text{Var}(R_i) + \cdots + 2w_i w_N \text{Cov}(R_i, R_N),$$

and so the derivative

$$\frac{d\text{Var}(R_p)}{dw_i} = 2w_1 \text{Cov}(R_i, R_1) + \cdots + 2w_i \text{Var}(R_i)$$

$$+ \cdots + 2w_N \text{Cov}(R_i, R_N) = 2\text{Cov}(R_i, R_p). \tag{3.3}$$

The ratio of the effect on mean, (3.1), to the effect on variance, (3.2), is

$$\frac{d\overline{R}_p / dw_i}{d\text{Var}(R_p) / dw_i} = \frac{\overline{R}_i - R_f}{2\text{Cov}(R_i, R_p)}. \tag{3.4}$$

If portfolio p is mean-variance efficient, this ratio should be the same for all individual assets i. To see why, consider adjusting two different portfolio weights, w_i and w_j, financing each adjustment using the riskless asset as before. The effects on the mean and variance of R_p are

$$d\overline{R}_p = (\overline{R}_i - R_f)\, dw_i + (\overline{R}_j - R_f)\, dw_j, \tag{3.5}$$

and

$$d\mathrm{Var}(R_p) = 2\mathrm{Cov}(R_i, R_p)\, dw_i + 2\mathrm{Cov}(R_j, R_p)\, dw_j. \tag{3.6}$$

Now consider setting dw_j so that the mean portfolio return is unchanged, $d\overline{R}_p = 0$:

$$dw_j = -\frac{(\overline{R}_i - R_f)}{(\overline{R}_j - R_f)}\, dw_i. \tag{3.7}$$

Then the portfolio variance must also be unchanged, because otherwise one could achieve a lower variance with the same mean, which would contradict the assumption that portfolio p is mean-variance efficient. We have

$$d\mathrm{Var}(R_p) = \left[2\mathrm{Cov}(R_i, R_p) - 2\mathrm{Cov}(R_j, R_p)\frac{(\overline{R}_i - R_f)}{(\overline{R}_j - R_f)} \right] dw_i = 0. \tag{3.8}$$

This requires

$$\frac{\overline{R}_i - R_f}{2\mathrm{Cov}(R_i, R_p)} = \frac{\overline{R}_j - R_f}{2\mathrm{Cov}(R_j, R_p)}. \tag{3.9}$$

This equation must hold for all assets j, including the original portfolio itself. Setting $j = p$, we get

$$\frac{\overline{R}_i - R_f}{2\mathrm{Cov}(R_i, R_p)} = \frac{\overline{R}_p - R_f}{2\mathrm{Var}(R_p)}, \tag{3.10}$$

or

$$\overline{R}_i - R_f = \frac{\mathrm{Cov}(R_i, R_p)}{\mathrm{Var}(R_p)}(\overline{R}_p - R_f) = \beta_{ip}(\overline{R}_p - R_f), \tag{3.11}$$

where $\beta_{ip} \equiv \mathrm{Cov}(R_i, R_p)/\mathrm{Var}(R_p)$ is the regression coefficient of asset i's return on portfolio p's return.

Equation (3.11) holds by construction for a mean-variance efficient portfolio p. In order to get a testable model with economic content, we impose the restriction of the CAPM that the market portfolio m is mean-variance efficient. Under this restriction (3.11) describes the market portfolio:

$$\overline{R}_i - R_f = \beta_{im}(\overline{R}_m - R_f), \tag{3.12}$$

where $\beta_{im} \equiv \mathrm{Cov}(R_i, R_m)/\mathrm{Var}(R_m)$ is the regression coefficient of asset i's return on the market portfolio m's return.[1]

Thus, if we consider the regression of excess returns on the market excess return,

$$R_{it} - R_{ft} = \alpha_i + \beta_{im}(R_{mt} - R_{ft}) + \epsilon_{it}, \tag{3.13}$$

the intercept $\alpha_i = \overline{R}_i - R_f - \beta_{im}(\overline{R}_m - R_f)$ should be zero for all assets. α_i is called *Jensen's alpha* and is used to try to find assets that are mispriced relative to the CAPM. The relationship

$$\overline{R}_i = R_f + \beta_{im}(\overline{R}_m - R_f) \tag{3.14}$$

is called the *security market line (SML)*, and α_i measures deviations from this line.

To simplify notation, in what follows we will often write the excess return on an asset over the riskless interest rate, $R_{it} - R_{ft}$, as R_{it}^e, and similarly for the market we will write $R_{mt} - R_{ft}$ as R_{mt}^e. The security market line then can be written more compactly as

$$\overline{R}_i^e = \beta_{im}\overline{R}_m^e. \tag{3.15}$$

3.1.2 The Black CAPM

What if we relax the assumption that investors can borrow at the riskfree interest rate? Then, more conservative investors may choose to combine the tangency portfolio with cash as in the basic Sharpe-Lintner model. They hold portfolios on the portion of the capital market line connecting the riskfree interest rate with the tangency portfolio. More aggressive investors might like to borrow at the riskfree rate, in order to move further up the capital market line beyond the tangency portfolio. If they are prevented from doing so by borrowing constraints, they will choose to hold different risky portfolios with higher expected returns. All these portfolios, however, will still be mean-variance efficient, and so Tobin's mutual fund theorem (with two risky mutual funds) still describes the set of risky portfolios chosen by all investors.

It follows that the market portfolio must be a combination of these mutual funds and must lie on the mean-variance frontier of risky assets. Since all investors hold either the tangency portfolio or a riskier portfolio with a higher expected return, the market portfolio lies on the portion of the mean-variance frontier above the tangency portfolio, where the slope of the frontier is smaller.

Our analysis of the covariance properties goes through as before, except that we replace the riskless interest rate R_f with the zero-beta rate for the market portfolio, that is, the expected return $\overline{R}_z$ on the mean-variance efficient portfolio z that is uncorrelated with the market portfolio. Black (1972) showed that we have

$$\overline{R}_i - \overline{R}_z = \beta_{im}(\overline{R}_m - \overline{R}_z). \tag{3.16}$$

Here $\overline{R}_z$ can be interpreted as the shadow cost of borrowing for the representative investor. It must exceed R_f, and this is guaranteed by the fact that the market portfolio lies on the portion of the mean-variance frontier above the tangency portfolio.

---

[1] β_{im} can also be interpreted as the weight on the market portfolio of the combination of the market portfolio and the riskless asset that most closely replicates the return on asset i.

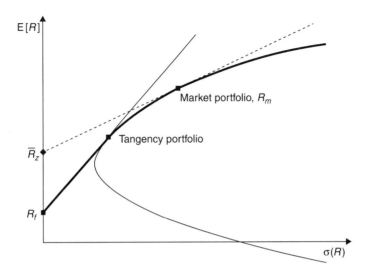

Figure 3.1. *The Black (1972) CAPM*

The geometry of the Black CAPM is illustrated in Figure 3.1. A line tangent to the efficient frontier of all risky assets that passes through the point corresponding to the market portfolio intersects the vertical axis at a point corresponding to the mean return on the zero-beta portfolio $\overline{R}_z$. The zero-beta portfolio itself can be found by drawing a horizontal line from this point to the efficient frontier, as in Problem 2.3 and the left panel of Figure 2.6.

3.1.3 Beta Pricing and Portfolio Choice

The beta pricing relations with or without a riskless asset, equation (3.11) or (3.16), can be used to evaluate the mean-variance efficiency of any portfolio, not just the market portfolio. This makes beta analysis a useful tool in portfolio construction.

As an informative example, consider the Harvard endowment. Each year the Harvard Management Company (HMC), which invests the endowment on behalf of the university, creates a "policy portfolio" with weights in about a dozen different asset classes. The policy portfolio weights do not pin down the actual weights in the endowment, but they serve as a guide. Figure 3.2 shows the history of weights over the two decades from 1991 through 2011. To reduce clutter in the figure, the asset classes have been aggregated into three broad categories: "plain vanilla" asset classes (US publicly traded stocks and bonds), international public stocks and bonds (including in emerging markets), and "exotic" asset classes (all others, including private equity, real estate, commodities, and absolute return strategies). It is immediately apparent from the figure that during this period HMC greatly reduced the weights in plain vanilla asset classes and expanded the allocations to exotic asset classes.

What beliefs about the world would justify such a change in portfolio allocation? To answer this question, Figures 3.3 and 3.4 summarize a mean-variance analysis that HMC periodically conducts. As part of this analysis, HMC writes down a mean return

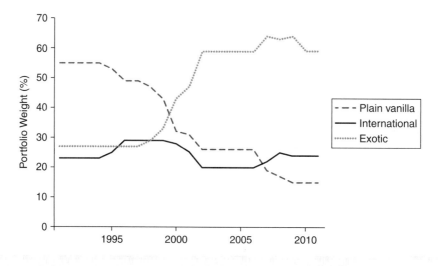

Figure 3.2.   *History of Harvard Policy Portfolio Weights*

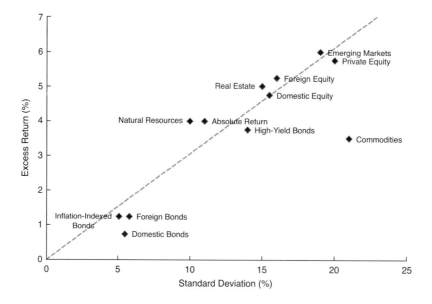

Figure 3.3.   *Harvard Investment Beliefs: Mean and Standard Deviation*

vector and variance-covariance matrix for the asset classes in the policy portfolio. These
numbers are determined subjectively on the basis not only of historical data, but also of
forward-looking forecasts by investment consultants and HMC's own staff. The figures
are based on numbers from 2004, during the extended period of portfolio reallocation
toward exotic asset classes.

Figure 3.3 is a mean-standard deviation diagram, with the assumed standard deviation
on the horizontal axis and mean excess return over cash on the vertical. The slope of a

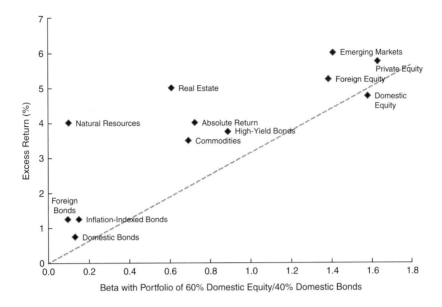

Figure 3.4. *Harvard Investment Beliefs: Mean and Beta*

line from the origin to each asset class is the assumed Sharpe ratio of that asset class. The solid line is drawn through the domestic stock market, so any point lying above that line corresponds to an asset class with a higher Sharpe ratio than the US stock market.

While a few asset classes, such as natural resources, have attractively high Sharpe ratios, many of the exotic asset classes have Sharpe ratios little better than US stocks or even lower in the case of commodities. This diagram does not make it easy to see why HMC would reallocate the portfolio so strongly away from public equities.

The difficulty with Figure 3.3 is that it tells one how attractive an asset class is on a stand-alone basis, but does not provide guidance for mixing asset classes into a portfolio with a high Sharpe ratio. To correct this, Figure 3.4 summarizes HMC's investment beliefs in a different way. Now the horizontal axis is the beta of each asset class with an assumed plain-vanilla initial portfolio that is invested 60% in domestic equities and 40% in domestic bonds. The solid line is drawn through the plain-vanilla portfolio. The distance of each asset class from the solid line is the alpha of the asset class with respect to the plain-vanilla portfolio. Whenever an asset class has a positive alpha, one can improve the portfolio (either increasing the mean with constant variance or reducing the variance with constant mean) by slightly increasing the portfolio weight in the asset class.

In Figure 3.4 all the exotic asset classes (indeed, all asset classes except domestic equity) have positive alphas. Thus the figure explains why an investor with an initially plain-vanilla portfolio would start to shift the portfolio into exotic asset classes. As the portfolio changes its weights, of course, the benchmark must be altered to current weights in order to decide whether to continue the process. As an informal exercise to test your understanding, explain how the figure will change as the benchmark is altered in this way. The answer to this is given at the end of the chapter. Problems 3.1 and 3.2 further explore portfolio implications of the CAPM and the incremental approach to portfolio construction following Treynor and Black (1973).

3.1.4 The Black-Litterman Model

Black and Litterman (1992) use the CAPM in a different way to assist portfolio construction in the context of asset allocation. Their starting point is the observation that
mean-variance analysis often produces unreasonable portfolios, with extreme long and
short positions, even when the inputs seem reasonable and the problem includes only a
relatively small number of asset classes that together make up the world market portfolio. (They consider an example with seven developed-country stock and bond markets,
including the US, together with six non-US currencies.)

To generate more reasonable results, Black and Litterman suggest the following
approach. If the market consists of N risky assets and a riskless asset is also available,
the N-element column vector of expected excess returns implied by the CAPM, $\overline{R}^e_{CAPM}$, is
written as

$$\overline{R}^e_{CAPM} = \delta \Sigma w_m, \tag{3.17}$$

where w_m is the column vector of asset class shares in the market portfolio which sum
to one, Σ is the $N \times N$ variance-covariance matrix of the excess returns on the asset
classes, and δ is a scale factor reflecting the average risk aversion of investors. This equation follows from inverting equation (2.61) in the previous chapter, imposing the CAPM
restriction that the market portfolio is mean-variance efficient, and using the notation
R^e to denote an excess return over the riskless asset. The i'th row of (3.17) says that
the expected excess return on asset i is proportional to its covariance with the market
portfolio.

Black and Litterman assume that the investor has views about returns that may differ
from those embodied in equation (3.17). These views can be written as a set of K linear
restrictions on the vector of expected excess returns $\overline{R}^e$, which are here interpreted as
the investor's subjective expectations:

$$P'\overline{R}^e = Q, \tag{3.18}$$

where P is an $N \times K$ matrix and Q is a K-element column vector. The investor wishes
to reflect these views in a fashion that deviates as little as possible from the CAPM.
Accordingly, the investor's expected returns minimize squared deviations from the
CAPM-implied expected excess returns π, weighted by the inverse of the covariance
matrix Σ (a natural measure of uncertainty about mean returns), while satisfying the
constraint (3.18). In other words, the investor's expected returns $\overline{R}^e$ solve the problem

$$\min \frac{1}{2}(\overline{R}^e - \overline{R}^e_{CAPM})' \Sigma^{-1} (\overline{R}^e - \overline{R}^e_{CAPM}) \quad \text{s.t.} \quad P'\overline{R}^e = Q. \tag{3.19}$$

Setting up the Lagrangian and solving this minimization problem, the solution can
be written as

$$\overline{R}^e = \overline{R}^e_{CAPM} + \Sigma P (P' \Sigma P)^{-1} (Q - P'\overline{R}^e_{CAPM}). \tag{3.20}$$

The investor's expected returns $\overline{R}^e$ will equal $\overline{R}^e_{CAPM}$ only if $(Q - P'\overline{R}^e_{CAPM})$ is a zero vector,
that is, if the investor's views happen to be consistent with the CAPM.

Conditional on these expected returns, the investor's vector of portfolio weights in
risky assets is

$$w = \theta \Sigma^{-1} \overline{R}^e = \theta \left[\delta w_m + P (P' \Sigma P)^{-1} (Q - P'\overline{R}^e_{CAPM}) \right], \tag{3.21}$$

where θ is a scale factor that depends on the investor's risk aversion. The weights in w need not sum to one because cash is a residual asset. If the investor's views are consistent with the CAPM, that is, if $(Q - P'\overline{R}^e_{CAPM}) = 0$, the investor holds the market portfolio of risky assets when $\theta\delta = 1$; when $\theta\delta < 1$, the investor is more conservative and combines the risky market portfolio with cash, and when $\theta\delta > 1$ the investor borrows cash to take a levered position in the market portfolio.

In general the investor's views in (3.20) cause his portfolio weights to deviate from these scaled market weights, but only for assets with nonzero elements in at least one row of the matrix P, that is, only for assets about which the investor has a view. This property holds for weights because it does not generally hold for expected returns: (3.20) adjusts the expected returns on all assets using the information in the variance-covariance matrix of returns, so even those assets for which no view is directly expressed will have their expected returns adjusted by the Black-Litterman method.

Black and Litterman generalize the above approach in a Bayesian spirit by assuming that the investor is willing to allow deviations from the constraints in (3.18), in other words, that the investor has less than perfect confidence in his views. Their general solution penalizes both deviations from the CAPM-implied risk premium vector $\overline{R}^e_{CAPM}$ and deviations from the investor's views (3.18), scaling the former by the empirically observed variance-covariance matrix Σ times a constant, and the latter by an assumed variance-covariance matrix Ω that embodies the investor's uncertainty about the restrictions in (3.18). The Black-Litterman approach has been popular among quantitatively oriented investment practitioners because it is a structured approach to asset allocation that allows investment views to affect portfolios while controlling the deviations of asset class weights from those of a broadly diversified market portfolio.

3.2 Arbitrage Pricing and Multifactor Models

In this section we present an alternative way to derive a beta pricing relationship like that of the CAPM, using asymptotic no-arbitrage arguments. This alternative approach generalizes straightforwardly to derive models with multiple risk factors.

3.2.1 Arbitrage Pricing in a Single-Factor Model

Suppose that we run the regression

$$R^e_{it} = \alpha_i + \beta_{im}R^e_{mt} + \epsilon_{it}, \tag{3.22}$$

where as before R^e_{it} denotes the excess return on asset i over the riskless interest rate. This relationship is called the *market model*. It is the leading example of a *single-factor model* with a single common factor moving stock returns.

Suppose further that the errors in this equation are uncorrelated across stocks:

$$\mathrm{E}[\epsilon_{it}\epsilon_{jt}] = 0 \tag{3.23}$$

for $i \neq j$. Then the residual risk in any stock is *idiosyncratic*, unrelated to the residual risk in any other stock.

These assumptions imply that covariances are easy to estimate for mean-variance analysis because

$$\text{Cov}(R_{it}^e, R_{jt}^e) = \beta_{im}\beta_{jm}\sigma_m^2. \tag{3.24}$$

Instead of $N(N+1)/2$ parameters in an unrestricted variance-covariance matrix, only $N+1$ parameters (N betas plus the variance of the market return) need to be estimated.

An even more striking implication of these assumptions is that if many assets are available, we should expect α_i typically to be very small in absolute value. This is the *arbitrage pricing theory* of Ross (1976).

To understand why this is the case, consider forming a portfolio of N assets i. The excess return on the portfolio will be

$$R_{pt}^e = \alpha_p + \beta_{pm}R_{mt}^e + \epsilon_{pt}, \tag{3.25}$$

where $\alpha_p = \sum_{j=1}^N w_j\alpha_j$, $\beta_{pm} = \sum_{j=1}^N w_j\beta_{jm}$, and $\epsilon_{pt} = \sum_{j=1}^N w_j\epsilon_{jt}$.

The variance of ϵ_{pt} will be

$$\text{Var}(\epsilon_{pt}) = \sum_{j=1}^N w_j^2\text{Var}(\epsilon_{jt}), \tag{3.26}$$

which will shrink rapidly with N provided that no single weight w_j is too large. In the benchmark case where the portfolio is equally weighted ($w_j = 1/N$) and all the stocks have the same idiosyncratic variance ($\text{Var}(\epsilon_{jt}) = \sigma^2$), we get

$$\text{Var}(\epsilon_{pt}) = \frac{\sigma^2}{N}. \tag{3.27}$$

Now suppose that the portfolio has enough stocks, with a small enough weight in each one, that the residual risk $\text{Var}(\epsilon_{pt})$ is negligible. We say that the portfolio is *well diversified*. For such a portfolio, we can neglect ϵ_{pt} and write the excess return as

$$R_{pt}^e = \alpha_p + \beta_{pm}R_{mt}^e. \tag{3.28}$$

But then we must have $\alpha_p = 0$. If not, there is an arbitrage opportunity: go short β_{pm} units of the market and go long one unit of portfolio p, while funding all positions with riskless borrowing and lending. This delivers a riskless excess return of α_p.

Ross (1976) exploits this insight, showing that $\alpha_p = 0$ for all well-diversified portfolios implies that "almost all" individual assets have α_i very close to zero. Intuitively, a few assets can be mispriced (have nonzero α_i), but if too many assets are mispriced then one can group them into a well-diversified portfolio and create an arbitrage opportunity. Technically, the result is that if idiosyncratic variances of individual assets are bounded above, then

$$\lim_{N\to\infty} \frac{1}{N}\sum_{i=1}^N \alpha_i^2 = 0. \tag{3.29}$$

To derive this result, consider forming an alpha-weighted portfolio by making dollar investments of

$$\frac{\alpha_i}{\sqrt{N \sum_{i=1}^{N} \alpha_i^2}}$$

in each asset $i = 1 \ldots N$. The payoff on this portfolio is

$$\frac{\sum_{i=1}^{N} \alpha_i R_{it}}{\sqrt{N \sum_{i=1}^{N} \alpha_i^2}} = \frac{\sum_{i=1}^{N} \alpha_i (R_{ft} + \alpha_i + \beta_{im} R_{mt}^e + \epsilon_{it})}{\sqrt{N \sum_{i=1}^{N} \alpha_i^2}}. \qquad (3.30)$$

Now consider what happens to this payoff as the number of assets becomes large. We will make two additional assumptions: first, that

$$\lim_{N \to \infty} \frac{\sum_{i=1}^{N} \alpha_i}{\sqrt{N \sum_{i=1}^{N} \alpha_i^2}} = 0. \qquad (3.31)$$

In other words, that as the number of assets increases, the alpha-weighted portfolio approaches an *arbitrage portfolio* with equal values of long and short positions, whose total initial dollar investment is zero. The second additional assumption is that

$$\lim_{N \to \infty} \frac{\sum_{i=1}^{N} \alpha_i \beta_{im}}{\sqrt{N \sum_{i=1}^{N} \alpha_i^2}} = 0. \qquad (3.32)$$

In other words, that as the number of assets increases, the alpha-weighted portfolio has a zero beta with the market. Shortly we will show how to justify these additional assumptions.

Under these assumptions the limiting payoff on the alpha-weighted portfolio has only two components:

$$\lim_{N \to \infty} \frac{\sum_{i=1}^{N} \alpha_i R_{it}}{\sqrt{N \sum_{i=1}^{N} \alpha_i^2}} = \sqrt{\frac{\sum_{i=1}^{N} \alpha_i^2}{N}} + \frac{\sum_{i=1}^{N} \alpha_i \epsilon_{it}}{\sqrt{N \sum_{i=1}^{N} \alpha_i^2}}. \qquad (3.33)$$

The first term is the expected payoff, and the second is the component of the payoff driven by idiosyncratic risk. The variance of the payoff is

$$\frac{\mathrm{Var}(\sum_{i=1}^{N} \alpha_i \epsilon_{it})}{N \sum_{i=1}^{N} \alpha_i^2} = \frac{\sum_{i=1}^{N} \alpha_i^2 \sigma_i^2}{N \sum_{i=1}^{N} \alpha_i^2}. \qquad (3.34)$$

If the idiosyncratic variances σ_i^2 are bounded above, then the variance of the payoff shrinks to zero as $N \to \infty$, while the dollar cost of the portfolio also approaches zero. To avoid an *asymptotic arbitrage opportunity* (an investment strategy that asymptotically in a large cross-section delivers a guaranteed positive payoff at zero cost), the expected payoff must approach zero, which implies that its square must approach zero. This is the desired result (3.29).

How can we justify the two additional assumptions (3.31) and (3.32) that were used to prove this result? Equation (3.31) follows from a parallel analysis of an equal-weighted portfolio that makes an equal dollar investment of

$$\frac{1}{\sqrt{N \sum_{i=1}^{N} \alpha_i^2}}$$

in each asset. Equation (3.32) follows from a parallel analysis of a beta-weighted portfolio that invests

$$\frac{(\beta_{im} - \overline{\beta}_{im})}{\sqrt{N \sum_{i=1}^{N} \alpha_i^2}}$$

in each asset. Each of these portfolios has a nonzero market beta, but the variance of the idiosyncratic component of each portfolio's excess return shrinks to zero as $N \rightarrow \infty$, so each portfolio becomes well diversified in the limit and must have a zero limiting alpha as in the discussion of (3.28) above, implying that (3.31) and (3.32) hold in the limit of a large cross-section.

Intuitively, if all assets in a large cross-section have a positive alpha and uncorrelated residual risk, then one can make riskless profits by holding an equal-weighted portfolio of these assets and hedging the market risk exposure by an appropriate short position in the market. The opposite strategy delivers riskless profits if all assets in the cross-section have a negative alpha and uncorrelated residual risk. And if there is a systematic relation between alphas and betas in a large cross-section of assets with uncorrelated residual risk, say a negative relation, then one can make riskless profits by going long low-beta assets and short high-beta assets and using the market to hedge any residual market exposure.

In this section we have derived the beta pricing equation of the Sharpe-Lintner CAPM, without using any of the apparatus of mean-variance analysis. The key assumption is that residual risk from the market model is uncorrelated across stocks. An advantage of this approach is that the "market" in the model can be any broadly diversified portfolio that produces uncorrelated residual risk; we do not have to worry about measuring the true market portfolio of all wealth, as the CAPM requires. However, the result is weaker than the CAPM because we have only a limiting result that nonzero alphas are rare, not the exact result that all alphas are zero. Problem 3.3 asks you to derive an explicit formula for alphas in a specific equilibrium example.

It is straightforward to generalize the above analysis of a single-factor model to eliminate the assumption that investors can borrow and lend at the riskfree interest rate. Just as in the Black (1972) version of the CAPM, a single-factor arbitrage pricing theory can allow a zero-beta rate that measures the shadow cost of borrowing and exceeds the Treasury bill rate.

The major difficulty with the analysis so far is that the assumption of uncorrelated residual risk from the market model is counterfactual. There are many other sources of common variation in stock returns, besides the common influence of the market return. Some of these sources are macroeconomic. For example, cyclical stocks are particularly sensitive to changes in industrial production, and highly leveraged firms are sensitive to changes in interest rates. More generally, firms with similar businesses, such as firms in the same industry or firms with similar market capitalization, also tend to move together. For these reasons no single-factor model can adequately fit the cross-section of stock returns and deliver uncorrelated residual returns.

3.2.2 Multifactor Models

To handle this, we can generalize the previous analysis to a multifactor model. If there are K "factor portfolios" capturing the common influence of K underlying sources of risk, and if riskless borrowing and lending are possible at the rate R_f, then we have

$$R_{it}^e = \alpha_i + \sum_{k=1}^{K} \beta_{ik} R_{kt}^e + \epsilon_{it}. \tag{3.35}$$

We assume that the residual is uncorrelated across stocks. The prediction of the model is again equation (3.29), which can be described informally as the statement that $\alpha_i = 0$ for almost all stocks. This is restrictive if $K \ll N$.

In the absence of riskless borrowing, we can replace R_f in equation (3.35) with the zero-beta rate for the K-factor model, now defined as the expected return on a portfolio that is uncorrelated with all the factor portfolios. Once again the model implies (3.29).

Alternatively, if we do not have factor portfolios but measure the factors directly as mean-zero shocks (e.g., innovations to macroeconomic variables), then we have

$$R_{it} = \mu_i + \sum_{k=1}^{K} \beta_{ik} f_{kt} + \epsilon_{it}, \tag{3.36}$$

and the prediction of the model is that (3.29) holds for alphas defined by

$$\alpha_i = \mu_i - \lambda_0 - \sum_{k=1}^{K} \beta_{ik} \lambda_k, \tag{3.37}$$

where λ_0 is the zero-beta rate (equal to the riskfree interest rate R_f if investors can borrow and lend freely), and λ_k is the *price of risk* of the k'th factor.[2] This use of the letter λ for risk prices is standard in the literature and distinct from the use of the letter to denote Lagrange multipliers in Chapter 2.

The analysis of this section has important implications for portfolio choice. First, consider the case where there are K traded factor portfolios and the K-factor model holds exactly, that is, $\alpha_i = 0$ for all i. Then the full mean-variance-efficient frontier can be constructed from the K factor portfolios and the zero-beta portfolio (the riskless asset in the case where riskless borrowing and lending are possible), so a mean-variance investor should always hold some combination of these portfolios. The dimension of mean-variance analysis is greatly reduced.

---

[2]In the version of the model with traded portfolios as factors, (3.35), the risk prices are captured by the mean returns on the traded portfolios, which is why we do not see them explicitly. In the alternative version (3.36), the prices of risk are implicitly defined by a cross-sectional regression of average returns onto a constant and betas, equation (3.48) below. From the properties of regression, alphas must then be mean-zero and uncorrelated with betas, which are the two additional assumptions we made in our discussion of the single-factor model above. Ingersoll (1987, Chapter 7) uses this framework and carefully derives equation (3.37).

Second, if the factors are measured directly as in equation (3.36), then we can construct "factor-mimicking portfolios" that have the highest correlation with a given factor among traded portfolios, and again we can construct the mean-variance-efficient frontier using only factor-mimicking portfolios and the zero-beta portfolio.

Third, any stock-level characteristic that predicts returns must be associated with some common risk factor—if not, a portfolio of stocks with that characteristic would have a high average return but no common variability, implying an asymptotic arbitrage opportunity. This means that an active asset manager using mean-variance optimization should always model the variance-covariance matrix of returns in a way that allows the risk model to estimate the common variation associated with the stock characteristics that the manager believes to be return predictors (MacKinlay 1995, Campbell, Lo, and MacKinlay 1997, Chapter 6).

The generality of arbitrage pricing theory is appealing, but the approach has several weaknesses. First, as already discussed the model predicts that nonzero alphas are rare in the limit of a large cross-section, and it is not clear how this prediction can be falsified in a finite cross-section of asset returns. Second, we know that some portfolio is always mean-variance efficient ex post. Thus we know that ex post, we can always get a single-factor model to fit the data if we happen to choose the ex post mean-variance efficient portfolio as the single factor. It must then be even easier to get a K-factor model to fit the data. This does not tell us anything about the world unless we can have some confidence that the K-factor model holds ex ante as well as ex post. In other words, we need theoretical reasons to believe that a K-factor model is structural.

Finally, arbitrage pricing theory does not determine the signs or magnitudes of the risk prices. Being a common factor is a necessary but not a sufficient condition to be a priced factor that helps determine the cross-section of average asset returns. Much recent work on general equilibrium asset pricing aims to pin down the risk prices more precisely from theoretical considerations.

3.2.3 The Conditional CAPM as a Multifactor Model

One important way to derive an unconditional multifactor model is from a conditional version of the CAPM (Hansen and Richard 1987). Suppose that the CAPM holds conditionally. For asset i, the conditional expected excess return is given by

$$E_t R^e_{i,t+1} = \beta_{imt} E_t R^e_{m,t+1}. \tag{3.38}$$

Taking unconditional expectations, and using the fact that the mean of a product is the product of the means plus the covariance,

$$
\begin{aligned}
E R^e_{i,t+1} &= (E\beta_{imt})(E R^e_{m,t+1}) + \mathrm{Cov}(\beta_{imt}, E_t R^e_{m,t+1}) \\
&= \beta_{im}(E R^e_{m,t+1}) + (E\beta_{imt} - \beta_{im})(E R^e_{m,t+1}) + \mathrm{Cov}(\beta_{imt}, E_t R^e_{m,t+1}),
\end{aligned} \tag{3.39}
$$

where $\beta_{im} = \mathrm{Cov}(R_{i,t+1}, R_{m,t+1})/\mathrm{Var}(R_{m,t+1})$ is the asset's unconditional beta. The second equality in (3.39) adds and subtracts the unconditional beta times the unconditional equity premium, that is, the unconditional CAPM's prediction of the asset's unconditional expected excess return. The second and third terms on the right-hand side of that equality represent deviations of the conditional CAPM from the unconditional CAPM that affect the unconditional average asset return.

The second term is positive if the time-series average of the asset's conditional beta is higher than its unconditional beta. This term is zero if the market return has constant variance but can be nonzero if the market return is heteroskedastic. Lewellen and Nagel (2006) and Boguth et al. (2011) show that $(E\beta_{imt} - \beta_{im})$ can be approximated as

$$(E\beta_{imt} - \beta_{im}) \approx -\frac{\text{Cov}(\beta_{imt}, \sigma_{mt}^2)}{\sigma_m^2}, \tag{3.40}$$

the negative of the covariance of conditional beta with conditional market volatility, divided by unconditional market volatility. Intuitively, the unconditional beta is a time-series regression coefficient that places high weight on periods in which there are large realizations in the market return of either sign. If an asset tends to have a high conditional beta when market volatility is low, the time-series average of its conditional beta will be higher than its unconditional beta. Such an asset will have a higher unconditional average return than predicted by the unconditional CAPM. Boguth et al. refer to this as the "volatility timing" effect.

The third term is positive if the asset's beta covaries positively with the equity premium. An asset can have a higher unconditional average return than predicted by the unconditional CAPM, if its beta tends to be high when the market risk premium is high. Intuitively, such an asset delivers market risk exposure at times when market risk is highly rewarded, and this increases its unconditional average return. This might be called the "equity premium timing" effect.

A simple way to test a conditional model is to parameterize the variables that shift betas over time. For example, we might write

$$\beta_{imt} = \beta_{i0} + \beta_{i1} z_t, \tag{3.41}$$

where z_t is a state variable. The conditional model can then be written as

$$E_t R_{i,t+1}^e = \beta_{i0} E_t R_{m,t+1}^e + \beta_{i1} E_t z_t R_{m,t+1}^e, \tag{3.42}$$

and now we can take unconditional expectations to get

$$E R_{i,t+1}^e = \beta_{i0} E R_{m,t+1}^e + \beta_{i1} E z_t R_{m,t+1}^e. \tag{3.43}$$

This is a multifactor model, where the factors are the excess market return and the excess market return scaled by the state variable z_t. The scaled excess market return can be interpreted as the return on a dynamic investment strategy that invests more aggressively in the market when z_t is high. The multifactor model, with a dynamic investment strategy as a second factor, incorporates both the volatility timing and equity premium timing effects discussed above.

3.3 Empirical Evidence

3.3.1 Test Methodology

Even if the CAPM is a correct model, it will never exactly describe sample moments in a finite sample. We need a statistical test to tell whether sample deviations from the model (mean-variance inefficiency of the market portfolio, or equivalently nonzero alphas) are statistically significant.

The two leading approaches are time-series and cross-sectional. At a deep level, they are much more similar than they appear to be at first.

Time-Series Approach

The time-series approach starts from the regression (3.13), which we write more compactly as

$$R_{it}^e = \alpha_i + \beta_{im} R_{mt}^e + \epsilon_{it}, \tag{3.44}$$

where $R_{it}^e = R_{it} - R_{ft}$ and $R_{mt}^e = R_{mt} - R_{ft}$. The null hypothesis is that $\alpha_i = 0$. This is a simple parameter restriction for any one asset; the challenge is to test it jointly for a set of N assets.

We will proceed under the assumption that the residuals ϵ_{it} in (3.44) are iid and independent of the excess return on the market. In other words, we are not allowing any changes in the investment opportunity set of the sort implied by a conditional asset pricing model. The assumption of iid residuals can be relaxed, as we show in the next chapter when we discuss the Generalized Method of Moments.

An asymptotic test is as follows. Define α as the N-vector of intercepts α_i, and Ω as the variance-covariance matrix of the regression residuals ϵ_{it}. (This is different from the matrix Σ, which is the variance-covariance matrix of the raw returns rather than the residuals.) Then as the sample size T increases, asymptotically

$$T \left[1 + \left(\frac{\overline{R}_m^e}{\widehat{\sigma}(R_{mt}^e)} \right)^2 \right]^{-1} \widehat{\alpha}' \widehat{\Omega}^{-1} \widehat{\alpha} \sim \chi_N^2. \tag{3.45}$$

Here and throughout this section, hats over variables denote sample estimates and bars over variables denote sample means, not true population means (whereas in earlier sections, explaining the asset pricing theory, we used bars to denote population means).

To see the intuition, suppose there were no market return in the model. Then the vector $\widehat{\alpha}$ would be a vector of sample mean excess returns, with variance-covariance matrix $(1/T)\Omega$ (or equivalently $(1/T)\Sigma$ since the regression residuals would equal the demeaned raw returns in this case). Thus the quadratic form $T\widehat{\alpha}'\widehat{\Omega}^{-1}\widehat{\alpha}$ is a sum of squared intercepts, divided by its estimated variance-covariance matrix, which has an asymptotic χ_N^2 distribution. The term in square brackets is a correction for the presence of the market return in the model. Uncertainty about the betas affects the alphas, and more so when the market has a high expected return relative to its variance.

A finite-sample test makes a further correction for the fact that the variance-covariance matrix Ω must be estimated. Under the additional assumption that the ϵ_{it} are normally distributed, we have

$$\left(\frac{T-N-1}{N} \right) \left[1 + \left(\frac{\overline{R}_m^e}{\widehat{\sigma}(R_{mt}^e)} \right)^2 \right]^{-1} \widehat{\alpha}' \widehat{\Omega}^{-1} \widehat{\alpha} \sim F_{N, T-N-1}. \tag{3.46}$$

Gibbons, Ross, and Shanken (GRS 1989) provide a geometric interpretation that relates this "GRS statistic" to mean-variance analysis. Define $\hat{S}_m^2$ as the estimated squared Sharpe ratio of the market and $\hat{S}_q^2$ as the squared Sharpe ratio of the estimated tangency portfolio (the highest squared Sharpe ratio available from the set of test assets together with the market). The GRS statistic is equivalent to

$$\left(\frac{T-N-1}{N}\right)\left(\frac{\hat{S}_q^2 - \hat{S}_m^2}{1 + \hat{S}_m^2}\right). \qquad (3.47)$$

Thus the GRS statistic measures how far the market is from the ex-post tangency portfolio in a mean-standard deviation diagram.

Cross-Sectional Approach
The cross-sectional approach first estimates betas from a time-series regression and then runs a cross-sectional regression

$$\overline{R}_i^e = \lambda \widehat{\beta}_{im} + a_i, \qquad (3.48)$$

where there is no intercept in the regression and λ is the cross-sectional reward for bearing market risk.[3] As the sample size increases, $T \to \infty$, $\overline{R}_i^e \to \mathrm{E}[R_{it}^e]$ and $\widehat{\beta}_{im} \to \beta_{im}$; taking unconditional expectations in (3.44) and (3.48), we see that $\lambda \to \mathrm{E}[R_{mt}^e]$ and $a_i \to \alpha_i$ so that the cross-sectional residuals are consistent estimates of the true alphas. We are, therefore, in the strange position of wanting to test that the residuals in a regression are close to zero, that is, that the regression has an almost perfect fit. We can do this only because the regressors, the betas, are generated by time-series regressions that tell us something about the size of the pricing errors.

Although our assumption that the residuals in the time-series regression (3.44) are uncorrelated over time is a direct implication of the CAPM, there is no restriction on the covariance structure of the cross-sectional residuals in (3.48). In practice, assets tend to be highly correlated with one another at a given point in time and thus on average, even after controlling for multiple factors.[4] Thus to get asymptotically efficient estimates (estimates with the lowest sampling variation), we can run Generalized Least Squares:

$$\widehat{\lambda}_{GLS} = (\widehat{\beta}_m' \widehat{\Omega}^{-1} \widehat{\beta}_m)^{-1} \widehat{\beta}_m' \widehat{\Omega}^{-1} \overline{R}^e \qquad (3.49)$$

$$\widehat{a}_{GLS} = \overline{R}^e - \widehat{\lambda}_{GLS} \widehat{\beta}_m, \qquad (3.50)$$

where $\widehat{\beta}_m = [\widehat{\beta}_{1m} \ldots \widehat{\beta}_{Nm}]'$. An asymptotic test statistic based on the GLS cross-sectional regression, and correcting for the fact that the betas are not known but are estimated from a prior time-series regression, is

$$T \left[1 + \left(\frac{\widehat{\lambda}_{GLS}}{\widehat{\sigma}(R_{mt}^e)}\right)^2\right]^{-1} \widehat{a}_{GLS}' \widehat{\Omega}^{-1} \widehat{a}_{GLS} \sim \chi_{N-1}^2. \qquad (3.51)$$

This is almost exactly the same as the asymptotic time-series test statistic but we have lost one degree of freedom by estimating the reward for beta in the cross-section rather than

---

[3]We can alternatively include an intercept in the regression and test that it is zero, or allow it to be free in the Black version of the CAPM.

[4]This makes it difficult to interpret cross-sectional plots of sample average returns against betas or predicted average returns, such as Figures 3.4–3.6 in this chapter, since many of the points may be generated by highly correlated underlying assets that are bound to plot near one another.

from the sample average excess market return. We can earn that degree of freedom back by adding the market to the set of assets in the cross-sectional GLS regression. Then the regression puts all the weight on the market in estimating the reward for market risk. (Since all other assets are just the market plus noise, the GLS regression understands that they are less informative about this parameter.) Thus $\widehat{\lambda}_{GLS} = \overline{R}_m^e$. The result is a test statistic that is exactly the same as the time-series test statistic, since $\widehat{a}_{GLS} = \overline{R}^e - \overline{R}_m^e \widehat{\beta}_m = \widehat{\alpha}$.

The cross-sectional approach has the advantage that it can be implemented even when the factor is not the return on a traded portfolio. In that case we need to use the cross-section to estimate the reward for bearing factor risk, as in equations (3.36) and (3.37) in section 3.2.2.

Fama-MacBeth Approach
A variant of the cross-sectional regression approach is the Fama-MacBeth approach (Fama and MacBeth 1973). This first estimates stock-level betas, then runs a series of period-by-period cross-sectional regressions of excess returns on estimated betas,

$$R_{it}^e - \lambda_t \widehat{\beta}_{im} + u_{it}. \tag{3.52}$$

Here the observations in each regression run from $i = 1 \ldots N$, and the regressions are run separately for each $t = 1 \ldots T$.

The coefficients $\widehat{\lambda}_t$ and residuals $\widehat{a}_{it}$ are then averaged over time to estimate the average reward for beta exposure $\widehat{\lambda}_{FM} \equiv (1/T) \sum \widehat{\lambda}_t$ and the average residuals $\widehat{a}_{i,FM} \equiv (1/T) \sum \widehat{a}_{it}$. Fama and MacBeth use the variability of the coefficients and residuals over time to estimate the standard errors of these averages (the variability of the estimates across different hypothetical samples) and to construct test statistics for the model. For example, under the standard assumption that all returns are iid over time,

$$\widehat{\sigma}^2(\widehat{a}_{i,FM}) = \frac{1}{T}\widehat{\sigma}^2(\widehat{a}_{it}) = \frac{1}{T^2}\sum_{t=1}^{T}(\widehat{a}_{it} - \widehat{a}_{i,FM})^2 \tag{3.53}$$

and similarly for $\widehat{\lambda}_{FM}$.

The Fama-MacBeth method for calculating standard errors does not adjust for the fact that stocks' betas are not known but must be estimated from time-series regressions. However, it does easily allow for changing betas over time ($\widehat{\beta}_{imt}$ instead of $\widehat{\beta}_{im}$ as explanatory variables in (3.52)). Thus it is more appropriate as a method to estimate the rewards to observable characteristics of firms (which can include their lagged historical betas), than as a method to test the CAPM.

Returns and Characteristics
The Fama-MacBeth method for estimating the return to a stock-level characteristic X_{it} is to run a series of cross-sectional regressions of excess returns on the characteristic, one for each date t:

$$R_{it}^e = \theta_t + \lambda_t X_{it} + a_{it}, \tag{3.54}$$

where θ_t is the intercept, λ_t is the slope coefficient, and a_{it} is the residual return on asset i at date t.

An appealing feature of the Fama-MacBeth regression is that the cross-sectional slope coefficients $\widehat{\lambda}_t$ can be interpreted as the payoffs on long-short portfolios with zero initial investment. This is easy to see from the formula for a simple OLS regression coefficient. In the case where the characteristic X_{it} has a zero cross-sectional mean at time t,

$$\widehat{\lambda}_t = \frac{\sum_{i=1}^{N} X_{it} R_{it}^e}{\sum_{i=1}^{N} X_{it}^2} = \frac{\sum_{i=1}^{N} X_{it} R_{it}}{\sum_{i=1}^{N} X_{it}^2}, \tag{3.55}$$

which is the payoff at time t on a long-short portfolio that invests in each stock in proportion to its characteristic X_{it}, financing long positions with short positions, and scaling the positions by the sum of squared characteristics so that the portfolio characteristic is one. Similarly, the estimated intercept $\widehat{\theta}_t$ is the excess return on an equal-weighted portfolio of all the assets, which has a zero value of the characteristic. In the case where the characteristic X_{it} has a nonzero cross-sectional mean, the slope is the payoff on a long-short portfolio that invests in each stock in proportion to its cross-sectionally demeaned characteristic, scaling such that the portfolio's characteristic is one, and the intercept is the excess return on a portfolio that has a zero value of the characteristic (but no longer an equal-weighted portfolio in this case).

These results generalize straightforwardly to a multiple Fama-MacBeth regression with several explanatory variables. In that case the cross-sectional regression coefficient on each characteristic is the payoff at time t to a long-short portfolio that has unit value of that characteristic and zero value of all other characteristics, while the intercept is the excess return on a portfolio with zero exposure to any of the characteristics. Problem 3.4 asks you to explore these portfolio properties of Fama-MacBeth regression.

An alternative way to estimate the rewards to observable characteristics is to estimate a panel regression. This requires adjusting the standard errors of the regression for the cross-sectional correlation of asset returns at a point in time, an adjustment that is now straightforward using clustered standard error commands in panel regression software packages. When the explanatory variables in the regression do not vary over time, the Fama-MacBeth estimates and standard errors are identical to those of the panel regression as well as those of the cross-sectional regression (3.48) (Cochrane 2005, Chapter 12).[5] When the explanatory variables do vary over time, Fama-MacBeth is different because it gives equal weight to each time period, even if the explanatory variables are more dispersed in one period than another.[6]

Linear regressions, estimated with either Fama-MacBeth or panel methodology, impose a linear relationship between characteristics and returns. The modern finance literature is often concerned that the true relationship may be nonlinear. To explore this, it is common to present tables of average returns (or alphas) for portfolios sorted by one or more characteristics. The idea is that such tables will reveal nonlinearity if it is present. In practice, a relationship between a characteristic and average return is regarded with particular suspicion if it is nonlinear enough to be nonmonotonic. This portfolio sorting methodology is a good exploratory tool for detecting nonlinearity, but it becomes unwieldy when more than two characteristics are being considered at a time. Regression methodology is a superior tool for understanding how multiple characteristics

---

[5]This statement assumes that no correction is made in any of these methods for heteroskedasticity or serial correlation of residuals, consistent with our assumption above that residual returns are iid over time.

[6]This distinction is related to the difference between the time-series average of conditional beta and the unconditional beta, stated in equation (3.40) above. The Fama-MacBeth estimate is analogous to the former, and the panel regression estimate is analogous to the latter.

affect stock returns, and it can accommodate nonlinearity where necessary by using non-linear transformations of raw characteristics as explanatory variables. Lewellen (2015) is a recent paper that illustrates this approach.

Choosing Test Assets

The different test approaches for the CAPM have important common features. Looking at more assets (increasing N) will tend to find larger deviations from the model. However, increasing N also increases the size of the deviations required to reject the CAPM statistically. Thus, to get a powerful test, one may wish to select a few test assets that one believes on prior grounds to be mispriced. However, a valid test cannot select assets using their average returns during the sample period used to test the model. This procedure, sometimes called "data snooping," leads to spurious rejections of the model (Lo and MacKinlay 1990a). Much of the debate about the empirical validity of the CAPM centers on this issue.

A separate issue concerns the grouping of test assets into portfolios on the basis of relevant characteristics. This procedure is commonly used because the diversification of idiosyncratic risk in portfolios increases the precision with which their factor loadings can be estimated and because it is easier to present summary statistics for a few portfolios than for a large cross-section of individual stocks. However, portfolio formation discards some of the information in the cross-section of individual stock returns and reduces the precision with which factor risk prices are estimated (Ang, Liu, and Schwarz 2016). In a linear regression context, it is natural to work with individual stocks as Brennan, Chordia, and Subrahmanyam (1998) and others have done.

3.3.2 The CAPM and the Cross-Section of Stock Returns

In this section I briefly summarize an enormous empirical literature on the cross-section of stock returns, with particular attention to characteristics of stocks that appear to predict returns in a way that cannot be explained by the CAPM. Most of this literature concentrates on the returns to US stocks since 1926, the starting date for the Center for Research in Securities Prices (CRSP) monthly database.

Beta. The earliest empirical studies of the CAPM grouped stocks into portfolios using their historical market betas and found a positive and close to linear relationship between the subsequent betas of these portfolios and their average returns (Black, Jensen, and Scholes 1972, Fama and MacBeth 1973). At the time, this was regarded as a success for the CAPM. The effect of beta on return was quite small, less than the excess return of the market over Treasury bills, which implies a zero-beta return higher than the Treasury bill rate. However, this can be explained by the Black (1972) version of the CAPM if stock market investors cannot borrow or can only borrow at a higher rate than the Treasury bill rate. Subsequent studies of the beta-return relationship have found an even weaker relationship between beta and return since the early 1960s, a period that tends to be much more challenging for the CAPM than the earlier part of the CRSP sample period.

Size. Banz (1981) found that firms with low market capitalization ("small" firms) tend to have higher average returns than their betas justify. In the period since World War II, the relationship between average return and market beta for size-sorted portfolios

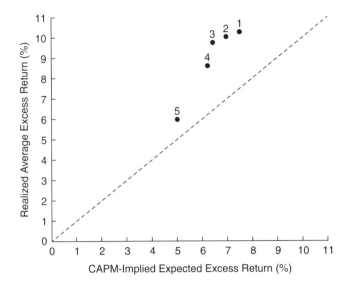

Figure 3.5. *The CAPM and the Size Effect*

is upward sloping and close to linear, but too steep rather than too flat as in the case of beta-sorted portfolios. Figure 3.5 illustrates this fact using data from 1963 through 2012.[7]

While size continues to be regarded as a relevant stock-level characteristic in empirical asset pricing, the size effect no longer commands so much attention for several reasons. First, large stocks outperformed small ones during the 1990s and part of the 2000s, reducing the average excess return on small stocks relative to the market index. Second, Keim (1983) and Reinganum (1983) pointed out that small stock outperformance was concentrated in January, a seasonal anomaly that began to disappear shortly after it was publicized.[8] Third, the profession has increasingly preferred to normalize market capitalization by other measures of the scale of the firm in order to isolate the component of size that is related to average return.

Value. Value investors seek to buy stocks with low market capitalization relative to accounting measures of their value, in the belief that such stocks will outperform. This approach to investing was popularized by Graham, Dodd, and Cottle (1934) several

---

[7]The five portfolios reported are aggregated from a five-by-five sort on size and value given on Kenneth French's website, with the smallest stocks in portfolio 1 and the largest stocks in portfolio 5. Because the aggregation equally weights across value portfolios, the resulting portfolios do not aggregate to the market, and thus all portfolios shown have positive alphas.

[8]One plausible explanation of the January size effect is that it is related to tax-loss selling of small stocks at the end of the year and subsequent buying of small stocks in January. While tax-loss selling should also occur among large stocks, it may have larger effects on small stock prices given the relative illiquidity of these stocks. Kang et al. (2015) point out that the incentive for tax-loss selling is greater when nominal interest rates and capital gains tax rates are high. Declines in both these variables may have contributed to the decline in the small-stock January effect since the 1980s. More general forms of seasonality have recently been measured in the returns on individual stocks and factor portfolios (Heston and Sadka 2008, Keloharju, Linnainmaa, and Nyberg 2016).

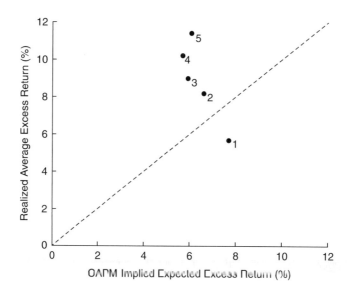

Figure 3.6.   *The CAPM and the Value Effect*

decades before the formulation of the CAPM. Academic studies have considered several alternative measures of value, including the dividend-price ratio or dividend yield (Litzenberger and Ramaswamy 1982, Miller and Scholes 1982), the earnings-price ratio (Basu 1977, 1983), and the book-market ratio (Stattman 1980, Rosenberg, Reid, and Lanstein 1985). Since the influential work of Fama and French (1992, 1993), attention now focuses mainly on the book-market ratio.

During the last 50 years, "value stocks" with high book-market ratios have had lower market betas than "growth stocks" with low book-market ratios, but higher average returns. Thus the slope of the relationship between average return and beta for value-sorted portfolios is actually negative, as shown in Figure 3.6.[9]

The returns to value stocks are much less anomalous in the early part of the CRSP sample period. During the Great Depression and the early postwar period, value stocks still outperformed growth stocks, but at that time they had higher betas than growth stocks so the pattern of average returns was consistent with the CAPM. Problem 3.5 asks you to estimate the returns to size and value and test the CAPM with a break in the sample period at the end of 1963.

Momentum. A very simple way to predict stock returns is to use the past history of stock returns, an approach that is discussed in greater detail in Chapter 5. While the autocorrelations of returns are tiny in any one stock, they imply meaningful outperformance of portfolios of stocks grouped by past returns. Return autocorrelations appear to be initially negative at horizons up to a month or two (possibly reflecting trading frictions), then positive for horizons from 3 to 12 months, then possibly negative again at horizons of several years. Long-term negative autocorrelation ("long-term reversal") was documented by DeBondt and Thaler (1985), but today it attracts less attention because

---

[9]The five portfolios shown are aggregated in the same manner as the previous figure, but over value categories rather than size categories, with extreme growth stocks having the lowest book-market ratios in portfolio 1 and extreme value stocks having the highest book-market ratios in portfolio 5.

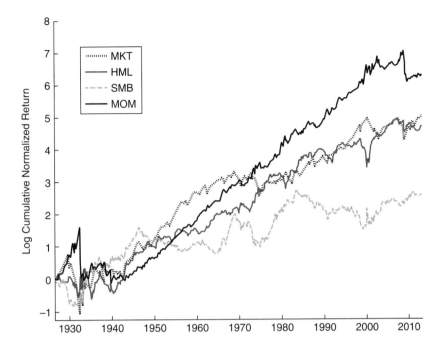

Figure 3.7. *Fama-French-Carhart Log Cumulative Normalized Factor Returns, 1926–2013*

the effect appears closely related to the value anomaly. Medium-term positive autocorrelation or "momentum" was discovered by Jegadeesh and Titman (1993) and appears to be a highly robust phenomenon.

Figure 3.7 summarizes the size, value, and momentum anomalies in relation to overall stock returns by plotting the cumulative returns on four long-short portfolios. The first (MKT or "Market") is long the aggregate market and short Treasury bills, the second (SMB or "Small Minus Big") is long small stocks and short large stocks, the third (HML or "High Minus Low") is long value (high book-market) stocks and short growth (low book-market) stocks, and the fourth (MOM or "Momentum") is long stocks that have performed well in the past year (excluding the last month to eliminate high-frequency reversal) and short stocks that have performed badly. These portfolios were introduced to the literature by Fama and French (1993) and Carhart (1997). Data on their returns are taken from Kenneth French's website, a standard data source for academic finance research.[10] In this figure, the returns on SMB, HML, and MOM are all scaled to have the

[10]A more precise description of portfolio construction is as follows. Stocks are allocated to portfolios at the end of each June, with stocks categorized as small if they have a market cap less than the median NYSE market cap at the portfolio formation date and large otherwise; and categorized as value if their book-market ratio (defined using book equity for the last fiscal year end in the previous calendar year divided by market equity for December of that calendar year) is greater than the 70th NYSE percentile, value if this ratio is less than the 30th NYSE percentile, and neutral if this ratio is between the 30th and 70th percentiles. Then, SMB is the equally weighted average return on the three small portfolios minus the return on the three large portfolios, while HML is the equally weighted average return on the two value portfolios minus the two growth portfolios. The momentum factor is constructed in a similar fashion to the HML factor, except that the lagged return over

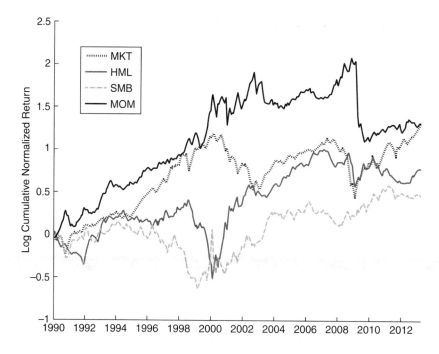

Figure 3.8.   *Fama-French-Carhart Log Cumulative Normalized Factor Returns, 1990–2013*

same standard deviation as MKT, so the height of each line at the right axis is proportional to the full-sample Sharpe ratio of each portfolio. The figure shows that MOM has a higher Sharpe ratio than the overall market, while HML has a similar Sharpe ratio to the market and SMB has a considerably lower Sharpe ratio. As mentioned above, SMB has had relatively poor performance since the academic literature first highlighted the size effect in the early 1980s.

Figure 3.8 is a similar plot for a shorter sample period starting in 1990. This figure highlights the fact that in recent data, value and momentum returns have generally been negatively correlated; this shows up particularly clearly during the technology boom of the late 1990s and bust of the early 2000s and during the global financial crisis of 2007–2009. For this reason, modern quantitative investment strategies in the equity market often try to combine value and momentum.

Two other points about the risk of these portfolios emerge from Figures 3.7 and 3.8. First, episodes of heightened volatility such as the Great Depression, the technology boom and bust, or the global financial crisis affect the returns not only on the market but also on these long-short portfolios. Second, cumulative momentum returns are subject to occasional particularly large drawdowns (declines from previous peaks), visible both at the onset of the Great Depression in the early 1930s and during the recovery from the global financial crisis in 2009.

---

the past year (excluding the most recent month) is used in place of the book-market ratio. Full details and data are available at http://mba.tuck.dartmouth.edu/pages/faculty/ken.french/data_library.html.

Although beta, value, size, and momentum are the core phenomena discussed in the literature on the cross-section of stock returns, many other variables have also been found to predict returns in the cross-section. A brief summary of some of the more salient phenomena follows.

Post-event drift. A number of papers have identified corporate events or changes in published views of stock analysts that cause an immediate stock price reaction, followed by subsequent drift in the same direction. This post-event drift is similar to price momentum in that higher initial returns are associated with higher subsequent returns, but different in that initial returns are measured conditional on the occurrence of an event.

The classic example is post-earnings announcement drift, upward for firms announcing unexpectedly high earnings and downward for firms announcing disappointingly low earnings (Ball and Brown 1968, Foster, Olsen, and Shevlin 1984, Bernard and Thomas 1989). Comparable results have been reported for analyst earnings forecast revisions (Gleason and Lee 2003), analyst recommendations (Womack 1996), dividend initiations and omissions (Michaely, Thaler, and Womack 1995), share repurchases (Ikenberry, Lakonishok, and Vermaelen 1995), stock splits (Desai and Jain 1997, Ikenberry, Rankine, and Stice 1996), and divestitures (Cusatis, Miles, and Woolridge 1993). There is also some intriguing evidence that the mere occurrence of earnings announcements, regardless of the content, is relevant for stock prices. Frazzini and Lamont (2006) point out that stocks tend to rise in months when they announce earnings, averaging over positive and negative announcements.

Turnover and volatility. Both turnover and idiosyncratic volatility appear to be negatively associated with returns at intermediate 3–12 month horizons (Lee and Swaminathan 2000, Ang et al. 2006), although turnover may have a shorter-term positive effect. These phenomena may be related to a negative effect of disagreement among equity analysts documented by Diether, Malloy, and Scherbina (2002), since investors who disagree about a firm's prospects are likely to trade more aggressively with one another and may create volatility in doing so.

Insider trading. There is some evidence that purchases and sales by corporate insiders predict future stock returns (Seyhun 1988), with stronger evidence for purchases (Jeng, Metrick, and Zeckhauser 2003) and for sales that are not part of a regular sale program (Cohen, Malloy, and Pomorski 2012).

Growth of the firm. Variables that capture growth of a firm's assets, such as capital expenditures and total asset growth (Titman, Wei, and Xie 2004, Cooper, Gulen, and Schill 2008), are negatively associated with subsequent returns. The same is true for variables that capture growth of a firm's liabilities, including measures of equity and debt issuance (Spiess and Affleck-Graves 1995, 1999) and the percentage change in shares outstanding (Daniel and Titman 2006). Poor returns following initial public offerings (IPOs) may be a related phenomenon (Carter, Dark, and Singh 1998, Ritter and Welch 2002).

Earnings quality. A large literature in accounting argues that different components of current earnings have different degrees of relevance for future earnings and hence may predict returns if investors do not fully appreciate these distinctions. A classic example is that accruals (roughly, growth in noncash current assets not accounted for by growth in current liabilities) are less persistent than the cash component of earnings and predict stock returns negatively (Sloan 1996). Dechow, Sloan, and Sweeney (1995) argue that corporate management can manipulate accruals to manage earnings, for example, by booking sales that have not been paid for by customers, and that investors are not fully aware of this. In related work, Hirshleifer et al. (2004) predict stock returns using net operating assets as a fraction of lagged total assets. This is a balance sheet measure that cumulates past accruals and past investment, and is therefore related to both earnings quality and growth of the firm.

Profitability. Novy-Marx (2013) shows that firms with higher ratios of gross profitability to book assets have higher subsequent returns. Gross profitability differs from current accounting earnings in that it adds back a number of corporate expenses that may enhance the long-run prospects of the firm, including advertising, sales commissions, and R&D.[11] Thus, while the accruals literature argues that the market gives firms too much credit for certain actions that do add to current earnings but are unproductive in the long run, the argument here is that the market gives insufficient credit for some actions that are productive in the long run but do not contribute to current earnings.

The existence of many empirically successful return predictors raises important questions about how these predictors interact with one another. Some newly reported predictors may simply be transformed versions of known effects, which disappear when those other effects are controlled for. However, the reverse is also possible. For example, a measure of profitability or earnings quality might have no predictive power on its own, but might predict returns jointly with the book-market ratio if it enables a more refined measure of the accounting value of a company.

In addition, some predictors may be more powerful for stocks with high or low values of another characteristic. Many predictive effects seem to be more important among small stocks, for example. This type of interaction is easily discovered with a double portfolio sort and can be represented in a Fama-MacBeth or panel regression by including the cross-product of two predictors in the regression along with the original predictors.[12]

3.3.3 Alternative Responses to the Evidence

Evidence that characteristics predict stock returns, while not proportionally predicting stocks' betas with the market index, presents a challenge to the CAPM. Such evidence has generated a variety of responses.

Data mining. The most conservative response is that the evidence has been found by a process of experimentation with many candidate explanatory variables. Of every 100 variables considered, 5 will appear to predict returns at the 5% significance level purely by chance. While any one paper may consider only a few variables, the finance profession as a whole has considered thousands, publishing and publicizing the few that pass conventional significance tests. The evidence summarized in the previous section could be, at least in part, the spurious outcome of this data-mining process.

---

[11] Gross profitability can be written as EBITDA (earnings before interest, taxes, depreciation, and amortization) plus SGA (selling, general, and administrative expenses). Eisfeldt and Papanikolaou (2013) find high returns to firms with high cumulated SGA, consistent with the results of Novy-Marx.

[12] Two caveats about this approach. First, cross-products of predictors often have fat tails which can lead to difficulties with the small-sample properties of regressions including them. Second, some predictors, notably value and momentum, have natural measures of scale (the book-market ratio and past returns, respectively). Portfolio sorts typically ignore the levels of these measures and simply sort stocks using their cross-sectional characteristic ranks at each point in time. If the measures of scale are more dispersed when a second predictor is high or low (e.g., among small stocks), then a portfolio sorting methodology may detect an interaction even when there is a fixed coefficient on the measure of scale in a regression (Bandarchuk and Hilscher 2013).

A variant of this argument is that test portfolios are chosen on the basis of characteristics that have been found to predict returns during the sample period. While the predictability might not create a statistically significant rejection of the CAPM in the full cross-section of assets, it may appear to do so once a few portfolios are constructed by sorting on these characteristics. This process is called "data snooping" by Lo and MacKinlay (1990a).

Anomaly elimination. Even if return predictability is the genuine result of investor behavior in the period during which it is measured, it is possible that publicizing the result leads investors to alter their behavior to weaken or even eliminate the phenomenon. In this case the CAPM remains a good description of the long-run behavior of the market once deviations from the model are brought to investors' attention. Anomaly elimination is consistent with evidence that institutional investors trade in line with anomalies (for example, Cohen, Gompers, and Vuolteenaho 2002) and by the growing popularity of "smart-beta" funds that allow less sophisticated investors to exploit anomalies at relatively low cost.

The January size effect, the excess return to small firms in January, provides a good example of anomaly elimination. Figure 3.9 reports the excess returns to small-cap stocks over the market in January and all other months, averaged over five years to smooth noisy annual variation. Figure 3.10 does the same thing for micro-cap stocks. The former category includes stocks in the middle 40% by market capitalization, and the latter category includes stocks in the bottom 30%, taken from Kenneth French's website. The figure includes a vertical dashed line in 1984, immediately after the publication of academic articles on the January size effect by Keim (1983) and Reinganum (1983). The disappearance of the seasonal anomaly in small and mid-cap stocks, and its substantial reduction in micro-cap stocks, are immediately obvious from these figures.

A recent paper by McLean and Pontiff (2016) evaluates the importance of both data mining and anomaly-elimination effects, systematically across many anomalies, by

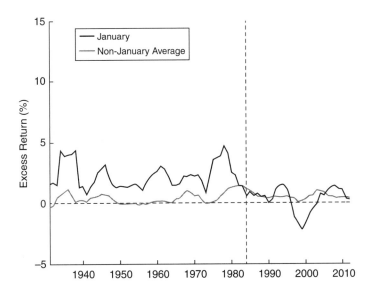

Figure 3.9. *Five-Year Moving Average Excess Returns to Small-Cap Stocks, January vs. Other Months*

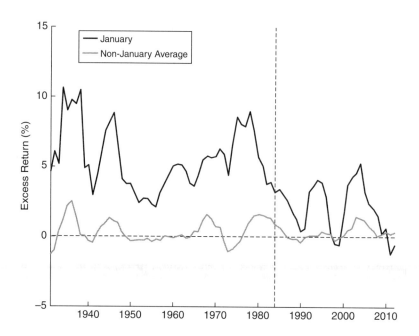

Figure 3.10. *Five-Year Moving Average Excess Returns to Micro-Cap Stocks, January vs. Other Months*

comparing the strength of return predictability in three sample periods: that used by the earliest academic studies, the period after publication of those studies, and the intermediate period after the research sample but before the publication date. This systematic approach is important because the strength of any one anomaly, such as the size effect in January, may be influenced by special factors, such as the decline in capital gains tax rates and nominal interest rates discussed by Kang et al. (2015). McLean and Pontiff find that return predictability declines by a statistically insignificant 10% between the end of the research sample and the publication date, and by a statistically significant 35% after the publication date. In addition, stocks favored by academic studies have higher trading volume and volatility after publication and move more closely with stocks favored by other academic studies. These results lead McLean and Pontiff to emphasize anomaly elimination over data mining.

Roll critique. Roll (1977) argued that CAPM tests are flawed because we do not know the composition of the true market portfolio, and so we use a broad stock index as an imperfect proxy. A rejection of the CAPM just tells us that our proxy is inadequate. This "Roll critique" can be regarded as a powerful defense of the CAPM (and critique of its detractors), but it can also be viewed as a devastating critique of the model itself, since if the market portfolio is unobservable the CAPM is not testable and cannot be regarded as a scientific model.

Empirical finance economists have responded to the Roll critique in several ways. One is to consider alternative proxies for the market portfolio and to see how results differ across these proxies. Adding bonds to the market index appears to have little effect (Stambaugh 1982), but imputing human capital may have a more important impact because of the size and volatility of labor income relative to capital income. Informally,

Fama and French (1996) have argued that the value effect might be explained by a high covariance between value stock returns and the value of human capital, if value stocks tend to be financially distressed and the failure of distressed firms is associated with destruction of human capital of the firms' employees.[13] We discuss this line of research in Chapter 10.

A second response to the Roll critique, developed by Kandel and Stambaugh (1987) and Shanken (1987), is to calculate an upper bound on the correlation between the true market portfolio and the proxy that is implied by a CAPM test statistic. If this upper bound is far below one, then only extreme mismeasurement of the return on the market index can reconcile the CAPM with the empirical test statistic.

Illiquidity. Some economists accept deviations from the CAPM as genuine but downplay their importance on the grounds that they are concentrated in small, illiquid stocks. It is certainly true that many portfolios have more anomalous returns, from the perspective of the CAPM, when they are equally weighted than when they are value weighted. In addition, illiquidity may itself influence the required return on a stock, requiring illiquidity adjustments before a risk-based model like the CAPM can be tested. We discuss this issue in greater detail in Chapter 12.

Conditional CAPM. Standard tests of the CAPM assume that stocks' betas and the market risk premium are constant over time. If this is not the case, then as discussed in section 3.2.3, the CAPM could hold conditionally at each point in time but could fail unconditionally (Hansen and Richard 1987). The model can be tested in the usual way using time-series or cross-sectional regressions following equations (3.41)–(3.43). If a cross-sectional regression is used, it is important to include the market itself, and the market scaled by the state variable z_t, in the set of test assets. This ensures that the model is able to price a managed portfolio that varies its exposure to the market in reaction to the state variable; equivalently, it ensures that cross-sectional estimates of the factor risk prices are reasonable, given the time-series behavior of the market return.

A well-known paper proposing a conditional asset pricing model as an explanation of the cross-section is Lettau and Ludvigson (2001b), which has particular success with a conditional consumption CAPM of the sort developed in Chapter 6. In the context of the CAPM, there is evidence that value stocks have higher betas at times when the market risk premium is high, but this effect does not appear to be powerful enough to explain the value premium (Lewellen and Nagel 2006). Recently, Cederburg and O'Doherty (2016) have argued that the anomalously low returns to high-beta stocks may be explained by the fact that the spread in betas between high- and low-beta stocks tends to increase when market volatility is high and when the equity premium is low; this generates both volatility timing and equity premium timing effects which give high-beta stocks lower returns than implied by the unconditional CAPM, even if they are well explained by a conditional CAPM.

Atheoretical multifactor risk model. Under quite weak conditions we should expect to be able to find a multifactor risk model that describes the cross-section of stock returns. A large literature seeks to do this empirically, without imposing any theoretical restrictions on risk prices. The first factor is almost always chosen to be the return on a broad

---

[13]Campbell, Hilscher, and Szilagyi (2008) counter that financially distressed firms have anomalously low returns relative to the CAPM, not anomalously high returns. However, it is possible that these firms have high idiosyncratic failure risk and that other firms have the highest exposure to aggregate failures and hence the highest beta with the omitted component of the market portfolio (George and Hwang 2010).

market index, so that the multifactor model nests the CAPM. The question then becomes how to choose additional factors that adequately describe the cross-section.

One approach is to model the covariance matrix of asset returns. During the 1980s a number of papers used statistical methods (factor analysis and principal component analysis of the covariance matrix) to find the most important common factors. This approach has fallen out of favor because it delivers little economic insight and tends to find more and more factors as the number of test assets increases. Alternatively, one can choose factors that seem likely on economic grounds to be important common influences on stock prices, such as the innovations to inflation, interest rates, and industrial production studied by Chen, Roll, and Ross (1986).

Fama and French (1993) originated an influential alternative approach. Instead of modeling the covariance matrix of returns directly, they constructed portfolios of stocks with common characteristics that are known to be related to average returns. The logic of the arbitrage pricing theory implies that such portfolios must be important risk factors for the covariance matrix of stock returns. The original Fama and French (1993) model has three factors: the excess return on the aggregate stock market over Treasury bills (MKT), the excess return on small stocks over large stocks (SMB), and the excess return on value stocks with high book-market ratios over growth stocks with low book-market ratios (HML). Subsequent work has added other factors such as the return on stocks that have recently performed well relative to stocks that have recently performed badly (Carhart's 1997 MOM factor). The cumulative historical returns on these four factor portfolios were plotted in Figure 3.7. The four-factor Fama-French-Carhart model asserts that all excess stock returns are explained by the betas of stocks on these portfolios.

Multifactor models with observed factors and free risk prices trivially fit a cross-section of average asset returns if there are as many observed factors as assets. They are also likely to have a good fit when a large number of test assets are used, if these test assets have a low-dimensional factor structure, in other words, if they are driven by a few common shocks. As a particularly relevant example, the realized returns of MKT, SMB, and HML have high explanatory power for the realized returns of 25 portfolios sorted by size and book-to-market ratios. This implies that any multifactor model whose factors correlate, even weakly, with the returns to the market, SMB, and HML, can deliver a good cross-sectional fit to the average returns on these 25 portfolios even if the model has no ability to explain the portfolios' alphas with respect to the Fama-French three-factor model. Lewellen, Nagel, and Shanken (2010) and Daniel and Titman (2012) emphasize this point and argue that one should test multifactor models using a combination of portfolios sorted by characteristics and by estimated firm-level factor exposures. Another response is to impose theoretical restrictions on factor risk prices, an approach we now discuss.

Equilibrium multifactor risk model. Even if an atheoretical multifactor risk model like the Fama-French or Fama-French-Carhart model provides a good empirical description of the cross-section of stock returns, it does not provide any economic explanation for the pricing of stocks. A satisfying economic explanation should at a minimum derive the risk prices of multiple factors from deeper equilibrium considerations, such as the preferences of investors and the production possibilities of the economy. The conditional CAPM, mentioned above, is one example of an equilibrium foundation for a multifactor model. Later in this book we discuss recent research that takes on this challenge in other ways, using a consumption-based approach (Chapter 6), a production-based approach (Chapter 7), or an intertemporal approach (Chapter 9).

In addition, one might hope to derive the factor loadings of stocks from features of firms' production technologies. A recent literature on structural modeling of the firm attempts to do this. Much of this work straddles the boundary between asset pricing and corporate finance, but we discuss some of it in Chapter 7.

Behavioral finance. Behavioral finance economists believe that investors with irrational beliefs (and/or highly nonstandard preferences) have an important influence on market equilibrium. While there may be rational investors who trade with irrational investors, and while one can certainly try to price assets from the perspective of these rational investors, in behavioral models the rational investors do not buy and hold the market portfolio and thus no model with a rational buy-and-hold investor can price assets. Thus, according to the behavioral perspective the logic of the CAPM is irredeemably flawed.

Behavioral models instead emphasize heterogeneity of beliefs, possibly in combination with restrictions on the trading strategies that investors can follow. We discuss models of this sort in Chapters 10 and 11. Assets can be priced using the first-order conditions of rational investors if one can find empirical proxies for their marginal utility that do not assume they buy and hold the market portfolio. We discuss this approach at the end of Chapter 12. A challenge for this literature, emphasized by Fama (1998), is to reconcile the evidence for medium-term stock price underreaction to fundamentals, as suggested by the phenomena of momentum and post-event drift, with evidence for long-term overreaction to fundamentals as suggested by the value effect.

3.4 Solution and Further Problems

As an informal exercise you were asked to explain what would change in Figure 3.4 as the benchmark portfolio is altered to include more exotic assets with positive alphas. The obvious answer is that the greater benchmark weights on these assets increase their betas with the benchmark portfolio, moving them to the right in Figure 3.4. This process should continue until all assets lie on the security market line and no assets have positive alphas. If the investor is large enough to move prices, or if a sizeable group of investors is pursuing a similar strategy, it may also be that increasing the weight on exotic assets raises their prices and lowers the investor's return expectations, in which case the points representing exotic assets would also shift downward.

Problem 3.1 Some Implications of the CAPM

Assume that the Sharpe-Lintner CAPM holds, so the mean-variance efficient frontier consists of combinations of Treasury bills and the market portfolio. Nonetheless, some households make the mistake of holding undiversified portfolios that contain only one stock or a few stocks. (Empirical evidence on such behavior is discussed in Chapter 10.)

(a) Show that the Sharpe ratio of any portfolio divided by the Sharpe ratio of the market portfolio equals the correlation of that portfolio with the market portfolio.

(b) Suppose the market is made up of identical stocks, each of which has the same market capitalization, the same mean and variance of return, and the same correlation

$\rho > 0$, with every other individual stock. Consider the limit as the number of stocks in the market increases. What is the Sharpe ratio of an equally-weighted portfolio that contains N stocks divided by the Sharpe ratio of the market portfolio? Interpret.

Problem 3.2 Appraisal Ratio

Consider a frictionless one-period economy with multiple risky assets and a riskfree asset with return R_f. Let R_p denote the return to the risky portfolio of an agent who trades off the mean against the variance of his (total) portfolio return, $\theta R_p + (1-\theta) R_f$, where θ denotes the share of initial wealth invested in risky assets.

Suppose the investor is in the process of constructing his optimal portfolio and has a candidate or "benchmark" portfolio of risky assets with return R_b that is optimal with respect to existing assets. But he becomes aware of a new investment opportunity (asset) with return R_n and wishes to adjust his portfolio in order to take advantage of this new opportunity.

(a) Explain intuitively why a portfolio adjustment policy that uses the Sharpe ratio of the existing portfolio, $SR_b = E[R_b - R_f]/\sigma_b$, and the Sharpe ratio of the new investment, $SR_n = E[R_n - R_f]/\sigma_n$, as sufficient statistics for the adjustment is not optimal. Here, $\sigma_b^2 = \text{Var}(R_b)$ and $\sigma_n^2 = \text{Var}(R_n)$.

(b) Let w denote the optimal weight of the risky portfolio on the new asset, so that $R_p = wR_n + (1-w)R_b$. Explain why the agent chooses w so as to maximize the Sharpe ratio of his risky portfolio, where the Sharpe ratio $SR_p = E[R_p - R_f]/\sigma_p$, with $\sigma_p^2 = \text{Var}(R_p)$. Show that

$$w = \frac{E[R_n - R_f]\sigma_b^2 - E[R_b - R_f]\sigma_{nb}}{E[R_n - R_f]\sigma_b^2 + E[R_b - R_f]\sigma_n^2 - (E[R_n - R_f] + E[R_b - R_f])\sigma_{nb}}, \qquad (3.56)$$

where $\sigma_{nb} = \text{Cov}(R_n, R_b)$.

(c) Suppose the investor believes that the return to the new asset is given by

$$R_n - R_f = \alpha + \beta(R_b - R_f) + \varepsilon, \qquad (3.57)$$

where α and β are constants, ε has mean zero and variance σ_ε^2, and $E[\varepsilon R_b] = 0$.

(i) Show that

$$w = \frac{\overline{w}}{1 + (1-\beta)\overline{w}}, \quad \text{where } \overline{w} \equiv \frac{\alpha/\sigma_\varepsilon^2}{E[R_b - R_f]/\sigma_b^2}. \qquad (3.58)$$

Explain intuitively why w is increasing in α and decreasing in σ_ε^2. Assuming $\alpha > 0$, why is it increasing in β?

(ii) Show that

$$SR_p^2 = SR_b^2 + AR_n^2, \qquad (3.59)$$

where $AR_n \equiv \alpha/\sigma_\varepsilon$ is the *appraisal ratio* of the new asset (Treynor and Black 1973).

How is the appraisal ratio different from and how is it similar to the Sharpe ratio? Why is it that the former performance measure captures the improvement in portfolio efficiency due to the new investment? Why does the formula involve the square of the appraisal ratio? Does the implied formula for AR_n^2 remind you of a test statistic? Explain.

(d) The Treynor and Black (1973) model is a classic model of active portfolio management. The authors argue that portfolio construction should begin with a passive benchmark (the market portfolio), and investors with superior information about certain assets (nonzero perceived alphas) should adjust their exposure to these assets (the active part of their portfolio) based on a generalization of the simple algorithm discussed in part (b). How is this approach similar to the Black and Litterman (1992) model of portfolio construction?

Problem 3.3 Arbitrage Pricing Theory

Consider a static frictionless economy with a riskless asset in zero net supply with return R_f, and n risky assets with jointly normal returns R_i, $i = 1 \ldots n$. Suppose the risky returns obey a linear K-factor model:

$$R_i = \overline{R}_i + \sum_{k=1}^{K} b_{ik} f_k + \epsilon_i, \tag{3.60}$$

where the factors and residuals are normally distributed, $\overline{R}_i$ and b_{ik} are constants, $\mathrm{Var}(\epsilon_i) = \sigma_i^2$, $\mathrm{Var}(f_i) = 1$, and $\mathrm{E}[\epsilon_i] = \mathrm{E}[f_k] = \mathrm{Cov}(\epsilon_i, \epsilon_k) = \mathrm{Cov}(\epsilon_i, f_i) = \mathrm{Cov}(f_i, f_k) = 0$, for all i and k with $k \neq i$. There is a representative investor who has exponential utility with coefficient of absolute risk aversion A. Assume that the representative investor has wealth $W = 1$.

For each asset i, define the deviation α_i from the average excess return predicted by arbitrage pricing theory as

$$\alpha_i \equiv \overline{R}_i - R_f - \sum_{k=1}^{K} b_{ik} \lambda_k, \tag{3.61}$$

where λ_k is the price of risk of factor k. Show that

$$\alpha_i = A w_i \sigma_i^2, \tag{3.62}$$

where w_i is the share of asset i in the market portfolio. Interpret this result.

Problem 3.4 Cross-Sectional Regressions

(a) Consider a cross-sectional regression of stock returns onto a constant (normalized to unity). Show that the regression coefficient is the return on a portfolio. What portfolio?

(b) Suppose that, for each stock, we have a measure of the stock's historical beta with the market. We run a cross-sectional regression of returns onto a constant and historical betas. Show that both the intercept and the slope coefficient are the returns on portfolios. Characterize each of these portfolios by stating the sum of the portfolio weights and the historical beta of the portfolio with the market. Relate the two portfolios to the portfolio from part (a).

(c) Assume that the CAPM holds conditionally and that true betas with the market are constant over time. What should the average excess return (over the riskfree rate) on the intercept portfolio from part (b) be? How could we calculate its standard error following the Fama-MacBeth approach?

(d) Suppose that we find historical average excess returns on the intercept portfolio to be significantly higher than the answer to part (c).

(i) If true betas with the market vary over time, would this constitute evidence against the conditional CAPM? Explain.

(ii) Suppose that we are confident in our measure of historical betas as a good proxy for current and future betas and interpret the finding above as evidence against the CAPM. We would like to start a quantitative hedge fund to exploit this mispricing, but a potential client objects that our profits will be eaten up by transactions costs. Explain why this objection may be reasonable and how we could adapt our trading strategy to address this concern.

Problem 3.5 Fama-French Portfolios

In this exercise, you are asked to explore some classic issues from the empirical literature on stock market returns. The data for this question can be found in an Excel spreadsheet on the textbook website.[14] To perform the analysis, we suggest using MATLAB or similar software that allows you to write flexible code.

We consider six assets: four Fama-French portfolios (small-low, small-high, big-low, big-high), the market portfolio, and the 30-day Treasury bill. The four Fama-French portfolios are the corners of the 2×3 size/value portfolios found on Kenneth French's website. The market portfolio is the value-weighted portfolio of stocks listed on NYSE, AMEX, and NASDAQ. The data set runs from July 1926 to June 2016.

(a) Download the data from the textbook website. Do the exercises described in parts (i), (ii), and (iii) for the whole sample and also for two subsamples: 7/26–12/63 and 1/64–6/16.

(i) Estimate the vector of sample mean excess returns and the covariance matrix of excess returns, for each of the samples. Use these estimates to compute two ex-post mean-variance efficient sets: one for portfolios not including the riskless asset and one including the riskless asset. Plot the two sets on a graph with the standard deviation of excess returns on the horizontal axis and the mean excess return on the vertical axis, and indicate where each of the four Fama-French portfolios and the market portfolio lie. Calculate the Sharpe ratios of the tangency portfolio and the market portfolio.

[14]http://press.princeton.edu/titles/11177.html.

(ii) Plot expected return against beta for each of the portfolios. Calculate alphas and discuss your results.

(iii) Test the hypothesis that the market portfolio is mean-variance efficient by calculating a Gibbons-Ross-Shanken test statistic. Interpret your results.

(b) In recent years there has been concern that the publicity given to value investing and the creation of quantitative investment strategies may alter the properties of value returns. One variant of this concern is that the excess return to value may disappear permanently as quantitative investors bid up the price of value stocks to efficient levels. Another variant is that the excess return to value may become less stable as capital flows in and out of value stocks in response to shifting sentiment of end investors about quantitative value strategies. Some have even argued that such shifting sentiment may cause the excess return to value to display a pattern of short-term positive autocorrelation ("style momentum") and longer-term negative autocorrelation ("style reversal").

(i) Plot a one-year moving average of the excess return to small value stocks over small growth stocks (small-high minus small-low, or "small HML") over the period 1/64–6/16. Compare the behavior of the plot in two subsamples: 1/64–12/93 and 1/94–6/16.

(ii) Calculate the mean, standard deviation, and Sharpe ratio of the excess return on the market portfolio over the Treasury bill, and the return on small HML, for each of the two subsamples.

(iii) Aggregate the small HML return to the quarterly data frequency and plot its autocorrelation function out to 12 quarters (3 years) in each of the two subsamples.

(iv) What do your results suggest about the changing behavior of value returns in recent years? Do they support any of the concerns described above?

4

The Stochastic Discount Factor

IN THIS CHAPTER we revisit many of the ideas discussed in the last chapter using an alternative paradigm. The modern literature on the stochastic discount factor (SDF) reformulates arbitrage-based and equilibrium asset pricing, building on the work of Ross (1978), Harrison and Kreps (1979), Hansen and Richard (1987), and Hansen and Jagannathan (1991, 1997). This is the dominant approach in contemporary academic research.

Section 4.1 develops the main ideas in the simplest possible context, a discrete-state model with complete markets. Section 4.2 extends the approach to incomplete markets, and Section 4.3 shows how the properties of asset returns can be used to infer properties of the SDF. Section 4.4 discusses Hansen's (1982b) Generalized Method of Moments, an econometric method widely used in finance because of its close relation with the SDF paradigm. These sections assume that trading is costless, allowing profit-seeking investors to exploit and eliminate arbitrage opportunities, but section 4.5 considers some of the costs and practical challenges that limit such trading. The last chapter of this book explores the determinants of trading costs in greater detail.

4.1 Complete Markets

4.1.1 The SDF in a Complete Market

Consider a simple discrete-state model with S states of nature $s = 1 \ldots S$, all of which have strictly positive probability $\pi(s)$. We assume markets are complete; that is, for each state s a contingent claim is available that pays \$1 in state s and nothing in any other state. Such a state-contingent claim is also known as an Arrow-Debreu security. We write the price of the contingent claim for state s as $q(s)$.

We assume that all contingent claim prices are strictly positive. If this were not true, if the contingent claim price for some state s were zero or negative, there would be an arbitrage opportunity in the sense that an investor could buy that contingent claim, paying nothing or even receiving a positive payoff today, while having some probability of receiving a positive payoff if state s occurs tomorrow, and having zero probability of a negative payoff in any future state of the world. Such an opportunity would be infinitely attractive to any investor who prefers more wealth to less, and so it is natural to assume it away.

Any asset, whether or not it is a contingent claim, is defined by its state-contingent payoffs $X(s)$ for states $s = 1 \ldots S$. The *law of one price* says that two assets with identical payoffs in every state must have the same price. If this were not true, again there would be an arbitrage opportunity, this time in the sense that an investor could go long the cheap asset and short the expensive one, receiving a positive payoff today while having guaranteed zero payoffs in all states in the future. The law of one price implies that we must have

$$P(X) = \sum_{s=1}^{S} q(s) X(s). \tag{4.1}$$

We now multiply and divide equation (4.1) by the probability of each state, $\pi(s)$:

$$P(X) = \sum_{s=1}^{S} \pi(s) \frac{q(s)}{\pi(s)} X(s) = \sum_{s=1}^{S} \pi(s) M(s) X(s) = \mathrm{E}[MX], \tag{4.2}$$

where $M(s) = q(s)/\pi(s)$ is the ratio of state price to probability for state s, the *stochastic discount factor* or SDF in state s. Our assumption of positive state prices implies that $M(s) > 0$ so the SDF is strictly positive.

The last equality in (4.2) uses the definition of an expectation as a probability-weighted average of a random variable to write the asset price as the expected product of the asset's payoff and the SDF. This equation is sometimes referred to rather grandly as the *fundamental equation of asset pricing*.

To understand the importance of this equation, we now explore a series of applications.

4.1.2 The Riskless Asset and Risk-Neutral Probabilities

Consider a riskless asset with payoff $X(s) = 1$ in every state. Its price is

$$P_f = \sum_{s=1}^{S} q(s) = \mathrm{E}[M], \tag{4.3}$$

so the riskless interest rate is

$$1 + R_f = \frac{1}{P_f} = \frac{1}{\mathrm{E}[M]}. \tag{4.4}$$

This tells us that the mean stochastic discount factor must be fairly close to one. A riskless real interest rate of 2%, for example, implies a mean stochastic discount factor of $1/1.02 \approx 0.98$.

Now define *risk-neutral probabilities* or *pseudo-probabilities*

$$\pi^*(s) = (1 + R_f) q(s) = \frac{M(s)}{\mathrm{E}[M]} \pi(s). \tag{4.5}$$

We have $\pi^*(s) > 0$ and $\sum_s \pi^*(s) = 1$, so the $\pi^*(s)$ can be interpreted as if they were probabilities. We can rewrite the asset pricing equation, (4.1) or (4.2), as

$$P(X) = \left(\frac{1}{1 + R_f}\right) \sum_{s=1}^{S} \pi^*(s) X(s) = \left(\frac{1}{1 + R_f}\right) \mathrm{E}^*[X]. \tag{4.6}$$

The price of any asset is the pseudo-expectation of its payoff, discounted at the riskless interest rate.

In a model with continuous states, the transformation from objective probabilities to risk-neutral probabilities is known as a change of measure. Valuation of assets using risk-neutral probabilities is a standard method in models of derivative pricing, and in finance models set in continuous time, both of which fall outside the scope of this book.

4.1.3 Utility Maximization and the SDF

Consider an investor with initial wealth W_0 who maximizes time-separable utility of consumption. Assume that the investor's subjective probabilities for states coincide with the objective probabilities $\pi(s)$. The investor's maximization problem is

$$\max \, u(C_0) + \sum_{s=1}^{S} \beta \pi(s) u(C(s)) \qquad (4.7)$$

subject to

$$C_0 + \sum_{s=1}^{S} q(s) C(s) = W_0, \qquad (4.8)$$

where initial wealth W_0 includes the present value of random future income, appropriately valued using contingent claim prices.

The first-order conditions for this problem can be written as

$$\beta \pi(s) u'(C(s)) = q(s) u'(C_0) \text{ for } s = 1 \ldots S. \qquad (4.9)$$

The left-hand side of this expression is the marginal increase in expected utility caused by buying one more unit of the contingent claim for state s, while the right-hand side is the marginal decrease in utility caused by reducing consumption at time 0 by $q(s)$, the time-0 cost of the contingent claim. At the optimum, these two marginal effects of an adjustment in the contingent claim holding for state s must exactly offset one another.

These first-order conditions imply that

$$M(s) = \frac{q(s)}{\pi(s)} = \frac{\beta u'(C(s))}{u'(C_0)}. \qquad (4.10)$$

The SDF is the discounted ratio of marginal utility tomorrow to marginal utility today. This representation of the SDF is the starting point for the large literature on consumption-based asset pricing, to be discussed in Chapter 6.

4.1.4 The Growth-Optimal Portfolio and the SDF

The above analysis gives particularly interesting results in the case where the investor has log utility. In this case, $u'(C) = 1/C$, so (4.10) becomes

$$M(s) = \frac{\beta C_0}{C(s)}. \qquad (4.11)$$

We write the return on the "growth-optimal" portfolio held by the log-utility investor, realized in state s, as $R_{GO}(s)$. For the growth-optimal portfolio, as for any other portfolio that satisfies the investor's budget constraint,

$$1 + R_{GO}(s) = \frac{C(s)}{W_0 - C_0}, \tag{4.12}$$

since the payoff of the investor's contingent-claim portfolio in state s is fully consumed in that state, and the total cost of the portfolio is $W_0 - C_0$.

With log utility the investor's first-order condition (4.9) implies that $\beta \pi(s) C_0 = q(s) C(s)$. Adding up across states and using the fact that the sum of the state probabilities equals one,

$$\beta C_0 = \sum_{s=1}^{S} q(s) C(s) = W_0 - C_0, \tag{4.13}$$

where the second equality follows from the budget constraint (4.8). Substituting into (4.12), we have

$$1 + R_{GO}(s) = \frac{C(s)}{\beta C_0}, \tag{4.14}$$

so (4.11) can be rewritten as

$$M(s) = \frac{1}{1 + R_{GO}(s)}. \tag{4.15}$$

Equation (4.15) says that in complete markets, the SDF is the reciprocal of the gross return on the growth-optimal portfolio. As we will discuss in section 4.2.2, this insight can be extended to incomplete markets.

4.1.5 Solving Portfolio Choice Problems

The logic of the SDF and utility maximization with complete markets can also be applied to solve portfolio choice problems. One can rearrange equation (4.10) to put the marginal utility of consumption in state s on the left-hand side:

$$u'(C(s)) = \frac{M(s) u'(C_0)}{\beta}. \tag{4.16}$$

Applying the inverse of the marginal utility function to both sides of this expression,

$$C(s) = u'^{-1}\left(\frac{M(s) u'(C_0)}{\beta}\right). \tag{4.17}$$

Consumption in state s, $C(s)$, equals the number of contingent claims for state s purchased by the investor. Thus, given the SDF and the investor's marginal utility at time 0, one can calculate the investor's asset purchases. The budget constraint can then be used to find the level of initial consumption C_0 that generates an affordable consumption and asset purchase plan.

This approach to portfolio choice was developed in continuous time by Cox and Huang (1989) and is known as the "martingale method" in the continuous-time finance literature. In general, it relies critically on the assumption of complete markets, which delivers a unique SDF $M(s)$ in equation (4.17). Problem 4.1 asks you to explore the properties of the martingale method in the special case where the investor has quadratic utility.

4.1.6 Perfect Risksharing

Let us consider two investors j and k, assuming that they share the same beliefs about the likelihood of each state. To simplify notation, we also assume that they have the same time discount factor β. Then equation (4.10) implies that

$$\frac{M(s)}{\beta} = \frac{u'_j(C_j(s))}{u'_j(C_{j0})} = \frac{u'_k(C_k(s))}{u'_k(C_{k0})}, \tag{4.18}$$

where the subscripts j and k denote the utility functions and consumption levels of investors j and k, respectively. Since this equation holds for any state s, it is also true that across any two states s and s^*,

$$\frac{u'_j(C_j(s))}{u'_j(C_j(s^*))} = \frac{u'_k(C_k(s))}{u'_k(C_k(s^*))}. \tag{4.19}$$

These conditions characterize perfect risksharing and will be satisfied in a complete markets economy with homogeneous beliefs. Perfect risksharing requires that the marginal utilities of different investors are perfectly correlated, which is a very strong statement about individual agents' consumption.

With perfect risksharing, the consumption allocation in the economy is Pareto optimal, since a social planner allocating aggregate consumption $\overline{C}(s)$ to the two investors would solve

$$\max \lambda_j \sum_s \pi(s) u_j(C_j(s)) + \lambda_k \sum_s \pi(s) u_k(C_k(s)) \tag{4.20}$$

subject to $C_j(s) + C_k(s) = \overline{C}(s)$, where λ_j and λ_k are Pareto weights on the utilities of investors j and k. The social planner's first-order condition

$$\lambda_j u'_j(C_j(s)) = \lambda_k u'_k(C_k(s)) \tag{4.21}$$

implies a common marginal utility ratio across states.

Empirical Tests

A naïve empirical test of perfect risksharing would assume a common utility function for all investors (e.g., power utility with a common coefficient of relative risk aversion), would calculate marginal utilities using microeconomic survey data on consumption, and would then test the null hypothesis that these marginal utilities are perfectly correlated across investors. Such a test would inevitably reject the null since correlations calculated from individual-level data are always imperfect.

Meaningful tests of perfect risksharing have been proposed by Cochrane (1991a) and Mace (1991), who allow for measurement error and idiosyncratic taste shocks that create noise in individual-level consumption. Under the assumption that measurement error and taste shocks are uncorrelated with idiosyncratic events that affect household income, the null hypothesis is that the growth rates of individual marginal utilities, calculated from measured consumption, are cross-sectionally uncorrelated with these events. Using data from the Panel Study of Income Dynamics (PSID), Cochrane is unable to reject the null for some events but does reject it for long-term illness and involuntary job loss.

A well-known study by Townsend (1994) uses a similar methodology to study risksharing in several Indian farming villages and finds only modest effects of idiosyncratic events on consumption. Building on this work, Ogaki and Zhang (2001) argue that households in poor farming villages have decreasing relative risk aversion, which they model using a power utility function with a positive subsistence level, and that risksharing is close to perfect within villages once one takes account of this fact. Of course, risksharing within small local groups of people may be easier to achieve than risksharing across a large economy.

Evidence that risksharing is imperfect has motivated a large literature modeling barriers to risksharing, which we review in Chapter 11.

4.1.7 Existence of a Representative Agent

The condition for perfect risksharing, equation (4.19), ensures that all agents have the same ordering of marginal utility across states. With declining marginal utility, this means that they all have the same ordering of consumption across states. Without loss of generality, we can then number states such that

$$C_j(1) \leq C_j(2) \leq \ldots \leq C_j(S) \tag{4.22}$$

for all agents j.

Define aggregate consumption in state s, $\overline{C}(s) = \sum_j C_j(s)$. Then we have

$$\overline{C}(1) \leq \overline{C}(2) \leq \ldots \leq \overline{C}(S). \tag{4.23}$$

Also, we have

$$M(1) \geq M(2) \geq \ldots \geq M(S). \tag{4.24}$$

Now we find a function $g(\overline{C}(s))$ s.t.

$$\frac{g(\overline{C}(s))}{g(\overline{C}(s^*))} = \frac{M(s)}{M(s^*)} \tag{4.25}$$

for all states s and s^*. The above ordering conditions ensure that this is always possible, with $g > 0$ and $g' \leq 0$. Since the ratios of $g(\overline{C}(s))$ across states equal the ratios of SDFs across states, $g(\overline{C}(s))$ can be interpreted as the marginal utility of a "composite consumer" or "representative agent" who consumes aggregate consumption and holds the market portfolio of all wealth.

Finally, we integrate to find a function $v(\overline{C}(s))$ such that

$$v'(\overline{C}(s)) = g(\overline{C}(s)). \tag{4.26}$$

The function $v(.)$ is the utility function of the representative agent.

This argument shows that with complete markets, the market portfolio is *efficient* (a generalization of the concept of mean-variance efficiency). That is, there exists some concave utility function that would induce an agent to hold the market portfolio. This is not true in general with incomplete markets (Ingersoll 1987).

The above construction is limited in several important respects (Constantinides 1982, Guvenen 2011). It does not tell us anything about the form of the representative agent's utility function. In general this utility function will not have the same form as the utility functions of individual agents, and so it is sometimes called a "mongrel" since mongrel (cross-bred) dogs need not resemble their parents. Only in tractable special cases (e.g., CARA with normal risks) do we get a representative-agent utility function in the same class as the utility functions of individual agents.

Moreover, economies with complete markets do not generally satisfy conditions for "demand aggregation." Any reallocation of wealth between agents can alter the utility function of the composite consumer, and aggregate demand for consumption and assets generally depends on the entire distribution of wealth in the economy, not just the aggregate level of wealth. Even under a fixed distribution of wealth, the representative agent's demand equals aggregate demand only at the equilibrium prices; his demand schedule need not coincide with the aggregate demand function. Thus, complete markets alone do not imply a representative consumer as defined in Mas-Colell, Whinston, and Green (1995, Chapter 4).

4.1.8 Heterogeneous Beliefs

So far we have assumed that all investors assign the same probabilities to the different states of the world. What happens if this is not the case?

Recall the maximization problem of investor j,

$$\max u(C_{j0}) + \sum_{s=1}^{S} \beta \pi_j(s) u(C_j(s)) \tag{4.27}$$

subject to

$$C_{j0} + \sum_{s=1}^{S} q(s) C_j(s) = W_{j0}. \tag{4.28}$$

We allow subjective probabilities $\pi_j(s)$ to differ across investors, but state prices $q(s)$ are given by the market. For simplicity and to highlight the effects of belief heterogeneity, in the remainder of this subsection we assume that all investors have the same utility function.

The first-order conditions for this optimization problem are

$$\beta \pi_j(s) u'(C_j(s)) = q(s) u'(C_{j0}) \text{ for } s = 1\ldots S. \tag{4.29}$$

Thus for any state s and investor j,

$$q(s) = \frac{\beta \pi_j(s) u'(C_j(s))}{u'(C_{j0})}. \tag{4.30}$$

The state price is related to the product of the investor's subjective probability of the state and the investor's marginal utility in that state. In other words, it is a composite "util-prob" to use the terminology of Samuelson (1969).

A similar observation applies to the SDF, the ratio of state price to objective probability:

$$M(s) = \frac{q(s)}{\pi(s)} = \left(\frac{\pi_j(s)}{\pi(s)}\right)\left(\frac{\beta u'(C_j(s))}{u'(C_{j0})}\right). \tag{4.31}$$

Volatility of the SDF across states may correspond either to volatile deviations of investor j's subjective probabilities from objective probabilities, or to volatile marginal utility across states. The usual assumption that investors have homogeneous beliefs rules out the first of these possibilities.

For any two states s and s^* and investors j and k,

$$\frac{q(s)}{q(s^*)} = \frac{\pi_j(s)\,u'(C_j(s))}{\pi_j(s^*)\,u'(C_j(s^*))} = \frac{\pi_k(s)\,u'(C_k(s))}{\pi_k(s^*)\,u'(C_k(s^*))}. \tag{4.32}$$

This equation tells us that the investors who have particularly low marginal utility in a state are the ones who give that state the highest probability. These investors perceive wealth in the state as relatively cheap and buy a lot of it. Thus the people who end up rich (with high consumption) are those who bet heavily on the state that occurs. One might caricature this result as "if you're so rich, you must be smart" (in the sense of assigning a high probability to a state that is likely to occur), although it is also possible that "if you're so rich, you must be lucky" (having assigned a high probability to a state that has occurred, even if it was unlikely to do so).

The results above are simplified by the assumption of this subsection 4.1.8 that all investors have the same utility function. If this is not the case, then marginal utilities as well as subjective probabilities and consumption levels must have investor-specific subscripts in equation (4.32). In the general case, investors may have relatively high consumption in states with low aggregate consumption because they are more risk-averse than average and have bought insurance from more risk tolerant investors. We return to this risksharing function of financial market trading in Chapter 11.

4.2 Incomplete Markets

What if markets are incomplete? Then the SDF is no longer unique, but under very weak conditions there exists a positive SDF that prices all financial assets. We present the arguments here following textbook treatments by Duffie (2001) and Cochrane (2005). For simplicity we continue to assume a discrete state space, although the arguments can be extended to a continuous state space. We proceed in two steps, first showing how to construct a linear combination of asset payoffs that satisfies the fundamental equation of asset pricing but may or may not be positive, and then discussing the conditions under which a positive SDF exists.

4.2.1 Constructing an SDF in the Payoff Space

We continue to observe a set of asset payoffs X and prices P. We write the set of all observed (traded) payoffs, the "payoff space," as Ξ. We make two assumptions:

Assumption 1 (portfolio formation). $X_1, X_2 \in \Xi \implies aX_1 + bX_2 \in \Xi$ for any real a, b. This says that any linear combination of asset payoffs in the payoff space can be achieved by holding the appropriate combination of assets. Since a and b can be negative, we are implicitly allowing short sales here.

Assumption 2 (law of one price). $P(aX_1+bX_2) = aP(X_1)+bP(X_2)$. This says that the price of an asset that delivers a linear combination of the payoffs on other assets must equal the same linear combination of the prices of those other assets. As discussed in section 4.1.1 for the special case of complete markets, if this were not true, there would be two investment strategies with the same payoffs but different prices. This would allow investors to go long the cheaper strategy and short the more expensive one, receiving the difference in cost today while having zero cash flows in all future states and dates.

Under these two assumptions, it can be shown that there exists a unique payoff X^* in the payoff space with the property $P(X) = E(X^*X)$ for all X in the payoff space. The payoff X^* thus satisfies equation (4.2), the fundamental equation of asset pricing, which is one of the two key properties of an SDF. We discuss the other property, the positivity of the SDF, in the next subsection. With slight abuse of terminology, but following the literature, we refer to any random variable that satisfies the fundamental equation of asset pricing as an SDF, whether or not it is positive.

The proof proceeds by construction. There are S discrete states and N basis payoffs $X_1 \ldots X_N$, where $N < S$ so markets are incomplete. We can represent the set of basis payoffs as a column vector $\mathbb{X}$ of the random variables X_1 through X_N, that is, $\mathbb{X} = [X_1 \ldots X_N]'$. Let $\mathbb{P} = [P(X_1) \ldots P(X_N)]' \in \mathbb{R}^N$ denote the column vector of prices of the basis payoffs. Using assumption 1, we can write the set of tradable payoffs as $\Xi = \{\mathbb{X}'c : c \in \mathbb{R}^N\}$. We want to construct a tradable payoff $X^* = \mathbb{X}'c^* \in \Xi$ that can serve as a valid stochastic discount factor. By the law of one price, this is true if and only if X^* prices the basis payoffs. That is, we require

$$\mathbb{P} = E[\mathbb{X}X^*] = E[\mathbb{X}\mathbb{X}'c^*], \tag{4.33}$$

which yields

$$c^* = E[\mathbb{X}\mathbb{X}']^{-1}\mathbb{P} \tag{4.34}$$

and

$$X^* = \mathbb{X}'E[\mathbb{X}\mathbb{X}']^{-1}\mathbb{P}. \tag{4.35}$$

This construction for X^* always exists and is unique provided that the matrix $E[\mathbb{X}\mathbb{X}']$ is nonsingular. Thus we have a recipe for deriving an SDF given payoffs and prices of a set of assets. While the recipe is given using uncentered second-moment matrices of payoffs, it is straightforward to subtract means and rewrite the above equations in terms of covariance matrices. We follow this alternative approach below when we discuss Hansen-Jagannathan volatility bounds on the SDF.

It is important to understand that only the SDF that is a linear combination of asset payoffs is unique. There may be many other SDFs of the form $M = X^* + \epsilon$, where $E[\mathbb{X}\epsilon] = E[\mathbb{X}(M-X^*)] = 0$. When a riskfree asset is traded these must all have higher variance than X^*, as discussed further below in the context of volatility bounds on the SDF. Equivalently, X^* is the projection of every SDF onto the space of tradable payoffs. Thus it can be thought of as the portfolio of available assets that best mimics the behavior of every SDF.

4.2.2 Existence of a Positive SDF

Equation (4.35) gives us an SDF, but it does not ensure that this SDF is positive. We now show that under slightly stronger (but still very weak) conditions, there exists a positive SDF in incomplete markets.

Definition. *Absence of arbitrage.* A payoff space Ξ and pricing function $P(X)$ have absence of arbitrage if $P(X) \geq 0$ for all $X \in \Xi$ such that $X \geq 0$ always, and if $P(X) > 0$ for all $X \in \Xi$ such that $X \geq 0$ always and such that $X > 0$ with positive probability.[1]

This is a stronger condition than the law of one price, given above as assumption 2. To see why, consider an economy with a (complete or incomplete) set of state-contingent claims or Arrow-Debreu securities, one of which has a negative price. This economy does not violate the law of one price, but it does violate absence of arbitrage because by buying the negative-priced Arrow-Debreu security an investor gets a payoff that is never negative and is strictly positive with positive probability, yet the investor pays a negative price today. Such an investment opportunity would attract infinite demand from all investors who prefer more to less. Therefore it is natural to assume that real-world economies have absence of arbitrage.

One can show that absence of arbitrage is equivalent to the conditions $P = \mathrm{E}(MX)$ *and* $M(s) > 0$ for some stochastic discount factor M. This requires two theorems to hold:

Theorem 1. $P = \mathrm{E}(MX)$ *and* $M(s) > 0 \implies$ *absence of arbitrage.*

Proof: Consider any $X \in \Xi$ such that $X \geq 0$ always. Then, $P(X) = \sum_s \pi(s)M(s)X(s) \geq 0$ since no terms in this expression are ever negative. Now consider any $X \in \Xi$ such that $X \geq 0$ always and such that $X > 0$ with positive probability. Then, $P(X) > 0$ since both $\pi(s)$ and $M(s)$ are strictly positive for all states, and $X(s) > 0$ for at least one state. It follows that there is no arbitrage.

Theorem 2. *Absence of arbitrage* $\implies \exists M$ *s.t.* $P = \mathrm{E}(MX)$ *and* $M(s) > 0$.

Proof: In our discrete-state framework, showing that there exists a strictly positive SDF is equivalent to showing that there exists a strictly positive state-price vector, that is, a vector $q \in \mathbb{R}_{++}^S$ such that $P(X) = q'X$ for all $X \in \Xi$. Recall that $q(s) = \pi(s)M(s)$, and $\pi(s)$ is strictly positive for all s.

Define $Z \equiv \{(-P(X), X) : X \in \Xi\}$, which is a linear subspace of $\mathbb{R} \times \mathbb{R}^S$. Also, define $C \equiv \mathbb{R}_+ \times \mathbb{R}_+^S$ as the subset of nonnegative vectors in $\mathbb{R} \times \mathbb{R}^S$. We can then translate the requirements for the absence of arbitrage into the condition that the intersection of subspaces Z and C contains only the zero vector: $Z \cap C = \overrightarrow{\{0\}}$. This condition, the fact that Z and C are closed and convex subsets of $\mathbb{R} \times \mathbb{R}^S$, and the fact that Z is a linear subspace give us, through an application of the Separating Hyperplane Theorem, that there exists a nonzero linear function $F : \mathbb{R} \times \mathbb{R}^S \to \mathbb{R}$ such that $F(a, b) = 0$ for all $(a, b) \in Z$ and $F(a, b) > 0$ for all $(a, b) \in C \backslash \overrightarrow{\{0\}}$, the subset of nonnegative vectors excluding the zero vector. Since any linear function can be represented by a vector through an inner product, these properties of the function F imply that there exists a strictly positive column vector $q \in \mathbb{R}_{++}^S$ such that $F(a, b) = a + q'b$. Finally, since $F(-P(X), X) = 0$ for all $X \in \Xi$, we have that $P(X) = q'X$ for all $X \in \Xi$, as desired.

---

[1]This definition follows Duffie (2001). Cochrane (2005) uses a slightly weaker definition that does not imply the law of one price.

The key step in the proof is the construction of a linear function F, represented by a strictly positive vector $(1, q)$, that can price any payoff X in $\mathbb{R}^S$, not just traded payoffs in the set Ξ, through $F(-P(X), X) = 0$ or $P(X) = q'X$. In other words, the theorem tells us that, as long as there is no arbitrage on the observed (traded) set of assets, we can always find an arbitrage-free complete-markets economy (in general, many such economies, one corresponding to each possible strictly positive state price vector) that could have generated the asset prices we observe.

An alternative way to understand this theorem is to recall the result that the reciprocal of the gross return on the growth-optimal portfolio equals the unique SDF in a complete-market setting. Even in an incomplete-market setting, where the SDF is no longer unique, the reciprocal of this return satisfies the fundamental equation of asset pricing $P = \mathrm{E}(MX)$. If there is absence of arbitrage, and if at least one asset is available whose lowest possible gross return is strictly positive, then the portfolio choice problem for log utility has a well-defined solution—the growth-optimal portfolio—with a strictly positive gross return whose reciprocal satisfies the conditions of the SDF in the theorem.[2]

An important caveat is that with incomplete markets, there also exist many SDFs that satisfy the fundamental equation of asset pricing but are not always positive. In particular, the unique SDF X^* that lies in the payoff space, constructed in equation (4.35), need not be positive. And the reciprocal of the gross return on the growth-optimal portfolio cannot generally be written as a linear function of asset payoffs when markets are incomplete.

4.3 Properties of the SDF

4.3.1 Risk Premia and the SDF

In this subsection we adapt the notation of the two-period discrete-state model to move in the direction of empirical research in finance. We use the subscript t for the initial date at which the asset's price is determined, and the subscript $t+1$ for the next period at which the asset's payoff is realized. This can easily be embedded in a multiperiod model, in which case the payoff is next period's price plus dividend. We add the subscript i to denote an asset. Then the fundamental equation of asset pricing can be written as

$$P_{it} = \mathrm{E}_t[M_{t+1}X_{i,t+1}] = \mathrm{E}_t[M_{t+1}]\mathrm{E}_t[X_{i,t+1}] + \mathrm{Cov}_t(M_{t+1}, X_{i,t+1}), \qquad (4.36)$$

where the t subscripts on the mean and covariance indicate that these are conditional moments calculated using probabilities perceived at time t. The price of the asset at time t is included in the information set at time t, hence there is no need to take a conditional expectation of this variable. Since the conditional mean of the SDF is the reciprocal of the gross riskless interest rate from (4.4), equation (4.36) says that the price of any asset is its expected payoff, discounted at the riskless interest rate, plus a correction for the conditional covariance of the payoff with the SDF.

---

[2]Long (1990) develops this argument, using the terminology "numeraire portfolio" for the growth-optimal portfolio. He emphasizes that expected net returns on all assets are zero if these returns are denominated in units of the numeraire portfolio.

For assets with positive prices, we can divide through by P_{it} and use $(1 + R_{i,t+1}) = X_{i,t+1}/P_{it}$ to get

$$1 = \mathrm{E}_t[M_{t+1}(1 + R_{i,t+1})]$$

$$= \mathrm{E}_t[M_{t+1}]\mathrm{E}_t[1 + R_{i,t+1}] + \mathrm{Cov}_t(M_{t+1}, R_{i,t+1}). \qquad (4.37)$$

Rearranging and using the relation between the riskless rate and the conditional mean of the SDF,

$$\mathrm{E}_t[1 + R_{i,t+1}] = (1 + R_{f,t+1})(1 - \mathrm{Cov}_t(M_{t+1}, R_{i,t+1})). \qquad (4.38)$$

This says that the expected return on any asset is the riskless return times an adjustment factor for the covariance of the return with the SDF.

Subtracting the gross riskless interest rate from both sides, the risk premium is the gross riskless interest rate times the covariance of the excess return with the SDF:

$$\mathrm{E}_t[R_{i,t+1} - R_{f,t+1}] = -(1 + R_{f,t+1})\mathrm{Cov}_t(M_{t+1}, R_{i,t+1} - R_{f,t+1}). \qquad (4.39)$$

We can rewrite this equation as

$$\mathrm{E}_t[R_{i,t+1} - R_{f,t+1}] = \beta_{iMt}\lambda_{Mt}, \qquad (4.40)$$

where $\beta_{iMt} \equiv \mathrm{Cov}_t(M_{t+1}, R_{i,t+1})/\mathrm{Var}_t(M_{t+1})$ is the regression coefficient of asset return i on the SDF and $\lambda_{Mt} \equiv -(1 + R_{f,t+1})\mathrm{Var}_t(M_{t+1})$. Therefore, returns always obey a linear factor pricing model with the SDF as the single factor. λ_{Mt}, the price of risk or factor risk premium of the SDF in the language of section 3.2.2, is equal to the conditional variance of the SDF multiplied by the gross riskfree interest rate.

Sometimes it is convenient to work with log versions of these equations, assuming joint lognormality of asset returns and the SDF (Hansen and Singleton 1983). Taking logs of (4.37) and using the formula for the conditional mean of a lognormal random variable, we have

$$0 = \mathrm{E}_t m_{t+1} + \mathrm{E}_t r_{i,t+1} + \frac{\sigma_{mt}^2}{2} + \frac{\sigma_{it}^2}{2} + \sigma_{imt}, \qquad (4.41)$$

where $m_{t+1} \equiv \log(M_{t+1})$, $r_{i,t+1} \equiv \log(1 + R_{i,t+1})$, $\sigma_{mt}^2 \equiv \mathrm{Var}_t(m_{t+1})$, $\sigma_{it}^2 \equiv \mathrm{Var}_t(r_{i,t+1})$, and $\sigma_{imt} \equiv \mathrm{Cov}_t(r_{i,t+1}, m_{t+1})$. For simplicity we omit brackets after the expectations operator where this does not lead to any ambiguity in the notation.

The return on the riskless asset has zero variance and zero covariance with the log SDF, so the riskless interest rate satisfies

$$r_{f,t+1} = -\mathrm{E}_t m_{t+1} - \sigma_{mt}^2/2. \qquad (4.42)$$

The log risk premium on any other asset, adjusted for Jensen's Inequality by adding one-half the variance of the asset's log return, is

$$\mathrm{E}_t r_{i,t+1} - r_{f,t+1} + \sigma_i^2/2 = -\sigma_{imt}, \qquad (4.43)$$

the negative of the covariance between the asset's log return and the log SDF. In this expression we no longer need to divide by the mean of the SDF (multiply by the gross riskless interest rate) as we do in equation (4.39), because the covariance here is with the log SDF, so it is a proportional rather than absolute covariance. In intertemporal equilibrium models, such as the representative-agent model with power utility, these logarithmic equations are often easier to work with.

4.3.2 Volatility Bounds

Asset pricing models place testable restrictions on the behavior of the SDF. Before considering specific models, however, one can use the observed properties of asset returns to characterize the SDF. One popular approach is to derive lower bounds on the volatility of the SDF from the risk premia observed in asset markets. In this section we consider a series of such lower bounds.

Simple Volatility Bound with a Risky and a Riskless Asset
We can use the fact that the correlation between the SDF and any excess return must be greater than minus one to obtain a lower bound on the volatility of the SDF. We have

$$
\begin{aligned}
\mathrm{E}_t[R_{i,t+1} - R_{f,t+1}] &= \frac{-\mathrm{Cov}_t(M_{t+1}, R_{i,t+1} - R_{f,t+1})}{\mathrm{E}_t[M_{t+1}]} \\
&= \frac{-\mathrm{Corr}_t(M_{t+1}, R_{i,t+1} - R_{f,t+1})\sigma_t(M_{t+1})\sigma_t(R_{i,t+1} - R_{f,t+1})}{\mathrm{E}_t[M_{t+1}]} \\
&\leq \frac{\sigma_t(M_{t+1})\sigma_t(R_{i,t+1} - R_{f,t+1})}{\mathrm{E}_t[M_{t+1}]}.
\end{aligned}
\tag{4.44}
$$

Rearranging, we get

$$
\frac{\sigma_t(M_{t+1})}{\mathrm{E}_t[M_{t+1}]} \geq \frac{\mathrm{E}_t[R_{i,t+1} - R_{f,t+1}]}{\sigma_t(R_{i,t+1} - R_{f,t+1})}.
\tag{4.45}
$$

The Sharpe ratio for asset i puts a lower bound on the volatility of the stochastic discount factor relative to its mean. The tightest lower bound is achieved by finding the risky asset, or portfolio of assets, with the highest Sharpe ratio. Bounds of this general type (although not the exact bound stated here) were first derived by Shiller (1982) and a conference discussion of his paper by Hansen (1982a). Problem 8.2 asks you to derive a related volatility bound in a setting where a candidate SDF from an asset pricing model misprices a single risky asset.

Logarithmic Volatility Bound with a Risky and a Riskless Asset
The logarithmic version of this bound, assuming lognormality, is even simpler. Since $-\sigma_{imt} \leq \sigma_{it}\sigma_{mt}$, equation (4.43) implies

$$
\sigma_{mt} \geq \frac{\mathrm{E}_t r_{i,t+1} - r_{f,t+1} + \sigma_i^2/2}{\sigma_{it}}.
\tag{4.46}
$$

The ratio on the right-hand side is in the range 0.33–0.5 for the aggregate US stock market in the 20th century, implying a large standard deviation for the SDF. Recall that the mean SDF must be close to 1 and the SDF is always positive, so a volatility of 0.33–0.5 implies that the lower bound of zero is only 2 or 3 standard deviations below the mean. It is surprising that marginal utility routinely changes this much in a year, implying that states of the world where people place almost no value on extra consumption have substantial probability weight. This is the most general way to understand the famous equity premium puzzle of Mehra and Prescott (1985), discussed further in Chapter 6.

Simple Volatility Bound without a Riskless Asset

Hansen and Jagannathan (HJ 1991) derive restrictions on the first two moments of any valid SDF given a set of observed asset payoffs even when there is no riskfree asset pinning down the mean of the SDF. They derive a frontier in SDF mean-standard deviation space that is closely related to the mean-standard deviation frontier of risky asset returns.

We return to the two-period framework of section 4.2.1. There are N risky assets in the vector $\mathbb{X}$ of basis payoffs, and no riskfree asset. The starting point of HJ's analysis is to treat the mean of the SDF $\overline{M}$ as an unknown parameter and, for each possible value of $\overline{M}$, augment the set of basis assets with a hypothetical riskfree payoff whose return equals $1/\overline{M}$. Each of these "augmented" economies is characterized by a basis payoff vector $\mathbb{X}_{\overline{M}} = [1/\overline{M}, \mathbb{X}']'$ and corresponding prices $\mathbb{P}_{\overline{M}} = [1, \mathbb{P}']'$.

The SDF that lies in the augmented payoff space, $M^*(\overline{M})$, is a linear combination of a constant (the riskfree payoff) and the risky payoffs. Since it must have mean $\overline{M}$ we can write it as

$$M^*(\overline{M}) = \overline{M} + (\mathbb{X} - \mathrm{E}[\mathbb{X}])'\beta_{\overline{M}}. \tag{4.47}$$

To simplify the notation where possible, we shall write this SDF simply as M^* in cases where this does not cause confusion. Note that M^* is a valid SDF for the original economy with only risky assets, as it prices these assets correctly. Also note that M^* is in general different from X^* in (4.35), the SDF that lies in the payoff space of the original economy.

Since M^* must correctly price the risky payoffs, we have

$$\mathbb{P} = \mathrm{E}[\mathbb{X}M^*] = \mathrm{E}[\mathbb{X}]\overline{M} + \mathrm{Cov}(\mathbb{X}, M^*) = \mathrm{E}[\mathbb{X}]\overline{M} + \Sigma\beta_{\overline{M}}, \tag{4.48}$$

where $\Sigma \equiv \mathrm{Var}(\mathbb{X})$. We can use this to solve for the coefficient vector $\beta_{\overline{M}}$ and the variance of M^* as

$$\beta_{\overline{M}} = \Sigma^{-1}(\mathbb{P} - \mathrm{E}[\mathbb{X}]\overline{M}), \tag{4.49}$$

and

$$\sigma^2(M^*) = \beta'_{\overline{M}}\Sigma\beta_{\overline{M}} = (\mathbb{P} - \mathrm{E}[\mathbb{X}]\overline{M})'\Sigma^{-1}(\mathbb{P} - \mathrm{E}[\mathbb{X}]\overline{M}). \tag{4.50}$$

The variance of M^* gives a lower bound on the variance of any other SDF with the same mean. To see this, note that any such SDF $M(\overline{M})$ can be written as

$$M(\overline{M}) = M^*(\overline{M}) + \varepsilon, \tag{4.51}$$

where $\mathrm{E}[\varepsilon] = 0$ so that $M(\overline{M})$ has the same mean $\overline{M}$, and $\mathrm{E}[\mathbb{X}\varepsilon] = 0$ so that $M(\overline{M})$ satisfies the fundamental equation of asset pricing. This implies that $\mathrm{Cov}(\mathbb{X}, \varepsilon) = 0$ and hence $\mathrm{Cov}(M^*(\overline{M}), \varepsilon) = 0$. Thus,

$$\sigma^2(M(\overline{M})) = \sigma^2(M^*(\overline{M})) + \sigma^2(\varepsilon)$$

$$\geq \sigma^2(M^*(\overline{M})). \tag{4.52}$$

Equivalently,

$$\frac{\sigma(M(\overline{M}))}{\mathrm{E}[M(\overline{M})]} \geq \frac{\sigma(M^*(\overline{M}))}{\overline{M}}. \tag{4.53}$$

The pairs $(\overline{M}, \sigma(M^*(\overline{M})))$ for all possible values of $\overline{M}$ comprise the HJ frontier, the set of SDF means and corresponding minimum SDF volatilities.

Geometry of the Hansen-Jagannathan Frontier

To understand the link between the SDF frontier and the mean-standard deviation frontier of asset returns, we can rederive the volatility bound (4.45) using (4.53) and the geometry of the mean-standard deviation diagram for asset returns. The top panel of Figure 4.1 plots the risky asset return frontier together with the return frontier corresponding to the augmented payoff space, for a particular value of $\overline{M}$. Recall from Chapter 2 that the frontier of an economy with a riskless asset is composed of two straight lines that are symmetric around an axis parallel to the horizontal axis. One of these lines is tangent to the risky asset frontier at a single point, the tangency portfolio return, $1 + R_q$.

Define the *benchmark return* of the augmented economy as the return to M^*, the SDF that is also a payoff:

$$1 + R^*(\overline{M}) \equiv \frac{M^*(\overline{M})}{P(M^*(\overline{M}))} = \frac{M^*(\overline{M})}{\mathrm{E}[(M^*(\overline{M}))^2]}. \tag{4.54}$$

This definition implies that

$$\frac{\sigma(1 + R^*(\overline{M}))}{\mathrm{E}[1 + R^*(\overline{M})]} = \frac{\sigma(M^*(\overline{M}))}{\overline{M}}. \tag{4.55}$$

Problem 4.3 asks you to derive Hansen and Richard's (1987) orthogonal decomposition of returns, which implies that the benchmark return is the traded return with the smallest second (uncentered) moment. In return mean-standard deviation space, the second moment of a return is given by the square of its distance from the origin, since $\mathrm{E}[(1 + R)^2] = \sigma^2(1 + R) + (\mathrm{E}[1 + R])^2$ (use Pythagoras' Theorem). Therefore, $1 + R^*$ is located at the point where a circle centered at the origin is tangent to the lower part of the frontier for the augmented payoff space, as can be seen in the top panel of Figure 4.1. It follows that the line from the origin to the benchmark return is perpendicular to the lower part of the frontier. Using the fact that the product of the slopes of two perpendicular lines equals –1 and that the slope of the lower part of the frontier equals the negative of the absolute value of the Sharpe ratio of the tangency portfolio, which is the maximum Sharpe ratio attainable in the augmented economy with the riskless asset, we have

$$\frac{\sigma(1 + R^*(\overline{M}))}{\mathrm{E}[1 + R^*(\overline{M})]} = \left| \frac{\mathrm{E}[1 + R_q - 1/\overline{M}]}{\sigma(1 + R_q)} \right|. \tag{4.56}$$

Combining (4.55) and (4.56), and using (4.53), we have rederived (4.45) for a given value of $\overline{M}$.

In a mean-standard deviation diagram with SDF mean on the horizontal axis and SDF standard deviation on the vertical axis (the orientation used in Hansen-Jagannathan volatility bound analysis), depicted in the bottom panel of Figure 4.1, the line from the origin to the SDF frontier at $\overline{M}$ has slope equal to the Sharpe ratio of the upper part of the return frontier. As we reduce $\overline{M}$ (increase $1/\overline{M}$), the Sharpe ratio declines given the hyperbolic shape of the risky asset frontier. The minimum Sharpe ratio occurs when the riskless interest rate equals the average return on the global minimum-variance risky portfolio, so the HJ frontier reaches its minimum in the neighborhood of this return. When $1/\overline{M}$ exceeds the average return on the global minimum-variance portfolio, the tangency portfolio lies in the lower part of the risky asset frontier. However, the maximum

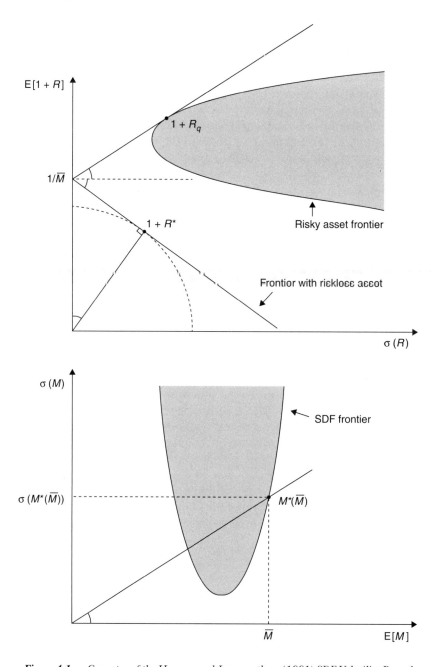

Figure 4.1.   *Geometry of the Hansen and Jagannathan (1991) SDF Volatility Bound*

attainable Sharpe ratio in the augmented payoff space is still given by the slope of the upper part of the V-shaped frontier, and equation (4.56) still holds. Thus, as we increase $1/\overline{M}$ past the average return on the minimum-variance risky portfolio the corresponding Sharpe ratio starts increasing again. This is why the line from the origin of the SDF graph with a given slope crosses the SDF frontier at two points.

We can confirm the duality between the risky asset return frontier and the SDF frontier algebraically. Assume that payoffs are given in the form of returns, $\mathbb{X} = \iota + R$ and $\mathbb{P} = \iota$. Then (4.50) can be written as

$$
\begin{aligned}
\sigma^2(M^*) &= (\iota - (\iota + \overline{R})\overline{M})' \Sigma^{-1} (\iota - (\iota + \overline{R})\overline{M}) \\
&= \overline{M}^2 (\iota + \overline{R})' \Sigma^{-1} (\iota + \overline{R}) - 2\overline{M}\iota' \Sigma^{-1} (\iota + \overline{R}) + \iota' \Sigma^{-1} \iota \\
&= A\overline{M}^2 - 2B\overline{M} + C,
\end{aligned}
\tag{4.57}
$$

where $A = (\iota + \overline{R})' \Sigma^{-1} (\iota + \overline{R})$, $B = \iota' \Sigma^{-1} (\iota + \overline{R})$ and $C = \iota' \Sigma^{-1} \iota$. Compare (4.57) with equation (2.47) from Chapter 2 giving the algebraic relationship between the mean and variance of any return p that lies on the risky asset return frontier:

$$
D\sigma_p^2 = A - 2B\overline{R}_p + C\overline{R}_p^2,
$$

where the constants A, B, and C are the same as in (4.57) and $D = AC - B^2$.[3]

The HJ frontier is commonly used as a quick check on the ability of a parametric asset pricing model to fit the properties of asset returns. The mean and volatility of the SDF can be calculated for different parameter values of the model, and if they fail to satisfy the SDF volatility bounds—that is, if they fall outside the shaded area in the lower panel of Figure 4.1—this indicates that the model fails to price the assets. For example, HJ calculate SDF volatility bounds using return data on Treasury bills and an aggregate stock index, and show that a simple consumption-based asset pricing model with a power-utility representative agent, of the sort we discuss in section 6.1, can only satisfy these bounds if very high risk aversion coefficients are used. This provides a simple way to understand the equity premium puzzle. HJ repeat this exercise using data on Treasury bills of various maturities and obtain even higher volatility bounds. As an informal exercise, you are asked to explain intuitively how this can occur and how this result should be interpreted.

The volatility bounds presented above, and plotted in Figure 4.1, are derived only from the condition $1 = \mathrm{E}[M(1 + R)]$. They do not impose positivity of the SDF. HJ show how to use positivity to tighten the volatility bounds; however, this greatly complicates the analysis and is rarely used in practice. SDF volatility bounds are typically used by empiricists as a convenient way to summarize the properties of an asset pricing dataset, and for this purpose a simple and easy procedure is appropriate. For the same reason, most applications of the methodology use point estimates rather than formal construction of test statistics.

---

[3]In Chapter 2 we defined these constants in terms of net returns, but they can also be expressed in terms of gross returns, as we do here, yielding the exact same formulas.

4.3.3 Entropy Bound

Stutzer (1995), Bansal and Lehmann (1997), Alvarez and Jermann (2005), and Backus, Chernov, and Martin (2011) have generalized the logarithmic approach discussed above to relax the assumption of lognormality.

Entropy and Cumulants
The *entropy* of a strictly positive random variable $\widetilde{X}$ is a measure of its randomness. We define it as

$$L(\widetilde{X}) = \log E\widetilde{X} - E\log(\widetilde{X}) \geq 0. \tag{4.58}$$

Jensen's Inequality implies that entropy is always nonnegative and strictly positive when $\widetilde{X}$ is random. Entropy is independent of scale, because for any constant a, $L(a\widetilde{X}) = L(\widetilde{X})$.

For a lognormal random variable, entropy equals one-half variance of the log, $L(\widetilde{X}) = \sigma_x^2/2$, but in general it depends also on higher moments as we now show using the useful concept of the *cumulant-generating function*.

The cumulant-generating function for any random variable z is defined as

$$\mathbf{c}(\theta, z) = \log E \exp(\theta z). \tag{4.59}$$

This function has the property that

$$\mathbf{c}(\theta, z) = \sum_{n=1}^{\infty} \frac{\kappa_n(z)\theta^n}{n!}, \tag{4.60}$$

where $\kappa_n(z)$ is the n'th cumulant of z. $\kappa_1(z)$ is the mean of z, κ_2 is the variance σ^2, κ_3/σ^3 is the skewness, κ_4/σ^4 is the excess kurtosis, and so forth. All cumulants above the second are zero when the random variable z is normally distributed.

Entropy can be related to cumulants as follows. If we write $x = \log(\widetilde{X})$ and set $z = x$, then

$$L(\widetilde{X}) = \log E \exp(x) - Ex = \mathbf{c}(1, x) - \kappa_1(x) = \sum_{n=2}^{\infty} \frac{\kappa_n(x)}{n!}. \tag{4.61}$$

Odd cumulants can be negative, but even ones are nonnegative, and the infinite weighted sum of all cumulants on the right-hand side of (4.61) is nonnegative. The first term on the right-hand side of equation (4.61) is one-half the variance of the log, but subsequent terms are zero only in the special case where $\widetilde{X}$ has a lognormal distribution.

Entropy of the SDF
Now consider a strictly positive SDF. We know from section 4.2 that such an SDF always exists given the absence of arbitrage. To interpret the entropy of the SDF, consider a two-period, discrete-state economy where a riskless asset is traded, and recall from section 4.1.2 that

$$M(s) = P_f \frac{\pi^*(s)}{\pi(s)}, \tag{4.62}$$

where $\pi^*(s)$ is the risk-neutral probability of state s. Since P_f is known in the first period, it drops out of the entropy formula so

$$L(M) = L\left(\frac{\pi^*}{\pi}\right) = \log E\left(\frac{\pi^*}{\pi}\right) - E\log\left(\frac{\pi^*}{\pi}\right) = -E\log\left(\frac{\pi^*}{\pi}\right). \tag{4.63}$$

The third equality holds because $E(\pi^*/\pi) = 1$, so $\log E(\pi^*/\pi) = 0$. Equation (4.63) allows us to interpret the entropy of the SDF as a measure of the deviation of the risk-neutral probabilities π^* from the objective probabilities π.

Alvarez and Jermann (2005) consider a multiperiod economy and derive a lower bound on the conditional entropy of the SDF:

$$L_t(M_{t+1}) \geq E_t[r_{j,t+1} - r_{f,t+1}], \tag{4.64}$$

for any risky asset j.

The first step in proving this inequality is to note, following Bansal and Lehmann (1997), that the product $M_{t+1}(1+R_{j,t+1})$ is a random variable with nonnegative conditional entropy and unit unconditional mean. Hence,

$$L_t(M_{t+1}(1 + R_{j,t+1})) = \log E_t[M_{t+1}(1 + R_{j,t+1})] - E_t m_{t+1} - E_t r_{j,t+1}$$
$$= -E_t m_{t+1} - E_t r_{j,t+1} \geq 0. \tag{4.65}$$

This implies that

$$E_t r_{j,t+1} \leq -E_t m_{t+1}. \tag{4.66}$$

The weak inequality becomes an equality for the growth-optimal portfolio, the portfolio chosen by an investor with log utility. As discussed above, the reciprocal of the gross return on the growth-optimal portfolio can always be used as an SDF.

Next we calculate the conditional entropy of the SDF itself and use the result (4.66):

$$L_t(M_{t+1}) = \log E_t M_{t+1} - E_t m_{t+1} = -r_{f,t+1} - E_t m_{t+1}$$
$$\geq E_t r_{j,t+1} - r_{f,t+1}. \tag{4.67}$$

The meaning of this result is that a high conditional log risk premium implies high conditional entropy of the SDF, but this does not require high conditional variance of the log SDF if the SDF has a nonlognormal distribution. The tightest lower bound on the conditional entropy of the SDF is given by the conditionally expected excess log return on the growth-optimal portfolio.

To move from a conditional entropy bound to an unconditional entropy bound, Alvarez and Jermann (2005) use the fact that, as is the case for variance, unconditional entropy equals the mean of conditional entropy plus the entropy of the conditional mean. That is, for any random variable $\tilde{X}_{t+1}$,

$$L(\tilde{X}_{t+1}) = EL_t(\tilde{X}_{t+1}) + L(E_t\tilde{X}_{t+1}). \tag{4.68}$$

Since the conditional mean of the SDF is the price of a riskfree asset $P_{ft} = 1/(1 + R_{f,t+1})$, applying (4.68) to (4.67) implies that

$$L(M_{t+1}) \geq E[r_{j,t+1} - r_{f,t+1}] + L\left(\frac{1}{1 + R_{f,t+1}}\right). \tag{4.69}$$

This result says that the SDF can have high unconditional entropy if either the average growth-optimal return is high relative to the riskfree interest rate, or the riskfree rate itself has high entropy over time. Alvarez and Jermann (2005) apply this analysis to the term structure of interest rates, and we return to this topic in Chapter 8.

4.3.4 Factor Structure

The SDF approach offers another way to understand the multifactor models introduced in section 3.2.2. Assume that the SDF is a linear combination of K common factors $f_{k,t+1}$, $k = 1 \ldots K$. For simplicity assume that the factors have conditional mean zero and are orthogonal to one another. If

$$M_{t+1} = a_t - \sum_{k=1}^{K} b_{kt} f_{k,t+1}, \tag{4.70}$$

then

$$E_t[R_{i,t+1} - R_{f,t+1}] = -\left(\frac{1}{a_t}\right) \text{Cov}_t(M_{t+1}, R_{i,t+1} - R_{f,t+1}) = \left(\frac{1}{a_t}\right) \sum_{k=1}^{K} b_{kt} \sigma_{ikt}$$

$$= \left(\frac{1}{a_t}\right) \sum_{k=1}^{K} \left(b_{kt} \sigma_{kt}^2\right) \left(\frac{\sigma_{ikt}}{\sigma_{kt}^2}\right) = \sum_{k=1}^{K} \lambda_{kt} \beta_{ikt}. \tag{4.71}$$

Here σ_{ikt} is the conditional covariance of asset return i with the k'th factor, σ_{kt}^2 is the conditional variance of the k'th factor, $\lambda_{kt} \equiv b_{kt} \sigma_{kt}^2 / a_t$ is the price of risk of the k'th factor, and $\beta_{ikt} \equiv \sigma_{ikt}/\sigma_{kt}^2$ is the beta or regression coefficient of asset return i on that factor. In other words, there is equivalence between a linear factor model written in return-beta form, and a linear factor model of the SDF with the same K factors.

As an informal exercise, you are asked to consider how this result is consistent with the insights about the CAPM and arbitrage pricing theory presented in Chapter 3. The answer is given at the end of this chapter.

Conditioning information is important here, as emphasized by Hansen and Richard (1987). A conditional multifactor model does not generally imply an unconditional multifactor model of the same form. The relevant covariance for an unconditional model is the unconditional covariance $-\text{Cov}(M_{t+1}, R_{i,t+1} - R_{f,t+1}) = -\text{Cov}(a_t - \sum_{k=1}^{K} b_{kt} f_{k,t+1}, R_{i,t+1} - R_{f,t+1})$, and this involves covariances of the coefficients a_t and b_{kt} with returns as well as covariances of the factors $f_{k,t+1}$ with returns. Proceeding as in section 3.2.3, one way to handle this problem is to model the coefficients themselves as linear functions of observable state variables. One might model $a_t = a'z_t$ and $b_{kt} = b'_k z_t$, where z_t is a vector of state variables including a constant. In this case one obtains an unconditional multifactor model in which the factors include the original $f_{k,t+1}$, the state variables z_t, and all cross-products of $f_{k,t+1}$ and z_t. In the case where the original factors are portfolio returns, the cross-products can be interpreted as the returns on managed portfolios that vary their exposure to the original factor portfolios in proportion to the values of the state variables.

4.3.5 Time-Series Properties

Predictability of asset returns requires predictability in the SDF. To get time-series variation in the riskless real interest rate, we need a changing conditional mean of the SDF. To get time-series variation in risk premia, we need changing covariances of asset returns with the SDF. To get time-series variation in the risk premium on an asset that is perfectly correlated with the SDF and has a constant return variance, we need time-variation in the variance of the SDF.

Thus dynamic asset pricing models often involve modeling both the first and second conditional moments of the SDF, drawing on both linear time-series analysis and non-linear models of conditional volatility. In Chapters 6, 8, and 9 we discuss numerous alternative specifications for the dynamic behavior of the SDF that attempt to capture the dynamics of real interest rates and risk premia.

4.4 Generalized Method of Moments

The Generalized Method of Moments (GMM) of Hansen (1982b) is an econometric approach that is particularly well suited for estimating and testing models of the SDF. In this section we present an introduction to GMM drawing on textbook treatments by Cochrane (2005) and Hall (2005).

In contrast to other econometric methods such as maximum likelihood that require a complete specification of the stochastic processes obeyed by the time series of the model, GMM allows the econometrician to estimate and evaluate a model based on particular features or predictions provided by the researcher in the form of moment conditions:

$$\mathrm{E}[u(v_t, b_0)] = 0, \tag{4.72}$$

where u is an N-dimensional function of the random variables v_t and the unknown K-dimensional vector of parameters b_0 to be estimated.

The Method of Moments approach in the statistics literature, going back to the work of Karl Pearson in the 1890s, estimates the parameter vector by setting to zero the corresponding sample moments to (4.72). That is, the estimate $\widehat{b}_{MM}$ is obtained by setting $g_T(\widehat{b}_{MM}) = 0$ where g_T is the sample counterpart to the moment conditions,

$$g_T(b) \equiv \frac{1}{T} \sum_{t=1}^{T} u(v_t, b). \tag{4.73}$$

Throughout this section, the subscript T indicates that the object may depend on the particular sample.

This construction is feasible only if $N = K$; that is, if there are exactly as many conditions as parameters. The Generalized Method of Moments extends this approach to settings where there are more moment restrictions than parameters, $N \geq K$. A GMM estimate is constructed by setting K linear combinations of the N sample moments to zero:

$$A_T g_T(\widehat{b}) = 0, \tag{4.74}$$

where A_T is a $K \times N$ selection matrix that converges in probability to a matrix of constants A that has full rank. As we will see, the information not used in estimation (the remaining $N - K$ linear combinations of the moments that are predicted to be zero) can be used to evaluate the model through a test of overidentifying restrictions. Equation (4.74) defines the broad class of GMM estimators, which includes many commonly used econometric procedures and specifically those discussed in Chapter 3.[4]

---

[4]In fact, since all results that follow are asymptotic, the GMM estimator condition (4.74) need only hold at the limit. Formally, any estimator $\widehat{b}$ such that $\sqrt{T} A_T g_T(\widehat{b})$ converges in probability to zero is a GMM estimator.

An important advantage of the GMM framework is that it can easily accommodate nonlinear, dynamic models of the kind studied in asset pricing (Hansen and Singleton 1982). Models of the SDF are a case in point. We can easily generate any desired number of moment restrictions from a conditional version of (4.37):

$$E[(\iota + R_{t+1})M_{t+1}(b_0)|I_t] = \iota, \tag{4.75}$$

where I_t denotes the information set at time t, ι is a J-vector of ones, and R_{t+1} is a vector of J asset returns on which estimation and testing will be based. Note that M_{t+1} may well be a nonlinear function of b_0. To turn (4.75) into a set of unconditional moments of the form (4.72) we can use instruments $z_t \in I_t$. For every instrument we have

$$E[z_t(\iota + R_{t+1})M_{t+1}(b_0) - z_t] = E[z_tE[(\iota + R_{t+1})M_{t+1}(b_0)|I_t] - z_t] = 0, \tag{4.76}$$

where the first equality follows from the law of iterated expectations. Summarizing all instruments through an $N \times J$ matrix of random variables $Z_t \in I_t$, the moment restrictions are:

$$E[u(v_{t+1}, b_0)] = E[Z_t((\iota + R_{t+1})M_{t+1}(b_0) - \iota)] = 0. \tag{4.77}$$

4.4.1 Asymptotic Theory

A central object in GMM theory is the covariance matrix of the sample moments $g_T(b_0)$, normalized for sample size:

$$S \equiv \lim_{T\to\infty} \text{Var}\left(\sqrt{T}g_T(b_0)\right)$$
$$= \lim_{T\to\infty} \frac{1}{T}[TE[u_t(b_0)u_t'(b_0)] + (T-1)(E[u_t(b_0)u_{t+1}'(b_0)] + E[u_t(b_0)u_{t-1}'(b_0)]) + \ldots]$$
$$= \sum_{s=-\infty}^{\infty} E[u_t(b_0)u_{t-s}(b_0)], \tag{4.78}$$

where $u_t(b_0) = u(v_t, b_0)$. Equation (4.78) is the reason S is referred to as the long-run covariance matrix of u_t. It is also known as the spectral density matrix of u_t at frequency zero in time-series theory.

Asymptotic tests and construction of confidence intervals for the parameters are based on the following asymptotic distributions of the estimator and the estimated sample moments under the null hypothesis that the model given by (4.72) is correct: as $T \to \infty$,

$$\widehat{b} \sim \mathcal{N}\left(b_0, \frac{1}{T}(AD)^{-1}ASA'(AD)^{-1'}\right) \tag{4.79}$$

$$g_T(\widehat{b}) \sim \mathcal{N}\left(0, \frac{1}{T}[I_N - D(AD)^{-1}A]S[I_N - D(AD)^{-1}A]'\right), \tag{4.80}$$

where

$$D \equiv E\left[\frac{\partial u(v_t, b_0)}{\partial b'}\right]. \tag{4.81}$$

To understand (4.80), note that the sample moments evaluated at the true parameter vector, $g_T(b_0)$, are asymptotically distributed as $\mathcal{N}(0, (1/T)S)$, consistent with the definition of S in (4.78). However, in any given sample K linear combinations of the sample moments evaluated at the GMM estimate are set to zero by construction of the GMM estimate. Therefore, the sampling variation of $g_T(\widehat{b})$ will be lower than that of $g_T(b_0)$ and the singular matrix $[I_N - D(AD)^{-1}A]$ captures the $N-K$ linear combinations of the sample moments that are not targeted in estimation and are the source of the sampling variation of $g_T(\widehat{b})$.

These $N-K$ linear combinations unused in estimation can be used to test the overall fit of the model through a χ^2 test of overidentifying restrictions: asymptotically,

$$g_T(\widehat{b})\,[\text{Cov}(g_T(\widehat{b}))]^+ g_T(\widehat{b}) \sim \chi^2_{N-K}, \tag{4.82}$$

where $[\text{Cov}(g_T(\widehat{b}))]^+$ denotes the pseudoinverse of the asymptotic covariance matrix of $g_T(\widehat{b})$ given in (4.80). The singularity of $\text{Cov}(g_T(\widehat{b}))$ is the reason why the pseudoinverse is needed and the χ^2 distribution has only $N-K$ degrees of freedom. To perform this test in a given sample, we need consistent estimators for D and S. A consistent estimator for D is, of course, $\widehat{D}_T \equiv \partial g_T(\widehat{b})/\partial b'$. Estimation of the long-run covariance matrix is far from a trivial matter, however, and we discuss it in more detail at the end of this section.

These asymptotic results require that the model (4.72) satisfies several regularity conditions, including conditions ensuring that all objects defined earlier exist and are finite. One crucial assumption is that the time series captured by v_t are stationary and ergodic. For asset pricing models, this requires that we formulate the pricing errors in terms of returns as in (4.77), price-dividend ratios, or related normalized payoffs. The form $E[M_{t+1}X_{t+1} - P_t] = 0$ cannot be used because the levels of prices and dividends are not stationary over time.

A second regularity condition is that the parameter vector is globally identified: $E[u(v_t, \bar{b})] \neq 0$ for all $\bar{b} \neq b_0$. This condition can be quite hard to check in nonlinear models. A necessary condition for global identification that is easier to check is local identification: matrix D must have rank equal to K, the dimension of the parameter vector.[5] In linear models, global and local identification are equivalent.

4.4.2 Important GMM Estimators

An important class of GMM estimators is defined through the solution to the minimization problem

$$\min_b g_T(b)' W_T g_T(b), \tag{4.83}$$

where the weighting matrix W_T is an $N \times N$ positive-semidefinite matrix converging asymptotically to a positive-definite matrix of constants, W. The minimand can be

---

[5]The parameter vector is clearly unidentified when $N < K$, but identification can fail even when $N > K$. For example, suppose we want to test a linear model of the SDF based on a set of *excess* returns so that our moment conditions are now $E[u_{t+1}(b_0)] = E[Z_t R^e_{t+1} M_{t+1}(b_0)] = 0$, where $M_{t+1}(b_0) = b_0[1, f_{1,t+1}, \ldots, f_{K,t+1}]'$ and $b_0 = [a, b_1, \ldots, b_K]$. Note that $E[u_t(\bar{b})] = 0$ for any $\bar{b}$ that is a multiple of b_0. In other words, the mean of the SDF a cannot be identified separately from the b's when the test asset payoffs are excess returns. Therefore, one has to normalize the parameter vector by setting a to an arbitrary value in order to proceed with estimation.

interpreted as a measure of how far the sample is from satisfying all moment conditions. The first-order condition for this minimization problem is

$$\frac{\partial g_T(\widehat{b})'}{\partial b} W_T g_T(\widehat{b}) = \widehat{D}'_T W_T g_T(\widehat{b}) = 0. \tag{4.84}$$

Comparing with (4.74), we can see that estimators based on (4.83) are GMM estimators with selection matrix $A_T = \widehat{D}'_T W_T$. Therefore, all asymptotic results based on (4.79) and (4.80) still apply with $A = D'W$. By choosing the weighting matrix W_T, the researcher dictates the relative importance of matching the different moments, but the construction of the estimator also takes into account the statistical informativeness of the different moments for the parameters through the dependence of the selection matrix on $\widehat{D}'_T$; $\partial g_{T,n}(\widehat{b})/\partial b'$ close to zero means that the n'th moment condition is largely uninformative about the parameters.[6]

Hansen (1982b) shows that one particular choice for the weighting matrix W is statistically optimal, in the sense that the resulting estimator has the lowest asymptotic covariance matrix among all possible GMM estimators given by (4.74). $W = S^{-1}$, the inverse of the long-run covariance matrix. Intuitively, the statistically efficient GMM estimator weighs most strongly the sample moments with the lowest sampling variation. Substituting $A = D'S^{-1}$ in (4.79) and (4.80), we see that the formulas simplify substantially: as $T \to \infty$,

$$\widehat{b} \sim \mathcal{N}\left(b_0, \frac{1}{T}D'S^{-1}D\right), \tag{4.85}$$

$$g_T(\widehat{b}) \sim \mathcal{N}\left(0, \frac{1}{T}[S - D(D'S^{-1}D)^{-1}D']\right). \tag{4.86}$$

The covariance matrix of $g_T(\widehat{b})$ is still singular, but in this particular case it turns out that the χ^2 test of overidentifying restrictions (4.82) is equivalent to the test

$$T g_T(\widehat{b}) S^{-1} g_T(\widehat{b}) \sim \chi^2_{N-K}. \tag{4.87}$$

Note that the test quantity is simply T times the minimand in (4.83).

Constructing the statistically efficient GMM estimator is complicated by the fact that any estimator of the long-run covariance matrix $\widehat{S}_T(\widehat{b})$ depends on the estimate $\widehat{b}$ itself. The most common algorithm to deal with this practical problem is Hansen and Singleton's (1982) two-stage procedure. First, solve (4.83) with an arbitrary weighting matrix to arrive at a parameter estimate $\widehat{b}_1$, known as the first-stage estimate of b_0. Then, construct an estimate of S using the first-stage parameter estimate. Finally, compute the second-stage estimate,

$$\widehat{b}_2 = \operatorname{argmin}_b : g_T(b)'\widehat{S}(\widehat{b}_1)g_T(b). \tag{4.88}$$

Other algorithms to arrive at a statistically efficient GMM estimate have been proposed, all of which have the same asymptotic properties, given by (4.85) and (4.86), but

---

[6]The majority of explicit GMM applications uses the minimization formulation, as opposed to directly choosing the selection matrix A_T. But the most general representation of the class of GMM estimators given by (4.74) is particularly useful when one wishes to study the properties of many standard econometric methods that are nested under GMM. We will follow precisely this route in the next subsection.

simulation evidence suggests that they may differ in their finite-sample performance, about which asymptotic theory is silent. One such variant is the iterated GMM estimator, which uses the second-stage estimate to reestimate S and arrive at a third-stage estimate, and repeats this process several times. This process reduces dependence on the fixed weighting matrix employed in the first stage. Another variant, proposed by Hansen, Heaton and Yaron (1996), is the continuously updated GMM estimator (CUE), which uses a different weighting matrix for every parameter vector considered. Formally,

$$\widehat{b}_{CUE} = \text{argmin}_b : g_T(b)'(\widehat{S}_T(b))^{-1} g_T(b). \tag{4.89}$$

This estimator is invariant to parameter-dependent transformations of the moment conditions ($\text{E}[C(b_0) u(v_t, b_0)] = 0$, where $C(b_0)$ is any nonsingular matrix of constants, yields the same estimator as $\text{E}[u(v_t, b_0)] = 0$ in a given sample) and has been argued to have better finite-sample properties (Newey and Smith 2004).[7]

4.4.3 Traditional Tests in the GMM Framework

In section 3.3.1 we discussed traditional econometric approaches using time-series and cross-sectional regressions to test single-factor and multifactor asset pricing models. The results reported there require the potentially restrictive assumption that pricing errors are iid over time and independent of the factors. We now show that these methods are nested under GMM and that one can use the flexibility of the GMM framework to derive asymptotic tests under more general assumptions regarding the error distribution. We will see that different distributional assumptions translate into different forms for the long-run covariance matrix, S. For simplicity, we focus the discussion on the market model, but the results extend to multifactor models in a straightforward way.

Time-Series Approach
Recall the time-series regression for the market model, equation (3.44), and write it in vector notation for N assets:

$$R_t^e = \alpha + \beta_m R_{mt}^e + \epsilon_t, \tag{4.90}$$

where R_t^e denotes the vector of excess returns on N test assets, and α and β_m are N-vectors. The CAPM hypothesis is that all alphas are zero, $\alpha = 0$.

The OLS regression coefficients for (4.90) solve the problem of minimizing the squared errors, whose first-order conditions are $\text{E}[(R_{it}^e - \alpha_i - \beta_{im} R_{mt}^e)] = 0$ and $\text{E}[(R_{it}^e - \alpha_i - \beta_{im} R_{mt}^e) R_{mt}^e] = 0$ with respect to α_i and β_{im}, respectively. Thus, OLS estimation easily maps to the GMM framework with the moment conditions

$$\text{E}\left[u_t\left(\begin{bmatrix}\alpha\\\beta_m\end{bmatrix}\right)\right] = \text{E}\left[\begin{matrix}R_t^e - \alpha - \beta_m R_{mt}^e\\(R_t^e - \alpha - \beta_m R_{mt}^e) R_{mt}^e\end{matrix}\right] = \text{E}\left[\begin{matrix}\epsilon_t\\\epsilon_t R_{mt}^e\end{matrix}\right] = 0. \tag{4.91}$$

---

[7]However, estimates based on CUE have been shown to be very sensitive to the starting values for the numerical minimization routine, which often diverges into regions of the parameter space with large $\widehat{S}_T(b)$ rather than small $g_T(b)$. Particular care is needed to ensure that the routine has actually found the global minimum.

This is an exactly identified system of $2N$ restrictions in $2N$ parameters. The selection matrix is irrelevant in this case since GMM reduces to the (unique) method of moments estimator, $g_T(\widehat{a}, \widehat{\beta}_m) = 0$.

We can now derive the matrices that appear in (4.79) and (4.80):

$$A = I_N \qquad D = -\begin{bmatrix} I_N & I_N \mathrm{E}[R^e_{mt}] \\ I_N \mathrm{E}[R^e_{mt}] & I_N \mathrm{E}[(R^e_{mt})^2] \end{bmatrix} \tag{4.92}$$

and

$$S = \sum_{-\infty}^{\infty} \begin{bmatrix} \mathrm{E}[\epsilon_t \epsilon'_{t-s}] & \mathrm{E}[\epsilon_t \epsilon'_{t-s} R^e_{m,t-s}] \\ \mathrm{E}[\epsilon_t \epsilon'_{t-s} R^e_{mt}] & \mathrm{E}[\epsilon_t \epsilon'_{t-s} R^e_{mt} R^e_{m,t-s}] \end{bmatrix}. \tag{4.93}$$

The long-run covariance matrix simplifies significantly under the standard assumptions that the errors have mean zero conditional on past errors and current and past factors and are conditionally homoskedastic,

$$\mathrm{E}[\epsilon_t | x_t, \epsilon_{t-1}, x_{t-1}, \epsilon_{t-2}, x_{t-2} \ldots] = 0 \tag{4.94}$$

$$\mathrm{E}[\epsilon_t \epsilon'_t | x_t, \epsilon_{t-1}, x_{t-1}, \epsilon_{t-2}, x_{t-2} \ldots] = \Omega. \tag{4.95}$$

(These are only slightly weaker than the assumption that the errors are iid over time and independent of the factor.) Assumption (4.94) implies that all terms in the sum with $j \neq 0$ are zero, and assumption (4.95) further simplifies the $j = 0$ term:

$$S = \begin{bmatrix} \Omega & \Omega \mathrm{E}[R^e_{mt}] \\ \Omega \mathrm{E}[R^e_{mt}] & \Omega \mathrm{E}[(R^e_{mt})^2] \end{bmatrix}. \tag{4.96}$$

Problem 4.4 asks you to show that, with this expression for S, the formula for the asymptotic variance of the parameter vector in (4.79) yields

$$\mathrm{Var}(\widehat{a}) = \frac{1}{T}\Omega \left[1 + \left(\frac{\mathrm{E}[R^e_{mt}]}{\sigma(R^e_{mt})} \right)^2 \right]. \tag{4.97}$$

We see that the χ^2 test statistic in (3.45), the asymptotic counterpart to the GRS statistic, is simply the test that the elements of vector a are all equal to zero:

$$(\widehat{a} - 0)' [\widehat{\mathrm{Var}}(\widehat{a})]^{-1} (\widehat{a} - 0) \sim \chi^2_N. \tag{4.98}$$

When we wish to allow for the possibility that the errors are serially correlated (e.g., if we run predictive regressions with overlapping horizons or if we suspect that the errors are serially correlated) or heteroskedastic, we follow the same steps to arrive at the test (4.98) with the appropriate (and less simplified) form for S.

Cross-Sectional Approach

We now consider the econometrics of the cross-sectional regression approach, again using the CAPM as an example. An issue complicating inference based on regression (3.48) is that the betas are not known but estimated. Regressions featuring generated regressors can be handled in the GMM framework by mapping all steps of the sequential estimation to the form (4.72).[8]

Consider the following 3N moment restrictions in $1 + 2N$ parameters (the scalar lambda, the alphas, and the betas):

$$\mathrm{E}\left[u_t \left(\begin{bmatrix} \lambda \\ \alpha \\ \beta_m \end{bmatrix} \right) \right] = \mathrm{E} \begin{bmatrix} R_t^e - \beta_m \lambda \\ R_t^e - \alpha - \beta_m R_{mt}^e \\ (R_t^e - \alpha - \beta_m R_{mt}^e) R_{mt}^e \end{bmatrix} = 0 \qquad (4.99)$$

and the selection matrix

$$A = \begin{bmatrix} \beta_m' \Omega^{-1} & 0_{(1\times N)} & 0_{(1\times N)} \\ 0_{(N\times N)} & I_N & 0_{(N\times N)} \\ 0_{(N\times N)} & 0_{(N\times N)} & I_N \end{bmatrix}. \qquad (4.100)$$

To see that this corresponds to the GLS cross-sectional estimators given by (3.49) and (3.50), note that $A_T g_T([\widehat{\lambda} \ \widehat{\alpha}' \ \widehat{\beta}_m']') = 0$ implies that $\widehat{\alpha}$ and $\widehat{\beta}$ are precisely the OLS coefficients from the time-series regression, and the top linear combination is $\widehat{\beta}_m' \widehat{\Omega}^{-1}(\overline{R}^e - \widehat{\beta}_m \widehat{\lambda}) = 0$, which yields $\widehat{\lambda} = [\widehat{\beta}_m' \widehat{\Omega}^{-1} \widehat{\beta}_m]^{-1} \widehat{\beta}_m' \widehat{\Omega}^{-1} \overline{R}^e = \widehat{\lambda}_{GLS}$. The estimates of the cross-sectional residuals are then $\widehat{a} = \overline{R}^e - \widehat{\beta}_m \widehat{\lambda}_{GLS} = \widehat{a}_{GLS}$.[9]

The null hypothesis of the CAPM is that $\mathrm{E}[R_t^e] = \beta_m \lambda$, that is, that the first N moments in (4.99) are indeed zero.[10] Given that the remaining $2N$ sample moments corresponding to the least squares estimation of α and β are zero by construction, testing the null hypothesis is equivalent to the χ^2 test of overidentifying restrictions, (4.82). One can show that, when errors are serially uncorrelated and homoskedastic, a pseudoinverse of $\mathrm{Cov}(g_T(\widehat{b}))$ is given by $T(1 + \lambda^2/\sigma^2(R_{mt}^e))^{-1}\Omega^{-1}$. Therefore, (4.82) reduces to the test statistic in (3.51).

4.4.4 GMM in Practice

In practical applications of GMM, researchers face a series of difficult choices for which there is no good guidance from theory. The main source of these challenges is the asymptotic character of GMM theory. Several econometric studies have found that asymptotic theory often provides a poor approximation to the finite-sample distribution of GMM estimators and test statistics. Thus, as a partial remedy, it is always good practice to approximate the finite-sample distribution of the estimators via simulation or bootstrap and check that the results are not too different from the predictions of asymptotic theory. Also, as we now discuss, the limitations of a finite sample often give rise to a tradeoff between employing the most statistically efficient choices and the researcher's desire to test the economically relevant predictions of an economic model.

---

[8]This is a useful approach in other contexts as well. For example, Campbell (1987) and Harvey (1989) use it to substitute out the variance of the aggregate stock market return from a model relating the equity premium to the conditional variance of the market return.

[9]The OLS cross-sectional estimators can be derived through the exact same steps except that the top-left block of matrix A should be set to β_m' rather than $\beta_m' \Omega^{-1}$.

[10]Recall that the cross-sectional regression can be used in factor models where the factors are not excess returns because it does not require the time-series intercepts α to be zero (see section 3.2.2).

A large econometric literature asks whether the poor approximation of GMM theory to finite-sample behavior can be ameliorated using appropriate moment selection procedures and weighting schemes. An important decision facing the researcher concerns which model predictions to test. There is usually an infinite number of possible moment conditions that a researcher can include in the vector of moment restrictions in (4.72) (e.g., any variable z_t in the information set at time t can be used as an instrument in (4.76)). The best advice is to choose the most economically relevant predictions of a given model. Econometric procedures that help choose the statistically optimal set of moments (or instruments) are often infeasible in dynamic economic models as they require knowledge of the exact data-generating process.[11]

The choice of the weighting matrix W_T in (4.83) (or the selection matrix A_T in (4.74)) is equivalent to the decision about which linear combinations of the sample moments will be used in the estimation of the parameter vector. The asymptotically efficient matrix $W_T = \widehat{S}_T^{-1}$ is an obvious choice. However, its efficiency may be compromised in finite samples due to sample variation in the estimate of S, and this may result in less efficient estimates than those obtained using a fixed weighting matrix.

The long-run covariance matrix can be poorly estimated when the number of moment conditions is large relative to the sample size. Even when this is not the case, in asset pricing applications the estimated S is often nearly singular due to the presence of apparent near-arbitrage opportunities. That is, certain linear combinations of the moments (basis assets) may appear to be nearly riskless and the efficient GMM estimator puts more weight precisely on these combinations since they appear to have the lowest sampling variation. Typically these combinations of assets involve leverage and short sales, so the researcher could respond by explicitly introducing leverage and short-sales constraints in the model (in the language of SDF theory, excluding such linear combinations of the basis assets from the space of tradable payoffs), but this may be too burdensome in models that are not specifically intended to study these constraints. In these cases, using a fixed weighting matrix allows the researcher to base the estimation of the model on its economically relevant predictions.

The tradeoff here between efficiency (provided the null of the model is indeed true) and robustness to "mild" forms of misspecification is the same that one faces when choosing between OLS regression estimates (or WLS estimates with exogenously specified weights) and GLS estimates. It is good practice to construct and test both the first-stage and the second-stage GMM estimates and to try to understand the reason for any significant differences between the two. Using fixed weighting matrices also facilitates transparent comparisons of the performance of different models.

A fixed GMM weighting matrix must be chosen thoughtfully. One simple choice is the identity matrix, which weighs each moment condition equally. In the context of SDF models, Hansen and Jagannathan (1997) suggest the use of the inverse of the second moment matrix of returns, $W = \mathrm{E}[(1+R_{t+1})(1+R_{t+1})']^{-1}$. They motivate this choice by showing that minimizing the resulting quadratic form corresponds to minimizing a measure of the (squared) distance, in a least-squares sense, between the SDF of the model and the nearest SDF that correctly prices the test assets. A potential disadvantage of this choice is that the second moment matrix, like the efficient weighting matrix discussed earlier, may be nearly singular in practice.

---

[11]Recent data-based methods for moment selection using information criteria (e.g., Andrews, 1999) are more promising and may help improve finite-sample behavior in certain settings.

Regardless of the weighting matrix used in estimation, model evaluation based on GMM theory requires that one estimates the long-run covariance matrix, which is in general a challenging task in light of the infinite sum in (4.78). Fortunately, in most asset pricing models the u_t's in the moment restrictions correspond to pricing errors, which are serially uncorrelated under the null of the model (the required condition is given formally by (4.94)). This is true of all models where $\{u_t\}$ is a martingale difference sequence with respect to past information sets, $E[u_{t+1}|I_{t-s}] = 0$ for $s = 0, 1, 2, \ldots$ In this case, S equals the contemporaneous covariance matrix of u_t and a consistent estimator of S is simply[12]

$$\widehat{S}_T(\widehat{b}) = \frac{1}{T} \sum_{t=1}^{T} \left(u_t(\widehat{b}) - \overline{u}(\widehat{b})\right)\left(u_t(\widehat{b}) - \overline{u}(\widehat{b})\right)'. \tag{4.101}$$

If theory does not predict that the u_t's are serially uncorrelated or if we want to construct tests that are robust to the presence of serial correlation, we can proceed either parametrically or nonparametrically. A parametric approach is to estimate a vector autoregressive moving average (VARMA) model for u_t, which will make S a function of the finite number of VARMA parameters. Alternatively, we can estimate S nonparametrically by a heteroskedasticity- and autocorrelation-consistent (HAC) covariance matrix estimator. HAC estimators take the form

$$\widehat{S}_{T,HAC}(\widehat{b}) = \widehat{\Gamma}_0 + \sum_{i=1}^{T-1} \omega_{i,T}(\widehat{\Gamma}_i + \widehat{\Gamma}_i'), \tag{4.102}$$

where

$$\widehat{\Gamma}_i = \frac{1}{T} \sum_{t=i+1}^{T} (u_t(\widehat{b}) - \overline{u}(\widehat{b}))(u_{t-i}(\widehat{b}) - \overline{u}(\widehat{b}))' \tag{4.103}$$

denotes the ith sample autocovariance matrix, and $\omega_{i,T}$ is the kernel or weight. Higher-order autocovariances need to be down-weighted by the kernel in order to ensure that the estimate is asymptotically consistent and also positive semi-definite in every sample. A common kernel choice is the Bartlett kernel used by Newey and West (1987),

$$\omega_{i,T} = \begin{cases} 1 - \dfrac{i}{m+1} & \text{for } i \leq m+1 \\ 0 & \text{for } i \geq m+1 \end{cases}. \tag{4.104}$$

The nonnegative integer m, known as the bandwidth of the kernel, controls the number of autocovariances included in the estimator and is the most important determinant of its finite-sample performance. As there is no direct theoretical guidance for choosing m in any finite sample, one should try different candidate values to ensure that adding more autocovariances will not affect the estimate significantly. Although HAC estimators are asymptotically consistent under much weaker conditions than parametric estimates, they can be very inefficient and tend to exhibit large sampling variation. The choice of how to estimate the long-run covariance matrix is another instance of the tradeoff between efficiency and robustness.

---

[12]Note that it does not matter for consistency whether we use sample second moments or sample covariances to estimate $E[u_t u_t']$ since $E[u_t] = 0$ under the null. However, it is good practice to subtract sample means, as this helps alleviate the singularity problem of the S estimate.

4.5 Limits of Arbitrage

The analysis of this chapter is based on the assumption that arbitrage opportunities do not exist. This assumption seems reasonable because if it were false—if arbitrage opportunities existed—then investors would wish to establish infinitely large security positions to exploit them.

A challenge to this reasoning is that apparent arbitrage opportunities are frequently visible in financial markets. It is instructive to consider a set of examples and to ask what allows these situations to arise. We do this in a preliminary fashion in this section, returning to the topic in Chapters 11 and 12.

A first example is that tax-exempt bonds of high-quality issuers normally trade at lower yields (higher prices) than US Treasury bonds, even though the promised payments may be identical and there may be almost no risk of default. This situation arises primarily because the US government does not tax the interest on tax-exempt bonds but does tax the interest on US Treasury bonds.[13] Furthermore, it is illegal for nontaxable entities such as universities to issue tax-exempt bonds in order to invest in taxable bonds, thus the "tax arbitrage" that would be required to exploit the yield differential is not feasible.

A second example, highlighted by Lamont and Thaler (2003), arises when one publicly traded company owns shares in a second publicly traded company. This naturally occurs when a division of a parent company is spun off in two stages, first issuing a small number of publicly traded shares to establish a market value and then distributing the remaining shares of the former division to shareholders of the parent company. In some cases the market value of the shares of the spinoff owned by each share of the parent company exceeds the market value per share of the parent company, implying a negative "stub value" for the rest of the parent company's business. This represents an arbitrage opportunity since the stock of the parent company has limited liability. A particularly famous example occurred in the spring of 2000 when 3Com spun out Palm, then a "hot" technology stock whose share value implied a negative stub value for 3Com for about eight weeks.

Exploiting a negative stub value requires holding shares of the parent company while shorting shares of the spinoff, and this can be difficult and costly to do in practice. Because of the decentralized structure of the share lending market, shareholders of the spinoff—who are often individual investors—may not make their shares available for lending even when attractive fees are offered for them to do so. High shorting costs can eliminate the apparent arbitrage profit resulting from a negative stub value.

In addition, arbitrageurs must consider two types of risk. First, the parent company may borrow, using its shares of the spinoff as collateral, and if the parent then defaults the long side of the arbitrage strategy no longer has a claim to shares of the spinoff to offset the open-market short position in the spinoff. Mitchell, Pulvino, and Stafford (2002) show that this happens surprisingly often, in about 30% of the negative-stub-value cases they consider. Second, even when this does not occur arbitrageurs must have enough capital to withstand losses resulting from periods when stub values become even more negative. Such losses generate margin calls, and if arbitrageurs cannot meet these margin calls their positions will be closed at a loss. The first type of risk is a fundamental risk, while

---

[13]Other factors also influence the relative pricing of tax-exempt and Treasury bonds, including state tax laws, the small risk of default, and liquidity.

the second arises from the nature of the trading process and is often referred to as noise trader risk (De Long et al. 1990a).

Noise trader risk is even more important in a third example of an arbitrage opportunity. "Siamese twins" are two stocks that are claims on the same cash flows but trade in different locations for different prices (Froot and Dabora 1999). The most famous case was the Royal Dutch Shell group, which until 2005 had distinct Royal Dutch shares, traded in the Netherlands, and Shell shares, traded in the UK. Royal Dutch shares traded as much 30% below their parity value with Shell in the early 1980s and 15% above in the mid-1990s. In this case there is no known date at which the two shares must reach parity, and arbitrageurs face the risk that deviations from parity may worsen for an indefinite period before correcting.

Shleifer and Vishny (1997) highlighted an amplification mechanism by which unusually severe mispricings (deviations from parity) may interact with limits on arbitrageurs' capital to force arbitrageurs to close their positions, worsening mispricing further and forcing more arbitrageurs out of the market. Many observers believe this mechanism was important during the 1998 failure of the arbitrage firm Long-Term Capital Management, and again during the global financial crisis in 2008–2009.

These examples are relevant for the theoretical literature on the stochastic discount factor discussed in this chapter. Ruling out arbitrage opportunities guarantees the existence of a positive SDF, which is more volatile the more state prices differ from probabilities. Near-arbitrage opportunities imply an extremely volatile SDF, which in turn implies extremely volatile marginal utility for investors with rational expectations. In applying these ideas, empirical finance economists must keep in mind the following considerations.

Return measurement. Many apparent arbitrage opportunities involve nonstandard components of returns such as taxes, transactions costs, short-selling fees, or liquidity services provided by certain assets. If these are not properly measured, an arbitrage opportunity may falsely appear to exist. However, not all investors may incur all these costs or benefits. In the Palm/3Com case, for example, individual investors who bought Palm shares could instead have bought shares in 3Com without paying shorting costs, or alternatively could have earned high fees by lending out their shares of Palm. Thus shorting fees cannot explain the behavior of these investors even if they can explain the limited response of arbitrageurs.

Risk. Subtle forms of risk, such as default by the parent company in a spinoff, convert apparent arbitrage opportunities into near-arbitrage opportunities with very high but finite Sharpe ratios. Then the puzzle is how such high Sharpe ratios, or "good deals," can exist in equilibrium (Cochrane and Saá-Requejo 2000). The main focus of the asset pricing literature has been on the Sharpe ratios implied by risky asset classes such as equities, but often small differences in the returns on assets with low return volatility, such as US Treasury bills and other money market instruments, imply even higher Sharpe ratios (Hansen and Jagannathan 1991).

Limits on the scale of arbitrage positions. In models with heterogeneous investors, arbitrageurs will be limited in the positions they can establish by the willingness of other investors to provide capital to them. Near-arbitrage opportunities in assets with low volatility require large gross positions to deliver high absolute returns, and it may be costly to obtain the necessary capital to establish these positions. The literature on margin-based asset pricing, such as Gârleanu, and Pedersen (2011), emphasizes this point which we explore in greater detail in Chapter 12. Of course, one still has to explain why capital is not provided cheaply to finance attractive opportunities that are almost certain to be profitable. There is also the question why all investors do not establish small positions to exploit the opportunity, in other words, why specialized arbitrageurs need to raise costly capital to do so.

Limited participation. One answer to the above question is that participation in certain risky markets requires investors to pay fixed costs, and may take time to arrange (Allen and Gale 1994, Duffie 2010). Such specialized markets may allow near-arbitrage opportunities to arise periodically. Limited participation is also a theme of the household finance literature reviewed in Chapter 10.

Heterogeneous beliefs. Finally, models with heterogeneous beliefs, such as the complete-markets example discussed in section 4.1.8 of this chapter, imply that a volatile SDF created by a near-arbitrage opportunity need not correspond to volatile marginal utility for investors who do not perceive the opportunity, in other words, whose subjective probabilities deviate from objective probabilities in line with state prices. There is a large recent literature exploring the implications of heterogeneous beliefs for asset markets, and we explore this in greater detail in Chapter 11.

4.6 Solutions and Further Problems

As an informal exercise you were asked to explain intuitively how Hansen and Jagannathan (1991) could obtain higher SDF volatility bounds using a set of Treasury bills of various maturities than using a single Treasury bill and an aggregate stock index. The explanation is that the HJ volatility bounds depend on the maximum Sharpe ratio that can be obtained by combining risky assets together with a hypothetical riskless asset. Since Treasury bills have very low return volatilities, tiny differences in their mean returns can imply large maximum Sharpe ratios from portfolios of bills. However, this result may not be economically meaningful if Treasury bill returns are slightly mismeasured because of market microstructure effects, of the sort discussed in Chapter 12, or if investors are unable to obtain the leverage they need to obtain attractive returns from these portfolios.

You were also asked to explain how the relationship between a factor structure for the SDF and a multifactor asset pricing model, presented in section 4.3.4, is consistent with insights about the CAPM and arbitrage pricing theory discussed in Chapter 3. A static model with quadratic utility implies that consumption equals wealth and marginal utility is linear. Thus the SDF must be linear in future wealth, or equivalently the market portfolio return. This in turn implies the static CAPM, which we derived in Chapter 3 using mean-variance analysis, noting in Chapter 2 that quadratic utility is one possible justification for this approach. We can understand the multifactor arbitrage pricing approach by noting that in a two-period model with K common shocks and completely diversifiable idiosyncratic risk, marginal utility and hence the SDF can depend only on the common shocks.

Problem 4.1 The Martingale Method with Quadratic Utility

The martingale method for portfolio choice, introduced in section 4.1.5, uses the SDF framework to characterize the optimal state-contingent payoffs that agents can attain through financial markets, given their wealth and asset prices, the latter summarized through the SDF.

Consider an economy with two dates, $t = 0, 1$. At date 0 an agent with wealth W solves the following optimization problem over his date-1 payoff:

$$\max_{X \in \Xi} \mathrm{E}[u(X)] \quad \text{s.t.} \, W = P(X) = \mathrm{E}[MX]. \tag{4.105}$$

Assume that a riskfree asset is traded, $1 \in \Xi$.[14]

(a) Let λ denote the Lagrange multiplier on the agent's budget constraint, and let $\hat{X}$ denote the optimal payoff. Show that the agent's first-order condition implies $\hat{X} = u'^{-1}(\lambda M)$.

Show that the optimal payoff for a power-utility investor with $u(X) = X^{1-\gamma}/(1-\gamma)$ is

$$\hat{X} = W \left(\frac{M^{-\frac{1}{\gamma}}}{\mathrm{E}[M^{1-\frac{1}{\gamma}}]} \right). \tag{4.106}$$

Show that the optimal payoff for a quadratic-utility investor with $u(X) = -(1/2)(X^b - X)^2$ is

$$\hat{X} = X^b - \left(\frac{\mathrm{E}[MX^b] - W}{\mathrm{E}[M^2]} \right) M, \tag{4.107}$$

where $X^b > 0$ is a constant corresponding to the investor's bliss point.[15]

(b) The martingale method has traditionally been applied under the assumption of complete markets. In this case, X^* defined in section 4.2.1 is the unique SDF and the optimal payoff formula in part (a) always yields a feasible (traded) payoff, $\hat{X} \in \Xi$. When markets are incomplete, however, there exist many valid SDFs. For a general utility function, such as power utility, $u'^{-1}(\lambda M)$ is in Ξ only for a particular M that is generically different from X^* and thus hard to pin down. Thus, the martingale method is in general of little use in incomplete-market settings.

An exception is the case of quadratic utility. Show that, under quadratic utility, $u'^{-1}(\lambda M) \in \Xi$ for $M = X^*$.

(c) Express the optimal payoff of a quadratic-utility investor as

$$\hat{X} = X^b - [X^b/(1 + R_f) - W](1 + R^*), \tag{4.108}$$

where $1 + R^* \equiv X^*/P(X^*)$ is the gross benchmark return. Explain the intuition behind this condition.

(d) Show that the return to the optimal payoff of a quadratic-utility investor, $\hat{R} = \hat{X}/P(\hat{X}) - 1$, is given by

$$\hat{R} = R_f + \frac{1}{\gamma}(R_f - R^*), \tag{4.109}$$

where $\gamma = \gamma((1 + R_f)W)$ is the coefficient of relative risk aversion evaluated at a value of consumption that can be obtained by investing all wealth in the riskfree payoff.

[14]Here 1 denotes the random variable whose realization is 1 in every state of nature.

[15]Throughout the exercise assume that the wealth of the quadratic utility agent is low enough that he cannot afford consumption equal to his bliss point with certainty.

(e) Conclude that quadratic-utility investors hold mean-variance efficient portfolios, regardless of the distribution of payoffs.

Note: This problem is based on Cochrane (2014).

Problem 4.2 A False SDF

Suppose that a set of assets are correctly priced by a stochastic discount factor M. An economist uses a false asset pricing model in which the stochastic discount factor is a random variable Y. M and Y have the same mean.

(a) Show that the false model correctly prices a riskless asset.

(b) In general the false model misprices risky assets. However, if Y moves closely with M, the mispricing cannot be very large. Define "Jensen's alpha" for risky asset i as the difference between the true expected return, $E[R_i]$, and the expected return implied by the false model, $E_Y[R_i]$. Show that Jensen's alpha per unit of standard deviation must satisfy the inequality

$$\frac{E[R_i] - E_Y[R_i]}{\sigma(R_i)} \leq \frac{\sigma(Y - M)}{E[M]}. \tag{4.110}$$

(c) You find an asset for which this inequality holds as an equality. What does this imply about the asset's return?

(d) How might you use the formula in part (b) to respond to the Roll critique, discussed in section 3.3.3?

Note: This question is based on Shanken (1987) and Hansen and Jagannathan (1997).

Problem 4.3 Hansen-Richard Decomposition

Hansen and Richard (1987) show that an arbitrary gross return $1 + R_i$ can be decomposed as

$$1 + R_i = 1 + R^* + w_i Z^* + \varepsilon_i, \tag{4.111}$$

where R^*, Z^*, and ε_i are random variables and w_i is a scalar. This decomposition is orthogonal in the sense that $E[(1 + R^*)Z^*] = E[\varepsilon_i(1 + R^*)] = E[\varepsilon_i Z^*] = 0$. The benchmark return $1 + R^* \equiv X^*/P(X^*)$ is the gross return on X^*, the SDF that is also a payoff, given by (4.35) when the payoff space is finite-dimensional. $Z^* \equiv \text{proj}(1|\underline{Z})$ is the projection of vector 1 (the random variable whose realization equals 1 almost surely) on the space of excess returns, $\underline{Z} = \{X \in \Xi \text{ s.t. } P(X) = 0\}$.[16] ε_i is a mean-zero residual.

---

[16]When the space of excess returns is finite-dimensional, the projection of a variable Y on the space of excess returns is

$$\text{proj}(Y|\underline{Z}) = E[YB]'E[BB']^{-1}B,$$

where B is a column vector of the basis payoffs of $\underline{Z}$. It is the excess return that best replicates variable Y in a least-squares sense.

(a) Show that the benchmark return is the gross return with the minimum second (uncentered) moment. Conclude from this result that, in mean-standard deviation space, $1 + R^*$ is the return on the mean-variance frontier that is closest to the origin.

(b) Use the definition of Z^* to show that Z^* is the "mean-generating" excess return in the sense that its second (uncentered) moment with any excess return yields the mean of that return, $E[Z] = E[Z^*Z]$ for all $Z \in \underline{Z}$. Then prove that Z^* is the excess return with the maximum Sharpe ratio in absolute value.

(c) Show that the mean-variance frontier is generated by the set of returns that satisfy $1 + R_i = 1 + R^* + w_i Z^*$ for some scalar w_i. Use this result to provide an alternative proof of the mutual-fund theorem of section 2.2.5: any mean-variance efficient return can be generated by any two portfolios on the frontier.

(d) Use the decomposition to show that any mean-variance efficient return R_{mv}, except the global minimum-variance return, can serve as the factor in a single-factor beta pricing model of the form

$$E[R_i] - E[R_{mv,z}] = \beta_{i,mv}(E[R_{mv}] - E[R_{mv,z}]), \tag{4.112}$$

where $E[R_{mv,z}]$ is the zero-beta rate for R_{mv}, defined in section 3.1.2 (for the case where $R_{mv} = R_m$, the market return).

Problem 4.4 GMM and Time-Series Regressions

This exercise asks you to complete the GMM derivation in section 4.4.3 of the standard asymptotic time-series test statistic (3.45). Use of the Kronecker product will be particularly useful. The Kronecker product, denoted by $\otimes$, is a matrix operation defined as follows: if A and B are $I \times J$ and $K \times L$ matrices, respectively, their Kronecker product is the $IK \times JL$ matrix:

$$A \otimes B = \begin{bmatrix} a_{11}B & \cdots & a_{1J}B \\ \vdots & \ddots & \vdots \\ a_{I1}B & \cdots & a_{IJ}B \end{bmatrix}, \tag{4.113}$$

where a_{ij} is the (i,j)th element of A.[17]

[17]The Kronecker product has the following properties:

$$A \otimes (B + C) = A \otimes B + A \otimes C$$
$$(A + B) \otimes C = A \otimes C + B \otimes C$$
$$(cA) \otimes B = A \otimes (cB) = c(A \otimes B)$$
$$(A \otimes B) \otimes C = A \otimes (B \otimes C)$$
$$(A \otimes B)(C \otimes D) = (AC) \otimes (BD)$$
$$(A \otimes B)^{-1} = A^{-1} \otimes B^{-1}$$
$$(A \otimes B)' = A' \otimes B',$$

where A, B, C, and D are arbitrary (conformable, where applicable) matrices and c is a scalar.

Write (4.92) and (4.96) as

$$A = I_N$$
$$D = -U \otimes I_N$$
$$S = U \otimes \Omega, \tag{4.114}$$

where

$$U \equiv \begin{bmatrix} 1 & E[R_{mt}^e] \\ E[R_{mt}^e] & E[(R_{mt}^e)^2] \end{bmatrix}. \tag{4.115}$$

Derive the formula for the asymptotic variance of the intercepts in the market model, (4.97).

Part II

Intertemporal Portfolio Choice and Asset Pricing

Present Value Relations

THE FIRST PART of this book considered static asset pricing models in which returns have exogenous second and higher moments, pinned down by the random distribution of terminal payoffs, and investors determine only the first moments of returns by setting initial asset prices. In a multiperiod context, however, investors trading in financial markets determine asset prices at every date and hence influence the random distribution of future prices as well as the initial level of prices. Handling this situation requires much more careful attention to the process by which both expected payoffs and required rates of return determine asset prices. In effect, one must move from "expected return" theory to "asset pricing" theory.

In this chapter we discuss models that map cash flows and discount rates into prices using present value relations. As a preliminary, we discuss the important concept of market efficiency in section 5.1, arguing that market efficiency is equivalent to rational expectations once a model of required returns has been specified. This section also summarizes the literature on autocorrelations of returns on individual stocks and stock indexes.

Section 5.2 discusses present value models with constant discount rates, and section 5.3 shows how to generalize such models to accommodate time-varying discount rates. This section also reviews the literature on the short- and long-term predictability of stock returns from the dividend-price ratio and other valuation ratios. Section 5.4 considers econometric problems with regressions that predict returns from valuation ratios, and section 5.5 introduces an alternative class of "drifting steady-state" models that may be useful when valuation ratios are highly persistent. Section 5.6 discusses some recent research that explores predictions of aggregate stock returns derived from the cross-section of stock prices at a point in time.

5.1 Market Efficiency

The intuition of market efficiency is that financial markets are competitive, so there should not be an easy way to profit by trading financial assets. The difficulty is to translate this compelling intuition into a testable hypothesis.

Fama (1970, p. 383) famously defines a market as *efficient* if "prices 'fully reflect' all available information." It is not obvious what these words mean, and Fama's use of quotation marks around the term "fully reflect" suggests his awareness of this problem.

122

5. *Present Value Relations*

Malkiel (1989, p. 127) usefully expands this definition in an article for the *New Palgrave Dictionary of Money and Finance*:

> A capital market is said to be efficient if it fully and correctly reveals all available information in determining security prices. Formally, the market is said to be efficient with respect to some information set, ϕ, if security prices would be unaffected by revealing that information to all participants. Moreover, efficiency with respect to an information set, ϕ, implies that it is impossible to make economic profits by trading on the basis of ϕ.

Malkiel's second sentence suggests an experiment that could be performed in principle but is difficult to conduct in practice (although event studies that measure market responses to news announcements can be interpreted as tests of market efficiency with respect to the announced information). Malkiel's third sentence describes an enormous literature in empirical asset pricing. This literature seeks to test whether

$$R_{i,t+1} - \Theta_{it} + U_{i,t+1}, \tag{5.1}$$

where Θ_{it} is the equilibrium return on asset i generated by some economic model, and $U_{i,t+1}$ is a fair game with respect to the information set at t (i.e., it has conditional expectation zero given that information set). Given the economic model, market efficiency is equivalent to rational expectations. Rejection of the specification (5.1) implies that the information set at t can be used to trade profitably in the asset, earning higher returns than those captured by the economic model in Θ_{it}.

The *joint hypothesis problem* is that market efficiency is not testable except in combination with a model of expected returns. The reverse is not true, however, because models of expected returns can also be made testable by combining them with survey data on expectations, or particular assumptions about irrational beliefs.

Even when we have a model of expected returns, we need to specify the variables that are included in the information set at t. Fama (1970) defines three forms of the efficient market hypothesis. The *weak form* includes past returns in the information set; the *semi-strong form* includes publicly available information such as stock splits, dividends, or earnings; and the *strong form* includes information available to some market participants but not necessarily available to all participants. This form can be tested by using measurable actions of the potentially better informed agents, such as trades or portfolio holdings, as information that may be useful for predicting returns.

The market efficiency literature contains two main branches. The cross-sectional literature averages returns over t and considers various assets i. The economic model for Θ_{it} is a cross-sectional asset pricing model. Tests of the CAPM that use average realized returns, for example, can be thought of as joint tests of the CAPM and market efficiency.

The time-series literature fixes i and models returns over t. The simplest economic model for Θ_{it} is then $\Theta_{it} = \Theta$, a constant, and the early literature concentrated on this model. However, equilibrium models with time-varying expected returns are the main focus of contemporary research. Also, early work concentrated on the behavior of an aggregate stock index, but much recent work considers multiple asset classes or moves to a panel structure, thereby combining the two branches of the literature in a more ambitious fashion.

To devise meaningful time-series tests and interpret the results, it is helpful to have an alternative hypothesis in mind. For example:

High-frequency noise. Market prices are contaminated by short-term noise caused by measurement errors or illiquidity (bid-ask bounce). This generates short-run reversals.

Imperfect information processing. The market reacts sluggishly to information. This generates short-run continuation of returns following information releases. In some variants of this story, the market may overreact to certain salient types of information, generating reversals.

Persistent mispricing. Market prices can deviate substantially from efficient levels, and the deviations are hard to arbitrage because they last a long time. This generates long-run reversal and predictability based on price levels but may be hard to detect in the short run.

Disposition effect. Individual investors are more willing to sell stocks they own that have increased in value (winners) than they are to sell stocks that have decreased in value since they were purchased (losers), unless the losses are extreme. That is, they display a disposition effect (Shefrin and Statman 1985) together with a capitulation effect. This implies that good news and extremely bad news cause increased trading volume and high expected future returns.

Short-term return predictability is easy to detect if it is present and is hard to explain using a risk-based asset pricing model. However, it has modest effects on prices, and it can disappear quickly if arbitrageurs discover the predictability or if transactions costs decline making arbitrage cheaper. Long-term return predictability can have large effects on prices but is hard to detect without very long time series and may be explained by a more sophisticated model of risk and return.

Michael Jensen (1978, p. 95) famously wrote:

There is no other proposition in economics which has more solid empirical evidence supporting it than the Efficient Markets Hypothesis.

Robert Shiller (1984, pp. 458–459) responded with equal vigor:

Returns on speculative assets are nearly unforecastable; this fact is the basis of the most important argument in the oral tradition against a role for mass psychology in speculative markets. One form of this argument claims that because real returns are nearly unforecastable, the real price of stocks is close to the intrinsic value, that is, the present value with constant discount rate of optimally forecasted future real dividends. This argument... is one of the most remarkable errors in the history of economic thought.

Paul Samuelson, in private correspondence discussed by Jung and Shiller (2005, p. 221), wrote:

Modern markets show considerable micro efficiency (for the reason that the minority who spot aberrations from micro efficiency can make money from those occurrences and, in doing so, they tend to wipe out any persistent inefficiencies). In no contradiction to the previous sentence, I had hypothesized considerable macro inefficiency, in the sense of long waves in the time series of aggregate indexes of security prices below and above various definitions of fundamental values.

The debate continues to this day, although most economists agree that market efficiency is a useful benchmark but does not hold perfectly. In other words, it is a half-full (or half-empty) glass.

5.1.1 Tests of Autocorrelation in Stock Returns

The most basic time-series test of market efficiency (as always, testing jointly with a model of expected return) is to test whether past deviations of returns from model-implied expected returns predict future return deviations. This is a test of *weak-form market efficiency* in Fama's terminology. For simplicity, we discuss the case where the model of expected return is that the expected return is an unknown constant. Then, we are testing whether past returns predict future returns.

The leading approach looks at the autocorrelations of stock returns. Under the null hypothesis that stock returns are iid, the standard error for any single sample autocorrelation is asymptotically given by $1/\sqrt{T}$, where T is the sample size. Unfortunately, this makes it extremely hard to detect small autocorrelations since the standard error is 0.1 when $T = 100$ and is still 0.02 when $T = 2500$.

Under the null hypothesis that stock returns are iid, different autocorrelations are uncorrelated with one another. This suggests that we may gain by combining different autocorrelations. For example, the Q statistic of Box and Pierce (1970) calculates a sum of K squared sample autocorrelations:

$$Q_K = T \sum_{j=1}^{K} \widehat{\rho}_j^2, \tag{5.2}$$

where $\widehat{\rho}_j = \widehat{\text{Corr}}(r_t, r_{t-j})$, and this is asymptotically distributed χ^2 with K degrees of freedom.

The Q statistic does not use the sign of the autocorrelations. Many plausible alternatives to the null hypothesis of constant expected returns imply that autocorrelations are each individually small but all have the same sign. To get power against such an alternative, we would like to average the levels of sample autocorrelations rather than their squares. One way to do this is the variance ratio statistic, the variance of K-period log returns divided by K times the variance of one-period log returns. This statistic was introduced to the finance literature by Lo and MacKinlay (1988) and Poterba and Summers (1988) and to the macroeconomics literature by Cochrane (1988a). The variance ratio is one when returns are serially uncorrelated, because then the K-period log return is the sum of K successive returns that are uncorrelated with one another, and its variance is K times the variance of each element of the sum. More generally, the variance ratio statistic can be related to the sample autocorrelations of returns as follows:

$$\widehat{V}(K) = \frac{\widehat{\text{Var}}(r_{t+1} + \cdots + r_{t+K})}{K\widehat{\text{Var}}(r_{t+1})} = 1 + 2 \sum_{j=1}^{K-1} \left(1 - \frac{j}{K}\right) \widehat{\rho}_j. \tag{5.3}$$

In other words, it is one plus a weighted average of the first $K-1$ sample autocorrelations, with linearly declining weights. A variance ratio statistic greater than one indicates that autocorrelations are predominantly positive, whereas a ratio less than one indicates that they are predominantly negative.

The asymptotic variance of the variance ratio statistic, under the null hypothesis of iid returns, is

$$\text{Var}(\widehat{V}(K)) = \frac{4}{T} \sum_{j=1}^{K-1} \left(1 - \frac{j}{K}\right)^2 = \frac{2(2K-1)(K-1)}{3KT}. \tag{5.4}$$

As K increases, this approaches $4K/3T$.

This result can be generalized when $K \to \infty$, $T \to \infty$, and $K/T \to 0$ (Priestley 1981, p. 463). In this case the true returns process can be serially correlated and heteroskedastic, and we still have

$$\text{Var}(\widehat{V}(K)) = \frac{4KV(K)^2}{3T}. \tag{5.5}$$

Note that this is larger when the true $V(K)$ is large. An econometric caveat is that the use of asymptotics assuming $K/T \to 0$ is dangerous when in practice K is often large relative to the sample size. Richardson and Stock (1989) develop alternative asymptotics assuming $K/T \to \delta$, where $\delta > 0$.

A related approach, implemented by Fama and French (1988b), is to regress the K-period return on the lagged K-period return. The coefficient in this K-period return regression, $\beta(K)$, is related to the variance ratio statistic by

$$\beta(K) = \frac{V(2K)}{V(K)} - 1, \tag{5.6}$$

and the R^2 statistic is just the square of the regression coefficient because the dependent and independent variables have the same variance.

5.1.2 Empirical Evidence on Autocorrelation in Stock Returns

Results from autocorrelation tests can be summarized as follows. In daily, weekly, and even monthly data, individual stocks have small negative autocorrelations, as shown most recently by Nagel (2012), who documents profits from a short-term reversal strategy that buys stocks that have underperformed the market in recent days and shorts stocks that have outperformed the market. This high-frequency reversal rewards investors who provide liquidity by buying (selling) individual stocks to accommodate exogenous selling (buying) pressure. We discuss it further in Chapter 12, as part of the literature on market microstructure.

Broader stock indexes, by contrast, have predominantly positive high-frequency auto-correlations. This results from positive cross-autocorrelations among individual stocks, particularly those between returns on larger and more liquid stocks and subsequent returns on smaller and less liquid stocks (Lo and MacKinlay 1988, 1990b). The positive autocorrelations of indexes have declined in recent decades, as illustrated by Figure 5.1, an update of a figure in Froot and Perold (1995) that reports the first-order daily autocorrelation of the excess return on the CRSP value-weighted index, estimated independently within each year from 1926 to 2012. As an informal exercise, you are asked to consider what economic forces might have driven the decline in index autocorrelations during the 1970s and 1980s; we return to this question at the end of the chapter.

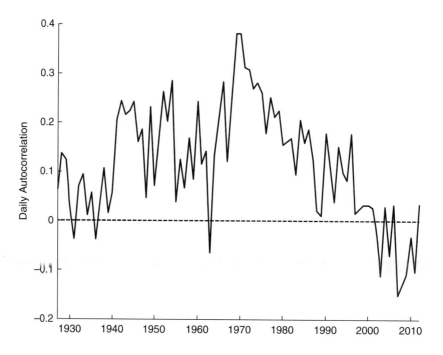

Figure 5.1. *Daily Autocorrelation of the Excess Market Return, 1926–2012*

Table 5.1. *Variance Ratio Statistics, 1926–2013*

Horizon	Normalized VR	Raw VR	Asymptotic SE
1 year	1.000	1.177	0.116
2 years	0.949	1.126	0.170
3 years	0.822	0.999	0.210
4 years	0.718	0.896	0.244
5 years	0.620	0.798	0.274
6 years	0.508	0.685	0.300
7 years	0.455	0.632	0.325
8 years	0.443	0.621	0.348

Autocorrelations of stock returns look quite different at horizons of several months or years. Both individual stocks and broad stock indexes have autocorrelations that tend to be positive for the first 12 months (possibly excluding the first month), then negative at longer horizons. The positive autocorrelations for individual stocks are the basis for the momentum effect discussed in Chapter 3, while negative longer-run autocorrelations for individual stocks were documented by DeBondt and Thaler (1985).

At the index level, Poterba and Summers (1988) used the variance ratio statistic, discussed above, to document long-run mean reversion in index returns. Table 5.1 updates their analysis, again using the CRSP value-weighted index, for the period July 1926–April 2013.

The data used to construct this table are monthly, so the raw variance ratio of 1.177 at a horizon of one year, reported at the top of the second column of the table, reflects predominantly positive autocorrelations between one month and one year. The raw variance ratios decline beyond one year, reaching 0.621 at a horizon of eight years, reflecting predominantly negative multiyear autocorrelations. Poterba and Summers highlighted the decline beyond one year by normalizing their variance ratios to be one at a one-year horizon, as shown in the first column of the table. At eight years, the normalized variance ratio is 0.443, indicating that the eight-year return has a variance only 8×0.443, or about 3.5 times as great as the one-year return. The asymptotic standard errors for these variance ratios are large, as reported in the final column of the table, so while these tests deliver point estimates of substantial mean reversion, they do not provide strong statistical evidence against the null hypothesis of serially uncorrelated returns. Also, variance ratios are closer to one when the Great Depression is excluded from the data, although they remain below one even in the most recent period since the end of Poterba and Summers' dataset.[1]

To interpret these results, we would like to have a better sense of what alternative models of time-varying expected returns would imply about the pattern of autocorrelations. This requires the use of present value models that determine prices, and thus realized returns, given alternative processes for expected returns. We discuss models of this sort in the next two sections.

5.2 Present Value Models with Constant Discount Rates

The simplest present value models assume that assets are priced by discounting payoffs at a rate that is constant over time. Despite substantial evidence for time-varying discount rates, such models are still useful for many purposes and remain a natural starting point for further theoretical development. We first present models in which dividends paid to investors are exogenous, and then discuss models that derive dividends from firms' profits and payout policies.

5.2.1 Dividend-Based Models

The gross simple return on a stock is given by

$$1 + R_{t+1} = \frac{P_{t+1} + D_{t+1}}{P_t}. \tag{5.7}$$

If the expected return on the stock is constant, $E_t R_{t+1} = R$, then

$$P_t = E_t \left[\frac{P_{t+1} + D_{t+1}}{1 + R} \right]. \tag{5.8}$$

Solving forward for K periods, we get

$$P_t = E_t \left[\sum_{k=1}^{K} \left(\frac{1}{1+R} \right)^k D_{t+k} \right] + E_t \left[\left(\frac{1}{1+R} \right)^K P_{t+K} \right]. \tag{5.9}$$

---

[1] There is a corresponding tendency for $\beta(K)$ to be negative, with maximum $R^2(K)$ of 25–45% at 3–5 years (Fama and French 1988b).

Dividend Discount Model

Letting $K \to \infty$, and assuming that the last term on the right-hand side converges to zero,

$$\lim_{K \to \infty} E_t \left[\left(\frac{1}{1+R} \right)^K P_{t+K} \right] = 0,$$ (5.10)

we have the dividend discount model of stock prices,

$$P_t = E_t \left[\sum_{k=1}^{\infty} \left(\frac{1}{1+R} \right)^k D_{t+k} \right].$$ (5.11)

This model, with a constant expected stock return, is sometimes called the *random walk* or *martingale model* of stock prices. But, in fact, the stock price is not a martingale in this model, since

$$E_t P_{t+1} = (1+R)P_t - E_t D_{t+1},$$ (5.12)

and a martingale process is defined by the property $E_t P_{t+1} = P_t$.

However, we can obtain a martingale process in this model as follows. If an investor reinvests all dividends in buying more shares, the number of shares owned is given by

$$N_{t+1} = N_t \left(1 + \frac{D_{t+1}}{P_{t+1}} \right).$$ (5.13)

The discounted value of the resulting portfolio, also known as the discounted gain process,

$$V_t = \frac{N_t P_t}{(1+R)^t},$$ (5.14)

follows a martingale.

Variance Bounds Tests

Shiller (1981) observed that if (5.11) holds, the realized discounted value of future dividends should equal the stock price plus unpredictable noise, and therefore should have greater variance than the stock price. He calculated a proxy for realized discounted dividends on an aggregate stock index, using a terminal condition to account for dividends not yet paid, and found that this series has much lower variance than the price of the index, contrary to the prediction of the model. LeRoy and Porter (1981) made a similar observation, and Shiller (1979) conducted a related analysis of long-term bond yields.

Shiller's critique generated a major controversy. Kleidon (1986) and Marsh and Merton (1986) emphasized that both dividends and stock prices follow highly persistent processes with unit roots, in which case the population variances of prices and of realized discounted dividends are undefined. Sample variances can be calculated in any sample, but they increase without limit as the sample size increases.

In response to this, Campbell and Shiller (1987) showed how to modify the variance calculations for the unit root case. A linear time-series model for dividends, in which the dividend process has a unit root, implies that prices and dividends are cointegrated (Engle and Granger 1987) with a cointegrating parameter that depends on the discount rate R in (5.11). Specifically, the dividend discount model can be rewritten as

$$P_t - \frac{D_t}{R} = \left(\frac{1}{R}\right) \mathrm{E}_t \left[\sum_{i=0}^{\infty} \left(\frac{1}{1+R}\right)^i \Delta D_{t+1+i}\right], \tag{5.15}$$

so there is a linear combination of stock prices and dividends, $P_t - D_t/R$, that is stationary, even though both the stock price and the dividend follow unit-root processes. Campbell and Shiller (1987) tested and rejected this form of the dividend discount model, once again finding excessive volatility—this time in the spread between prices and current dividends rather than in the level of prices.

Linearity-Generating Processes
Gabaix (2009) has proposed a broader class of models in which the level of prices, normalized by some measure of current fundamentals (typically the current dividend), is linearly related to time-varying factors such as the contemporaneous growth rate of cash flows and the contemporaneous discount rate.

To derive the simplest linearity-generating process, let us assume a constant discount rate and model the dividend as

$$\mathrm{E}_t D_{t+1} = (1 + G_t) D_t, \tag{5.16}$$

where g_t is the dividend growth rate. We assume that shocks to this growth rate and shocks to the level of dividends are independent of one another.

Leading equation (5.16) by one period and taking expectations, we have

$$\mathrm{E}_t D_{t+2} = \mathrm{E}_t (1 + G_{t+1}) D_{t+1} = \mathrm{E}_t (1 + G_{t+1}) \mathrm{E}_t D_{t+1}, \tag{5.17}$$

where the second equality follows from the independence of shocks to the level and growth rate of dividends.

The linearity-generating process for the dividend growth rate takes a specific nonlinear form:

$$\mathrm{E}_t G_{t+1} = \frac{\rho G_t}{1 + G_t}. \tag{5.18}$$

Here the division by $(1 + G_t)$ is the "linearity-generating twist" that converts a linear AR(1) process for dividend growth into a nonlinear process that has just the right form to make the price-dividend ratio linear in dividend growth.

Substituting into the expression for the expected two-period-ahead dividend and simplifying, we have

$$\mathrm{E}_t D_{t+2} = (1 + G_t(1 + \rho)) D_t. \tag{5.19}$$

Thus the nonlinear model for the dividend growth rate is a linear model for the level of dividends, or equivalently for changes in dividends, with expected changes decaying geometrically at rate ρ:

$$\mathrm{E}_t \Delta D_{t+2} = \rho \mathrm{E}_t \Delta D_{t+1}. \tag{5.20}$$

This is a special case of the dividend discount model, and we can use equation (5.15) to verify that the price-dividend ratio is linear in the dividend growth rate,

$$\frac{P_t}{D_t} = \left(\frac{1}{R}\right)\left[1 + \left(\frac{1+R}{1+R-\rho}\right)G_t\right].$$

(5.21)

Gabaix's contribution is to show that a similar trick can be used more generally, even in models with time-varying discount rates. Problem 5.1 asks you to follow his approach in a richer example with a time-varying discount rate, and an application to a consumption-based asset pricing model with disaster risk is presented in section 6.3.1.

The Gordon Growth Model

A particularly useful special case of the dividend discount model assumes that the expected dividend growth rate is a constant G, so that $E_t D_{t+k} = (1 + G)^{k-1} E_t D_{t+1}$. Then we get the Gordon growth model (Gordon and Shapiro 1956, Williams 1938):

$$P_t = \frac{E_t D_{t+1}}{R - G},$$

(5.22)

often written more simply, omitting time subscripts, as

$$\frac{D}{P} = R - G,$$

(5.23)

where D denotes the next-period dividend. Rearranging this, we have

$$R = \frac{D}{P} + G,$$

(5.24)

which says that returns come from income and capital gains (equal to dividend growth in steady state).

Taken literally, the Gordon growth model implies that all the variables in equation (5.24) are constant over time. Obviously this is counterfactual, and practical implementations of the model work either with a point-in-time value for D/P and contemporaneous estimates of R and G or with sample averages of all these variables estimated over long historical samples.

Summary statistics reported in Siegel (2007) illustrate the usefulness of the latter approach. Siegel calculates statistics for a broad index of US stocks, using Cowles indexes before 1925 and data from the Center for Research in Security Prices (CRSP) at the University of Chicago since 1926. Over the period 1871–2006, the geometric average real stock return on US stocks was 6.7%, the average dividend-price ratio was 4.5%, and the geometric average rate of real capital appreciation was 2.1%.[2] Thus about 2/3 of total return came from income, and 1/3 from capital gains. The average rate of real dividend growth, which should equal the rate of real capital appreciation in steady state, was somewhat lower at 1.3%, reflecting a tendency for stock prices to grow faster than dividends over this period. Later in this chapter we discuss several ways to modify the Gordon growth model to explicitly incorporate time-variation in R and G.

---

[2]The use of geometric averages is important in this context and is explained in greater detail below in section 5.5.2.

5.2.2 Earnings-Based Models

So far we have treated dividends and their growth rate as exogenous. Alternatively, we may ask how dividends are determined by a firm's payout policy and profitability.

We write earnings as X_t and the book equity of the firm as B_t. We assume that reinvested earnings, $X_t - D_t$, augment book equity one-for-one:

$$B_t = B_{t-1} + X_t - D_t. \tag{5.25}$$

This is exactly true under so-called clean-surplus accounting and approximately true under real-world accounting.

We define the firm's accounting return on equity (ROE) as earnings divided by lagged book equity,

$$ROE_t = X_t / B_{t-1}. \tag{5.26}$$

We define the retention or plowback ratio λ_t as the fraction of earnings that is retained for reinvestment, so that

$$D_t = (1 - \lambda_t) X_t. \tag{5.27}$$

In the steady state of the Gordon growth model, book equity, earnings, and dividends all grow at the common rate G. Thus we have

$$G = \frac{B_t - B_{t-1}}{B_{t-1}} = \frac{X_t - D_t}{B_{t-1}} = \lambda \frac{X_t}{B_{t-1}} = \lambda ROE. \tag{5.28}$$

Substituting these expressions into the Gordon growth model, we have

$$P_t = \frac{(1 - \lambda) E_t X_{t+1}}{R - \lambda ROE} \tag{5.29}$$

or, omitting time subscripts,

$$\frac{X}{P} = \frac{R - \lambda ROE}{1 - \lambda}, \tag{5.30}$$

where X denotes next-period earnings. This shows that stock prices increase with the retention ratio when $ROE > R$, since then the firm's investments more than cover their cost of capital. However, stock prices decline with the retention ratio when $ROE < R$. Firms with ROE below R cannot make adequately profitable investments and should distribute cash to shareholders rather than retaining earnings for reinvestment.

Rearranging (5.30), we have

$$R = (1 - \lambda) \frac{X}{P} + \lambda ROE, \tag{5.31}$$

so the return can be written as a weighted average of the earnings yield and profitability. Profitability is important only to the extent that the firm is reinvesting earnings to generate growth.

In the long run, we might expect investments to continue until *ROE* is driven to equality with *R*. In this case, the earnings-price ratio equals the discount rate, regardless of payout policy:

$$\frac{X}{P} = R. \tag{5.32}$$

Siegel (2007) reports that the average price-earnings ratio on US stocks over the period 1871–2006 was 14.45. This corresponds to an earnings-price ratio of 6.9%, close to the geometric average real return of 6.7%, which suggests that corporate profitability may indeed be close to the cost of capital on average over the long run.

This framework can also be used to explain the determinants of the firm's book-market ratio, the most commonly used measure of value in cross-sectional analysis of stock returns. We have

$$\frac{B}{P} = \frac{R - \lambda ROE}{(1 - \lambda) ROE} = 1 + \left(\frac{R/ROE - 1}{1 - \lambda} \right), \tag{5.33}$$

so the book-market ratio is above one and increasing in the retention ratio when *ROE* < *R*, and below one and decreasing in the retention ratio when *ROE* > *R*. This is consistent with the previous conclusion that stock prices increase with the retention ratio when *ROE* > *R* and decline otherwise. In a long-run steady state where *ROE* equals *R*, the book-market ratio equals one for any payout policy.

5.2.3 Rational Bubbles

Models of rational bubbles drop the assumption (5.10) that the limit of the discounted stock price equals zero, while retaining the assumption that the expected stock return is constant. We then get an infinity of possible solutions

$$P_t = P_{Dt} + Q_t, \tag{5.34}$$

where P_{Dt} is the price implied by the dividend discount model (5.11), and the rational bubble Q_t is any stochastic process satisfying

$$Q_t = \mathrm{E}_t \left[\frac{Q_{t+1}}{1 + R} \right]. \tag{5.35}$$

For example, Blanchard and Watson (1982) suggested the following bubble process: $Q_{t+1} = ((1 + R)/\pi) Q_t + \zeta_{t+1}$ with probability π, and $Q_{t+1} = \zeta_{t+1}$ with probability $1 - \pi$, where $E_t \zeta_{t+1} = 0$. This bubble process either grows rapidly or bursts. The more likely it is to burst, the faster it must grow before bursting in order to satisfy equation (5.35).

The conditions for rational bubbles to exist are restrictive. Some of these restrictions can be stated in partial equilibrium. For example, rational bubbles cannot exist on finite-lived assets, because at the terminal date *T* the asset value is given by its terminal payoff and the terminal bubble Q_T must be zero. Working backward using (5.35), the bubble must be zero at all earlier periods as well. Similar logic tells us that negative rational bubbles cannot exist if there is a lower bound on the asset price (e.g., zero, for assets with limited liability); and positive rational bubbles cannot exist if there is an upper bound on the asset price (e.g., a high-priced substitute in perfectly elastic supply). Furthermore, in the case where positive bubbles can exist but negative bubbles are ruled out, then a bubble can never start because from (5.35), $Q_t = 0$ and $Q_{t+1} \geq 0$ imply $Q_{t+1} = 0$. In this case, any bubble must have existed from the moment when the asset first began to be traded (Diba and Grossman 1987).

Other restrictions arise from the nature of general equilibrium. First, rational bubbles cannot exist in a representative-agent economy with an infinite-lived agent because the agent's investment in a bubble violates the transversality condition, so a bubble cannot be consistent with infinite-horizon rational-expectations equilibrium. Second, Tirole (1985) showed that rational bubbles cannot exist in a deterministic over-lapping generations (OLG) economy where the interest rate exceeds the growth rate of the economy, because in such an economy a bubble growing at the interest rate will eventually exhaust the wealth of the young generation that must purchase assets from the old generation. In a deterministic economy, an interest rate lower than the growth rate of the economy implies that the economy is dynamically inefficient, in other words, that a social planner can achieve a Pareto improvement by reallocating resources intertem-porally. Tirole's result then implies that rational bubbles cannot exist in a dynamically efficient economy.

Matters become more complicated in OLG models with random shocks to output and asset returns. Here the growth rate of a bubble will depend on the fundamental risk of the underlying asset and the stochastic properties of the bubble itself, and the condi-tions for dynamic efficiency cannot be reduced to the comparison of a single interest rate with the growth rate of the economy. Farhi and Tirole (2012) show that with incomplete markets and imperfect risksharing, an OLG economy can have a low riskless interest rate (because of precautionary saving) even if it is dynamically efficient. Abel et al. (1989) provide a sufficient condition for dynamic efficiency in a stochastic economy, that capital income always exceeds investment. They argue that this condition is satisfied empiric-ally, but Geerolf (2013) challenges this finding. These considerations and the low level of real interest rates in the early 21st century have revived interest in bubbles among macroeconomists and monetary economists.

Empirical tests for rational bubbles have traditionally compared the time-series beha-vior of prices and dividends on the same asset, looking for evidence that prices deviate from dividends in a nonstationary (explosive) fashion. These tests have mixed results because it is difficult to distinguish stationary but highly persistent processes from non-stationary processes in the available data samples (Diba and Grossman 1988, Evans 1991, Phillips, Wu, and Yu 2011). Giglio, Maggiori, and Stroebel (2016)) instead compare the prices of two related assets and find that no rational bubble exists in a particular asset class, residential real estate. This is possible because in the UK and Singapore, very long real estate leases (leaseholds) are traded alongside outright ownership claims (free-holds). Some leaseholds have maturities of over seven centuries, and Giglio et al. show that their prices are indistinguishable from those of comparable freeholds, implying that the discounted real estate value 700 years in the future is a negligible component of real estate value today.

Even if one does not believe that rational bubbles exist in reality, the rational bubble literature is informative because it tells us something about the phenomena we may observe in a world of irrational bubbles. As we shall see in the next section, large move-ments in asset prices relative to fundamentals generate only a small amount of return predictability if the movements in prices (and the corresponding movements in expected returns) are persistent. A rational bubble, whose constant expected growth rate equals the underlying asset's constant discount rate, is the extreme case, where a deviation of price from fundamentals is so persistent (indeed, explosive) that it implies no return predictability at all. Popular discussion of bubbles seems generally to be referring to irrational bubbles that do generate a small amount of return predictability.

5.3 Present Value Models with Time-Varying Discount Rates

5.3.1 The Campbell-Shiller Approximation

The models discussed in the previous section have constant expected returns, but to account for evidence of stock return predictability we need to allow for time-varying expected returns. In this case, the exact present value model becomes nonlinear and difficult to work with. This is another example of the problems caused by the simultaneous presence of additive and multiplicative terms in asset pricing models.

Return Approximation
Campbell and Shiller (1988a) responded by proposing an approximate loglinear present value model. Their approach starts from the definition of the log stock return,

$$r_{t+1} = \log(1 + R_{t+1}) = \log(P_{t+1} + D_{t+1}) - \log(P_t)$$
$$= p_{t+1} - p_t + \log(1 + \exp(d_{t+1} - p_{t+1})), \tag{5.36}$$

where p_{t+1} and d_{t+1} denote log prices and dividends.

A first-order Taylor approximation of the nonlinear function is

$$\log(1 + \exp(d_{t+1} - p_{t+1})) = f(d_{t+1} - p_{t+1})$$
$$\approx f(\overline{d-p}) + f'(\overline{d-p})(d_{t+1} - p_{t+1} - (\overline{d-p})). \tag{5.37}$$

Here the function $f(z) = \log(1 + \exp(z))$ and $f'(z) = \exp(z)/(1 + \exp(z))$. The resulting approximation for the log return is

$$r_{t+1} \approx k + \rho p_{t+1} + (1 - \rho) d_{t+1} - p_t, \tag{5.38}$$

where

$$\rho = \frac{1}{1 + \exp(\overline{d-p})}, \tag{5.39}$$

and

$$k = -\log(\rho) - (1 - \rho)\log(1/\rho - 1). \tag{5.40}$$

This approximation replaces the log of a sum with an average of logs, where the relative weights depend on the average relative magnitudes of dividend and price. Given a long-run historical average dividend-price ratio between 4% and 5%, a reasonable value for the loglinearization parameter ρ is in the range 0.95–0.96 if the time period is one year. If the period length is shorter, ρ must be adjusted accordingly, for example, from 0.96 to $0.96^{1/4} = 0.990$ per quarter.

The accuracy of the Campbell-Shiller approximation depends on the variability of the log dividend-price ratio around its mean, so unlike the loglinear approximation to log portfolio return discussed in section 2.1.4, it does not become more accurate as the period length becomes shorter. Campbell and Shiller (1988a) present evidence that accuracy is good in historical aggregate US stock market data. More generally, the approximation delivers insights that survive in numerical solutions to asset pricing models, including several of the consumption-based models discussed in Chapter 6.

Price Decomposition
The approximate expression for the log stock return is a difference equation in log price, dividend, and return. Solving forward and imposing the terminal condition that

$$\lim_{j \to \infty} \rho^j p_{t+j} = 0, \tag{5.41}$$

we get

$$p_t = \frac{k}{1-\rho} + \sum_{j=0}^{\infty} \rho^j [(1-\rho) d_{t+1+j} - r_{t+1+j}]. \tag{5.42}$$

This equation holds ex post, as an accounting identity. It should therefore hold ex ante, not only for rational expectations but also for irrational expectations that respect identities. Taking conditional expectations of (5.42) and using the fact that $E_t p_t = p_t$ because the current price is in the information set, we have

$$p_t = \frac{k}{1-\rho} + p_{CF,t} + p_{DR,t}, \tag{5.43}$$

where

$$p_{CF,t} = E_t \sum_{j=0}^{\infty} \rho^j (1-\rho) d_{t+1+j} \tag{5.44}$$

and

$$p_{DR,t} = -E_t \sum_{j=0}^{\infty} \rho^j r_{t+1+j} \tag{5.45}$$

are the components of the log stock price driven by cash flow (dividend) expectations and discount rate (return) expectations, respectively.

Dividend-Price Ratio Decomposition
If log dividends follow a unit root process, then log dividends and log prices are cointegrated with a known cointegrating vector. The log dividend-price ratio is stationary and is linearly related to realized future dividend growth and returns. Subtracting the formula (5.42) from the current log dividend, we have

$$d_t - p_t = \frac{-k}{1-\rho} + \sum_{j=0}^{\infty} \rho^j [-\Delta d_{t+1+j} + r_{t+1+j}]. \tag{5.46}$$

Once again we can take expectations to get

$$d_t - p_t = \frac{-k}{1-\rho} + dp_{CF,t} + dp_{DR,t}, \tag{5.47}$$

where

$$dp_{CF,t} = d_t - p_{CF,t} = -E_t \sum_{j=0}^{\infty} \rho^j \Delta d_{t+1+j} \tag{5.48}$$

and

$$dp_{DR,t} = -p_{DR,t} = E_t \sum_{j=0}^{\infty} \rho^j r_{t+1+j} \tag{5.49}$$

are the cash-flow and discount-rate components of the log dividend-price ratio.

This decomposition shows why the log dividend-price ratio is a natural candidate to predict stock returns. If there is any predictable variation in stock returns, it will be reflected in the component $dp_{DR,t}$. While the log dividend-price ratio also reflects expectations of dividend growth in the component $dp_{CF,t}$, aggregate US dividend payments have been relatively smooth and close to a random walk at least since World War II (Lintner 1956). Hence, forecasts of future growth rates of dividends may not be too volatile, allowing return forecasts to be the primary influence on the ratio $d_t - p_t$.

Since the decomposition (5.47) holds for irrational expectations that respect identities as well as for rational expectations, it shows how different cash flow forecasts can lead different investors to interpret stock market valuations differently. An investor with a higher than rational long-term cash flow forecast must also have a higher than rational long-term return forecast, given the level of the log dividend-price ratio. Thus, irrational optimism about cash flows makes optimistic investors willing to hold stocks at prices that are unattractive for rational investors.

Book-Market Ratio Decomposition
The above models are dynamic versions of the Gordon growth model (5.23). Vuolteenaho (2002) uses a similar loglinear approximation to derive a dynamic version of the profitability-based formula for the book-market ratio (5.33):

$$b_t - v_t = \mu + E_t \sum_{j=0}^{\infty} \rho^j [-roe_{t+1+j} + r_{t+1+j}], \tag{5.50}$$

where b_t is the log book value of the firm, v_t is its log market value, and $roe_t = \log(1 + ROE_t)$. It is natural to use this formula in studies of individual firms, since firm-level dividend policy may be unstable over time and some firms do not pay dividends at all in historical data.

Return Decomposition
Campbell (1991) used the Campbell-Shiller loglinearization to decompose the variation in stock returns, rather than prices, into revisions in expectations of dividend growth and future returns:

$$r_{t+1} - E_t r_{t+1} = N_{CF,t+1} - N_{DR,t+1}, \tag{5.51}$$

where

$$N_{CF,t+1} = (E_{t+1} - E_t) \sum_{j=0}^{\infty} \rho^j \Delta d_{t+1+j} \qquad (5.52)$$

and

$$N_{DR,t+1} = (E_{t+1} - E_t) \sum_{j=1}^{\infty} \rho^j r_{t+1+j} \qquad (5.53)$$

are revisions in expectations or "news" about cash flows (dividends) and discount rates (expected future returns). Discount-rate news $N_{DR,t+1}$ is defined to be positive when expected future returns increase, hence it has a negative effect on the current return.

In equation (5.51) the time index in the cash-flow sum starts at zero, whereas the time index in the discount-rate sum starts at one. If one were to bring discount-rate news to the left-hand side of the equation, it would say that including both the current period and all future periods, discount-rate news must exactly equal cash-flow news.

The return decomposition (5.51) implies that better information about future dividends reduces the volatility of returns. The reason is that news about dividends must enter prices at some point; the earlier it does, the more heavily the effect is discounted. West (1988) emphasizes this point, which is often misunderstood.

This return decomposition does not require a researcher to take a stand on which valuation ratio (the dividend-price ratio, earnings-price ratio, book-market ratio, or some other ratio of total payout to market value) best characterizes the stock market. Any of these ratios can be used in a predictive analysis that constructs empirical proxies for the return components $N_{CF,t+1}$ and $N_{DR,t+1}$. These return components are also relevant for intertemporal asset pricing theory as discussed in Chapter 9.

5.3.2 Short- and Long-Term Return Predictability

The formulas in the previous section imply that predictable variation in returns can be negligible at short horizons in relation to the overall variation of returns, and yet can be an important determinant of the level of asset prices and the volatility of returns. This idea has been important in the work of Eugene Fama and particularly of Robert Shiller, and contributed significantly to their 2013 Nobel Prize award as surveyed in Campbell (2014).

Price and Return Decomposition with an AR(1) Discount Rate
To understand this, we follow Campbell, Lo, and MacKinlay (1997) and consider a specific model of time-varying expected returns, in which the expected return is an AR(1) process:

$$r_{t+1} = \bar{r} + x_t + u_{t+1}, \qquad (5.54)$$

$$x_{t+1} = \phi x_t + \xi_{t+1}. \qquad (5.55)$$

Here $\bar{r}$ is the unconditional mean return. The conditional mean return is $\bar{r} + x_t$, where x_t is a zero-mean AR(1) process (unrelated to uses of the letter x earlier in this book). The unexpected return is u_{t+1}, and the innovation in the expected return is ξ_{t+1}. The goal of the analysis is to derive the price and return variation that is attributable to variation in the expected return, and ultimately to understand what determines the variance of the unexpected return u_{t+1} and its covariance with ξ_{t+1}.

The process for x_t implies that the component of the log dividend-price ratio that is driven by changes in future expected returns, $dp_{DR,t}$ from equation (5.49), is

$$dp_{DR,t} = \frac{\bar{r}}{1-\rho} + \frac{x_t}{1-\rho\phi}. \tag{5.56}$$

The variance of this component is

$$\text{Var}(dp_{DR,t}) = \frac{\sigma_x^2}{(1-\rho\phi)^2}, \tag{5.57}$$

so the expected return may have a very small volatility yet may still have a very large effect on the log dividend-price ratio (or equivalently the stock price) if it is highly persistent. This is the point made by Shiller (1984) when he wrote that the claim that "because real returns are nearly unforecastable, the real price of stocks is close to the intrinsic value. . .is one of the most remarkable errors in the history of economic thought."

We get a similar insight if we calculate the component of the stock return that is driven by news about future discount rates, $N_{DR,t+1}$ from equation (5.53):

$$N_{DR,t+1} = \frac{\rho\xi_{t+1}}{1-\rho\phi} \approx \frac{\xi_{t+1}}{1-\phi}. \tag{5.58}$$

A 1% increase in the expected return today is associated with a capital loss of about 2% if the AR coefficient is 0.5, a loss of about 4% if the AR coefficient is 0.75, and a loss of about 10% if the AR coefficient is 0.9. Thus, for a given variance of the expected return innovation ξ_{t+1}, the variance of discount-rate news is increasing in the persistence of the expected return.

Return Autocovariances with an AR(1) Discount Rate
This example can also be used to calculate the implied autocovariances of realized returns:

$$\text{Cov}(r_{t+1}, r_{t+1+i}) = \phi^{i-1}\left[\text{Cov}(\xi_{t+1}, N_{CF,t+1}) + \left(\frac{\phi}{1-\phi^2} - \frac{\rho}{1-\rho\phi}\right)\sigma_\xi^2\right], \tag{5.59}$$

where ξ_{t+1} is the innovation in the return predictor and cash-flow news $N_{CF,t+1}$ was defined in equation (5.52).[3] This expression has several interesting properties. Under the assumption that expected returns are persistent ($\phi > 0$), all autocovariances have the same sign, and they die off at rate ϕ. This suggests that they may be detectable using the variance ratio statistics described in section 5.1.2 and illustrated in Table 5.1, particularly when ϕ is relatively large.

The sign of the autocovariances depends on three effects: the positive effect of covariance between dividend news and revisions in expected returns ($\text{Cov}(\xi_{t+1}, N_{CF,t+1})$); the

[3]If desired, it is straightforward to use equation (5.58) to rewrite (5.59) in terms of cash-flow and discount-rate news N_{CF} and N_{DR}. However, this does not yield additional insights.

direct positive effect of autocorrelated expected returns ($\phi\sigma_\xi^2/(1-\phi^2)$); and the negative effect from the capital loss that occurs when expected returns unexpectedly increase ($-\rho\sigma_\xi^2/(1-\rho\phi)$). If these three terms cancel one another out, all autocovariances can be zero even if expected returns vary through time. This illustrates the general point that prices can be weak-form efficient even if they are not semistrong form efficient: Past returns are not a sufficient statistic for the information that investors may be able to use to predict returns. However, reasonable parameter values in this model (no strong positive covariance between expected return innovations and cash flow news, and ϕ positive but not too large) tend to generate negative autocovariances consistent with the empirical results reported in Table 5.1.

Short- and Long-Horizon Predictive Regressions with an AR(1) Discount Rate
The AR(1) example also shows us what happens if we regress the stock return onto the predictor variable x_t. (To fix ideas, one might suppose that the log dividend-price ratio is a good proxy for x_t, which will be the case in the AR(1) example if dividend growth is unpredictable.)

For simplicity, assume that discount-rate news and cash-flow news are uncorrelated: $\text{Cov}(\xi_{t+1}, N_{CF,t+1}) = 0$. Then the unconditional variance of the stock return is

$$\text{Var}(r_{t+1}) = \sigma_{CF}^2 + \sigma_x^2 \left(\frac{1 + \rho^2 - 2\rho\phi}{(1-\rho\phi)^2} \right) \approx \sigma_{CF}^2 + \frac{2\sigma_x^2}{1-\phi}, \qquad (5.60)$$

where $\sigma_{CF}^2 = \text{Var}(N_{CF,t+1})$, and the approximate equality holds when ρ is close to one and ϕ is not too close to one.

The R^2 of a single-period return regression onto x_t is

$$R^2(1) = \frac{\text{Var}(E_t r_{t+1})}{\text{Var}(r_{t+1})} \approx \frac{\sigma_x^2}{\sigma_{CF}^2 + 2\sigma_x^2/(1-\phi)} = \left(\frac{\sigma_{CF}^2}{\sigma_x^2} + \frac{2}{1-\phi} \right)^{-1} \leq \frac{1-\phi}{2}. \qquad (5.61)$$

When x_t is extremely persistent, the one-period return regression must have a low R^2, even if there is no cash flow news at all. To understand this point, consider what would happen if the asset were an inflation-indexed perpetuity with constant cash flows. Persistent movements in interest rates would be the only influence on the perpetuity's price, but its single-period return would not be very predictable because most of its variation would result from unpredictable innovations in interest rates, not the slowly time-varying required return.

Now consider a long-horizon regression of the K-period return onto the predictor variable x_t:

$$r_{t+1} + \cdots + r_{t+K} = \beta(K) x_t, \qquad (5.62)$$

where

$$\beta(K) = 1 + \phi + \cdots + \phi^{K-1} = \frac{1-\phi^K}{1-\phi}. \qquad (5.63)$$

The ratio of the K-period R^2 to the 1-period R^2 is

$$\frac{R^2(K)}{R^2(1)} = \left[\frac{\text{Var}(\text{E}_t r_{t+1} + \cdots + \text{E}_t r_{t+K})}{\text{Var}(r_{t+1} + \cdots + r_{t+K})}\right] \Bigg/ \left[\frac{\text{Var}(\text{E}_t r_{t+1})}{\text{Var}(r_{t+1})}\right] \tag{5.64}$$

$$= \frac{\beta(K)^2}{\beta(1)^2} \frac{1}{KV(K)} = \left(\frac{1-\phi^K}{1-\phi}\right)^2 \frac{1}{KV(K)}.$$

This grows at first with K if ϕ is large, then eventually dies away to zero. The reason for this hump-shaped pattern in the R^2 statistic is that expected returns at multiple future dates are positively correlated with one another, so the variance of their sum grows faster than the sum of their variances, while realized returns at multiple future dates have small autocorrelations that (as discussed above) may well be negative, so the variance of their sum grows more slowly than the sum of their variances. In the very long run, however, the variance of expected returns in the distant future diminishes to zero, driving down the extremely long-horizon R^2 statistic.

Long-horizon return regressions were used by Fama and French (1988a) and attracted subsequent interest because empirically, as suggested by the above example, they have much higher R^2 statistics than short-horizon regressions, and the usual asymptotic t-statistics (calculated allowing for overlap in the residuals following Hansen-Hodrick or Newey-West) deliver stronger rejections. However, these t-statistics tend to have size distortions when the overlap is large relative to the sample size, so the long-horizon regression evidence is tenuous statistically.

Pástor and Stambaugh (2009) have argued for the use of a "predictive system," in which an AR(1) model for the expected return is combined with a vector of return predictors that are used to deliver filtered estimates of the unobservable expected return. Thus the AR(1) example has applications beyond the simple calculations reported here.

5.3.3 Interpreting US Stock Market History

The formulas in the previous section can be used to interpret the historical fluctuations of the US stock market.

Dividend-Price Ratio

Figure 5.2 plots the history of the dividend-price ratio on the S&P 500 index over the period 1871–2013, using data from Robert Shiller's website. Following standard convention in the finance literature, dividends are summed over each year to eliminate seasonality, and then divided by the end-of-year stock price. The long-run historical average for this ratio is 4.4%, but the dividend-price ratio has been below this average for almost 30 years since the early 1980s, and in early 2013 was close to 2%.

In the steady state of the Gordon growth model, equation (5.23), a decline of 2.4 percentage points in the dividend-price ratio implies a decline of 2.4 percentage points in the gap between the discount rate and the dividend growth rate. If the discount rate has not changed, the dividend growth rate must have increased by 2.4 percentage points; or, if the dividend growth rate has not changed, the discount rate must have declined by 2.4 percentage points. In a dynamic model where discount rates and dividend growth rates vary through time, the Campbell-Shiller formula (5.47) implies that the discounted present values of period-by-period discount rates and dividend growth rates must have moved in a comparable fashion.

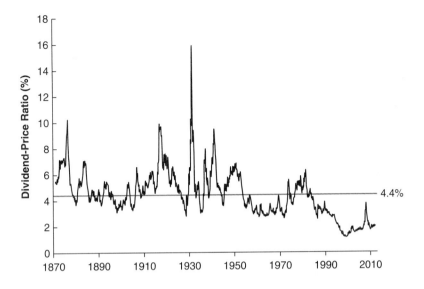

Figure 5.2. *The S&P 500 Dividend-Price Ratio, 1871–2013*

An extensive empirical literature has found that in US historical data, the dividend-price ratio has little ability to forecast dividend growth. This is particularly true since World War II, when corporations began to smooth dividends in the manner documented by Lintner (1956), but even in the earlier part of the Shiller sample period dividend growth is forecastable only over a year or two. There is little evidence of long swings in the dividend growth rate that could justify the long swings in the dividend-price ratio shown in Figure 5.2. The dividend-price ratio does, however, predict returns in historical US data. This suggests that most of the variation in the series should be attributed to changing discount rates rather than changing expectations of dividend growth—at least if we take the perspective of rational investors.

One caveat is that changing corporate payout policy can distort the behavior of the dividend-price ratio. The Gordon growth model or the Campbell-Shiller formula can be applied in two different ways. Either the dividend can be interpreted as total cash paid by the firm to investors, and the price can be interpreted as the total market value of the firm, or the dividend can be interpreted as a dividend per share and the price can be interpreted as the price per share. In the former case, dividends should include share repurchases. In the latter case, dividends need not include share repurchases but one must keep in mind that a permanent repurchase program increases the growth rate of dividends per share by steadily shrinking the number of shares. Since the data plotted in Figure 5.2 do not include repurchases, the latter interpretation is appropriate for the figure. A shift toward repurchases in the 1980s might have increased the growth rate of expected dividends per share in a persistent manner that is not easily captured by historical regression analysis. However, such an effect probably accounts for no more than 1 percentage point of the decline in the dividend-price ratio shown in Figure 5.2 (Liang and Sharpe 1999).[4]

---

[4]Robertson and Wright (2006) make a related point that at the aggregate level, cash- or debt-financed acquisitions distribute cash to shareholders and should be taken into account in calculating payouts to shareholders.

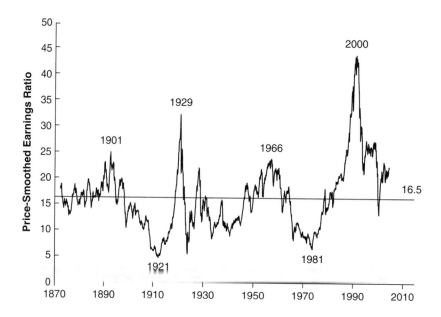

Figure 5.3. *The S&P 500 Price-Smoothed Earnings Ratio, 1881–2013*

Price-Smoothed Earnings Ratio

To the extent that share repurchases are important and variable, it becomes less appealing to measure the level of stock prices in relation to dividends. Two alternative approaches are to look at the aggregate market value of stocks in relation to their book value (Kothari and Shanken 1997, Pontiff and Schall 1998), which is a time-series analogue of the standard procedure for measuring value in the cross-section, or to measure stock prices in relation to earnings. Since earnings are subject to short-run cyclical fluctuations even at an annual frequency, Campbell and Shiller (1988b) proposed smoothing earnings over a number of years (an approach that was advocated much earlier by Graham and Dodd, and that investment practitioners have adopted in recent years under the name of the cyclically adjusted PE ratio, or CAPE). Figure 5.3 plots the history of the ratio of prices to smoothed earnings, averaged over 10 years. Spikes in this figure correspond to peaks in the stock market, with 1929 and 2000 showing up as the extremes. This figure, like the previous one, shows that the great bull market of the late 20th century was not fully reversed during the early 21st century, so that in early 2013 the price-smoothed earnings ratio was well above its historical average of 16.5.

Historical regressions show that the price-smoothed earnings ratio has had little ability to forecast future earnings growth, and much greater ability to forecast long-run returns. Campbell and Shiller (2005) is an accessible summary of this work.[5] A typical regression uses the log of the price-smoothed earnings ratio as the forecasting variable (taking logs to reduce the tendency for the level of the ratio to be most volatile when it is

[5]Campbell and Shiller (2005) is an update of earlier analyses presented to the Federal Reserve Board in December 1996, just before Fed Chairman Alan Greenspan gave a well-known speech coining the phrase "irrational exuberance." During the late 1990s, this work suggested low future stock returns, a pessimistic forecast with initially large forecast errors. Undeterred, Robert Shiller published his book *Irrational Exuberance* in March 2000, almost exactly at the peak of the market.

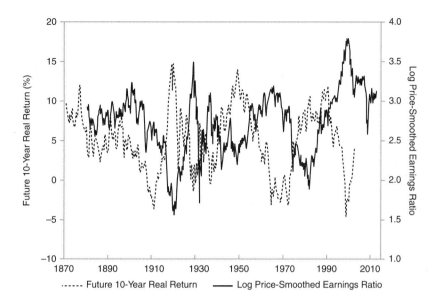

Figure 5.4. *The Log Price-Smoothed Earnings Ratio and the 10-Year Future Real Return on the S&P 500, 1881–2013*

high), and a longer-term real return, measured over 10 years, as the dependent variable. A time-series plot of the forecasting and dependent variables is shown in Figure 5.4. The strong negative correlation between the log price-smoothed earnings ratio and the future 10-year real return is clearly visible, at least since the early 20th century, but of course one must keep in mind that even in a century of data there are only 10 independent observations of 10-year returns, so the effective sample size is small.

5.3.4 VAR Analysis of Returns

An alternative to direct long-horizon return regression is to use a time-series model and calculate its implications for long-horizon return behavior. Most obviously, if one is willing to assume that a vector autoregression (VAR) describes the data, then the news components of returns can be calculated directly from the VAR coefficients (Campbell and Shiller 1988a, Campbell 1991).

Define z_t as a vector of state variables, and assume that

$$z_{t+1} = Az_t + \epsilon_{t+1}. \tag{5.65}$$

The assumption that z_t follows a first-order VAR is not restrictive because one can always rewrite a higher-order VAR as a first-order VAR with an expanded state vector and a singular variance-covariance matrix of innovations. This model implies that

$$\mathrm{E}_t z_{t+1+j} = A^{j+1} z_t. \tag{5.66}$$

Suppose that the stock return is the first element of the VAR, and the other variables help to predict returns. Then

$$r_{t+1} - \mathrm{E}_t r_{t+1} = e1'\epsilon_{t+1}, \tag{5.67}$$

where $e1' = [1 \ 0 \cdots 0]$, a vector with first element one and all other elements zero. Discount-rate news is

$$N_{DR,t+1} = e1' \sum_{j=1}^{\infty} \rho^j A^j \epsilon_{t+1} = e1' \rho A (I - \rho A)^{-1} \epsilon_{t+1}, \tag{5.68}$$

and cash-flow news is

$$N_{CF,t+1} = r_{t+1} - E_t r_{t+1} + N_{DR,t+1} = e1' (I + \rho A (I - \rho A)^{-1}) \epsilon_{t+1}. \tag{5.69}$$

The methodology outlined above predicts returns, and then constructs cash-flow forecasts as a residual. However, provided that the log dividend-price ratio is included in the system, results are not sensitive to this choice because log dividends, returns, and the log dividend-price ratio are linked by the approximate identity (5.38), which implies that

$$r_{t+1} \approx k + (d_t - p_t) - \rho (d_{t+1} - p_{t+1}) + \Delta d_{t+1}. \tag{5.70}$$

Thus forecasts of either returns or dividend growth along with the log dividend-price ratio imply forecasts of the missing variable, and returns and dividend growth should not both be included in the system along with the log dividend-price ratio, because the resulting system will have perfectly collinear variables (except for a small approximation error in (5.38)). Even in systems that replace the dividend-price ratio with another persistent valuation ratio such as the price-smoothed earnings ratio, results are similar when forecasting returns or dividend growth. Engsted, Pedersen, and Tanggaard (2012) provide a clear explanation of these points, which are sometimes misunderstood.

While the VAR methodology is robust to the decision whether to predict returns or dividend growth, results can be sensitive to the choice of explanatory variables, a point emphasized by Chen and Zhao (2009).

Empirical work starting with Campbell (1991) typically finds that for broad stock indexes, the standard deviation of discount-rate news is about twice the standard deviation of cash-flow news. This finding is related to the inability of valuation ratios to predict dividend or earnings growth, discussed earlier. Results are quite different for individual stocks as shown by Vuolteenaho (2002) and Cohen, Polk, and Vuolteenaho (2009). Although there is predictability in individual stock returns, related to the stock-level characteristics discussed in Chapter 3, the explanatory power of a time-series regression of an individual stock's return on characteristics is very small even at long horizons, implying that most stock-level return variation is attributed to cash-flow news. This finding for individual stocks does not contradict the evidence for aggregate stock indexes because much of the stock-level cash-flow news is idiosyncratic, so it diversifies away at the aggregate level; whereas the stock-level discount-rate news has an important aggregate component that does not diversify away but accounts for a large part of the variation in aggregate stock returns.

5.4 Predictive Return Regressions

The previous section argued that aggregate stock returns can be predicted using valuation ratios such as the log dividend-price ratio. However, predictive regressions of this sort encounter tricky econometric issues when the predictor is both persistent and contemporaneously correlated with returns, as is certainly the case for standard valuation ratios.

5.4.1 Stambaugh Bias

Kendall (1954) showed that there is a downward finite-sample bias in the estimated auto-correlation coefficient of a first-order autoregression. Specifically, in the autoregression

$$x_{t+1} = (1 - \phi)\overline{x} + \phi x_t + \xi_{t+1},$$
(5.71)

the bias is

$$\mathrm{E}[\widehat{\phi} - \phi] = -\left(\frac{1 + 3\phi}{T}\right) + o\left(\frac{1}{T^2}\right),$$
(5.72)

where the notation $o(1/T^2)$ indicates that remaining terms shrink with the square or higher powers of the sample size. This downward bias in the estimated persistence of x_t arises both because the regressor is predetermined but not exogenous (i.e., x_t is uncorrelated with ξ_{t+1} and its leads but not with ξ_t and its lags), and because the mean of x_t is unknown and must be estimated. In a small sample, the observations of x_t may be far away from the true mean and the process may never cross its true mean; but by construction it must cross its sample mean at least once, suggesting a transitory process with a propensity to cross its mean.

Stambaugh (1999) shows that Kendall bias creates finite-sample bias in the coefficient of a single-period predictive regression for returns whenever return innovations are correlated with innovations in the predictor variable. Consider the regression

$$r_{t+1} = \alpha + \beta x_t + u_{t+1}.$$
(5.73)

Stambaugh's bias formula, under the assumption that the predictor follows (5.71), is

$$\mathrm{E}[\widehat{\beta} - \beta] = \gamma \, \mathrm{E}[\widehat{\phi} - \phi],$$
(5.74)

where $\gamma = \sigma_{u\xi}/\sigma_\xi^2$, the regression coefficient of the innovation to return on the innovation to the predictor variable.

When return innovations are negatively correlated with innovations in the predictor variable, as is the case for a regression of stock return on dividend yield, we have $\gamma < 0$, so downward bias in $\widehat{\phi}$ produces upward bias in $\widehat{\beta}$:

$$\mathrm{E}[\widehat{\beta} - \beta] = -\gamma \left(\frac{1 + 3\phi}{T}\right) > 0.$$
(5.75)

There are similar problems with the distribution of the t-statistic when ϕ is close to one (Cavanagh, Elliott, and Stock 1995).

In other finance applications, Stambaugh bias is less of a problem. Persistent predictor variables whose innovations are only weakly correlated with stock returns, such as inflation and interest rates, have minimally biased coefficients and test statistics. Also, when bond returns are regressed on the yield spread as in the term structure literature discussed in Chapter 8, the correlation between bond returns and yield spread innovations is positive rather than negative, so the predictive coefficient is biased downward rather than upward. In this case the standard test results are conservative, and the evidence for bond return predictability is stronger than it appears rather than weaker (Bekaert, Hodrick, and Marshall 1997).

5.4.2 Recent Responses Using Financial Theory

A number of papers have responded to the econometric issue identified by Stambaugh (1999) by using additional information derived from finance theory. A theme of this literature is that theory allows one to improve on the obvious procedure of running OLS predictive regressions of returns on predetermined predictors. In the words of Shiller (2014, p. 1491), "testing market efficiency by regressing excess returns on information variables makes no use of the terminal condition that requires that all movements in prices need to be justified by information about subsequent movements in fundamentals."

Lewellen's Response

Lewellen (2004) starts by conditioning the Stambaugh bias formula on the estimated persistence $\widehat{\phi}$ and the true persistence ϕ:

$$\mathrm{E}[\widehat{\beta} - \beta \,|\, \widehat{\phi}, \phi] = \gamma \,[\widehat{\phi} - \phi]. \qquad (5.76)$$

At first sight this expression does not seem particularly useful because we do not know the true persistence coefficient. However, Lewellen argues on the basis of theory that ϕ cannot be larger than one—the dividend-price ratio is not explosive—so the largest bias occurs when $\phi = 1$. He proposes the conservative approach of adjusting the estimated coefficient using this worst-case bias:

$$\widehat{\beta}_{adj} = \widehat{\beta} - \gamma \,(\widehat{\phi} - 1). \qquad (5.77)$$

He shows that the bias-adjusted coefficient has variance $\sigma_v^2 / (T\widehat{\sigma}_x^2)$, regardless of the true value of ϕ, where T is the sample size, $\widehat{\sigma}_x^2 = \sum_T (x_t - \widehat{\overline{x}})^2 / T$ is the (biased) sample variance of x_t, and v is the residual in the regression of u on ξ: $u = \gamma \xi + v$.

Empirically, Lewellen finds that in historical US data, the estimated autoregressive coefficient $\widehat{\phi}$ is close to one so the bias-adjusted coefficient $\widehat{\beta}_{adj}$ is not far below the unadjusted coefficient. However, the bias-adjusted coefficient has a much lower variance so Lewellen's test strongly rejects the hypothesis that stock returns are unpredictable. Put another way, samples that generate spuriously high predictive coefficients for stock returns are samples with spuriously low persistence of the dividend-price ratio. Since the persistence of the dividend-price ratio is close to the upper bound of one in the historical US data, this cannot be a sample with a large degree of spurious return predictability.

Cochrane's Response

Cochrane (2008) responds to Stambaugh by directing attention to the inability of the log-dividend price ratio to forecast dividend growth.[6] At first sight this response does not seem connected to Lewellen's, but in fact it is closely related. The Campbell-Shiller

---

[6]The amusing title of Cochrane's article, "The Dog That Does Not Bark," refers to the Sherlock Holmes story "The Hound of the Baskervilles." in which Holmes solves the mystery by focusing on something that does not occur rather than on something that does occur.

loglinearization (5.38) implies that r_{t+1}, $d_t - p_t$, Δd_{t+1}, and $d_{t+1} - p_{t+1}$ are deterministically linked by $r_{t+1} \approx k + (d_t - p_t) + \Delta d_{t+1} - \rho(d_{t+1} - p_{t+1})$. It follows that if we regress r_{t+1}, Δd_{t+1}, and $d_{t+1} - p_{t+1}$ onto $d_t - p_t$, the coefficients β, β_d, and ϕ are related by

$$\beta = 1 + \beta_d - \rho\phi. \tag{5.78}$$

If we have prior knowledge about ϕ, then β and β_d are linked. For example, if $\rho = 0.96$ and we know that $\phi \leq 1$, then $\beta_d \leq \beta - 0.04$. If $\beta = 0$, then β_d must be negative and less than -0.04. The fact that regression estimates of β_d are close to zero is therefore indirect evidence that $\beta > 0$, in other words, that stock returns are predictable—given our prior knowledge, based on theory, that the log dividend-price ratio is not explosive.

Another way to express Cochrane's point is that if the dividend-price ratio fails to predict stock returns, it will be explosive unless it predicts dividend growth. Since the dividend-price ratio cannot be explosive, the absence of predictable dividend growth strengthens the evidence for predictable returns.

Campbell and Yogo's Response

Campbell and Yogo (2006) offer a third response to Stambaugh. They point out that if we knew persistence ϕ, we could reduce noise by adding the innovation to the predictor variable to the predictive regression, estimating

$$r_{t+1} = \alpha + \beta x_t + \gamma(x_{t+1} - \phi x_t) + v_{t+1}. \tag{5.79}$$

The additional regressor, $(x_{t+1} - \phi x_t)$, is a constant plus the innovation in x_{t+1}; thus it is uncorrelated with the original regressor x_t but in general is correlated with the dependent variable r_{t+1}. Thus we still get a consistent estimate of the original predictive coefficient β, but with increased precision because we have controlled for some of the noise in unexpected stock returns.

Of course, in practice we do not know the persistence coefficient ϕ, but Campbell and Yogo argue that we can construct a confidence interval for it by inverting a unit root test statistic. The resulting procedure "de-noises" the return and delivers a more powerful test. The evidence for predictability is particularly strong if we rule out a persistence coefficient $\phi > 1$ on prior grounds. Polk, Thompson, and Vuolteenaho (2006) implement a related approach using results of Jansson and Moreira (2006).

Other Responses

Several other recent papers also use restrictions from financial theory to improve forecasts of stock returns. Welch and Goyal (2008) direct attention to the poor out-of-sample performance of return predictions based on regressions that include both a constant and time-varying explanatory variables such as the dividend-price ratio. The difficulty with these regressions is partly that they must estimate the unconditional mean of stock returns using noisy historical data. In reply, Campbell and Thompson (2008) show that out-of-sample performance is improved by imposing theoretically motivated sign restrictions on the regression coefficient and the fitted value, and improved further by using a drifting steady-state valuation model (discussed in section 5.5.2) to avoid directly estimating the unconditional mean of stock returns. Problem 5.2 invites you to implement this approach empirically.

Fama and French (2002) estimate the unconditional mean stock return, not the predictive coefficient that is the focus of the other papers we have discussed. They argue that the unconditional mean stock return can be better estimated by correcting historical average returns for the historical change in valuation ratios, because finance theory implies that such changes cannot be expected to continue. Avdis and Wachter (2017) make a similar correction in a formal maximum likelihood framework.

5.4.3 Other Predictors

The discussion so far has concentrated on prediction of stock returns from persistent valuation ratios such as the dividend-price ratio, the price-smoothed earnings ratio, or the aggregate book-market ratio. However, the empirical literature has also considered a number of other potential predictors.

Bond markets. One class of predictors comes from the bond markets, including the yields on short- and long-term Treasury securities (Campbell 1987, Fama and French 1989, Hodrick 1992) and the yield spreads or excess returns of lower rated corporate bonds relative to higher rated corporate bonds or Treasuries (Keim and Stambaugh 1986, Fama and French 1989). The short-term interest rate appears to predict market returns negatively, while yield spreads of long-term over short-term Treasuries and credit spreads of lower rated corporate bonds over higher rated bonds predict returns positively.[7]

The macroeconomy. Other predictors capture the state of the macroeconomy, including the inflation rate (Fama and Schwert 1977) and the aggregate investment rate expressed as a ratio of investment to the capital stock (Cochrane 1991b), motivated by the q theory of investment as discussed in Chapter 7. Both these variables predict market returns negatively.

Equity issuance. Aggregate stock returns have been predicted negatively using the equity issuance of corporations, in relation either to total issuance of equity and debt (Baker and Wurgler 2000) or to the market value of stocks (Boudoukh, Michaely, Richardson, and Roberts 2007). Both investment and equity issuance are aggregate versions of variables that have been shown to predict returns in the cross-section as discussed in Chapter 3.[8]

Consumption and wealth. Lettau and Ludvigson (2001a) propose a return predictor based on an estimated cointegrating relationship between aggregate consumption, the aggregate value of household financial wealth, and labor income. This cointegrating relationship reflects the intertemporal budget constraint of households, which links their consumption spending to the financial and human wealth available to support it. Lettau and Ludvigson call the stationary linear combination of consumption, financial wealth, and labor income *cay*. Cointegration implies that an unusually high value of *cay*—a high level of consumption relative to financial wealth and labor income—must predict slow consumption growth, rapid growth of financial wealth generated by high returns, or rapid growth of labor income. Lettau and Ludvigson find that most of the predictability is in fact in financial wealth, corresponding to an ability of *cay* to predict aggregate stock returns positively.

---

[7]Since the Treasury yield spread also predicts excess bond returns positively, as discussed in Chapter 8, these predictor variables imply some common variation in predicted excess returns on bonds and stocks (Fama and French 1989). We discuss joint modeling of the bond and stock markets in section 9.4.2.

[8]However, not all cross-sectional predictors work in the same direction at the aggregate level. Hirshleifer, Hou, and Teoh (2009) find that aggregate accruals predict market returns positively even though firm-level accruals predict returns negatively in the cross-section.

Option markets. Several recent papers use the prices of equity index options to predict the future realized return on the index. A standard predictor is the variance risk premium, defined as the difference between option-implied volatility and lagged realized volatility (Bollerslev, Tauchen, and Zhou 2009) or a rational forecast of realized volatility (Drechsler and Yaron 2011). Option-implied volatility is calculated using a model-free option pricing methodology that does not impose the Black-Scholes or any other parametric model. A limitation of this predictor is that it is only available for a relatively short sample period starting in 1990. Problem 5.3 asks you to consider an alternative option-based return predictor proposed by Martin (2017).

The cross-section of stock returns. The aggregate stock market can also be predicted using information on the relative pricing of different types of stocks. Eleswarapu and Reinganum (2004), for example, use the lagged three-year return on an equal-weighted index of growth stocks orthogonalized to the lagged three-year market return, while Campbell and Vuolteenaho (2004) use the difference in log book-market ratios of small value stocks and small growth stocks, and Polk, Thompson, and Vuolteenaho (2006) use the relative pricing of high- and low-beta stocks. We discuss the latter paper, and the recent work of Kelly and Pruitt (2013), in section 5.6.2.

Alternative Predictors and the Log Dividend-Price Ratio

It is natural to combine these alternative predictors with a valuation ratio such as the log dividend-price ratio. When this is done, the identity linking the log dividend-price ratio to future returns and dividend growth restricts the way in which the alternative predictors can enter. Recall from equation (5.46) that the log dividend-price ratio approximately equals an infinite discounted sum of future realized returns, less an infinite discounted sum of future realized dividend growth. A regression of the infinite discounted sum of future realized returns less dividend growth onto the log dividend-price ratio must then deliver a regression coefficient of one and a perfect fit (ignoring approximation error). No other variables can enter this regression because there is no residual error to be explained. If one now runs two separate regressions, first the infinite discounted sum of future realized returns onto the log dividend-price ratio to obtain a coefficient β_1, and then the infinite discounted sum of future realized dividend growth onto the log dividend-price ratio to obtain a coefficient β_2, the difference $\beta_1 - \beta_2$ must equal one. Adding other variables to these two separate regressions, they can only enter the two regressions with equal signs so that the difference of coefficients across the regressions is zero. In the presence of the log dividend-price ratio, any variable that predicts infinite-horizon returns must also predict infinite-horizon cash-flow growth with the same coefficient.

While this restriction is meaningful, it is limited in two respects. First, it does not tell us how alternative predictors correlate with either the dividend growth component or the return component of the log dividend-price ratio. A predictor that is correlated only with the dividend growth component, for example, can still predict returns in combination with the log dividend-price ratio by controlling for the variation in the log dividend-price ratio that is driven by expected dividend growth. Second, the restriction applies only to regressions whose dependent variables are sums of realized returns and dividend growth discounted to an infinite horizon. Alternative predictors can enter short-horizon regressions without obeying the restriction, if they forecast near-term returns or dividend growth differently from longer-term returns or dividend growth. Cochrane (2011) argues, for example, that Lettau and Ludvigson's *cay* predicts short-term returns positively and longer-term returns negatively, so that it has no effect on either the infinite discounted sum of returns or the infinite discounted sum of dividend growth.

5.5 Drifting Steady-State Models

The previous section discussed econometric problems that arise when valuation ratios are highly persistent. We now go further and consider the possibility that valuation ratios change permanently.

5.5.1 Volatility and Valuation

Pástor and Veronesi (2003) point out that uncertainty about growth rates increases firm value. One way to understand this is to augment the Gordon growth model, in which the growth rate of expected dividends is known and constant, with a limited form of uncertainty. Suppose that the growth rate is random today, but in the next instant all uncertainty about it will be resolved once and for all. This is an extreme special case of a permanent change in the growth rate. Then the Gordon growth formula becomes

$$\frac{P}{D} = \mathrm{E}\left[\frac{1}{R-G}\right] > \frac{1}{R-\mathrm{E}[G]}. \tag{5.80}$$

The inequality in (5.80) follows from Jensen's Inequality given that the reciprocal is a convex function.

Another way to understand Pástor and Veronesi's point is that the returns that appear in the Campbell-Shiller dividend growth formula (5.43) or the Vuolteenaho ROE formula (5.50) are log returns. Uncertainty lowers the average log return or geometric average return corresponding to any arithmetic average return. (Recall that the difference between these two averages is one-half the variance of log returns when log returns are normally distributed.) Thus, if uncertainty does not increase the required arithmetic average return too much (which will be the case, for example, if the uncertainty is idiosyncratic), then higher uncertainty lowers the required average log return on an asset and increases its price today.

Pástor and Veronesi develop this idea in a structural model of a young firm for which uncertainty is unusually high. They consider a firm that is born at time 0 with book equity B_0. The firm grows at a constant rate g until time T, at which point book equity is $B_T = B_0 \exp(gT)$. At time T, the firm is mature and competition eliminates abnormal profits, so at that date the market-book ratio is driven to one: $M_T/B_T = 1$. At earlier dates, the market value of the firm is the terminal book value discounted at the required rate of return r.

In the simplest version of Pástor and Veronesi's model, the growth rate g is unknown at date 0 and normally distributed with mean $\overline{g}$ and variance σ^2. These assumptions imply that

$$\frac{M_0}{B_0} = \mathrm{E}\{\exp(g-r)T\} = \exp[(\overline{g}+\sigma^2/2-r)T]. \tag{5.81}$$

This formula shows that higher uncertainty increases the firm's market-book ratio, holding constant the mean growth rate $\overline{g}$ and discount rate r.

Pástor and Veronesi enrich their model with a number of other features. Specifically, they assume that investors can observe realized profitability each period, which equals true mean profitability plus serially correlated noise. Investors use observed profitability to update their priors about true mean profitability, as in the models of Bayesian learning discussed in section 9.5. Also, the firm can have both systematic and idiosyncratic risk in its profitability, and it can make higher or lower dividend payments.

In the Pástor-Veronesi model, the market-book ratio for young firms tends to decrease with age as uncertainty about true mean profitability diminishes over time. Return volatility declines with firm age for the same reason. Both the market-book ratio and return volatility are higher for firms that pay no dividends, because profitability has a greater effect on firm value when earnings are reinvested than when they are paid out to shareholders. All these properties are consistent with data on stocks in the first 10 years after initial listing.

Pástor and Veronesi (2006) argue that the volatility effect helps to justify high prices for technology stocks in the late 1990s. Not only was there an unusual degree of uncertainty about the profitability of young technology companies during the internet boom, but also the discount rate was plausibly low at that time. A low discount rate increases the term $\exp(-rT)$ that multiplies the volatility term $\exp(\sigma^2 T/2)$ in equation (5.81), thereby amplifying the volatility effect on the market-book ratio.

5.5.2 Drifting Steady-State Valuation Model

Another way to understand the importance of uncertainty in valuation is to consider what happens when the log dividend-price ratio follows a random walk. In this case valuation is always at steady state and does not revert to a fixed mean, but the steady state itself drifts over time. By analyzing this case we can develop a modification of the Gordon growth model that is applicable in a world where the dividend-price ratio changes over time. This also provides an alternative methodology to predictive regressions for constructing stock return forecasts.

Assume that the dividend is known one period in advance. Then we can write

$$\frac{D_{t+1}}{P_t} = \exp(x_t), \tag{5.82}$$

where x_t now denotes the log dividend-price ratio using a forward or indicated dividend rather than a historical dividend. Assume that x_t follows a random walk:

$$x_t = x_{t-1} + \varepsilon_t. \tag{5.83}$$

Since the dividend growth rate is known one period in advance, we can write

$$\frac{D_{t+1}}{D_t} = 1 + G_t = \exp(g_t). \tag{5.84}$$

Finally, assume that x_{t+1} and g_{t+1} are conditionally normal and homoskedastic given time t information, with conditional variances σ_x^2 and σ_g^2, and conditional covariance σ_{gx}.

The definition of the stock return implies that

$$1 + R_{t+1} = \frac{P_{t+1} + D_{t+1}}{P_t} = \frac{D_{t+1}}{P_t} + \frac{D_{t+2}}{D_{t+1}} \frac{D_{t+1}}{P_t} \left(\frac{D_{t+2}}{P_{t+1}}\right)^{-1}$$
$$= \exp(x_t)[1 + \exp(g_{t+1} - x_{t+1})]. \tag{5.85}$$

The conditionally expected stock return can be calculated using the formula for the conditional expectation of lognormally distributed random variables and the martingale property that $E_t x_{t+1} = x_t$:

$$E_t(1 + R_{t+1}) = \exp(x_t)\left[1 + E_t \exp(g_{t+1} - x_{t+1})\right]$$

$$= \exp(x_t)\left[1 + \exp\left(E_t g_{t+1} - x_t + \sigma_g^2/2 + \sigma_x^2/2 - \sigma_{gx}\right)\right]$$

$$= \frac{D_{t+1}}{P_t} + \exp(E_t g_{t+1})\exp(\text{Var}_t(p_{t+1} - p_t)/2). \tag{5.86}$$

Finally, the right-hand side can be approximated using the facts that for small y, $\exp(y) \approx 1 + y$, and that over short time intervals unexpected log stock returns are approximately equal to unexpected changes in log stock prices.[9] The result is

$$E_t(1 + R_{t+1}) \approx \frac{D_{t+1}}{P_t} + \exp(E_t g_{t+1}) + \frac{1}{2}\text{Var}_t(r_{t+1}). \tag{5.87}$$

This equation is a modification of the Gordon growth model that expresses the expected simple stock return (arithmetic average return) as the level of the dividend yield, plus geometric average dividend growth, plus one-half the variance of stock returns. If we subtract half the variance of stock returns from each side, use the approximate conditional lognormality of returns, and rearrange terms, we find that the level of the dividend-price ratio equals the geometric average stock return less the geometric average dividend growth rate:

$$\frac{D_{t+1}}{P_t} \approx \exp(E_t r_{t+1}) - \exp(E_t g_{t+1}). \tag{5.88}$$

This corresponds exactly to the calculation by Siegel (2007) reported at the end of section 5.2.1, which related the historical average dividend-price ratio to historical geometric average returns and dividend growth rates.

In the Gordon growth model, the dividend-price ratio is constant over time so the variance of stock returns equals the variance of dividend growth. Under this assumption Siegel's geometric average implementation of the model would be equivalent to an arithmetic average implementation because stock returns and dividend growth would have the same variance so their geometric and arithmetic averages would differ by the same amount. In the data, however, the dividend-price ratio moves over time, making stock returns much more volatile than the dividend growth rate, so the geometric implementation and the arithmetic implementation are different. The analysis here shows that the geometric implementation is correct.

The drifting steady-state valuation model is an appealing alternative to long-horizon return regressions for generating forecasts of long-term stock returns. While return regressions capture the effect of mean reversion in valuations if such mean reversion is present, they require the forecaster to estimate the unconditional mean stock return which can be challenging given the volatility of returns. Equation (5.87) requires as inputs only the current dividend-price ratio, the conditional mean of dividend growth,

---

[9]When the time period is small enough, $D_{t+1}/P_t \approx 0$, so that $\text{Var}_t(\log(1 + R_{t+1})) \approx \text{Var}_t(\log(P_{t+1}/P_t))$. The approximate equality of these conditional variances becomes exact in the continuous-time limit.

and the conditional variance of returns. Campbell and Thompson (2008) show that variants of this approach forecast US stock index returns quite well out of sample, whereas Welch and Goyal (2008) find poor out-of-sample results for standard return regressions.

5.5.3 Inflation and the Fed Model

The Gordon growth model can be written as $D/P = R - G$, equation (5.23), or as $X/P = (R - \lambda ROE)/(1 - \lambda)$, where λ is the reinvestment ratio, equation (5.30). The so-called Fed model is the claim that these valuation ratios should move one-for-one with the long-term Treasury bond yield, used as a proxy for R.

This model has never been endorsed by the Federal Reserve Board, although during the 1990s Fed staff reports included time-series charts of valuation ratios and bond yields. Such charts, with the logic above, have sometimes been used by Wall Street firms to justify rising stock prices in periods of declining nominal bond yields.

The Fed model fits the rise in the dividend yield from the 1960s to the early 1980s, when nominal bond yields were increasing, and the decline from the early 1980s to the early 2000s as nominal bond yields declined. The model does not explain the high dividend yield during the Great Depression of the 1930s, as Treasury yields were very low at that time. However, Asness (2003) shows that the Fed model can be extended to fit this period too if one adjusts the discount rate R in line with the volatility of stock returns relative to the volatility of bond returns (which was particularly high in the 1930s).

The apparent empirical success of the Fed model is puzzling. If a nominal interest rate is used as a proxy for R in equation (5.23), then for consistency a nominal growth rate G must also be used. While real growth rates appear to be fairly stable over time, nominal growth rates move with inflation just as nominal bond yields do, so inflation-driven variation in nominal G should offset the effect on stock prices of inflation-driven variation in nominal R. Put another way, one should expect the dividend-price ratio to move with the real interest rate, not the nominal interest rate. While real and nominal interest rates have moved in parallel in the early 21st century—so low real interest rates help to explain high stock prices in recent years—this was not generally the case in the 20th century.

There are several possible explanations for the empirical success of the Fed model. It is possible that high inflation predicts low real growth or a high equity risk premium (although innovations in inflation are not strongly correlated with innovations in stock returns, and this correlation appears to have shifted over time as we discuss in Chapter 9). Alternatively, Modigliani and Cohn (1979) made the radical suggestion that investors have inflation illusion; that is, they confuse real and nominal interest rates and mistakenly discount real cash flows at nominal interest rates.

5.6 Present Value Logic and the Cross-Section of Stock Returns

Several recent papers have studied the cross-section of stock returns using present value relations to structure the investigation. In this section I briefly summarize some of the interesting findings of this literature. Not all of these findings are firmly established, but they do illustrate how present value logic can guide research.

5.6.1 Quality as a Risk Factor

Asness, Frazzini, and Pedersen (AFP 2013) use a profitability-based version of the Gordon growth model to form a list of characteristics that are valued by investors and help to justify high stock prices. They start from the relationship

$$\frac{P}{B} = \frac{ROE(1-\lambda)}{R-G},$$ (5.89)

where λ is the reinvestment ratio as in section 5.2.2, so $(1-\lambda)$ is the payout ratio. In this expression high profitability ROE, high growth G, a low discount rate R justified by low risk, and a high payout ratio all imply a high price-book ratio. Note that AFP take growth as exogenous rather than as the endogenous outcome of profitability and reinvestment.

AFP create empirical proxies for all the above quantities, using cross-sectional z-scores (deviations of firm-level characteristics from the cross-sectional mean, divided by the cross-sectional standard deviation). They create a profitability measure by z-scoring individual profitability measures (return on equity, return on assets, etc.) and then z-scoring the sum. In a similar fashion they construct a growth measure from individual five-year growth rates of profitability measures; a measure of safety, which they treat as a predictor of a low discount rate, using low volatility, low beta etc.; and a payout measure using equity and debt issuance and net payout over profits. Finally, they z-score the sum of all the above and call the resulting measure "quality."

AFP find that high-quality firms do have higher prices, but there is a great deal of valuation noise. Hence, there is an excess return to buying high-quality firms and shorting low-quality ("junk") firms. In other words, quality can be regarded as a characteristic associated with higher average returns. Following the familiar methodology of Fama and French, AFP construct a QMJ (quality minus junk) return factor and add it to the Fama-French factor list. They find that the QMJ return is positive on average but it declines with the average price of quality, just as the return on the HML value factor declines when value stocks become more expensive, that is, when the value spread narrows. AFP also find that covariance with the QMJ return helps to explain the average return on individual stocks. These results are related to several phenomena discussed in Chapter 3, such as the high return to firms with high gross profitability (Novy-Marx 2013), as well as the low return to financially distressed stocks documented by Campbell, Hilscher, and Szilagyi (2008).

5.6.2 Cross-Sectional Measures of the Equity Premium

Polk, Thompson, and Vuolteenaho (PTV 2006) consider the cross-sectional implications of the Gordon growth model where firms may differ in both their growth rates and their discount rates. If the CAPM holds, the discount rate for a firm at any point of time should be the riskless interest rate plus the firm's beta times the equity premium. If the equity premium is highly persistent, as suggested by the literature summarized earlier in this chapter, and if firms have highly persistent betas, then the long-run discount rate that determines stock prices is also approximately equal to the firm's current beta times the current equity premium. Then in a cross-sectional regression of dividend-price ratios on betas and expected growth rates,

$$\left(\frac{D}{P}\right)_{it} = \lambda_{0t} + \lambda_{1t}\beta_i + \lambda_{2t}E_t(g_{it}),$$ (5.90)

the coefficient on the firm's beta, λ_{1t}, should equal the equity premium at time t. PTV run a version of this regression and study the ability of the time-series of cross-sectional coefficients to predict subsequent returns on the aggregate stock market.

PTV encounter several challenges in implementing this idea. The use of dividend-price ratios can be problematic in studying individual firms because some firms do not pay dividends, and more generally valuation ratios can have extreme outliers in the cross-section. Accordingly, in their main specification PTV replace the dividend-price ratio with a composite value measure based on dividend-price, book-market, earnings-price, and cash flow-price ratios. They also calculate percentile ranks, not levels of the composite value measure, and calculate a rank correlation, not a regression coefficient. PTV control for the expected growth rate using several empirical proxies for firm-level payout policy and profitability.

PTV find that their estimate of the equity premium declines over time. This reflects the fact that value stocks (cheap stocks) had high betas during the Great Depression, whereas in the last few decades they have had lower betas than growth stocks (expensive stocks). Equivalently, high-beta stocks used to be cheaper than they are now, suggesting a decline in the equity premium. The cross-sectional estimate of the equity premium moves quite closely with aggregate valuation ratios for the stock market, such as the dividend-price ratio or smoothed earnings-price ratio, except during the late 1970s and early 1980s when the cross-sectional estimate is low while these valuation ratios are quite high.

PTV's use of asset pricing theory is appealing, although the strong empirical evidence against the CAPM in recent decades suggests that a richer asset pricing model may be needed. In Chapter 9 we discuss subsequent work that uses intertemporal asset pricing theory to study the cross-section of stock returns.

Cohen, Polk, and Vuolteenaho (2005) present an intriguing explanation for the deviation of the cross-sectional equity premium estimate from aggregate valuation ratios in the late 1970s and early 1980s. They argue that it results from inflation illusion among investors of the sort postulated by Modigliani and Cohn (1979). With inflation illusion, investors incorrectly discount real cash flows at nominal interest rates and hence undervalue stocks when inflation is high. Undervaluation implies a high dividend-price ratio and smoothed earnings-price ratio, and a high equity premium from a rational observer's perspective, but investors use a lower subjective equity premium to price high-beta stocks in relation to low-beta stocks, generating the pattern observed by PTV during the period of particularly high US inflation. A further implication of CPV's story is that high-beta stocks are relatively overpriced when inflation is high, and ex post, they will underperform relative to the CAPM. Consistent with this, CPV find that the CAPM security market line is particularly flat when inflation is high.

Kelly and Pruitt (2013) also use the cross-section of stock returns to predict the equity premium, but their approach is very different. Rather than rely on an asset pricing model such as the CAPM, they allow the data to tell them which firms' valuation ratios have historically predicted either high returns or rapid cash-flow growth on the market. This requires that such relationships reflect some underlying economic structure that is stable over time.

Kelly and Pruitt proceed in three steps. First, for each stock or portfolio, they run time-series regressions of valuation ratios on future aggregate market returns or cash-flow growth to estimate loadings. Second, for each time-period, they run cross-sectional regressions of valuation ratios on the two loadings to estimate current forecasts of market returns and cash-flow growth. Third, to validate the method they regress future market returns or cash-flow growth on forecasts from the second step.

Kelly and Pruitt work primarily with Fama-French size and value portfolios. They suggest that individual stocks are best handled without using accounting data (using levels of stock prices relative to historical moving averages, rather than conventional valuation ratios such as the book-market ratio). They report good in-sample and out-of-sample predictive power for their approach, although it is not yet clear what economic structure is responsible for this forecasting success.

5.7 Solution and Further Problems

As an informal exercise, you were asked to consider what economic forces might have caused the first daily autocorrelation of stock indexes, such as the index illustrated in Figure 5.1, to decline during the 1970s and 1980s. Various factors are relevant. The underlying progress of information technology reduced the cost of trading and financial innovation, leading to the elimination of fixed commissions in the mid-1970s and making it easier for arbitrageurs to enforce short-term market efficiency. In addition, the introduction of stock index futures contracts in 1982 made it possible to trade the whole index, rather than the constituent stocks, while creating incentives for arbitrageurs to bring futures prices and cash market prices into line.

It is also possible that illiquidity in the stock market as a whole, combined with volatile aggregate shocks, can create reversals in daily index returns as seen in the 1930s and the 2000s, first during the technology downturn in the early 2000s and again during the global financial crisis in the late 2000s. Such an effect is an index-level version of "bid-ask bounce" discussed in section 12.2.1.

Problem 5.1 A Linearity-Generating Process

Consider an economy where the dividends on the aggregate stock market are expected to grow at a constant rate:

$$\frac{D_{t+1}}{D_t} = 1 + G + \eta_{t+1}, \tag{5.91}$$

where η_{t+1} has mean zero and variance σ^2.

The stochastic discount factor (SDF) in the economy can be written as

$$M_{t+1} = k \left(1 - \frac{\pi_t}{\sigma^2} \eta_{t+1} \right), \tag{5.92}$$

where the parameter k satisfies the restriction $1/k > 1 + G$.

The state variable π_t determines the equity premium. It follows the process

$$\pi_{t+1} = \frac{\phi}{1 + G - \pi_t} \pi_t + \varepsilon_{t+1}, \tag{5.93}$$

where the shock ε_{t+1} is independent of the dividend growth shock η_{t+1}.

(a) Write the coefficient k as a function of the riskless interest rate. Interpret the restriction $1/k > 1 + G$.

(b) Write an expression relating the price-dividend ratio, P_t/D_t, to the expected time $t + 1$ SDF, price-dividend ratio, and dividend growth rate.

(c) Conjecture a solution for the price-dividend ratio of the form $P_t/D_t = \alpha + \beta \pi_t$. Solve for the intercept α and slope β of this relationship.

(d) Interpret the intercept you obtained in part (c).

(e) Interpret the slope you obtained in part (c). What is its sign? How does its magnitude depend on the persistence of the π_t process? Explain.

(f) What assumptions in this example make the price-dividend ratio linear in the state variable π_t even though the risk premium is time-varying? How might you generalize this example?

Note: This problem is based on Gabaix (2009).

Problem 5.2 Predicting Stock Returns Out of Sample

In this exercise we study empirically whether the out-of-sample stock market return predictability of well-known valuation ratios can be improved by imposing simple theoretical restrictions on the predictive regressions. The data for this question can be found in an Excel spreadsheet on the textbook website[10] together with an accompanying explanatory document offering more details on the suggested implementation of the predictive regressions.

Consider the regression

$$R_{t+1} - R_{f,t+1} = \alpha + \beta x_t + u_{t+1}, \tag{5.94}$$

where R_{t+1} denotes the one-quarter-ahead return to the S&P 500 index and x_t is a predictor variable. Motivated by the claim of Welch and Goyal (2008) that the historical average excess stock return forecasts future excess stock returns out of sample better than regressions of excess returns on predictor variables, we evaluate the out-of-sample performance of forecasts based on predictor variable x_t using the out-of-sample R^2 statistic computed as

$$R_{OS}^2 = 1 - \frac{\sum_{t=0}^{T-1} (R_{t+1} - \widehat{R}_{t+1})^2}{\sum_{t=0}^{T-1} (R_{t+1} - \overline{R}_{t+1})^2}, \tag{5.95}$$

where $\widehat{R}_{t+1}$ is the fitted value from regression (5.94) estimated from the start date $-T_{IE}$ of the initial estimation sample through date t and $\overline{R}_{t+1}$ is the historical arithmetic average return estimated from $-T_{IE}$ through t. Here T_{IE} is the length of the initial estimation period, and T is the length of the out-of-sample forecast evaluation period. A positive value for R_{OS}^2 means that the predictive regression has lower average mean-squared prediction error than the historical average return.

(a) Calculate the in-sample R^2 statistics for the dividend yield, $x_t = D_t/P_t$, and the smoothed earnings yield, $x_t = X_t/P_t$, when regression (5.94) is estimated by standard ordinary least squares (OLS) over the full sample from 1872 to 2016.

[10]http://press.princeton.edu/titles/11177.html

(b) Calculate the out-of-sample R^2 statistics for the two valuation ratios when regression (5.94) is estimated by standard OLS, with 1872–1926 as the initial estimation period and 1927–2016 as the out-of-sample forecast evaluation period.

Compare the values you obtained for the in-sample and out-of-sample R^2 statistics. Are your results consistent with Welch and Goyal's (2008) claim?

(c) Repeat the calculations of the previous part for the out-of-sample R^2 statistics but now impose the (rather weak) theoretical restrictions that the slope β in the predictive regression and the forecast for the excess return are both nonnegative. That is, calculate the return forecast as

$$\widehat{R}_{t+1} = R_{f,t+1} + \max\{0, \widehat{a}_{t+1} + \max\{0, \widehat{\beta}_{t+1}\}\bar{x}_{t+1}\}, \tag{5.96}$$

where $\widehat{a}_{t+1}$ and $\widehat{\beta}_{t+1}$ denote the intercept and slope estimates from the standard OLS regression and $\bar{x}_{t+1}$ is the historical arithmetic average value of x, all estimated through period t.

Is there a significant improvement in the out-of-sample explanatory power of the two valuation ratios?

In the remaining parts of the exercise, we examine whether the forecasting performance of the dividend yield improves once we impose the theoretical restrictions of the drifting steady-state valuation model of section 5.5.2. Following equation (5.87), we use a version of the dividend yield adjusted for dividend growth and the real rate as our predictor variable:

$$x_t = \frac{D_t}{P_t}(1 + G_t) + \exp(\mathrm{E}_t[g_{t+1}]) + \frac{1}{2}\mathrm{Var}_t(r_{t+1}), \tag{5.97}$$

where $\mathrm{E}_t[g_{t+1}]$ and $\mathrm{Var}_t(r_{t+1})$ denote market participants' conditional expectation of future log dividend growth and the conditional variance of log returns.

(d) Construct an estimate of (5.97) using the historical sample mean of dividend growth and the historical sample variance of log stock returns up to date t. Even though the model assumes that market participants know the value of D_{t+1} at date t, to avoid any look-ahead bias construct a real-time estimate of x_t assuming that D_{t+1} is not in the econometrician's information set at date t.

Discuss alternative procedures that you could use to construct real-time estimates of $\mathrm{E}_t[g_{t+1}]$ and $\mathrm{Var}_t(r_{t+1})$.

(e) Repeat the calculations of parts (b) and (c) for x_t given by (5.97). Compare the forecasting performance of this adjusted version of the dividend yield with that of the (unadjusted) dividend yield.

(f) Finally, fully impose the theoretical restriction of equation (5.97) by calculating the predicted return as[11]

$$\widehat{R}_{t+1} = R_{f,t+1} + x_t, \tag{5.98}$$

where x_t is given by (5.97). What is the out-of-sample R^2 statistic now? Discuss your conclusions from this exercise.

Note: This problem is based on Campbell and Thompson (2008).

---

[11]Equivalently, impose a zero intercept and a unit slope in predictive regression (5.94).

Problem 5.3 A Market Return Predictor: the SVIX

In this problem we derive and explore the theoretical and empirical implications of a lower bound on the forward-looking expected equity premium, derived by Martin (2017). The lower bound is the *risk-neutral* conditional variance of equity returns divided by the gross risk-free rate.

Martin (2017) introduces a volatility index, $\text{SVIX}_{i,t,T}$, defined in terms of the time-t prices of put and call options on an underlying asset or portfolio i, usually a market index, with different strike prices and the same maturity T. It turns out that the square of the SVIX equals the (normalized) risk-neutral conditional variance of the gross simple return $R_{i,t,T}$ on the underlying asset i,

$$\text{SVIX}_{i,t,T}^2 = \frac{1}{T-t}\text{Var}_t^*\left(\frac{R_{i,t,T}}{R_{f,t,T}}\right), \tag{5.99}$$

The asterisk denotes moments of the risk-neutral distribution of returns. The fact that SVIX is directly observable at time t from the cross section of option prices implies that the lower bound on the equity premium that we will derive below is directly observable. In general, moments of the risk-neutral (conditional) distribution of asset returns can be backed out from option prices.

(a) Show that

$$\frac{\text{Var}_t^*(R_{i,t+1})}{R_{f,t+1}} = \text{E}_t R_{i,t+1} - R_{f,t+1} + \text{Cov}_t(M_{t+1}R_{i,t+1}, R_{i,t+1}), \tag{5.100}$$

where M_{t+1} denotes the stochastic discount factor.

Conclude that $\text{Var}_t^*(R_{i,t+1})/R_{f,t+1} = R_{f,t+1}\text{SVIX}_{i,t+1}^2$ is a lower bound on the equity premium, $\text{E}_t R_{i,t+1} - R_{f,t+1}$, provided that the *negative correlation condition*,

$$\text{Cov}_t(M_{t+1}R_{i,t+1}, R_{i,t+1}) \leq 0 \tag{5.101}$$

holds[12].

(b) Although SVIX has not yet been put to practical use, a well-known volatility index that is closely related to the SVIX is the VIX. It turns out that the VIX satisfies

$$\text{VIX}_{i,t,T}^2 = \frac{2}{T-t}L_t^*\left(\frac{R_{i,t,T}}{R_{f,t,T}}\right), \tag{5.102}$$

where $L^*(\cdot)$ is the risk-neutral entropy of returns.
  (i) What risk-neutral distribution of returns would approximately equate the VIX and the SVIX (for short maturities T)?

  (ii) Assume that returns and the stochastic discount factor are jointly conditionally lognormal (with respect to the objective probability measure). Show that

$$\text{SVIX}_{i,t+1}^2 = \exp\left(\sigma_{it}^2\right) - 1, \tag{5.103}$$

$$\text{VIX}_{i,t+1}^2 = \sigma_{it}^2, \tag{5.104}$$

---

[12]For ease of exposition we suppress the indices denoting the initial period t when this is obvious. For example, $\text{SVIX}_{i,t+1}$ should be interpreted as $\text{SVIX}_{i,t,t+1}$.

where $\sigma_{i,t}^2$ is the conditional variance of $r_{i,t+1} = \log R_{i,t+1}$. To derive the expression for the VIX you will need to make use of Stein's Lemma: if X and Y are two jointly normally distributed variables, $\mathrm{Cov}(h(X), Y) = \mathrm{E}[h'(X)]\mathrm{Cov}(X, Y)$, for any differentiable function $h(\cdot)$ such that $\mathrm{E}[h'(X)]$ and $\mathrm{Cov}(h(X), Y)$ exist.

   (iii) In recent data the VIX is always higher than the SVIX. What does this tell us about the usual assumption of conditionally lognormal returns?

(c) We now investigate the theoretical relevance of the negative correlation condition. Take asset i to be the market portfolio of risky assets. Show whether or not (NCC) holds in each of the following settings, or whether additional assumptions need to be imposed:

   (i) An economy where there exists an unconstrained risk-neutral investor.

   (ii) An economy where there exists a CRRA agent who lives only for periods t and $t + 1$ and who holds the market.

   (iii) An economy where the stochastic discount factor and the market return are conditionally jointly lognormal and where the market's conditional Sharpe ratio, $\log \mathrm{E}_t[R_{m,t+1}/R_{f,t+1}]/\sigma_t(\log R_{m,t+1})$, exceeds the conditional volatility of the market, $\sigma_t(\log R_{m,t+1})$.

   In light of these results, do you think that (NCC) imposes rather strong or weak restrictions on preferences?

(d) Empirical estimates of $\mathrm{Cov}_t(M_{t+1}R_{m,t+1}, R_{m,t+1})$ in linear factor models are negative and close to zero. Indeed, the time-series average of the lower bound in recent data is around 5%, quite close to the typical estimates of the unconditional equity premium. If the lower bound is approximately satisfied with equality, what would this imply about the relative risk aversion of a marginal investor who holds the market? Consider, for example, the setting of part (c)(ii).

(e) The risk-neutral variance (SVIX) approach presents an alternative to the large literature seeking to estimate the equity premium via predictive regressions based on valuation ratios discussed in this chapter. Compare and discuss the advantages and disadvantages of each approach.

(f) A notable divergence of forecasts between the risk-neutral variance approach and the valuation-ratios approach occurred in the late 1990s. The monthly and quarterly forecasts for the SVIX bound were high from late 1998 until the end of 1999, consistent with the high equity premia subsequently realized during that period. In contrast, valuation ratios were so low that predictive regressions forecasted a negative equity premium. Is it possible to reconcile these contrasting forecasts?

   Hint: use the the Campbell-Shiller approximation to the dividend yield to think about what the dividend yield forecasts.

6

Consumption-Based Asset Pricing

THIS CHAPTER EXPLORES the enormous literature on consumption-based asset pricing. Section 6.1 begins by writing down the simplest consumption-based model, making the traditional assumptions that a representative agent has power utility and that consumption is conditionally lognormally distributed. Section 6.2 shows how this model leads to three puzzles: the equity premium puzzle (why is the average return on stocks so high relative to the riskless real interest rate?), the riskfree rate puzzle (why is the riskless real interest rate relatively stable over time and across economies?), and the equity volatility puzzle (why are stocks so much more volatile than aggregate consumption growth?).

The remainder of the chapter considers alternative models that have been developed to address these puzzles. Section 6.3 asks what happens if consumption growth is not lognormally distributed but has fat tails as will be the case if economies are vulnerable to rare disasters. Section 6.4 presents Epstein-Zin preferences, a popular generalization of power utility that disentangles the coefficient of relative risk aversion from the elasticity of intertemporal substitution. Section 6.5 discusses long-run risk models, a recently popular class of representative-agent models in which investors have Epstein-Zin preferences with a high elasticity of intertemporal substitution, and both expected consumption growth and consumption volatility fluctuate persistently over time. Section 6.6 summarizes recent literature on ambiguity aversion, conservative behavior by investors who are uncertain of the true model of the economy. This section shows that a particular form of ambiguity aversion provides an alternative microfoundation for Epstein-Zin preferences. Section 6.7 shows how models of habit formation can generate time-varying risk aversion that helps to explain equity volatility even if consumption growth is lognormally distributed with low and constant volatility. Section 6.8 discusses recent work on models with nonseparable utility over both nondurable and durable goods.

The models in this chapter treat the stochastic process for consumption as exogenous, but the investors' first-order conditions that restrict asset prices are equally valid if investors choose consumption in response to time-varying production opportunities. We explore models with nontrivial production decisions in Chapter 7.

Throughout this chapter, we discuss applications of consumption-based models to the cross-section of stock returns as well as to the behavior of the aggregate stock market. The main limitation of the chapter is that we use the representative-agent approach throughout, deferring consideration of models with heterogeneous agents until Part III of the book.

6.1 Lognormal Consumption with Power Utility

We start by assuming that a representative agent has time-separable power utility with time discount factor δ and constant relative risk aversion γ defined over aggregate consumption C_t. The utility of consumption received at time t can be written as

$$U(C_t) = \frac{C_t^{1-\gamma} - 1}{1 - \gamma}. \tag{6.1}$$

This utility function has several desirable properties that make it popular in macrofinance models. First, it is scale-invariant, so risk premia do not alter with aggregate wealth given constant return distributions. Second, and related to the first point, investors with different levels of wealth but the same risk aversion coefficient have the same portfolio shares. The utility function is restrictive in that it imposes that the elasticity of intertemporal substitution or EIS, ψ, is the reciprocal of the CRRA γ. Epstein-Zin preferences, discussed in section 6.4, relax this restriction.

Power utility implies that marginal utility

$$U'(C_t) = C_t^{-\gamma} \tag{6.2}$$

and the stochastic discount factor

$$M_{t+1} = \delta (C_{t+1}/C_t)^{-\gamma}. \tag{6.3}$$

The SDF will be conditionally lognormal if consumption is conditionally lognormal. We assume lognormality here but relax this assumption in section 6.3. Then the log SDF is

$$m_{t+1} = \log(\delta) - \gamma \, \Delta c_{t+1}, \tag{6.4}$$

where $c_t = \log(C_t)$.

We now assume that consumption and asset returns are jointly conditionally homoskedastic. Substituting (6.4) into the lognormal version of the fundamental equation of asset pricing from Chapter 4, equation (4.41), we have

$$0 = E_t r_{i,t+1} + \log \delta - \gamma \, E_t \Delta c_{t+1} + \left(\frac{1}{2}\right) \left[\sigma_i^2 + \gamma^2 \sigma_c^2 - 2\gamma \, \sigma_{ic}\right]. \tag{6.5}$$

Here conditional second moments have no time subscripts because of the assumption of conditional homoskedasticity. σ_c^2 denotes the conditional variance of consumption growth, which under homoskedasticity equals the unconditional variance of log consumption innovations $\mathrm{Var}(c_{t+1} - E_t c_{t+1})$. Similarly, σ_{ic} denotes the conditional covariance between log asset returns and consumption growth, which under homoskedasticity equals the unconditional covariance of innovations $\mathrm{Cov}(r_{i,t+1} - E_t r_{i,t+1}, c_{t+1} - E_t c_{t+1})$.

The riskfree rate can be obtained from (6.5), or by substituting (6.4) into equation (4.42), as

$$r_{f,t+1} = -\log \delta + \gamma \, E_t \Delta c_{t+1} - \frac{\gamma^2 \sigma_c^2}{2}. \tag{6.6}$$

It is linear in expected consumption growth, with slope coefficient equal to the coefficient of relative risk aversion. The conditional variance of consumption growth has a negative effect on the riskless rate which can be interpreted as a precautionary savings effect.

The risk premium on any other asset, from (6.5) or by substituting (6.4) into equation (4.43), is

$$E_t[r_{i,t+1} - r_{f,t+1}] + \frac{\sigma_i^2}{2} = \gamma \sigma_{ic}. \tag{6.7}$$

An asset with a high consumption covariance tends to have low returns when consumption is low, that is, when the marginal utility of consumption is high. Such an asset is risky and commands a large risk premium.

6.2 Three Puzzles

We now summarize empirical evidence on the fit of equation (6.7). Updating an empirical analysis in Campbell (2003), we present data from the US over the period 1947–2011, together with some international evidence on a broader set of developed markets over a shorter sample period. At this stage we treat the consumption covariance σ_{ic} as exogenous and measured from the data, in the manner of Hansen and Singleton (1983), rather than asking what generates this covariance in equilibrium. Models discussed later in the chapter endogenize σ_{ic}, in the manner of Mehra and Prescott (1985).

Table 6.1 reports basic moments for quarterly log equity returns r_e, short-term log interest rates r_f, and per capita log consumption growth Δc, all measured in real terms and on an annualized basis. For each variable the table has three columns reporting the mean and standard deviation in percentage points and the first autocorrelation (denoted by ρ) in natural units. The basic message of the table is that stock returns are high on average, highly volatile, and only weakly autocorrelated; ex post real interest rates are much lower on average, modestly volatile, and positively autocorrelated; and real consumption growth is also low and stable on average with autocorrelations that vary considerably across countries.

In interpreting these results, an important caveat is that the standard deviation of the ex post real return on short-term nominal debt, reported in Table 6.1, exceeds

Table 6.1. *International Stock and Bill Returns and Consumption Growth*

Country	Sample period	$\overline{r_e}$	$\sigma(r_e)$	$\rho(r_e)$	$\overline{r_f}$	$\sigma(r_f)$	$\rho(r_f)$	$\overline{\Delta c}$	$\sigma(\Delta c)$	$\rho(\Delta c)$
USA	1947Q2–2011Q2	6.85	15.98	0.10	0.72	1.78	0.36	1.74	1.64	0.04
Australia	1970Q1–2011Q2	3.84	20.75	0.03	2.00	2.18	0.55	1.82	1.77	−0.09
Canada	1970Q1–2011Q2	5.47	17.85	0.15	2.07	1.64	0.66	1.69	1.93	0.07
France	1973Q2–2011Q2	7.06	23.10	0.08	2.08	1.53	0.74	1.38	1.80	−0.13
Germany	1978Q4–2011Q2	7.54	23.85	0.04	2.38	1.09	0.40	1.74	4.19	−0.07
Italy	1971Q2–2011Q2	1.51	25.74	0.07	1.86	2.06	0.77	2.18	2.23	0.47
Japan	1970Q2–2011Q2	2.70	21.41	0.09	1.03	1.91	0.29	1.72	2.92	−0.10
Netherlands	1977Q2–2011Q2	8.57	19.76	0.09	2.29	1.42	0.45	1.05	2.21	−0.11
Sweden	1970Q1–2011Q2	8.93	25.16	0.12	1.68	2.23	0.40	1.23	1.81	−0.15
Switzerland	1982Q2–2011Q2	8.14	20.05	0.01	0.87	1.32	0.03	0.75	1.30	−0.22
UK	1970Q1–2011Q2	6.33	19.85	0.10	1.34	2.60	0.46	2.14	2.68	−0.03

the standard deviation of the ex ante real interest rate to the extent that there are unpredictable quarterly shocks to inflation. Thus one should not calibrate asset pricing models to deliver a real interest rate volatility comparable to the numbers in Table 6.1, but should require a lower real interest rate volatility than this. This is an important point because many asset pricing models that fit the equity premium also imply excessive volatility of the real interest rate.

The Equity Premium Puzzle

Table 6.2 uses the sample moments from Table 6.1 to calculate the implied risk aversion coefficient from equation (6.7). The equity premium puzzle of Mehra and Prescott (1985) is that implied risk aversion is implausibly high.

The third column of Table 6.2 (labeled $\overline{aer_e}$) reports the arithmetic average excess stock return, calculated by adding one-half the variance of the excess log stock return to the average excess log stock return as on the left-hand side of equation (6.7). The average excess log stock return is the difference between the third and sixth columns of Table 6.1, and the variance correction can be calculated from the standard deviation of the excess log stock return reported in percentage points (labeled $\sigma(er_e)$) in the fourth column of Table 6.2. The fifth column reports a lower bound on the implied standard deviation of the log stochastic discount factor from equation (4.46) in section 4.3.2. This lower bound is just the third column of Table 6.2 divided by the fourth column, and multiplied by 100 to express it in annualized percentage points. In most countries the lower bound is above 30% per year, a surprisingly high standard deviation as discussed in Chapter 4.

Table 6.2 presents two alternative calculations of risk aversion. The first method divides the equity premium on the left-hand side of (6.7) by the measured consumption covariance σ_{ic} to get an implied relative risk aversion coefficient labeled RRA(1) and reported in the eighth column of the table. This number is extremely high in all countries where it is positive, but in a few countries the measured consumption covariance is actually negative.

The second method deliberately ignores the measured low correlation between stock returns and consumption, and uses only their relative volatilities. We can write

Table 6.2.   *The Equity Premium Puzzle*

Country	Sample period	$\overline{aer_e}$	$\sigma(er_e)$	$\sigma(m)$	$\sigma(\Delta c)$	$\rho(er_e, \Delta c)$	RRA(1)	RRA(2)
USA	1947Q2–2011Q2	7.39	15.86	46.57	1.64	0.18	154.98	28.42
Australia	1970Q1–2011Q2	3.95	20.58	19.21	1.77	−0.11	<0	10.89
Canada	1970Q1–2011Q2	5.01	17.93	27.94	1.93	0.09	166.97	14.51
France	1973Q2–2011Q2	7.68	23.22	33.06	1.80	0.00	<0	18.34
Germany	1978Q4–2011Q2	8.03	23.94	33.54	4.19	−0.01	<0	8.01
Italy	1971Q2–2011Q2	2.96	25.71	11.51	2.23	0.08	66.96	5.15
Japan	1970Q2–2011Q2	3.95	21.33	18.49	2.92	0.05	118.09	6.32
Netherlands	1977Q2–2011Q2	8.22	19.70	41.72	2.21	0.13	141.29	18.90
Sweden	1970Q1–2011Q2	10.44	25.28	41.32	1.81	0.07	314.53	22.87
Switzerland	1982Q2–2011Q2	9.27	20.01	46.33	1.30	0.07	483.74	35.60
UK	1970Q1–2011Q2	6.99	19.96	35.00	2.68	−0.04	<0	13.07

the consumption covariance for any asset i as $\sigma_{ic} = \sigma_i \sigma_c \rho_{ic}$, where ρ_{ic} is the correlation between the asset's excess return and consumption. The sample standard deviations for log excess returns and consumption growth are reported in the fourth and sixth columns of the table. The sample correlation for aggregate stock returns, reported in the seventh column of Table 6.2, is low; but if we set it equal to its maximum of one, the implied consumption covariance becomes $\sigma_i \sigma_c$. The ninth column labeled RRA(2) reports risk aversion coefficients obtained by dividing the arithmetic average equity premium by $\sigma_i \sigma_c$. Equivalently, the RRA(2) column is the RRA(1) column multiplied by the correlation in the seventh column. The RRA(2) coefficients are still implausibly high in most countries, indicating that the equity premium puzzle results in large part from the smoothness of consumption growth, not just from its low measured correlation with stock returns.

Both these calculations estimate the second moments of stock returns from historical data, but it is also possible to derive equilibrium stock returns from assumptions on the dividends paid by stocks. The classic approach, dating back to Mehra and Prescott (1985), is to model stocks as a claim to consumption. In this case, if consumption growth is serially uncorrelated then the unexpected return on stocks is equal to unexpected consumption growth, implying that stock returns and consumption have the same standard deviation and are perfectly correlated. Risk aversion coefficients calculated this way are of the same order of magnitude as the RRA(1) coefficients reported in Table 6.2. Mehra and Prescott (1985) calibrate a model with persistent consumption growth, increasing the volatility of stock returns and reducing their estimate of relative risk aversion closer to the RRA(2) value. Other papers model stocks as leveraged claims to consumption (Campbell 1986, Abel 1990) or as claims to dividends that are imperfectly correlated with consumption.

The Riskfree Rate Puzzle
One response to the equity premium puzzle is simply to accept that investors are more risk averse than commonly believed. However, high risk aversion has implausible implications for the riskless real interest rate in equilibrium, a fact described as the riskfree rate puzzle by Weil (1989). Equation (6.6) is quadratic in risk aversion, with the level of risk aversion multiplying average consumption growth, and the negative square of risk aversion multiplying one-half the variance of consumption growth. Since consumption growth has a very small variance, the linear term dominates for small to moderate levels of risk aversion, implying that a high risk aversion coefficient increases the average real interest rate for a fixed rate of time preference. Intuitively, risk averse consumers are keen to smooth consumption intertemporally to achieve a flat consumption path, so they react to trend economic growth by seeking to borrow and driving up the equilibrium real interest rate. However, if risk aversion becomes large enough, the negative quadratic term dominates. Extremely risk averse consumers react to even modest uncertainty about future consumption with aggressive precautionary saving, driving down the equilibrium real interest rate for a fixed rate of time preference.

Table 6.3 illustrates these offsetting effects using the risk aversion numbers from Table 6.2. The power utility model has a free parameter, the time discount factor δ, that can be used to fit the average riskless interest rate. The rate of time preference, $-\log \delta$, is the riskless real interest rate that would be observed in a hypothetical economy without growth or uncertainty. Table 6.3 shows that the rate of time preference must typically be negative to fit the mean real interest rate with risk aversion coefficients in the RRA(2) range, and it must be extremely large and positive to fit the mean real interest rate with higher risk aversion coefficients in the RRA(1) range.

Table 6.3.   *The Riskfree Rate Puzzle*

Country	Sample period	$\overline{r_f}$	$\overline{\Delta c}$	$\sigma(\Delta c)$	RRA(1)	TPR(1)	RRA (2)	TPR(2)
USA	1947Q2–2011Q2	0.72	1.74	1.64	154.98	53.08	28.42	–37.97
Australia	1970Q1–2011Q2	2.00	1.82	1.77	<0	N/A	10.89	–15.93
Canada	1970Q1–2011Q2	2.07	1.69	1.93	166.97	236.67	14.51	–18.55
France	1973Q2–2011Q2	2.08	1.38	1.80	<0	N/A	18.34	–17.80
Germany	1978Q4–2011Q2	2.38	1.74	4.19	<0	N/A	8.01	–5.97
Italy	1971Q2–2011Q2	1.86	2.18	2.23	66.96	–32.42	5.15	–8.73
Japan	1970Q2–2011Q2	1.03	1.72	2.92	118.09	394.17	6.32	–8.15
Netherlands	1977Q2–2011Q2	2.29	1.05	2.21	141.29	340.11	18.90	–8.86
Sweden	1970Q1–2011Q2	1.68	1.23	1.81	314.53	1230.28	22.87	–17.84
Switzerland	1982Q2–2011Q2	0.87	0.75	1.30	483.74	1617.47	35.60	–15.24
UK	1970Q1–2011Q2	1.34	2.14	2.68	<0	N/A	13.07	–20.48

Even if one could accept the time preference rates reported in Table 6.3, the real interest rate would still be extremely sensitive to any small change in expected consumption growth or consumption volatility. In a power utility model with high risk aversion, reasonable behavior of the real interest rate is a knife-edge case achieved by offsetting strong effects of intertemporal substitution and precautionary saving on the equilibrium real interest rate.

The Equity Volatility Puzzle

Table 6.1 shows that stock returns are far more volatile than consumption growth. This is a puzzle if stocks are a claim to aggregate consumption (i.e., if stock dividends equal consumption), consumption growth is iid, and investors have power utility, because then the consumption-wealth ratio should be constant, and stock returns and consumption growth should have the same volatility. Campbell (2003) calls this the equity volatility puzzle and argues that it is just as fundamental a challenge for consumption-based asset pricing models as either of the other two puzzles. Volatility can be explained if dividends or consumption growth have predictable long-run components, as in the long-run risks model of Bansal and Yaron (2004), or if preferences induce persistent fluctuations in risk premia, as in the Campbell and Cochrane (1999) model of habit formation. Models with these features must however also explain the comparative stability of the riskless real interest rate, which tells us that while the SDF may have variation over time in its conditional volatility (generating variation in Sharpe ratios and risk premia), it has relatively little variation in its conditional mean.

6.2.1 Responses to the Puzzles

The enormous literature on consumption-based asset pricing has responded to these three puzzles in various ways. Here we present a brief summary, and elaborate on some of the responses later in this chapter and in following chapters.

Sampling error. The risk aversion coefficients reported in Table 6.2 do not come with standard errors. In some cases, a confidence interval includes more modest values that are easier to reconcile with intuition.

Sample selection. We may be looking at an unusual sample drawn from the right tail of the ex ante distribution of stock returns. Dimson, Marsh, and Staunton (2002) have argued that the late 20th century was a particularly fortunate period for economic growth and investors in long-term assets. Fama and French (2002) and McGrattan and Prescott (2005) have argued that this period saw a decline in the required real stock return (attributed by McGrattan and Prescott to declining capital income taxation) that drove up stock prices in a manner that was not expected ex ante.

Mismeasurement of returns. McGrattan and Prescott (2003) emphasize that capital income taxation reduces average after-tax returns to taxable investors, although it also reduces the volatility of these returns.

Mismeasurement of consumption. Measured consumption is a flow over a period of time, whereas the theoretical concept required to test a consumption-based asset pricing model is instantaneous consumption at a point in time, which is then used to construct consumption growth over a discrete interval (Breeden, Gibbons, and Litzenberger 1989). In addition, the usual National Income and Product Accounts (NIPA) consumption series have been filtered to reduce measurement error and seasonally adjusted, and this may distort the covariance of stock returns with consumption. Savov (2011) works with the volume of garbage, a side-effect of consumption that is measured without filtering or seasonal adjustment, and obtains lower—although still substantial—estimates of risk aversion; Kroencke (2017) obtains similar results by unfiltering NIPA consumption.

Long-run consumption covariances. Perhaps stock market risk should be measured by the covariance between stock returns and long-run consumption growth, not short-run consumption growth (Daniel and Marshall 1997, Parker and Julliard 2005). This might be because measurement issues are less serious at long horizons, or because there are costs of processing information that lead to infrequent adjustment of consumption (Gabaix and Laibson 2001). Jagannathan and Wang (2007) find that annual consumption growth explains the cross-section of stock returns better when it is measured in the fourth quarter, which is both the holiday season and the end of the tax year and hence a plausible time for investors to make consumption and portfolio decisions.

Rare disasters. Consumption growth is not lognormal but has a fat-tailed distribution. Standard preferences imply that expected returns are higher than for a lognormal consumption distribution with the same variance. The fat tail in consumption growth may arise from a small probability of a disaster (Rietz 1988, Barro 2006) or from parameter uncertainty (Weitzman 2007).

Epstein-Zin preferences. It may be that the power utility model does not adequately represent preferences. A popular alternative is Epstein-Zin utility (Epstein and Zin 1989, 1991), which retains the basic scale independence of power utility but abandons the restriction that the elasticity of intertemporal substitution is the reciprocal of the coefficient of relative risk aversion. At the very least, this allows one to increase risk aversion (to fit the equity premium) without encountering the riskfree rate puzzle.

Ambiguity aversion. The engineering literature on robust optimal control proposes to handle model uncertainty by optimizing in a manner that delivers satisfactory results even if an unfavorable model is true. In economics, this approach can be used as a model of optimizing behavior by investors who are uncertain about the true model. Maenhout (2004) and Hansen and Sargent (2008) have shown how this can provide an alternative microfoundation for Epstein-Zin preferences, increasing the parameter of risk aversion in the Epstein-Zin model.

Long-run risks. Even if consumption is adjusted continuously, investors are averse to covariance with long-run consumption growth if they have Epstein-Zin preferences with a relatively high elasticity of intertemporal substitution (Restoy and Weil 2011, Bansal and Yaron 2004, Bansal, Kiku, and Yaron 2012). Models with such preferences and persistent variation in the consumption growth rate and the volatility of consumption have come to be known as long-run risk models.

Habit formation. Models in which investors get utility from consumption relative to a gradually adjusting habit level can generate gradual adjustment in consumption (Constantinides 1990) and time-varying risk aversion (Campbell and Cochrane 1999). Time-varying risk aversion contributes to an explanation of the equity volatility puzzle.

Nonseparable utility. The standard assumption in the literature is that marginal utility derived from consumption of nondurables and services (the consumption series used in most empirical tests) does not depend on the consumption of leisure or of services provided by a stock of durable goods. If this assumption fails—that is, if utility is nonseparable across nondurables and services, on the one hand, and leisure or durable goods, on the other—then standard tests are misspecified (Dunn and Singleton 1986, Eichenbaum and Hansen 1990, Yogo 2006).

All the responses above can be discussed in a representative agent model, and will be covered in this chapter. Other responses invoke heterogeneity of investors, and will be discussed in Chapters 10 and 11.

Uninsurable idiosyncratic risk. Constantinides and Duffie (1996) show that in principle, with an arbitrary distribution of uninsurable background risk, the equity premium can be arbitrarily large with an arbitrary coefficient of risk aversion for investors.

Portfolio restrictions. The effects of heterogeneity can be amplified if there are restrictions on investor portfolios, for example, participation constraints that prevent some consumers from holding stocks, borrowing constraints that limit the risk exposures of some investors, or barriers to capital flows across countries.

6.3 Beyond Lognormality

In this section we explore the "rare disasters" explanation for the equity premium puzzle proposed originally by Rietz (1988), and further developed by Barro (2006, 2009) and his coauthors. We use the approach of Martin (2013) to calculate the risk premium on a consumption claim for an arbitrary distribution of consumption growth, using only the assumptions that consumption growth is iid and that a representative agent has power utility.[1]

Consider an asset that pays $D_t = C_t^\lambda$. The parameter λ scales the volatility of dividends, and can be thought of as a proxy for leverage (Campbell 1986, Abel 1990). When $\lambda = 0$, the asset is riskless. When $\lambda = 1$, the asset is a claim to aggregate consumption; equivalently, it is the aggregate wealth portfolio.

With power utility, the present value formula for the asset price is

$$P_t = \mathrm{E}_t \sum_{j=1}^{\infty} \delta^j \left(\frac{C_{t+j}}{C_t} \right)^{-\gamma} C_{t+j}^\lambda$$

---

[1]Martin (2013) presents the formulas for the more general Epstein-Zin preference specification that we discuss in the next section.

$$= D_t \mathrm{E}_t \sum_{j=1}^{\infty} \delta^j \left(\frac{C_{t+j}}{C_t} \right)^{\lambda-\gamma}. \tag{6.8}$$

Now define $\delta = \exp(-r^*)$, so r^* is the pure rate of time preference. Also, define g as a random variable with the distribution of $c_{t+1} - c_t$. There is no time subscript on g because of the assumption that consumption growth is iid. Then we have

$$P_t = D_t \sum_{j=1}^{\infty} \exp(-r^* j)\{\mathrm{E}[(\exp(\lambda-\gamma)g)]\}^j, \tag{6.9}$$

where we can use an unconditional expectation, and write the power j outside the expectation operator, because of the assumption that consumption is iid.

Recall from Chapter 4 that the cumulant-generating function for any random variable x, with parameter θ, is

$$\mathbf{c}(\theta) = \log \mathrm{E} \exp(\theta x)$$

$$= \sum_{n=1}^{\infty} \frac{\kappa_n \theta^n}{n!}, \tag{6.10}$$

where κ_n is the n'th cumulant of x. In our application $x = g$, log consumption growth—so κ_1 is the mean of log consumption growth, κ_2 is the variance σ^2, κ_3/σ^3 is the skewness, κ_4/σ^4 is the excess kurtosis, and so forth. All cumulants above the second are zero when log consumption growth is normal. Also, $\mathbf{c}(0) = 0$ and $\mathbf{c}(1)$ is the log of the mean of simple gross consumption growth.

Martin (2013) shows how to relate asset prices and returns to the cumulant-generating function for consumption growth, and hence to the cumulants that summarize the distribution of consumption risk. We begin by rewriting the asset price equation (6.9) as

$$P_t = D_t \sum_{j=1}^{\infty} \exp[-(r^* - \mathbf{c}(\lambda-\gamma))j]$$

$$= D_t \frac{\exp[-(r^* - \mathbf{c}(\lambda-\gamma))]}{1 - \exp[-(r^* - \mathbf{c}(\lambda-\gamma))]}, \tag{6.11}$$

where the second equality evaluates the infinite geometric sum. We see from equation (6.11) that the price-dividend ratio is constant, an implication of our iid setting.

To simplify this expression we can define $dp = \log(1 + D_t/P_t)$, the log gross dividend yield. We write $dp(\lambda)$ to indicate the dependence of the log gross dividend yield on the leverage parameter λ. Equation (6.11) implies that

$$dp(\lambda) = r^* - \mathbf{c}(\lambda-\gamma). \tag{6.12}$$

The gross return on the asset is

$$1 + R_{t+1} = \frac{P_{t+1}}{P_t} \left(1 + \frac{D_{t+1}}{P_{t+1}} \right)$$

$$= \frac{D_{t+1}}{D_t} \exp(r^* - \mathbf{c}(\lambda-\gamma)). \tag{6.13}$$

Thus the expected gross return is

$$1 + ER_{t+1} = E \exp(g\lambda) \exp(r^* - \mathbf{c}(\lambda - \gamma))$$
$$= \exp(r^* - \mathbf{c}(\lambda - \gamma) + \mathbf{c}(\lambda)). \tag{6.14}$$

Again, we can simplify this expression by defining $er = \log(1 + ER_{t+1})$, the log of the expected gross return. Then

$$er(\lambda) = r^* - \mathbf{c}(\lambda - \gamma) + \mathbf{c}(\lambda). \tag{6.15}$$

Putting these results together, we have a logarithmic Gordon growth model of the sort discussed in Chapter 5. For any leverage parameter λ,

$$dp(\lambda) = er(\lambda) - \mathbf{c}(\lambda). \tag{6.16}$$

This equation says that the log gross dividend yield is the log expected gross return minus the log expected gross dividend growth rate. The Gordon growth model holds here because this is a steady-state model with iid dividend (consumption) growth and constant discount rates.

Now consider the two special cases $\lambda = 0$, corresponding to a riskless asset, and $\lambda = 1$, corresponding to a consumption claim or equivalently the aggregate wealth portfolio. For the riskless asset, we have $er(0) = dp(0) = r_f$. Using this property and equation (6.12) we have

$$r_f = r^* - \mathbf{c}(-\gamma) = r^* - \sum_{n=1}^{\infty} \frac{\kappa_n(-\gamma)^n}{n!}. \tag{6.17}$$

For the consumption claim, the log gross dividend yield

$$dp(1) = \log\left(1 + \frac{C}{W}\right) \equiv cw, \tag{6.18}$$

since aggregate wealth is just a claim to the infinite stream of aggregate consumption, so the dividend-price ratio of a consumption claim equals the aggregate consumption-wealth ratio. The notation cw is a simple way to denote the log gross consumption-wealth ratio. Setting $\lambda = 1$ in equation (6.12), we have

$$dp(1) = cw = r^* - \mathbf{c}(1 - \gamma) = r^* - \sum_{n=1}^{\infty} \frac{\kappa_n(1-\gamma)^n}{n!}. \tag{6.19}$$

The equity premium eqp, defined as the log expected gross return for the consumption claim less the riskless interest rate, is given by (6.15) and (6.17) as

$$eqp = er(1) - r_f = \mathbf{c}(1) + \mathbf{c}(-\gamma) - \mathbf{c}(1 - \gamma)$$
$$= \sum_{n=2}^{\infty} \frac{\kappa_n}{n!}\{1 + (-\gamma)^n - (1-\gamma)^n\}. \tag{6.20}$$

This result generalizes the familiar formula for a consumption-based model with iid lognormal consumption growth, $eqp = \gamma\sigma^2$, to allow for the influence of higher moments. The term $\mathbf{c}(1)$ is the log of the arithmetic mean of gross consumption growth, which is quite small. The other two terms are the change in the value of the cumulant-generating function between the points $(1-\gamma)$ and $-\gamma$. Since the cumulant-generating function is always convex, this change is increasing in γ. Features of the consumption growth distribution that increase the convexity of the cumulant-generating function increase the equity premium for any given value of γ, and therefore lower the γ value that is needed to fit any given equity premium.

The form of (6.20) makes it tempting to work with the first few terms on the right-hand side, considering, for example, the mean, variance, skewness, and kurtosis of consumption growth, and ignoring all moments beyond the fourth. Unfortunately, Martin (2013) shows that the convergence of the infinite sum of cumulants is extremely slow in realistic examples, so this approach would require many more moments that are effectively impossible to estimate nonparametrically.

The cumulant-generating function has a tractable closed form in a special case considered by Barro (2006, 2009). This special case is a continuous-time jump-diffusion for log consumption, where the diffusion has mean μ and variance σ^2, jumps follow a Poisson process with arrival rate ω, and if a jump occurs, log consumption drops by a random amount x. In this case,

$$\mathbf{c}(\theta) = \mu\theta + \frac{1}{2}\sigma^2\theta^2 + \omega(\mathrm{E}[\exp(-\theta x)]-1)$$

$$= \mu\theta + \frac{1}{2}\sigma^2\theta^2 + \omega\left(\exp\left(-\theta m + \frac{1}{2}\theta^2 s^2\right) - 1\right), \qquad (6.21)$$

where the second line follows under the further special assumption that x is distributed normal with mean m and variance s^2. This formula shows clearly how jumps increase the convexity of the cumulant-generating function. If ω is small, and m is positive and large relative to s^2, this is a model of occasional "disasters" in which a large fraction of consumption is lost.

Applying the general equity premium formula (6.20) to this special case, we have

$$eqp = \gamma\sigma^2 + \omega\left\{\mathrm{E}[\exp(-x)] + \mathrm{E}[\exp(\gamma x)] - \mathrm{E}[\exp((\gamma-1)x)] - 1\right\}$$

$$= \gamma\sigma^2 + \omega\mathrm{E}[(1-B)(B^{-\gamma}-1)], \qquad (6.22)$$

where the random variable $B \equiv \exp(-x)$ is the proportion of consumption that survives a disaster (this might be called the economy-wide recovery rate). The second line of (6.22), derived by Barro (2009), shows that the increase in the equity premium caused by the risk of disasters equals the disaster probability ω multiplied by the product of the disaster loss $(1-B)$ and the proportional increase in the marginal utility of consumption caused by a disaster, $(B^{-\gamma}-1)$.

This model illustrates the important general point that a small probability of a large disaster can greatly increase the equity premium. Martin (2013) calibrates the diffusion mean $\mu = 2.5\%$, the diffusion standard deviation $\sigma = 2.0\%$, the arrival rate of jumps $\omega = 1.7\%$, the mean drop in the event of a jump $m = 39\%$, and the standard deviation

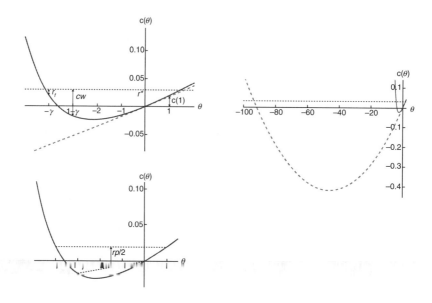

Figure 6.1. *Consumption Cumulant-Generating Function and Asset Prices* (Martin, Ian W. R., 2013, "Consumption-Based Asset Pricing with Higher Cumulants," *Review of Economic Studies* 80, 745–773; reprinted by permission of Oxford University Press.)

of this drop $s = 25\%$. With a time discount rate of 3% and risk aversion of 4, these parameters imply a 1.0% riskless interest rate and an equity premium of 5.7%.

The cumulant-generating function with these parameters is illustrated in Figure 6.1, taken from Martin's (2013) Figures 1 and 2. The top left panel plots the cumulant-generating function for two illustrative consumption-growth distributions, one with jumps (the solid line) and one without (the dashed line). For a relative risk aversion parameter equal to 4, the panel shows how to read the riskfree interest rate $r^* - \mathbf{c}(-\gamma)$ and the log consumption-wealth ratio $r^* - \mathbf{c}(1-\gamma)$ off the figure. The panel shows that jumps help the model produce a reasonable riskfree rate and consumption-wealth ratio given a pure rate of time preference of 3%. In the absence of jumps, the cumulant-generating function is much less convex, so a much higher value of risk aversion is needed to deliver these properties as illustrated by the top right panel of the figure which extends the horizontal axis far to the left.

The bottom panel of Figure 6.1 shows how to read the equity premium off the figure, again for the canonical example with jumps. A rearrangement of equation (6.20), using $c(0) = 0$, shows that the equity premium is $\mathbf{c}(1) + \mathbf{c}(-\gamma) - \mathbf{c}(1 - \gamma) = 2\{(\mathbf{c}(1) + \mathbf{c}(-\gamma))/2 - (c(0) + \mathbf{c}(1-\gamma))/2\}$, a difference between two averages that is increasing in the convexity of the cumulant-generating function. The figure makes the role of convexity visually obvious.

The powerful effect of rare disasters on asset prices is a double-edged sword. Small changes in the parameters can have very large effects on both the riskless interest rate and the equity premium. For example, a slight increase in the disaster arrival rate ω to 2.2% implies a riskless interest rate of –2.4% and an equity premium of 7.4%, while a slight decrease in ω to 1.2% produces a riskless interest rate of 4.5% and an equity premium of 4.1%. Changes in m or s of 5 percentage points have similarly dramatic effects. This suggests that it will be very difficult to find external evidence on the probability and magnitude of disaster risk that is sufficient to generate precise implications for asset prices. Instead, disaster risk must be backed out from observed asset prices; in effect, the model has several additional free parameters.[2]

6.3.1 Time-Varying Disaster Risk

The disaster models discussed so far have iid consumption growth, so they imply that the riskless interest rate, the price-dividend ratio for a consumption claim, and the equity premium are all constant, and the volatility of the return on a consumption claim equals the volatility of consumption growth. Thus, these models have nothing to say about the equity volatility puzzle. A natural extension of the rare disasters framework is to allow the probability of a disaster, or the effects of a disaster on asset payoffs, to be time-varying. Time-variation in disaster risk can generate time-varying risk premia and increase the volatility of risky asset returns.

Gabaix (2012) presents a particularly tractable framework for the analysis of time-varying disaster risk, using the linearity-generating processes discussed in section 5.2.1. In Gabaix's model, aggregate consumption growth is deterministic except when a disaster occurs. With probability $(1 - p_t)$, no disaster occurs and consumption growth is

$$\frac{C_{t+1}}{C_t} = \exp(\mu). \tag{6.23}$$

With probability p_t, a disaster occurs and consumption growth is

$$\frac{C_{t+1}}{C_t} = \exp(\mu) B_{t+1}. \tag{6.24}$$

Here, as before, the random variable $B_{t+1} > 0$ is the macroeconomic recovery rate, the proportion of consumption that survives a disaster.

Gabaix assumes power utility with time preference rate r^* and relative risk aversion γ, so the stochastic discount factor in this economy is $M_{t+1} = \exp(-r)$ if no disaster occurs, and $M_{t+1} = \exp(-r) B_{t+1}^{-\gamma}$ if a disaster occurs, where $r = r^* + \gamma \mu$ is the log riskless interest rate that would prevail if the disaster probability were zero.

Gabaix considers assets whose dividend processes are exposed to disaster risk. For asset i, dividend growth is given by

$$\frac{D_{i,t+1}}{D_{it}} = \exp(g_i) \tag{6.25}$$

if no disaster occurs, and

$$\frac{D_{i,t+1}}{D_{it}} = \exp(g_i) F_{i,t+1} \tag{6.26}$$

---

[2]For this reason I referred to rare disasters as "dark matter for economists" in my 2008 Princeton Lectures in Finance (http://scholar.harvard.edu/campbell/presentations/risk-and-return-stocks-and-bonds-princeton-finance-lecture-slides). The analogy is with dark matter in cosmology, which can only be detected by its gravitational interactions with ordinary matter.

if a disaster occurs, where $F_{i,t+1} > 0$ is the asset-specific recovery rate, the proportion of the dividend stream that survives a disaster.[3]

The key variable in Gabaix's model summarizes the ability of an asset to protect investors against disasters. The "resilience" of asset i is defined as

$$H_{it} = p_t E_t^* \left[B_{t+1}^{-\gamma} F_{i,t+1} - 1 \right], \tag{6.27}$$

where E_t^* denotes an expectation conditional on the occurrence of a disaster. Resilience is increasing in the asset-specific recovery rate $F_{i,t+1}$, it may be positive or negative, and it varies more strongly with $F_{i,t+1}$ when a disaster is more likely or is expected to be more severe.

In order to obtain closed-form solutions for asset prices and returns, Gabaix assumes that the resilience of each asset follows a linearity-generating process. Writing

$$H_{it} = \overline{H}_i + \widehat{H}_{it}, \tag{6.28}$$

where $\overline{H}_i$ is the unconditional mean of H_{it} and $\widehat{H}_{it}$ is the deviation from that mean, the process is

$$\widehat{H}_{i,t+1} = \frac{1 + \overline{H}_i}{1 + \overline{H}_{it}} \exp(-\phi_H) \widehat{H}_{it} + \eta_{i,t+1}. \tag{6.29}$$

As in equation (5.18), this is an AR(1) process with a "linearity-generating twist" (division by $1 + \overline{H}_{it}$) that delivers tractable asset pricing formulas. The shock $\eta_{i,t+1}$ is assumed to be uncorrelated with the disaster event.[4]

Asset prices in this model take a particularly simple form when the time interval is short. Here we present the solutions without repeating the derivations in Gabaix (2012). Define $\overline{h}_i = \log(1 + \overline{H}_i)$. Then with a short time interval,

$$P_{it} \approx \frac{D_{it}}{r - \overline{h}_i - g_i} \left(1 + \frac{\widehat{H}_{it}}{r - \overline{h}_i - g_i + \phi_H} \right). \tag{6.30}$$

This can be understood as a modified Gordon growth model with linear variation in prices driven by demeaned resilience $\widehat{H}_{it}$. It implies that when a disaster occurs, the asset price drops in proportion to the dividend given that $\widehat{H}_{it}$ variation is negligible over short time intervals. Hence, the gross asset return in a disaster is just the asset-specific recovery rate $F_{i,t+1}$.

The expected return on an asset, conditional on no disaster occurring, is

$$E_t' R_{i,t+1} = r - p_t E_t^* \left[B_{t+1}^{-\gamma} (1 + R_{i,t+1}) - 1 \right] = r - H_{it}, \tag{6.31}$$

where the second equality follows from the equality of the gross asset return and the recovery rate $F_{i,t+1}$ in a disaster, and the definition of resilience (6.27). This equation is

---

[3]Random shocks uncorrelated with disasters can be added to these expressions for dividend growth, but they do not affect risk premia given the assumption that consumption risk is deterministic in the absence of disasters.

[4]The distribution of $\eta_{i,t+1}$ does not affect asset prices and therefore need not be fully specified, but it must be heteroskedastic in order to keep the process (6.29) stable and guarantee that $F_{i,t+1} > 0$.

intuitive: a more resilient asset has a lower expected return because it better protects investors when disasters occur.

The unconditional expected return on an asset further subtracts the loss in a disaster times the probability of a disaster:

$$E_t R_{i,t+1} = r - H_{it} - p_t E_t^*(1 - F_{i,t+1}). \tag{6.32}$$

As Barro (2006) has emphasized, the correction $p_t E_t^*(1 - F_{i,t+1})$ is typically small relative to the resilience term H_{it} when disasters are large and investors have moderate coefficients of risk aversion. Disaster risk is more important for its effect on the equity premium than for its distortion of average returns in samples where disasters do not occur.

An important question is what factors drive time-variation in resilience. The most obvious possibility, emphasized by Gourio (2012) and Wachter (2013), is that the disaster probability p_t varies over time. This generates correlated movements in resilience, and hence in price-dividend ratios and risk premia, across all risky assets. Changes in the distribution of the macroeconomic recovery rate B_{t+1} have similar effects. A difficulty with this story is that if disasters are interpreted as wars (which historically have been the largest observed disasters), then the movements in asset prices do not seem to line up well with changing probabilities of global conflict.[5] Broadening the definition of disasters to include financial crises certainly improves the correlation with stock prices, but also shrinks the average magnitude of disasters to a level that may be too low to explain the equity premium. It is possible that larger effects can be obtained in a model with limited participation and shocks to factor shares of the sort discussed by Lettau and Ludvigson (2013). In such a model, expropriation of stockholders by nonstockholders will be priced as a disaster even in the absence of a collapse in consumption for the economy as a whole. Such an approach would also allow the use of political data to discipline the modeling of changing disaster probabilities.

An alternative view, emphasized by Gabaix (2012), is that resilience is driven by investors' changing beliefs about asset-specific recovery rates $F_{i,t+1}$. This allows price-dividend ratios and risk premia to vary idiosyncratically in different risky asset classes, so it is a more flexible model, but for this reason is even harder to discipline with external data. It is not at all clear how to test this hypothesis as opposed to merely backing out implied recovery rates from asset prices.

Rare disaster models have interesting implications for the prices of equity index options (Backus, Chernov, and Martin 2011, Gabaix 2012, Seo and Wachter 2016). While such implications are beyond the scope of this book, Problem 6.1 asks you to consider the general problem of recovering consumption growth processes and preference parameters from data on contingent claims prices following Ross (2015) and Borovička, Hansen, and Scheinkman (2016).

The disasters discussed in this section are instantaneous downward jumps in consumption, but this assumption can be relaxed. Nakamura et al. (2013) allow for disasters to unfold over several years rather than occurring instantaneously, and for some recovery in consumption afterward. They also allow for uncertainty about future consumption

---

[5]Such probabilities are hard to measure (Russett and Slemrod 1993), but one possible proxy is the number of minutes to midnight in the nuclear clock produced by the Bulletin of Atomic Scientists. This proxy indicates a relatively low probability of disaster during the 1970s and a much higher probability during the mid-1980s, the opposite of the pattern in stock prices. Nuclear proliferation increased this proxy for disaster probability during the late 1990s, again contrary to the boom in stock prices at that time.

growth to increase during a disaster, and they distinguish between global and country-specific disasters in an international dataset assembled by Barro and Ursúa (2008). Their model shares some features with the long-run risk model discussed in section 6.5 below. Tsai and Wachter (2015) survey this literature within a continuous-time framework.

6.4 Epstein-Zin Preferences

The simple power-utility model discussed in section 6.1 has the desirable property of scale invariance, implying that interest rates and risk premia remain stationary even in a growing economy. However, it tightly links risk aversion and the elasticity of intertemporal substitution (EIS), making one the reciprocal of the other. Within the power-utility framework, risk aversion cannot be increased to solve the equity premium puzzle without lowering the EIS. A very low value for the EIS implies implausible behavior of the riskless interest rate, a fact highlighted by Weil (1989) in his discussion of the riskfree rate puzzle.

The preferences proposed by Epstein and Zin (1989, 1991), building on the work of Kreps and Porteus (1978), escape this dilemma by decoupling the coefficient of relative risk aversion and the EIS. The Epstein-Zin objective function is a member of a class of preferences defined recursively by

$$U_t = f(C_t, \mu(U_{t+1})), \qquad (6.33)$$

where $f(\cdot)$ is an aggregator function that evaluates tradeoffs between present and future, and $\mu(\cdot)$ is a certainty-equivalent function that encodes attitudes toward risk. The Epstein-Zin objective function gives $f(\cdot)$ a CES form, and $\mu(\cdot)$ a power form to retain the scale-independence of power utility:

$$
\begin{aligned}
U_t &= \left\{ (1-\delta) C_t^{1-\frac{1}{\psi}} + \delta \left(\mathrm{E}_t \, U_{t+1}^{1-\gamma} \right)^{\frac{1-\frac{1}{\psi}}{1-\gamma}} \right\}^{\frac{1}{1-\frac{1}{\psi}}} \\
&= \left\{ (1-\delta) C_t^{\frac{1-\gamma}{\theta}} + \delta \left(\mathrm{E}_t \, U_{t+1}^{1-\gamma} \right)^{\frac{1}{\theta}} \right\}^{\frac{\theta}{1-\gamma}},
\end{aligned}
\qquad (6.34)
$$

where γ is risk aversion, ψ is the elasticity of intertemporal substitution, and the composite parameter $\theta \equiv (1-\gamma)/(1-1/\psi)$.[6] When $\gamma = 1/\psi$, $\theta = 1$ and the recursion becomes linear; it can then be solved forward to yield the familiar time-separable power utility model.

The case where $\psi = 1$ is particularly tractable. As $\psi \to 1$, $\theta \to \infty$ and the Epstein-Zin objective function is rewritten as

$$U_t = C_t^{1-\delta} \left(\mathrm{E}_t U_{t+1}^{1-\gamma} \right)^{\frac{\delta}{1-\gamma}}. \qquad (6.35)$$

---

[6] It is standard in the literature to describe the Epstein-Zin parameter γ as risk aversion and the parameter ψ as the elasticity of intertemporal substitution, and we will see that these parameters affect asset pricing in a manner that is intuitively consistent with this description. However, Garcia, Renault, and Semenov (2006) and Hansen et al. (2007) point out that this interpretation may not be strictly correct when γ differs from the reciprocal of ψ.

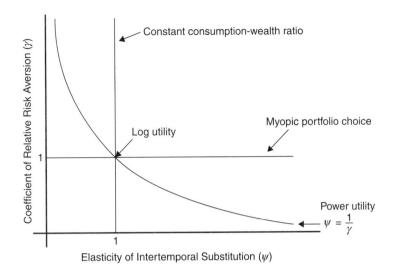

Figure 6.2. *Epstein-Zin Parameter Space*

Defining $V_t = (\log U_t)/(1 - \delta)$, we have

$$V_t = c_t - \delta\lambda \log \mathrm{E}_t \exp\left(\frac{-V_{t+1}}{\lambda}\right), \tag{6.36}$$

where $\lambda \equiv -1/((1 - \delta)(1 - \gamma))$ has the same sign as $(\gamma - 1)$. Hansen and Sargent (2008) call this a "risk-sensitive recursion" for reasons that we discuss in section 6.5. If we now let γ approach 1, $\lambda \to \infty$ and the recursion becomes linear: $V_t = c_t + \delta\mathrm{E}_t V_{t+1}$. This is the familiar case of log utility.

Figure 6.2 illustrates the parameter space for Epstein-Zin preferences. The elasticity of intertemporal substitution ψ is on the horizontal axis, and the coefficient of relative risk aversion is on the vertical axis. The hyperbola with $\gamma = 1/\psi$ is the case of power utility. The cases $\psi = 1$ and $\gamma = 1$, drawn as vertical and horizontal lines, respectively, are both important. When $\psi = 1$ the consumption-wealth ratio is constant, while when $\gamma = 1$ the investment horizon has no effect on portfolio choice (portfolio choice is "myopic"), as discussed in Chapter 9. The special case of log utility has $\psi = \gamma = 1$ and is the point where all these lines cross.

Epstein-Zin preferences violate the independence axiom of von Neumann-Morgenstern utility discussed in Chapter 1. Agents with Epstein-Zin preferences are not indifferent to the timing of the resolution of uncertainty as the independence axiom requires. However, these preferences do imply dynamically consistent decision making (Backus, Routledge, and Zin 2004).

When $\gamma > 1/\psi$ (i.e., we are above or to the right of the hyperbola in Figure 6.2), agents are more concerned about uncertainty than they are about predictable variation in consumption. They therefore prefer early resolution of uncertainty about future consumption paths, because early resolution transforms uncertainty into predictable consumption variation. Epstein, Farhi, and Strzalecki (2014) argue that points far above the hyperbola in the figure (e.g., the cases of $\psi = 1$ or 1.5 and $\gamma = 7.5$ or 10 proposed by

Bansal and Yaron 2004) imply that investors have unrealistically high willingness to pay for early resolution. Problem 6.2 asks you to recreate some parts of their analysis.

Conversely, if $\gamma < 1/\psi$ (i.e., we are below or to the left of the hyperbola in Figure 6.2), agents prefer late resolution of uncertainty. However, the empirical literature has concentrated on the case $\gamma > 1/\psi$ for reasons that we now discuss.

6.4.1 Deriving the SDF for Epstein-Zin Preferences

Because Epstein-Zin preferences are time-nonseparable, we need to write the first-order conditions for intertemporal choice in a more general way than has been required thus far. In a discrete-state contingent-claim model of the sort we considered in Chapter 4, the first-order condition for an investor who can freely trade in the contingent claim for state s at price $q(s)$ (where s indexes the possible states at time $t+1$ conditional on the state at time t) is

$$q(s) \frac{\partial U_t}{\partial C_t} = \frac{\partial U_t}{\partial C_{t+1}(s)}, \tag{6.37}$$

since the investor equates the marginal utility of consumption today with the marginal utility, evaluated today, of an extra dollar spent on the state-s contingent claim.

Under Epstein-Zin preferences (6.34), and using the fact that $q(s) = \pi(s)M_{t+1}(s)$, this condition becomes

$$M_{t+1} = \delta \left(\frac{C_{t+1}}{C_t}\right)^{-\frac{1}{\psi}} \left(\frac{U_{t+1}}{E_t(U_{t+1}^{1-\gamma})^{\frac{1}{1-\gamma}}}\right)^{-\left(\gamma-\frac{1}{\psi}\right)}$$

$$= \delta\Gamma_t \left(\frac{C_{t+1}}{C_t}\right)^{-\gamma} \left(\frac{U_{t+1}}{C_{t+1}}\right)^{-\left(\gamma-\frac{1}{\psi}\right)}, \tag{6.38}$$

where

$$\Gamma_t \equiv E_t \left[\left(\frac{C_{t+1}}{C_t}\right)^{1-\gamma} \left(\frac{U_{t+1}}{C_{t+1}}\right)^{1-\gamma}\right]^{\frac{1-\theta}{\theta}}. \tag{6.39}$$

The first equality in (6.38) shows that marginal utility at time $t+1$ is affected not only by shocks to consumption C_{t+1}, but also by shocks to continuation utility U_{t+1} relative to its expectation. The second equality writes all time-varying quantities known at time t in a single variable Γ_t, and renormalizes shocks to continuation utility by the level of consumption C_{t+1}. In the case where $\gamma = 1/\psi$, or equivalently $\theta = 1$, the extra terms involving continuation utility disappear.

Equation (6.38) has straightforward implications for the innovation in the log SDF (which determines risk premia in a lognormal model). We take logs of (6.38) and use a tilde to denote innovations relative to one-period-ahead expectations, that is, $\tilde{x}_{t+1} \equiv x_{t+1} - E_t x_{t+1}$, obtaining

$$\tilde{m}_{t+1} = -\gamma\tilde{c}_{t+1} - \left(\gamma - \frac{1}{\psi}\right)(\tilde{u}_{t+1} - \tilde{c}_{t+1}). \tag{6.40}$$

Using the Intertemporal Budget Constraint

The SDF stated in (6.38) and (6.40) is not usable for empirical work because continuation utility is unobservable. However, Epstein and Zin (1989, 1991) show that one can use the intertemporal budget constraint and dynamic programming methods to substitute out continuation utility, replacing it with realized consumption growth and the realized return on total wealth, both of which are in principle observable. Specifically, the intertemporal budget constraint for a representative agent can be written as

$$W_{t+1} = (1 + R_{w,t+1})\,(W_t - C_t),\tag{6.41}$$

where W_{t+1} is the representative agent's wealth, and $(1 + R_{w,t+1})$ is the gross simple return on the portfolio of all invested wealth. This form of the budget constraint is appropriate for a complete-markets model in which wealth includes human capital as well as financial assets.

Assuming this budget constraint, Epstein and Zin rewrite the SDF as

$$M_{t+1} = \left(\delta \left(\frac{C_{t+1}}{C_t}\right)^{-\frac{1}{\psi}}\right)^{\theta} \left(\frac{1}{1 + R_{w,t+1}}\right)^{1-\theta}.\tag{6.42}$$

In logs, and again using a tilde to denote innovations, this becomes

$$\widetilde{m}_{t+1} = -\theta \left(\frac{\widetilde{c}_{t+1}}{\psi}\right) - (1-\theta)\widetilde{r}_{w,t+1}.\tag{6.43}$$

The log SDF is negatively related to consumption growth scaled by the reciprocal of the EIS and to the return on aggregate wealth or equivalently the return on a claim on the infinite stream of all future consumption. These two terms are combined in a weighted average with weights θ and $1 - \theta$, respectively. In the power utility case where $\gamma = 1/\psi$, $\theta = 1$ and we have the standard consumption CAPM with power utility. In the case where the parameter $\gamma = 1$ and $\psi \neq 1$, $\theta = 0$ and the SDF places all the weight on the wealth portfolio return, in the spirit of the static CAPM.

Equation (6.43) is not suitable for analyzing the case where $\psi = 1$ and $\gamma \neq 1$, because in this case the composite parameter θ becomes infinite. This case must be analyzed using equation (6.36), or equations (6.49) or (6.53) derived below.

If asset returns and consumption are homoskedastic and jointly lognormal (an assumption we make for the rest of this subsection), equation (6.42) implies that the riskless real interest rate is

$$r_{f,t+1} = -\log \delta + \frac{1}{\psi}\,\mathrm{E}_t[\Delta c_{t+1}] - \frac{\theta}{2\psi^2}\,\sigma_c^2 + \frac{\theta-1}{2}\,\sigma_w^2,\tag{6.44}$$

where σ_c^2 is the variance of the innovation in log consumption and σ_w^2 is the variance of the innovation in the log return on wealth.

In the special case where $\psi = 1$, we have

$$r_{f,t+1} = -\log \delta + \mathrm{E}_t[\Delta c_{t+1}] - \left(\gamma - \frac{1}{2}\right)\sigma_c^2,\tag{6.45}$$

which depends only linearly on the coefficient of risk aversion γ and is a reasonable specification given empirical moments of consumption growth of the sort reported in

Table 6.1. This illustrates the possibility of using Epstein-Zin preferences to address the equity premium puzzle by increasing risk aversion, while avoiding the riskfree rate puzzle by leaving the EIS at or close to unity. Such a model has $\gamma > 1/\psi$ and hence involves a preference for early resolution of uncertainty.

The premium on risky assets, including the wealth portfolio itself, follows directly from (6.43) as

$$\mathrm{E}_t[r_{i,t+1}] - r_{f,t+1} + \frac{\sigma_i^2}{2} = \theta\,\frac{\sigma_{ic}}{\psi} + (1-\theta)\sigma_{iw}, \qquad (6.46)$$

where σ_{ic} and σ_{iw} denote the covariances between innovations in log returns on asset i and log consumption growth and the log wealth return, respectively. This again writes the Epstein-Zin model as a nesting of the consumption CAPM with power utility ($\theta = 1$) and the traditional static CAPM ($\theta = 0$).

Extended Consumption CAPM
This is not the end of the story, because the budget constraint restricts the behavior of consumption in relation to the wealth portfolio return, so innovations in consumption are linked to innovations in wealth, and consumption covariances σ_{ic} are linked to wealth covariances σ_{iw}. Once we take account of this, we can derive expressions for the log SDF and for risk premia that deliver new insights and that, unlike equation (6.46), are well behaved even in the case where $\psi = 1$ and $\gamma \neq 1$, and hence θ is infinite.

Specifically, the loglinear return approximation developed in section 5.3.1 can be used to write the unexpected log return on the wealth portfolio as

$$\widetilde{r}_{w,t+1} = (\mathrm{E}_{t+1} - \mathrm{E}_t)\sum_{j=0}^{\infty}\rho^j\Delta d_{w,t+1+j} - (\mathrm{E}_{t+1} - \mathrm{E}_t)\sum_{j=1}^{\infty}\rho^j r_{w,t+1+j}$$

$$= \widetilde{c}_{t+1} + \left(1 - \frac{1}{\psi}\right)\widetilde{g}_{t+1}, \qquad (6.47)$$

where $\widetilde{g}_{t+1}$ is news about future consumption growth:

$$\widetilde{g}_{t+1} = (\mathrm{E}_{t+1} - \mathrm{E}_t)\sum_{j=1}^{\infty}\rho^j\Delta c_{t+1+j}. \qquad (6.48)$$

The first equality in (6.47) applies equation (5.51) to the wealth portfolio return. The second equality uses the fact that the dividend on the wealth portfolio is aggregate consumption, and the implication of equations (6.44) and (6.46) that the expected log return on the wealth portfolio is a constant, plus $(1/\psi)$ times expected consumption growth.

The economic interpretation of equation (6.47) is that current consumption, the current dividend on the wealth portfolio, affects the value of wealth one-for-one if we hold fixed future consumption (dividend) growth. News about future consumption growth has offsetting effects on the value of wealth. It increases dividend growth one-for-one, but also increases the discount rate (the log expected return on wealth) $(1/\psi)$-for-one. The former effect dominates, so upward revisions in expected future consumption growth increase the value of wealth, if $(1/\psi) < 1$, that is, if the EIS $\psi > 1$. The latter effect dominates if the EIS $\psi < 1$, and the two effects cancel when $\psi = 1$, the special case where the wealth-consumption ratio is constant.

Substituting into equation (6.43), and using the relation between the parameters θ, γ, and ψ, we have

$$\widetilde{m}_{t+1} = -\gamma \, \widetilde{c}_{t+1} - \left(\gamma - \frac{1}{\psi} \right) \widetilde{g}_{t+1}. \tag{6.49}$$

The economic interpretation is that with Epstein-Zin utility, marginal utility moves not only with current consumption innovations but also with revisions in long-run expected future consumption growth. Whenever $\gamma > 1/\psi$, an increase in expected future consumption growth lowers marginal utility.

Equation (6.49) implies that in a conditionally lognormal model, the risk premium on any asset can be written as

$$\mathrm{E}_t[r_{i,t+1}] - r_{f,t+1} + \frac{\sigma_i^2}{2} = \gamma \, \sigma_{ic} + \left(\gamma - \frac{1}{\psi} \right) \sigma_{ig}, \tag{6.50}$$

where σ_{ig} is the covariance of the unexpected return on asset i with the revision in expected future consumption growth. This might be called an "extended consumption CAPM" because it nests the consumption CAPM with power utility and adds a term reflecting long-run growth risk. Restoy and Weil (2011), in a paper first written in the 1990s, originally derived this formula. It has attracted much more attention since Bansal and Yaron (2004), building on the work of Kandel and Stambaugh (1991), proposed a version of this model that adds changing variance (the "long-run risk" model, discussed in section 6.5).

Intertemporal CAPM
Campbell (1993) uses these relations in a different way. Instead of substituting the wealth return out of the Epstein-Zin model, he substitutes consumption out of the model to get a discrete-time version of the intertemporal CAPM of Merton (1973). The innovation in consumption is

$$\widetilde{c}_{t+1} = \widetilde{r}_{w,t+1} + (1 - \psi)\widetilde{h}_{t+1}, \tag{6.51}$$

where $\widetilde{h}_{t+1}$ is the innovation in expected future wealth returns, discount-rate news for the wealth portfolio:

$$\widetilde{h}_{t+1} = (\mathrm{E}_{t+1} - \mathrm{E}_t) \sum_{j=1}^{\infty} \rho^j r_{w,t+1+j}. \tag{6.52}$$

The economic intuition is that the current wealth return has a one-for-one effect on desired consumption, holding fixed future returns, which follows from the scale independence of the Epstein-Zin utility function. Expected future wealth returns have offsetting income and substitution effects on desired consumption, with strength 1 and $-\psi$, respectively. The two effects cancel in the special case $\psi = 1$ where the consumption-wealth ratio is constant. The letter h is used here as a mnemonic for hedging demand (Merton 1973), a term commonly used in the finance literature to describe the component of asset demand that is determined by investors' responses to changing investment opportunities.

Substituting (6.51) into (6.43), the innovation in the log SDF can be written as

$$\tilde{m}_{t+1} = -\gamma\,\tilde{r}_{w,t+1} - (\gamma - 1)\tilde{h}_{t+1}. \tag{6.53}$$

It follows immediately that the risk premium on any asset can be written as

$$\mathrm{E}_t[r_{i,t+1}] - r_{f,t+1} + \frac{\sigma_i^2}{2} = \gamma\sigma_{iw} + (\gamma - 1)\sigma_{ih}. \tag{6.54}$$

This is an intertemporal CAPM as in Merton (1973), which nests the traditional CAPM and adds a term reflecting covariance with changing investment opportunities. The risk premium on any asset is the coefficient of risk aversion γ times the covariance of that asset with the return on the wealth portfolio, plus $(\gamma - 1)$ times the covariance of the asset with revisions in expected future returns on wealth. The second term is zero if $\gamma = 1$; in this case, it is well known that intertemporal hedging demands are zero and asset pricing is myopic. We discuss this model further in Chapter 9.

6.5 Long-Run Risk Models

Bansal and Yaron (2004) have argued that the extended consumption CAPM of section 6.4.1 can solve the equity premium, riskfree rate, and equity volatility puzzles if one assumes that a representative agent has Epstein-Zin preferences with moderately high risk aversion and a high EIS greater than one, and that aggregate consumption growth is both persistent and conditionally heteroskedastic. Models with these features have come to be called "long-run risk" models. The long-run risk literature is voluminous, with an early foundation by Kandel and Stambaugh (1991) and notable contributions by Hansen, Heaton, and Li (2008) and Bansal, Kiku, and Yaron (2012) among others. To develop understanding of the long-run risk paradigm, we first explore the implications of predictable consumption growth in a homoskedastic model, then discuss the effect on asset prices of a permanent once-and-for-all change in consumption volatility, and finally discuss empirical specifications with both predictable consumption growth and conditional heteroskedasticity of consumption.

6.5.1 Predictable Consumption Growth

We return to the extended consumption CAPM of section 6.4.1 and assume that there are shocks to expected future consumption growth so that revisions in the present discounted value of expected consumption growth rates, $\tilde{g}_{t+1}$ from equation (6.48), have a nonzero volatility. For simplicity assume that these shocks to expected future consumption growth are uncorrelated with shocks to current consumption. Then, from equations (6.47) and (6.50), the risk premium on the aggregate wealth portfolio is

$$\mathrm{E}_t[r_{w,t+1}] - r_{f,t+1} + \frac{\sigma_w^2}{2} = \gamma\sigma_c^2 + \left(\gamma - \frac{1}{\psi}\right)\left(1 - \frac{1}{\psi}\right)\sigma_g^2. \tag{6.55}$$

The first term is small for moderate levels of risk aversion, given the low volatility of aggregate consumption growth. However, the second term can be large if the present value of revisions in expected consumption growth has a large variance σ_g^2. Given that the revision in the expectation of any single future consumption growth rate cannot be more volatile than the consumption growth rate itself, this requires revisions in the same direction in many future consumption growth rates; that is, it requires persistent shocks to consumption growth.

In order for such shocks to increase the risk premium on the wealth portfolio, we require that $\gamma > 1/\psi$ so investors are averse to assets whose returns covary positively with expected future consumption growth, and that $1 - 1/\psi > 0$ (or equivalently the EIS $\psi > 1$) so the aggregate wealth return covaries positively with expected consumption growth.[7]

The second condition is needed because, as discussed earlier in explaining equation (6.47), an increase in future consumption growth has offsetting effects on the value of wealth. On the one hand, consumption is the dividend of the aggregate wealth portfolio, so rapid future consumption growth increases future dividends and increases the value of wealth today. On the other hand, rapid consumption growth increases interest rates (and all other discount rates given that the model is homoskedastic so risk premia are constant). This discount-rate effect is inversely proportional to the EIS. When the EIS is one, the two effects cancel; the wealth-consumption ratio is constant and the wealth portfolio has zero covariance with expected future consumption growth given the sim-plifying assumption that current consumption innovations are uncorrelated with growth innovations. When the EIS is less than one, the discount-rate effect dominates so the wealth-consumption ratio falls when expected consumption growth increases. Only if the EIS is greater than one does an expected consumption boom increase the value of wealth today.

These results can be generalized to claims whose log dividends are proportional to log consumption rather than equal to it, including real bonds that pay fixed log dividends. Problem 6.3 asks you to analyze the pricing of such claims—which are sometimes interpreted as levered equities—in the context considered here.

A homoskedastic model with consumption growth shocks and an EIS greater than one faces two empirical difficulties that are discussed by Campbell (2003) and Beeler and Campbell (2012). First, this model implies that the log wealth-consumption ratio, or equivalently the log price-dividend ratio on the aggregate wealth portfolio, satisfies

$$w_t - c_t = \left(1 - \frac{1}{\psi}\right) \mathrm{E}_t \sum_{j=0}^{\infty} \rho^j \Delta c_{t+1+j}, \qquad (6.56)$$

where a constant has been omitted for simplicity. This equation follows from the Campbell-Shiller formula (5.47), applied to the wealth portfolio whose dividend is consumption and whose expected return is a constant plus $(1/\psi)$ times expected consumption growth.

Unfortunately, there is little evidence that either the dividend-price ratio on the stock market or the consumption-wealth ratio measured directly (Lettau and Ludvigson 2001a), predict long-run consumption growth in the manner required by the model. Beeler and Campbell (2012), for example, report a 0.0% R^2 statistic in a regression of five-year aggregate consumption growth on the log price-dividend ratio in US data over the period 1930–2008. Simulations of the calibrated model of Bansal and Yaron (2004)

---

[7]The opposite pair of assumptions, $\gamma < 1/\psi$ and $\psi < 1$, would also work but these assumptions force risk aversion to be quite low unless the EIS is extremely small.

have a median R^2 statistic of 28.5%, and only 0.1% of these simulations have explanatory power as low as in the data.

Second, a high EIS in a homoskedastic consumption-based model implies that the real interest rate should be perfectly correlated with, but less volatile than, predictable consumption growth. Hansen and Singleton (1983), followed by Hall (1988), Campbell and Mankiw (1989), and others, used an instrumental variables (IV) regression approach to estimate the elasticity of intertemporal substitution from the homoskedastic Euler equation. One way to run the regression is as

$$r_{i,t+1} = \mu_i + \left(\frac{1}{\psi}\right) \Delta c_{t+1} + \eta_{i,t+1}. \tag{6.57}$$

In general, the error term $\eta_{i,t+1}$ will be correlated with realized consumption growth, so OLS is not an appropriate estimation method. However, $\eta_{i,t+1}$ is uncorrelated with any variables in the information set at time t. Hence, any lagged variables correlated with asset returns can be used as instruments in an IV regression to estimate $1/\psi$. Alternatively, one can reverse the regression and estimate

$$\Delta c_{t+1} = \tau_i + \psi r_{i,t+1} + \zeta_{i,t+1}. \tag{6.58}$$

If the orthogonality conditions hold, then the estimate of ψ in (6.58) will asymptotically be the reciprocal of the estimate of $1/\psi$ in (6.57). In a finite sample, however, Staiger and Stock (1997) have shown that the IV estimator is poorly behaved if the right-hand-side variable is difficult to predict. If the Euler equation holds and ψ is small, there is little predictable variation in consumption growth relative to the predictable variation in the real interest rate, so it is better to estimate (6.58); however, if ψ is large, the opposite is true and it is better to estimate (6.57).

Hall (1988) estimated an extremely small value of ψ using this approach. Campbell and Mankiw (1989) found some predictability of consumption growth associated with predictable income growth, but little predictable variation associated with interest rates, again implying a low ψ. Campbell (2003) summarizes these results and finds similar patterns in international data.

Both these problems have the same root cause, namely that there is no strong evidence for the persistent predictable variation in consumption growth that is needed to increase the Epstein-Zin equity premium above the low value implied by a standard model with power utility.

6.5.2 Heteroskedastic Consumption

The model of Bansal and Yaron (2004) allows for conditional heteroskedasticity in consumption, and this turns out to be extremely important for the empirical performance of the model. Subsequent work, for example by Lettau, Ludvigson, and Wachter (2008) and Bansal, Kiku, and Yaron (2012), has increased the persistence of consumption volatility to further increase its effect on asset prices.

To understand the importance of changing consumption risk, in this subsection we look at the effect on asset prices of a once-and-for-all permanent change in consumption volatility. This comparative static analysis provides insight into the numerical results that the literature reports for conditionally heteroskedastic consumption models.

We consider a simple case where c_t follows a random walk with drift:

$$\Delta c_t = g + \varepsilon_t. \tag{6.59}$$

Thus we are abstracting from the persistent growth shocks considered in the previous subsection. The variance of the consumption shock is written as σ^2.

With Epstein-Zin utility and a random walk for consumption, the expected return on the aggregate wealth portfolio is

$$\mathrm{E}_t r_{w,t+1} = -\log \delta + \frac{g}{\psi} - \frac{\sigma^2}{2}\left(1 - \frac{1}{\psi}\right)(1-\gamma). \tag{6.60}$$

Once again we apply the Campbell-Shiller formula (5.47) to the wealth portfolio, whose dividend is consumption and whose expected return is given by (6.60). Suppressing terms unrelated to the consumption growth process for economy of notation, we have

$$p_{wt} - d_{wt} = w_t - c_t = \left(\frac{1}{1-\rho}\right)\left(1 - \frac{1}{\psi}\right)\left(g + \frac{\sigma^2}{2}(1-\gamma)\right). \tag{6.61}$$

If we increase variance σ^2 while holding g constant, the wealth-consumption ratio increases if $(1 - 1/\psi)$ and $(1 - \gamma)$ have the same sign, as will be the case under power utility. To get consumption claim prices to fall when variance increases, we need $(1-1/\psi)$ and $(1 - \gamma)$ to have opposite signs; that is, we need $\psi > 1$ if $\gamma > 1$, and $\psi < 1$ if $\gamma < 1$.

What is the intuition for this requirement? If volatility increases, holding geometric mean consumption growth constant, the arithmetic mean consumption growth rate increases. As discussed in section 2.1.4, a representative agent perceives an improvement in investment opportunities if $\gamma < 1$ (because the arithmetic mean growth rate increase outweighs the increase in risk) and a deterioration if $\gamma > 1$. If $\psi > 1$, the agent has strong intertemporal substitution in response to improved investment opportunities and lowers her consumption relative to wealth, driving up wealth for given consumption. If $\psi < 1$, intertemporal substitution is weak and the income effect of improved investment opportunities dominates; the agent increases her consumption relative to wealth, driving down wealth for given consumption. Combining these considerations, we need ψ and γ to be on the same side of unity to get wealth to fall when volatility increases.

This analysis simplifies if we fix arithmetic average consumption growth, $g + \sigma^2/2$, rather than geometric average consumption growth g. In this case stock prices increase with volatility if $(1 - 1/\psi)$ is negative and decrease if it is positive, that is, if $\psi > 1$. The intuition is that with fixed arithmetic average consumption growth, an increase in volatility is unambiguously a deterioration in investment opportunities, so we need only look at ψ to sign the effect. However, the magnitude of the effect is increasing in risk aversion as one would expect.

The fact that consumption volatility drives down wealth only when the EIS $\psi > 1$ is perhaps the most powerful argument for this parameter choice. The recent experience of the global financial crisis, when consumption volatility increased while aggregate wealth declined, has contributed to the popularity of this preference specification. However, financial assets may not correspond directly to aggregate wealth but may be better modeled as a levered claim on aggregate consumption. Problem 6.4 asks you to consider how leverage, modeled as a log dividend proportional to log consumption rather than equal to it, alters the effect of volatility on financial asset prices in a simple model with power utility.

6.5.3 Empirical Specification

The empirical model calibrated by Bansal and Yaron (BY 2004) and Bansal, Kiku, and Yaron (BKY 2012) can be written as follows:

$$\Delta c_{t+1} = \mu_c + x_t + \sigma_t \eta_{t+1},$$

$$x_{t+1} = \rho_x x_t + \varphi_e \sigma_t e_{t+1},$$

$$\sigma_{t+1}^2 = \overline{\sigma}^2 + \nu\left(\sigma_t^2 - \overline{\sigma}^2\right) + \sigma_w w_{t+1},$$

$$\Delta d_{t+1} = \mu_d + \phi x_t + \varphi \sigma_t u_{t+1} + \pi \sigma_t \eta_{t+1}. \tag{6.62}$$

Here, the shocks w_{t+1}, e_{t+1}, u_{t+1}, and η_{t+1} are iid standard normal random variables. Consumption and dividend growth are modeled as separate processes denoted by Δc_{t+1} and Δd_{t+1}, respectively. x_t is a persistently varying component of the expected consumption growth rate. σ_t^2 is the conditional variance of consumption, also persistently time-varying, with unconditional mean $\overline{\sigma}^2$. The variance process can take negative values, but this will happen only with small probability if the mean is high enough relative to the volatility of variance. Dividends are imperfectly correlated with consumption, but their growth rate Δd_{t+1} shares the same persistent and predictable component x_t scaled by a parameter ϕ, and the conditional volatility of dividend growth is proportional to the conditional volatility of consumption growth.[4] The representative investor is assumed to have Epstein-Zin preferences with risk aversion of 10 and EIS of 1.5.

The literature solves the model using loglinear analytical approximations of the sort used elsewhere in this chapter and in earlier chapters. These approximations imply that the log wealth-consumption ratio for a consumption claim and the log price-dividend ratio for a dividend claim are linear in the conditional mean and variance of consumption growth, the two state variables of the model. The unknown parameters of these linear relationships can be solved analytically given parameters of loglinearization, and the parameters of loglinearization can be solved numerically given the other parameters of the model. One can iterate until convergence to obtain an accurate approximate solution.

Two key parameters of the empirical model (6.62) are the persistence of expected consumption growth, ρ_x, and the persistence of consumption variance, ν. The first parameter is calibrated to about 0.98 per month in both BY and BKY, implying a half-life for expected consumption growth between two and three years. The second parameter is about 0.99 per month in BY, implying a half-life for variance of about four years, and 0.999 per month in BKY, implying a half-life of almost 60 years. The greater persistence of volatility in BKY makes conditional heteroskedasticity much more important for asset prices in that model. This improves the fit of the BKY model to several aspects of the data.

---

[4]This process does not impose cointegration between consumption and dividends. Some more recent research, notably Bansal, Dittmar, and Kiku (2009) and Hansen, Heaton, and Li (2008), emphasizes such cointegration.

First, changing volatility affects the equity premium and the price-dividend ratio. This weakens the tight relationship between the price-dividend ratio and expected consumption growth in the homoskedastic model, illustrated in equation (6.56). Beeler and Campbell (2012) report that simulations of the BKY model have a median R^2 statistic of 8.5% in a regression of five-year consumption growth onto the price-dividend ratio, and 1.5% of the simulations have explanatory power as low as in the data. These results are better than those for the original BY model.

Second, the same mechanism helps to explain the ability of the price-dividend ratio to predict excess stock returns, discussed in Chapter 5. The R^2 of a regression of five-year excess stock returns onto the log price-dividend ratio is 26.9%, whereas the median simulated R^2 in the BKY model is 4.3%, and 4.4% of the simulations have a greater explanatory power than in the data. Thus the long-run predictability of excess returns is fairly modest in the BKY model.

Third, there is direct evidence that the price-dividend ratio predicts consumption volatility negatively. Beeler and Campbell report a 20.4% R^2 for a regression of five-year realized consumption volatility on the log price-dividend ratio, as compared with a median simulated R^2 in the BKY model of 13.2%. 34.7% of the simulations give higher explanatory power for consumption volatility than in the data, indicating that the BKY model captures this feature of the data well. A puzzle, however, is that the log price-dividend ratio does not predict stock return volatility well in the data, whereas it does do so in simulations of the BKY model.

Fourth, conditional heteroskedasticity invalidates the use of IV regressions like (6.58) and (6.57) to estimate the EIS. In the presence of conditional heteroskedasticity, the intercept of these equations should be time-varying, reflecting a time-varying desire for precautionary savings. This can lead to downward bias in the estimate of the EIS, although Beeler and Campbell find that the downward bias is negligible in the BY model and still modest even in the BKY model.

A final property of both the BY and BKY models is that they imply a downward-sloping term structure of real interest rates, because a decrease in expected future consumption growth lowers interest rates and increases bond prices; hence, bonds are good hedges against bad news about future consumption growth. We discuss this further in section 8.3.2.

The long-run risk literature has devoted increasing attention to a broader cross-section of assets beyond just the aggregate stock market and the term structure of real bonds. Parker and Julliard (2005), for example, observe that the covariance of stock returns with current and future consumption growth increases with the interval over which consumption growth is measured, and more steeply for value stocks than for growth stocks. This implies a higher risk premium for value stocks than in a power utility model whenever $\gamma > 1/\psi$ (and for this effect we do not need $\psi > 1$). Hansen, Heaton, and Li (2008) similarly analyze long-run consumption covariances for a variety of equity portfolios.

6.6 Ambiguity Aversion

The literature on ambiguity aversion, building on the insights of Knight (1921) and the experimental evidence of Ellsberg (1961), argues that investors handle uncertainty about models differently from uncertainty about outcomes within a model. Within a model, outcomes can be described by a probability distribution, but investors do not behave as if they have a subjective probability distribution over alternative models and therefore cannot be described as Bayesians in their response to model uncertainty or "ambiguity." Instead, authors such as Gilboa and Schmeidler (1989) and Klibanoff, Marinacci, and Mukerji (2005) have argued that investors behave conservatively with respect to ambiguity, acting as if a worst-case model is true. Epstein and Schneider (2010) offer a recent review.

In a series of papers summarized in a recent book, Hansen and Sargent (2008) have adapted an engineering literature on robust optimal control to develop one of the major paradigms of this literature. Strzalecki (2011) discusses the axiomatic foundation of their approach. The Hansen-Sargent specification of ambiguity aversion provides an alternative micro-foundation for Epstein-Zin preferences with EIS equal to one and risk aversion greater than one.

In the Hansen-Sargent framework, an investor has a reference model of the economy but chooses the actions that maximize expected utility in a "worst-reasonable-case" model that delivers the lowest expected utility within a set of models that do not deviate too far from the reference model. This can be interpreted as the outcome of a hypothetical game in which an investor chooses a decision rule and then a malevolent opponent chooses a model (subject to a penalty for unreasonable models) to minimize the expected utility that the investor derives from that decision rule. In such a game the investor chooses the decision rule that maximizes expected utility subject to the model choices of the malevolent player.

The Hansen-Sargent approach can also be justified intuitively as a way to find choices that will perform well within a set of models in the neighborhood of the reference model. In the words of Cagetti et al. (2002, p. 373), "As a vehicle to explore the directions in which a candidate decision rule is most fragile, the decision maker considers the model that delivers the worst utility. We are not saying that he believes that the true model is the worst one, but that by planning a best response against it, he can devise a rule that is robust under a set of models surrounding his approximating [reference] model."

A key issue is how the set of alternative models is constrained. Hansen and Sargent use relative entropy to measure the deviation of a model from the reference model. In a two-period discrete-state setting, if the reference model has state probabilities π_s and an alternative model has probabilities $\widehat{\pi}_s$, the relative entropy of the alternative model is defined as

$$\sum_{s=1}^{S} \widehat{\pi}_s \log \left(\frac{\widehat{\pi}_s}{\pi_s} \right) = \widehat{\mathrm{E}} \left[\log \left(\frac{\widehat{\pi}}{\pi} \right) \right] = \mathrm{E} \left[\left(\frac{\widehat{\pi}}{\pi} \right) \log \left(\frac{\widehat{\pi}}{\pi} \right) \right], \qquad (6.63)$$

which is always positive and increases with the variability of state-probability deviations between the two models. Hansen and Sargent impose a penalty on the malevolent player that is increasing in relative entropy, thereby keeping the model chosen by the malevolent player in the neighborhood of the reference model.

To understand the implications of this framework, first consider a static partial-equilibrium portfolio choice problem with a risky asset and a safe asset, where the reference model assigns a positive risk premium to the risky asset. If an investor chooses a large position in the risky asset, the malevolent agent will choose a model with a very low or even negative risk premium, implying very low expected utility. A small position in the risky asset, however, reduces the gain to the malevolent agent from distorting the risk premium (and in the extreme of a zero risky-asset position, there would be no gain).

Hence, given the entropy penalty on the malevolent agent, the solution features a small positive investment in the risky asset, just as if the investor were more risk-averse.[8]

To apply their framework to a consumption-based general-equilibrium asset pricing model with exogenous consumption, Hansen and Sargent assume that a representative agent has specified a reference model and uses it to form expectations. They define a nonnegative martingale $D_{t+1} = d_{t+1}D_t$, where $E_t d_{t+1} = 1$ and $d_{t+1} \geq 0$. (We use the letter d here as a mnemonic for "distortion.") They assume that the representative agent evaluates a given consumption path $\{c_t\}$, that is, a given process for consumption under the reference model, using log utility and a "worst-case" assumption about the shocks d_{t+1} with a penalty for the entropy of the shocks:

$$V_0\left(\{c_t\}\right) = \min_{\{d_{t+1}\}} E_0 \sum_{t=0}^{\infty} \delta^t D_t [c_t + \delta \lambda E_t (d_{t+1} \log d_{t+1})], \tag{6.64}$$

where expectations are taken under the reference model. The constraints on the problem are the properties of d_{t+1}: $E_t d_{t+1} = 1$ and $d_{t+1} \geq 0$.

To understand this expression, note first that it is a minimization problem because a malevolent player is assumed to pick the shocks to minimize the representative agent's utility. Note second that multiplying a random variable ε_{t+1} by d_{t+1} can be interpreted as changing the conditional probabilities of each possible realization of ε_{t+1} to distorted pseudo-probabilities. This is true because of the restrictions $E_t d_{t+1} = 1$ and $d_{t+1} \geq 0$. (In the two-period, discrete-state setting of equation (6.63), $d(s) = \widehat{\pi}_s / \pi_s$.)

According to the definition of the entropy of a random variable that we discussed in section 4.3.3, the entropy of d_{t+1} is $\log E_t d_{t+1} - E_t \log d_{t+1} = -E_t \log d_{t+1}$ given that $E_t d_{t+1} = 1$. Here we use the version of entropy introduced in equation (6.63), $\widehat{E}_t \log d_{t+1} = E_t d_{t+1} \log d_{t+1}$, where $\widehat{E}_t$ denotes the pseudo-expectation calculated using distorted probabilities. Both these versions of entropy are positive: as an informal exercise, we ask you to construct a simple argument showing this. The objective function penalizes entropy by multiplying it by a penalty coefficient λ that can be interpreted as a Lagrange multiplier on an entropy constraint.

For simplicity, assume that the reference model is a random walk with drift for log consumption:

$$c_{t+1} = c_t + \mu + \sigma \varepsilon_{t+1}, \tag{6.65}$$

where ε_{t+1} is a standard normal random variable.

Under this assumption, the only state variable of the problem is c_t, so we can write the Bellman equation as

$$V(c_t) = c_t + \delta \min_{\{d_{t+1}\}} E_t [d_{t+1} V(c_t + \mu + \sigma \varepsilon_{t+1}) + \lambda d_{t+1} \log d_{t+1}], \tag{6.66}$$

or more compactly as

$$V_t = c_t + \delta \min_{\{d_{t+1}\}} E_t [d_{t+1} V_{t+1} + \lambda d_{t+1} \log d_{t+1}]. \tag{6.67}$$

---

[8]An alternative implementation of ambiguity aversion, due to Gilboa and Schmeidler (1989) and Epstein and Wang (1994), can even generate a worst-case model with a zero equity premium, implying nonparticipation in risky asset markets—which would require infinite risk aversion in a standard model. We discuss nonparticipation in section 10.2.

Now we rewrite the constrained minimization problem in Lagrangian form as

$$\min_{\{d_{t+1}\}} E_t[d_{t+1} V_{t+1} + \lambda d_{t+1} \log d_{t+1} + \kappa(d_{t+1} - 1)], \tag{6.68}$$

where κ is the Lagrange multiplier on the constraint that $E_t d_{t+1} = 1$. The first-order condition for this minimization problem is

$$E_t[V_{t+1} + \lambda \log d_{t+1} + (\lambda + \kappa)] = 0, \tag{6.69}$$

which implies

$$\log d_{t+1} = \frac{-V_{t+1}}{\lambda} - \frac{(\lambda + \kappa)}{\lambda}. \tag{6.70}$$

Exponentiating, we have

$$d_{t+1} \frac{\exp(-V_{t+1}/\lambda)}{E_t \exp(-V_{t+1}/\lambda)}, \tag{6.71}$$

where the denominator imposes the constraint that $E_t d_{t+1} = 1$.

We can substitute this solution for d_{t+1} into the Bellman equation and simplify. We obtain

$$V_t = c_t - \delta \lambda \log E_t \exp\left(\frac{-V_{t+1}}{\lambda}\right), \tag{6.72}$$

which is exactly the same formula as for Epstein-Zin preferences with EIS = 1, equation (6.36). Since $\lambda > 0$ here, the ambiguity-averse model corresponds to relative risk aversion greater than one in the Epstein-Zin model. Maenhout (2004) makes a similar point, and Hansen and Sargent (2008, Chapter 14) show how to generalize this argument for an arbitrary loglinear consumption process.

If we guess that V_t takes the linear form $V_t = A + Bc_t$, we can solve the above recursion for A and $B = 1/(1-\delta)$. It follows that

$$V_{t+1} = A + \frac{c_t + \mu + \sigma \varepsilon_{t+1}}{1-\delta}, \tag{6.73}$$

and

$$d_{t+1} = K \exp\left(\frac{-\sigma \varepsilon_{t+1}}{(1-\delta)\lambda}\right), \tag{6.74}$$

where K is a constant.

Recall that multiplying ε_{t+1} by d_{t+1} is equivalent to changing the probabilities of different realizations of ε_{t+1}. The probability density for ε_{t+1} is the standard normal density $\pi(\varepsilon_{t+1})$ which is proportional to $\exp(-\varepsilon_{t+1}^2/2)$. The distorted probability density $\widehat{\pi}(\varepsilon_{t+1})$ then satisfies

$$\widehat{\pi}(\varepsilon_{t+1}) \propto \exp\left(\frac{-\varepsilon_{t+1}^2}{2}\right) \exp\left(\frac{-\sigma \varepsilon_{t+1}}{(1-\delta)\lambda}\right) \propto \exp\left(\frac{-\left(\varepsilon_{t+1} + \frac{\sigma}{(1-\delta)\lambda}\right)^2}{2}\right), \tag{6.75}$$

so the distorted beliefs lower the mean of the standard normal random variable ε_{t+1} from zero under the reference model to $-\sigma/(1-\delta)\lambda$ under the worst-case model. (Multiplying by d_{t+1} does not change the variance of ε_{t+1} because we have made assumptions to get a linear value function. A similar result holds in continuous-time diffusion models, where changes of measure affect only drifts and not diffusion coefficients.) The worst-case model is more pessimistic when consumption volatility is greater, and when the entropy penalty parameter λ is smaller. This result illustrates the point made in Chapter 4 that the stochastic discount factor reflects both preferences and beliefs, so that ambiguity aversion can be thought of either as an increase in effective risk aversion, or as a pessimistic shift in beliefs about the process generating consumption.

In the example above, ambiguity aversion alters the investor's assumption about mean consumption growth but does not affect the assumed serial correlation of consumption growth. Bidder and Dew-Becker (2016) present an alternative framework in which an investor with Epstein-Zin preferences, whose reference model has unpredictable consumption growth, uses a worst-reasonable-case model that resembles the Bansal and Yaron (2004) long-run risk model, where shocks to consumption growth are persistent.

The literature on ambiguity aversion blurs the distinctions between positive and normative economics, and between rational and irrational decision-making. Conservative pessimism can be treated as a positive prediction about investor behavior, but some authors have defended it as a normatively justifiable ("robust") response to model uncertainty. This contrasts with the behavioral finance literature, in which some investors are regarded as having beliefs or behaviors that do objective damage to their interests.

Related to this, Hansen and Sargent suggest that a statistical approach can be used to choose the size of the entropy penalty in their framework. The worst-case model can be chosen to be rejectable at some critical value, say 5%, given a sample of a fixed size generated by the reference model. In this way the deviation of investor beliefs from the reference model can be kept at a normatively defensible level given the data available to the investor. This, and the related issue of how conservatism varies over time in a dynamic model, are active areas of current research.

6.7 Habit Formation

We now consider models of habit formation, in which the marginal utility of consumption depends not on the absolute level of consumption, but on consumption relative to a stochastic "habit" process that is related to the history of consumption.

Several modeling issues arise at the outset. Writing the period utility function as $u(C_t, X_t)$, where X_t is the time-varying habit or subsistence level, the first issue is the functional form for $u(\cdot)$. Abel (1990, 1999) proposed that $u(\cdot)$ should be a power function of the ratio C_t/X_t, while Constantinides (1990), Campbell and Cochrane (1999), and others have used a power function of the difference $C_t - X_t$. The second issue is the effect of an agent's own decisions on future levels of habit. In standard "internal habit" models such as Constantinides (1990), habit depends on an agent's own consumption and the agent takes account of this when choosing how much to consume. In "external habit" models such as those in Abel (1990, 1999) and Campbell and Cochrane (1999), habit depends on aggregate consumption which is unaffected by any one agent's decisions. Abel calls this "catching up with the Joneses." The third issue is the speed with which habit reacts to individual or aggregate consumption. Analysis is often more tractable if habit depends on a single lag of consumption, but slower adjustment enables habit-formation models to better fit asset price fluctuations at business-cycle and lower frequencies.

6.7.1 A Ratio Model of Habit

The choice between ratio models and difference models of habit is important because ratio models have constant risk aversion whereas difference models have time-varying risk aversion. To see this, consider Abel's (1990) specification in which an agent's utility can be written as a power function of the ratio C_t/X_t,

$$U_t = \sum_{j=0}^{\infty} \delta^j \frac{(C_{t+j}/X_{t+j})^{1-\gamma} - 1}{1 - \gamma}, \tag{6.76}$$

where X_t summarizes the influence of past consumption levels on today's utility. For simplicity and to keep the model conditionally lognormal, specify X_t as an external habit depending on only one lag of aggregate consumption:

$$X_t = \overline{C}_{t-1}^{\kappa}, \tag{6.77}$$

where $\overline{C}_{t-1}$ is aggregate past consumption and the parameter κ governs the degree of time-nonseparability. Since there is a representative agent, in equilibrium aggregate consumption equals the agent's own consumption, so

$$X_t = C_{t-1}^{\kappa}. \tag{6.78}$$

With this specification of utility, in equilibrium the stochastic discount factor is

$$M_{t+1} = \delta \left(\frac{C_t}{C_{t-1}} \right)^{\kappa(\gamma-1)} \left(\frac{C_{t+1}}{C_t} \right)^{-\gamma}. \tag{6.79}$$

Assuming homoskedasticity and joint lognormality of asset returns and consumption growth, this implies the following riskless real interest rate:

$$r_{f,t+1} = -\log \delta - \gamma^2 \sigma_c^2/2 + \gamma \, \mathrm{E}_t \Delta c_{t+1} - \kappa (\gamma - 1) \Delta c_t, \tag{6.80}$$

Equation (6.80) says that the riskless real interest rate equals its value under power utility, less $\kappa (\gamma - 1) \Delta c_t$. Holding consumption today and expected consumption tomorrow constant, an increase in consumption yesterday increases the marginal utility of consumption today whenever risk aversion $\gamma > 1$. This makes the representative agent want to borrow from the future, driving up the real interest rate.

Although the ratio model of habit alters the riskless real rate, it does not change the risk premium because the innovation in the log SDF implied by equation (6.79) is just the usual

$$\widetilde{m}_{t+1} = -\gamma \, \Delta \widetilde{c}_{t+1}, \tag{6.81}$$

which implies that the expected excess return on any risky asset over the riskless rate, adjusted for Jensen's Inequality, satisfies the standard risk premium formula for power utility: $E_t[r_{i,t+1} - r_{f,t+1}] + \sigma_i^2/2 = \gamma \sigma_{ic}$. The external habit simply adds a term to the SDF (6.79) which is known at time t, and this does not affect the risk premium for an asset with a given consumption covariance.

The volatility of the riskless real interest rate in (6.80) illustrates a challenge for habit formation models as Abel (1999) points out. Time-nonseparable preferences make marginal utility volatile even when the path of consumption is smooth, because consumers derive utility from consumption relative to its recent history rather than from the absolute level of consumption. But unless the consumption and habit processes take particular forms, time-nonseparability also creates large swings in expected marginal utility at successive dates, and this implies large movements in the real interest rate. I now present an alternative specification in which it is possible to solve this problem, and in which risk aversion varies over time.

6.7.2 The Campbell-Cochrane Model

Campbell and Cochrane (CC 1999) argue that many aspects of aggregate stock market behavior can be explained by a representative agent model in which utility arises from the difference between consumption and a time-varying habit level. To simplify the calculation of marginal utility they assume that habit is external, and to highlight the effects of habit formation on asset prices they assume that there is no predictable variation or heteroskedasticity in consumption growth so that the consumption-wealth ratio would be constant in a power-utility model. The consumption growth process is

$$\Delta c_{t+1} = g + \epsilon_{c,t+1}, \tag{6.82}$$

where $\epsilon_{c,t+1}$ is a normal homoskedastic innovation with variance σ_c^2.

The utility function of the representative agent takes the form

$$E_t \sum_{j=0}^{\infty} \delta^j \frac{(C_{t+j} - X_{t+j})^{1-\gamma} - 1}{1 - \gamma}. \tag{6.83}$$

Here X_t is the level of habit, δ is the subjective discount factor, and γ is the utility curvature parameter. Utility depends on a power function of the difference between consumption and habit; it is only defined when consumption exceeds habit.

It is convenient to capture the relation between consumption and habit by the surplus consumption ratio S_t, defined by

$$S_t \equiv \frac{C_t - X_t}{C_t}. \tag{6.84}$$

The surplus consumption ratio is the fraction of consumption that exceeds habit and is therefore available to generate utility in (6.83).

If habit X_t is held fixed as consumption C_t varies, the local coefficient of relative risk aversion is

$$\frac{-Cu_{CC}}{u_C} = \frac{\gamma}{S_t}, \tag{6.85}$$

where u_C and u_{CC} are the first and second derivatives of period utility with respect to consumption. Risk aversion rises as the surplus consumption ratio S_t declines—that is, as consumption approaches the habit level—because given proportional movements in consumption have larger effects on surplus consumption and hence on utility when the surplus consumption ratio is low. Importantly γ, the curvature parameter in utility, is no longer the coefficient of relative risk aversion in this model.

To complete the description of preferences, one must specify how the habit X_t evolves over time in response to aggregate consumption. CC suggest an AR(1) model for the log surplus consumption ratio, $s_t \equiv \log(S_t)$:

$$s_{t+1} = (1 - \varphi)\bar{s} + \varphi s_t + \lambda(s_t)\epsilon_{c,t+1}. \tag{6.86}$$

The parameter $\bar{s}$ defines the value of the log surplus consumption ratio in steady state. The parameter φ governs the persistence of the log surplus consumption ratio, while the "sensitivity function" $\lambda(s_t)$ controls the sensitivity of s_{t+1} and thus of log habit x_{t+1} to innovations in consumption growth $\epsilon_{c,t+1}$.

Linear Approximation of the Model
Equation (6.86) specifies that today's habit is a complex nonlinear function of current and past consumption. A linear approximation may help to understand it. If we substitute the definition $s_t \equiv \log(1 - \exp(x_t - c_t))$ into (6.86) and linearize around the steady state, we find that (6.86) is approximately a traditional habit-formation model in which log habit responds slowly and linearly to log consumption,

$$x_{t+1} \approx (1 - \varphi)\alpha + \varphi x_t + (1 - \varphi)c_t = \alpha + (1 - \varphi)\sum_{j=0}^{\infty} \varphi^j c_{t-j}. \tag{6.87}$$

The linear model (6.87) has two serious problems. First, when consumption follows an exogenous process such as (6.82) there is nothing to stop consumption falling below habit, in which case utility is undefined. This problem does not arise when one specifies a process for s_t, since any real value for s_t corresponds to positive S_t and hence $C_t > X_t$. Second, the linear model typically implies a highly volatile riskless real interest rate. The process (6.86) with a nonconstant sensitivity function $\lambda(s_t)$ allows one to control or even eliminate variation in the riskless interest rate.

Stochastic Discount Factor and Riskless Real Interest Rate
The marginal utility of consumption in the CC model is

$$u'(C_t) = (C_t - X_t)^{-\gamma} = S_t^{-\gamma} C_t^{-\gamma}, \tag{6.88}$$

and the stochastic discount factor is

$$M_{t+1} = \left(\frac{S_{t+1}}{S_t}\right)^{-\gamma} \left(\frac{C_{t+1}}{C_t}\right)^{-\gamma}. \tag{6.89}$$

This SDF can be volatile, generating significant risk premia, even if consumption growth is smooth, provided that the surplus consumption ratio varies sufficiently over time. The innovation in the log SDF is

$$\widetilde{m}_{t+1} = -\gamma(\widetilde{s}_{t+1} + \widetilde{c}_{t+1}) = -\gamma(1 + \lambda(s_t))\epsilon_{c,t+1}, \tag{6.90}$$

where the second equality uses equations (6.82) and (6.86).

Solving for the log riskless real interest rate in the usual fashion, we have

$$r_{f,t+1} = -\log(\delta) + \gamma g - \gamma (1 - \varphi)(s_t - \bar{s}) - \frac{\gamma^2 \sigma_c^2}{2}(1 + \lambda(s_t))^2. \tag{6.91}$$

The first two terms on the right-hand side of (6.91) are familiar from the power utility model (6.6), while the last two terms are new. The third term (linear in $(s_t - \bar{s})$) reflects intertemporal substitution. As an informal exercise, you are asked to explain how there can be an intertemporal substitution effect on the riskless interest rate given that log consumption growth is unpredictable in the CC model. The answer is given at the end of the chapter.

The fourth term (linear in $(1 + \lambda(s_t))^2$) reflects precautionary savings. As uncertainty increases, consumers become more willing to save and this drives down the equilibrium riskless interest rate. Note that what determines precautionary savings is uncertainty about marginal utility, not uncertainty about consumption itself. In this model the consumption process is homoskedastic so there is no time-variation in uncertainty about consumption; but habit formation makes a given level of consumption uncertainty more or less serious for marginal utility depending on the position of consumption relative to habit.

Equation (6.91) can be made to match the observed stability of the real interest rate in two ways. First, it is helpful if the habit persistence parameter φ is close to one, since this limits the strength of the time-varying intertemporal substitution effect (the third term in (6.91)). Second, this effect is offset by the precautionary savings effect (the fourth term in (6.91)) if $\lambda(s_t)$ declines with s_t. In fact, CC parameterize the $\lambda(s_t)$ function so that these two effects exactly offset each other everywhere, implying a constant riskless real interest rate and a degenerate term structure of interest rates.[9] With this parameterization, a given degree of consumption uncertainty has a more powerful effect on marginal utility when the surplus consumption ratio s_t is low and $\lambda(s_t)$ is high; this in turn implies a more volatile SDF and higher risk premia when surplus consumption is low.

Specification of the Sensitivity Function
The sensitivity function $\lambda(s_t)$ is not fully determined by the requirement of a constant riskless interest rate. CC choose the function to satisfy two additional conditions: (1) Habit is predetermined with respect to infinitesimal consumption shocks at the steady state, that is, $dx/dc = 0$ at $s_t = \bar{s}$. (2) Habit is predetermined with respect to such shocks near the steady state, that is, $d(dx/dc)/ds = 0$ at $s_t = \bar{s}$. These two conditions also guarantee that infinitesimal positive shocks to consumption may increase habit but never reduce it, that is, $dx/dc \geq 0$ everywhere, because $d^2(dx/dc)/ds^2 > 0$ so dx/dc is a U-shaped function of s_t that is tangent to the horizontal axis at the steady state $s_t = \bar{s}$.

To understand these conditions more intuitively, recall that the traditional notion of habit makes it a predetermined variable. On the other hand habit cannot be predetermined everywhere, or a sufficiently low realization of consumption growth would leave consumption below habit. To make habit "as predetermined as possible," CC assume

---

[9]The working paper version (Campbell and Cochrane 1995) shows how to generalize the model to make the log real interest rate linear in s_t. Wachter (2006) and Verdelhan (2010) develop this idea further, and we discuss Verdelhan's model in Chapter 8. See also Menzly, Santos, and Veronesi (2004).

that habit is predetermined at and near the steady state. This also ensures that positive infinitesimal shocks to consumption always increase welfare and never cause habit to decline.

CC use these conditions to show that the steady-state surplus consumption ratio must be a function of the other parameters of the model,

$$\overline{S} = \sigma_c \sqrt{\frac{\gamma}{1 - \phi}}, \tag{6.92}$$

and the sensitivity function $\lambda(s_t)$ must take the particular form

$$\lambda(s_t) = \frac{1}{\overline{S}} \sqrt{1 - 2(s_t - \overline{s})} - 1, \tag{6.93}$$

provided that $\lambda(s_t) \geq 0$, and $\lambda(s_t) = 0$ otherwise. The surplus consumption ratio has a lower bound at zero, and an upper bound at the point where the right-hand side of (6.93) equals zero.

The calibrated sensitivity function is illustrated in Figure 6.3. The sensitivity function declines with the surplus consumption ratio, reaches zero at the upper bound, and increases to infinity as the surplus consumption ratio approaches its lower bound. The steady-state surplus consumption ratio is marked with a vertical line in the figure. The derivative of habit with respect to contemporaneous consumption shocks, dx/dc, is zero at the steady state, and increases on either side of it, reaching one at the lower and upper bound. This implies that whenever consumption gets too close to habit or too far away from it, habit becomes more sensitive to consumption shocks so that consumption can never fall below habit or violate the upper bound for the surplus consumption ratio.

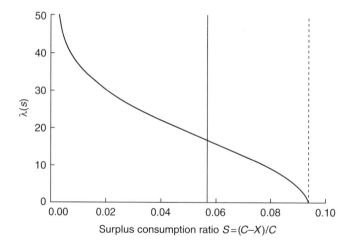

Figure 6.3. *Sensitivity Function* (Campbell, John Y., and John H. Cochrane, 1999, "By Force of Habit: A Consumption-Based Explanation of Aggregate Stock Market Behavior," *Journal of Political Economy* 107, 205–251; reprinted by permission of the University of Chicago Press.)

Ljungqvist and Uhlig (2015) point out that the nice properties of the CC specification apply only to infinitesimal consumption shocks. A social planner who has the ability
to create a large temporary downward jump in consumption through a discrete destruction of endowment might choose to do so, in part because habit may decline both as
the endowment falls and as the endowment recovers afterward. Campbell and Cochrane
(2015) respond by showing how the model can be rewritten in continuous time to avoid
such problems.

Fitting Asset Prices
With the above specification of the sensitivity function, equations (6.90), (6.92), and
(6.93) imply that the standard deviation of the innovation to the log SDF is

$$\sigma_m = \gamma \, \sigma_c (1 + \lambda(s_t)) = \frac{\gamma \, \sigma_c}{\bar{S}} \sqrt{1 - 2(s_t - \bar{s})}. \tag{6.94}$$

At the steady state, this equals $\gamma \, \sigma_c / \bar{S} = \sqrt{\gamma \, (1 - \phi)}$, and at the upper bound for the surplus
consumption ratio it falls to $\gamma \, \sigma_c$, which would be the value under power utility with relative risk aversion γ. As the surplus consumption ratio approaches zero, the right-hand
side of (6.94) increases without limit. Thus the upper bound on the Sharpe ratio of any
asset varies with the surplus consumption ratio and can be arbitrarily higher than under
power utility.

CC calibrate their model to fit postwar quarterly US data, choosing the mean consumption growth rate $g = 1.89\%$ per year and the standard deviation of consumption
growth $\sigma_c = 1.50\%$ per year. In their basic analysis, they assume that the stock market pays
a dividend equal to consumption, although they also consider a more realistic model
in which the dividend is a random walk whose innovations are imperfectly correlated
with consumption growth. They show that results in this model are very similar because
the implied regression coefficient of dividend growth on consumption growth is close to
one, which produces similar asset price behavior. They use numerical methods to find the
price-dividend ratio for the stock market as a function of the state variable s_t. They set the
persistence of the state variable, φ, equal to 0.87 per year to match the persistence of the
log price-dividend ratio. They choose $\gamma = 2$ to match the ratio of unconditional mean to
unconditional standard deviation of return in US stock returns. These parameter values
imply that at the steady state, the surplus consumption ratio $\bar{S} = 0.057$ (as illustrated in
Figure 6.3), so habit is about 94% of consumption. Finally, CC choose the discount factor
$\delta = 0.89$ to give a riskless real interest rate of just under 1% per year.

With these parameter values the model uses high average risk aversion to fit the high
unconditional equity premium. Steady-state risk aversion is $\gamma / \bar{S} = 2.00/0.057 = 35$, and
this corresponds to a steady-state Sharpe ratio of $\sqrt{2(1 - 0.87)} = 0.51$. In this respect the
model resembles a power utility model with a very high risk aversion coefficient, and does
not "solve" the equity premium puzzle.

There are however two important differences between the CC habit formation model
and the power utility model with high risk aversion. First, the model with habit formation
avoids the riskfree rate puzzle. Evaluating equation (6.91) at the steady-state surplus consumption ratio and using the restrictions on the sensitivity function $\lambda(s_t)$, the constant
riskless interest rate in the CC model is

$$r^f_{t+1} = -\log(\delta) + \gamma \, g - \left(\frac{\gamma}{\bar{S}}\right)^2 \frac{\sigma_c^2}{2}. \tag{6.95}$$

In the power utility model the same large coefficient γ would appear in the consumption growth term and the consumption volatility term (equation (6.6)); in the CC model the curvature parameter γ appears in the consumption growth term, and this is much lower than the steady-state risk aversion coefficient $\gamma/\bar{S}$ which appears in the consumption volatility term. Thus a much lower value of the discount factor δ is consistent with the average level of the risk free interest rate, and the model implies a less sensitive relationship between mean consumption growth and interest rates. This property of the model is similar to that of an Epstein-Zin model with an elasticity of intertemporal substitution ψ that exceeds the reciprocal of risk aversion.

Second, the CC model has risk aversion that varies with the level of consumption, whereas a power utility model has constant risk aversion. The time-variation in risk aversion generates large predictable movements in excess stock returns like those discussed in Chapter 5, enabling the model to match the volatility of stock prices even with a smooth consumption series and a constant riskless interest rate. Risk premia are high and stock prices are low when a sequence of negative consumption shocks has lowered consumption relative to habit, so the model implies countercyclical risk premia, consistent with the evidence of Fama and French (1989), and procyclical stock prices. The model also generates time-varying and countercyclical volatility in stock returns even though consumption is homoskedastic.

6.7.3 Alternative Models of Time-Varying Risk Aversion

It is instructive to compare the Campbell-Cochrane (1999) and Constantinides (1990) models of habit formation. Both these models use a difference specification of habit formation, but they make different assumptions about the economic environment. The CC model assumes unforecastable exogenous consumption growth and implies negative autocorrelation of stock returns. The Constantinides model, by contrast, assumes unforecastable exogenous asset returns and implies positive autocorrelation of consumption growth. In both cases habit formation increases the autocorrelation of consumption growth relative to that of stock returns, but in the CC model both sets of autocorrelations are lower than they are in the Constantinides model. This is the important empirical distinction between the two models; the distinction between an endowment economy with exogenous consumption and external habit, as assumed by CC, and a storage economy with exogenous asset returns and internal habit, as assumed by Constantinides, is not essential because production economies can generate either types of dynamics, as we discuss in Chapter 7, and because external and internal habit models typically have similar empirical implications.

In any model with nonstationary but cointegrated wealth and consumption, the long-run volatilities of wealth and consumption growth rates are equal. Empirically, the short-run volatility of wealth returns is much higher than the short-run volatility of consumption growth as illustrated in Table 6.1. Any model must take a stand on how to reconcile these volatilities. The CC model assumes that the low short-run volatility of consumption growth is an accurate representation of the true long-run risk in the economy, as consumption growth is iid, but wealth is mean-reverting so its long-run risk is lower than its short-run risk (a theme we develop further in Chapter 9). The Constantinides model assumes that the high short-run volatility of wealth is an accurate representation of the true long-run risk in the economy, as wealth returns are iid, but habit formation artificially smooths consumption so its short-run risk is lower than its long-run risk. The Constantinides assumption of high long-run risk enables the model to fit the equity premium with low risk-aversion, but it achieves this success at the cost of a positively serially correlated consumption process that contradicts the empirical findings of Cochrane (1994) and Lettau and Ludvigson (2001a).

Both the CC and Constantinides models tightly link time-varying risk aversion to the level of consumption relative to its recent past history. Some researchers have advocated a looser specification in which risk aversion can move independently of consumption. Bekaert, Engstrom, and Grenadier (2010) and Dew-Becker (2012) are two notable examples.

Recent work in behavioral finance has explored similar themes. Barberis, Huang, and Santos (2001) combine a standard power utility function in consumption with the prospect theory of Kahneman and Tversky (1979). Appealing to experimental evidence of Thaler and Johnson (1990), they argue that aversion to losses varies with past outcomes; past success reduces effective risk aversion as investors feel they are "gambling with house money." This creates a time-varying price of risk which explains aggregate stock market volatility in a similar manner to CC. The Barberis et al. model has a lower aversion to consumption risk than the CC model, because it generates risk-averse behavior from direct aversion to wealth fluctuations as well as from standard aversion to consumption fluctuations.

Finally, some researchers have pointed out that a stochastic discount factor similar to that in the CC model can arise in a model with heterogeneous agents. Chan and Kogan (2002) consider differences in risk aversion, and find that positive shocks transfer resources to investors with low risk aversion, lowering the effective risk aversion of a representative agent. They also assume habit formation at the microeconomic level to prevent agents with log utility from taking over the economy in the long run as would be the case in an economy with power-utility investors and heterogeneous risk aversion (see section 2.1.5). Guvenen (2009) considers a model in which some agents do not participate in risky asset markets and have predetermined consumption. In such a model, the consumption of nonparticipants must be subtracted from aggregate consumption to obtain the consumption of participants. If participants have power utility, the resulting equilibrium resembles that of the CC model where nonparticipants' consumption is equivalent to habit. We discuss this further in section 10.2.2.

6.8 Durable Goods

All the models we have discussed so far assume that a representative investor's marginal utility can be measured from the consumption of nondurable goods and services ("nondurables"). This will be the case if there are no durable goods or if utility is separable in the consumption of durables and nondurables. With nonseparable utility, however, one must also measure the stock of durable goods and calculate its influence on marginal utility as pointed out by Dunn and Singleton (1986) and Eichenbaum and Hansen (1990).

A recent paper by Yogo (2006) develops a nonseparable model and shows that incorporating durable goods into a consumption-based asset pricing model improves its ability to fit the cross-section of stock returns. The same model has been used to fit foreign-currency returns by Lustig and Verdelhan (2007) and to fit commodity futures returns by Dhume (2010).

In the Yogo model, a representative investor has constant-elasticity-of-substitution (CES) period utility over nondurables consumption C_t and the stock of durables D_t, with a weight α on durables and an intratemporal elasticity of substitution η between nondurables and durables:

$$u(C_t, D_t) = \left[(1-\alpha) C_t^{1-1/\eta} + \alpha D_t^{1-1/\eta} \right]^{1/(1-1/\eta)}. \tag{6.96}$$

In the case $\eta = 1$, this becomes a model with Cobb-Douglas period utility.

Yogo assumes that intertemporal preferences take the Epstein-Zin form (6.34):

$$U_t = \left\{ (1-\delta) u(C_t, D_t)^{(1-\gamma)/\theta} + \delta (\mathrm{E}_t [U_{t+1}^{1-\gamma}])^{1/\theta} \right\}^{\theta/(1-\gamma)}. \tag{6.97}$$

Here, as before, the parameter $\theta \equiv (1-\gamma)/(1-1/\psi)$, where γ is the coefficient of relative risk aversion and ψ is the elasticity of intertemporal substitution.

Yogo derives conditions under which the marginal utility of nondurables is decreasing in the ratio of the durables stock to nondurables consumption. He shows that if the EIS $\psi < 1$ and the coefficient of relative risk aversion $\gamma > 1$, which he finds to be the empirically relevant case, then the ratio D_t/C_t is inversely related to the marginal utility of nondurables if $\psi < \eta$. In this case the intratemporal elasticity of substitution between durables and nondurables is large enough that a high stock of durables can substitute for nondurable consumption. On the other hand, if $\psi > \eta$ then durables and nondurables are complements in the Pareto-Edgeworth sense, that is, a high durables stock drives up the marginal utility of nondurables consumption.

Figure 6.4, taken from Yogo (2006), plots the growth rates of nondurable consumption and the stock of durables in US quarterly data over the period 1951Q1–2001Q4. The shaded regions are NBER recessions. It is apparent that both nondurable consumption and the stock of durables are procyclical, but the latter more so than the former so the ratio D_t/C_t is procyclical. Also, nondurable consumption tends to fall at the onset of a recession and rise at the beginning of a boom, whereas the stock of durables is slower

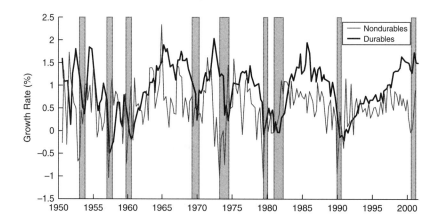

Figure 6.4. *Growth Rates of Nondurable Consumption and the Stock of Durables, 1951–2001* (Yogo, Motohiro, 2006, "A Consumption-Based Explanation of Expected Stock Returns," *Journal of Finance* 61, 539–580; reprinted by permission of John Wiley & Sons, Inc.)

moving and so its troughs and peaks occur later in recessions and booms. This behavior implies that nonseparable utility can both increase the volatility of marginal utility of nondurables and alter the timing of its variation relative to NBER recessions.

To analyze the asset pricing implications of his model, Yogo derives an approximate linear factor representation:

$$E[R_{it} - R_{ft}] = b_1 \text{Cov}(\Delta c_t, R_{it} - R_{ft}) + b_2 \text{Cov}(\Delta d_t, R_{it} - R_{ft})$$
$$+ b_3 \text{Cov}(r_{wt}, R_{it} - R_{ft}), \tag{6.98}$$

where $d_t = \log(D_t)$, r_{wt} is the log return on the aggregate wealth portfolio, and the risk prices are related to the preference parameters by

$$b_1 = \theta[1/\psi + \alpha(1/\eta - 1/\psi)],$$
$$b_2 = \theta\alpha(1/\psi - 1/\eta),$$
$$b_3 = 1 - \theta. \tag{6.99}$$

Yogo estimates the restricted factor model using the 25 Fama-French portfolios (equity portfolios sorted by market capitalization and the book-market ratio). He finds a risk price on the wealth return b_3 of about 2/3, implying that $\theta \approx 1/3$. He finds a very large positive value of the risk price on the growth rate of durables b_2. The positive sign of b_2 implies that $\psi < \eta$, so the marginal utility of nondurables is low when the stock of durables is high. The large magnitude of b_2 implies that the EIS ψ is extremely low. To fit the estimated value of θ, risk aversion must then be very high. Yogo's estimates are $\psi = 0.002$, $\gamma = 189$, and $\alpha = 0.907$.

These parameter values obviously do not "solve" the equity premium puzzle since they imply an extreme degree of risk aversion and an EIS close to zero. What they do show is that cross-sectional patterns in stock prices can be fit using parameter values similar to those that fit aggregate stock returns in an Epstein-Zin model extended to include durables and nondurables consumption. The results of Lustig and Verdelhan (2007) and Dhume (2010) suggest that the model can fit returns in other asset classes as well. The consumption-based asset pricing literature, like other branches of empirical asset pricing, increasingly takes the ability to fit the cross-section of equity and nonequity test assets as the standard for a successful model.

6.9 Solutions and Further Problems

In section 6.5 you were asked to show that two definitions of entropy, $-E_t \log d_{t+1}$ and $E_t d_{t+1} \log d_{t+1}$, are both positive given that $E_t d_{t+1} = 1$. A simple way to show this is to note that the functions $-\log d$ and $d \log d$ are both convex, so they both lie above tangents to these functions drawn at any point. A convenient point to choose is $d = 1$. Then for a convex function $f(d)$, we know that $f(d) \geq f(1) + f'(1)(d - 1)$. Applying this to the function $f(d) = -\log d$, we find that $-\log d \geq 1 - d$. Taking expectations and using $Ed = 1$ gives the desired result. Applying this to the function $f(d) = d \log d$, we find that $d \log d \geq d - 1$. Taking expectations and using $Ed = 1$ again gives the desired result.

In section 6.7.2 you were asked to explain how there can be an intertemporal substitution effect on the riskless real interest rate in the Campbell-Cochrane habit formation model, given that the model assumes unpredictable log consumption growth. The answer is that when the surplus consumption ratio is low, the marginal utility of consumption is high but is expected to revert to its steady-state value in the future. This occurs not through predictable consumption growth but through predictable adjustment of habit to the new level of consumption. Over time the consumer becomes accustomed to reduced circumstances, and the habit level declines. Anticipating this adjustment, the consumer wishes to borrow from the future to increase consumption in the period when habit is still high; to prevent this, the equilibrium real interest rate increases.

Problem 6.1 The Recovery Theorem

In this problem we explore what information about the underlying economy we can recover from Arrow-Debreu state prices.[10] Assume the existence of a representative agent with time separable utility $U(\cdot)$ over consumption and time discount factor δ whose Euler equations price the assets.

(a) First consider a stationary economy with no growth. Suppose there are two consumption states C_H and C_L. Transitions between the two states follow a Markov process with transition probabilities given by $f_{ij} > 0$ for $i, j \in \{H, L\}$. The four Arrow-Debreu securities are denoted by $p_{ij} > 0$ for $i, j \in \{H, L\}$. Note that p_{ij} is the price of the claim to one unit of consumption in state j tomorrow given state i today. Write down the four optimality (first-order) conditions of the representative agent. Then solve for the ratio of marginal utilities, the time discount factor, and the transition probabilities as functions of the state prices.

(b) Now suppose that there are three consumption states. Suppose also that $p_{13} = 0$, $p_{21} = 0$, and $p_{32} = 0$. What is the implication of a zero state price for the associated natural probability? Repeat the analysis of part (a). You don't need to explicitly solve the equation for δ.

(c) In parts (a) and (b), what is the relationship between the time discount factor and the matrix of state prices?

(d) We now introduce consumption growth. Assume that given the current level, consumption grows at either the rate g_H or g_L. The rate of consumption growth follows a Markov process with transition probabilities given by $f_{ij} > 0$ with $i, j \in \{H, L\}$. Moreover, assume that the representative agent has power utility with coefficient of relative risk aversion γ.

  (i) Show that the four Arrow-Debreu prices are independent of the current level of consumption. Solve for the risk aversion parameter, the time discount factor, and the transition probabilities as functions of the state prices and the growth rates g_H and g_L.

  (ii) Suppose that $p_{LH} = p_{HH}$ and $p_{LL} = p_{HL}$. Show that recovery breaks down.

This result illustrates a general point. In a model with growth, state dependence of Arrow-Debreu prices is crucial for recovery of economic fundamentals.

---

[10]Under general conditions and the assumption of complete markets, it is possible to use asset prices to recover Arrow-Debreu state prices. This is often done using the prices of options (Breeden and Litzenberger 1978).

(e) Finally, continue to assume two possible growth rates g_H or g_L but allow for an arbitrary utility function. State prices will now depend on the current level of consumption in general. Show that given state prices $p_{ij}(C)$, where C is current consumption, we can recover the natural probabilities as well as $\delta U'(g_j C)/U'(C)$ for $j \in \{H, L\}$. In other words, we can recover the transition probabilities, but we cannot independently recover both the ratio of marginal utilities and the time discount factor.

Note: This problem is based on Ross (2015) and Borovička, Hansen, and Scheinkman (2016).

Problem 6.2 Timing Premia in the Long-Run Risk Model

Long-run risk models offer a solution to the main asset pricing puzzles by assuming that there exists a representative agent with Epstein-Zin preferences with moderately high risk aversion and a high elasticity of intertemporal substitution and that aggregate consumption growth is persistent and conditionally heteroskedastic. In this problem we explore the implications of such a setting (preference and endowment specification) for the representative agent's attitudes toward the temporal resolution of uncertainty.

Consider an infinite-horizon endowment economy. The representative agent has Epstein-Zin utility, defined recursively in (6.34) and (6.35). Consumption follows an exogenous process given by

$$\Delta c_{t+1} = \mu_c + x_t + \sigma \eta_{t+1}, \tag{6.100}$$

$$x_{t+1} = \rho_x x_t + \varphi_e \sigma e_{t+1}, \tag{6.101}$$

where $c_t \equiv \log C_t$, and η_t and e_t are standard normal variables, mutually independent and iid over time.[11]

(a) Explain intuitively why $\gamma - 1/\psi > 0$ implies a preference for early resolution of uncertainty.

(b) Recall the discussion of the risk premium in section 1.2. The *timing premium*, π^*, can be defined analogously as the (maximum) fraction of the consumption stream that one would give up at date 0 in order to have all risk resolved at date 1. That is, the agent is indifferent between consuming the stream $C = \{C_t\}_{t=0}^{\infty}$ given by (6.100) and (6.101) with risk resolved gradually and consuming the stream $(1 - \pi^*) C = \{(1 - \pi^*) C_t\}_{t=0}^{\infty}$ while learning the realizations of $C_1, C_2, C_3, \ldots$ with certainty at date 1.

Let U_0 denote the utility at date 0 from consuming C with risk resolved gradually and let U_0^* denote the utility at date 0 from consuming C with risk resolved at date 1. Show that, for Epstein-Zin preferences, the timing premium can be written as

$$\pi^* = 1 - \frac{U_0}{U_0^*}. \tag{6.102}$$

[11]Note that, for tractability reasons, our specification (referred to as Case 1 in Bansal and Yaron (2004)) abstracts from stochastic volatility of consumption growth, but the results turn out to be very similar in the general case.

For the remaining parts assume that $\psi = 1$, a case that admits a closed-form solution.

(c) Guess and verify that U_0 is given by

$$\log U_0 = c_0 + \frac{\delta}{1-\delta\rho_x} x_0 + \frac{\delta}{1-\delta} \mu_c + \frac{1-\gamma}{2} \frac{\delta\sigma^2}{1-\delta} \left(1 + \frac{\varphi_e^2 \delta^2}{(1-\delta\rho_x)^2}\right). \tag{6.103}$$

(d) Calculate U_0^* by first solving for U_1^*, the utility from a deterministic consumption stream, as $\log U_1^* = c_0 + \Sigma_{t=1}^{\infty} \delta^{t-1} \Delta c_t$ and then solving for U_0^* given the date-0 conditional distribution of U_1^*. Show that the timing premium, (6.102), equals

$$\pi^* = 1 - \exp\left[\frac{1-\gamma}{2} \frac{\delta^2\sigma^2}{1-\delta^2} \left(1 + \frac{\varphi_e^2 \delta^2}{(1-\delta\rho_x)^2}\right)\right]. \tag{6.104}$$

Explain why, for $\gamma > 1$, the timing premium is increasing in γ, δ, σ, φ_e, and ρ_x.

(e) Give a numerical estimate for the timing premium given the following parameter values from Bansal and Yaron (2004): $\sigma = 0.0078$, $\varphi_e = 0.044$, $\rho_x = 0.979$, $\delta = 0.998$, and $\gamma = 7.5$. Repeat with $\gamma = 10$. Assess these estimates through introspection: would you be willing to give such a fraction of your entire consumption stream in order to know your consumption stream with certainty earlier in your life? Note that the question at hand is about consumption risk, not about income or return risk; that is, there is no instrumental value in knowing your consumption in advance.

(f) Finally, we ask whether a high EIS necessarily implies very high timing premia or whether the results of part (e) are due to the particular combination of preferences and endowment process frequently assumed in the long-run risk literature. Repeat part (e) under the assumption of an iid consumption growth process, that is, by setting $\rho_x = \varphi_e = 0$. How do these estimates compare to those of part (e)? Explain intuitively why, given the assumed preferences (high γ and $\gamma > 1/\psi$), a persistent process for consumption growth is associated with high timing premia.

Note: This problem is based on Epstein, Farhi, and Strzalecki (2014).

Problem 6.3 Pricing Levered Equity with the Extended Consumption CAPM

Consider an infinite-horizon representative-agent economy. The representative agent has Epstein-Zin utility. Consumption, expected future consumption, and returns on all assets are jointly lognormally distributed and homoskedastic.

(a) Show that the expected log return on any asset i can be written as

$$\mathrm{E}_t[r_{i,t+1}] = \mu_i + \frac{1}{\psi} \mathrm{E}_t[\Delta c_{t+1}], \tag{6.105}$$

where μ_i is constant over time and c_{t+1} denotes log consumption.

(b) We define levered equity as an infinitely-lived asset with dividend equal to $D_t = C_t^\lambda$, where λ can be interpreted as a measure of leverage. Use the Campbell-Shiller return decomposition (5.51) to show that the unexpected return to levered equity can be written as

$$\tilde{r}_{le,t+1} = \lambda \tilde{c}_{t+1} + \left(\lambda - \frac{1}{\psi}\right) \tilde{g}_{t+1}, \tag{6.106}$$

where $\tilde{x}_{t+1} \equiv (\mathrm{E}_{t+1} - \mathrm{E}_t) x_{t+1}$ for any variable x and $\tilde{g}_{t+1}$, defined in equation (6.48), captures revisions in expected future consumption growth.

(c) Use the preceding result to derive an expression for the unexpected return on an inflation-indexed perpetuity (real consol bond), an asset with a fixed real dividend every period.

For the remaining parts, assume that aggregate consumption follows an exogenous process given by

$$\Delta c_{t+1} = \mu_c + x_t + \varepsilon_{c,t+1}, \tag{6.107}$$

$$x_{t+1} = \varphi_x x_t + \varepsilon_{x,t+1}, \tag{6.108}$$

where $\varepsilon_{c,t+1}$, $\varepsilon_{x,t+1}$ are iid with zero means with variances σ_c^2 and σ_x^2, and covariance σ_{cx}.

(d) Show that the risk premium on levered equity over the riskfree interest rate is given by

$$\mathrm{E}_t[r_{le,t+1}] - r_{f,t+1} + \frac{\sigma_{le}^2}{2} = \gamma \left[\lambda \sigma_c^2 + \left(\lambda - \frac{1}{\psi}\right) \frac{\rho}{1 - \rho\varphi_x} \sigma_{cx} \right] + \left(\gamma - \frac{1}{\psi}\right) \left[\frac{\lambda\rho}{1 - \rho\varphi_x} \sigma_{cx} \right]$$
$$+ \left(\gamma - \frac{1}{\psi}\right)\left(\lambda - \frac{1}{\psi}\right)\left(\frac{\rho}{1 - \rho\varphi_x}\right)^2 \sigma_x^2. \tag{6.109}$$

(e) Use the preceding result to obtain expressions for the consol bond risk premium over the riskfree rate and for the risk premium of levered equity over the real consol bond. Interpret each of the terms appearing in the two expressions and give the economic intuition for their sign. What determines the sign of the term premium and the equity premium?

(f) If σ_c^2 and σ_{cx} are small, as the smooth path of observed consumption growth implies, what restrictions on preference parameters γ and ψ imply both large equity premia and small real term premia (positive or negative)?

Problem 6.4 Levered Equity and Consumption Volatility

A representative agent in an endowment economy has power utility with time discount factor δ and coefficient of relative risk aversion γ. The log of the endowment, c_t, follows a random walk with drift:

$$\Delta c_t = g + \varepsilon_t. \tag{6.110}$$

The shock to endowment growth rate is iid over time, distributed normally with mean zero and variance σ^2.

(a) Solve for the log riskless interest rate. Explain the forces that determine it.

(b) Consider an infinite-lived asset whose log dividend is λc_t in each period. The coefficient λ can be loosely thought of as a measure of leverage, and the asset can be called "levered equity." Solve for the arithmetic risk premium on levered equity and the arithmetic average growth rate of the dividend on levered equity.

(c) Now suppose the volatility of endowment growth increases, while the parameter g changes to maintain the same arithmetic average growth rate of the endowment. What is the effect on the riskless interest rate? What is the effect on the arithmetic risk premium of levered equity? What is the effect on the arithmetic average growth rate of the dividend on levered equity?

(d) With power utility, higher endowment volatility with an unchanged arithmetic average endowment growth rate lowers the price of unlevered equity only if $\gamma > 1$. Show that it lowers the price of levered equity only if $\lambda - 1 < \gamma < \lambda$. Explain the economic forces that cause endowment volatility to raise the price of levered equity if risk aversion is lower than $\lambda - 1$ or greater than λ.

(e) Relate your answer to the debate about the magnitude of the elasticity of intertemporal substitution and the relative merits of Epstein-Zin utility and power utility as descriptions of investor preferences.

7

Production-Based Asset Pricing

IN THIS CHAPTER we discuss production-based asset pricing, the study of asset prices in relation to the production decisions of firms. We start with the q theory of Tobin (1969), which relates firms' investment to their stock prices, and the related observation of Cochrane (1991b, 1996) that the returns on firms' physical investments should equal the financial returns on claims to the firm. Section 7.1 develops these ideas, emphasizing that adjustment costs in investment are needed to explain volatile stock returns. We review a recent empirical literature estimating the parameters of firms' production and adjustment cost functions that best match these two types of returns. We also discuss models that derive the factor loadings of firms' stock prices from fundamental features of the firms' production technologies.

In section 7.2 we examine dynamic stochastic general equilibrium (DSGE) models that explicitly model production along with technology shocks. Previously discussed models of preferences interact with the production possibilities of the economy to determine a consumption process and hence a stochastic discount factor, which in turn pins down asset prices. DSGE models can include flexible labor supply, which influences the effective degree of risk aversion in the economy as emphasized by Swanson (2012).

It is tempting to treat consumption and production symmetrically. If asset prices reveal consumers' marginal rate of substitution across states of the economy, do they not also reveal producers' marginal rate of transformation across states? For this approach to be fruitful, firms must have some ability to shift output across states, and in section 7.3 we discuss a recent model with this feature due to Belo (2010).

7.1 Physical Investment with Adjustment Costs

The q theory of investment (Tobin 1969, Hayashi 1982) relates the decision of a firm to invest in physical capital to convex adjustment costs of physical investment and the valuation of already installed capital in financial markets. Building on this framework, Cochrane (1991b, 1996) introduces the idea of investment returns, defined as the returns generated by a firm's investment decision. He shows that these returns must equal the financial returns to owners of the firm. Therefore, it should be possible to relate variation in stock returns to the determinants of investment returns, including sales-capital ratios, investment-capital ratios, and adjustment costs in investment.

7.1.1 A q-Theory Model of Investment

To explain these ideas, we first set up a standard q-theoretic model of investment following the exposition in Kogan and Papanikolaou (2012). We consider a firm producing
output X_t with a Cobb-Douglas production technology subject to productivity shocks Z_t:

$$X_t = Z_t K_t^\alpha L_t^{1-\alpha}. \tag{7.1}$$

Here K_t is the firm's capital stock, and L_t is the firm's employment.

We assume, here and throughout this chapter, that the firm employs the optimal
quantity of labor at the going wage to maximize profits. As we consider variation in investment and the capital stock, we will always take these optimal adjustments in labor supply
as given. This practice is standard in the production-based asset pricing literature. The
firm's first-order condition for optimal choice of labor supply equates the wage ω_t to the
marginal product of labor, $\omega_t = \partial X_t / \partial L_t$, and this implies that optimal labor supply L_t^* is
given by

$$L_t^* = \left(\frac{(1-\alpha) Z_t}{\omega_t} \right)^{\frac{1}{\alpha}} K_t. \tag{7.2}$$

Substituting into the production function (7.1), and writing Y_t for the firm's output
conditional on the optimal labor input, we have

$$Y_t = \left(Z_t^{\frac{1}{\alpha}} \left(\frac{1-\alpha}{\omega_t} \right)^{\frac{1}{\alpha}-1} \right) K_t, \tag{7.3}$$

which is proportional to the capital stock. We also have that the gross profits paid to the
owners of the firm's capital, $\Pi_t = Y_t - \omega_t L_t^*$, satisfy

$$\Pi_t = \alpha Y_t. \tag{7.4}$$

Thus we have the standard result that the capital exponent α is the capital share.

The capital stock follows

$$K_{t+1} = I_t + (1 - \delta) K_t, \tag{7.5}$$

where I_t is investment and δ is the depreciation rate. The cost of investment Φ_t is deducted from profits as in Lucas (1967), implying that the firm can pay a dividend each
period of

$$D_t = \Pi_t - \Phi_t. \tag{7.6}$$

The cost of investment includes adjustment costs and is scaled so that the ratio of the
total cost of investment to the capital stock depends only on the ratio of investment to
the capital stock. In this sense, adjustment costs have constant returns to scale. We write

$$\Phi_t = \phi \left(\frac{I_t}{K_t} \right) K_t, \tag{7.7}$$

where $\phi(.)$ is a convex function, increasing for positive levels of investment, so $\phi'(I_t/K_t) >$
0 when $I_t > 0$ and $\phi''(I_t/K_t) \geq 0$ everywhere. A model without adjustment costs would
have $\phi(I_t/K_t) = I_t/K_t$, $\phi'(I_t/K_t) = 1$, and $\phi''(I_t/K_t) = 0$.

Implications of Firm Optimization

The firm chooses investment to maximize firm value V_t, the risk-adjusted present value of current and future dividends using the term structure of stochastic discount factors:

$$V_t = \max \mathrm{E}_t \sum_{s=0}^{\infty} M_{t,t+s} D_{t+s}, \qquad (7.8)$$

where $M_{t,t+s}$ is the multiperiod SDF from time t to time $t+s$ (discussed in greater detail in Chapter 8), and $M_{t,t} = 1$. Note that the summation here starts at zero because the current dividend is included in the firm value; that is, V_t is the cum-dividend value of the firm at time t. This notational convention eases the presentation of the firm's optimization problem, but it differs from the standard convention in empirical asset pricing, which is to write valuations ex-dividend, that is, excluding the current dividend.

The solution to the firm's optimization problem satisfies the Bellman equation:

$$V_t = \max_{I_t}\{D_t + \mathrm{E}_t[M_{t+1} V_{t+1}]\}, \qquad (7.9)$$

where as always, the firm is assumed to set employment optimally in each period in relation to its capital stock and productivity.

At the optimal level of investment, the derivative of the value function with respect to investment is zero. Hence, from (7.9) the marginal reduction in today's dividend caused by the cost of investment must exactly equal the marginal expected discounted increase in the firm's future value created by additional future capital resulting from investment:

$$\phi'\left(\frac{I_t}{K_t}\right) = \mathrm{E}_t\left[M_{t+1}\frac{\partial V_{t+1}}{\partial K_{t+1}}\right]. \qquad (7.10)$$

In other words, the marginal cost of investment must equal the expected discounted marginal benefit, adjusting for risk using the SDF.

We can obtain further insight by applying the envelope theorem to equation (7.9). Differentiating the left- and right-hand sides of (7.9) with respect to capital K_t, and leading one period, we have

$$\begin{aligned}
\frac{\partial V_{t+1}}{\partial K_{t+1}} &= \frac{\partial D_{t+1}}{\partial K_{t+1}} + \mathrm{E}_{t+1}\left[M_{t+2}\frac{\partial V_{t+2}}{\partial K_{t+1}}\right] \\
&= \alpha\frac{\partial Y_{t+1}}{\partial K_{t+1}} - \frac{\partial \Phi_{t+1}}{\partial K_{t+1}} + (1-\delta)\mathrm{E}_{t+1}\left[M_{t+2}\frac{\partial V_{t+2}}{\partial K_{t+2}}\right] \\
&= \alpha\frac{\partial Y_{t+1}}{\partial K_{t+1}} - \frac{\partial \Phi_{t+1}}{\partial K_{t+1}} + (1-\delta)\phi'\left(\frac{I_{t+1}}{K_{t+1}}\right).
\end{aligned} \qquad (7.11)$$

Here the second equality uses the firm's budget constraint for dividend payments, (7.6), and the fact that with constant investment a unit of extra capital at time $t+1$ depreciates to $(1-\delta)$ units of extra capital at time $t+2$. The third equality uses (7.10), led one period. The interpretation of equation (7.11) is that the realized marginal benefit of an extra unit of capital for the firm is the profit share times the marginal effect on output, less the marginal effect on investment adjustment costs, plus the value of the undepreciated capital that enters the following period, which can be calculated from the marginal cost of investment. This realized marginal benefit is random, and so investment decisions are based on averaging across possible future states.

The derivatives in equation (7.11) are calculated conditional on optimal adjustment of labor supply. Note in particular that the derivative $\partial Y_{t+1}/\partial K_{t+1} \neq \partial X_{t+1}/\partial K_{t+1}$, the marginal product of capital taking labor input as given.[1] The constant-returns-to-scale production function (7.3) implies that the output-capital ratio does not depend on the capital stock once the firm adjusts its employment optimally taking wages as given. Thus the derivative $\partial Y_{t+1}/\partial K_{t+1} = Y_{t+1}/K_{t+1}$, and the first term on the right-hand side of (7.11) can be rewritten as $\alpha Y_{t+1}/K_{t+1}$.

Implications of Constant Returns to Scale

Hayashi (1982) shows that constant returns to scale in both production and adjustment costs, equations (7.1) and (7.7), imply that the marginal effect of an additional unit of capital on the firm's value equals the average ratio of the firm's value to its capital stock:

$$\frac{\partial V_t}{\partial K_t} = \frac{V_t}{K_t}. \tag{7.12}$$

The left-hand side of equation (7.12) is sometimes called "marginal q," and the right-hand side is one measure of "average q" or "Tobin's q."

Substituting (7.12) into (7.10), and then using (7.9) and the fact that K_{t+1} is known at time t, we have

$$\phi'\left(\frac{I_t}{K_t}\right) = E_t\left[M_{t+1}\frac{V_{t+1}}{K_{t+1}}\right] = \frac{V_t - D_t}{K_{t+1}}. \tag{7.13}$$

The left-hand side is the marginal cost of investment, and the right-hand side is the ratio of the ex-dividend value of the firm to its next-period capital stock, an alternative measure of average or Tobin's q.

Empirical measures of the right-hand side of (7.13) are highly variable across firms and over time (just as the market-book ratio is highly variable as discussed in earlier chapters), so to fit the data this relation requires some combination of variable investment rates I_t/K_t and a high derivative ϕ' that makes adjustment costs extremely sensitive to the level of investment. Early research on aggregate and firm-level investment found it hard to explain investment behavior with reasonable parameters in equation (7.13) (see, e.g., Chirinko 1993). This may be due in part to financial frictions, fixed costs of investment, or decision lags omitted from the simple neoclassical investment model with convex adjustment costs (Fazzari, Hubbard, and Petersen 1988, Abel and Eberly 1994, Lamont 2000), or to inframarginal fixed assets that affect average but not marginal values of capital, or to measurement errors in average q (Erickson and Whited 2000). Merz and Yashiv (2007) find that a model with adjustment costs in both labor and capital inputs, and with greater-than-quadratic convexity in adjustment costs, fits aggregate investment of the US nonfinancial corporate sector considerably better than the classic models discussed in this chapter.

---

[1] This is related to the distinction between the marginal revenue product of capital, the marginal effect of capital on profits with optimal choice of labor supply, $\partial \Pi_{t+1}/\partial K_{t+1} = \alpha \partial Y_{t+1}/\partial K_{t+1}$, and the marginal product of capital $\partial X_{t+1}/\partial K_{t+1}$.

We can do more with the relationship (7.13) if we note that

$$\frac{V_t - D_t}{K_{t+1}} = \frac{D_t}{K_{t+1}} \frac{V_t - D_t}{D_t}. \tag{7.14}$$

The first term on the right-hand side is the dividend divided by the capital stock, which can be regarded as a measure of current profitability. The second term is the ratio of the firm's ex-dividend value to its dividend, in other words, the conventionally defined price-dividend ratio for the firm. Taking logs of both sides of (7.13) and using (7.14) and the Campbell-Shiller formula for the log price-dividend ratio, equation (5.47), we obtain

$$\log\left(\phi'\left(\frac{I_t}{K_t}\right)\right) = (d_t - k_{t+1}) + E_t \sum_{j=0}^{\infty} \rho^j \Delta d_{t+1+j} - E_t \sum_{j=0}^{\infty} \rho^j r_{t+1+j}. \tag{7.15}$$

This equation says that a firm that is investing heavily, and hence has high marginal cost for investment, must either make high payouts relative to capital today or have payouts that grow rapidly (in either case supported by underlying profitability of investment), or else it will deliver low returns in the future. Controlling for profitability, firms with high investment must have low average future returns, and controlling for investment, profitable firms must have high average future returns. Of course, this is merely a reduced-form relationship, and it is consistent with various structural interpretations. For example, a firm may have a low cost of capital—equivalently, a low expected return—because the market overvalues its stock or because its investment projects are fundamentally less risky. In either case the firm's managers should respond by investing more for any given level of profitability, enforcing the equality (7.15).

This analysis provides a theoretical motivation for the empirical findings, discussed in Chapter 3, that firms with rapidly growing assets tend to have low average stock returns (Titman, Wei, and Xie 2004, Cooper, Gulen, and Schill 2008), while firms with high gross profitability have high average returns (Novy-Marx 2013). Hou, Xue, and Zhang (HXZ 2015) use these ideas to propose a "q-factor" model, in the spirit of Fama and French (1993), but dropping value and adding two investment-inspired factors. Alongside the Fama-French market and size factors, HXZ use the returns on low-investment minus high-investment firms, and the returns on high-profitability minus low-profitability firms, where investment is measured by the growth rate of assets and profitability is measured by accounting return on equity (ROE). This model reduces the magnitude of many cross-sectional anomalies, in the sense that long-short anomaly portfolios have smaller alphas with respect to this model than with respect to the Fama-French model. Notably, the HXZ model fits various anomalies better even than the Carhart four-factor model, which includes an explicit momentum factor. A caveat is that HXZ confront their model with value-weighted anomaly portfolios and thus do not require it to fit cross-sectional return patterns among small stocks where these patterns are typically more extreme.

Fama and French (2015) similarly extend the Fama-French three-factor model, retaining value and adding investment and profitability factors. They offer an alternative motivation that can be understood by reference to equation (5.50). As an informal exercise, you are asked to explain how that equation might justify the inclusion of both value and profitability factors in a multifactor model. The answer is given at the end of this chapter.

7.1.2 Investment Returns

We can rearrange equations (7.12) and (7.13) to show that the gross market return on a financial claim to the firm,

$$(1 + R_{t+1}) = \frac{V_{t+1}}{V_t - D_t},$$ (7.16)

equals the investment return defined as

$$(1 + R_{t+1}^I) = \frac{\frac{\partial V_{t+1}}{\partial K_{t+1}}}{\phi'\left(\frac{I_t}{K_t}\right)},$$ (7.17)

the ratio of the marginal benefit of investment to its marginal cost. That is,

$$(1 + R_{t+1}) = (1 + R_{t+1}^I).$$ (7.18)

This relationship holds ex post, in every realized state, not just ex ante. Naturally it is also true that investment returns, like financial returns, satisfy the fundamental equation of asset pricing:

$$1 = E_t[M_{t+1}(1 + R_{t+1}^I)].$$ (7.19)

Cochrane (1991b, 1996) uses the relationship between financial and investment returns to test q theory in a manner that is more sensitive to high-frequency variation in investment and stock returns, and less sensitive to low-frequency variation in q that may be particularly affected by measurement error or by the presence of inframarginal fixed assets. Instead of testing the relationship between the level of investment and the level of stock prices, (7.13), this approach effectively differences the data to look at the relationship between investment returns (closely related to investment growth) and financial returns (closely related to stock price growth).

Ex post equality of financial and investment returns in every state is too much to ask of the data, so different papers look at different implications of this equality. Cochrane (1991b), for example, studies a single investment return derived from aggregate investment. He shows that high adjustment costs are needed to match the volatility of stock returns (to make Tobin's q variable) and that expected investment returns appear to move with expected stock returns (because aggregate investment is low when stock prices are depressed). Cochrane (1996) uses two investment returns derived from aggregate residential and nonresidential investment. He uses them as factors in a multifactor representation of the SDF and asks whether they explain the size effect in stock returns.

A recent empirical literature uses this approach to estimate the parameters of firms' production functions and to relate cross-sectional patterns in stock returns to firms' investment decisions. A well-known example is Liu, Whited, and Zhang (LWZ 2009). LWZ assume a specific functional form for adjustment costs, which we write as:

$$\phi\left(\frac{I_t}{K_t}\right) = \frac{I_t}{K_t} + \frac{a}{2}\left(\frac{I_t}{K_t}\right)^2.$$ (7.20)

In addition they enrich the above framework by allowing for taxes and corporate debt. Leaving these elements aside for simplicity of notation, LWZ obtain that the marginal cost of investment is

$$\phi'\left(\frac{I_t}{K_t}\right) = 1 + a\left(\frac{I_t}{K_t}\right), \tag{7.21}$$

and the marginal benefit of investment from equation (7.11) is

$$\frac{\partial V_{t+1}}{\partial K_{t+1}} = \alpha \frac{Y_{t+1}}{K_{t+1}} + \frac{a}{2}\left(\frac{I_{t+1}}{K_{t+1}}\right)^2 + (1-\delta)\left[1 + a\left(\frac{I_{t+1}}{K_{t+1}}\right)\right]. \tag{7.22}$$

As in (7.11), the three terms on the right-hand side of (7.22) represent first, higher output next period; second, the reduction in adjustment costs next period for a given level of future investment; and third, the shadow value of undepreciated capital carried forward from next period into subsequent periods. This shadow value of undepreciated capital is the same as the marginal cost of investment next period.

Taken literally, equations (7.17), (7.18), (7.21), and (7.22) imply a very tight relationship between realized returns on the firm and current and future sales-capital and investment-capital ratios:

$$(1 + R_{t+1}) = \frac{\alpha \frac{Y_{t+1}}{K_{t+1}} + \frac{a}{2}\left(\frac{I_{t+1}}{K_{t+1}}\right)^2 + (1-\delta)\left[1 + a\left(\frac{I_{t+1}}{K_{t+1}}\right)\right]}{1 + a\left(\frac{I_t}{K_t}\right)}. \tag{7.23}$$

Such a relationship certainly does not describe the data, so LWZ test weaker implications of this equality that still may be informative.

LWZ consider portfolios of stocks and estimate the model's parameters, using GMM, to minimize the weighted average difference between the means and variances of stock returns and levered investment returns (not the average difference between the levels of returns period by period). The model is extremely parsimonious because it has only two parameters, the capital share α and the adjustment cost a. The test assets are portfolios of stocks sorted by capital investment (high-investment firms have been found empirically to deliver low financial returns), earnings surprises (high-earnings-surprise firms have been found to deliver high financial returns in the literature on post-earnings-announcement drift), and value (firms with a high book-to-market ratio have been found empirically to deliver high financial returns).

LWZ obtain a reasonable capital share estimate in the range of 0.2–0.5. Their adjustment cost estimate is low for investment-sorted portfolios, intermediate for earnings-surprise-sorted portfolios, and very high for value-sorted portfolios. This is because high-investment portfolios have extremely high investment today and much lower investment tomorrow, which would imply hugely negative investment returns if adjustment costs were high. Growth portfolios, on the other hand, have high investment both today and tomorrow, and high sales-capital ratios, so much larger adjustment costs are needed to explain their low returns. This problem, that different parameters are needed to fit each anomaly, is a pervasive one in the q-theoretic asset pricing literature.

7.1.3 Explaining Firms' Betas

Another strand of the production-based literature continues to treat the SDF as exogenous but seeks to explain why particular types of firms have returns that covary more strongly with the SDF than other firms do. Much of this literature seeks to explain the relative pricing of value and growth firms.

A well-known example is Zhang (2005). Zhang assumes a heteroskedastic single-factor SDF. In logs,

$$m_{t+1} = \log \beta - \gamma_t (x_{t+1} - x_t), \tag{7.24}$$

and

$$\gamma_t = \gamma_0 + \gamma_1 (x_t - \overline{x}), \tag{7.25}$$

where x_t is an aggregate productivity shock that follows an AR(1) process. These assumptions imply that the conditional CAPM holds, as in section 8.2.8, since the SDF has a single-factor structure with time-varying volatility. When $\gamma_1 < 0$, the price of risk increases when productivity is low.

The model also includes idiosyncratic productivity shocks for each firm j, z_{jt}, that follow AR(1) processes with a common degree of persistence. Value firms are those that currently have low z_{jt} and hence low productivity, investment, and profits, while growth firms currently have high realizations of z_{jt}.

As in the paper by LWZ discussed in section 7.1.2, firms pay a quadratic adjustment cost of investment, deducted from profits, similar to equation (7.20):

$$\phi_{jt} = \frac{I_{jt}}{K_{jt}} + \frac{a_{jt}}{2} \left(\frac{I_{jt}}{K_{jt}} \right)^2. \tag{7.26}$$

However, in Zhang's model the adjustment cost depends on whether the firm is investing or disinvesting. The parameter a_{jt} equals a^+ if firm j's investment is positive, and a^- if investment is negative, where $a^- > a^+$.

Zhang calibrates his model so that both value and growth firms are investing in good times, but growth firms are investing more. However, in bad times, growth firms continue to invest modestly whereas value firms disinvest. This implies that adjustment costs are higher for growth firms in good times but for value firms in bad times.

Firms with low adjustment costs react to aggregate productivity shocks by adjusting their investment in the same direction, which not only increases the expected value of future dividends but also lowers their volatility. Firms with high adjustment costs are less able to make use of this dividend-smoothing, risk-reducing mechanism. Hence, growth firms are riskier in good times and value firms are riskier in bad times. The unconditional return on value firms is higher because the specification of the SDF (7.24) implies that the risk of value firms in bad times commands a higher price than the risk of growth firms in good times.

The Zhang (2005) model can generate a sizeable excess return to value firms, but it imposes the conditional CAPM by assumption and generates only modest deviations from the unconditional CAPM. Thus it does not fit the fact, discussed in Chapter 3, that in recent decades value firms have had lower CAPM betas than growth firms. Other more recent papers in this literature, such as Bazdresch, Belo, and Lin (2013), Kogan and Papanikolaou (2014), and McQuade (2013), work with alternative exogenous SDF specifications that deviate more importantly from the CAPM. Bazdresch et al., consider shocks to the adjustment costs of investment, and Kogan and Papanikolaou consider investment-specific technology shocks that lower the cost of investment goods. These shocks are assumed to increase marginal utility, despite the improvement in investment opportunities. Similarly, McQuade assumes that positive volatility shocks increase marginal utility. Growth firms with options to invest are particularly sensitive to these shocks and therefore provide insurance against them. A full explanation of this literature is beyond the scope of this book, as the valuation of growth options requires derivative pricing methods.

7.2 General Equilibrium with Production

We now consider asset pricing in full general equilibrium with production. The goal is to understand the ingredients that a representative-agent dynamic stochastic general equilibrium (DSGE) model needs in order to generate realistic asset prices along with realistic behavior for macroeconomic aggregates. The consumption-based literature, discussed in Chapter 6, already considers the joint modeling of asset prices and aggregate consumption. The production-based literature adds aggregate output and investment, and uses technology shocks as the primary driving process of macroeconomic uncertainty. Some models also allow for variable labor supply, and recent work has considered a wider variety of economic shocks.

As one would expect from Chapter 6, one needs at least moderate levels of risk aversion to generate realistic prices of risk. As discussed in section 7.1, one needs adjustment costs in investment to match asset price volatility. The remaining issues concern the elasticity of intertemporal substitution, which need not equal the reciprocal of risk aversion in a model with Epstein-Zin preferences, and the possibility of time-variation in risk aversion, caused perhaps by habit formation in utility. We first explore a model with Epstein-Zin preferences, following Kaltenbrunner and Lochstoer (2010), and then discuss models with habit formation (Jermann 1998, Dew-Becker 2012).

7.2.1 Long-Run Consumption Risk in General Equilibrium

Kaltenbrunner and Lochstoer (KL 2010) show that persistent variation in consumption growth arises naturally when capital accumulation is endogenous. They work with a general equilibrium model in which aggregate output Y_t is produced with capital K_t. The production function is Cobb-Douglas with multiplicative technology Z_t and a capital exponent α as in equation (7.1) but now describing the output of the whole economy rather than a single firm.

Technology is subject to random shocks that may be more or less persistent. We have

$$Z_t = \exp(\mu t + z_t), \qquad (7.27)$$

where

$$z_t = \rho_z z_{t-1} + \varepsilon_t. \qquad (7.28)$$

KL consider $\rho_z = 1$ (a random walk for technology) and $\rho_z = 0.95$ (a stationary but persistent technology process with a half-life of 13.5 quarters or 3.4 years).

KL model adjustment costs in investment as a reduction to the accumulation of physical capital, rather than as a subtraction from profits as in section 7.1. In other words they define investment as investment expenditure, gross of adjustment costs, rather than the accumulation of capital. Thus the capital accumulation equation is

$$K_{t+1} = (1 - \delta) K_t + \phi \left(\frac{I_t}{K_t} \right) K_t, \tag{7.29}$$

and output is divided between consumption and investment expenditure with nothing being lost to adjustment costs:

$$Y_t = C_t + I_t. \tag{7.30}$$

KL choose the functional form of the adjustment cost as

$$\phi(X) = a_1 + a_2 \frac{X^{1-1/\xi}}{1 - 1/\xi}, \tag{7.31}$$

where ξ is the elasticity of investment to Tobin's q, and the parameters a_1 and a_2 are set so that adjustment costs are zero in the nonstochastic steady state.

These assumptions allow KL to write the investment return, which as always satisfies $E_t[M_{t+1}(1 + R_{t+1}^I)] = 1$ (see equation (7.19)) as

$$1 + R_{t+1}^I = \phi' \left(\frac{I_t}{K_t} \right) \alpha \left(\frac{Z_{t+1}}{K_{t+1}} \right)^{1-\alpha}$$
$$+ \phi' \left(\frac{I_t}{K_t} \right) \frac{1 - \delta + \phi(I_{t+1}/K_{t+1}) - \phi'(I_{t+1}/K_{t+1}) I_{t+1}/K_{t+1}}{\phi'(I_{t+1}/K_{t+1})}. \tag{7.32}$$

This captures the output effect next period and the value of capital carried forward. The formula is different from equations (7.17) and (7.23) because here I_t denotes investment expenditure, not capital accumulation.

To close the model, KL assume that a representative agent has Epstein-Zin preferences with relative risk aversion γ and elasticity of intertemporal substitution ψ, as given by equation (6.34) in Chapter 6. Given a homoskedastic lognormal technology process and an approximate loglinear solution (to be discussed next), all variables in their model are lognormal and homoskedastic, so the loglinear formulas for the SDF with Epstein-Zin preferences, equations (6.40) and (6.49), can be used to price assets.

Model Solution

To solve the model, KL follow a method originally proposed by King, Plosser, and Rebelo (1987) and commonly used in the real business cycle literature. The idea is to transform the model into a system of loglinear difference equations for key aggregate variables, using loglinear approximations around the model's steady state. This approach is closely related to the Campbell-Shiller approximation of the return on a dividend-paying asset, introduced in Chapter 5 and applied to consumption-based asset pricing models in Chapter 6. Because the model solution is first-order around the steady state, the coefficient of risk aversion does not affect the dynamics of any of the variables; however, risk aversion does affect expected asset returns and asset prices in the sta ndard fashion of lognormal asset pricing models.[2]

In the loglinear solution, the logs of utility, consumption, and next period's capital, u_t, c_t, and k_{t+1}, are all linear in the logs of this period's capital and technology, k_t and z_t, which are the two state variables of the model:

$$u_t = A_1 k_t + A_2 z_t,$$

$$c_t = B_1 k_t + B_2 z_t,$$

$$k_{t+1} = D_1 k_t + D_2 z_t. \tag{7.33}$$

The unknown parameters of these equations can be solved analytically using the method of undetermined coefficients (Campbell 1994, Uhlig 1999). Problem 7.1 asks you to develop this solution method in a simple example.

Understanding Model Dynamics
The dynamics of the model can be understood by reference to the first-order condition relating the real interest rate to expected consumption growth in a model with Epstein-Zin utility, equation (6.44) in Chapter 6. This equation can be written as

$$E_t \Delta c_{t+1} = \mu_c + \psi \, r_{f,t+1}, \tag{7.34}$$

where the constant μ_c incorporates time preference and precautionary savings effects that are constant in a homoskedastic model. Equation (7.34) says that the representative agent is willing to tilt his planned consumption path in response to the riskless interest rate (or the expected marginal product of capital, which equals the riskless rate plus a constant in a homoskedastic model). The willingness to do this is proportional to the elasticity of intertemporal substitution.

Figure 7.1, a reproduction of Figure 1 in KL, shows the consumption response to two alternative technology shocks in a version of the model without adjustment costs in investment. The first shock, the dotted line in the top panel, is a transitory AR(1) with a half-life of 13 quarters; the second shock, the dotted line in the bottom panel, is a random walk. The dashed line in each figure is the consumption path corresponding to a very low EIS of 0.1, and the solid line is the consumption path for a much higher EIS of 1.5. In each case, the dashed line is flatter than the solid line, because an agent with a low EIS is willing to allow only very small tilts in his planned consumption path in response to changes in the marginal product of capital generated by a technology shock. Such an agent's consumption is close to a random walk, a general equilibrium version of the permanent income theory of consumption.

In both panels of Figure 7.1, the solid line initially rises less than the dashed line in response to a technology shock. This is because an agent with a high EIS is willing to defer consumption and increase saving to exploit high rates of return implied by a positive technology shock. The longer run dynamics depend on the nature of the shock. With a transitory shock, the economy first accumulates capital while capital is productive and then decumulates it later when productivity deteriorates; accordingly there is a hump in

---

[2]Tallarini (2000) works with a special case of this model, assuming a unit elasticity of intertemporal substitution and no capital adjustment costs. In this case the result that risk aversion does not affect the dynamics of the model holds exactly rather than to a first-order approximation.

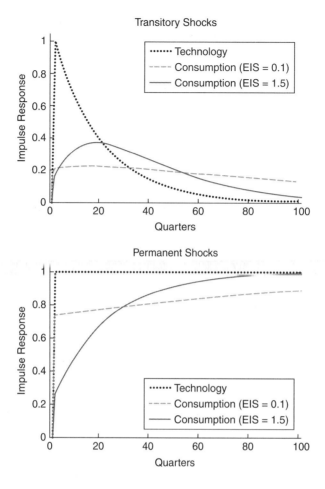

Figure 7.1. *Consumption Dynamics in General Equilibrium* (Kaltenbrunner, Georg, and Lars A. Loch-stoer, 2010, "Long-Run Risk through Consumption Smoothing," *Review of Financial Studies* 23, 3190–3224; reprinted by permission of Oxford University Press.)

consumption, which is more pronounced when the EIS is high. With a permanent shock, the economy converges to a new steady state with higher capital and technology, and this convergence is more rapid when the EIS is high.

An important stylized fact of macroeconomic data is that consumption growth is about half as volatile as output growth. To match this behavior, one can reintroduce adjustment costs into the model; these inhibit variation in investment and make consumption dynamics more similar to output dynamics. KL find that high capital adjustment costs in a model with a low EIS and a transitory technology shock generate a consumption path that resembles a dampened version of the technology shock (the dotted line) in the top panel of Figure 7.1, first spiking up and then declining gradually. Low capital adjustment costs in a model with a high EIS and a permanent technology path generate a consumption path that is similar to the one illustrated (the solid line) in the bottom panel of Figure 7.1, jumping up and then continuing to rise gradually. In both these cases the model matches the relative volatility of consumption and output, and generates a realistic maximum Sharpe ratio between 0.3 and 0.4.

However, the mechanism generating risk premia is different in these two calibrations. In the first calibration, innovations to consumption growth are negatively correlated with revisions in expected future consumption growth. From equation (6.49), this increases the volatility of the SDF if $\gamma < 1/\psi$, which is the case when $\gamma = 5$ and $\psi = 0.1$. In the second calibration, innovations to consumption growth are positively correlated with revisions in expected consumption growth. This increases the volatility of the SDF if $\gamma > 1/\psi$, which is the case when $\gamma = 5$ and $\psi = 1.5$. The second calibration is a general equilibrium version of the long-run risk model of Bansal and Yaron (2004).

Although these two calibrations have similar implications for maximum Sharpe ratios, they differ in other ways. The first calibration has a highly volatile riskless interest rate, reflecting the representative agent's aversion to the variation in expected consumption growth created by transitory technology shocks and adjustment costs in investment that limit consumption smoothing.

The second calibration has a relatively stable riskless interest rate but also a very stable return to risky assets such as consumption claims or claims to the physical capital stock. (Consumption claims and claims to physical capital are different in a production-based model, since a portion of output is paid to labor, that is, to the owners of human capital rather than physical capital.) These two properties of the second calibration are related, since the homoskedastic general equilibrium model generates asset price variation through revisions in expected future dividend growth (which are modest in realistic calibrations given smooth consumption and capital) or revisions in riskless interest rates. Risk premia are constant in this model so they cannot contribute to asset price variation. Thus volatile long-term real interest rates are needed to generate volatile prices on long-term risky claims. The stability of the capital return in the second calibration can also be understood, following the analysis of section 7.1, as the result of low adjustment costs to investment.

Other Shocks

The types of productivity shocks considered by KL are not the only ones that can be considered in a general equilibrium model with production. Campbell (1994) shows how an anticipated persistent change in productivity growth, with no effect on the level of productivity today, can be modeled as a combination of a permanent productivity shock and an offsetting transitory shock with the opposite sign (effectively subtracting the top panel of Figure 7.1 from the bottom panel or vice versa). Beaudry and Portier (2006) argue for the empirical relevance of such "news shocks." It is also possible to allow for rational learning or irrational expectations about productivity growth: Hirshleifer, Li, and Yu (2015), for example, assume that agents extrapolate past productivity growth rates when forecasting future productivity growth.

Papanikolaou (2011) considers shocks to the relative cost of investment goods, as in Justiniano, Primiceri, and Tambalotti (2010). A positive "investment shock" that reduces this relative cost causes the economy to reduce the production of consumption goods and increase the production of investment goods. Current consumption decreases, but investment opportunities are good and future consumption increases. Marginal utility may either be low or high in this situation but is high with Epstein-Zin utility when the elasticity of intertemporal substitution is less than the reciprocal of risk aversion (the opposite of the assumption made in the long-run risk literature). Bazdresch, Belo, and Lin (2013) and Kogan and Papanikolaou (2014) use this model to motivate their empirical research on the cross-section of stock returns (see section 7.1.3).

Finally, the empirical literature on the long-run risk model, discussed in Chapter 6, strongly suggests that shocks to volatility help a model with Epstein-Zin preferences match the dynamics of asset prices and consumption. In a similar spirit, Christiano, Motto, and Rostagno (2014) introduce shocks to the idiosyncratic volatility of individual firms in a macroeconomic model with incomplete markets.

7.2.2 Variable Labor Supply

The general equilibrium model considered above assumes that households provide a fixed supply of labor, so the only decision variable in the model is consumption (or equivalently investment). Many DSGE models allow households to vary their labor supply subject to a time endowment and disutility of labor, thereby introducing a second decision variable. Flexible labor supply provides households with an additional margin on which they can adjust to negative shocks. A decline in wealth, for a given wage, will induce households to increase labor supply and thereby labor income, partially offsetting the effect of the shock on consumption. Unsurprisingly then, models with flexible labor supply tend to generate smoother consumption and lower risk premia for a given curvature of the utility function over consumption. Lettau and Uhlig (2000) and Rudebusch and Swanson (2008) provide numerical results illustrating this point for DSGE models with habit formation.

Swanson (2012) presents an analytical characterization of risk aversion in a DSGE model with variable labor supply. He shows that if a nonstochastic steady state (or, more generally, a nonstochastic balanced growth path) exists, then risk aversion in the steady state can be characterized using the first-order conditions of a representative agent.

Swanson's results can be stated as follows. He assumes that utility is time-separable with time discount factor β and a twice-differentiable concave period utility function $U(C_t, L_t)$, where C_t is consumption and L_t is labor supply. He assumes that a value function $V(A_t, Z_t)$ exists, where A_t is beginning-of-period wealth and Z_t is a vector of state variables. The value function satisfies the usual Bellman equation. The coefficient of absolute risk aversion is given by

$$ARA(A_t, Z_t) = -\frac{V_{11}}{V_1}, \tag{7.35}$$

where V_1 and V_{11} are the first and second derivatives of the value function with respect to wealth, its first argument. Swanson shows that the classic Arrow-Pratt results from the static theory of choice under uncertainty, discussed in Chapter 1, hold in a dynamic model with this definition of absolute risk aversion.

Optimal choice implies that

$$V_1 = (1 + R_{ft}) U_1, \tag{7.36}$$

since a marginal increment to beginning-of-period wealth can be invested at the riskless rate and then consumed at the end of the period, and at the optimum this use of wealth has the same marginal value as any other. Differentiating the left- and right-hand sides of equation (7.36) with respect to wealth A_t, we have

$$V_{11} = (1 + R_{ft}) \left(U_{11} \frac{\partial C_t}{\partial A_t} + U_{12} \frac{\partial L_t}{\partial A_t} \right). \tag{7.37}$$

The intratemporal first-order condition for optimal labor supply implies that

$$-U_2 = W_t U_1, \tag{7.38}$$

since a marginal increase in labor supply has disutility $-U_2$ but finances W_t units of consumption, where W_t denotes the wage, and each unit of consumption has marginal utility U_1. Differentiating the left- and right-hand sides of (7.38) with respect to A_t, rearranging terms, and using (7.38) to substitute out the wage, we have

$$\frac{\partial L_t}{\partial A_t} = -\left(\frac{U_1 U_{12} - U_2 U_{11}}{U_1 U_{22} - U_2 U_{12}}\right)\frac{\partial C_t}{\partial A_t} = -\lambda \frac{\partial C_t}{\partial A_t}, \tag{7.39}$$

where the coefficient λ is defined in this equation.

Finally, the intertemporal Euler equation and budget constraint together imply that in the nonstochastic steady state,

$$\frac{\partial C_t}{\partial A_t} = \frac{R_f}{1 + W\lambda}. \tag{7.40}$$

When wealth increases in steady state, the agent permanently adjusts consumption upward and labor supply downward. In the absence of a labor supply adjustment, the agent could permanently consume the interest rate on the additional wealth. The factor $1/(1 + W\lambda)$ adjusts for the decrease in labor income caused by reduced labor supply in the proportion given by equation (7.39).

Combining these equations delivers the main result, that absolute risk aversion in steady state satisfies

$$ARA = \frac{-U_{11} + \lambda U_{12}}{U_1}\frac{R_f}{1 + W\lambda}. \tag{7.41}$$

Swanson shows that the right-hand side of this expression is always less than $-U_{11}R_f/U_1$, the equivalent expression for absolute risk aversion in a model with fixed labor supply ($\lambda = 0$). Also, absolute risk aversion can be arbitrarily small as $U_{11}U_{22} - U_{12}^2$ approaches zero, implying that risk aversion depends on the concavity of utility in both the consumption and labor supply dimensions, not just the concavity of utility with respect to consumption. In a model with separable utility over consumption and leisure, for example, where $U_{12} = 0$, risk aversion is zero when $U_{22} = 0$, that is, when the agent is risk-neutral with respect to labor supply, regardless of the magnitude of consumption concavity U_{11}.

Swanson also discusses the measurement of relative risk aversion in a DSGE model. If wealth is defined as the present discounted value of consumption, which must equal C/R_f in steady state, then, from equation (7.41)

$$RRA = \frac{C}{R_f}ARA = \frac{-U_{11} + \lambda U_{12}}{U_1}\frac{C}{1 + W\lambda}. \tag{7.42}$$

It is important to understand the meaning of these results. In a model with flexible labor supply, risk aversion with respect to wealth shocks (given by the curvature of the value function) is lower than it would be in a model with fixed labor supply and the same preferences over consumption and leisure. However, this does not necessarily mean that it is harder to explain risk premia in such a model. Instead, one may wish to consider greater curvature of the utility function $U(C_t, L_t)$, understanding that such curvature may correspond to reasonable risk aversion in a model with flexible labor supply.

DSGE models with flexible labor supply and highly concave utility of consumption face a challenge, however. Recall that the intratemporal first-order condition for optimal labor supply, equation (7.38), equates the marginal disutility of labor to the product of the wage and the marginal utility of consumption. When a positive shock hits the economy, the wage tends to rise but the marginal utility of consumption tends to fall. If the wage effect dominates, labor supply will be realistically procyclical; if the marginal utility effect dominates, labor supply will be unrealistically countercyclical. If utility over consumption is highly concave, shocks have very strong effects on the marginal utility of consumption, which will tend to induce countercyclical labor supply.

7.2.3 Habit Formation in General Equilibrium

A number of authors have embedded habit-formation preferences within a production model. Jermann (1998) works with a fixed-labor DSGE model like that of Kaltenbrunner and Lochstoer (2010) and a power utility function of $C_t - \theta C_{t-1}$ (one-period habit formation). He can explain the equity premium and the smoothness of consumption relative to output but at the cost of far too volatile a riskless interest rate. Boldrin, Christiano, and Fisher (2001) continue to assume one-period habit formation but introduce flexible labor supply. They show that the Jermann model implies countercyclical labor supply, and propose instead a two-sector model with a one-period lag in capital reallocation across sectors. This short-term rigidity makes labor supply procyclical while retaining other desirable properties of the solution.

Melino and Yang (2003) and Dew-Becker (2012) suggest an alternative way to model habit formation. They generalize Epstein-Zin preferences to allow time-variation in the curvature parameter over next-period value. That is, the fixed risk aversion coefficient γ in equation (6.34) becomes a time-varying coefficient γ_t. Dew-Becker motivates this assumption as the result of habit formation in next-period value, which, however, does not affect the valuation of current consumption. In bad times, next-period value is close to habit and the agent becomes highly averse to fluctuations in this value but remains able to tolerate short-term fluctuations in consumption. This specification of utility generates time-varying risk aversion, with important effects on the valuation of consumption claims, without implying unrealistic variation in the riskless interest rate or unrealistic autocorrelation of consumption growth in a standard DSGE model.

7.3 Marginal Rate of Transformation and the SDF

Belo (2010) implements a suggestion made by Cochrane (1988b) that producers' decisions reveal the marginal rate of transformation across states, and thereby the SDF, if producers have the ability to shift output across states. This requires a different specification of technology than the usual aggregate production function. The usual specification is

$$Y_{t+1}(s) = \varepsilon_{t+1}(s) F(K_{t+1}), \tag{7.43}$$

where firms choose K_{t+1} in advance, by investing at time t, but are then subject to an exogenous state-dependent technology shock $\varepsilon_{t+1}(s)$, which multiplies output and cannot be affected by firms.

In the Belo model, firms also choose ε_{t+1} subject to a constraint

$$\mathrm{E}_t\left[\left(\frac{\varepsilon_{t+1}}{\Theta_{t+1}}\right)^{\alpha}\right]^{1/\alpha} \leq 1, \tag{7.44}$$

where the parameter α is greater than one. The limit as $\alpha \to \infty$ is the standard model, since then ε_{t+1} must always equal Θ_{t+1}, which is exogenous and random at time t. Even when α is finite, the choice of ε_{t+1} is still conditional on the state of the world Θ_{t+1} that is realized at time $t+1$; that is, ε_{t+1} is still a random variable from the perspective of time t.

Figure 7.2, taken from Figure 1 in Belo (2010), illustrates the difference between the conventional representation of technology and the representation advocated by Belo and Cochrane. Each panel of the figure plots production possibility frontiers across two states of nature that may be realized in the next period. There are two such frontiers in each panel, corresponding to two different levels of the capital stock. In the top panel of the figure, illustrating the standard model, the technology for producing output is Leontief across the states of nature (and in fact produces equal output in the two states, although this is not essential). An increase in the capital stock shifts the frontier out, but there is no way for the firm to trade off output in one state for output in another. In the bottom panel of the figure, production is flexible, so the production possibility frontier is differentiable and concave. The firm can choose a point on the frontier as well as the overall position of the frontier, and optimality implies that the slope of the frontier at the equilibrium point (the marginal rate of transformation) should equal the marginal rate of substitution across states and hence should reveal the SDF.

Belo considers the optimization problem of a competitive producer j who takes as given an SDF M_t denominated in a numeraire good, and a relative price for its own output P_{jt}. The producer chooses investment I_{jt} and the technology shock $\varepsilon_{j,t+1}$. The Bellman equation is

$$V(x_{jt}) = \max\{D_{jt} + \mathrm{E}_t M_{t+1} V(x_{j,t+1})\}, \tag{7.45}$$

where $x_{jt} = (K_{jt}, \varepsilon_{jt}, P_{jt}, Z_{jt})$, and Z_{jt} is a vector of forecasting variables.

There are four constraints on the maximization problem:

$$D_{jt} = P_{jt} Y_{jt} - I_{jt}, \tag{7.46}$$

$$Y_{jt} = \varepsilon_{jt} F^j(K_{jt}), \tag{7.47}$$

$$\mathrm{E}_t\left[\left(\frac{\varepsilon_{j,t+1}}{\Theta_{j,t+1}}\right)^{\alpha}\right]^{1/\alpha} \leq 1, \tag{7.48}$$

$$K_{jt+1} = (1 - \delta_j) K_{jt} + I_{jt}. \tag{7.49}$$

Equation (7.46) writes the dividend as the value of output in units of the numeraire, less the cost of investment (the model abstracts from other variable inputs). Equations (7.47) and (7.48) relate output to capital and technology, both of which are choice variables. The parameter α, which determines the flexibility of technology, is assumed to be

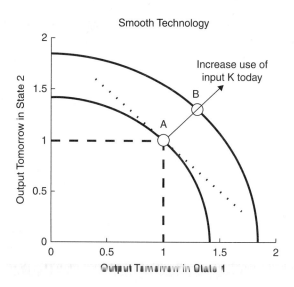

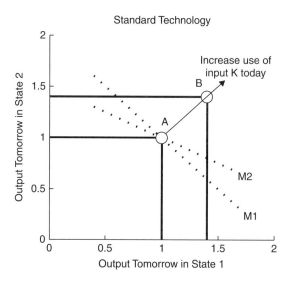

Figure 7.2. *Two Production Possibility Frontiers* (Reprinted from Belo, Frederico, 2010, "Production-Based Measures of Risk for Asset Pricing," *Journal of Monetary Economics* 57, 146–163; reprinted by permission of Elsevier.)

constant across firms, time, and states of nature. Equation (7.49) shows how investment augments the capital stock (the model abstracts from adjustment costs of investment).

The first-order condition for the choice of $\varepsilon_{j,t+1}$ is

$$\frac{\varepsilon_{j,t+1}}{\varepsilon_{jt}} = \phi_{jt}^{\frac{1}{1-a}} \left(\frac{M_{t+1}P_{j,t+1}}{P_{jt}}\right)^{\frac{1}{a-1}} \left(\frac{\Theta_{j,t+1}}{\Theta_{jt}}\right)^{\frac{a}{a-1}}, \qquad (7.50)$$

where ϕ_{jt} captures other terms known at t that play no role in the subsequent analysis. In words, technologies are chosen to be productive in states with high marginal utility of the numeraire good, a high relative price for the producer's output, or high baseline technology. The higher is α, the more important is the baseline technology level as the firm finds it more costly to shift productivity across states.

This first-order condition can be rearranged to express the SDF as

$$
\begin{aligned}
M_{t+1} &= \phi_{jt} \left(\frac{P_{j,t+1}}{P_{jt}} \right)^{-1} \left(\frac{\varepsilon_{j,t+1}}{\varepsilon_{jt}} \right)^{\alpha-1} \left(\frac{\Theta_{j,t+1}}{\Theta_{jt}} \right)^{-\alpha} \\
&= \overline{\phi}_{jt} \left(\frac{P_{j,t+1}}{P_{jt}} \right)^{-1} \left(\frac{Y_{j,t+1}}{Y_{jt}} \right)^{\alpha-1} \left(\frac{\Theta_{j,t+1}}{\Theta_{jt}} \right)^{-\alpha},
\end{aligned} \tag{7.51}
$$

where the second equality holds (with a different factor $\overline{\phi}_{jt}$ known at time t) since $\varepsilon_{j,t+1}$ is the only component of $Y_{j,t+1}$ that is not known at time t.

Next, Belo assumes that $\Theta_{j,t+1}$ has a single-factor structure. Writing $\theta_{j,t+1}$ for the log of $\Theta_{j,t+1}$,

$$
\alpha \Delta \theta_{j,t+1} = \lambda_j f_{t+1}. \tag{7.52}
$$

The factor f_{t+1} captures the state of the business cycle. Some firms, or sectors, with high λ_j coefficients have inherently more cyclical productivities than others. Sector 1 produces the numeraire good, and its factor loading is normalized to one: $\lambda_1 = 1$.

This assumption implies that for any two firms or sectors, the numeraire sector and another sector 2 with $\lambda_2 = \lambda$,

$$
\widetilde{f}_{t+1} = \frac{1}{1-\lambda} \Delta \widetilde{p}_{2,t+1} - \frac{\alpha-1}{1-\lambda} (\Delta \widetilde{y}_{2,t+1} - \Delta \widetilde{y}_{1,t+1}), \tag{7.53}
$$

and

$$
\begin{aligned}
\widetilde{m}_{t+1} &= -\frac{1}{1-\lambda} \Delta \widetilde{p}_{2,t+1} + \frac{\alpha-1}{1-\lambda} (\Delta \widetilde{y}_{2,t+1} - \Delta \widetilde{y}_{1,t+1}) \\
&\quad + (\alpha - 1) \Delta \widetilde{y}_{1,t+1},
\end{aligned} \tag{7.54}
$$

where lowercase letters denote logs of the corresponding uppercase letters, and tildes denote the innovations at time $t+1$ with respect to information available at time t.

Belo implements a test of this relationship, assuming sector 1 to be durables producers and sector 2 to be nondurables producers. The test consists of GMM estimation using excess returns on various equity test assets (e.g., portfolios of stocks sorted by size and book-market ratio, or by estimated betas with respect to the relative price and output growth of durables and nondurables), and two instruments (a constant and the aggregate dividend-price ratio). Returns are measured annually over the period 1930–2007. The model is not rejected by any sets of test assets considered (although it should be noted that the CAPM performs relatively well in the earlier part of this sample period).

Belo estimates α only slightly greater than one (implying that producers can choose technologies to adapt to exogenous shocks) and λ slightly less than one to capture the less cyclical nature of nondurables production. With these parameters, a high SDF (high marginal utility, or a bad state of the economy) is implied by low prices of nondurables relative to durables, high output growth of nondurables, and low output growth of durables. The model is empirically successful for some of the same reasons that Yogo (2006) is successful when he uses consumption (rather than production) of durables to price assets as discussed in Chapter 6. The production of durables decreases, and their price

increases (so nondurables become relatively cheaper), when the economy does unexpectedly badly. These results are also consistent with the finding of Gomes, Kogan, and Yogo
(2009) that the stocks of durable goods producers have higher systematic risk and hence
higher average returns than the stocks of nondurable goods or services producers.

7.4 Solution and Further Problem

You were asked to explain how equation (5.50) might justify Fama and French's (2015)
inclusion of both value and profitability in a multifactor model. That equation shows
that a stock with a high book-market ratio must either have low return on equity (ROE)
or deliver high returns over the infinite future. Thus, ROE should predict returns controlling for value and vice versa. Equation (5.50) is a statement about the characteristics
of an individual firm, so in order to justify a factor model it must be the case that profitable firms tend to move together with other profitable firms, just as value stocks tend
to move together with other value stocks. A caveat is that (5.50), unlike the *q*-theory
model developed in section 7.1.1, does not explain the role of an investment factor. Also,
Fama and French find that the value factor is relatively unimportant for explaining the
cross-section of stock returns once investment and profitability factors are included in
the model.

Problem 7.1 Inspecting the Mechanism

Consider a stochastic growth model with fixed labor supply and labor-augmenting
technological shocks. Output Y_t is

$$Y_t = A_t^{1-\alpha} K_t^\alpha, \tag{7.55}$$

for technology A_t and capital stock K_t.

Capital is accumulated without adjustment costs:

$$K_{t+1} = (1 - \delta) K_t + Y_t - C_t, \tag{7.56}$$

where δ is the capital depreciation rate and C_t is consumption. Consumption is chosen by
a representative agent maximizing power utility with time discount factor β, coefficient
of relative risk aversion γ, and elasticity of intertemporal substitution $\psi = 1/\gamma$.

(a) Write an expression relating the one-period gross return on an investment in capital, $1 + R_{t+1}$, to the marginal product of capital in production and the depreciation
rate.

(b) Consider the steady state (the nonstochastic balanced growth path) of the model in
which technology is growing at a constant rate G:

$$\frac{A_{t+1}}{A_t} = 1 + G. \tag{7.57}$$

(i) Use the equations for output and capital accumulation, and the first-order condition of the representative agent, to solve for the steady-state ratios A/K, Y/K,
and C/Y as functions of the log technology growth rate $g = \log(1 + G)$, the log

real return on capital $r = \log(1 + R)$, the capital share of output α, and the capital depreciation rate δ. You may assume $g \approx G$ and $r \approx R$. In this exercise, what is implicitly being assumed about the parameters β and γ?

(ii) In a calibrated annual model with $g = 0.02$, $r = 0.06$, $\alpha = 0.333$, and $\delta = 0.10$, what values for Y/K and C/Y are implied?

(c) Now consider fluctuations around the steady state, writing lowercase letters for log deviations from steady state. We have

$$y_t = (1 - \alpha) a_t + \alpha k_t \tag{7.58}$$

from the production function, and can loglinearize the capital accumulation equation as

$$k_{t+1} = \lambda_1 k_t + \lambda_2 a_t + (1 - \lambda_1 - \lambda_2) c_t \tag{7.59}$$

and

$$r_{t+1} = \lambda_3 (a_{t+1} - k_{t+1}), \tag{7.60}$$

where $\lambda_1 = (1 + r)/(1 + g)$, $\lambda_2 = (1 - \alpha)(r + \delta)/(\alpha(1 + g))$, and $\lambda_3 = (1 - \alpha)(r + \delta)/(1 + r)$.

(i) In the calibrated example above, what are the values of λ_1, λ_2, and λ_3? Give an intuitive explanation for the magnitudes of $1 - \lambda_1 - \lambda_2$ and λ_3.

(ii) Show that the representative agent's first-order condition makes $E_t \Delta c_{t+1}$ proportional to $E_t(a_{t+1} - k_{t+1})$. What is the coefficient of proportionality? Explain.

(d) We close the model by assuming an AR(1) process for log technology deviations:

$$a_t = \phi a_{t-1} + \varepsilon_t. \tag{7.61}$$

(i) We conjecture a solution of the form

$$c_t = \eta_{ck} k_t + \eta_{ca} a_t. \tag{7.62}$$

Show that this implies a similar solution for the dynamics of the capital stock:

$$k_{t+1} = \eta_{kk} k_t + \eta_{ka} a_t. \tag{7.63}$$

Write η_{kk} and η_{ka} as functions of η_{ck}, η_{ca}, λ_1, and λ_2.

(ii) Conditional on the conjecture, derive a quadratic equation that η_{ck} must satisfy, and a linear equation for η_{ca} given η_{ck}.

(e) The parameters have the following properties. In each case, explain the intuition:

(i) η_{ck} is increasing and η_{kk} is decreasing in the elasticity of intertemporal substitution ψ. In the limit as ψ increases, η_{kk} approaches zero.

(ii) η_{ca} is increasing in persistence ϕ for low values of ψ, but decreasing in ϕ for high values of ψ.

(iii) When $\phi = 1$, $\eta_{ck} + \eta_{ca} = 1$ and $\eta_{kk} + \eta_{ka} = 1$.

(iv) High values of ψ amplify the short-run response of output and dampen the longer-run response of output to a transitory technology shock.

(v) High values of ψ lead output to adjust more quickly to the new steady-state level of output when there is a permanent technology shock.

Note: This problem is based on Campbell (1994).

8
Fixed-Income Securities

THIS CHAPTER EXPLORES the pricing of fixed-income securities or bonds, defined as securities that make credible promises of deterministic payoffs at one or more dates in the future. (Thus we exclude from consideration risky debt instruments, which embed options to default and thus require more advanced analysis using derivatives pricing methods.) One might ask why such securities deserve separate treatment in a chapter of their own, given that they are just a special case of the more general securities with risky payoffs that we have analyzed extensively in earlier chapters. There are several reasons for such a treatment. From the perspective of academic finance, a set of fixed-income securities with payoffs at each future date reveals information about the time-series process of the stochastic discount factor. From the perspective of finance practice, fixed-income securities have their own terminology and conventions of market analysis.

The yield on a bond is the average rate of return if the bond is held to maturity. The analysis of fixed-income securities centers on the comparison of yields across maturities and the relation of these yields to the expected returns if bonds are held for a single period. Bonds may be nominal, making fixed dollar payments, or real, making dollar payments that are indexed to inflation and hence fixed in real terms. Two simple facts about nominal bonds motivate many of the models explored in this chapter: first, yields tend to increase with maturity; and second, unusually high yields at a given maturity forecast unusually high single-period returns on a bond with that maturity.

Section 8.1 begins the chapter by reviewing basic fixed-income concepts, including yield to maturity, the holding-period return, forward rates, and duration. We discuss both zero-coupon bonds, which make payments at a single future date, and coupon bonds, which make a stream of payments over time. This section documents the tendency for nominal yields to increase with maturity.

Section 8.2 examines the evidence on a simple empirical hypothesis about the expected returns on fixed-income securities, that they are all equal up to a constant. This "expectations hypothesis of the term structure" has been empirically rejected many times and in many different ways, but it remains a useful benchmark just as the CAPM remains a good starting point for cross-sectional equity analysis. This section summarizes the evidence that, contrary to the expectations hypothesis, spreads between yields of different maturities predict excess bond returns.

Section 8.3 presents affine term structure models, a class of bond pricing models with an exogenous time-series process for the SDF that has proven to be remarkably flexible and tractable. To build intuition, we develop simple special cases in which bond prices are driven by single factors, either with constant variance or with suitably specified stochastic volatility, and then discuss the general multivariate affine framework. We discuss the properties that the SDF must have in an affine model in order to explain the main facts about bond returns. This section ends by discussing the possibility that certain factors may be "hidden," relevant for predicting future bond prices but without any impact on the current term structure.

Section 8.4 relates affine models to the consumption-based equilibrium asset pricing models discussed in Chapter 6. In consumption-based models the persistence of consumption growth determines the sign and magnitude of risk premia on real (inflation-indexed) bonds. This motivates a presentation of the Alvarez and Jermann (2005) decomposition of the stochastic discount factor into permanent and transitory components. This section also highlights the distinction between real and nominal bonds and the effects of inflation on nominal bond risk premia.

Section 8.5 reviews the literature on pricing bonds that are denominated in different currencies. The key empirical observation in this literature is that high interest rates in a currency are associated with high excess returns on short-term bonds denominated in that currency. This observation has led researchers to use portfolios of currencies, sorted by interest rates, as test assets for evaluating equilibrium asset pricing models.

The concepts used in fixed-income analysis have been fruitfully applied not just to fixed-income securities but to other financial instruments as well. Several recent papers apply the notion of a term structure of yields on zero-coupon claims to equity and real estate markets. We defer a discussion of this literature until Chapter 9.

This chapter draws on Campbell, Lo, and MacKinlay (1997), suitably updated to reflect new data and advances in research over the past two decades, and on recent surveys by Piazzesi (2010), Gürkaynak and Wright (2012), and Duffee (2013). Consistent with the rest of this book, we remain in discrete time throughout even though much of the literature is set in continuous time.

8.1 Basic Concepts

8.1.1 Yields and Holding-Period Returns

We start by defining units, either current dollars (nominal units), or inflation-adjusted dollars (real units). Nominal units are appropriate for conventional government bonds that promise fixed nominal payments, and real units are appropriate for inflation-indexed bonds, such as US Treasury inflation-protected securities (TIPS), that promise fixed payments after adjustment for inflation. The basic concepts to be discussed in this section apply for either choice, and we will be explicit when one or another is intended.

A *zero-coupon bond* of maturity n at time t pays one unit at time $t + n$. We write its price at time t as P_{nt}.

The bond's *yield to maturity* Y_{nt} is defined by

$$P_{nt} = \frac{1}{(1 + Y_{nt})^n}. \tag{8.1}$$

The yield to maturity is the discount rate that equates the price to the present value of the final payoff. Equivalently, the yield is the annualized return if the bond is held to maturity.

It is convenient to take logs and write

$$p_{nt} = -n y_{nt}, \tag{8.2}$$

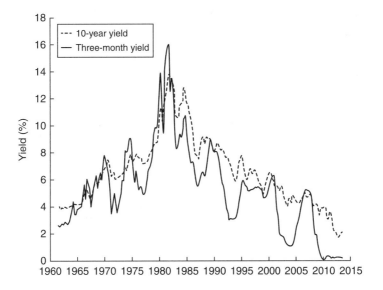

Figure 8.1. *Three-Month and 10-Year Log Zero-Coupon US Treasury Yields, 1961–2013*

or

$$y_{nt} = -\left(\frac{1}{n}\right) p_{nt}. \tag{8.3}$$

Figure 8.1 plots the history of the log yields on two US Treasury nominal zero-coupon securities over the period June 1961–June 2013. The solid line shows the log three-month yield, and the dashed line shows the log 10-year yield. It is immediately apparent that the 10-year yield is normally above the three-month yield, and shows less transitory variation.

The *yield curve* summarizes the behavior of yields at a point in time by plotting yield against maturity at a particular date. As implied by Figure 8.1, the yield curve for nominal US Treasury bonds is normally upward sloping (i.e., the yield y_{nt} normally increases with n), but there are periods where the yield curve inverts (slopes downward so that y_{nt} decreases with n). Other shapes are occasionally observed, including a hump-shaped curve that first slopes up and then down and, rarely, a reverse hump-shaped curve that first slopes down and then up.[1]

The *yield spread* or *term spread* is the difference between a long-term yield and a short-term yield. In logs,

$$s_{nt} = y_{nt} - y_{1t}. \tag{8.4}$$

When the yield curve is upward sloping, yield spreads are positive.

The bottom row of Table 8.1 reports average log yield spreads, relative to a one-quarter (three-month) US Treasury bill, on zero-coupon Treasury bills and bonds of

---

[1] A good way to get an intuitive feel for the dynamics of the yield curve is to watch a "yield curve movie" such as those available online at https://www.youtube.com/watch?v=RzKJP129DUg or https://www.youtube.com/watch?v=6z8g9xaj3g8.

Table 8.1. *Means and Standard Deviations of Term-Structure Variables, 1961–2013*

Variable	Long bond maturity (n), quarterly intervals					
	2	3	4	8	20	40
Excess return	0.117	0.283	0.426	0.865	1.650	2.173
$r_{n,t+1} - y_{1t}$	(0.878)	(1.591)	(2.284)	(4.696)	(10.030)	(17.052)
Change in yield	–0.012	–0.013	–0.013	–0.015	–0.014	–0.009
$y_{n,t+1} - y_{nt}$	(0.737)	(0.714)	(0.694)	(0.626)	(0.502)	(0.422)
Change in yield	–0.064	–0.081	–0.079	–0.065	–0.042	–0.024
$y_{n-1,t+1} - y_{nt}$	(0.802)	(0.748)	(0.723)	(0.645)	(0.512)	(0.426)
Yield spread	0.052	0.121	0.187	0.410	0.846	1.259
$y_{nt} - y_{1t}$	(0.253)	(0.368)	(0.458)	(0.713)	(1.119)	(1.456)

maturities 2, 3, 4, 8, 20, and 40 quarters, during the period June 1961 to June 2013. These average log yield spreads are all positive, increasing from 0.05% (5 basis points) at two quarters to 1.26% (126 basis points) at 40 quarters or 10 years. This confirms the average upward slope of the nominal yield curve in this period.

Although the yield is the average annualized return if a bond is held to maturity, it cannot be used to compare returns on bonds of different maturities, because a valid comparison requires the use of a common holding period. The *holding-period return* on a bond of any maturity is the return if it is held for a single period and sold before maturity. The gross simple holding-period return is given by

$$1 + R_{n,t+1} = \frac{P_{n-1,t+1}}{P_{nt}} = \frac{(1 + Y_{nt})^n}{(1 + Y_{n-1,t+1})^{n-1}}, \tag{8.5}$$

where the first equality uses the fact that the return on a zero-coupon bond is pure capital appreciation with no cash payment until the final date (at which time the price must equal the unit payment). The notation is complicated by the fact that after one period, the remaining maturity of the bond has shortened from n periods to $n-1$ periods, so the bond's price at time $t+1$ is $P_{n-1,t+1}$ rather than $P_{n,t+1}$. The second equality converts bond prices to yields using equation (8.1).

Equation (8.5) is easier to work with if we take logs:

$$r_{n,t+1} = p_{n-1,t+1} - p_{nt}$$
$$= ny_{nt} - (n-1)y_{n-1,t+1}$$
$$= y_{nt} - (n-1)(y_{n-1,t+1} - y_{nt}). \tag{8.6}$$

Here the first equality relates log returns to log prices, the second uses the relation between log prices and log bond yields, and the third rearranges terms to express the log holding-period return as the initial yield, less a multiple (maturity minus one) of the change in the log bond yield over the holding period. To earn a high return, a bondholder needs a high yield at purchase but a declining yield during the holding period.

This relation can also be understood geometrically. In Figure 8.2, time from the current date t is plotted on the horizontal axis and log bond prices are plotted on the

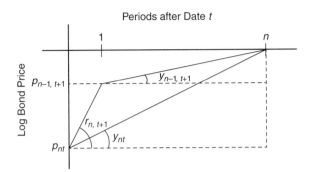

Figure 8.2. *Log Bond Prices, Yields, and Holding-Period Return*

vertical axis. Since bond prices are below one when yields are positive, log bond prices are negative. The log bond yield y_{nt} is the slope of the line from the point $(0, p_{nt,})$ to the point $(n, 0)$. The log holding-period return $r_{n,t+1}$ is the slope of the line from the point $(0, p_{nt,})$ to the point $(1, p_{n-1,t+1})$. If this exceeds y_{nt}, then because the log bond price must be zero at the terminal date, the slope of the remaining line from $(1, p_{n-1,t+1})$ to $(n, 0)$—equivalently, the yield $y_{n-1,t+1}$—must be below y_{nt}.

We can take this analysis one step further if we add and subtract a multiple $(n-1)$ of $y_{n,t+1}$ on the right-hand side of equation (8.6) to obtain

$$r_{n,t+1} = y_{nt} - (n-1)(y_{n,t+1} - y_{nt}) + (n-1)(y_{n,t+1} - y_{n-1,t+1}). \tag{8.7}$$

This breaks the change in the log bond yield over the holding period into a change over time in a constant-maturity yield and a change at a point in time as maturity decreases. The former captures the pure effect of a shift in the yield curve, and the latter captures a movement along the yield curve (sometimes known as "riding the yield curve").

The excess log holding-period return on a bond just subtracts the current short rate from both sides of equation (8.6) and uses (8.4):

$$r_{n,t+1} - y_{1t} = s_{nt} - (n-1)(y_{n-1,t+1} - y_{nt}). \tag{8.8}$$

Although log holding-period returns are linear in log bond yields, investors are often interested in simple returns. To convert from average log returns to average simple returns one must take account of Jensen's Inequality effects. If bond returns are conditionally lognormal, then the log of the mean simple excess return on a bond is given by (8.8) plus one-half the conditional variance of the bond return. The fact that long-term bond returns are more volatile than short-term bond returns, discussed below, implies that the correction becomes larger as one moves out along the yield curve.

To understand the relationships between these concepts, consider the data presented in Table 8.1 for nominal US Treasury bonds over the period June 1961–June 2013.

The top row presents average excess log holding-period returns over the three-month bill for longer-term nominal US Treasury securities. The average excess log returns are positive and increasing in maturity, from 0.12% for six-month bills to 2.17% for 10-year zero-coupon bonds. These numbers are greater than the average log yield spreads in the bottom row of the table, and the difference between the two rows is increasing in maturity.

Mechanically, the difference between the average log excess return and the average yield spread is accounted for by the change in the log bond yield over the holding period, shown in the third row of the table, multiplied by $(n-1)$. The numbers in the third row of the table are all negative. They are generally declining in magnitude with maturity (with the exception of the very short end of the yield curve), but the multiplying number is strongly increasing in maturity, which explains why the gap between the top row and the bottom row of the table increases with maturity. Small changes in bond yields have large effects on the prices of long-term bonds, and these effects have been positive on average over this sample period.

The second row of the table provides further information on the bond yield change effect. This row reports the average change in the yield on a bond of constant maturity, for each maturity shown in the table. The numbers here are negative, reflecting the fact that bond yields ended up slightly lower in June 2013 than they began in June 1961. But they are all extremely small, on the order of 1 to 1.5 basis points per quarter corresponding to a roughly 2% decline in yields over 52 years. The difference between the small negative numbers in the second row and the larger negative numbers in the third row reflects the additional impact of declining maturity on yields and hence on log holding-period returns. Since the yield curve is typically upward sloping, declining maturity normally reduces yield beyond the change in constant-maturity yield. This "riding the yield curve" effect further increases the average returns on long-term bonds over short-term bonds.

The numbers shown in parentheses beneath each row of the table are the standard deviations of the corresponding quantities. The standard deviations of log yield changes decline with maturity, but these yield changes affect returns in proportion to $(n-1)$, so the standard deviations of returns are strongly increasing in maturity from 0.88% at six months to 17.05% at 10 years. These standard deviations imply that the Jensen's Inequality correction from average log excess returns to the log of average simple returns is negligible (less than half a basis point) at six months and very far from negligible (1.45% or 145 basis points) at 10 years.

8.1.2 Forward Rates

Bonds of different maturities can be combined to guarantee an interest rate on a fixed-income investment to be made in the future; the interest rate on this investment is called a *forward rate*. To guarantee at time t the interest rate on a one-period investment to be made at time $t+n$, the investor proceeds as follows. First, she buys one $(n+1)$-period bond. This pays \$1 at time $t+n$ and costs $P_{n+1,t}$ today. To offset the cost, she sells $(P_{n+1,t}/P_{nt})$ n-period bonds today. This costs $(P_{n+1,t}/P_{nt})$ at time $t+n$ when the bonds mature. The cash flows on this strategy are illustrated in Figure 8.3 below.

The implied forward rate is

$$1 + F_{nt} = \frac{1}{(P_{n+1,t}/P_{nt})} = \frac{(1+Y_{n+1,t})^{n+1}}{(1+Y_{nt})^n}. \tag{8.9}$$

In logs,

$$
\begin{aligned}
f_{nt} &= p_{nt} - p_{n+1,t} \\
&= (n+1)y_{n+1,t} - ny_{nt} \\
&= y_{nt} + (n+1)(y_{n+1,t} - y_{nt}).
\end{aligned} \tag{8.10}
$$

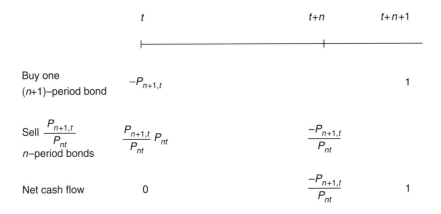

Figure 8.3. *Cash Flows on Forward Investment Strategy*

The first equality in (8.10) expresses the log forward rate as the proportional decline in zero-coupon bond prices when maturity increases. The second and third equalities show that the forward rate at maturity n exceeds the yield at the same maturity when the yield is increasing with maturity. In other words, the forward curve lies above the yield curve when the yield curve is rising and below it when the yield curve is falling. The two curves cross when the yield curve is flat. These are exactly the properties of marginal cost and average cost curves in elementary microeconomics; one can think of the yield as the average cost of borrowing at a particular maturity, and the forward rate as the marginal cost of extending the maturity of a loan.

Forward rates can also be related to bond returns. From the definition of return,

$$r_{n,t+1} = p_{n-1,t+1} - p_{nt}$$
$$= (p_{n-1,t+1} - p_{n,t+1}) + (p_{n,t+1} - p_{nt})$$
$$= f_{n-1,t+1} - n\Delta y_{n,t+1}. \qquad (8.11)$$

Since changes in log bond yields must have zero unconditional mean to avoid upward or downward trends in interest rates, this equation implies that in the absence of an interest rate trend, the unconditional average log return on a bond of maturity n equals the unconditional average log forward rate at maturity $(n-1)$.

To understand the implications of this result, consider a stylized model in which the average simple bond return is equal across maturities and the distribution of simple bond returns is lognormal. In such a model the average log bond return at maturity n—and hence, from equation (8.11), the average log forward rate at maturity $(n-1)$—is a constant, less one-half the variance of log bond returns at maturity n. When long-term bond returns are more volatile than short-term bond returns, as they are in the data, this implies that unconditional average forward rates decline with maturity. Even in a model where average simple bond returns differ across maturities, this effect tends to lower forward rates at long maturities. It can be understood as another manifestation of Jensen's Inequality in the bond pricing context.

8.1.3 Coupon Bonds

Many bonds pay a stream of coupons at rate C up to and including the maturity date, as well as one unit (the principal) at maturity. Such *coupon bonds* can be treated as packages of zero-coupon bonds, whose value equals the sum of the values of its constituents. However, it is sometimes convenient to model them directly.

The yield to maturity on an n-period coupon bond, Y_{cnt}, is defined implicitly from the bond's price P_{cnt} by

$$P_{cnt} = \sum_{i=1}^{n} \frac{C}{(1+Y_{cnt})^i} + \frac{1}{(1+Y_{cnt})^n}. \tag{8.12}$$

Once again the yield is the discount rate that equates the present value of the bond's cash flows to its price. This formula always has a unique solution, because bonds make only positive payments, but in general the solution must be obtained numerically. However, it simplifies in two special cases. If $P_{cnt} = 1$, the bond is said to be selling at par and the yield equals the coupon rate. $Y_{cnt} = C$. If maturity is infinite, the bond is a perpetuity or *consol* and we have $Y_{c\infty t} = C/P_{c\infty t}$, a formula that can be understood as a special case of the Gordon growth model in which the growth rate of cash flows is zero.

Macaulay's duration is a measure of the average length of time for which money is invested in a coupon bond, where the present values of each payment, evaluated using the coupon bond yield, are used to construct the average. The formula is

$$D_{cnt} = \frac{\sum_{i=1}^{n} \frac{iC}{(1+Y_{cnt})^i} + \frac{n}{(1+Y_{cnt})^n}}{P_{cnt}}. \tag{8.13}$$

The numerator of (8.13) is a sum of times to repayment (1, 2, and so forth up to the maturity date n), weighted by the present values $C/(1+Y_{cnt})^i$ for all coupon payment dates before maturity, and by the present value $(1+C)/(1+Y_{cnt})^n$ for the maturity date. The denominator P_{cnt} divides by the sum of the weights in the numerator to obtain a weighted average.

Macaulay's duration trivially equals maturity for zero-coupon bonds but is always less than maturity for coupon bonds. Duration declines as yield increases for coupon bonds. Duration normally increases in maturity, but for high yield and low coupon, the relation between duration and maturity may be nonmonotonic. The reason for this counterintuitive possibility is that increasing maturity has offsetting effects: it increases duration by adding a distant future payment and shifting the large principal payment one period further from the present, but it decreases duration by reducing the weight placed on the final payment relative to the weights on the coupon payments. When a bond's yield is high enough relative to its coupon, the latter effect may dominate.

The formula for Macaulay's duration simplifies in the two special cases discussed above. For a par bond,

$$D_{cnt} = \frac{1-(1+Y_{cnt})^{-n}}{1-(1+Y_{cnt})^{-1}}. \tag{8.14}$$

For a perpetuity,

$$D_{c\infty t} = (1+Y_{c\infty t})/Y_{c\infty t} = 1 + P_{c\infty t}/C. \tag{8.15}$$

Macaulay's duration has the important property that it is the negative of the elasticity of a coupon bond's price with respect to its gross yield. Equivalently, it is the negative of the derivative of the log price with respect to the log yield. Thus the previously stated relations between holding-period returns, forward rates, and yields for zero-coupon bonds can be generalized to approximate relations for coupon bonds if we replace maturity with duration (Shiller, Campbell, and Schoenholtz 1983). For example,

$$r_{c,n,t+1} \approx D_{cnt} y_{cnt} - (D_{cnt} - 1) y_{c,n-1,t+1}. \tag{8.16}$$

Practitioners often work with *modified duration,*

$$D^*_{cnt} = \frac{D_{cnt}}{(1 + Y_{cnt})}. \tag{8.17}$$

Modified duration is the negative of the derivative of log price with respect to the level of the yield. Equivalently, modified duration gives the proportional response in a bond's price to a given infinitesimal change in yield or the effect of a small change in the yield Y_{cnt} on a bond's realized log return $r_{c,n,t+1}$.

Modified duration declines with yield for all bonds, even zero-coupon bonds whose Macaulay's duration is constant. Hence, large increases in yield have a dampened effect on bond returns as modified duration declines, while large decreases in yield have an amplified effect on bond returns as duration increases. The relation between bond returns and yield changes is therefore convex. This *convexity* implies that for a given level of the bond yield, the average simple return on a long-term bond is higher when its yield change is volatile. If investors understand convexity and do not require a higher average simple return as compensation for volatility, bond prices rise and bond yields fall in response to volatility. This is another way to understand the Jensen's Inequality effect that drives down long-term forward rates in models with interest rate volatility.

8.2 The Expectations Hypothesis of the Term Structure

The *expectations hypothesis* (EH) says that expected excess returns on long-term bonds over short-term bonds are constant over time, so there is no particularly good time to hold long- or short-term bonds. The *pure expectations hypothesis* (PEH) says that expected excess returns on long-term bonds over short-term bonds are zero, but this is of less empirical interest.

Both these hypotheses must specify the holding period over which excess returns are measured and whether excess returns are simple or log. If one works in simple returns, one has the problem that the PEH for a particular holding period is inconsistent with the PEH for any other holding period, because of Jensen's Inequality. For example, equality of expected one-period holding returns on one- and two-period zero-coupon bonds requires

$$1 + Y_{1t} = E_t[1 + R_{2,t+1}] = (1 + Y_{2t})^2 E_t\left[\frac{1}{1 + Y_{1,t+1}}\right], \tag{8.18}$$

whereas equality of expected two-period holding returns on one- and two-period bonds requires

$$(1 + Y_{2t})^2 = (1 + Y_{1t}) E_t[1 + Y_{1,t+1}]. \tag{8.19}$$

Equations (8.18) and (8.19) are inconsistent with one another whenever interest rates are random, because the reciprocal is a nonlinear function, so

$$\frac{1}{E_t[1 + Y_{1,t+1}]} \neq E_t\left[\frac{1}{1 + Y_{1,t+1}}\right]. \tag{8.20}$$

Most empirical work studies log excess returns; this has the advantage that if the log EH or PEH holds for all maturities at a single holding period, it also holds for all other holding periods. The log EH can be written for a one-period holding period as

$$E_t[r_{n,t+1} - y_{1t}] = \mu_n, \tag{8.21}$$

where μ_n is an unrestricted constant that can depend on maturity n but not time t. Alternatively, the log EH can be written for an n-period holding period as

$$E_t\left[y_{nt} - \left(\frac{1}{n}\right)\sum_{i=0}^{n-1} y_{1,t+i}\right] = \theta_n. \tag{8.22}$$

The first term on the left-hand side of (8.22) is the return on an n-period bond held to maturity, and the second term is the return on a sequence of single-period bonds rolled over for n periods. The expected difference between these two returns is an unrestricted constant θ_n that can depend on maturity but not time. Equation (8.22) holds for all maturities n if equation (8.21) holds for all maturities and vice versa.

The log EH can be tested using the usual methodology for testing unpredictability of expected excess returns, by regressing realized log excess returns on variables known at time t and testing the null hypothesis that coefficients on all variables other than a constant are zero. A natural choice of regressor is the yield spread $s_{nt} = y_{nt} - y_{1t}$.

8.2.1 Restrictions on Interest Rate Dynamics

The log EH has interesting implications for the dynamics of interest rates, and tests of the model can be interpreted as tests of these implications. The implications can be stated in three different ways. First, if one substitutes the relation between excess returns and yields, equation (8.8), into equation (8.21) and drops the constant for notational simplicity, the log EH implies that

$$s_{nt} = (n - 1)E_t[y_{n-1,t+1} - y_{nt}]. \tag{8.23}$$

The log EH says that when the yield spread is unusually high, the yield on the long-term bond must be expected to increase slightly to generate a capital loss that will offset the bond's higher initial yield. This can be tested by a regression of the scaled single-period change in the yield on a long-term bond onto the yield spread:

$$(n - 1)(y_{n-1,t+1} - y_{nt}) = \alpha + \beta s_{nt} + u_{t+1}, \tag{8.24}$$

where the null hypothesis is that $\beta = 1$ and the intercept α is unrestricted.

This implication of the log EH seems counterintuitive at first because it seems to imply that when the yield spread is unusually high, the increase in the long-term yield will increase the spread even further, preventing any return to a normal level of the spread.

Naturally this is not the case; as an informal exercise, you are asked to explain why not. The answer is given at the end of the chapter.

Second, equation (8.22) can be rearranged, again dropping the constant for simplicity, to state that:

$$s_{nt} = E_t \left(\frac{1}{n}\right) \sum_{i=0}^{n-1} (y_{1,t+i} - y_{1t}) = E_t \sum_{i=0}^{n-1} \left(1 - \frac{i}{n}\right) \Delta y_{1,t+i}. \tag{8.25}$$

The log EH says that when the yield spread is unusually high, the average short-term interest rate over the life of the long-term bond must be substantially higher than the current short rate. The second equality in (8.25) restates this in terms of expected single-period changes in short rates. This can be tested by a regression,

$$\sum_{i=0}^{n-1} \left(1 - \frac{i}{n}\right) \Delta y_{1,t+i} = \alpha + \beta s_{nt} + v_{t+n}, \tag{8.26}$$

where again the EH implies that $\beta = 1$ and the intercept is unrestricted. This regression has overlapping errors because the residual v_{t+n} is not known until time $(t + n - 1)$, so the standard error of the estimated coefficient must be corrected for this using standard methods.

Third, recall from equation (8.10) that the n-period-ahead forward rate, $f_{nt} = (n + 1)y_{n+1,t} - ny_{nt}$. Combining this with the n-period form of the log EH, equation (8.22), we have

$$f_{nt} = \phi_n + E_t y_{1,t+n}. \tag{8.27}$$

The log EH says that the log forward rate is a constant plus the expected future short-term interest rate, so the forward curve can be used to read off market expectations of future short rates after correcting for constant risk premia. Subtracting the current short rate from each side of (8.27), this can be tested by a regression

$$y_{1,t+n} - y_{1t} = \alpha + \beta (f_{nt} - y_{1t}) + \varepsilon_{t+n}, \tag{8.28}$$

where again the the EH implies that $\beta = 1$ but does not restrict the intercept, and the regression has overlapping errors that must be taken into account in calculating the standard error of the estimated coefficient.

8.2.2 Empirical Evidence

Campbell and Shiller (1991) implement the first two regression tests above and contrast the results of these tests. Here we update Campbell and Shiller's findings. Table 8.2 reports estimated slope coefficients from regressions (8.24) (first row) and (8.26) (second row), using quarterly data on US Treasury zero-coupon bond yields over the period 1961Q3–2013Q2.

The two rows of this table present a striking contrast. The regression (8.24) that looks at the relation between yield spreads and short-run changes in long-term yields rejects the EH strongly, with an estimated slope coefficient that not only fails to equal one but is actually negative. The standard errors in this regression are small enough to reject not

Table 8.2.   *Slope Coefficients from Single-Period and Multiperiod Regression Tests of the Log Expectations Hypothesis, 1961–2013*

| Variable | Long bond maturity (n), quarterly intervals | | | | | |
	2	3	4	8	20	40
Long-yield changes	−1.277 (0.319)	−1.082 (0.432)	−1.170 (0.489)	−1.505 (0.619)	−2.283 (0.736)	−3.133 (0.895)
Short-rate changes	0.252 (0.137)	0.232 (0.143)	0.253 (0.132)	0.427 (0.142)	0.835 (0.117)	0.554 (0.126)

only the EH null that the slope coefficient is one, but even the hypothesis that the slope coefficient is zero. In other words, unusually high yield spreads predict declines in the yields on longer-term bonds rather than increases.

The regression that looks at long-run changes in short-term interest rates, (8.26), also rejects the EH but with a coefficient that is statistically significantly positive for most maturities. Unusually high yield spreads do predict increases in short rates, albeit smaller increases than those implied by the EH. Fama and Bliss (1987) report similar findings using the regression (8.28), emphasizing that the ability of forward rates to predict changes in short rates is strongest at horizons beyond one year.

Campbell and Shiller (1991) argue that the pattern of coefficients shown in Table 8.2 can be explained by any force that causes temporary variation in the yield on long-term bonds, unrelated to expected future short-term interest rates. This force could be a time-varying rational risk premium, changing investor sentiment in a behavioral model, or even measurement error in the long-term bond yield (which is minimal in practice given highly liquid markets for Treasury bonds). Any temporary variation in the long yield will bias the coefficient in (8.26) toward zero, because it adds noise to the explanatory variable but does not affect the dependent variable, so it attenuates the regression coefficient. However, the same temporary variation in the long yield will affect both the explanatory variable and the dependent variable in (8.24), moving them in opposite directions, and thus can cause the estimated coefficient to be negative as seen in Table 8.2.

More recent research on equilibrium bond pricing models has fleshed out this idea by modeling the driving force that moves long yields. Gabaix (2012), for example, assumes that inflation jumps when a rare consumption disaster occurs and that the magnitude of this jump itself varies over time. In periods where a large increase in inflation is expected in the event of a disaster, long-term nominal bonds are expected to perform extremely poorly in a disaster and are therefore regarded as unusually risky. The yield and risk premium are unusually high in such periods, but subsequently expectations of disaster inflation return to normal, generating the empirical patterns documented by Fama and Bliss (1987) and by Campbell and Shiller (1991).

All the tests of the EH that we have considered so far in this section treat different bond maturities independently of one another, predicting excess returns on n-period bonds over one-period bonds using only the yields on bonds with these specific maturities. An alternative approach is to use the entire yield curve to predict excess bond returns. Cochrane and Piazzesi (2005) work with annual returns on bonds of maturities two through five years and regress the excess returns on bonds at each maturity onto the current one-year rate and forward rates for years two through five. They find a high correlation between the fitted values at all maturities and cannot reject the hypothesis that predicted excess returns on bonds of all these maturities are proportional to a single predictor, a linear combination of forward rates.

Cochrane and Piazzesi report two other intriguing results about their return predictor. First, the return predictor has a tent shape, placing positive weight on the three-year forward rate but declining weights as the maturity moves away from three years toward one year or five years. Equivalently, the predictor measures the concavity of the yield curve between maturities one and five years. This has stimulated interest in equilibrium models whose yield curves are concave at times when risk premia are high, although the tent shape turns out to be less robust in an extended sample period than the basic finding of a single return predictor. Second, the return predictor is cyclical, tending to increase during recessions when the Fed lowers the short-term interest rate and creates a yield curve that is steep at maturities between one and three years. This finding suggests the possibility that bond return predictability can be linked to cyclical predictability of other assets, as suggested by early empirical work of Fama and French (1989) and equilibrium asset pricing models with cyclical variation in risk or risk aversion.

8.3 Affine Term Structure Models

Pricing models for zero-coupon bonds exploit the fact that returns are given by ratios of successive prices. For an n-period zero-coupon bond, the return $(1 + R_{n,t+1}) = P_{n-1,t+1}/P_{nt}$, so the standard pricing equation (4.37), $1 = \mathrm{E}_t[(1 + R_{n,t+1})M_{t+1}]$, implies

$$P_{nt} = \mathrm{E}_t[P_{n-1,t+1}M_{t+1}]. \tag{8.29}$$

Solving this equation forward and using the terminal condition $P_{0t} = 1$, we obtain

$$P_{nt} = \mathrm{E}_t[M_{t+1}M_{t+2}\ldots M_{t+n}] = \mathrm{E}_t[M_{t,t+n}]. \tag{8.30}$$

Just as the one-period riskless bond price is the expectation of the single-period SDF, a result we discussed in Chapter 4, so the n-period riskless bond price is the expectation of the product of n successive SDFs or, equivalently, the expectation of the n-period SDF (written $M_{t,t+n}$ in the above equation).

Equation (8.30) shows that a term structure model is actually a time-series model for the SDF. Modeling the dynamics of the SDF and inferring bond prices guarantees that there will be no arbitrage opportunities in the bond market, whereas reduced-form econometric models for bond yields may inadvertently allow such arbitrage opportunities to arise. Problem 8.1 asks you to explore this possibility in the case of a popular reduced-form specification due to Nelson and Siegel (1987).

Given the multiplicative nature of equations (8.29) and (8.30), it is natural to take logs. We can do this straightforwardly if we assume that the SDF and bond prices are jointly conditionally lognormal. Then equation (8.29) becomes

$$p_{nt} = \mathrm{E}_t[m_{t+1} + p_{n-1,t+1}] + \frac{1}{2}\mathrm{Var}_t[m_{t+1} + p_{n-1,t+1}]$$

$$= p_{1t} + \mathrm{E}_t p_{n-1,t+1} + \frac{1}{2}\mathrm{Var}_t p_{n-1,t+1} + \mathrm{Cov}_t(p_{n-1,t+1}, m_{t+1}), \tag{8.31}$$

where the second equality uses the implication of equation (4.42) that $p_{1t} = -y_{1t} = \mathrm{E}_t m_{t+1} + (1/2)\mathrm{Var}_t m_{t+1}$.

Affine term structure models make assumptions to ensure that all log bond prices (equivalently, log bond yields) are linear in state variables, which themselves follow linear time-series processes. *Completely affine* models require that the conditional expectations and the variance-covariance matrix of log bond returns and the log SDF are both linear in the state variables. *Essentially affine* models (Duffee 2002) allow nonlinearity in the SDF specification while retaining linearity in log bond prices.

We present a sequence of illustrative single-factor models to build intuition and then discuss more general multivariate affine term structure models.

8.3.1 Completely Affine Homoskedastic Single-Factor Model

The simplest affine model, originally formulated in continuous time by Vasicek (1977), has a homoskedastic AR(1) process for a single state variable:

$$x_{t+1} = \mu + \phi x_t + \sigma \varepsilon_{t+1}, \tag{8.32}$$

where ε_{t+1} is a standard normal random variable. We assume that the stochastic process for the log SDF can be written as

$$m_{t+1} = -x_t - \frac{1}{2}\left(\frac{\lambda}{\sigma}\right)^2 - \left(\frac{\lambda}{\sigma}\right)\varepsilon_{t+1}. \tag{8.33}$$

To understand this expression, start by considering the last term on the right-hand side of (8.33). This shows that the shock to the state variable x_{t+1} also moves the log SDF. There can be additional shocks to the log SDF that are uncorrelated with ε_{t+1}, but given the process (8.32), such shocks will not affect bond prices. For simplicity we therefore ignore all other shocks.

Next consider the first term on the right-hand side of (8.33). This shows that the state variable captures movements in the expected log SDF and hence movements in the interest rate.

Finally, the second term on the right-hand side of (8.33) is a Jensen's Inequality adjustment that eliminates effects of SDF volatility on the level of interest rates. To see the effect of this term, we solve (8.32) and (8.33) for the price of a one-period real bond:

$$p_{1t} = E_t m_{t+1} + \frac{1}{2}\mathrm{Var}_t m_{t+1} = -x_t - \frac{1}{2}\left(\frac{\lambda}{\sigma}\right)^2 + \frac{1}{2}\left(\frac{\lambda}{\sigma}\right)^2 = -x_t. \tag{8.34}$$

This implies that the one-period log interest rate, $y_{1t} = -p_{1t}$, is exactly equal to the state variable x_t:

$$y_{1t} = x_t. \tag{8.35}$$

Given the linearity of the model, it is natural to guess a linear functional form for the log prices (equivalently, yields) on all longer-term bonds:

$$p_{nt} = -ny_{nt} = A_n + B_n x_t, \tag{8.36}$$

where A_n and B_n are unknown coefficients to be determined by the equilibrium conditions of the model. Under this conjecture the pricing equation (8.31) can be rewritten as

$$A_n + B_n x_t = -x_t + [A_{n-1} + B_{n-1}(\mu + \phi x_t)] + \frac{B_{n-1}^2 \sigma^2}{2} - B_{n-1}\lambda. \tag{8.37}$$

To solve for the unknown coefficients A_n and B_n and verify the assumed linearity of log bond prices, we first equate coefficients on the state variable x_t in equation (8.37) and solve for B_n:

$$B_n = -1 + \phi B_{n-1} = -\left(\frac{1 - \phi^n}{1 - \phi}\right), \tag{8.38}$$

where the second inequality uses the initial condition $B_1 = -1$. As maturity n increases, the coefficient B_n approaches $-1/(1 - \phi)$.

Next we equate the remaining coefficients (constant terms) in equation (8.37) and obtain a recursive solution for A_n:

$$A_n = A_{n-1} + B_{n-1}\mu + \frac{B_{n-1}^2 \sigma^2}{2} - B_{n-1}\lambda. \tag{8.39}$$

This equation can be rearranged to combine the second and the fourth terms:

$$A_n = A_{n-1} + B_{n-1}(\mu - \lambda) + \frac{B_{n-1}^2 \sigma^2}{2}. \tag{8.40}$$

Equation (8.40) shows that risk in this model (a nonzero coefficient λ in the expression for the SDF) affects bond prices in the same way as a change in the intercept μ of the process for the short-term interest rate. Bond prices in the presence of risk are the same as those in a model without risk but with an average short rate of $(\mu - \lambda)/(1 - \phi)$ rather than $\mu/(1 - \phi)$. This is an example of the general proposition, discussed in Chapters 4 and 6, that risk aversion and distorted beliefs have the same effect on the SDF and hence on asset prices.

To understand more deeply the economic forces at work in this model, we next solve for bond risk premia and forward rates.

Bond Risk Premia

The risk premium on an n-period bond over a one-period bond (the term premium) is a constant,

$$\mathrm{E}_t r_{n,t+1} - y_{1t} + \frac{\mathrm{Var}_t r_{n,t+1}}{2} = \mathrm{E}_t p_{n-1,t+1} - p_{nt} + \frac{\mathrm{Var}_t p_{n-1,t+1}}{2} + p_{1t}$$

$$= -\mathrm{Cov}_t(p_{n-1,t+1}, m_{t+1}) = B_{n-1}\lambda. \tag{8.41}$$

Since B_{n-1} is negative, this has the opposite sign to the coefficient λ in the equation describing the stochastic discount factor, (8.33). The Sharpe ratio for an n-period bond, S_n, is also constant:

$$S_n = \frac{B_{n-1}\lambda}{-B_{n-1}\sigma} = -\frac{\lambda}{\sigma}. \tag{8.42}$$

When $\lambda > 0$, a positive shock ε_{t+1}, which drives interest rates up and bond prices down, also drives down the SDF (the marginal utility of investors). In this case bonds do badly in good times and well in bad times; they are hedges with negative risk premia. When $\lambda < 0$, however, high interest rates and low bond prices coincide with high marginal utility, and in this case bonds are risky assets with positive risk premia.

Because bond risk premia are constant in this model, the expectations hypothesis of the term structure holds. The response of bond prices to interest rate movements, given by the coefficients B_n, can be understood using the expectations hypothesis. When the short rate x_t increases by ε_t, the expected future short rate i periods ahead increases by $\phi^i \varepsilon_t$. The effect on the n-period bond price is the negative of the sum of these short rate effects, $-[1 + \phi + \phi^2 + \cdots + \phi^{n-1}] = -(1 - \phi^n)/(1 - \phi) = B_n$. The effect on the n-period log bond yield is the average of these short rate effects, as in the expectations hypothesis, $[1 + \phi + \phi^2 + \cdots + \phi^{n-1}]/n = -B_n/n$.

Forward Rates
The forward rate at maturity n is

$$f_{nt} = p_{nt} - p_{n+1,t} = -(A_{n+1} - A_n) - (B_{n+1} - B_n)x_t$$
$$= \frac{\mu - \lambda}{1 - \phi} - \left(\frac{1 - \phi^n}{1 - \phi}\right)^2 \frac{\sigma^2}{2} + \phi^n \left(x_t - \frac{\mu - \lambda}{1 - \phi}\right). \tag{8.43}$$

Here the first equality is definitional, the second holds in any affine model, and the third holds in this particular model after substituting in the solutions (8.38) and (8.39) for the coefficients B_n and A_n.

Equation (8.43) illustrates once again that the effect of risk can be represented as a shift in the long-run average level of the short-term interest rate, from $\mu/(1 - \phi)$ to $(\mu - \lambda)/(1 - \phi)$. The expression for the forward rate contains three terms: the risk-adjusted long-run average short rate; a Jensen's Inequality or convexity term, which is negative and increasing in magnitude with n; and the effect of the deviation of the current short rate from its long-run risk-adjusted average. The last term can be either positive or negative depending on the current value of the short rate, so the term structure of forward rates can be upward sloping, downward sloping, or hump shaped.

As n increases, the forward rate approaches the limit

$$f_{\infty t} = \frac{\mu - \lambda}{1 - \phi} - \left(\frac{1}{1 - \phi}\right)^2 \frac{\sigma^2}{2}. \tag{8.44}$$

The limiting forward rate is constant unless $\phi = 1$, in which case it does not exist but instead forward rates become ever more negative as maturity n increases. The property that the limiting forward rate is either constant or diverges to negative infinity is much more general, as highlighted by Dybvig, Ingersoll, and Ross (1996). It is a difficulty for empirical term structure modeling, since observed long-term forward rates do seem to vary over time but do not seem to diverge to negative infinity as maturity increases (although we do not observe maturities beyond about 30 years in practice).

In the stationary case where the limiting forward rate is constant, it is determined by the long-run average short rate $\mu/(1 - \phi)$, the long-run risk adjustment $-\lambda/(1 - \phi)$, and the Jensen's Inequality or convexity term $-(1/(1 - \phi))^2\sigma^2/2$. The last term is negative because, as discussed in section 8.1.3, long bonds have convexity: they rise in value more when rates decline than they decline in value when rates rise. Investors, understanding this, are willing to hold long bonds at high prices and correspondingly low yields and forward rates. The convexity effect becomes more powerful as maturity increases because long bond returns are more volatile than short bond returns, but in the stationary case where $\phi < 1$, bond volatility approaches a constant so the convexity effect converges to a finite constant. In the nonstationary case where $\phi = 1$, bond volatility and the convexity effect become ever more powerful as maturity increases, which prevents the long-term forward rate from converging to any finite limit.

8.3.2 Completely Affine Heteroskedastic Single-Factor Model

The model just discussed has constant bond risk premia. Given the evidence for time-varying risk premia presented in section 6.2, it is natural to consider models that can capture this feature of the data. One particularly well-known single-factor model, proposed by Cox, Ingersoll, and Ross (CIR 1985) in continuous time, has time-varying volatility in both the state variable and the log SDF, where the state variable controls the level of this volatility. In order to retain an affine term structure, this requires that the standard deviations of shocks are proportional to the square root of the state variable so the variances and covariances of shocks remain linear in the state variable.

Specifically, we change equation (8.32) to

$$x_{t+1} = \mu + \phi x_t + \sigma x_t^{1/2} \varepsilon_{t+1}. \tag{8.45}$$

This process has the property that x_t will always remain nonnegative in continuous time, provided that $\mu > 0$, because as x_t declines toward zero the volatility of shocks disappears and the process reverts deterministically toward its positive mean. Hence, the square root of x_t will always be a real number in the continuous-time version of this model.

Also, we change equation (8.33) to

$$m_{t+1} = -x_t - \frac{1}{2}\left(\frac{\lambda}{\sigma}\right)^2 x_t - \left(\frac{\lambda}{\sigma}\right) x_t^{1/2} \varepsilon_{t+1}. \tag{8.46}$$

The second term in equation (8.46) is the Jensen's Inequality correction, which now must be proportional to the state variable rather than constant.

Like the previous model, the CIR model implies that the one-period log bond yield equals the state variable x_t, and the prices of longer-term bonds are linear in the state variable with intercept A_n and slope B_n at maturity n. However, the recursions for A_n and B_n are different from before. We have

$$B_n = -1 + \phi B_{n-1} + \frac{B_{n-1}^2}{2} - B_{n-1}\lambda$$

$$= -1 + (\phi - \lambda)B_{n-1} + \frac{B_{n-1}^2}{2}. \tag{8.47}$$

This is no longer a linear recursion, but is straightforward to solve numerically. Note that risk adjustment through the parameter λ now affects the solution for B_n, and is equivalent to altering the persistence of the state variable.

While the B_n solution is more complex because variances and covariances of shocks are proportional to x_t in this model, the solution for A_n given B_n is simpler for the same reason:

$$A_n = A_{n-1} + B_{n-1}\mu. \tag{8.48}$$

Bond Risk Premia
In the CIR model the risk premium on long bonds is proportional to the state variable x_t and hence to the short-term interest rate:

$$\mathrm{E}_t r_{n,t+1} - y_{1t} + \frac{\mathrm{Var}_t r_{n,t+1}}{2} = -\mathrm{Cov}_t(p_{n-1,t+1}, m_{t+1}) = B_{n-1}\lambda x_t. \qquad (8.49)$$

The Sharpe ratio for long bonds is proportional to the square root of the interest rate:

$$S_n = \frac{B_{n-1}\lambda x_t}{-B_{n-1}\sigma x_t^{1/2}} = -\left(\frac{\lambda}{\sigma}\right) x_t^{1/2}. \qquad (8.50)$$

The ratio of mean to variance of return is, however, constant in this model.

Although the CIR model generates time-varying risk premia on long bonds, it cannot explain the predictability of excess bond returns from the yield spread. In the CIR model, the risk premium is increasing in the state variable x_t if it is positive on average. Empirically, however, the yield spread is negatively correlated with the short-term interest rate and hence with the state variable x_t. Thus, the CIR model predicts that low yield spreads should predict high returns on long bonds, contrary to the empirical evidence reported in Table 8.2.

The assumption that interest rate volatility is proportional to the square root of the interest rate is theoretically convenient but does not fit historical US data well. Data from the 1960s through the 1980s suggested that volatility increases with a higher power of the short rate than the square root, while more recent data, with very low short rates and continuing interest rate volatility, suggest the opposite. This suggests that a more flexible model of volatility is needed, one in which interest rate volatility is not tied so closely to the level of the short-term interest rate.

8.3.3 Essentially Affine Models

In the Cox, Ingersoll, and Ross (1985) model, bond risk premia vary in proportion to the variance of the interest rate. However, Duffee (2002) pointed out that it is possible to write down an affine term structure model in which risk premia vary independently of interest rate volatility. Doing this sacrifices the linearity of the mean and variance of the log SDF, but log bond prices can still be linear in the state variable, which is the essential property of an affine term structure model. (Hence, Duffee calls this broader class of affine models essentially affine and the models discussed above completely affine.)

Single-Factor Essentially Affine Model with Homoskedastic Bond Yields
The simplest essentially affine model retains a single homoskedastic state variable, as in section 8.3.1, but multiplies innovations to the SDF by that state variable. We have $x_{t+1} = \mu + \phi x_t + \sigma \varepsilon_{t+1}$ as in equation (8.32) but a new specification for the SDF:

$$m_{t+1} = -x_t - \frac{1}{2}\left(\frac{\lambda}{\sigma}\right)^2 x_t^2 - \left(\frac{\lambda}{\sigma}\right) x_t \varepsilon_{t+1}. \qquad (8.51)$$

With this specification the short interest rate again equals the state variable x_t, and long bond prices again obey a linear recursion. Bond yields are homoskedastic even though the log SDF is now heteroskedastic. The solution for B_n becomes

$$B_n = -1 + (\phi - \lambda) B_{n-1} = -\frac{1 - (\phi - \lambda)^n}{1 - (\phi - \lambda)}, \tag{8.52}$$

which is the solution from the fully homoskedastic model with a risk adjustment to the persistence of the short interest rate. The solution for A_n becomes:

$$A_n = A_{n-1} + B_{n-1}\mu + \frac{B_{n-1}^2}{2}. \tag{8.53}$$

In this model the risk premium on long bonds is $B_{n-1}\lambda x_t$, just as in the CIR model (equation (8.49)), but bonds have constant return volatility, so both the Sharpe ratio and the mean-variance ratio for long bonds are proportional to the level of the interest rate. The Sharpe ratio is given by

$$S_n = \frac{B_{n-1}\lambda x_t}{-B_{n-1}\sigma} = -\left(\frac{\lambda}{\sigma}\right) x_t. \tag{8.54}$$

More generally, essentially affine models decouple time-variation in bond risk premia from time-variation in the level or volatility of the short interest rate. It is straightforward to write down a two-factor model in which the first factor is the short rate while the second factor governs the volatility of shocks to the SDF and hence the level of bond risk premia but need not have any influence on the volatility of shocks to the interest rate. A problem at the end of this chapter asks you to analyze such a model. Here we instead discuss the general form of essentially affine term structure models with an arbitrary number of factors.

Multivariate Essentially Affine Model with Homoskedastic Bond Yields
Single-factor models imply that all bond returns are perfectly correlated, since the term structure is driven by only a single shock. Recent literature therefore concentrates on multifactor models. The extension is particularly straightforward when the state variables, and hence bond yields, are homoskedastic.

A multifactor version of the previous essentially affine model, with a homoskedastic vector of state variables and a heteroskedastic SDF, can be written as

$$x_{t+1} = \mu + \Phi x_t + \Sigma \varepsilon_{t+1}, \tag{8.55}$$

where x_{t+1}, μ, and ε_{t+1} are now vectors (with the variance-covariance matrix of ε_{t+1} equal to the identity matrix) and Φ and Σ are matrices. The stochastic process for the log SDF is

$$m_{t+1} = -(\delta_0 + \delta_1' x_t) - \frac{1}{2}\Lambda_t'\Lambda_t - \Lambda_t'\varepsilon_{t+1}, \tag{8.56}$$

where δ_0 is a scalar and δ_1 and Λ_t are vectors. Finally, we parameterize Λ_t as

$$\Lambda_t = \Sigma^{-1}(\lambda_0 + \lambda_1' x_t), \tag{8.57}$$

where λ_0 is a vector and λ_1 is a matrix.

To price bonds, we follow the same procedure as before, guessing a linear solution

$$p_{nt} = A_n + B_n' x_t, \tag{8.58}$$

where B_n is now a vector. Substituting this into the pricing recursion (8.31) and equating coefficients on the state vector, we find that

$$B_n' = B_{n-1}'(\Phi - \lambda_1) - \delta_1'$$
$$= -\delta_1'(I - (\Phi - \lambda_1))^{-1}(I - (\Phi - \lambda_1)^n). \tag{8.59}$$

Similarly, we find that

$$A_n = A_{n-1} + B_{n-1}'(\mu - \lambda_0) - \delta_0 + \frac{B_{n-1}'\Sigma\Sigma'B_{n-1}}{2}. \tag{8.60}$$

Equations (8.59) and (8.60) can be solved recursively, using $A_1 = -\delta_0$ and $B_1 = -\delta_1$. These equations are the multivariate generalization of the solutions for the homoskedastic single-factor model and the essentially affine single-factor model, which can be obtained by setting the matrix Σ equal to a scalar σ, setting $\delta_0 = 0$ and $\delta_1 = 1$, and setting either $\lambda_0 = \lambda$ and $\lambda_1 = 0$ for the homoskedastic model, or $\lambda_0 = 0$ and $\lambda_1 = \lambda$ for the essentially affine single-factor model.

These equations once again illustrate how the vector of risk coefficients λ_0 shifts the mean of the state vector, while the matrix of risk coefficients λ_1 shifts the transition matrix describing the dynamics of the state vector. Bond prices in this model satisfy

$$P_{nt} = \exp(-y_{1t})E_t^Q P_{n-1,t+1}, \tag{8.61}$$

where risk-neutral expectations E_t^Q are calculated using risk-adjusted dynamics for the state vector,

$$x_{t+1} = (\mu - \lambda_0) + (\Phi - \lambda_1)x_t + \Sigma\varepsilon_{t+1}^Q. \tag{8.62}$$

In other words, the price of any bond today is the risk-neutral expectation of its price tomorrow, discounted at the riskless interest rate.

Multivariate Essentially Affine Model with Heteroskedastic Bond Yields

Multivariate affine models are more difficult to specify when the state variables, and hence bond yields, are heteroskedastic. In a natural extension of equation (8.55), a heteroskedastic model can be written as

$$x_{t+1} = \mu + \Phi x_t + \Sigma S(t)\varepsilon_{t+1}. \tag{8.63}$$

Here the matrix $S(t)$ captures heteroskedasticity in the state variables, and as before, the variance-covariance matrix of the vector ε_{t+1} is the identity matrix. The fixed matrix Σ renormalizes the state variables and can be set to the identity matrix in cases where the state variables are observed only indirectly through bond yields.

This model requires that $S(t)S(t)'$ is positive definite so that innovations to the state variables have a well-defined variance-covariance matrix. We also require that

$$S(t)S(t)' = \Theta_0 + \Theta_1 x_t \tag{8.64}$$

to preserve the affine structure of the model. Finally, covariances with the SDF must be affine.

These requirements impose many restrictions on the form of heteroskedasticity, which have been explored in a large literature following Dai and Singleton (2000). The standard approach is to specify multiple square-root (CIR) processes that govern heteroskedasticity. Each square-root process is independent of all other processes in the model. Each square-root process also appears in the SDF (multiplied by a constant that governs the price of risk for that process). There can also be multiple homoskedastic factors, which can be arbitrarily correlated with one another.[2]

This framework is general enough to accommodate specifications that might at first seem to fall outside the affine class. Problem 8.2 asks you to analyze one simple example with discrete states. As another example, suppose we have a scalar variable y_t that follows an AR(1) and we need both y_t and y_t^2 to be state variables. Since in continuous time, $d(y_t^2) = 2y_t dy_t = 2(y_t^2)^{1/2} dy_t$, we can include y_t^2 in the model as a square-root process.[3] The conditional variance of dy_t is constant, the conditional variance of dy_t^2 is linear in y_t^2, and the conditional covariance of dy_t and dy_t^2 is linear in y_t. With suitable restrictions on the SDF, it is possible to preserve the affine structure of the model. Duffie and Kan (1996), followed by Cheng and Scaillet (2007) and others, have developed this strategy of expanding the state vector to incorporate nonlinearities within affine models. Their work has greatly increased the flexibility and usefulness of this class of models.

8.3.4 Strong Restrictions and Hidden Factors

Despite their apparent generality, multivariate affine models with K factors have some surprisingly strong implications. Most obviously, with K factors the variance-covariance matrix of all bond returns has rank K. Empirically this restriction can always be rejected, and the standard approach is to assume small measurement errors in bond prices to escape this implication. Literal measurement errors are likely to be negligible in Treasury bond prices, so the errors assumed in affine models should be interpreted as small unmodeled variations in bond prices caused perhaps by trading frictions.

Equally importantly, in a general K-factor affine model any K bond yields capture all the predictability of future bond yields and returns, hence no other current or lagged variables can add to the predictive power of these bond yields. Related to this, if the model includes macroeconomic variables as factors (which is desirable to link bond pricing with the macroeconomy), K bond yields capture all predictability of these variables too, so again no other current or lagged variables can add predictive power.

The problem is that these implications are counterfactual. Cochrane and Piazzesi (2005) find that additional lags of forward rates help predict bond returns. And there is evidence that lagged macro variables and survey forecasts predict macro variables even conditional on bond yields (Ang, Bekaert, and Wei 2007, Ludvigson and Ng 2009).

One possible solution, proposed by Duffee (2011) and Joslin, Priebsch, and Singleton (2014), is to impose a knife-edge parameter restriction that a "hidden factor" moves risk premia and expected future interest rates in opposite directions, with no effect on the current term structure. To see how this works, return to the multivariate homoskedastic affine model and recall that bonds are priced using risk-adjusted dynamics for the state vector, $x_{t+1} = (\mu - \lambda_0) + (\Phi - \lambda_1)x_t + \Sigma \varepsilon_{t+1}^Q$. If risk adjustment eliminates the ability of

---

[2]A convenient special case of this approach has only factors that are independent of one another. In this case we can simply "add up" the implied term structures for each factor to obtain the multifactor term structure.

[3]Here, dy_t denotes the change in variable y_t over an infinitesimal interval of time dt.

one of the state variables to predict the short-term interest rate and all other state variables that predict the short rate, then this state variable is irrelevant for bond pricing and does not affect the current term structure of interest rates. It may still be relevant, however, in the actual physical dynamics of the state variables, and in this case it will predict future interest rates and excess bond returns when added to a vector of bond yields. Problem 8.3 asks you to work out a specific example of a two-factor model in which one factor is hidden.

Hidden factors can result from other mechanisms as well. Offsetting predictability of interest rates and excess bond returns will arise if the bond market is inefficient, so some information about future interest rates that is available to investors is not priced into the current term structure. Similarly, econometric problems or data mining will generate spurious predictability of interest rates, which again will show up in both excess bond returns and interest rate movements, since spurious information is not priced into the current term structure. This possibility has been highlighted by Bauer and Hamilton (2016).

8.4 Bond Pricing and the Dynamics of Consumption Growth and Inflation

8.4.1 Real Bonds and Consumption Dynamics

The affine models discussed in the previous section vary in their specifications of SDF dynamics, but in all these models bond risk premia have the opposite sign from that of the covariance between innovations to the current level of the SDF and innovations to its expected future value. The reason is that the interest rate is negatively related to the expectation of the SDF, so $\text{Cov}_t(m_{t+1}, \text{E}_{t+1} m_{t+2})$ and $\text{Cov}_t(m_{t+1}, y_{1,t+1})$ have opposite signs. When current SDF innovations covary negatively with innovations to the expected future SDF, interest rates tend to rise and bond prices tend to fall in bad times with a high current SDF; in this case bonds are risky assets with positive risk premia. Conversely, when current SDF innovations covary positively with expected future SDF innovations, bonds tend to do well in bad times and carry negative risk premia. These effects on risk premia also influence the average slope of the term structure, which is negative unless bond risk premia are sufficiently positive to overcome the downward slope caused by bond convexity.

It is instructive to relate these properties to the consumption-based models discussed in Chapter 6. In this subsection, we assume that there is zero inflation, or equivalently, that bonds are inflation indexed; in subsection 8.4.3, we consider the effects of random inflation on nominal bonds.

Power Utility

In the simplest consumption-based asset pricing model with power utility and homoskedastic consumption growth, presented in section 6.1, the short-term interest rate y_{1t} is linearly increasing in expected consumption growth (equation (6.6)), and the innovation to the SDF is $-\gamma$ times the innovation to realized consumption growth (equation (6.4)). This is equivalent to the homoskedastic single-factor affine term structure model of section 8.3.1 (equations (8.32) and (8.33), where $x_t = y_{1t}$) if expected consumption growth follows an AR(1) process, whose innovations are perfectly negatively correlated with current consumption innovations if $\lambda < 0$ and perfectly positively correlated if $\lambda > 0$.

In the $\lambda < 0$ case, consumption is mean-reverting: a positive shock today is expected to be followed by unusually slow consumption growth, which drives interest rates down and bond prices up. In this case bonds do well when good shocks occur and badly when bad shocks occur, so they are risky assets with positive risk premia.

In the $\lambda > 0$ case, consumption growth is persistent: a positive shock today is expected to be followed by further rapid consumption growth. The expectation of rapid consumption growth in the future drives interest rates up and bond prices down, so that bonds do badly when good shocks occur. Conversely, bonds do well when bad shocks occur; they provide insurance against consumption shocks and have negative risk premia.

The inverse relationship between the persistence of consumption growth and the sign of bond risk premia holds more generally in consumption-based models with power utility. For example, Campbell (1986) assumes power utility and considers an arbitrary univariate stochastic process for realized consumption growth. In this case, risk premia may be positive for some maturities and negative for others. The sign of risk premia depends on whether the impulse response function for the level of consumption following a consumption innovation is above or below one (the normalized level of consumption immediately following the innovation) at the given maturity, as illustrated in Figure 8.4.

Epstein-Zin Preferences

If investors have Epstein-Zin preferences as in section 6.4, the analysis becomes more complicated, because innovations to the SDF reflect not only innovations in current consumption, but also innovations in expected future consumption growth. When risk aversion exceeds the reciprocal of the EIS ($\gamma > 1/\psi$), equation (6.49) shows that a positive innovation to expected future consumption growth directly lowers the SDF. Since expected future consumption growth raises interest rates and lowers bond prices, this creates a positive covariance between bond returns and the SDF, even when innovations to expected future consumption growth are uncorrelated with innovations to current consumption growth. Bonds are hedges, with negative risk premia, because they do poorly at times when consumption is expected to grow rapidly; even with unchanged current consumption, such times are good times for Epstein-Zin investors with $\gamma > 1/\psi$.

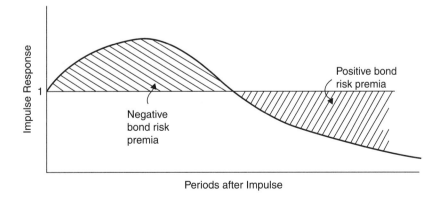

Figure 8.4. *Consumption Impulse Response Function and Bond Risk Premia* (Campbell, John Y., 1986, "Bond and Stock Returns in a Simple Exchange Model," *Quarterly Journal of Economics* 101, 785–804; reprinted by permission of Oxford University Press.)

Stochastic Volatility and Rare Disasters
The long-run risk literature, discussed in section 6.5, adds persistent variation in volatility to the stochastic process for consumption growth. This also tends to generate negative bond risk premia, because an increase in volatility stimulates precautionary saving, driving real interest rates down and real bond prices up. Since the increase in volatility is bad news for a conservative investor, bonds hedge the risk of volatility shocks and for this reason also command negative risk premia. A similar effect generates negative bond risk premia in models with a time-varying probability of a rare disaster (section 6.3.1), where an increase in the disaster probability works like an increase in consumption volatility.[4]

Habit Formation
The Campbell-Cochrane model of habit formation, discussed in section 6.7, has offsetting effects of consumption on interest rates. On the one hand, when consumption falls toward the habit level marginal utility is temporarily high and is expected to revert toward a normal level as habit adjusts; this tends to raise the equilibrium real interest rate. On the other hand, when consumption is close to habit marginal utility is volatile, stimulating precautionary saving and lowering the equilibrium real interest rate. Campbell and Cochrane (1999) make these effects exactly cancel so that the real interest rate is constant. However, it is straightforward to generalize the model to make the real interest rate either procyclical (implying negative bond risk premia) or countercyclical (implying positive bond risk premia) as shown by Campbell and Cochrane (1995), Wachter (2006), and Verdelhan (2010). We discuss Verdelhan's (2010) model, which assumes a procyclical interest rate and hence a negative bond risk premium, in section 8.5.2.

8.4.2 Permanent and Transitory Shocks to Marginal Utility

Alvarez and Jermann (AJ 2005) have developed a more general framework that clarifies how temporary and permanent shocks to the level of marginal utility (or consumption in the specific case of a consumption-based model) can be separated by looking at the behavior of the term structure of interest rates. AJ work with the cumulative SDF or pricing kernel

$$Q_t = M_1 M_2 \ldots M_t, \tag{8.65}$$

which can be interpreted as the marginal utility of a representative investor, discounted to a fixed initial date. The SDF at a point in time is given by the growth rate of the pricing kernel:

$$M_{t+1} = \frac{Q_{t+1}}{Q_t}. \tag{8.66}$$

Using this notation, the standard pricing equation for an n-period bond can be written as

$$Q_t P_{nt} = E_t[Q_{t+n}]. \tag{8.67}$$

AJ consider what happens as the maturity of the bond increases. As $n \to \infty$, standard models with discounting and consumption growth imply that P_{nt} and $E_t[Q_{t+n}]$ approach

---

[4]See Wachter (2013), footnote 10 and Appendix B.

zero. However, it is typically the case (as in the affine models considered earlier) that there exists some β such that P_{nt}/β^n and $E_t[Q_{t+n}]/\beta^n$ approach a finite nonzero limit, and AJ assume this. Dividing (8.67) by β^{t+n}, we have

$$Q_t \frac{P_{nt}}{\beta^{t+n}} = E_t \left[\frac{Q_{t+n}}{\beta^{t+n}} \right]. \tag{8.68}$$

AJ define the permanent component of the pricing kernel, Q_t^P, as the limit of the right-hand side of (8.68) as n increases:

$$Q_t^P = \lim_{n \to \infty} E_t \left[\frac{Q_{t+n}}{\beta^{t+n}} \right]. \tag{8.69}$$

That is, Q_t^P is the expected value of the pricing kernel in the long run relative to its long-term drift β^{t+n}. Q_t^P is unaffected by new information at date t that does not lead to a revision of the expected value of the pricing kernel in the long run, and in this sense it is the pricing kernel's permanent component.

The transitory component of the pricing kernel, Q_t^T is defined such that $Q_t = Q_t^P Q_t^T$, or equivalently

$$Q_t^T = \frac{Q_t}{Q_t^P} = \lim_{n \to \infty} \frac{\beta^{t+n}}{P_{nt}}, \tag{8.70}$$

where the second equality follows from (8.68).

Because this permanent-transitory decomposition of the pricing kernel is multiplicative, it implies a similar decomposition for the SDF. Using (8.66),

$$M_{t+1} = \frac{Q_{t+1}^P}{Q_t^P} \frac{Q_{t+1}^T}{Q_t^T} = M_{t+1}^P M_{t+1}^T. \tag{8.71}$$

The permanent and transitory components of the pricing kernel and the SDF have several interesting properties. First, because Q_t^P in (8.69) is the conditional expectation of a random variable infinitely far in the future, one would expect it to follow a martingale process, and AJ make technical assumptions that imply this.[5] This implies that $E_t M_{t+1}^P = 1$.

Second, the definition of Q_t^T in (8.70) shows that the price of an infinite-maturity bond depends only on Q_t^T and not on Q_t^P. The gross return on the bond satisfies

$$1 + R_{\infty,t+1} = \lim_{n \to \infty} \frac{P_{n-1,t+1}}{P_{nt}} = \frac{1}{M_{t+1}^T}. \tag{8.72}$$

It follows immediately that in a model where there is no time variation in the permanent component of the pricing kernel, $Q_t^P = Q_{t+1}^P$, implying $M_t^P = 1$ for all t (e.g., a consumption-based model where the level of consumption is stationary), the gross return on an infinite-horizon bond is the reciprocal of the SDF and therefore is the growth-optimal portfolio. More generally, the properties of infinite-horizon bond returns reveal the corresponding properties of the transitory component of the SDF.

---

[5] The law of iterated expectations implies that the conditional expectation of a random variable at a fixed future date follows a martingale. The technical issue here is that the future date in the conditional expectation in (8.69) is not fixed but is infinitely far in the future.

Third, AJ use these results to derive a relation between the conditional entropy of the SDF M_{t+1} and of its permanent component M_{t+1}^P. We have

$$L_t(M_{t+1}) = \log \mathrm{E}_t M_{t+1} - \mathrm{E}_t \log \left(M_{t+1}^P M_{t+1}^T \right)$$

$$= -r_{f,t+1} - \mathrm{E}_t \log \left(M_{t+1}^P \right) - \mathrm{E}_t \log \left(M_{t+1}^T \right)$$

$$= -r_{f,t+1} + L_t\left(M_{t+1}^P\right) + \mathrm{E}_t r_{\infty,t+1}, \qquad (8.73)$$

where the third line uses the fact that $\mathrm{E}_t M_{t+1}^P = 1$ and the relation (8.72) between the temporary component of the SDF and the infinite-horizon bond return. Rearranging,

$$L_t\left(M_{t+1}^P\right) = L_t(M_{t+1}) - \left(\mathrm{E}_t r_{\infty,t+1} - r_{f,t+1}\right). \qquad (8.74)$$

The conditional entropy of the permanent component of the SDF is less than the conditional entropy of the SDF itself when infinite-maturity bonds have positive risk premia, and greater when infinite-maturity bonds have negative risk premia. The former case corresponds to predominantly negative autocorrelations in the SDF or mean reversion in the pricing kernel, and the latter case to predominantly positive autocorrelations in the SDF or persistence in the pricing kernel. This result generalizes the discussion of consumption-based models in the previous subsection, and specifically the finding for univariate homoskedastic consumption processes illustrated in Figure 8.4.

Fourth, the equality (8.74) can be combined with the lower bound on the entropy of the SDF stated in equation (4.67) of Chapter 4, $L_t(M_{t+1}) \geq \mathrm{E}_t r_{j,t+1} - r_{f,t+1}$ for any asset j, to derive a lower bound on the conditional entropy of the permanent component of the SDF:

$$L_t\left(M_{t+1}^P\right) \geq \mathrm{E}_t r_{j,t+1} - \mathrm{E}_t r_{\infty,t+1}. \qquad (8.75)$$

This lower bound is tighter, the greater the difference in average log return between the growth-optimal portfolio and an infinite-horizon bond. As already stated, in a model with only transitory shocks, the infinite-horizon bond is the growth-optimal portfolio, and the lower bound on $L_t(M_{t+1}^P)$ is zero. While we do not directly observe infinite-maturity bonds, bonds with long maturities have much lower average returns than equities and other risky assets, suggesting that permanent shocks are an important contributor to the overall volatility of the SDF and hence to risk premia in financial markets.

The entropy bounds stated here are all for conditional entropy, which is not directly observable unless an econometrician has the same information set as investors. AJ also derive bounds for unconditional entropy, but these are more complex to state and we do not reproduce them here. The decomposition of the pricing kernel into permanent and temporary shocks is an area of current research interest, with important contributions by Hansen, Heaton, and Li (2008) and Hansen and Scheinkman (2009).

8.4.3 Real Bonds, Nominal Bonds, and Inflation

The consumption-based models discussed in subsection 8.4.1 treat bonds as claims to fixed amounts of consumption and therefore are appropriate for real (inflation-indexed) bonds or for nominal bonds in an economy without inflation. In this subsection we compare the stylized facts on inflation-indexed and nominal bonds and discuss consumption-based bond pricing models that allow for random inflation.

Inflation-indexed bonds make nominal coupon and principal payments that are adjusted for inflation. They have been issued in many countries, including the US since 1997, where they are called Treasury inflation-protected securities or TIPS, and the UK since 1982, where they are called index-linked gilts. Inflation-indexed bonds account for a modest share (less than 10%) of marketable public debt in the US and a somewhat larger share (about 25%) in the UK. These bonds have long maturities at issue, so they enable direct measurement of the long-term real interest rate.

Inflation-indexed bond yields have not been stable over time, but have trended downward since the 1990s when they averaged about 3.5% in both the US and the UK. In recent years the 10-year TIPS yield has varied between 0% and 1%. The difference between nominal and inflation-indexed bond yields, also known as the breakeven inflation rate, has also varied over time, with a particularly large decline to almost zero during the global financial crisis and movements between 1.5% and 2.5% since 2009. Nominal bond returns are typically somewhat more volatile than inflation-indexed bond returns, and the two types of bond returns are positively but not perfectly correlated (Campbell, Shiller, and Viceira 2009).

The slope of the inflation-indexed yield curve is hard to measure because no short-term inflation-indexed instrument exists. However, one can impute a short-term real interest rate by subtracting a measure of expected inflation (calculated from a survey or from a forecasting regression) from the nominal Treasury bill rate. Pflueger and Viceira (2011) report that the average spread of the long-term inflation-indexed bond yield over this short-term real interest rate is positive in the US (where it is comparable to the nominal yield spread) and slightly negative in the UK. Excess returns on inflation-indexed bonds are positive on average, but these returns may be biased upward by a decline in real interest rates during the relatively short period in which inflation-indexed bonds have been issued. The inflation-indexed yield spread predicts excess returns on inflation-indexed bonds in a manner similar to that documented for nominal bonds in section 8.2.2.

These empirical patterns carry several lessons for financial economists. First, pricing models for real bonds, of the sort discussed in the previous subsection, must generate persistent variation in the real interest rate and time-varying risk premia on real bonds. Second, these models should not imply a steeply downward-sloping real yield curve. Third, pricing models for nominal bonds cannot ignore random time variation in inflation.

The Nominal SDF
One approach to pricing nominal bonds is to work with a "nominal SDF" that is stated in nominal units. To understand this approach, consider an n-period zero-coupon nominal Treasury bond. The bond's nominal price can be written $P_{nt}^{\$}$ to indicate that it is measured in current-dollar units. The real price of the bond is $P_{nt}^{\$}/CPI_t$, where CPI_t is the consumer price index at time t. Inflation from time t to time $t+1$ is written as $\Pi_{t+1} = CPI_{t+1}/CPI_t$.

The standard pricing equation for real returns on any asset implies that

$$1 = \mathrm{E}_t\left[M_{t+1} \frac{P_{n-1,t+1}^{\$}/CPI_{t+1}}{P_{nt}^{\$}/CPI_t} \right] = \mathrm{E}_t\left[\frac{M_{t+1}}{\Pi_{t+1}} \frac{P_{n-1,t+1}^{\$}}{P_{nt}^{\$}} \right] = \mathrm{E}_t\left[M_{t+1}^{\$} \frac{P_{n-1,t+1}^{\$}}{P_{nt}^{\$}} \right], \quad (8.76)$$

where M_{t+1} is the real SDF and $M_{t+1}^{\$} = M_{t+1}/\Pi_{t+1}$ is the nominal SDF that prices nominal returns.

It is immediate that the nominal price of a nominal bond satisfies the recursion

$$P_{nt}^{\$} = \mathrm{E}_t\big[P_{n-1,t+1}^{\$} M_{t+1}^{\$}\big] = \mathrm{E}_t\big[M_{t+1}^{\$} M_{t+2}^{\$} \ldots M_{t+n}^{\$}\big] = \mathrm{E}_t\big[M_{t,t+n}^{\$}\big]. \tag{8.77}$$

This equation is the nominal analog of equation (8.30) for real bonds, using the terminal condition that a nominal Treasury bond has terminal nominal value of one (where a real bond would have a terminal real value of one and a terminal nominal value equal to cumulative inflation over the life of the bond).

Equation (8.77) implies that any model that prices real bonds using assumptions about the time series properties of the real SDF can be repurposed to price nominal bonds using the same assumptions for the time series properties of the nominal SDF. Indeed, some of the affine term structure models we discussed in section 8.3 are more natural descriptions of the nominal SDF than of the real SDF. The square-root single-factor model, for example, implies that the short-term interest rate is always positive in the limit of continuous time. Such a zero lower bound is broadly reasonable for the nominal interest rate given that the existence of currency, which pays a zero nominal rate, limits the extent to which investors will accept negative rates on other safe nominal assets. However, a zero lower bound is grossly counterfactual for the real interest rate, which was substantially negative in the 1970s and has been persistently negative since 2009.

Inflation and Consumption Growth
An alternative approach to pricing nominal bonds is to derive their real returns from assumptions about inflation, real interest rates, and the real SDF. For example, Campbell and Viceira (2001) estimate a two-factor affine model that adds a homoskedastic AR(1) process for expected inflation to the AR(1) process for the real interest rate assumed in the single-factor model of section 8.3.1. We discuss this model in section 9.2.2. Gabaix (2012) proposes a rare disaster model in which inflation jumps up when disasters occur, implying that nominal bonds are risky assets with positive risk premia and an upward-sloping nominal yield curve.

Piazzesi and Schneider (PS 2006) argue that expected inflation is negatively correlated with expected consumption growth and show that this can make the nominal yield curve upward sloping, even if the real yield curve is downward sloping. They work with Epstein-Zin preferences, assuming that risk aversion γ exceeds the reciprocal of the EIS $1/\psi$. With homoskedastic consumption growth, the risk premium on any asset is given by equation (6.50) from section 6.4.1 as γ times the covariance with current consumption growth innovations $\Delta \tilde{c}_{t+1}$ plus $(\gamma - 1/\psi)$ times the covariance with revisions in expected future consumption growth $\tilde{g}_{t+1}$.

To understand the implications of the PS model for the pricing of bonds, we can compare inflation-indexed perpetuities with nominal perpetuities. When expected real consumption growth increases by 1 percentage point, the equilibrium real interest rate increases by $1/\psi$ percentage points, and thus the unexpected inflation-indexed perpetuity return is given by[6]

$$\tilde{r}_{IIP,t+1} = -\frac{1}{\psi}\tilde{g}_{t+1}. \tag{8.78}$$

The return on nominal perpetuities is also influenced directly by real interest rates, but in addition it responds to expected inflation. PS assume that expected inflation is

[6]This is a special case of equation (6.106), which you were asked to derive in Problem 6.3.

negatively related to expected consumption growth. If expected inflation declines by ϕ percentage points when expected real consumption growth increases by 1 percentage point, then the unexpected real return on a nominal perpetuity is

$$\widetilde{r}_{NOMP,t+1} = \left(\phi - \frac{1}{\psi} \right) \widetilde{g}_{t+1}. \tag{8.79}$$

One can also allow for shocks to inflation unrelated to consumption growth, but these will not affect the risk premium on nominal bonds, and thus we do not consider them here.

Combining equation (6.50) with (8.78), the risk premium on an inflation-indexed perpetuity over the short-term riskless real interest rate is

$$RP_{IIP} = \gamma \left(-\frac{1}{\psi} \right) \sigma_{cg} + \left(\gamma - \frac{1}{\psi} \right) \left(-\frac{1}{\psi} \right) \sigma_g^2. \tag{8.80}$$

With power utility, only the first term is nonzero. As described in the previous subsection, persistent consumption growth implies a positive covariance between current consumption growth shocks and expected future consumption growth, and hence a negative real term premium. The second term is also negative when $\gamma > 1/\psi$, and its sign does not depend on the persistence of the consumption process. Hence, this model generates a strong prediction that the real term premium is negative.

Combining equation (6.50) with (8.79), the risk premium on a nominal perpetuity is

$$RP_{NOMP} = \gamma \left(\phi - \frac{1}{\psi} \right) \sigma_{cg} + \left(\gamma - \frac{1}{\psi} \right) \left(\phi - \frac{1}{\psi} \right) \sigma_g^2. \tag{8.81}$$

If the inflation effect is large enough, $\phi > 1/\psi$, nominal bonds can have positive risk premia even when real bonds have negative premia. The reason is that good news about expected future consumption reduces expected inflation and thus causes nominal interest rates to decline and nominal bond prices to increase. Nominal bonds become procyclical, risky assets even though real bonds are countercyclical assets that hedge against weak economic growth.

Summarizing, PS argue that inflation is negatively related to the long-run prospects for consumption growth. Thus nominal bonds, whose real payoffs are negatively related to inflation, are more similar to equities, whose dividends respond positively to consumption, than they are to inflation-indexed bonds. The negative correlation between inflation and consumption growth also implies a negative correlation between stock returns and inflation, despite the fact that stocks are real assets.[7] In section 9.4 in the next chapter, we discuss in greater detail models that simultaneously price the term structures of bonds and stocks.

8.5 Interest Rates and Exchange Rates

In this section we review the literature comparing the returns on bonds denominated in different currencies. For simplicity, we work with short-term interest rates and suppress subscripts indicating bond maturity. Thus the log short-term interest rate in the domestic

---

[7]Fama and Schwert (1977) and other authors in the late 1970s noted a negative correlation between inflation and stock returns. Geske and Roll (1983) attributed this to a negative effect of real economic growth on inflation. The PS model is similar in spirit.

currency (which we will refer to as the dollar) is written y_t. We use stars to indicate foreign variables, so the log short-term interest rate in a foreign currency (which we will refer to as the euro) is written y_t^*. The foreign exchange rate, expressed as dollars per euro, is written as Q_t and its log as q_t. With this notational convention, an increase in q_t corresponds to an appreciation of the euro against the dollar.

Just as in single-country bond analysis, these variables can be defined either in nominal terms or in real (inflation-adjusted) terms. Most of the empirical literature works with nominal interest rates and exchange rates, although some theoretical models are specified in real terms. In recent years nominal and real exchange rates have been highly correlated with one another, at least in developed countries.

8.5.1 Interest Parity and the Carry Trade

A forward exchange contract commits an investor to exchange one euro for F_t dollars, where F_t is determined at time t, but money does not change hands until time $t+1$. There are then two ways for the investor to obtain dollars risklessly at time $t+1$. One is to invest in the domestic riskless asset and earn the log return y_t. The other is to convert dollars to euros today, invest in the foreign riskless asset, and convert the proceeds back to dollars using a forward contract. The log return on this "forward euro" investment is $y_t^* + f_t - q_t$, where $f_t = \log(F_t)$.

Covered interest parity (CIP) is the statement that these two riskless investment strategies must offer the same return, hence

$$y_t^* - y_t = -(f_t - q_t). \tag{8.82}$$

This no-arbitrage condition has historically held to a high degree of accuracy, although deviations from it have increased since the global financial crisis (Du, Tepper, and Verdelhan 2016). Despite these recent deviations, we will assume covered interest parity throughout the remainder of this section.

An alternative way to invest in money markets at time t, receiving dollars at time $t + 1$, is to convert dollars to euros today, invest in the foreign riskless asset, and convert the proceeds back to dollars at the spot exchange rate that prevails at time $t + 1$. The log return on this "spot euro" or foreign exchange investment is $y_t^* + q_{t+1} - q_t$, which is random, given information available at time t. The excess log return on the spot euro investment over the domestic riskless interest rate is $y_t^* - y_t + q_{t+1} - q_t = q_{t+1} - f_t$, where the equality follows from CIP.

Uncovered interest parity (UIP) is the statement that the excess log return on a spot euro investment over the domestic riskless interest rate is unpredictable; that is, the expected excess log return on foreign exchange is zero:

$$E_t q_{t+1} - f_t = 0. \tag{8.83}$$

This trivially implies that the log forward exchange rate equals the expected future log spot exchange rate:

$$f_t = E_t q_{t+1}. \tag{8.84}$$

UIP requires that the interest differential between the euro and the dollar is exactly offset by an expected depreciation of the euro, a negative change in the log exchange rate:

$$y_t^* - y_t = -(E_t q_{t+1} - q_t). \tag{8.85}$$

UIP is comparable to the expectations hypothesis of the term structure, in that it is an ad hoc statement about the expected returns on alternative fixed-income investment strategies. Like the expectations hypothesis, it is normally written in log form to avoid problems with Jensen's Inequality.[8] And like the expectations hypothesis, constant terms are often added to equations (8.85) or (8.84) to accommodate a constant risk premium on one currency relative to the other.

Tests of Uncovered Interest Parity

A natural way to test UIP is to regress the realized excess log return on a spot euro investment, $y_t^* - y_t + q_{t+1} - q_t = q_{t+1} - f_t$, onto the interest differential $y_t^* - y_t$:

$$y_t^* - y_t + q_{t+1} - q_t = \mu + \beta (y_t^* - y_t) + \varepsilon_{t+1}. \tag{8.86}$$

The UIP null hypothesis (allowing for a free constant term μ) is that the slope coefficient $\beta = 0$ in this regression. Alternatively, if the log spot exchange rate is a random walk whose changes are unforecastable, then $\beta = 1$.

Equivalently, one can regress the realized change in the spot exchange rate, $q_{t+1} - q_t$, onto the forward-spot exchange rate differential $f_t - q_t$:

$$q_{t+1} - q_t = \theta + \gamma (f_t - q_t) + \varepsilon_{t+1}. \tag{8.87}$$

The UIP null hypothesis, again allowing for a free constant term, is that the slope coefficient $\gamma = 1$ in this regression. Alternatively, if changes in the log spot exchange rate are unforecastable, then $\gamma = 0$.

Fama (1984) found that in the data, the estimated coefficient in equation (8.86), $\widehat{\beta} > 1$, implying that a high euro interest rate is associated with appreciation of the euro, not depreciation as required by UIP. Equivalently, in the data, the estimated coefficient in equation (8.87), $\widehat{\gamma} < 0$, implying that a high forward-spot differential predicts an exchange rate movement with the opposite sign. This finding implies that there is a time-varying risk premium on the euro relative to the dollar, which must be sufficiently variable and positively correlated with predictable increases in the spot exchange rate (predictable appreciation of the euro).

To understand this implication of Fama's regression results, note that the forward-spot differential can always be decomposed into the expected movement in the spot exchange rate less the log risk premium on foreign exchange:

$$f_t - q_t = (E_t q_{t+1} - q_t) - (E_t q_{t+1} - f_t). \tag{8.88}$$

Hence, the estimated regression coefficient $\widehat{\gamma}$ in equation (8.87) can only be negative if

$$\text{Cov}((E_t q_{t+1} - q_t), (E_t q_{t+1} - q_t) - (E_t q_{t+1} - f_t)) < 0, \tag{8.89}$$

which requires $\text{Cov}((E_t q_{t+1} - q_t), (E_t q_{t+1} - f_t)) > \text{Var}((E_t q_{t+1} - q_t))$. The positive covariance between predictable exchange rate increases and the risk premium must exceed the variance of predictable exchange rate movements. A necessary, but not sufficient condition,

---

[8]If written in levels, the equality $F_t = E_t Q_{t+1}$ cannot hold both for exchange rates expressed as dollars per euro and for exchange rates expressed as euros per dollar, when the spot exchange rate is random. This consequence of Jensen's Inequality is known as Siegel's paradox (Siegel 1972).

for this is that the variance of the risk premium exceeds that of predictable exchange rate movements: $\text{Var}(\text{E}_t q_{t+1} - f_t) > \text{Var}(\text{E}_t q_{t+1} - q_t)$.

Subsequent research surveyed by Engel (2014) has not always found the strong results that $\widehat{\beta} > 1$ and $\widehat{\gamma} < 0$. However, it is reliably the case that $\widehat{\beta} > 0$ and $\widehat{\gamma} < 1$, which implies the existence of a time-varying foreign exchange risk premium.

The Carry Trade

So far we have discussed a single pair of currencies, which we have called the dollar and the euro for concreteness. An alternative approach is to consider many currencies simultaneously. The foreign exchange carry trade is an investment strategy that goes long currencies with high short-term interest rates and goes short (borrows) in currencies with low interest rates. The carry trade may be implemented in a US dollar-neutral fashion, in which case only currencies other than the US dollar are included in the long and short currency portfolios. Alternatively, the carry trade may allow US dollar positions, in which case the dollar tends to be a "funding currency" on the short side of the strategy, because US dollar interest rates are typically lower than the global average interest rate.

The carry trade would not be profitable on average if UIP held across all currency pairs with constant terms equal to zero, but the empirical failure of UIP discussed above translates into positive historical average returns on the carry trade. Lustig and Verdelhan (2007) initiated an academic literature on the carry trade that studies the average returns on portfolios of currencies sorted by their levels of interest rates. This methodology, which is analogous to the construction of portfolios of stocks sorted by characteristics such as book-market ratios, has shifted the focus of recent academic work from time-series regressions for specific currency pairs to cross-sectional analysis of currency returns.

Since interest rate differentials across countries are extremely persistent in the data, carry-trade portfolios contain persistent long and short positions. For example, Japan has had low interest rates since the 1990s, while Australia has had high interest rates, so the carry trade has been short Japan and long Australia for an extended period of time. Hassan and Mano (2015) show that persistent positions are important contributors to the overall profitability of the carry trade. This is particularly true for the US dollar-neutral carry trade, as failures of UIP (in tests that allow for free constant terms) are strongest when the US dollar is one of the currencies in the pair.

The carry trade responds to cross-currency differences in short-term interest rates. It would also be possible to invest in longer-term bonds denominated in currencies where yield curves are steep, but Lustig, Stathopoulos, and Verdelhan (2016) find that such a strategy does not deliver high average returns. Problem 8.4 asks you to analyze the implications of this fact.

8.5.2 The Domestic and Foreign SDF

The above analysis can be restated in the language of the stochastic discount factor (Backus, Foresi, and Telmer 2001). For any asset return denominated in dollars, recall that the fundamental equation of asset pricing is

$$1 = \text{E}_t[M_{t+1}(1 + R_{t+1})],$$

where M_{t+1} is the usual dollar-denominated SDF. Similarly, for any asset return denominated in euros, the fundamental equation describes the euro stochastic discount factor.

Using stars to denote euro returns and the euro SDF, we have

$$1 = \mathrm{E}_t[M^*_{t+1}(1 + R^*_{t+1})].\tag{8.90}$$

Euro-denominated assets can also be used to obtain dollar-denominated returns by converting dollars to euros at the spot exchange rate Q_t at time t, receiving a euro return at time $t+1$, and converting euros back to dollars at the time $t+1$ spot exchange rate Q_{t+1}. This implies that

$$1 = \mathrm{E}_t\left[M_{t+1}\left(\frac{Q_{t+1}}{Q_t}\right)(1 + R^*_{t+1})\right].\tag{8.91}$$

Equations (8.90) and (8.91) link the dollar- and euro-denominated stochastic discount factors. In complete markets, the SDF denominated in any unit is unique so we have the stronger statement that

$$M^*_{t+1} = M_{t+1}\left(\frac{Q_{t+1}}{Q_t}\right),\tag{8.92}$$

or in logs,

$$m^*_{t+1} - m_{t+1} = q_{t+1} - q_t.\tag{8.93}$$

Movements in log exchange rates are then equivalent to relative movements in log SDFs denominated in different currencies.

Buying euros on the forward market and selling them on the spot market is a zero-cost investment strategy with a realized dollar return $(Q_{t+1} - F_t)$ for each euro purchased. Accordingly the fundamental equation of asset pricing implies that

$$0 = \mathrm{E}_t[M_{t+1}(Q_{t+1} - F_t)] = \mathrm{E}_t\left[M_{t+1}\left(\frac{Q_{t+1}}{Q_t} - \frac{F_t}{Q_t}\right)\right],\tag{8.94}$$

where the second equality holds because one can divide the zero-cost return in (8.94) by any variable known at time t (effectively rescaling the investment strategy) without altering the equality.

Rearranging and using the complete-markets condition (8.92),

$$\left(\frac{F_t}{Q_t}\right)\mathrm{E}_t[M_{t+1}] = \mathrm{E}_t\left[M_{t+1}\left(\frac{Q_{t+1}}{Q_t}\right)\right] = \mathrm{E}_t[M^*_{t+1}].\tag{8.95}$$

Taking logs and assuming conditional lognormality,

$$\begin{aligned}
f_t - q_t &= \log \mathrm{E}_t[M^*_{t+1}] - \log \mathrm{E}_t[M_{t+1}]\\
&= \left(\mathrm{E}_t m^*_{t+1} - \mathrm{E}_t m_{t+1}\right) + L_t\left(M^*_{t+1}\right) - L_t(M_{t+1})\\
&= \left(\mathrm{E}_t m^*_{t+1} - \mathrm{E}_t m_{t+1}\right) + \left(\sigma^{*2}_{mt} - \sigma^2_{mt}\right)/2,
\end{aligned}\tag{8.96}$$

where the second line uses the definition of entropy, equation (4.58), and the third line uses the fact that entropy equals one-half the variance of the log for a lognormally distributed random variable.

Equation (8.96) relates the log forward-spot differential to cross-country differences in the conditional means and variances of log SDFs. The first term on the right-hand side of (8.96) is, from equation (8.93), the expected change in the log spot exchange rate. The second term, from equation (8.88), must then be the negative of the log risk premium on foreign exchange.

Fama's conditions can now be restated in terms of the SDFs. To explain deviations from uncovered interest parity, there must be sufficiently large movements in the cross-country difference of conditional log SDF variances, and these movements must be sufficiently correlated with the cross-country difference of conditional log SDF means. Recent equilibrium exchange rate models, such as Farhi and Gabaix (2016) using a rare disasters framework, are deliberately calibrated to meet these conditions.

Multicountry Endowment Models

One class of equilibrium models assumes a representative agent in each country with a standard utility function defined over an endowment of a consumption good. Financial markets are complete, but there are no opportunities for the two countries to trade their goods (or equivalently, the endowment processes are the outcome of already exploited trade opportunities). The domestic- and foreign-currency SDFs are interpreted as the SDF of the domestic agent in units of the domestic good, and the SDF of the foreign agent in units of the foreign good, respectively. This type of model is specified in real terms and assumes that there is no inflation in either country.

Verdelhan (2010) presents an equilibrium model of this sort in which Fama's conditions hold. Verdelhan works with the Campbell and Cochrane (1999) habit formation model discussed in Chapter 6, modified to allow real interest rates to vary as proposed by Campbell and Cochrane (1995). In the modified model, the steady-state surplus consumption ratio satisfies

$$\overline{S} = \sigma_c \sqrt{\frac{\gamma}{1 - \phi - B/\gamma}}, \tag{8.97}$$

where σ_c is the standard deviation of consumption growth, ϕ is the persistence of the log surplus consumption ratio, γ is the curvature of utility, and B is a free parameter set to zero in the original Campbell-Cochrane model. All other equations of the model are unchanged. The short-term domestic real interest rate equals

$$y_t = \overline{y} - B(s_t - \overline{s}), \tag{8.98}$$

which is linear in the log surplus consumption ratio s_t, and the analogous equation holds in the foreign country. In each country the conditional variance of the log SDF is linear in that country's log surplus consumption ratio as in the original Campbell-Cochrane model.[9]

Verdelhan assumes that two symmetric countries have the same preference parameters and the same dynamics for their endowment processes. Under these assumptions the log interest differential is

$$y_t^* - y_t = -B(s_t^* - s_t) \tag{8.99}$$

---

[9]Taking the square of equation (6.94) in Chapter 6 delivers a linear relation between the conditional variance of the log SDF and the log surplus consumption ratio.

(or equivalently, the log forward-spot differential $f_t - q_t = B(s_t^* - s_t)$), and the risk premium on foreign exchange is

$$\mathrm{E}_t q_{t+1} - f_t = \frac{\gamma^2 \sigma_c^2}{\overline{S}^2}(s_t^* - s_t).\qquad(8.100)$$

The first of Fama's regression tests of UIP, equation (8.86), is a regression of the realized excess log return on foreign exchange onto the interest differential. The regression coefficient is $-\gamma^2 \sigma_c^2 / B\overline{S}^2 = 1 - \gamma(1-\phi)/B$. This will exceed one, matching Fama's empirical evidence, whenever $B < 0$. The intuition is that with a negative value of B in (8.99), a recession in one country lowers the interest rate in that country so a high interest differential tends to be associated with a domestic recession. A domestic recession also increases the risk premium on foreign exchange by making the log SDF at home more volatile than the log SDF abroad, and hence making the log exchange rate more highly correlated with domestic marginal utility than with foreign marginal utility. Thus, a high interest differential is associated with a high risk premium on foreign exchange.[10]

Despite the appeal of multicountry endowment models with complete markets, they face some challenges. Measured Sharpe ratios on risky assets and the volatility bounds developed in Chapter 4 imply that log SDFs have annual standard deviations on the order of 0.5, regardless of the currency of denomination. Brandt, Cochrane, and Santa-Clara (2006) observe that with such volatile log SDFs, real exchange rates will be far too volatile unless the log SDFs are highly correlated across countries. Equation (8.93) implies that the conditional variance of the log exchange rate is the sum of the variances of the log SDFs denominated in euros and in dollars, less twice the covariance between them. Equivalently, with equal variances of the two log SDFs, the conditional variance of the log exchange rate is $2\sigma_m^2(1 - \mathrm{Corr}(m, m^*))$. To obtain a realistic conditional standard deviation of the log exchange rate of, say, 0.1, the conditional variance of the log exchange rate must be 0.01. With a 0.5 standard deviation for each of the log SDFs, the correlation between them must then be 0.98. Such a high cross-country correlation of log SDFs seems hard to reconcile with the much lower correlations of measured consumption growth and macroeconomic conditions across countries, although Colacito and Croce (2011) argue that this can be done in a long-run risk model, where investors in each country have Epstein-Zin preferences and where long-run expected consumption growth is highly correlated across countries.

A related point is that these models are silent on the forces that limit trade between countries. If the endowment falls at home relative to the foreign country and financial markets are complete, why do goods not flow from the foreign country to the home country? Richer models from international economics with nontradable goods, or shipping costs for tradable goods, are needed to address these questions. With plausible shipping costs, flows of goods tend to increase the correlation between log SDFs at home and abroad, thereby helping to explain the relative stability of exchange rates.[11]

---

[10]If the coefficient B is positive, it must be sufficiently small that the steady-state surplus consumption ratio in equation (8.97) is defined. This requires that $\gamma(1-\phi)/B > 1$, delivering a negative coefficient in Fama's regression test (8.86). Thus, the Verdelhan model cannot generate a regression coefficient in (8.86) between zero and one.

[11]Brandt, Cochrane, and Santa-Clara (2006, pp. 673–674) describe the issue as follows: "Risksharing requires frictionless goods markets. The container ship is a risksharing innovation as important as 24-hour trading. Suppose that Earth trades assets with Mars by radio, in complete and frictionless capital markets. If

Finally, multicountry endowment models do not capture the interaction between real and nominal exchange rate behavior. Mussa (1986) famously observed that fixed nominal exchange rate regimes are associated with stable real exchange rates, while flexible nominal exchange rate regimes are associated with volatile real exchange rates. It remains an unresolved challenge to build an asset pricing model that explains currency risk premia in a way that is consistent with this pattern.

Pricing Foreign Currency from the Domestic SDF

An alternative way to understand the pricing of foreign exchange risk is to use the SDF of a domestic investor and empirical measures of exchange rate covariance with this SDF. While this leaves to one side the question of how real and nominal exchange rates are determined in general equilibrium, it can deliver useful insights. Lustig and Verdelhan (2007), for example, use Yogo's (2006) consumption CAPM with durable goods, discussed in section 6.8, and show that the SDF from this model prices currency portfolios sorted by interest rates. In a similar spirit, Campbell, Serfaty-de Medeiros, and Viceira (2010) show that currencies such as the Australian dollar that have high average interest rates also tend to have high betas with global equity markets. Portfolios of currencies, sorted by their interest rates, have become increasingly popular test assets that can be used to evaluate the performance of any of the asset pricing models discussed in this book.

8.6 Solution and Further Problems

As an informal exercise, you were asked to explain how, under the log EH, an unusually high yield spread returns to normal even though the model implies that a high yield spread predicts a rising long-term bond yield (equation (8.23)). The answer is that according to the second implication of the log EH, equation (8.25), the short-term interest rate rises even faster, so the yield spread reverts toward its mean.

Problem 8.1 The Nelson-Siegel Model of the Yield Curve

The first three principal components of the yield curve are empirically known to account for almost all of the cross-sectional variation in bond yields. These principal components approximately correspond to the average level, slope, and curvature of the yield curve. Nelson and Siegel (1987) propose the following functional form as an approximation of the yield curve:[12]

$$y_{nt} = x_{1t} + x_{2t}\frac{1}{\lambda n}(1 - (1 - \lambda)^n) + x_{3t}\left(\frac{1}{\lambda n}(1 - (1 - \lambda)^n) - (1 - \lambda)^{n-1}\right). \qquad (8.101)$$

Mars enjoys a positive shock, Earth-based owners of Martian assets rejoice in anticipation of their payoffs. But trade between Earth and Mars is still impossible, so the real exchange rate between Mars and Earth must adjust exactly to offset any net payoff. In the end, Earth marginal utility growth must reflect Earth resources, and the same for Mars." Ready, Roussanov, and Ward (2016) model shipping costs and Powers (2015) and Farhi and Gabaix (2016) model nontradable goods production in relation to evidence on the carry trade.

[12]Nelson and Siegel (1987) originally offered a static, continuous-time model of the yield curve. Diebold, Li, and Yue (2008) showed that x_{1t}, x_{2t}, and x_{3t} can be interpreted as latent dynamic factors.

The Nelson-Siegel (NS) specification of the yield curve is a parsimonious approximation of the yield curve that is flexible enough to capture a wide range of observed shapes of the yield curve and has been found to provide a remarkably good fit to the cross-section of yields in many countries. As a result, it is widely used among finance practitioners and central banks.

(a) Plot the loadings of factors x_{1t}, x_{2t}, and x_{3t} as a function of maturity n (in months), $n \geq 1$, for $\lambda = 0.06$. Describe their shapes and their values at $n = 1$ and as $n \to \infty$. What is the short rate y_{1t} and the rate on an infinite-maturity bond, $\lim_{n \to \infty} y_{nt}$?

(b) For each factor, explain whether it mainly affects the short-term, the medium-term, or the long-term component of the yield curve. Explain why x_{1t}, x_{2t}, and x_{3t} are known, respectively, as the level, slope, and curvature factors of the yield curve. How does the parameter λ affect the role of each factor?

(c) Even though the original NS specification (8.101) does not impose absence of arbitrage, Christensen, Diebold, and Rudebusch (2011) show that, with a small adjustment, the NS yield curve corresponds to a class of arbitrage-free essentially affine three-factor models.

Assume that a state vector $x_t = [x_{1t}, x_{2t}, x_{3t}]'$ evolves under the risk-neutral measure according to

$$x_{t+1} = \mu^* + \begin{bmatrix} 1 & 0 & 0 \\ 0 & 1-\lambda & \lambda \\ 0 & 0 & 1-\lambda \end{bmatrix} x_t + \Sigma \varepsilon_{t+1}^Q, \tag{8.102}$$

where μ^* and Σ are unrestricted. Moreover, $y_{1t} = x_{1t} + x_{2t}$. Use the results of section 8.3.3 to show that under these assumptions the yield curve is given by the NS curve (the right-hand side of (8.101)) plus a maturity-specific constant, C_n. Characterize C_n.

Hint: use the fact that x_{1t} in (8.102) follows a random walk, while the evolution of x_{2t} and x_{3t} does not depend on the level of x_{1t}.

Problem 8.2 A Term Structure Model with Regime Switching

Consider the following model for the log stochastic discount factor, m_{t+1}:

$$m_{t+1} = -x_t - \beta \xi_{t+1}, \tag{8.103}$$

$$x_{t+1} = \phi x_t + \xi_{t+1}, \tag{8.104}$$

where ξ_{t+1} is randomly drawn from one of two distributions. With probability π, state 1 occurs at time $t+1$ and $\xi_{t+1} = \xi_{1,t+1}$, where $\xi_{1,t+1} \sim \mathcal{N}(0, \sigma_1^2)$; with probability $1-\pi$, state 2 occurs at time $t+1$ and $\xi_{t+1} = \xi_{2,t+1}$, where $\xi_{2,t+1} \sim \mathcal{N}(0, \sigma_2^2)$.

(a) Is the stochastic discount factor M_{t+1} lognormally distributed, conditional on information available at time t? Is it lognormally distributed, conditional on information available at time t and knowledge of the state (1 or 2) that occurs at time $t+1$?

(b) Solve for the one-period zero-coupon bond yield, $1 + Y_{1t}$, in this economy. Show that the log short yield, $y_{1t} \equiv \log(1 + Y_{1t})$, is linear in the state variable x_t.

(c) Use the recursive pricing equation for bonds (8.29) to show that all log bond yields are linear in x_t. Derive an expression for the slope coefficient B_n relating the log n-period bond price to the state variable x_t, as in (8.36). What is the standard name for models with log bond yields linear in state variables? What makes this model different from other models you have seen with this property?

(d) Which of the following phenomena are displayed by this model? Explain.
   (i) Time-varying risk premia in the term structure of interest rates.

   (ii) Changing volatility of interest rates.

   (iii) Excess kurtosis of interest rate movements.

   (iv) Imperfect conditional correlation of returns on bonds with different maturities.

Problem 8.3 Hiding a Factor

Consider the following two-factor essentially affine term structure model,

$$m_{t+1} = -x_t - \frac{1}{2}\left(\alpha^2 + \beta^2\right)z_t^2 - \alpha z_t \varepsilon_{t+1} - \beta z_t \eta_{t+1}, \tag{8.105}$$

$$x_{t+1} = \mu_x + \varphi_{xx}x_t + \varphi_{xz}z_t + \sigma_x \varepsilon_{t+1}, \tag{8.106}$$

$$z_{t+1} = \mu_z + \varphi_{zx}x_t + \varphi_{zz}z_t + \sigma_{z\varepsilon} \varepsilon_{t+1} + \sigma_{z\eta} \eta_{t+1}, \tag{8.107}$$

where ε_{t+1} and η_{t+1} are independent standard normal variables. Assume $\sigma_x, \sigma_{z\varepsilon}, \sigma_{z\eta} > 0$ and that x_{t+1} and z_{t+1} are stationary processes.

(a) Why do we call such a model "essentially affine"? Calculate the short rate, y_{1t}, and the conditional variance of the log SDF, $\text{var}_t(m_{t+1})$. Explain that z_t can be interpreted as the price of aggregate market risk. Does the expectations hypothesis hold in this model?

(b) Conjecture that log bond prices are affine in the state variables,

$$p_{nt} = A_n + B_{x,n}x_t + B_{z,n}z_t. \tag{8.108}$$

Derive the law of motion of the state variables under the risk-neutral measure Q that prices bonds (the equivalent martingale measure).

(c) Explain intuitively why factor z_t is hidden from (unspanned by) the current term structure if and only if it does not affect the dynamics of x_t under the risk-neutral measure. What is the restriction on the parameters of equations (8.105)–(8.107) such that factor z_t is hidden from the term structure? Is it possible that the current term structure can help forecast future values of z_t if z_t is hidden?
   For the rest of this problem, assume that z_t is hidden.

(d) Use the recursive pricing equation for bonds (8.29) to solve for the coefficients in the price function (8.108).

(e) Calculate excess returns, $r_{n,t+1} - r_{1,t+1}$. Show that the conditional term premium, $E_t[r_{n,t+1} - r_{1,t+1}] + (1/2)\text{Var}_t(r_{n,t+1})$, is proportional to z_t. Interpret the terms in the expression for the term premium and their signs. Why do $\sigma_{z\varepsilon}$ and $\sigma_{z\eta}$ not affect the term premia? Finally, explain the intuition for the parameter restriction you derived in part (c).

Problem 8.4 The Term Structure of Carry Trade Risk Premia

Lustig, Stathopoulos, and Verdelhan (2016) investigate the profitability of carry-trade strategies with long-maturity bonds. One such strategy involves going long (short) long-maturity government bonds in currencies with high (low) local-currency term premia, that is, steep (flat) yield curves. They find that, across G10 countries, average returns to these strategies are close to zero, in sharp contrast to the high risk premia of the classic carry trade at the short end of the yield curve (with short-maturity bonds).[13] Equivalently, they find that differences in long-term government bond risk premia expressed in the same currency are insignificant.

In this exercise we explore the implications of this finding for the comovement of marginal utility across countries under the assumption that international financial markets are complete.

(a) Show that the log risk premium (one-period-ahead expected excess log return) on a foreign long-maturity bond over the domestic riskfree rate expressed in domestic currency (US dollars) can be written as the the bond's log risk premium in local (foreign) currency plus the log risk premium on foreign exchange:

$$\mathrm{E}_t\left[r_{n,t+1}^{*\$} - r_{f,t+1}\right] = \mathrm{E}_t\left[r_{n,t+1}^{*} - r_{f,t+1}^{*}\right] + \mathrm{E}_t\left[q_{t+1} - f_t\right]. \tag{8.109}$$

(b) Show that, when financial markets are complete, the difference between the dollar log risk premium on infinite-maturity (zero-coupon) foreign bonds and the log risk premium on infinite-maturity domestic bonds is given by

$$\mathrm{E}_t\left[r_{\infty,t+1}^{*\$} - r_{f,t+1}\right] - \mathrm{E}_t\left[r_{\infty,t+1} - r_{f,t+1}\right] = L_t\left(M_{t+1}^{P}\right) - L_t\left(M_{t+1}^{*P}\right), \tag{8.110}$$

where $L_t(M_{t+1}^{P}) - (L_t(M_{t+1}^{*P}))$ is the entropy of the permanent component of the domestic (foreign) SDF, defined through the Alvarez and Jermann (2005) decomposition of the SDF discussed in section 8.4.2.

Conclude that transitory shocks to the SDF are irrelevant for the log risk premia of the carry trade with bonds of very long maturity.

(c) Explain the economic intuition behind this result by considering a world where there are no permanent innovations to the pricing kernel of any country. How do exchange rates and returns to infinite-maturity bonds respond if a country experiences unexpectedly high marginal utility growth relative to other countries?

---

[13]The result also holds for other currency sorts, for example, when the groups of investment and funding currencies are chosen based on their short-term interest rates.

(d) Suppose that the SDFs of all countries are exposed to the same set of global risk factors; for example, this exposure may be captured by an affine multifactor model as in section 8.3. However, countries may have asymmetric exposures to these factors (and there are no country-specific factors). Some of these factors only affect the permanent component of the SDFs, and the remaining ones affect only the temporary component of the SDFs. What assumption on countries' exposures to these sources of risk is consistent with the empirical finding that carry trade risk premia are high at the short end of the yield curve but become insignificant as bond maturity increases?

9

Intertemporal Risk

THIS CHAPTER CONSIDERS models of portfolio choice for long-term investors and discusses their implications for asset pricing in equilibrium. Section 9.1 begins by asking when portfolio choice does not depend on the investment horizon, that is, when it is myopic. We assume scale-independent Epstein-Zin preferences, in which relative risk aversion is independent of wealth, in order to rule out effects of the investment horizon that arise from changes in wealth during intermediate periods as returns are reinvested over time. Given such preferences, portfolio choice is myopic if the coefficient of relative risk aversion equals one or if returns are independently distributed over time. In the case of power utility, these results have been known since the classic analysis of Samuelson (1969). We build intuition for them by considering the special case of an investor with power utility over terminal wealth, investing over two periods in an environment with lognormal returns.

Section 9.2 characterizes the portfolio choice of an infinitely lived investor with Epstein-Zin preferences over consumption and risk aversion not equal to one, in response to time-varying interest rates and risk premia. This section assumes that asset returns are conditionally lognormal and homoskedastic. The analysis closely follows Campbell and Viceira (2002).

Section 9.3 discusses how the first-order conditions of an infinitely lived Epstein-Zin investor can be used to price the cross-section of asset returns. This section develops an approximate closed-form discrete-time version of Merton's (1973) intertemporal capital asset pricing model (ICAPM), following Campbell (1993) and Campbell and Vuolteenaho (2004). The model is developed first in a homoskedastic environment, and then generalized to handle a specific type of heteroskedasticity as in Campbell et al. (2017).

Section 9.4 integrates ideas from Chapters 6 and 8 with this chapter. The section introduces the concept of a term structure of yields on risky assets, by analogy with the yields on fixed-income securities defined in Chapter 8. There is evidence that the term structure of risky yields is downward sloping, and as Lettau and Wachter (2007) point out, such evidence challenges many of the asset pricing models we have developed earlier in the book. This section also discusses the integrated modeling of stock and bond returns, with special emphasis on the covariance between these asset classes.

Section 9.5 studies the effects of learning on long-term portfolio choice and intertemporal asset pricing, drawing on work by Pástor and Stambaugh (2012) and Collin-Dufresne, Johannes, and Lochstoer (2016).

9.1 Myopic Portfolio Choice

Portfolio choice is said to be myopic if, at a given point in time, an investor with given preferences has the same optimal portfolio regardless of the investor's horizon. This is conceptually different from constant portfolio choice over time, in which an investor with given preferences and a given investment horizon holds the same optimal portfolio in each period. Portfolio choice can be myopic even if it is not constant over time.

Log Utility and Unit Risk Aversion

Investors with log utility of terminal wealth have myopic portfolio choice. To see this, consider an investor with log utility of wealth two periods from now. Such an investor maximizes the expected two-period log return on his portfolio, which we write as $E_t[r_{p,2,t+2}]$ to denote that it is a two-period log return received two periods from now, and which is the sum of two successive expected one-period log returns:

$$\max E_t[r_{p,2,t+2}] = E_t r_{p,t+1} + E_t r_{p,t+2}, \tag{9.1}$$

Portfolio weights at time t only affect the first term in this expression, while portfolio weights at time $t+1$ only affect the second term. Hence, at time t the investor maximizes the first term, which is the same objective function that a single-period log-utility maximizer would have. In other words, portfolio choice is myopic. It need not, however, be constant over time if investment opportunities are time-varying.

   This result generalizes straightforwardly to the case of an investor with log utility of consumption in each period and to an Epstein-Zin investor with unit relative risk aversion but an arbitrary elasticity of intertemporal substitution.

Independent Returns Over Time

If return distributions are independent over time, investors with power utility of terminal wealth have myopic portfolio choice. The argument is one of backward induction. In the last period of a T-period investment problem, the investor makes a single-period optimal portfolio choice. The resulting value function at the end of period $T-1$ is a power function of wealth with the same curvature parameter and a scale factor that depends on investment opportunities. This value function can be used to solve the portfolio choice problem for period $T-1$, and the scale factor does not affect the solution because, under the assumption of independent returns, the scale factor is independent of decisions made at $T-1$. Hence, the investor will make a single-period optimal choice in that period also. Proceeding backward in time, portfolio choice in each period is myopic.

   This result generalizes straightforwardly to the case of an investor with power or Epstein-Zin utility of consumption in each period. It requires returns to be independent over time but not necessarily identically distributed. If returns are iid over time, then portfolio choice is constant over time as well as myopic.

   To build intuition about portfolio choice with iid returns, consider an investor with power utility of terminal wealth who faces iid lognormally distributed returns. We will use the portfolio return approximation (2.24) developed in Chapter 2, so that both portfolio returns and the returns on individual assets are lognormal. The power utility investor with a two-period horizon solves a two-period mean-variance problem:

$$\max E_t[r_{p,2,t+2}] + \frac{1}{2}\text{Var}_t(r_{p,2,t+2}) - \frac{\gamma}{2}\text{Var}_t(r_{p,2,t+2}), \tag{9.2}$$

where the first two terms equal the log of the mean gross simple return on the portfolio, and the third term is a risk correction.

With power utility, portfolio choice does not depend on wealth, so past returns are irrelevant. In addition, the assumption of iid returns means that there are no state variables relevant for forecasting future returns. Without loss of generality, therefore, we can confine attention to deterministic portfolio shares chosen in advance. We want to show that these deterministic portfolio shares are optimally constant.

Consider the simple case where the investor allocates wealth between a riskless asset and a single risky asset whose portfolio share at time t is written as α_t. The two-period excess log portfolio return over the riskless asset is the sum of two successive one-period excess log portfolio returns:

$$r_{p2,t+2} - 2r_f = (r_{p,t+1} - r_f) + (r_{p,t+2} - r_f)$$

$$= \alpha_t(r_{t+1} - r_f) + \frac{1}{2}\alpha_t(1 - \alpha_t)\sigma^2 + \alpha_{t+1}(r_{t+2} - r_f) + \frac{1}{2}\alpha_{t+1}(1 - \alpha_{t+1})\sigma^2, \qquad (9.3)$$

where the second equality uses the portfolio return approximation (2.24). Then the two-period variance in (9.2) is

$$\text{Var}_t(r_{p,2,t+2}) = \left(\alpha_t^2 + \alpha_{t+1}^2\right)\sigma^2, \qquad (9.4)$$

and the log of the mean gross simple return is

$$\text{E}_t[r_{p,2,t+2}] + \frac{1}{2}\text{Var}_t(r_{p,2,t+2}) = 2r_f + (\alpha_t + \alpha_{t+1})(\text{E}r - r_f + \sigma^2/2). \qquad (9.5)$$

Equation (9.5) shows that the log of the mean gross return depends only on the sum of the risky shares $(\alpha_t + \alpha_{t+1})$. Fixing this sum, the variance in (9.4) is minimized by $\alpha_t = \alpha_{t+1}$, a constant portfolio rule. With a constant portfolio rule, both mean and variance in the two-period problem are twice their values in the one-period problem, so the optimal choice of α_t is the same as in the one-period problem.

Kritzman (2000) presents the above argument in an essay succinctly entitled "Half Stocks All the Time or All Stocks Half the Time?" He points out that both strategies have the same expected return, but the former is safer.

Myopic Investing without Rebalancing
The models we have considered so far allow the investor to rebalance her portfolio each period. While this is a realistic assumption, it is worth briefly considering what happens if rebalancing is prohibited. In this case, changes in investment opportunities over time will cause long-term investors to choose different initial portfolio weights than short-term investors even if they have log utility, because long-term investors must choose weights that deliver the best results on average over the investment horizon, not necessarily those that are initially optimal.

Even if single-period returns are iid over time, the distribution of returns to any investment strategy will vary with the investment horizon as the returns are compounded, and this can again generate horizon effects on portfolio choice. Such effects disappear if we assume that investors have Epstein-Zin preferences, that the returns on individual assets are lognormally distributed, and that we can use the approximate formula for portfolio returns (2.24) developed in Chapter 2. Under these assumptions, both individual asset returns and the returns on arbitrary portfolios are lognormally distributed. As the horizon increases, both the mean and the variance of log returns increase in proportion to the horizon, and this has no effect on optimal portfolio rules for Epstein-Zin investors, which depend on the ratio of mean to variance when returns are lognormal. Hence, portfolio choice is invariant to the horizon, that is, myopic.

Unfortunately the portfolio approximation used in the above argument is accurate only for short intervals of time and deteriorates as longer investment horizons are considered. Empirically, however, Barberis (2000) shows that nonrebalancing investors are very close to myopic in realistic examples with iid returns.

9.2 Intertemporal Hedging

9.2.1 A Simple Example

To understand how portfolio choice is affected by a long horizon, we begin by considering the portfolio choice problem of a K-period investor with power utility over final wealth facing lognormal return distributions. Rewrite this as

$$\max_{\alpha_t} \; E_t[r_{p,t+1}] - \frac{\gamma - 1}{2}\text{Var}_t(r_{p_{t+1}})$$

$$+ \left\{E_t[r_{p,K,t+K}] - E_t[r_{p,t+1}]\right\} - \frac{\gamma - 1}{2}\left\{\text{Var}_t(r_{p,K,t+K}) - \text{Var}_t(r_{p,t+1})\right\}. \qquad (9.6)$$

The maximization is only over short-term portfolio choice, α_t, because we take as given the (generally state-contingent) portfolio choice rules for α_{t+j-1}, $j = 2, \ldots, K$, using the fact that portfolio choice with scale-independent preferences is purely forward-looking and independent of past returns. If $K = 2$, α_{t+1} is given by the short-term portfolio choice rule from Chapter 2, equation (2.28). If $K > 2$ we can calculate the future portfolio choice rules using backward induction.

It is clear from equation (9.6) that the optimal choice for α_t will still be given by the optimal rule (2.28) for the one-period problem unless α_t affects the terms in curly brackets. The first term in curly brackets is the difference between K-period and 1-period expected portfolio returns and is in fact unaffected by α_t due to the independence of portfolio choice from past returns and the linearity of the expectation operator. However, short-term portfolio choice α_t in general does affect the long-term riskiness of portfolio returns beyond its impact on the variance of next-period returns, the second term in curly brackets, and this is the source of the deviation of the optimal long-horizon rule from the myopic rule (2.28).

We can rewrite the difference between long-run and short-run variances, using the relation $r_{p,K,t+K} = r_{p,t+1} + r_{p,K-1,t+K}$, as $\text{Var}_t(r_{p,K-1,t+K}) + 2\text{Cov}_t(r_{p,t+1}, r_{p,K-1,t+K})$. Noting that $\text{Var}_t(r_{p,K-1,t+K})$ is unaffected by α_t due to the independence of portfolio choice from past returns, we can derive the optimal portfolio rule from the first-order condition of the maximization problem (9.6):

$$\alpha_t = \frac{E_t r_{t+1} - r_{f,t+1} + \sigma_t^2/2}{\gamma \sigma_t^2} - \frac{\gamma - 1}{\gamma \sigma_t^2}\frac{d\text{Cov}_t(r_{p,t+1}, r_{p,K-1,t+1})}{d\alpha_t}. \qquad (9.7)$$

The first term in (9.7) is just the short-term portfolio choice rule derived in Chapter 2, equation (2.28). The second term, known as the "intertemporal hedging" component of the portfolio rule, has a sign that depends on whether the coefficient of relative risk aversion is above or below one, for the reasons discussed in section 2.1.4: under our assumptions, the investor trades off the log of the arithmetic mean K-period return linearly against the variance of the log K-period return. Higher portfolio risk is penalized by risk-averse agents, but higher variance also results in a higher arithmetic mean return for a given expected log return. The net impact of higher portfolio variance on utility is positive if $\gamma < 1$ and negative if $\gamma > 1$, and the portfolio rule is adjusted accordingly.

To gain further insight about the intertemporal hedging term, consider a simple two-period setting with constant log risk premia and constant second moments. The only source of uncertainty is that the expectation of the risky asset return in the second period depends on the realization of the first-period risky asset return: $E_{t+1}[r_{t+2}] = \bar{r} + \varphi(r_{t+1} - \bar{r})$, where $\bar{r}$ is the unconditional mean risky asset return, and $r_{f,t+2}$ varies in the same fashion with r_{t+1} to keep the risk premium constant. In this setting $\text{Cov}_t(r_{p,t+1}, r_{p,t+2}) = \alpha_t \varphi \sigma^2$, so the intertemporal hedging component in portfolio demand is simply $-(\gamma - 1)\varphi/\gamma$. Intuitively, if $\varphi > 0$, the risky asset's first-period return is positively correlated with the quality of future investment opportunities. Thus, investing in the risky asset at t increases the two-period volatility of the portfolio, as the investor at the beginning of the second period will have more wealth to invest when investment opportunities going forward are good and less wealth to invest when investment opportunities are bad. This effect on volatility increases initial investment in the risky asset if $\gamma < 1$ and decreases it if $\gamma > 1$.

9.2.2 Hedging Interest Rates

We now study the implications of intertemporal hedging in a more sophisticated environment. A single investor, with an infinite horizon and Epstein-Zin preferences over consumption, finances a consumption stream entirely from invested wealth and faces exogenous asset returns. The analysis parallels the discussion in section 6.4 of consumption-based asset pricing with an infinitely lived Epstein-Zin representative agent and an exogenous consumption process, but the perspective here is different. In Chapter 6 we took consumption as given and derived implications for asset returns; here, we take asset returns as given and derive implications for consumption and, particularly, for portfolio choice.

Following Campbell and Viceira (2001), we first consider an environment with changing interest rates, but constant risk premia and second moments of returns. The Campbell-Shiller loglinear approximation to the investor's budget constraint implies that

$$\widetilde{c}_{t+1} = c_{t+1} - E_t c_{t+1}$$

$$= (E_{t+1} - E_t) \sum_{j=0}^{\infty} \rho^j r_{p,t+1+j} - (E_{t+1} - E_t) \sum_{j=1}^{\infty} \rho^j \Delta c_{t+1+j}, \tag{9.8}$$

where, as before, tildes denote innovations to random variables. As always, ρ is a coefficient of loglinearization, which here equals $1 - \exp(E(c_t - w_t))$. In the special case where the elasticity of intertemporal substitution equals one, the consumption-wealth ratio is constant at $(1 - \delta)$ and the loglinearization coefficient $\rho = \delta$, where δ is the investor's time discount factor.

Because variances and covariances of asset returns are constant, expected consumption growth satisfies

$$E_t[\Delta c_{t+1}] = \mu + \psi E_t r_{p,t+1},\qquad(9.9)$$

where the intercept μ captures all precautionary savings effects. Then the budget constraint can be rewritten as

$$\widetilde{c}_{t+1} = \widetilde{r}_{p,t+1} + (1-\psi)(E_{t+1} - E_t)\sum_{j=1}^{\infty}\rho^j r_{p,t+1+j}.\qquad(9.10)$$

The first-order condition for portfolio choice with Epstein-Zin utility, equation (6.46), is

$$E_t r_{i,t+1} - r_{f,t+1} + \frac{\sigma_t^2}{2} = \theta\frac{\mathrm{Cov}_t(r_{i,t+1}, c_{t+1})}{\psi} + (1-\theta)\mathrm{Cov}_t(r_{i,t+1}, r_{p,t+1}).\qquad(9.11)$$

Substituting out consumption using (9.10) and simplifying using the definition of $\theta = (1-\gamma)/(1-1/\psi)$, we find that

$$E_t r_{i,t+1} - r_{f,t+1} + \frac{\sigma_t^2}{2} = \gamma\,\mathrm{Cov}_t(r_{i,t+1}, r_{p,t+1}) + (\gamma-1)\mathrm{Cov}_t\left(r_{i,t+1}, (E_{t+1}-E_t)\sum_{j=1}^{\infty}\rho^j r_{p,t+1+j}\right).$$

$$(9.12)$$

The first term relates the required risk premium on any asset to the covariance of the asset's return with the return on the agent's whole portfolio, as in static mean-variance analysis. The second term captures the intertemporal hedging effect that is the focus of this chapter. Its sign depends on whether risk aversion γ is greater than or smaller than one, for reasons discussed in the previous subsection.

Equation (9.12) has an important property that will recur throughout this chapter. The required risk premium depends on the investor's coefficient of relative risk aversion γ but does not directly depend on the elasticity of intertemporal substitution ψ.[1] While ψ does directly affect risk prices when risks are measured from consumption covariances, as in equation (9.11), this parameter cancels out when consumption is substituted out of the model.

We have assumed that risk premia are constant, so returns on all assets move in parallel with the riskfree interest rate. Hence,

$$(E_{t+1} - E_t)\sum_{j=1}^{\infty}\rho^j r_{p,t+1+j} = (E_{t+1} - E_t)\sum_{j=1}^{\infty}\rho^j r_{f,t+1+j},\qquad(9.13)$$

and intertemporal hedging demand in this model depends on the covariance of an asset's return with revisions in expected future riskfree interest rates.

---

[1] There is an indirect effect of ψ because in general the loglinearization coefficient ρ depends on ψ. Campbell and Viceira (1999) show numerically that in a related model discussed in the next subsection, this indirect effect is small.

In a simplified portfolio choice problem with a single risky asset with return r_{t+1} and portfolio weight α_t,

$$\text{Cov}_t(r_{t+1}, r_{p,t+1}) = \alpha_t \sigma_t^2. \tag{9.14}$$

Substituting (9.13) and (9.14) into (9.12), we find that

$$\alpha_t = \frac{1}{\gamma} \frac{\text{E}_t r_{t+1} - r_{f,t+1} + \sigma_t^2/2}{\sigma_t^2} + \left(1 - \frac{1}{\gamma}\right) \frac{\text{Cov}_t\left(r_{t+1}, -(\text{E}_{t+1} - \text{E}_t)\sum_{j=1}^{\infty} \rho^j r_{f,t+1+j}\right)}{\sigma_t^2}. \tag{9.15}$$

The first term in (9.15) is the myopic portfolio weight from Chapter 2, (2.28), and the second term is an interest rate hedging term. As noted above, both terms involve risk aversion γ but not the elasticity of intertemporal substitution ψ. The second term drops out when risk aversion $\gamma = 1$, but comes to dominate the solution as risk aversion increases. In other words, conservative investors' risky holdings are primarily driven by intertemporal hedging and not by a speculative desire to earn a risk premium.

What is the Riskless Asset for a Long-Term Investor?
An investor who cares about single-period returns reduces his portfolio weight in single-period risky assets to zero as his risk aversion increases. However, this is not generally the case for the infinite-horizon investor considered here. In the limiting case of infinite risk aversion, the infinite-horizon investor's portfolio share in the single-period risky asset is not zero but

$$\alpha_t = \frac{\text{Cov}_t\left(r_{t+1}, -(\text{E}_{t+1} - \text{E}_t)\sum_{j=1}^{\infty} \rho^j r_{f,t+1+j}\right)}{\sigma_t^2}. \tag{9.16}$$

We can interpret this result using loglinear pricing formulas for real (inflation-indexed) perpetuities based on the analysis of coupon bonds in section 8.1.3. When risk premia are constant, the yield on an inflation-indexed perpetuity, denoted by *IIP*, is related to expected future riskless real interest rates by

$$y_{IIP,t} = \mu_{IIP} + (1 - \rho_{IIP})\text{E}_t \sum_{j=0}^{\infty} \rho_{IIP}^j r_{f,t+1+j}, \tag{9.17}$$

and the return on the perpetuity is

$$\begin{aligned} r_{IIP,t+1} &= \frac{1}{1 - \rho_{IIP}} y_{IIP,t} - \frac{\rho_{IIP}}{1 - \rho_{IIP}} y_{IIP,t+1} \\ &= r_{f,t+1} + \mu_{IIP} - (\text{E}_{t+1} - \text{E}_t)\sum_{j=1}^{\infty} \rho_{IIP}^j r_{f,t+1+j}. \end{aligned} \tag{9.18}$$

Here μ_{IIP} captures a constant risk premium and $\rho_{IIP} \equiv 1 - \exp\{\text{E}(-p_{IIP,t})\}$, where $p_{IIP,t}$ is the log "cum-dividend" price of the perpetuity including its current coupon. The first equality in (9.18) is equivalent to equation (8.16) with the duration of the perpetuity equal to $1/(1 - \rho_{IIP})$.

Hence, if the asset that is risky from a single-period perspective is an inflation-indexed perpetuity, and if $\rho = \rho_{IIP}$, we get $\alpha = 1$ for an infinitely risk-averse investor. We can show that $\rho = \rho_{IIP}$ for the case $\psi = 0$, where the infinitely risk-averse investor also has a zero elasticity of intertemporal substitution (as will be the case with power utility). In this case the investor demands a riskless and flat consumption path, which is provided by a perpetuity with a fixed stream of real coupons. This shows that an infinite-lived investor perceives risk quite differently from a single-period investor. The riskless asset for an infinite-lived investor is not a real Treasury bill but a real perpetuity.

Multiple Risky Assets
It is straightforward to generalize the above analysis to handle a portfolio choice problem with multiple risky assets and no short-term asset that is entirely safe in real terms. In this case we can define an arbitrary asset to be a benchmark asset and write its return as $r_{0,t+1}$. A natural choice for the benchmark is a Treasury bill, which has no nominal short-term risk and only modest real short-term risk. The vector of portfolio weights in other assets, α_t, is given by

$$\alpha_t = \frac{1}{\gamma} \Sigma_t^{-1} (\mathrm{E}_t r_{t+1} - r_{0,t+1} \iota + \sigma_t^2/2) + \left(1 - \frac{1}{\gamma}\right) \Sigma_t^{-1} (\sigma_{ht} - \sigma_{0t}), \tag{9.19}$$

where Σ_t is the variance-covariance matrix of the excess returns on risky assets over the benchmark asset, σ_t^2 is the vector of variances of these excess returns (the main diagonal of Σ_t), σ_{0t} is the vector of covariances of each risky asset's excess return over the benchmark with the benchmark return, and σ_{ht} is the vector of covariances of risky asset returns with revisions in expected future benchmark returns:

$$\sigma_{ht} \equiv \mathrm{Cov}_t \left(r_{t+1}, -(\mathrm{E}_{t+1} - \mathrm{E}_t) \sum_{j=1}^{\infty} \rho^j r_{0,t+1+j} \right). \tag{9.20}$$

We can further allow for borrowing and short-sales constraints by shrinking the menu of available assets. Since portfolio weights are constant, the solution for a problem with borrowing and short-sales constraints is also the solution for an unconstrained problem with a smaller set of available assets.

Application to the Asset Allocation Puzzle
Campbell and Viceira (2001) apply the above analysis to the asset allocation puzzle of Canner, Mankiw, and Weil (1997). Recall from Table 2.1 that financial advisers tend to recommend a higher ratio of bonds to stocks for more conservative investors. In a single-period model, this violates the mutual fund theorem of Tobin (1958). In an infinite-horizon model, however, it may simply reflect the ability of long-term bonds to hedge against declines in real interest rates, or equivalently, to provide a stable long-term stream of real income.

In order to capture realistic dynamics of nominal and real interest rates, inflation, and stock returns, Campbell and Viceira estimate a simple affine term structure model of the sort discussed in Chapter 8. The model has constant risk premia but multiple factors. As in the single-factor homoskedastic model of section 8.3.2, the conditional expectation of the log stochastic discount factor is driven by an AR(1) state variable x_t that equals the log riskless real interest rate. Similarly, expected log inflation is driven by an AR(1) state variable z_t. Shocks to the log SDF, to the log real interest rate, and to realized and expected log inflation can all be correlated with one another. Equities are modeled in reduced form as having returns that are linear in shocks to the log SDF and the log real interest rate.

Table 9.1. *Long-Term Asset Allocation in the Campbell and Viceira (2001) Model*

γ	Long sample		Short sample	
	Stocks	Bonds	Stocks	Bonds
1	100	0	100	0
2	100	0	87	13
5	73	6	36	64
10	35	8	19	81
5000	0	10	1	98

Campbell and Viceira estimate this model using quarterly data in two sample periods, a long sample 1952Q1–1999Q2 and a shorter sample 1983Q1–1999Q2. In the long sample, which includes the extended increase in inflation during the 1970s and decrease in inflation during the 1980s, the expected inflation rate is estimated to be highly persistent, while fluctuations in the real interest rate are relatively transitory. In the short sample, which contains only the period of strongly anti-inflationary monetary policy after the appointment of Paul Volcker as Federal Reserve chairman, the real interest rate is estimated to be more persistent and expected inflation less so. The contrast between these two sample periods illustrates the influences on long-term portfolio choice.

Table 9.1 reports the optimal portfolio weights calculated by Campbell and Viceira using the long-sample and short-sample models, and imposing short-sales and borrowing constraints. In each case the asset classes available to investors are equities, long-term nominal bonds, and Treasury bills ("cash"). In both models log utility investors are fully invested in equities, but as risk aversion increases, these relatively risky assets become less attractive. The difference between the two models concerns the alternative asset that conservative long-term investors shift into. In the long-sample model, uncertainty about future real interest rates is quite limited, while persistent inflation makes long-term bonds risky at all horizons; hence, conservative long-term investors hold mostly cash. In the short-sample model, persistent variation in real interest rates makes cash risky for long-term investors, while inflation is mostly transitory, so nominal bonds are good substitutes for inflation-indexed bonds; hence, conservative long-term investors hold a portfolio that is almost fully invested in long-term bonds. Campbell and Viceira also show that if offered inflation-indexed bonds, such as the Treasury Inflation Protected Securities (TIPS) that were first issued in 1997, conservative long-term investors hold this asset regardless of the inflation or real interest rate processes. Thus, long-term portfolio choice theory has the potential to explain the asset allocation puzzle if either bonds are inflation-indexed, or inflation is relatively well controlled by the monetary authority.

9.2.3 Hedging Risk Premia

In general, long-term investors may want to hedge time-variation in risk premia as well as time-variation in riskless real interest rates. In this section we begin by illustrating the point using a simple example based on Kim and Omberg (1996) and Campbell and Viceira (1999), where the riskfree interest rate is constant but the risk premium on a single risky asset is time-varying. We then generalize to consider time-variation in the expected returns on multiple risky assets and briefly discuss alternative approaches to the long-term portfolio choice problem.

A Single Risky Asset with an AR(1) Risk Premium

We assume a constant log riskless rate r_f and a single risky asset with log return r_{t+1}. The unexpected risky return is written as

$$r_{t+1} - E_t r_{t+1} = u_{t+1}. \tag{9.21}$$

We write the risk premium as x_t, and assume it follows an AR(1) process:

$$E_t r_{t+1} - r_f + \frac{\sigma_u^2}{2} = x_t. \tag{9.22}$$

$$x_{t+1} = \mu + \phi(x_t - \mu) + \eta_{t+1}. \tag{9.23}$$

We allow the shocks u_{t+1} and η_{t+1} to be correlated. If $\sigma_{\eta u} < 0$, then stock returns display mean reversion—negative autocorrelations and a long-horizon unconditional variance ratio less than one—as discussed in section 5.1.1 of Chapter 5.

Risk and the Investment Horizon

Pastor and Stambaugh (2012) point out that even in the presence of mean reversion, and even when all model parameters are known, the annualized conditional variance of the risky asset return need not decline monotonically with the investment horizon. The distinction between horizon effects on conditional variance and on unconditional variance arises from variability in the conditional mean over time. Formally, we have $(r_{t+1} - E r_{t+1}) = (r_{t+1} - E_t r_{t+1}) + (E_t r_{t+1} - E r_{t+1})$, and these components are unconditionally uncorrelated with one another, so

$$\mathrm{Var}(r_{t+1} - E r_{t+1}) = \mathrm{Var}(r_{t+1} - E_t r_{t+1}) + \mathrm{Var}(E_t r_{t+1} - E r_{t+1}). \tag{9.24}$$

Condensing the notation,

$$\sigma_1^2 = \sigma_{u1}^2 + \sigma_{e1}^2. \tag{9.25}$$

Similarly, at a K-period horizon,

$$\frac{\mathrm{Var}(r_{t,t+K} - E r_{t,t+K})}{K} = \frac{\mathrm{Var}(r_{t,t+K} - E_t r_{t,t+K})}{K} + \frac{\mathrm{Var}(E_t r_{t,t+K} - E r_{t,t+K})}{K}, \tag{9.26}$$

or

$$\sigma_K^2 = \sigma_{u,K}^2 + \sigma_{eK}^2. \tag{9.27}$$

We know from equation (5.3) in Chapter 5 that in the presence of mean reversion, the unconditional variance ratio σ_K^2/σ_1^2 is less than one:

$$\frac{\sigma_K^2}{\sigma_1^2} = V(K) < 1. \tag{9.28}$$

A more relevant question for a long-term investor is how the multiperiod risk ratio $\sigma_{u,K}^2/\sigma_{u,1}^2$ behaves, since this captures risk relative to the investor's information set at the time a portfolio decision is made. This ratio can be written as

$$\frac{\sigma_{u,K}^2}{\sigma_{u,1}^2} = V(K) \frac{(1 - R^2(K))}{(1 - R^2(1))}. \tag{9.29}$$

The analysis of section 5.3.2 in Chapter 5 showed that the multiperiod R^2 statistic in an AR(1) predictive model is hump shaped, increasing at first and then declining toward zero in the very long run. It follows that $(1 - R^2(K))$ declines at first and then eventually increases toward one. Thus, the multiperiod risk ratio declines at first but then can increase, eventually rising above one if the limit of $V(K)$ is not too low and if the single-period explanatory power $R^2(1)$ is high enough.

It is an empirical question whether the multiperiod risk ratio is monotonic or not. Campbell and Viceira (2002) and Campbell, Chan and Viceira (2003) present estimates in which the multiperiod risk ratio is monotonically declining for the aggregate stock market, but Pástor and Stambaugh (2012) use a model with a higher single-period R^2 statistic in which the multiperiod risk ratio first declines and then increases above its initial level.

We now show that regardless of whether the multiperiod risk ratio is monotonic, mean reversion in this AR(1) model implies a positive intertemporal hedging demand for the risky asset by conservative long-term investors.

Solving for Portfolio Choice
To solve for the portfolio choice of an infinite-horizon Epstein-Zin investor, we guess the form of the solution and equate terms to solve for implied coefficients and verify the form of the solution. We guess that the portfolio rule is linear in the state variable, while the consumption rule and log value function are quadratic:

$$\alpha_t = a_0 + a_1 x_t, \tag{9.30}$$

$$c_t - w_t = b_0 + b_1 x_t + b_2 x_t^2. \tag{9.31}$$

These guesses imply a quadratic value function:

$$V_t = \exp\left[b_0^* + b_1^* x_t + b_2^* x_t^2\right]. \tag{9.32}$$

As an informal exercise, you are asked to consider why the quadratic form for the value function makes sense, conditional on the linear portfolio rule.

The coefficient $b_0 = (1 - \psi)b_0^* + \psi \log(1 - \delta)$. As ψ approaches one, b_0 approaches $\log(1 - \delta)$. The coefficients $b_1 = (1 - \psi)b_1^*$ and $b_2 = (1 - \psi)b_2^*$, and b_1^* and b_2^* do not directly depend on ψ.[2] Hence, as ψ approaches one, the coefficients b_1 and b_2 approach zero, implying a constant consumption-wealth ratio.

The value function coefficients b_1^* and b_2^* determine the properties of the portfolio choice solution. It can be shown that $b_2^* > 0$ and does not depend on μ, while $b_1^* = 0$ when $\mu = 0$ and normally has the same sign as μ.[3] To understand these results, first consider the case where $\mu = 0$. Then the value function is a symmetric quadratic function with a minimum when x_t equals its unconditional mean of zero. At this point in the state space, the risk premium is zero, so no expected profits can be made by going either long or short the risky asset. Furthermore, the risk premium is not expected to move either up or

[2]They do depend on the loglinearization coefficient ρ, which in turn depends on ψ, but Campbell and Viceira (1999) show that this indirect effect of ψ is very small in realistic examples.

[3]The property that b_1^* has the same sign as μ is verified numerically but not proved analytically by Campbell and Viceira (1999). Kim and Omberg (1996) prove the analogous result in a simpler finite-horizon model with power utility of terminal wealth.

down from this point. Thus, the opportunity to invest in the risky asset is least valuable, and accordingly the value function is lowest, when x_t is zero.

Now consider the case where $\mu > 0$. Then there is a positive linear term in the value function, implying that the minimum is reached when $x_t < 0$. The explanation is that x_t is expected to revert toward its positive mean, so it is expected to spend more time in the future close to zero when it starts from a negative value than when it starts from zero. This means that the minimum of the value function, where the opportunity to invest in the risky asset is least valuable, occurs at a slightly negative risk premium, not a zero risk premium.

Solving for the coefficients in the portfolio rule, Campbell and Viceira (1999, 2002) show that

$$a_0 = \left(1 - \frac{1}{\gamma}\right)(b_1^* + 2\mu(1-\phi)b_2^*)\left(-\frac{\sigma_{\eta u}}{\sigma_u^2}\right), \tag{9.33}$$

$$a_1 = \frac{1}{\gamma\sigma_u^2} + \left(1 - \frac{1}{\gamma}\right)(2\phi b_2^*)\left(-\frac{\sigma_{\eta u}}{\sigma_u^2}\right) \tag{9.34}$$

The myopic portfolio rule is $a_0 = 0$ and $a_1 = 1/\gamma\sigma_u^2$. The solutions (9.33) and (9.34) differ from this only when $\gamma \neq 1$ (so investors desire to intertemporally hedge) and $\sigma_{\eta u} \neq 0$ (so the risky asset is useful in intertemporal hedging).

Intertemporal hedging demand in general affects both the intercept and slope of the portfolio rule. Considering the intercept first, when $\mu = 0$ then $a_0 = 0$. However, when $\gamma > 1$, $\mu > 0$ and $\sigma_{\eta u} < 0$, then $a_0 > 0$. A positive intercept a_0 implies that the investor holds the risky asset even when the risk premium is zero, something that can never happen in a static model as shown in section 2.1.1.

The explanation is that when $\mu = 0$, the slope of the value function is zero at $x_t = 0$. The investor is indifferent to marginal changes in the risk premium and thus has no incentive to hedge against either increases or decreases. When $\mu > 0$, on the other hand, the value function is increasing at $x_t = 0$. A conservative investor, with $\gamma > 1$, will try to hedge against declines in x_t by holding an asset that increases in value when x_t declines. Under the assumption of mean reversion, $\sigma_{\eta u} < 0$, the risky asset has this property. Thus intertemporal hedging can lead risk-averse investors to hold a risky asset with a zero risk premium.

Turning to the slope of the portfolio rule, when $\gamma > 1$ and $\sigma_{\eta u} < 0$, a_1 exceeds the myopic value of $1/\gamma\sigma_u^2$ (the first term in (9.34)). This implies that a long-term investor should time the market more aggressively than a short-term investor. The reason is that the magnitude of intertemporal hedging demand increases with the slope of the value function, which is always increasing in x_t. Putting the intercept and slope results together, mean reversion increases the average demand for stocks by conservative long-term investors relative to short-term investors with the same level of risk aversion.

Jeremy Siegel, in the first edition of his well-known book *Stocks for the Long Run* (1994, pp. 29–30), writes:

> It is widely known that stock returns, on average, exceed bonds in the long run. But it is little known that in the long run, the risks in stocks are *less than* those found in bonds or even bills! .... Real stock returns are substantially more volatile than the returns of bonds and bills over short-term periods. But as the horizon increases, the range of stock returns narrows far more quickly than for fixed-income assets ....

Stocks, in contrast to bonds or bills, have never offered investors a negative real holding-period return yield over 20 years or more. Although it might appear riskier to hold stocks than bonds, precisely the opposite is true: the safest long-term investment has clearly been stocks, not bonds.

Siegel concludes from this that long-term investors should buy and hold stocks, increasing their constant portfolio allocation to stocks above the level that would be appropriate for short-term investors. As a further informal exercise, you are asked to comment on this conclusion.

Multiple Risky Assets with Vector Autoregressive Risk Premia
The results of this section can be generalized to a multivariate model (Campbell, Chan and Viceira 2003). We can define a state vector z_{t+1} that contains a reference return $r_{0,t+1}$ (not necessarily riskless), a vector of excess returns on other assets over the reference return $r_{t+1} - r_{0,t+1}\iota$, and a vector of other state variables s_{t+1} relevant for forecasting these returns:

$$z_{t+1} \equiv \begin{bmatrix} r_{0,t+1} \\ r_{t+1} - r_{0,t+1}\iota \\ s_{t+1} \end{bmatrix}. \tag{9.35}$$

We assume that the state vector follows a VAR(1) process:

$$z_{t+1} = \Phi_0 + \Phi_1 z_t + v_{t+1}. \tag{9.36}$$

Then the previous example generalizes as follows:

$$\alpha_t = a_0 + A_1 z_t, \tag{9.37}$$

$$c_t - w_t = b_0 + b_1' z_t + z_t' B_2 z_t. \tag{9.38}$$

Here α_t is a vector of portfolio weights, a_0 and b_1 are vectors, and A_1 and B_2 are matrices. A system of nonlinear equations can be solved numerically to obtain these coefficient vectors and matrices.

Campbell, Chan and Viceira (2003) estimate a model like this for equities, nominal Treasury bonds, and Treasury bills. Their estimates from quarterly US data over the period 1953Q2–1999Q4 imply that there is mean reversion in both bond and stock returns, but that the risk of Treasury bill investing increases with the horizon because of uncertainty about the rates at which Treasury bills can be rolled over in the future. The implied portfolio rule features an average intertemporal hedging demand for stocks that is hump shaped in risk aversion. Log utility investors have no intertemporal hedging demand, while extremely conservative investors do not invest in stocks in any case, so variation in the equity premium is not a relevant feature of their investment opportunity set and need not be intertemporally hedged.

Conversely, the intertemporal hedging demand for bonds is U-shaped. For intermediate levels of risk aversion at which intertemporal hedging demand for stocks is large, bonds are crowded out because in the 1953Q2–1999Q4 sample period, bonds and stocks are positively correlated. For high levels of risk aversion, the demand for stocks disappears and bonds are held as intertemporal hedges. This implies that total demand for bonds is nonmonotonic in risk aversion.

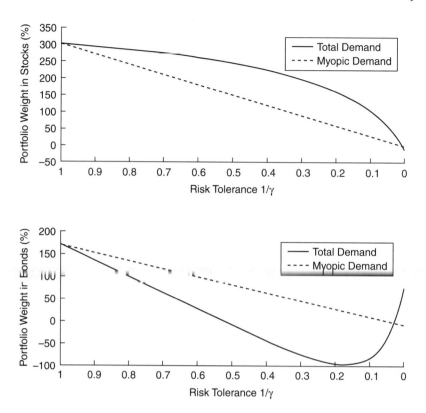

Figure 9.1. *Average Estimated Optimal Portfolio Weights in Stocks and Bonds* (Reprinted from Campbell, John Y., Y. Lewis Chan, and Luis M. Viceira, 2003, "A Multivariate Model of Strategic Asset Allocation," *Journal of Financial Economics* 67 (1), 41–80; reprinted by permission of Elsevier.)

Figure 9.1 illustrates these effects. The figure contains two panels, the upper one illustrating stock demand and the lower one illustrating bond demand. Each panel plots the portfolio weight, calculated conditional on mean values for all state variables, against relative risk tolerance, the reciprocal of relative risk aversion. The highest risk tolerance shown is one, implying risk aversion of one, and risk tolerance declines (risk aversion increases) as one moves to the right in the figure. The dotted lines show the myopic demand of a single-period investor, which is linear in risk tolerance and decreases for both bonds and stocks. At risk tolerance of zero (infinite risk aversion), myopic demand is almost exactly zero for both bonds and stocks, and would be exactly zero if Treasury bills were riskless in real terms. The solid lines show total demand, so the gap between the two lines is intertemporal hedging demand.

Hedging Volatility
The model discussed here can be further extended to allow for stochastic volatility. In a lognormal framework, the investment opportunity set is summarized by the maximum available Sharpe ratio on risky assets. Hence, fluctuations in volatility are associated with intertemporal hedging demand if the maximum Sharpe ratio also fluctuates, but not if it

is constant over time—as will be the case if the conditional risk premium and conditional standard deviation of a single risky asset return move in proportion to one another. With a constant Sharpe ratio and time-varying volatility for a single risky asset, the optimum portfolio weight on the risky asset is time-varying but is the same as in a single-period portfolio choice model.

Chacko and Viceira (2005) explore volatility hedging in a continuous-time lognormal framework assuming a univariate AR(1) process for volatility. They find relatively modest intertemporal hedging demands given the volatility process they estimate, which decays relatively quickly and thus is of limited relevance for long-term investors. We defer a full discussion of volatility hedging to section 9.3.2, where we summarize results from an implementation of the ICAPM incorporating a multivariate volatility process that picks up persistent fluctuations in volatility.

9.2.4 Alternative Approaches

A caveat about the linear-quadratic approach to intertemporal portfolio choice is that it relies on the log approximation to portfolio returns in discrete time, which rules out bankruptcy even when portfolio weights on risky assets are negative or exceed one. In reality, short sales and leverage create the possibility of bankruptcy in discrete time (or in continuous time when asset prices can jump). While it is straightforward to modify the linear-quadratic approach to impose short-sales and leverage constraints in the case where only interest rates are time-varying, so optimal portfolio weights are constant, this is no longer true in the general case where risk premia and optimal portfolio weights are time-varying.

An alternative approach to intertemporal portfolio choice, developed by Brandt (1999) and Aït-Sahalia and Brandt (2001), is to use the Euler equation for optimal portfolio choice together with assumed functional forms for portfolio rules (that can include short-sales and leverage constraints). The data can then be used to estimate the portfolio rule parameters that minimize the Euler equation errors, using Generalized Method of Moments. This approach is highly flexible and straightforward to implement, although it does not deliver analytic results or insights about the mapping from the data generating process for asset returns to the portfolio decisions of investors.

Cochrane (2014) instead assumes time-separable quadratic utility of consumption and derives propositions about optimal payoff streams in relation to the stochastic discount factor. The idea here is to carry over the intuition of static mean-variance optimization to a dynamic environment. Cochrane's analysis is the basis of Problem 9.1.

9.3 The Intertemporal CAPM

9.3.1 A Two-Beta Model

Intertemporal portfolio choice theory can be used to study the cross-section of stock returns. Consider a model in which the expected return on the market portfolio varies. What average returns on individual stocks, or portfolios of stocks sorted by characteristics such as value, would make a long-term investor content to hold the market portfolio rather than overweighting stocks with high expected returns?

For a short-term investor, or a long-term investor with log utility, the answer is given by the CAPM: average excess stock returns over the riskless interest rate must be proportional to the betas of stocks with the market portfolio. Merton (1973) first extended the CAPM to a setting with intertemporal hedging demand, formulating an intertemporal CAPM or ICAPM. He showed that innovations to variables that predict market returns are priced risk factors, with risk prices that are pinned down by the derivatives of the investor's value function. Here we follow Campbell (1993) and Campbell and Vuolteenaho (CV 2004) and develop a discrete-time approximate version of the ICAPM in which risk prices can be solved in closed form.

We begin by using the loglinear return decomposition (5.51) to break the unexpected log return on the market, $\tilde{r}_{m,t+1} = r_{m,t+1} - E_t\,r_{m,t+1}$, into two components, revisions in expected future dividends ("cash-flow news," or N_{CF}) and revisions in discount rates ("discount-rate news," or N_{DR}):

$$\tilde{r}_{m,t+1} = (E_{t+1} - E_t) \sum_{j=0}^{\infty} \rho^j \Delta d_{t+1+j} - (E_{t+1} - E_t) \sum_{j-1}^{\infty} \rho^j r_{m,t+1+j}$$

$$= N_{CF,t+1} - N_{DR,t+1}. \tag{9.39}$$

If an investor with Epstein-Zin preferences holds the market portfolio, whose return is homoskedastic, equation (9.12) can be rewritten as

$$E_t[r_{i,t+1}] - r_{f,t+1} + \frac{\sigma_{i,t}^2}{2} = \gamma\,\mathrm{Cov}_t(r_{i,t+1}, r_{m,t+1}) + (1 - \gamma)\,\mathrm{Cov}_t(r_{i,t+1}, -N_{DR,t+1})$$

$$= \gamma\,\mathrm{Cov}_t(r_{i,t+1}, N_{CF,t+1}) + \mathrm{Cov}_t(r_{i,t+1}, -N_{DR,t+1}), \tag{9.40}$$

where the first equality puts the contemporaneous return covariance in the first term and the intertemporal hedging effect in the second term, while the second equality shows that of the two elements of the contemporaneous return, cash flow news is more serious for long-term investors (because it is permanent), and so it carries a higher risk price.

CV multiply and divide each term on the right-hand side of (9.40) by the variance of the market return, $\sigma_{mt}^2 = \mathrm{Var}_t r_{t+1}$ and define the beta with cash-flow news as

$$\beta_{i,CF,t} = \mathrm{Cov}_t(r_{i,t+1}, N_{CF,t+1}) / \sigma_{mt}^2 \tag{9.41}$$

and the beta with discount-rate news as

$$\beta_{i,DR,t} = \mathrm{Cov}_t(r_{i,t+1}, -N_{DR,t+1}) / \sigma_{mt}^2. \tag{9.42}$$

Defined this way, the two betas sum up to the traditional CAPM beta. In the intertemporal theory, however, they have different risk prices because (9.40) implies

$$E_t[r_{i,t+1}] - r_{f,t+1} + \frac{\sigma_{i,t}^2}{2} = \gamma\,\sigma_{mt}^2\beta_{i,CF,t} + \sigma_{mt}^2\beta_{i,DR,t}. \tag{9.43}$$

The cash-flow beta has a risk price γ times higher than the discount-rate beta, because conservative long-term investors fear permanent declines in wealth driven by cash-flow news more than temporary declines in wealth driven by increases in discount rates. Accordingly CV call the cash-flow beta "bad beta" and the discount-rate beta "good beta."[4]

---

[4]The terminology reflects an analogy with cholesterol. Decades ago, cholesterol was used as a measure of cardiovascular risk. Today, two types of cholesterol are separately measured, LDL ("bad") and HDL ("good").

Empirical Implementation

CV test the unconditional implications of this model, using simple average excess returns on test assets and relating them to the two betas. The discount-rate beta has a risk price that is pinned down by the theory, and the ratio of the cash-flow beta's risk price to the discount-rate beta's risk price identifies the investor's coefficient of relative risk aversion.

CV use a VAR methodology, as developed in Chapter 5, to estimate the two components of the market return. They assume that a state vector z_{t+1}, the first element of which is the market return, follows a VAR(1) process:

$$z_{t+1} = a + \Gamma z_t + u_{t+1}. \tag{9.44}$$

Then the two news terms are given by

$$N_{CF,t+1} = (e1' + e1'\lambda) u_{t+1} \tag{9.45}$$

$$N_{DR,t+1} = e1'\lambda u_{t+1}, \tag{9.46}$$

where $\lambda \equiv \rho\Gamma(I - \rho\Gamma)^{-1}$. $e1'\lambda$ captures the long-run significance of each individual VAR shock to discount-rate expectations. The greater the absolute value of a variable's coefficient in the return prediction equation (the top row of Γ), the greater the weight the variable receives in the discount-rate-news formula. More persistent variables should also receive more weight, which is captured by the term $(I - \rho\Gamma)^{-1}$.

CV estimate a VAR system including the smoothed P/E ratio, the term spread, and the small-stock value spread. They include the value spread because it is suggested by the logic of the ICAPM as applied to the value anomaly. For the ICAPM to explain the low returns to growth stocks, the high CAPM beta of growth stocks must be disproportionately discount-rate beta; that is, growth stocks must do particularly well when the expected return on the market declines. This in turn implies that expensive growth stocks (a high value spread) should predict low returns on the aggregate stock market. CV report evidence for this effect, in line with the empirical findings of Eleswarapu and Reinganum (2004). The estimated VAR system implies that value stocks have higher bad betas than growth stocks, even though growth stocks have higher good betas and higher total CAPM betas during the last 50 years. This enables the intertemporal model to explain the value effect by choosing a large coefficient of relative risk aversion (about 24). Problem 9.2 asks you to replicate parts of this empirical work.

Caveats and Interpretation

Several caveats apply to this analysis. First, the cross-sectional pattern of bad and good betas is sensitive to the variables included in the VAR system, as pointed out by Chen and Zhao (2009). Some other specifications reverse this result and imply that growth stocks have higher bad betas. In a sense this should not be surprising, since growth stocks have higher overall betas and thus any decomposition of market returns that implies a constant proportional split of market returns into cash-flow and discount-rate components will imply that growth stocks have higher betas with both components. However, it does seem to be a fairly robust result across specifications that the ratio of bad beta to good beta is higher for value stocks; this is enough to enable the intertemporal model

---

These have different effects on cardiovascular risk. However, the analogy is imperfect because HDL cholesterol actually reduces risk, whereas the "good beta" is still risky for long-term investors, albeit less so than the "bad beta."

to generate a positive CAPM alpha for value stocks, even if not a higher absolute return. In addition, Campbell, Polk, and Vuolteenaho (2010) use direct long-horizon measurement of cash flows and recover the result that value stocks have higher cash-flow betas than growth stocks.

A second issue is theoretical. CV test only the unconditional implications of their model. If the expected return on the aggregate stock market is time-varying and homoskedastic, then an Epstein-Zin investor with constant risk aversion will optimally hold a constant position in the market portfolio only if the riskfree interest rate moves in parallel with the expected market return to keep the equity premium constant over time. But this is counterfactual because the predictor variables in the VAR system predict the excess return over the riskfree interest rate, in line with the evidence of a time-varying equity premium discussed in Chapter 5. The CV model cannot explain why the investor under consideration does not follow a market timing strategy; equivalently, the average return to a managed market-timing portfolio is higher than predicted by its cash-flow and discount-rate betas. Nonetheless, the two-beta model does explain why a conservative, long-term equity investor (whose desire to hold equity is not modeled) may avoid taking a value tilt in her equity portfolio.

Third, the two-beta model does not help to explain the equity premium puzzle. The evidence for mean reversion of the aggregate market return, discussed in Chapter 5, implies that a large fraction of the volatility of stock returns is accounted for by discount-rate news rather than cash-flow news. In other words, most of the unit beta of the aggregate stock market consists of discount-rate beta whose price is constrained to equal the variance of the market return. The cash-flow beta of the market is only a small fraction of the total beta, and only the price of this component increases with risk aversion. Hence, a larger coefficient of relative risk aversion is needed to account for the equity premium than would be the case in a traditional static model where all market risk is cash-flow risk. This is another way to express the finding, stated earlier in this chapter, that a conservative long-term investor facing mean-reverting stock returns is willing to hold a larger average equity position than an equally conservative short-term investor. CV need a coefficient of relative risk aversion over 20 to fit both the average equity premium and the excess return to value stocks.

There is an intimate connection between the intertemporal model presented here and the consumption-based model with Epstein-Zin utility discussed in Chapter 6. Both models describe an infinitely lived investor with constant relative risk aversion. The intertemporal model assumes that the investor holds the market portfolio and explains risk premia using the dynamics of market returns, but it does not necessarily assume that the investor is a representative agent whose consumption equals aggregate consumption. Both models require a relatively large coefficient of relative risk aversion to fit the equity premium: the intertemporal model because stock returns are mean-reverting and the consumption-based model because aggregate consumption growth is smooth.[5]

---

[5]Given mean-reverting market returns, the investor will choose a smooth consumption path if the elasticity of intertemporal substitution is low, as illustrated by equation (6.51) and discussed by Campbell (1996). The intertemporal model reconciles the low estimate of risk aversion of 2 calculated by Friend and Blume (1975), using a static model in which the optimal portfolio weight is the equity premium divided by risk aversion times market return variance, with the much higher estimates of risk aversion that emerge from consumption-based models. The intertemporal model achieves this by adjusting the Friend and Blume estimate of risk aversion upward to account for mean reversion in stock returns.

9.3.2 Hedging Volatility: A Three-Beta Model

A difficulty with the Campbell-Vuolteenaho model is that it assumes a constant variance for the market return. This is counterfactual and potentially important. Time-varying volatility affects the quality of investment opportunities and should influence intertemporal hedging demand.

Campbell et al. (CGPT 2017) address this issue. They show that with time-varying second moments, the innovation to the log stochastic discount factor (calculated from the marginal utility of an infinitely lived investor with Epstein-Zin preferences, as in the previous section), can be written as

$$\widetilde{m}_{t+1} = -\gamma \, N_{CF,t+1} + N_{DR,t+1} + \frac{1}{2} N_{RISK,t+1}, \tag{9.47}$$

where "risk news" $N_{RISK,t+1}$ is defined as

$$N_{RISK,t+1} = (\mathrm{E}_{t+1} - \mathrm{E}_t) \sum_{j=1}^{\infty} \rho^j \mathrm{Var}_{t+j}[m_{t+1+j} + r_{t+1+j}]. \tag{9.48}$$

The definition of risk news in equation (9.48) contains the log stochastic discount factor itself, so the representation (9.47) does not express risk in relation to measurable exogenous variables. To accomplish this, CGPT make the additional assumption that market returns and their conditional variance are described by a first-order VAR system

$$z_{t+1} = \bar{z} + \Gamma\,(z_t - \bar{z}) + \sigma_{mt} u_{t+1}, \tag{9.49}$$

where z_{t+1} is a vector of state variables that has $r_{m,t+1}$ as its first element and $\sigma_{m,t+1}^2$ as its second element. The shock vector u_{t+1} has a constant variance-covariance matrix Σ, scaled so that its first diagonal element is one.

In the system (9.49), a scalar random variable, σ_{mt}^2, equal to the conditional variance of market returns, also governs time-variation in the variance of all shocks to this system. Both market returns and state variables, including variance itself, have innovations whose variances move in proportion to one another. This assumption makes the stochastic volatility process affine, as in Heston (1993). It also implies that the conditional variance of returns plus the stochastic discount factor is proportional to the conditional variance of returns themselves.[6]

In this system, cash-flow and discount-rate news terms can be calculated using analogous expressions to equations (9.45) and (9.46). More importantly, news about risk is proportional to news about future market return variance, discounted over an infinite horizon:

$$N_{RISK,t+1} = \omega (\mathrm{E}_{t+1} - \mathrm{E}_t) \sum_{j=1}^{\infty} \rho^j \sigma_{m,t+j}^2 = \omega N_{V,t+1}. \tag{9.50}$$

---

[6]The VAR system (9.49) is a multivariate generalization of the square-root single-factor affine model discussed in section 8.3.3. A single-factor square-root process is guaranteed to remain nonnegative when specified in continuous time (and strictly positive if the Feller condition is satisfied); unfortunately, this is not true for a multivariate process because, although the process becomes deterministic as the zero boundary is approached, the drift in volatility depends on all the state variables and may be negative at the boundary. However, discrete-time simulations of the multivariate affine process do show that it is much less likely to go negative than the analogous process with homoskedastic volatility. Homoskedastic volatility processes have often been used in the long-run risk literature.

Variance news can be calculated directly from the VAR system, and the coefficient ω is obtained by solving a quadratic equation in γ and the second moments of the news terms. When $\gamma = 1$, $\omega = 0$ and ω increases quadratically with γ. There is an upper bound on γ beyond which there is no longer a real solution for ω, and the agent's value function is ill-defined. This is a common property of infinite-horizon models with stochastic volatility, such as (9.49), in which volatility itself becomes more volatile as its level increases.[7]

Putting these results together, the expected excess return on any asset is given by

$$\mathrm{E}_t[r_{i,t+1}] - r_{f,t+1} + \frac{\sigma_{i,t}^2}{2} = \gamma\,\sigma_{mt}^2 \beta_{i,CF,t} + \sigma_{mt}^2 \beta_{i,DR,t} - \frac{\omega\sigma_{mt}^2}{2}\beta_{i,V,t}, \qquad (9.51)$$

where by analogy with cash-flow and discount-rate betas, the variance beta is defined as $\beta_{i,V,t} = \mathrm{Cov}_t(r_{i,t+1}, N_{V,t+1})/\sigma_{mt}^2$. This model relates the risk premium on any asset to three separate betas, but importantly there is only one free parameter in the model, the coefficient of relative risk aversion γ, because the variance risk price ω is pinned down by the VAR dynamics and γ.

Empirical Implementation

To implement the three-beta model, CGPT estimate a VAR that includes the explanatory variables from the two-beta model as well as the default spread on risky corporate bonds relative to high-grade corporate bonds. The default spread is a natural forecasting variable for long-term volatility, because corporate bonds have long maturities and are more exposed to negative shocks than to positive shocks, so their prices will fall and their yields will increase when long-term volatility is expected to be high. CGPT find that the default spread indeed plays an important role in forecasting low-frequency movements in aggregate market volatility.

CGPT study test assets that include equity portfolios sorted by characteristics such as value and by estimated betas, as well as managed portfolios that alter risk exposures in response to changes in volatility. They find that growth stocks tend to outperform value stocks when long-term volatility forecasts increase (as during the technology boom of the late 1990s and the global financial crisis of the late 2000s). This implies that growth stocks have positive variance betas—they insure long-term investors against increases in market risk—which contributes to an explanation of their low average returns. The three-beta model fits the value premium and other cross-sectional patterns in stock returns with a lower coefficient of relative risk aversion, around 7, than that required by the two-beta model.

In CGPT's implementation, the aggregate stock market has a positive variance beta during the last 50 years (although it had a negative variance beta in an earlier sample period including the Great Depression). This implies that the three-beta model requires a large coefficient of risk aversion to fit the equity premium, because the aggregate stock market is a variance hedge, which makes stocks more appealing to conservative long-term investors. This pattern contrasts with that estimated by Bansal et al. (BKSY 2014) in an alternative empirical model of variance risk. In the BKSY model, the aggregate market falls when volatility increases, so variance risk helps to explain the equity premium, but value stocks have higher variance betas than growth stocks, so variance risk effects go the

---

[7]The online appendix to CGPT presents a simple example with unit elasticity of intertemporal substitution that can be used to study this issue in greater detail.

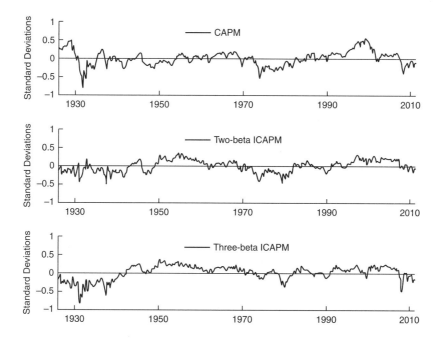

Figure 9.2. *History of SDF Shocks Implied by the CAPM, Two-Beta ICAPM, and Three-Beta ICAPM* (Campbell, John Y., Stefano Giglio, Christopher Polk, and Robert Turley, 2017, "An Intertemporal CAPM with Stochastic Volatility," forthcoming *Journal of Financial Economics.*)

wrong way to explain the value premium.[8] The contrast in results is likely to stimulate further debate and empirical research.

As a summary of the models discussed in this section, Figure 9.2 plots the history of the SDF shocks $m_{t+1} - E_t m_{t+1}$ that drive the investor's marginal utility in the single-beta CAPM, the two-beta ICAPM, and the three-beta ICAPM. To improve visibility and highlight longer-term movements, the shocks are exponentially smoothed with a decay factor of 0.08 per quarter, corresponding to a half-life of about two years. The top panel of the figure shows the history of the CAPM shock $\widetilde{r}_{m,t+1} = N_{CF,t+1} - N_{DR,t+1}$. This traces out the familiar history of stock market fluctuations, including the very poor returns of the early 1930s and late 1970s, the extended bull market during the 1990s, and the two downturns of the early 2000s and late 2000s. The middle panel shows the history of the two-beta ICAPM shock $\gamma N_{CF,t+1} - N_{DR,t+1}$, with γ estimated at 16.5. The increased weight on cash-flow news highlights bad times throughout the 1930s and good times in the 1950s, and dampens the runup in the 1990s, which is attributed more to a decline in discount rates than to an increase in expected cash flows. The bottom panel shows the history of the three-beta ICAPM shock $\gamma N_{CF,t+1} - N_{DR,t+1} - (\omega/2) N_{V,t+1}$, with γ estimated at 7.2 implying

---

[8]Related to this, in BKSY the equity premium is modeled as proportional to variance, whereas in CGPT this is not imposed, implying that CGPT cannot explain why an investor with constant risk aversion does not time the market in response to changes in the equity premium and market return variance. The hypothesis that the equity premium is proportional to variance was proposed by Merton (1980) and has been rejected empirically by Campbell (1987), Harvey (1989), Ang and Timmermann (2012), and Moreira and Muir (2017) among others.

ω = 24.9. The inclusion of volatility shocks in the model worsens the bad times in the volatile Great Depression, extends the good times in the stable period after World War II, and accentuates the bad news that arrived during the global financial crisis in 2008.

9.4 The Term Structure of Risky Assets

9.4.1 Stylized Facts

The previous section discussed the pricing of cash-flow, discount-rate, and variance betas, and emphasized the empirical finding that growth stocks have high discount-rate betas with correspondingly modest risk premia. One plausible explanation for the high discount-rate betas of growth stocks is that these stocks have growing cash flows, so a high proportion of their value comes from dividends to be paid in the distant future. In the fixed-income language of Chapter 8, growth stocks have a relatively long duration. As discussed in section 8.1.3, duration is the elasticity of market valuation with respect to yield, so the returns of long-duration growth stocks will be particularly sensitive to persistent movements in discount rates unless there is some offsetting pattern in their cash flows.

A recent empirical literature has attempted to measure the term structure of risky prices more directly, by calculating the prices of zero-coupon claims to dividends to be paid at specific dates in the future. Short-term equity assets, for example, are claims to the first few years of equity dividends. Van Binsbergen, Brandt, and Koijen (BBK 2012) show how to impute their prices using S&P 500 index options to create synthetic index futures, then comparing the futures prices (which have no claim to early dividends) to spot index prices (which do). They calculate monthly returns on short-term S&P 500 dividend claims, bought and sold monthly to maintain a dividend maturity between one and two years, over the period 1996–2010. They find that these returns are surprisingly volatile, with a standard deviation about two-thirds greater than the S&P 500 index itself. Short-term dividend claims also have a Sharpe ratio almost twice as high as the index, and therefore expected returns more than three times higher.

The high volatility of short-term dividend claim returns is at first surprising since S&P 500 index dividends are very smooth and predictable, and only adjusted substantially in extreme circumstances such as the global financial crisis of 2008. However, it is important to note that BBK do not calculate a buy-and-hold claim on dividends to be paid within a fixed interval of time but instead calculate a monthly return whose volatility is increased by fluctuations in the short-term claim price itself. To the extent that these fluctuations are mean-reverting, as may be the case in an illiquid market, average monthly returns are biased upward by this effect (Blume and Stambaugh 1983, Boguth et al. 2011). Despite this concern, BBK's results are striking and suggest that short-term claims are exposed to a source of risk with a high price.

Van Binsbergen et al. (2013) and van Binsbergen and Koijen (2015) present comparable results for dividend futures contracts, claims to near-term dividends that have been traded for several global stock indexes since the early 2000s. These contracts also have average returns and Sharpe ratios several times higher than those on the underlying indexes, although there is no consistent pattern of decline in returns or Sharpe ratios as dividend futures maturities vary between one and seven years.

At the long end of the risky term structure, a recent paper by Giglio, Maggiori, and Stroebel (GMS 2015) calculates the value of a claim to extremely distant cash flows. GMS look at residential real estate, an asset class that while not as risky as equities, is risky enough to be typically priced at a rent-price ratio (the analog of a dividend-price ratio) of around 5% (Davis, Lehnert, and Martin 2008). In the UK and Singapore, comparable properties are traded both as freeholds, which convey permanent ownership, and as leaseholds, which convey ownership for very long but finite periods of time that often exceed 100 years. GMS find that in both countries, 100-year leaseholds are discounted by 10–15% relative to freeholds. In a Gordon growth model of the sort considered in Chapter 5, the rent-price ratio on a freehold would be $(r - g)$ and the discount for a T-year leasehold would be $-\exp(-(r - g)\,T)$, where r is the continuously compounded real discount rate and g is the real growth rate of rents. To obtain a 15% discount at $T = 100$ requires $(r - g) = 1.9\%$, but this is inconsistent with the much higher rent-price ratio on freeholds. To match both freehold and leasehold prices then requires a different model in which the term structure of real estate discount rates is not flat, as in the Gordon growth model, but downward sloping.

Putting these results together, several sources of evidence suggest that claims to risky payments in the distant future—such as growth stocks—have relatively low discount rates, while claims to near-term risky payments—such as value stocks—have higher discount rates. In other words, the risky term structure is downward sloping, at least at longer maturities beyond the first few years.

9.4.2 Asset Pricing Theory and the Risky Term Structure

A recent literature has asked how to reconcile a downward-sloping risky term structure with asset pricing theory. The standard power-utility model with iid consumption growth makes trivial predictions regarding the risky term structure. Letting V_{nt} denote the price at time t of a claim to aggregate consumption at time $t + n$ (a consumption strip with maturity n), we can calculate its one-period-ahead return as:

$$\frac{V_{n-1,t+1}}{V_{n,t}} = \frac{\mathrm{E}_{t+1}[M_{t+1,t+n}C_{t+n}]}{\mathrm{E}_t[M_{t,t+n}C_{t+n}]} = \frac{\mathrm{E}_{t+1}\left[(C_{t+n}/C_{t+1})^{1-\gamma}C_{t+1}\right]}{\mathrm{E}_t\left[\beta(C_{t+n}/C_t)^{1-\gamma}C_t\right]}$$
$$= \frac{C_{t+1}/C_t}{\mathrm{E}_t\left[\beta(C_{t+1}/C_t)^{1-\gamma}\right]}, \tag{9.52}$$

where the last equality follows from the fact that one-period-ahead consumption growth is independently distributed over time. Since this expression is independent of n, the standard model predicts a flat term structure for the risk premia $\mathrm{E}_t[R_{n,t+1} - R_{f,t+1}]$ on consumption claims. Intuitively, since equity premia and riskfree rates are constant over time in this model, all price-consumption ratios $V_{n,t}/C_t$ are constant over time. This implies that the prices of all consumption strips move one-for-one with realized consumption, and hence their expected and realized returns are equal. Even in this case the limiting behavior of consumption strip prices has some interesting properties, which are explored in Problem 9.3 following Martin (2012).

It is not easy to obtain a downward-sloping risky term structure as can be seen by considering the leading asset pricing models discussed earlier in this book. The long-run risk model, most obviously, has a downward-sloping term structure for real fixed-income securities but an upward-sloping term structure for risky securities. In that model a shock that decreases expected future consumption growth increases marginal utility, lowers interest rates driving bond prices up, and decreases future dividends driving stock prices down. Similarly, a shock that increases the volatility of consumption growth increases marginal utility, lowers interest rates and increases bond prices through a precautionary savings effect, but lowers the price of risky dividend claims. Hence, in the long-run risk model bonds are intertemporal hedges while stocks are intertemporally risky, and the two asset classes are negatively correlated with each other. Both these effects are more powerful for long-term claims, so the riskless and risky term structures have opposite slopes.

The Campbell-Cochrane model of external habit formation also features an upward-sloping term structure of risky discount rates. The reason is that a negative shock to consumption today increases marginal utility not only today but also in the future by bringing the level of the entire future consumption stream closer to habit, even though consumption growth is iid. This implies that in response to a negative consumption shock the prices of long-maturity dividend strips will fall by more than those of short-maturity strips due to the cumulative effect of the persistent increase in the price of consumption risk. As a result, long-maturity strips are riskier and command a higher risk premium.

The rare disasters model of Gabaix (2012), which fits the behavior of aggregate stock returns by introducing time variation in the probability and magnitude of disasters, does somewhat better under two assumptions: agents have power utility as opposed to Epstein-Zin preferences so that time variation in the probability and magnitude of disasters is not directly priced; and the stochastic processes for the probability and magnitude of future disasters are unaffected by the occurrence of a disaster today. These assumptions ensure that consumption strips of all maturities fall by the same proportional amount during a disaster and thus command identical risk premia ex ante. At the same time, the prices of longer-maturity strips will be more sensitive to the unpriced shocks to the disaster probability and magnitude if these are persistent, so the model is able to produce a downward-sloping term structure for Sharpe ratios. Even in this model, however, the term structure of risk premia is flat rather than declining with maturity.

Lettau and Wachter (LW 2007, 2011) propose and calibrate reduced-form asset pricing models to address this puzzle. These models are essentially affine term structure models of the sort discussed in section 8.3.3, extended to price risky claims as in Brennan, Wang, and Xia (2004). The LW (2007) model has a constant riskfree rate so the riskless term structure is trivially flat, but the risky term structure is downward sloping. The model is driven by two homoskedastic AR(1) processes, one for expected dividend growth and one for the volatility of the stochastic discount factor (equivalently, the price of risk).

Dividend growth is given by

$$\Delta d_{t+1} = z_t + \sigma_d \varepsilon_{d,t+1}, \tag{9.53}$$

where expected dividend growth z_t follows an AR(1) process:

$$z_{t+1} = (1 - \phi_z)\bar{z} + \phi_z z_t + \sigma_z \varepsilon_{z,t+1}. \tag{9.54}$$

A second AR(1) variable x_t controls the volatility of the SDF:

$$x_{t+1} = (1 - \phi_x)\bar{x} + \phi_x x_t + \sigma_x \varepsilon_{x,t+1}. \tag{9.55}$$

$$m_{t+1} = -r_f - \frac{x_t^2}{2} - x_t \varepsilon_{d,t+1}. \tag{9.56}$$

The shocks $\varepsilon_{d,t+1}$, $\varepsilon_{z,t+1}$, and $\varepsilon_{x,t+1}$ are jointly standard normal. The log riskless interest rate is a constant r_f, and the maximum Sharpe ratio in the economy is time-varying and approximately equal to $|x_t|$. Because $\varepsilon_{d,t+1}$ is the only shock that enters equation (9.56), only contemporaneous dividend risk is directly priced. Other shocks can carry risk premia only to the extent that they correlate with shocks to current dividends.

LW (2007) calibrate this model to have persistent shocks to both expected dividend growth and the price of risk ($\phi_z = 0.91$ and $\phi_x = 0.87$ per year). The shocks $\varepsilon_{d,t+1}$ and $\varepsilon_{z,t+1}$ have a strong negative correlation of -0.83, implying a mean-reverting process for dividend growth.[9] However, the shock to the price of risk $\varepsilon_{x,t+1}$ is uncorrelated with the other shocks and hence is itself unpriced. The annualized standard deviations of the shocks are 14.5% for $\varepsilon_{d,t+1}$, 0.32% for $\varepsilon_{z,t+1}$, and 24% for $\varepsilon_{x,t+1}$.

The persistence of dividend growth z_{t+1} implies that the prices of long-term claims to distant future dividends are more sensitive to dividend growth shocks $\varepsilon_{z,t+1}$ than are the prices of short-term dividend claims. Since dividend growth shocks are negatively correlated with current dividend shocks $\varepsilon_{d,t+1}$, long-term dividend claims are relatively safer than short-term claims. In addition, shocks to the price of risk $\varepsilon_{x,t+1}$ have a greater impact on longer-term and particularly on intermediate-term dividend claims than on near-term claims.[10] Since these shocks are unpriced, they contribute to volatility but not to risk premia, lowering the Sharpe ratios on intermediate-term and longer-term dividend claims. This contrasts with the habit models of Campbell and Cochrane (1999) and Menzly, Santos, and Veronesi (2004) and with long-run risk models, where shocks to the price of risk are themselves priced and increase the risk premia on longer-term risky claims. Problem 9.4 asks you to analyze the LW (2007) model in greater detail.

Integrated Pricing of Bonds and Stocks
LW (2011) enrich this framework to price real and nominal bonds. They retain equations (9.53)–(9.55) but alter equation (9.56) to have a time-varying riskless real interest rate that also follows a homoskedastic AR(1) process:

$$m_{t+1} = -r_{f,t+1} - \frac{x_t^2}{2} - x_t \varepsilon_{d,t+1}, \tag{9.57}$$

$$r_{f,t+1} = (1 - \phi_r)\overline{r}_f + \phi_r r_{f,t} + \sigma_r \varepsilon_{r,t+1}. \tag{9.58}$$

In addition, to price nominal bonds LW (2011) assume that expected inflation is driven by a fourth AR(1) process:

$$\pi_{t+1} = q_t + \sigma_\pi \varepsilon_{\pi,t+1}, \tag{9.59}$$

$$q_{t+1} = (1 - \phi_q)\overline{q} + \phi_q q_t + \sigma_q \varepsilon_{q,t+1}, \tag{9.60}$$

where π_{t+1} is realized inflation and q_t is expected inflation.

---

[9]Belo, Collin-Dufresne, and Goldstein (2015) argue that this pattern can be generated by corporate financial policies that maintain a stationary leverage ratio given an underlying process for unlevered corporate cash flows.

[10]The response to $\varepsilon_{x,t+1}$ is nonmotonic because, although longer-term claims have higher duration and thus higher sensitivity to persistent discount-rate shocks, they also have lower cash-flow risk than shorter-term claims. As maturity increases in the risky term structure, the duration effect initially dominates but is eventually more than offset by the cash-flow risk effect.

The calibration for this model makes the shocks $\varepsilon_{\pi,t+1}$ and $\varepsilon_{q,t+1}$ perfectly correlated, reducing the dimensionality of the model and implying that realized inflation is an ARMA(1,1) process. In addition, the three new shocks in this model, $\varepsilon_{r,t+1}$, $\varepsilon_{\pi,t+1}$, and $\varepsilon_{q,t+1}$, all have a correlation of –0.3 with the dividend shock $\varepsilon_{d,t+1}$ whose risk is priced. This implies that both real interest rates and realized and expected inflation tend to rise in bad times when negative dividend shocks occur. This drives up real and nominal interest rates in bad times, making bonds risky and creating upward-sloping term structures of real and nominal interest rates.

The variable price of risk in this model implies that scaled prices predict excess returns, both for stocks and for real and nominal bonds. The model approximately captures several of the predictability patterns discussed in earlier chapters, including the ability of the log dividend-price ratio to predict excess stock returns and the ability of the yield spread and the Cochrane-Piazzesi factor to predict excess bond returns. At the same time, it retains the ability to fit the return patterns on value and growth stocks, interpreted as short-duration and long-duration dividend claims.

Despite these successes, the Lettau-Wachter framework has some weaknesses. Theoretically, it uses a reduced-form representation of the SDF, and it is not clear what structural model of the economy is consistent with this reduced form. The unpriced variation in the price of risk is particularly hard to derive from underlying preferences and technology, although a low price for discount-rate shocks is consistent with the logic of the intertemporal CAPM as discussed in the previous section.

The Time-Varying Correlation Between Bond and Stock Returns
Empirically, the LW (2011) model implies a strong positive correlation of 0.83 between the returns on stocks and nominal bonds whereas the average correlation in monthly data from 1952 to 2004 is only 0.15. In fact, the conditional correlation between stock and nominal bond returns in US historical data is time-varying, as emphasized by Campbell, Sunderam, and Viceira (CSV 2017) and illustrated in Figure 9.3. The figure

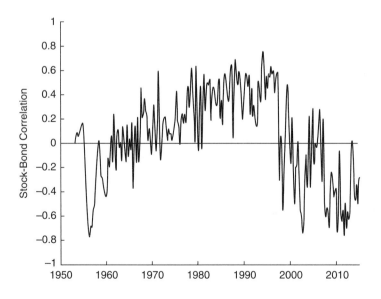

Figure 9.3.   *Historical Correlation of US Stocks and Bonds*

plots the correlation between stocks and nominal bonds estimated from daily data within each quarter, a series that contains short-run noise but also moves systematically at lower frequencies. The correlation was modestly positive in the 1960s and 1970s, strongly positive in the 1980s and early 1990s, and has been negative since the year 2000, implying that Treasury bonds hedge stock market risk in modern conditions. Campbell, Shiller, and Viceira (2009) report a similar negative covariance between stocks and US inflation-indexed bonds (TIPS) in the period since TIPS were first issued in 1997.

CSV estimate a term structure model with an additional state variable that captures the bond-stock covariance and can switch sign. Their model has a constant volatility of the SDF but stochastic volatility of nominal and real bond returns and a time-varying covariance of nominal and real bond returns with the SDF, both driven by a single state variable. CSV find that this model of time-varying bond risk implies a bond risk premium that was unusually high in the early 1980s, when bonds moved strongly with stocks, and negative in the 21st century, when bonds move opposite stocks. However, their model does not have a time-varying price of risk and does not capture many of the other asset pricing phenomena modeled by LW (2011). This is an active area, with recent contributions by Adrian, Crump, and Moench (2015) and Koijen, Lustig, and Van Niewerburgh (2017), but the literature has not yet reached consensus even on a reduced-form model with an exogenous SDF, still less a structural model that derives the SDF from economic fundamentals.

9.5 Learning

The models described so far assume that investors know the parameters of the process driving asset returns, even though economists observing the markets may have to estimate them. If this is not the case, investors must learn about asset returns, and this can lead to a new set of intertemporal effects. The basic intuition is that if an investor is learning about the mean of an asset return from realized returns on the asset, then the conditional expected return will update positively whenever the realized return is high. This tends to make long-run returns riskier than short-run returns and generates a negative intertemporal hedging demand for risky assets by conservative long-term investors. Similarly, if an investor is learning about the mean of consumption growth from realized consumption growth, consumption growth will be positively correlated with revisions in expected future consumption growth, as in a long-run risk model, even if true consumption growth is iid over time.

The simplest framework in which these effects can be understood has an iid normal process generating a random variable y_{t+1}:

$$y_{t+1} = \mu + \sigma \varepsilon_{t+1}, \tag{9.61}$$

where $\varepsilon_{t+1} \sim N(0, 1)$. We assume that an investor knows the standard deviation σ but does not know the mean μ. The investor starts with a prior distribution for μ that is normal with mean μ_0 and variance $A_0 \sigma^2$,

$$p_0(\mu) = N(\mu_0, A_0 \sigma^2), \tag{9.62}$$

and updates this prior using Bayes' Law after observing realizations of y. The resulting posterior distribution can be written as

$$p_t(\mu) = p(\mu \mid y_1, \dots, y_t) = N(\mu_t, A_t \sigma^2). \tag{9.63}$$

Because the investor does not know the true mean μ, the investor does not perceive the true process for y_{t+1} given in equation (9.61) but instead perceives y_{t+1} as following

$$y_{t+1} = \mu_t + \sigma \sqrt{1 + A_t} \tilde{\varepsilon}_{t+1}, \tag{9.64}$$

where the perceived shock $\tilde{\varepsilon}_{t+1}$ is distributed standard normal conditional on the investor's information.

When there are two normally distributed signals for an unobservable variable x (or a prior distribution for x and a signal for x), the posterior distribution for x given by Bayes' Law takes a particularly tractable form. Letting $s_1 = x + u_1$ and $s_2 = x + u_2$ denote the two signals, where $u_1 \sim N(0, \tau_1^{-1})$ and $u_2 \sim N(0, \tau_2^{-1})$ and u_1 and u_2 are independently distributed, the posterior distribution for x is normal with mean and variance

$$E[x|s_1, s_2] = \frac{\tau_1 s_1 + \tau_2 s_2}{\tau_1 + \tau_2} \tag{9.65}$$

and

$$\mathrm{Var}(x|s_1, s_2) = (\tau_1 + \tau_2)^{-1}, \tag{9.66}$$

respectively. Here the notation τ_i is used to denote the reciprocal of the conditional variance of s_i, also known as the precision of s_i.

As an informal exercise, you are asked to explain how the Bayesian updating formula for two normally distributed independent signals, equation (9.65), relates to the formula for the global minimum-variance portfolio with two uncorrelated risky assets, equation (2.35) in Chapter 2. The answer to this is given at the end of the chapter.

In our model, each observation y_{t+1} is a new signal for μ, with precision $1/\sigma^2$, which is combined with the previous period's conditional mean μ_t, with precision $1/(A_t \sigma^2)$. Using formulas (9.65) and (9.66), the mean and variance of the posterior conditional distribution $p_{t+1}(\mu)$ are

$$\mu_{t+1} = \frac{\frac{\mu_t}{A_t \sigma^2} + \frac{y_{t+1}}{\sigma^2}}{\frac{1}{A_t \sigma^2} + \frac{1}{\sigma^2}} = \frac{\mu_t + A_t y_{t+1}}{1 + A_t} = \mu_t + \frac{\sigma A_t}{\sqrt{1 + A_t}} \tilde{\varepsilon}_{t+1} \tag{9.67}$$

and

$$A_{t+1} = \left(\frac{1}{A_t} + 1 \right)^{-1}. \tag{9.68}$$

The updating rule for the conditional variance is linear in precision. If the initial prior is very diffuse (A_0 is very large), then $1/A_0$ is very close to zero and we have $1/A_t \approx t$ or equivalently $A_t \approx 1/t$.[11] Thus, the variance of the investor's posterior distribution for the parameter μ declines hyperbolically over time, decreasing rapidly at first and then much more slowly.

In the updating rule for the posterior mean, realizations of y_{t+1} that are surprises to the investor, $\tilde{\varepsilon}_{t+1}$, have an effect on the posterior mean that eventually declines in proportion to A_t, that is, hyperbolically over time.

---

[11]This result also allows us to interpret $1/A_0$ as the number of observations that would be needed to generate the same precision from data as the investor has in his prior.

Learning about Portfolio Returns

What are the implications of this framework for long-term investors? First interpret y_{t+1} as a log asset return, and consider a K-period log return $y_{t,t+K} = y_{t+1} + \cdots + y_{t+K}$. Write the conditional variance of this return, conditional on the investor's information set, as $\text{Var}_t^*(y_{t,t+K})$. Then we have

$$\text{Var}_t^*(y_{t,t+K}) = \text{E}_t^*\text{Var}(y_{t,t+K} \mid \mu) + \text{Var}_t^*(\text{E}(y_{t,t+K} \mid \mu))$$

$$= K\sigma^2 + K^2\text{Var}_t^*(\mu)$$

$$= K\sigma^2(1 + KA_t), \tag{9.69}$$

where E_t^* denotes a mean conditional on the investor's information set.

The first equality in (9.69) is the usual statement that variance conditional on less information (in this case the history of the process until time t) equals the mean of variance conditional on more information (in this case the true parameter μ) plus the variance of the mean conditional on more information. The first term in the second equality uses the fact that given knowledge of μ, the variance of the K-period return grows linearly with K, while the second term expresses the variance of the conditional mean of the K-period return as K^2 times the variance of the conditional mean of the single-period return. The scale factor in the second term is K^2 rather than K because the conditional mean affects each term in the sum of single-period returns in the same way. The third equality in (9.69) uses the fact that the variance of the conditional mean of the single-period return is $A_t\sigma^2$ from equation (9.63).

The annualized conditional variance of the K-period return is $\text{Var}_t^*(y_{t,t+K})/K$. In a model with iid returns and no parameter uncertainty, this is independent of K as we discussed in section 5.1.1, but equation (9.69) shows that uncertainty about the mean return causes the annualized conditional variance to increase with K. In other words, risk is increasing in the investment horizon rather than invariant to the investment horizon as would normally be the case in an iid model. While this effect diminishes as learning proceeds, it diminishes only slowly because of the hyperbolic decline in A_t.

More importantly for long-run portfolio choice, the conditional covariance between a surprise return today and revisions in expected future returns is positive in this model. Equations (9.64) and (9.67) imply that

$$\text{Cov}_t^*\left(y_{t+1}, \left(\text{E}_{t+1}^* - \text{E}_t^*\right)\sum_{j=1}^{\infty}\rho^j y_{t+1+j}\right) = \text{Cov}_t^*\left(\sigma\sqrt{1 + A_t}\widetilde{\varepsilon}_{t+1}, \left(\frac{\rho}{1-\rho}\right)\frac{\sigma A_t}{\sqrt{1 + A_t}}\widetilde{\varepsilon}_{t+1}\right)$$

$$= \left(\frac{\rho}{1-\rho}\right)\sigma^2 A_t > 0. \tag{9.70}$$

If y_{t+1} is the log return on the investor's portfolio, the covariance in (9.70) determines the intertemporal component of the risk premium that the investor requires on the portfolio, as in equation (9.12). When the covariance is positive and the investor has risk aversion greater than one, the required risk premium is greater—so this type of learning makes it easier to explain the equity premium puzzle. Equivalently, learning about the mean return on a risky asset generates negative intertemporal hedging demand for the asset.

The simple analytical model presented here has no time-variation in investment opportunities other than those arising from learning. In richer dynamic models of asset returns, it is an empirical question how important learning is relative to the mean-reversion that was emphasized earlier in this chapter. Papers by Stambaugh (1999) and Barberis (2000) analyze this question. Using models in which observed predictor variables perfectly capture the variation in expected return, they find relatively modest effects of parameter uncertainty on the relative magnitudes of perceived short-run and long-run variance. Pástor and Stambaugh (2009, 2012), however, use a "predictive system," in which the expected return is persistent and time-varying but not perfectly captured by observed variables. This system allows a greater role for learning, and Pástor and Stambaugh (2012) argue that the investor's perceived variance increases with the investment horizon. Their model also displays nonmonotonic behavior of the multiperiod risk ratio, discussed in section 9.2.3, which is not related to learning.

All these models of rational learning have the property that learning about fixed model parameters diminishes in importance over time as the precision of the investor's posterior distribution increases. In models where persistent unobserved state variables drive returns, learning about these state variables can remain important indefinitely; but the persistence of state variables creates positive return autocorrelations conditional on knowing the underlying parameters of the model, which makes it harder for such models to match the mean reversion observed in historical US data and discussed in Chapter 5. Investors might also form their beliefs about future asset returns drawing on information other than the history of returns—for example, the Gordon growth model combined with information on the growth rate of dividends, as in section 5.5.2—and this would weaken the learning effect of returns on expected future returns.

Learning about Consumption Growth
Collin-Dufresne, Johannes, and Lochstoer (CJL 2016) use the same learning model but apply it to consumption growth. Reinterpreting the process y_{t+1} as consumption growth rather than an asset return, the positive covariance between consumption surprises today and revisions in expected future consumption growth given in equation (9.70) implies that an investor who is uncertain about mean consumption growth perceives consumption growth as persistent, even if true consumption growth is iid.

Recall from equation (6.49) in Chapter 6 that the log SDF under Epstein-Zin preferences can be written as $\widetilde{m}_{t+1} = -\gamma \, \widetilde{c}_{t+1} - (\gamma - 1/\psi)\widetilde{g}_{t+1}$, where $\widetilde{c}_{t+1}$ is the innovation in consumption growth today, and $\widetilde{g}_{t+1}$ is the revision in the present discounted value of expected future consumption growth. In the model with learning, these innovations are perfectly correlated so we have

$$\widetilde{m}_{t+1} = \left(-\gamma \, \sigma \sqrt{1 + A_t} - \left(\gamma - \frac{1}{\psi}\right)\left(\frac{\rho}{1-\rho}\right)\frac{\sigma A_t}{\sqrt{1 + A_t}}\right)\widetilde{\varepsilon}_{t+1}. \qquad (9.71)$$

This log SDF is more volatile than the log SDF with known mean consumption growth ($A_t = 0$) for two reasons. First, the investor perceives single-period consumption growth as riskier than he would if the mean were known. Second, the investor increases expected future consumption growth in response to positive consumption surprises today, and this amplifies the response of the log SDF whenever risk aversion γ exceeds the reciprocal of the EIS $1/\psi$. The latter effect is very powerful because the revisions in expected future consumption growth are permanent, so their discounted sum is $\rho/(1-\rho)$ times the single-period effect. CJL show that this effect can be quantitatively very important in models with realistic parameter uncertainty.

The CJL model is related to the long-run risk model of Bansal and Yaron (2004) discussed in section 6.5.3, but it differs in several important respects. First, shocks to long-run expected consumption growth are driven by learning, so they diminish over time as in all models of rational learning. Second, these shocks are perfectly correlated with current consumption growth; there are no independent shocks to the expected growth rate of the sort assumed in the long-run risk literature. Third, the equilibrium real interest rate varies with expected consumption growth and subjective consumption volatility in the CJL model, but this variation diminishes over time as learning proceeds, and the real interest rate also drifts upward because learning decreases precautionary saving. Fourth, because true consumption growth is iid in the CJL model, an ex post econometric analysis will find that risky asset prices do not predict consumption growth, and the real interest rate varies despite unpredictable consumption growth, thus resolving two empirical criticisms of the long-run risk model.

9.6 Solutions and Further Problems

As an exercise, you were asked to state why the quadratic form of the value function makes sense given the linear form for the portfolio rule. The answer is that an increase in the equity premium has two effects. First, it increases the expected portfolio return for any given investment in the risky asset. Second, it increases the optimal portfolio weight on the risky asset. The interaction of these two effects is quadratic.

You were also asked to comment on Jeremy Siegel's portfolio advice to buy and hold stocks for the long run, given his view that stocks are relatively safer in the long run. This advice is internally inconsistent, because stocks can only be safer in the long run if there is mean reversion in stock returns, which implies a time-varying expected stock return that should induce changes over time in the allocation to stocks. In fact, the optimal long-term portfolio rule responds more aggressively than a short-term portfolio rule to changes in the equity premium. However, Siegel's rule might be justified if the long-run investor has relatively low risk aversion and faces binding leverage constraints, in which case the constrained solution may be 100% equity investment all (or at least most) of the time.

Finally, you were asked to explain the relation between the Bayesian updating formula for two normally distributed independent signals, equation (9.65), and the formula for the global minimum-variance portfolio with two uncorrelated risky assets, equation (2.35) in Chapter 2. These formulas are equivalent, as can be seen by rewriting (9.65) in terms of variances using the fact that precision is the reciprocal of variance. The equivalence results from the fact that with normally distributed signals, the Bayesian formula chooses an average of uncorrelated signals to minimize the error variance, and this is the same problem that is solved by equation (2.35).

Problem 9.1 The Payoff Approach to Intertemporal Portfolio Choice

In Problem 4.1 we showed that the martingale method for portfolio choice can be applied to static incomplete market settings under the special assumption of quadratic utility. Cochrane (2014) extends this method to study intertemporal portfolio choice under incomplete markets by treating dates and states of nature symmetrically. This approach

contrasts with the standard approach to intertemporal portfolio choice because it characterizes the investor's optimal stream of final payoffs, that is, the ultimate dividend stream
that the investor receives from financial markets, without specifying the dynamic portfolio
strategy that supports these payoffs in a given market structure.

Consider the following generalization of the setting of Problem 4.1. A payoff $X = \{X_t\}_{t=1}^{\infty} \in \Xi$ now denotes the stream of dividends purchased at price $P(X) = P(\{X_t\})$ at
time 0. The intertemporal analog of payoff returns is the payoff yield, $Y = X/P(X)$, the
stream of dividend yields or coupon rates that correspond to payoff X.

Following Hansen (1987), define a generalized "long-run expectation" operator $\tilde{E}[\cdot]$
that sums over time, weighted by a number $\beta < 1$, as well as over states of nature, weighted
by probabilities,[12]

$$\tilde{E}[X] \equiv \frac{1-\beta}{\beta} E\left[\sum_{t=1}^{\infty} \beta^t X_t\right]. \tag{9.72}$$

Then, the intertemporal analog of the pricing equation $P_t = E[M_{t+1} X_{t+1}]$ is

$$P(X) = E\left[\sum_{t=1}^{\infty} \beta^t M_t X_t\right] = k\tilde{E}[MX], \tag{9.73}$$

where $k \equiv \beta/(1-\beta)$. Under this generalized notion of the expectation operator all
results derived for the static framework of Problem 4.1 directly carry over to the corresponding infinite-horizon framework and, once again, do not hinge on a particular payoff
distribution.

(a) Define the riskfree yield as $Y_f = 1/P(1)$. What is the riskfree asset corresponding to
this definition?

(b) Reinterpret the results from Problem 4.1 to conclude that the yield to the optimal
payoff of an infinite-horizon quadratic-utility investor with only financial wealth is
a linear and time-invariant combination of two yields: the riskfree yield and a long-
run mean-variance efficient yield. Moreover, these two yields are the same regardless
of the agent's risk aversion. Why do hedging demands and state variables affecting
investment opportunities not appear in this characterization?

(c) Cochrane (2014) argues that a focus on final payoffs in asset management can be
welfare improving, as it helps separate the investor's risk and return decisions from
the financial engineering of how to achieve optimal portfolios in a given market
structure. Individual investors will be better served if they focus on specifying the
payout streams that are optimal for them and leave the dynamic portfolio implementation of these payoffs to the professional asset management industry. Evaluate
this claim.

[12]Other "long-run" moments are defined in the same manner. For example, the long-run variance of X,

$$\tilde{\sigma}^2(X) \equiv \tilde{E}[X^2] - (\tilde{E}[X])^2$$

captures stability over time as well as across states of nature.

Problem 9.2 GMM Analysis of the Two-Beta ICAPM

This problem asks you to use the GMM framework, presented in section 4.4, to analyze the two-beta asset pricing model of Campbell and Vuolteenaho (CV 2004). The data for this question can be found in an Excel spreadsheet on the textbook website, together with an accompanying explanatory document.[13] The data include the excess return on the market together with the expected excess return and two components of the unexpected excess return, the news about cash flows $N_{CF,t}$ and the news about discount rates $-N_{DR,t}$. The news terms were estimated from a VAR as in CV. The data also include the riskless interest rate R_{ft} and the returns R_{it} on a set of test assets, 9 of the 25 Fama-French portfolios sorted by size and book-to-market ratios.

We suggest using MATLAB or similar software that allows you to write flexible code. For all parts, document in detail the results and formulas from section 4.4 that you use in each step.

(a) Estimate the parameters of the linear stochastic discount factor model

$$M_t = a + b(-N_{DR,t}) + cN_{CF,t}. \qquad (9.74)$$

Use 10 moment conditions (one for the risk-free asset and nine for the stock portfolios) of the form $0 = E[M_t(1 + R_{it}) - 1]$ and the identity weighting matrix $W_T = I_{10}$.

(b) Estimate the long-run covariance matrix of the moments both under the null of the model that pricing errors are serially uncorrelated and by using the Newey-West HAC covariance matrix estimator. Estimate the covariance matrix of the parameter estimates under both estimates of the long-run covariance matrix. Do your results suggest pricing errors are serially correlated?

For the remaining parts, use the Newey-West estimator.

(c) For each parameter, report the t-statistic and p-value for the hypothesis that the parameter is zero.

(d) Assume the following approximate and unconditional version of the first-order condition (9.40):

$$E[R_{it} - R_{ft}] = \gamma \, \text{Cov}((R_{it} - R_{ft}), N_{CF,t}) + \text{Cov}((R_{it} - R_{ft}), -N_{DR,t}). \qquad (9.75)$$

(i) What restriction does this condition impose on the parameters of SDF specification (9.74)?

(ii) Test this restriction using a Wald test. Is it rejected?

(iii) Provide an estimate of γ and the standard error of this estimate. Hint: Use the delta method.

(e) Return to the general model and compute the second-stage estimates of the parameters in (9.74). Repeat parts (c), (d)(ii), and (d)(iii) for the second-stage estimates. How do your answers differ?

---

[13]http://press.princeton.edu/titles/11177.html.

(f) Finally, perform a χ^2-test of overidentifying restrictions using the second-stage estimates. What is the p-value of the test? Comment on the empirical success of the model.

Problem 9.3 The Valuation of Long-Term Risky Assets

Let $Y_1, Y_2, \ldots$ be independent and identically distributed (iid) non-negative random variables with mean one. For t greater than or equal to one, define $X_t = Y_1 Y_2 \cdots Y_t$.

(a) Show that $EX_t = 1$ for all t.

(b) Let $a = E\sqrt{Y_t}$. Show that $0 < a \leq 1$. Under what conditions does $a = 1$?

(c) X_t is a non-negative martingale, so its limit as t increases exists and is finite almost surely. Call this limit X_∞. A result of Kakutani, applied to finance by Martin (2012), can be stated as follows in this example. If $a = 1$, $X_\infty = 1$. Otherwise, $X_\infty = 0$. Explain intuitively how it is possible to have both $EX_t = 1$ for all t and $X_\infty = 0$.

(d) Consider an asset with iid gross returns $(1 + R_1), (1 + R_2), \ldots$ and an iid stochastic discount factor $M_1, M_2, \ldots$ Define the risk-adjusted value of the asset at time t as $V_t = M_1 M_2 \ldots M_t (1 + R_1)(1 + R_2) \ldots (1 + R_t)$. Define the limiting risk-adjusted value in the infinite future as V_∞. Show that there is a unique asset and SDF for which $V_\infty = 1$. Otherwise, $V_\infty = 0$. For what asset and SDF do we have $V_\infty = 1$?

(e) For any other asset, explain intuitively how it is possible to have $EV_t = 1$ for all t despite the fact that $V_\infty = 0$. Illustrate your mechanism by reference to the properties of the gross return series, and then by reference to the properties of the SDF series. Discuss the economic difference between these two cases.

Note: This problem is based on Martin (2012).

Problem 9.4 The Risky Term Structure

Consider the risky term structure model of Lettau and Wachter (LW 2007), given by equations (9.53)–(9.56). The model is closely related to the class of essentially affine term structure models with homoskedastic bond yields studied in section 8.3.3. Let $\sigma_{dz} \equiv \mathrm{Cov}_t(d_{t+1}, z_{t+1})$ and denote other covariances similarly.

(a) The prices of dividend strips (zero-coupon equity) V_{nt} follow the same recursion as bond prices P_{nt}, (8.29) but subject to a different terminal condition, $V_{0t} = D_t$ instead of $P_{0t} = 1$. Conjecture that the log price-to-current-dividend ratio of dividend strips is affine in the state variables:

$$v_{nt} - d_t = A_n + B_{x,n} x_t + B_{z,n} z_t, \tag{9.76}$$

the analogue of (8.58). Derive the recursive equations defining the price coefficients A_n, $B_{x,n}$, and $B_{z,n}$.

(b) Solve for the risk premium, $E_t[r_{n,t+1}] - r_f + \sigma_n^2/2$, and volatility of log returns, σ_n^2, on zero-coupon equity as a function of the price coefficients.

(c) Suppose that the price of risk and expected dividend growth have zero contemporaneous covariance with one-period-ahead dividend growth, $\sigma_{dx} = \sigma_{dz} = 0$. Are the term structures of risk premia and Sharpe ratios for zero-coupon equity upward sloping, flat, or downward sloping? Explain.

(d) LW obtain lower risk premia for long-horizon equity than short-horizon equity by assuming that the price of risk is contemporaneously uncorrelated with one-period-ahead dividend growth and that dividend growth follows a mean-reverting process, $\sigma_{dz} < 0$. If we instead assume $\sigma_{dz} = 0$, how can we obtain a downward-sloping term structure of risk premia for zero-coupon equity in the LW model? Explain.

Part III

Heterogeneous Investors

10

Household Finance

THE ASSET PRICING models presented in earlier parts of this book abstract from differences across financial market participants in objectives, resources, constraints, and beliefs. In this last part of the book, we focus on such differences and begin in this chapter by studying the financial decisions of households.

Recent years have seen an explosion of research in this field of household finance. The growth of the field is driven by several factors, among them an increased appreciation for the importance of labor income in determining optimal investment strategies, the maturing of behavioral finance with its emphasis on measuring and modeling individuals' decisions, and the availability of large administrative datasets on household assets and liabilities.

We begin in section 10.1 by discussing the effect of labor income on optimal portfolio choice. We present stylized models that can be solved analytically and discuss the standard features of a life-cycle model that is solved numerically. This section also describes empirical evidence on household investment behavior in relation to income and discusses asset pricing models that incorporate income risk. Although we focus on labor income in line with the focus of this chapter on households, the theoretical insights can be applied to other forms of nonfinancial income and the policies of other actors such as firms and financial intermediaries.

Many households make financial decisions that are hard to rationalize on the basis of rational optimizing models of the sort presented earlier in this book. The remainder of the chapter discusses some of these important behaviors and their potential effects on asset pricing. In section 10.2 we consider nonparticipation (the avoidance of all risky financial assets); in section 10.3 underdiversification (the holding of concentrated portfolios that are exposed to idiosyncratic risk); and in section 10.4 responses to changing market conditions including portfolio inertia, extrapolation of personal experience, mortgage refinancing inertia, and the disposition effect (the tendency for investors to realize gains rather than losses). This part of the chapter can be read as an abbreviated introduction to the behavioral finance literature, although it cannot do justice to that important field. An important theme in behavioral finance is that agents may have heterogeneous beliefs and speculate against one another: we take up this topic in Chapter 11. As in the earlier part of the chapter, some of the ideas presented here—for example, the implications of market segmentation—are important in other areas of finance and not only for households.

10.1 Labor Income and Portfolio Choice

Chapter 9 considered the implications of time-varying investment opportunities for the optimal portfolio choice of long-term investors. Another, entirely separate source of horizon effects has to do with labor income. Long-term investors often have claims to a stream of income, and this should alter their portfolio decisions. In this section we explore such effects. While this analysis could be done in a model with a representative agent who receives aggregate labor income (Campbell 1996, Lustig, Van Nieuwerburgh, and Verdelhan 2013), the most interesting issues concerning labor income arise when we allow for heterogeneous agents; for this reason, we have deferred discussion of labor income until this chapter.

10.1.1 Static Portfolio Choice Models

We develop intuition by considering a sequence of stylized static models where an investor receives random future income and allocates wealth between a riskless asset and a risky asset. These models allow us to understand the separate portfolio choice effects of mean labor income, the risk in labor income that is unhedgeable because it is uncorrelated with asset returns, and the risk in labor income that is hedgeable because it is correlated with asset returns.

Constant Absolute Risk Aversion

Models of portfolio choice with labor income sometimes assume constant absolute risk aversion (CARA) for convenience. However, this assumption eliminates any effect of mean labor income and of unhedgeable income risk on risky asset holdings. The reason is the usual one that wealth and uncorrelated additive background risk only affect riskless asset holdings, not risky asset holdings, in a CARA model as we now show formally.

A minor modification of the portfolio analysis in section 2.1.3 states the portfolio choice problem for a CARA investor as

$$\max - \log \mathrm{E}\left[\exp(-A(W(1+R_f) + \widetilde{Y} + \theta(\widetilde{R}-R_f)))\right]$$

$$= AW(1+R_f+\overline{Y}+\theta(\overline{R}-R_f) - \frac{1}{2}A^2\sigma_Y^2 - \frac{1}{2}A^2\theta^2\sigma_R^2 - A\theta\sigma_{YR}, \qquad (10.1)$$

where A is the coefficient of absolute risk aversion, W is initial financial wealth, R_f is the riskless interest rate, $\widetilde{Y}$ is risky labor income with mean $\overline{Y}$ and variance σ_Y^2, θ is the dollar investment in a risky asset, $\widetilde{R}$ is the risky asset return with mean $\overline{R}$ and variance σ_R^2, and σ_{YR} is the covariance between labor income and the excess risky return.

The solution to this problem is

$$\theta^* = \frac{(\overline{R}-R_f)-\sigma_{YR}}{A\sigma_R^2} = \left(\frac{1}{A}\right)\left(\frac{(\overline{R}-R_f)}{\sigma_R^2} - \beta_{YR}\right). \qquad (10.2)$$

Neither the mean of labor income $\overline{Y}$ nor the variance σ_Y^2 appear in this formula, which is influenced only by the covariance σ_{YR} or equivalently the regression coefficient of labor income on the excess risky asset return $\beta_{YR} = \sigma_{YR}/\sigma_R^2$. A CARA investor alters risky asset holdings to hedge labor income risk but not for any other reason.

Constant Relative Risk Aversion and Riskless Labor Income
Things are more complicated in the empirically more relevant case where an investor
has constant relative risk aversion. In this case, even riskless labor income alters portfolio
choice. To see this, write the discounted value of riskless labor income as H and call this
human wealth. A holding of human wealth is an implicit holding of safe assets. Financial
wealth consists of safe bonds B and risky stocks S. Bonds deliver a riskless return R_f, while
stocks deliver a risky return $\widetilde{R}$. The risky share in total wealth, including both financial
and human wealth, is

$$\alpha^* = \frac{S}{S + B + H}. \tag{10.3}$$

If financial returns are lognormally and independently distributed over time, then as
discussed in section 9.1 the usual static portfolio solution applies:

$$\alpha^* = \frac{\overline{R} - R_f}{\gamma \, \sigma_R^2} \tag{10.4}$$

Although this formula is standard, the implication for the share of stocks in financial
wealth is not. Equations (10.3) and (10.4) imply that the share of risky assets in financial
wealth is given by

$$\alpha = \frac{S}{S + B} = (1 + h)\alpha^* = (1 + h)\left(\frac{\overline{R} - R_f}{\gamma \, \sigma_R^2}\right), \tag{10.5}$$

where h is the ratio of human to financial wealth,

$$h = \frac{H}{S + B}. \tag{10.6}$$

An investor with high human wealth relative to financial wealth should invest a greater
share of financial wealth in stocks, because human wealth is implicitly invested in the
riskless asset. This can explain the standard rule of thumb in financial planning that
young investors can afford to take greater financial risk than older investors, especially
those who are already retired and therefore have no remaining human wealth.[1]

Although equation (10.5) is a very simple modification of the standard portfolio
choice rule, it has some striking implications. First, the investor should reduce the risky
portfolio share in response to positive stock returns that lower the ratio h. That is, realized returns now affect portfolio choice going forward despite the fact that the investor
has scale-independent preferences. Second, because the ratio h can be large for young
investors, the portfolio solution (10.5) can easily imply a risky portfolio share greater than
one, which requires the use of leverage to implement. If borrowing to finance risky investment is ruled out, investors with high labor income should invest all their financial wealth
in the risky asset but cannot take as much risk as the unconstrained solution would imply.

---

[1] The rule of thumb is particularly applicable to older investors who have defined-contribution pensions.
A retired investor with a defined-benefit pension has a safe income stream that should be thought of as an
alternative form of human capital.

Constant Relative Risk Aversion and Risky Labor Income
The analysis of risky labor income is more difficult under constant relative risk aversion, because income risk is additive but CRRA utility functions are tractable for multiplicative risks. One way to handle this is to use a loglinear approximation of the sort discussed earlier in this book. Following Viceira (1998) and Campbell and Viceira (2002), consider an investor who chooses a portfolio to solve the following problem at time t:

$$\max \mathrm{E}_t \left[\delta \frac{C_{t+1}^{1-\gamma}}{1-\gamma} \right] \tag{10.7}$$

subject to

$$C_{t+1} = W_t(1 + R_{p,t+1}) + Y_{t+1}. \tag{10.8}$$

For simplicity, the investor consumes nothing at time t but merely decides the composition of the portfolio that will, along with income, determine consumption at time $t+1$.

We divide by future income to rewrite the budget constraint as

$$\frac{C_{t+1}}{Y_{t+1}} = \frac{W_t}{Y_{t+1}}(1 + R_{p,t+1}) + 1 \tag{10.9}$$

and assume that $(1 + R_{p,t+1})$ and Y_{t+1} are lognormally distributed.

Next we loglinearize (10.9) to get

$$c_{t+1} - y_{t+1} \approx k + \rho \left[w_t + r_{p,t+1} - y_{t+1} \right], \tag{10.10}$$

where

$$\rho \equiv \frac{\exp\{\overline{r}_p + w_t - \overline{y}\}}{1 + \exp\{\overline{r}_p + w_t - \overline{y}\}} < 1. \tag{10.11}$$

This can be rewritten as

$$c_{t+1} \approx k + \rho(w_t + r_{p,t+1}) + (1 - \rho)y_{t+1}. \tag{10.12}$$

Log consumption is approximately linear in log wealth and log income, and the loglinearization parameter ρ is the elasticity of consumption with respect to financial wealth. The parameter ρ increases toward its upper bound of one as financial wealth increases relative to labor income.

Now consider the investor's portfolio choice problem between a safe asset and a single risky asset. If α_t is the share in the risky asset, the usual portfolio return approximation implies

$$r_{p,t+1} - \mathrm{E}_t r_{p,t+1} \approx \alpha_t(r_{t+1} - \mathrm{E}_t r_{t+1}). \tag{10.13}$$

The cross-sectional Euler equation for power utility is

$$\mathrm{E}_t[r_{t+1} - r_f] + \frac{1}{2}\sigma_r^2 = \gamma \, \mathrm{Cov}_t(c_{t+1}, r_{t+1})$$
$$= \gamma \, \mathrm{Cov}_t(\rho r_{p,t+1} + (1 - \rho)y_{t+1}, r_{t+1})$$
$$= \gamma \rho \alpha_t \sigma_r^2 + \gamma(1 - \rho)\sigma_{yr}, \tag{10.14}$$

where σ_r^2 is the variance of the log risky asset return and σ_{yr} is the covariance of log income with the log risky return. Rearranging,

$$\alpha_t = \frac{1}{\rho}\frac{E_t[r_{t+1} - r_f] + \frac{1}{2}\sigma_r^2}{\gamma\,\sigma_r^2} + \left(1 - \frac{1}{\rho}\right)\beta_{yr}, \tag{10.15}$$

where $\beta_{yr} = \sigma_{yr}/\sigma_r^2$. The second term on the right-hand side of equation (10.15) is the adjustment to the portfolio weight caused by the ability of the risky asset to hedge labor income risk. This is analogous to the income hedging effect for CARA utility shown in equation (10.2).

In the CRRA case, however, the portfolio weight is affected by labor income even when $\sigma_{yr} = \beta_{yr} = 0$. With no income hedging effect, the solution simplifies to

$$\alpha_t = \frac{1}{\rho}\frac{E_t[r_{t+1} - r_f] + \frac{1}{2}\sigma_r^2}{\gamma\,\sigma_r^2} > \frac{E_t[r_{t+1} - r_f] + \frac{1}{2}\sigma_r^2}{\gamma\,\sigma_r^2} \tag{10.16}$$

since $\rho < 1$. An investor with risky but uncorrelated labor income always invests a larger share of his financial wealth in the risky asset than an investor with no labor income (a "retired" investor).

To understand the effect of labor income risk in the CRRA case, consider a mean-preserving spread of labor income that increases the variance of income while holding the mean fixed. Since

$$\overline{Y} = \exp\left(\overline{y} + \frac{1}{2}\sigma_y^2\right), \tag{10.17}$$

the mean of log income, $\overline{y}$, must decline when income risk σ_y^2 increases in order to keep the mean of income, $\overline{Y}$, fixed. This increases ρ in (10.11), which in turn reduces α, moving the risky share closer to the case with no labor income.[2] An interpretation of this result is that uncorrelated labor income risk reduces the investor's valuation of labor income relative to financial wealth, reducing the positive impact of labor income on the willingness to take financial risk.

A summary of these results is that with constant relative risk aversion, riskless labor income crowds out riskless financial assets and tilts portfolios toward risky assets. Uncorrelated labor income risk reduces but does not reverse this effect. Sufficiently correlated labor income risk can reverse the effect and tilt portfolios toward riskless assets.

Subsistence Needs
Finally, we consider how these results are altered when a consumer has a habit level as in the Campbell-Cochrane (1999) model. Write the objective function as

$$U(C_{t+1}, X_{t+1}) = \frac{(C_{t+1} - X_{t+1})^{1-\gamma}}{1 - \gamma} = \frac{S_{t+1}^{1-\gamma}}{1 - \gamma}, \tag{10.18}$$

---

[2]A minor caveat is that ρ also depends on mean log portfolio return and hence on α. Viceira (1998) does a full analysis and finds that it is possible to reverse the effect on α stated above if γ is very low. However, the typical result is that increased labor income risk reduces the tendency for working investors to take more equity risk than retired investors.

where X_{t+1} is habit and surplus consumption $S_{t+1} = C_{t+1} - X_{t+1}$. The budget constraint is

$$C_{t+1} = W_{t+1} = (1 + R_{p,t+1})\,W_t, \tag{10.19}$$

which can be rewritten as

$$S_{t+1} = (1 + R_{p,t+1})\,W_t - X_{t+1}. \tag{10.20}$$

Equations (10.18) and (10.20) show that subsistence needs are like negative labor income. They have all the effects on optimal portfolio choice that we have just discussed for labor income but with the opposite sign. If we assume that subsistence needs are known one period in advance, the optimal portfolio choice is to invest $X_{t+1}/(1 + R_f)$ in the riskless asset and invest surplus wealth $W_t - X_{t+1}/(1 + R_f)$ using the standard formula for power utility. The risky share of financial wealth is always smaller than in the absence of subsistence needs, and the risky share increases with wealth. These results are the opposite of those with labor income.

As an informal exercise, you are asked to relate this analysis to issues faced by Harvard University and other wealthy universities during the last years of the 20th century and the first years of the 21st century. During the prolonged stock market boom of that period, the university's endowment grew faster than other sources of income. The endowment share of Harvard's budget was about 15% in the early 1990s, but this share had doubled by the mid-2000s. At the same time, the university made large fixed commitments to faculty and campus expansion during the mid-2000s. How should this have affected the university's investment strategy for the endowment? This question is discussed at the end of the chapter.

10.1.2 Multiperiod Portfolio Choice Models

The static models discussed in the previous section do not include an intertemporal tradeoff between consumption today and consumption in the future. Multiperiod models endogenize the consumption decision, and this leads to interesting new effects on portfolio choice. While a full account of the modern literature on the consumption function is beyond the scope of this book, in this section we briefly review that literature. We assume power or Epstein-Zin utility, although many of the results hold for other utility functions with a precautionary saving motive.[3]

For simplicity, consider first a context with riskless borrowing and lending, riskless labor income, and a constant riskfree interest rate. In this setting, a long-lived consumer obeys the permanent income hypothesis, choosing a flat consumption path if the rate of time preference equals the interest rate, and tilting the consumption path up or down in response to any difference between these two parameters. The elasticity of intertemporal substitution governs the magnitude of any such tilt, as discussed in Chapter 6. The marginal propensity to consume out of current income is low in this model unless a

---

[3]An agent engages in precautionary saving if he reduces current consumption in favor of savings, referred to as precautionary savings, in response to uncertainty about future consumption. Using Jensen's Inequality, we can see from the standard Euler equation (assuming a concave period utility function over consumption) that current consumption $C_t = u'^{-1}(\delta(1 + R_{f,t+1})E[u'(C_{t+1})])$ is decreasing in the volatility of future consumption, all else equal, if and only if the third derivative of the utility function is positive, that is, if the marginal utility function is convex.

consumer is extremely impatient. For example, with time preference equal to the interest rate and an infinite horizon, the marginal propensity to consume equals the riskless interest rate.

If one adds a borrowing constraint to this model, the marginal propensity to consume out of income remains low unless the borrowing constraint binds, in which case all current income is consumed and the marginal propensity to consume equals one.

These properties change if labor income is risky, as emphasized by Zeldes (1989), Kimball (1990), Deaton (1991), and Carroll (1997). With risky labor income and either a borrowing constraint or a positive probability of zero income in any period, the consumer maintains positive financial assets in all periods and uses them as a "buffer stock" to smooth fluctuations in labor income. A lower buffer stock implies more volatile consumption and hence a steeper planned consumption path and greater precautionary saving. In such a model the consumption function is concave in financial wealth (Carroll and Kimball, 1996), with a high marginal propensity to consume (close to but below one) at low levels of financial asset holdings and a lower marginal propensity to consume at higher levels. An increase in income risk stimulates precautionary saving and reduces consumption today, and this effect is stronger when the buffer stock of financial assets is low.

If one adds portfolio choice to this model, labor income risk has two effects beyond those discussed in the previous section. First, income risk stimulates precautionary saving and induces an accumulation of wealth over time. This increases the importance of financial return shocks relative to proportional labor income shocks, reducing the portfolio share in risky assets through the mechanism discussed in the previous section (an increase in the parameter ρ in equation (10.16)). Viceira (2001) explores this effect in a stationary model with no fixed horizon but a constant probability of retirement.

Second, if the variance of labor income is itself a random variable, an unexpected increase in income risk stimulates precautionary saving, inducing an unexpected decrease in current consumption and an unexpected increase in expected future consumption growth. If the consumer has power utility, the reduction in current consumption increases current marginal utility; hence, the consumer will lower risky asset holdings ex ante if risky returns are negatively correlated with shocks to labor income risk.[4] Storesletten, Telmer, and Yaron (STY 2004, 2007) have emphasized this "income risk covariance" effect on long-term portfolio choice.

Multiperiod portfolio choice models can also allow endogenous labor supply. Bodie, Merton, and Samuelson (1992) emphasize that the ability to adjust to negative financial returns by increasing labor supply makes households more willing to invest in risky assets, consistent with the general equilibrium analysis of Swanson (2012) discussed in section 7.2.2. Farhi and Panageas (2007) model endogenous labor supply in a different fashion by allowing a working household to continue working or to retire. They assume that retirement is an irreversible decision and show that it is triggered by a sufficient accumulation of wealth. As retirement approaches, the incentive to save increases and the willingness to take financial risk may also increase.

---

[4]The increase in expected future consumption growth may, however, have an offsetting negative effect on current marginal utility if the consumer has Epstein-Zin preferences with risk aversion greater than the reciprocal of the elasticity of intertemporal substitution.

Life-Cycle Models

A recent empirical literature explores these effects within the context of life-cycle models of consumption and portfolio choice. A canonical life-cycle model specifies log income during working life as the sum of a deterministic component with a hump shape in age, a permanent random component following a random walk, and a transitory white noise component:

$$y_t = f(Z_t) + v_t + \varepsilon_t, \tag{10.21}$$

where Z_t captures age and other household characteristics, $v_t = v_{t-1} + u_t$, and u_t and ε_t are white noise shocks that have permanent and transitory effects on log income, respectively. In some versions of this model (Zeldes 1989, Carroll 1997), the level of income can temporarily equal zero, which requires $\exp(\varepsilon_t) = 0$ with some probability. This distributional assumption ensures that a consumer with power utility never borrows to consume today; alternatively, a borrowing constraint can be imposed exogenously. The shocks u_t and ε_t can be further decomposed into aggregate components, common to all households, and idiosyncratic components that are uncorrelated across households.

Gourinchas and Parker (2002) calibrate and solve this model under the assumption that only a riskless asset is available for saving. Because the deterministic component of income is hump-shaped in age, younger consumers hold only a small buffer-stock of assets, but middle-aged consumers accumulate financial wealth in anticipation of retirement. Consumption volatility and precautionary savings are therefore higher for young adults, and income risk is relatively unimportant for middle-aged retirement savers.

Angeletos et al. (2001) and Kaplan and Violante (2014) escape this conclusion by enriching the model to include two riskless assets, one liquid and one illiquid. The illiquid asset earns a higher return but deposits to or withdrawals from this asset incur a fixed cost. The illiquid asset is attractive for retirement saving, both because of its high return and because it helps households resist the temptation to consume accumulated savings too early (Angeletos et al. 2001), but it is less suitable for use as a buffer stock to smooth consumption in the face of temporary income shocks. This specification implies that households save for retirement in illiquid form and may have only a small buffer stock of liquid assets even in middle age when they have accumulated substantial wealth. Such "wealthy hand-to-mouth" consumers have a high marginal propensity to consume out of income even though their total wealth is high.

Cocco, Gomes, and Maenhout (2005) extend the life-cycle model to incorporate portfolio choice between two liquid assets, one safe and one risky. Their model excludes leverage so the maximum feasible risky portfolio share is one. They estimate relatively low correlations between income shocks and risky asset returns. Accordingly they find that the risky share should be one early in working life and should fall only in middle age as financial wealth increases and the value of remaining future income decreases with the approach of retirement.

These predictions have been compared with panel data on risky investment over the life cycle by Ameriks and Zeldes (2004), using a US sample of contributors to TIAA-CREF, a US provider of retirement financial services, and by Fagereng, Gottlieb, and Guiso (2017), using Norwegian administrative records. The results are summarized by Guiso, and Sodini (2013). This empirical research faces several difficulties, notably the need to restrict age, cohort, and time effects in some fashion to identify the model.[5] However, the data do appear consistent with a relatively high risky share (albeit much less than one) among younger stock market participants and a decline in this share among participants after age 45 or so. This is also consistent with the asset allocation rules of target date funds that have been increasingly popular retirement savings vehicles in the US in recent years. However, many households do not own any risky assets at all—that is, stock market participation is limited—a fact we discuss in the next section.

All the life-cycle models discussed so far assume that income shocks have fixed variances that may vary across groups of households but do not evolve stochastically over time. STY (2004) challenge this assumption. They present indirect evidence that the variance of idiosyncratic income shocks is itself random and increases during recessions. The evidence is indirect because panel data on income are available only since the late 1960s and therefore do not include many recessions. However, older cohorts have lived through more, and more serious, recessions; and STY show that the cross-sectional dispersion of income is greater for these cohorts in a fashion that is difficult to explain unless idiosyncratic income variance is countercyclical. Such a negative covariance between stock returns and idiosyncratic income risk might deter young households from stockholding.

Borrowing Constraints and Risk Perceptions

Models with risky income and borrowing constraints have interesting implications for the risk assessment of standard financial contracts. An important example is the choice between an adjustable-rate mortgage (ARM) and a fixed-rate mortgage (FRM). An adjustable-rate mortgage is a floating-rate instrument whose interest rate is reset in response to movements in the short-term interest rate; accordingly, it has a low duration and its market value is always close to its principal value. A fixed-rate mortgage is a long-term fixed-rate instrument with a level stream of nominal payments specified in advance; like a long-term bond, it has a high duration and an unstable market value. While US FRMs can be refinanced without penalty, limiting the increase in market value that can be caused by a decline in interest rates, they can fall in value considerably if interest rates increase. Conventional risk analysis with a short-term perspective would therefore describe an FRM as a risky mortgage and an ARM as a safe mortgage. Even a risk analysis with a long-term perspective, of the sort discussed in Chapter 9, will deliver the same conclusion if the real interest rate is constant while inflation varies over time.[6]

A borrowing-constrained household may view mortgage risks very differently, as emphasized by Campbell and Cocco (2003). For simplicity, continue to assume a constant real interest rate and a stochastic inflation rate. An increase in inflation, with a corresponding increase in the short-term nominal interest rate, increases the required

---

[5]Unrestricted age, cohort, and time effects are unidentified because age equals current year less birth year, so there is perfect collinearity among age, cohort, and time dummies. A recently popular approach is to restrict cohort effects by relating them to lifetime experiences of the cohort, as in Malmendier and Nagel (2011, 2016).

[6]A decline in the value of an FRM caused by an increase in inflation is, of course, beneficial to a mortgage borrower. However, this benefit is priced ex ante, and so the mortgage is risky in the sense that its real cost is highly sensitive to the random realization of inflation.

real payments on an ARM to offset the inflationary erosion of the mortgage's real principal. If the household is able to borrow elsewhere to offset the increase in required mortgage payments, then the household's real budget is unaffected, and the household can perfectly smooth its real consumption over time using an ARM. However, if this is not possible, then the increase in inflation forces a reduction in consumption for ARM borrowers. Hence, a household considering an ARM should take into account the risk that future interest-rate increases will interact with future borrowing constraints to destabilize consumption. Problem 10.1 at the end of this chapter asks you to work out a simple analytical model of this effect.

10.1.3 Labor Income and Asset Pricing

Relative to models in which investors live only off financial wealth, models with labor income typically predict a greater willingness to take financial risk at any level of risk aversion. Hence, the first-order effect of labor income is to make the equity premium harder to explain. Put another way, models with labor income imply less volatile consumption for any given portfolio allocation, consistent with consumption-based models in which smooth consumption leads to an equity premium puzzle.

The distribution of income across households can affect this result, however. The life-cycle models discussed in the previous section imply that young investors with a high ratio of human to financial wealth should wish to hold leveraged risky portfolios. If leverage is ruled out, young investors can take relatively little financial risk because they have accumulated little wealth, so they cannot buy many stocks even if they hold no riskless assets at all. This forces middle-aged investors to take almost all the financial risk in the economy. The consumption of older investors becomes highly sensitive to aggregate risk, and the implied equity premium is high. Constantinides, Donaldson, and Mehra (2002) model this effect in an overlapping generations model and argue that it is substantial.

Who Takes Risk?

Models of income risk have interesting implications for cross-sectional patterns of financial behavior. One of these is that households with riskier labor income should take less financial risk if they have the same risk preferences. Guiso, Jappelli, and Terlizzese (1996) report a negative unconditional correlation between income risk and financial risktaking in Italian survey data, but Ranish (2013) finds that in the US Survey of Consumer Finances, households whose characteristics suggest they have risky income also tend to take greater financial risk, an effect that may result from self-selection of risk-tolerant individuals into risky occupations.

Hedging Idiosyncratic Income Risk

Regardless of risk preferences, households should increase their demand for risky assets that can hedge their nonfinancial income risks and should reduce demand for assets that are positively correlated with those risks. In contrast to this, many US households have large holdings in the stock of their employer, particularly within their 401(k) retirement savings accounts (Mitchell and Utkus 2003). While some of these holdings result from employer policies, Benartzi (2001) shows that a substantial fraction of unrestricted employee contributions go to employer stock rather than diversified alternatives.[7] Furthermore, both Massa and Simonov (2006) and Døskeland and Hvide (2011) report that individual Scandinavian investors overweight other stocks in the industries they work for. Massa and Simonov (2006) find positive abnormal returns on own-industry investments and attribute this to an informational advantage in own-industry investing, but Døskeland and Hvide (2011) report underperformance of these investments and argue that investors' tendency to "anti-hedge" results from a behavioral bias in favor of familiar companies.

Individual investors also overweight local companies from their own country and region, and this is also a form of anti-hedging to the extent that local shocks affect both local stock returns and local income growth. There is a debate about informational advantage versus behavioral bias in this context also (Lewis 1999, Grinblatt and Keloharju 2001, Huberman 2001, Ivković and Weisbenner 2005, Bekaert et al. 2015).[8] We discuss models of informational advantage in section 12.1.4 of Chapter 12.

Hedging Aggregate Income Risk

Even if investors do not pick assets to hedge their occupation-specific risks, they may prefer to hold assets that hedge aggregate income risk. This could lead in equilibrium to lower returns on such assets and higher returns on assets that covary with income. One way to understand this, following Mayers (1972), is as a modification of the CAPM to include human capital along with financial wealth in the market portfolio.

This idea has been explored by numerous papers over the years. For example, Liew and Vassalou (2000) show that the returns on country-specific portfolios that go long small and value stocks, and short large and growth stocks, predict GDP growth rates in 10 developed markets, even controlling for aggregate country returns. This finding makes it plausible that such portfolios are correlated with the value of human capital in each country, contributing to an explanation of their high returns. In a similar spirit, Koijen, Lustig, and Van Niewerburgh (2017) show that the Cochrane-Piazzesi combination of forward rates predicts US GDP growth and that value stocks covary with innovations in this variable.

A recent paper by Betermier, Calvet, and Sodini (2017) presents evidence that the demand for growth stocks varies across investors in a way that one would expect if investors are using these stocks to hedge aggregate income risk. In Swedish administrative data, young investors with more human capital than financial wealth, and investors working in more cyclical sectors, tend to hold more growth stocks; whereas value stocks are preferred by older investors with greater financial wealth who work in more stable sectors.

Gârleanu, Kogan, and Panageas (GKP 2012) offer a structural interpretation of the income-hedging property of growth stocks, in the spirit of production-based asset pricing. In their overlapping generations model, technological progress increases output but lowers the value of human capital for current workers (as opposed to new workers entering the economy). Growth firms do well in times of rapid technological progress, when entering cohorts are gaining at the expense of currently active cohorts. Growth

---

[7]This is especially true when the employer stock has performed well over the previous decade, suggesting that households extrapolate the past performance of the employer.

[8]In the local context, another possibility arises: it could be rational for investors to mimic the portfolios of other local investors if they derive utility from relative consumption or consume local goods that are in fixed supply, whose prices therefore depend on the wealth of local investors (DeMarzo, Kaniel, and Kremer 2004).

stocks are therefore valuable hedges against this "displacement risk." GKP show that in a basic version of their model, the CAPM holds when risky human capital is included in the market portfolio.

10.2 Limited Participation

10.2.1 Wealth, Participation, and Risktaking

An important stylized fact of household finance is that many households do not participate in risky asset markets, thereby violating the principle of participation discussed in section 2.1.1. We illustrate the prevalence of this behavior across the wealth distribution using the 2001 Survey of Consumer Finances as in Campbell (2006).

Figure 10.1 presents the cross-sectional wealth distribution for US households. The horizontal axis in this figure shows the percentiles of the distribution of total assets, defined broadly to include both financial assets and nonfinancial assets (durable goods, real estate, and private business equity but not defined benefit pension plans or human capital). The vertical axis reports dollars on a log scale. The three lines in the figure show the average levels of total assets, financial assets, and net worth (total assets less debts, including mortgages, home equity loans, credit card debt, and other debt) at each percentile of the total assets distribution. It is clear from the figure that many households have negligible financial assets. Even the median household has financial assets of only $35,000, net worth of $86,000, and total assets of $135,000.

The figure also shows the extreme skewness of the wealth distribution. Wealthy households at the right of the figure have an overwhelming influence on aggregate statistics. To the extent that these households behave differently from households in the middle of the wealth distribution, the aggregates tell us very little about the financial decision making of a typical household.

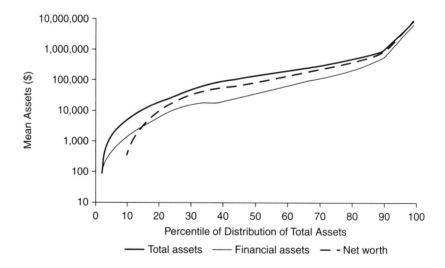

Figure 10.1. *The US Wealth Distribution in 2001* (Campbell, John Y., 2006, "Household Finance," Presidential Address, *Journal of Finance* 61, 1553–1604; reprinted by permission of John Wiley & Sons, Inc.)

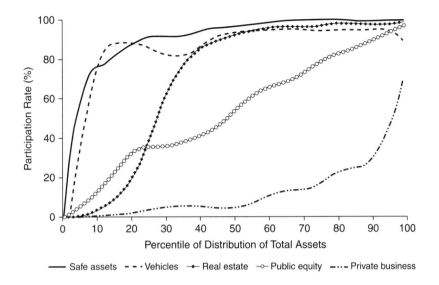

Figure 10.2. *Participation Rates by Asset Class* (Campbell, John Y., 2006, "Household Finance," Presidential Address, *Journal of Finance* 61, 1553–1604; reprinted by permission of John Wiley & Sons, Inc.)

Figure 10.2 illustrates the participation decisions of households with different levels of wealth. The horizontal axis is the same as in Figure 10.1, but the vertical axis now shows the fraction of households that participate in particular asset classes. This figure aggregates the SCF asset data into several broad categories, namely, safe assets, vehicles, real estate, public equity, and private business assets.[9]

Given the negligible financial assets held by households at the left of the figure, it should not be surprising that most households in the bottom quartile of the wealth distribution hold only safe assets and vehicles, with a minority participating in real estate through homeownership. As we move to the right in the figure we see that an increasing fraction of households participate in equity markets. Participation is far from universal, however, even among quite wealthy households. Limited participation among the wealthy poses a significant challenge to financial theory and is one of the main stylized facts of household finance. At the 80th percentile of the wealth distribution, for example, a typical household has about $200,000 in financial assets, but almost 20% of these households own no public equity.

Many wealthy households have significant private business assets. Figure 10.2 shows that the fraction of business owners increases from 22% at the 80th percentile of the wealth distribution to 70% at the right tail of the distribution. Heaton and Lucas (2000) emphasize that private business assets substitute for public equity in the portfolios of some wealthy households. The fraction of households at the 80th percentile of the wealth distribution that hold neither private business assets nor public equity is just under 10%. Thus,

---

[9]Safe assets include checking, saving, money market, and call accounts, CDs, and US savings bonds. Public equity includes stocks and mutual funds held in taxable or retirement accounts or trusts. Bonds are omitted from the figure: they include Treasury bonds other than US savings bonds, municipal, corporate, foreign, and mortgage-backed bonds, cash-value life insurance, and amounts in mutual funds, retirement accounts, trusts, and other managed assets that are not invested in stock.

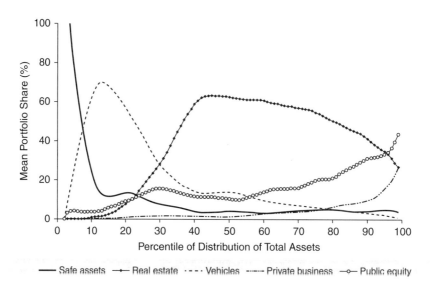

Figure 10.3. *Asset Class Shares in Household Portfolios* (Campbell, John Y., 2006, "Household Finance," Presidential Address, *Journal of Finance* 61, 1553–1604; reprinted by permission of John Wiley & Sons, Inc.)

private business assets can explain much of the nonparticipation in public equity markets by wealthy households, but there remains a significant number of these households who have no exposure to equity risk of any kind.

Figure 10.3 illustrates the asset allocation decisions of households with different levels of wealth. The horizontal axis is the same as in the two previous figures, but the vertical axis now depicts the weight of an asset class in the aggregate portfolio of households at each level of wealth (this is almost identical to the mean share for households within a given wealth range). The figure illustrates the dominant role of liquid assets and vehicles for the poor and real estate—primarily owner-occupied housing—for middle-class households. Equity has some importance for the middle class but represents the largest portfolio share only for wealthier households at the right of the figure.

Figure 10.3 shows that wealthy households are willing to take greater risk in their portfolios. This is partly the result of greater participation in risky asset classes but also partly the result of higher portfolio shares conditional on participation. Carroll (2002) emphasizes this phenomenon and shows that similar patterns obtain in several European countries.

Interpretation

How can we make sense of the above empirical results? Textbook financial theory, summarized in section 2.1.1, implies that all households, no matter how risk averse, should hold some equities as long as the equity premium is positive. It follows that limited participation in the equity market must be due to a failure of one of the standard assumptions.

One possibility is that households have nonstandard preferences. Models with a kink in the utility function at a reference level of wealth, for example, imply nonparticipation if the reward for risktaking is small enough (Epstein and Zin 1990, Segal and Spivak

1990). Similarly, the models of ambiguity aversion due to Gilboa and Schmeidler (1989) and Epstein and Wang (1994) imply that investors who are uncertain about the true value of the equity premium may make a worst-case assumption that the equity premium is zero, in which case they will rationally choose not to participate in the stock market. These models can explain nonparticipation at all levels of wealth and do not predict that participation rates increase with wealth.

An alternative possibility is that households face fixed costs, for example, one-time entry costs or ongoing participation costs. Fixed costs can explain why participation increases with wealth, since a larger portfolio is more likely to justify the payment of a fixed cost to increase return. One-time entry costs imply strong positive age effects, since a household will continue to participate once a fixed entry cost has been paid; ongoing participation costs produce limited participation with weaker age effects. Haliassos and Bertaut (1995) and Vissing-Jørgensen (2003) show that moderate ongoing participation costs can explain the nonparticipation of many US households, although not the richest households.

Fixed participation costs can be interpreted in different ways. One approach is to think of fixed costs as capturing time and money that must be spent in order to invest in the stock market. Alternatively, fixed costs may be an economist's description of psychological factors that make equity ownership uncomfortable for some households.[10] Consistent with this view, education has a strong positive effect on equity market participation after controlling for age, income, and wealth (Campbell 2006, Calvet, Campbell, and Sodini 2007). Even more strikingly, Grinblatt, Keloharju, and Linnainmaa (2011) find that IQ, measured early in life for Finnish males entering military service, has a similar positive effect on participation. According to this interpretation, nonparticipation can be regarded as an investment mistake, one that less educated households with lower cognitive skills are more likely to make.

An interesting question is whether stock market participants are more risk tolerant than nonparticipants. If nonparticipants are relatively risk averse, then small fixed costs suffice to deter them from participation. Carroll (2002) proposes a model in which all agents have a common utility function with declining relative risk aversion and argues that this model explains the high participation rate and more aggressive asset allocation of wealthy households. However, Gomes and Michaelides (2005, 2008) argue that more risk-averse households have a stronger precautionary saving motive, which leads them to accumulate more wealth. If there is exogenous cross-sectional variation in risk aversion and the precautionary saving effect is sufficiently strong, those households that are wealthy enough to pay the fixed costs of stock market participation may actually be more risk averse than nonparticipating households.

Other features of the data can be explained by the effect of background risk on portfolio choice. Self-employed households and households with significant private business assets are exposed to private business risk that, as explained in section 10.1, increases their effective risk aversion even if it is uncorrelated with returns on publicly traded equities. Private business risk has an even stronger discouraging effect on equity ownership if, as seems plausible, it is positively correlated with public equity risk. Poor health also predicts

---

[10] Hong, Kubik, and Stein (2004), for example, find that households that interact less with other households in their community are less likely to own stocks, suggesting that households prefer to follow financial practices that they know they share with others. Similarly, Guiso, Sapienza, and Zingales (2008) find that households that express reluctance to trust others are less likely to own stocks.

a conservative asset allocation. This can also be understood as a background risk effect; in this case the risk is to spending needs rather than to income.

Finally, there are interesting age effects on participation. Life-cycle studies such as Ameriks and Zeldes (2004) and Fagereng, Gottlieb, and Guiso (2017) find a hump shape when the participation rate is plotted against age and a risky share that declines with age among participants. This may be explained by some combination of a life-cycle hump in financial wealth, a one-time entry cost and small ongoing participation costs, increasing risk aversion with age, and possibly a life-cycle hump in financial competence (Agarwal et al. 2009).

10.2.2 Asset Pricing Implications of Limited Participation

What are the consequences of limited participation for asset pricing? We can begin to understand this issue by considering a representative-agent model with a single risky asset and iid returns. Under the standard assumptions of constant relative risk aversion and lognormally distributed returns, the optimal risky share is the usual formula given in equation (10.4), $\alpha = (\overline{R}-R_f)/\gamma\sigma_R^2$. With full participation and a zero net supply of riskless assets, equilibrium requires $\alpha = 1$. Hence,

$$\overline{R} - R_f = \gamma\sigma_R^2. \tag{10.22}$$

Also, with a constant consumption-wealth ratio and all wealth invested in risky assets, the conditional variance of consumption growth equals the variance of risky returns:

$$\sigma_c^2 = \sigma_R^2. \tag{10.23}$$

Now suppose only a fraction k of wealth belongs to investors who can hold stocks (participants denoted by P). The remaining wealth belongs to nonparticipants (denoted by NP) who can only hold safe assets. Nonparticipants lend to participants at the riskless interest rate. Equilibrium now requires $\alpha_P = 1/k$ for participants. Hence,

$$\overline{R} - R_f = \frac{\gamma\sigma_R^2}{k}. \tag{10.24}$$

The consumption growth of participants is more volatile because they hold a leveraged risky portfolio. Its variance σ_{cP}^2 is

$$\sigma_{cP}^2 = \frac{\sigma_R^2}{k^2}. \tag{10.25}$$

Since aggregate consumption growth $\Delta c = k\Delta c_P + (1-k)\Delta c_{NP}$ (a relation that would be exact in levels and is approximate in logs), and nonparticipants have deterministic consumption growth with zero variance, the variance of aggregate consumption growth is the same as before:

$$\sigma_c^2 = k^2\sigma_{cP}^2 = \sigma_R^2. \tag{10.26}$$

Thus, limited participation increases the equity premium by a factor $1/k$ without any increase in aggregate risk. Limited participation is equivalent to a decline in aggregate risk tolerance.

The fraction of households investing in equity markets has increased over the last 100 years, and it is tempting to relate this to the evidence discussed in Chapter 5 that the equity premium declined during the late 20th century. A difficulty in doing this is that the effect of limited participation is more powerful for low values of k, and k is the share of wealth controlled by participants, not the share of the population that participates. This makes it challenging to get a large effect from expanding participation, because wealth-weighted participation rates have always been higher than equally weighted participation rates. However, models where human wealth is a large fraction of total wealth, such as Constantinides, Donaldson, and Mehra (2002), make it easier for limited participation to have an important effect on the equity premium.

The static model described above is extreme in that nonparticipants achieve riskless consumption, but similar effects operate in multiperiod models where nonparticipants are exposed to some risk. As an example, Guvenen (2009) builds a model with two infinite-lived agents, one allowed to participate and one exogenously restricted from participation. Nonparticipants have a low elasticity of intertemporal substitution while participants have a high EIS (consistent with empirical evidence in Vissing-Jørgensen 2002). The economy has technology shocks that affect labor income as well as capital income. Nonparticipants use the bond market to smooth their income, so participants' consumption is highly procyclical even if the wealth share of nonparticipants is small on average. Finally, in a recession, nonparticipants have an even stronger desire to smooth their income because they are poorer (and the value function is concave in wealth when markets are incomplete), so stockholders' consumption volatility rises, increasing the equity premium. In Guvenen's model, the consumption of nonparticipants acts like habit in the Campbell-Cochrane (1999) model, implying a more volatile stochastic discount factor when aggregate consumption is low.

It is more challenging to get large effects of nonparticipation on asset returns in models where the participation decision is endogenous. Gomes and Michaelides (2008) build a life-cycle model with two groups of agents, idiosyncratic income risk within each group, and a fixed cost of participation. In their model the equity premium is explained primarily by idiosyncratic risk among participants that reduces the willingness to take financial risk and only secondarily by limited participation itself.

Endogenous participation can affect the relationship between stock market volatility and the equity premium. With constant participation, equation (10.24) shows the usual result that the equity premium is proportional to variance, and the market's Sharpe ratio is proportional to standard deviation; but if an increase in the Sharpe ratio induces more investors to pay the fixed cost of participation, the expansion of risk-bearing capacity will dampen the increase in the equity premium, an effect modeled by Hirshleifer (1988) in the context of commodity futures trading.

10.3 Underdiversification

A major question in household finance is how well households diversify their portfolios within each asset class. Accurate measurement is significantly more challenging in this context because it requires the holdings of each individual asset, and survey data do not generally give this much detail. Since Blume and Friend (1975), surveys and sometimes tax returns have been used to show that many households own relatively few individual stocks (the median number of stocks held is only two or three in the Survey of Consumer Finances, depending on the year). However, many households own equity indirectly, through mutual funds or retirement accounts, and these indirect holdings tend to be much better diversified. Thus, it is not clear that concentrated individual stockholdings have a large effect on household portfolio risk.

10.3.1 Empirical Evidence

Calvet, Campbell, and Sodini (CCS 2007) use Swedish administrative data, which report a complete breakdown of all asset holdings outside defined-contribution retirement accounts, to look more directly at portfolio diversification. CCS construct a sample of 100,000 households and measure the composition of their portfolios at the end of 2002, down to the level of individual stocks and mutual funds. They calculate the risk properties of these portfolios by estimating a variance-covariance matrix Σ for the returns of all stocks and mutual funds held by Swedish households. Then, if a household h has portfolio weight vector w_h in risky assets, the variance of its portfolio return is estimated as $w_h'\Sigma w_h$. This procedure captures the risk in household portfolios at a point in time; it does not track the trading decisions of households within the year.

The median household in the CCS sample has a risky portfolio with a standard deviation of 21%. Part of this standard deviation comes from exposure to systematic risk in the world equity market, and part comes from unsystematic risk. As a measure of systematic risk, CCS calculate the standard deviation of the fitted value in a regression of each household's portfolio return on the dollar excess return of the MSCI All World Index. For the median household, this systematic standard deviation is 14%. The standard deviation of the residual, a measure of unsystematic risk, is 16%, implying that more than half of the median Swedish household's portfolio variance is idiosyncratic.

Although Swedish households can obtain the dollar excess return on international stocks by hedging their currency exposure when they invest internationally, this may be an unrealistic benchmark given that international equity funds widely marketed in Sweden are not currency hedged. When CCS repeat the above exercise with the Swedish krona excess return on the MSCI index, they find that slightly less than half of the median household's portfolio variance is idiosyncratic.

While the median standard deviation of the risky portfolio return is 21%, there is wide variation in this number across households. Some households take low risk and hold primarily bond funds; others take high risk. The 95th percentile of the risky portfolio standard deviation is 51%. Portfolios with this level of risk tend to have betas above one, but they also have extremely high shares of idiosyncratic as opposed to systematic risk.

In the Swedish data, portfolios with high idiosyncratic risk tend to have high shares of directly owned stocks, and the directly owned portfolios tend to be concentrated in one or two volatile stocks. Concentration, however, can be a misleading statistic; many portfolios with low idiosyncratic risk also contain one or two directly owned stocks, but these portfolios are dominated by mutual funds and contain only a small share of directly owned stocks. This pattern illustrates the danger of looking only at the number of directly held stocks in a portfolio without considering the broader context within which those stocks are held. Correlation across stocks in the portfolio contributes very little to the cross-sectional risk pattern in Swedish portfolios.

Portfolio Efficiency under the International CAPM

In order to evaluate the consequences of underdiversification for household welfare, CCS assume that mean returns on stocks and mutual funds obey an international CAPM.[11] This assumption avoids the difficult task of estimating average returns on individual stocks and mutual funds from short historical time series, while enabling CCS to plot Swedish household portfolios on a mean-standard deviation diagram. By assumption, all portfolios must fall below the efficient frontier, which in the case of the international CAPM is a straight line connecting the riskless rate to the currency-hedged return on the MSCI world index.

Figure 10.4 illustrates the diversification of a random subsample of 10,000 Swedish portfolios. The top panel looks only at directly held stocks, while the bottom panel also includes mutual funds.[12] It is immediately obvious that mutual funds improve diversification considerably. Many household portfolios in the bottom panel come close to the Sharpe ratio of the unhedged world index (estimated at 35%), although almost none attain the efficient Sharpe ratio of the currency-hedged world index (estimated at 45%). The Swedish domestic equity index has an estimated Sharpe ratio of 27%, comparable to that of many household portfolios.

There are several ways to measure portfolio inefficiency within this framework. One is to calculate the percentage difference between a household portfolio's Sharpe ratio S_h and the Sharpe ratio of a benchmark index S_B, $1 - S_h/S_B$. An alternative approach is to calculate the return lost, at the portfolio's given standard deviation, by the lower Sharpe ratio of the household portfolio. This return loss RL_h is given by

$$RL_h = \alpha_h(S_B\sigma_h - \mu_h) = \alpha_h\beta_h\left(\frac{S_B}{S_h} - 1\right) E R_m^e, \tag{10.27}$$

where α_h is the portfolio's weight in risky assets, σ_h is the standard deviation of the household's risky portfolio return, and μ_h is the mean of that return. The second equality in (10.27) relates the return loss to the aggressiveness of household investments, as captured by the risky share and the beta of the household's assets, and to a transformation of the relative Sharpe ratio.

CCS find that the median Swedish household gives up about a third of the maximum available Sharpe ratio. This Sharpe ratio loss is reduced by more than half if one uses as a benchmark the world index in Swedish kronas rather than the currency-hedged world index. The median Swedish household portfolio has a higher Sharpe ratio than the Swedish equity index, reflecting the fact that many Swedish households hold global equity mutual funds.

Reductions in Sharpe ratios have little effect on portfolio returns if households invest conservatively. Return loss, the second measure of portfolio inefficiency, places greater weight on low Sharpe ratios that are accompanied by aggressive investment strategies. The median Swedish household loses almost 1.2% or about $130 per year relative to the currency-hedged world index under the CAPM. Relative to the unhedged

---

[11]CCS do not subtract fees from mutual fund returns; hence, they implicitly assume that funds earn a pre-fee alpha sufficient to cover their fees. If this is not the case, then return losses relative to the benchmark are increased by the difference between fees and alpha on the portion of the portfolio held in mutual funds.

[12]A hyperbola of two-stock portfolios is visible in the top panel. This results from a common tendency to hold only Ericsson and TeliaSonera, a privatized telecommunications stock, but typically these two stocks are held along with mutual funds, so the hyperbola does not show up in the bottom panel.

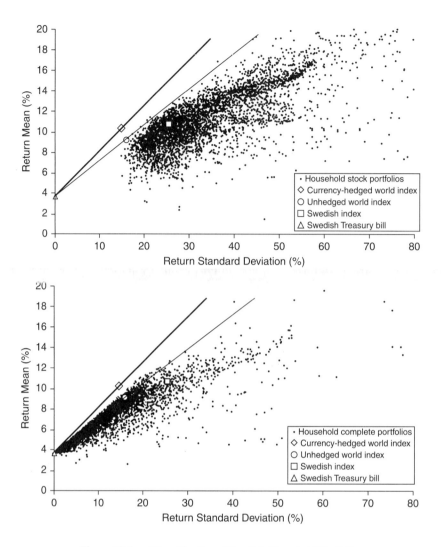

Figure 10.4. *Diversification of Swedish Household Portfolios*

world index, the median household loses only one-quarter as much. Clearly portfolio underdiversification has only modest effects on the welfare of the median Swedish household.

Once again, however, there is wide variation in these numbers across households. At the right tail of the distribution of return losses, these losses are substantial. The 95th percentile of the return loss is 5.0% relative to the hedged world index and about half this relative to the unhedged index. In dollar units, the 95th percentile of the loss is over $2,200 per year relative to the hedged world index and almost $850 per year relative to the unhedged index.

These numbers suggest that underdiversification is a problem for only a minority of households. A natural next question is which households lose the most by inefficient investing. To investigate this, CCS take logs of equation (10.27) and then regress the log return loss and its three household-specific components onto demographic characteristics of households. They find offsetting effects on return losses. On the one hand, financially sophisticated households with high disposable income, wealth, education, private pension savings, and financial liabilities tend to invest more aggressively. They invest a higher fraction of their wealth in risky assets, and those assets have higher betas. On the other hand, these households also tend to invest more efficiently, consistent with results reported by Goetzmann and Kumar (2008) for US brokerage account data and by Grinblatt, Keloharju, and Linnainmaa (2011) for Finnish data. In the Swedish data the first effect dominates, so financially sophisticated households actually have higher overall return losses.

An important question is how well these results describe household behavior in other countries. While Scandinavian portfolio data are more complete than data available elsewhere, the evidence reviewed in section 10.1.3, that investors tend to hold the stocks of the company they work for, other companies in the same industry, and other local companies, suggests that underdiversification is at least as great a problem elsewhere in the world. One would expect Scandinavian investors to be comparatively well diversified, since these countries have high average levels of education and a well-developed mutual fund industry with an international orientation.

Diversification and Participation

The demographic predictors of portfolio inefficiency are similar to the demographic predictors of nonparticipation and cautious investing. This suggests that some households may fail to invest in stocks, or may invest only cautiously in stocks, in part because they are aware that they lack the skills to invest efficiently. They may correctly calculate lower welfare benefits of participation given their investment skills, or they may simply feel uncomfortable participating in an activity for which they are poorly prepared (this can be interpreted as a higher psychological fixed cost of participation). To demonstrate the relevance of the first channel, CCS calculate the extra return that stock market participation can provide a household with the typical demographic characteristics of nonparticipants, assuming that this household invests with the efficiency predicted by a demographic regression. The implied increase in portfolio return is slightly lower than the increase for a household that invests with the average efficiency of Swedish households and only about half the increase for a household that invests fully efficiently. Put another way, the fixed costs that are needed to deter participation are smaller if households correctly anticipate their own limited ability to diversify their portfolios.

10.3.2 Effects on the Wealth Distribution

Recent research seeks to understand the implications of underdiversification for the wealth distribution. Household underdiversification can help explain the puzzling dispersion of wealth at retirement reported in US data by Venti and Wise (2001). Venti and Wise argue that differences in lifetime earnings or asset allocation do not explain dispersion and conclude that it must be caused by differences in savings propensities. However, poorly diversified stock investments can also explain a great deal of dispersion. This is particularly true if wealthier people diversify more effectively or earn higher returns for other reasons, as argued by Piketty (2014, Chapter 12).

Campbell (2016) lays out a framework in which these effects can be quantified. Consider a set of households, indexed by i, with heterogeneous investment strategies. In the absence of income and consumption (and hence in the absence of saving), the evolution of household i's wealth is given by $W_{i,t+1} = W_{it}(1 + R_{i,t+1})$, where $(1 + R_{i,t+1})$ is the gross return on household i's portfolio. Taking logs,

$$w_{i,t+1} = w_{it} + r_{i,t+1}$$
$$= w_{it} + E_t r_{i,t+1} + \tilde{r}_{i,t+1}, \tag{10.28}$$

where $E_t r_{i,t+1}$ is the rational (econometrician's) expectation of the log portfolio return for household i, and $\tilde{r}_{i,t+1} = r_{i,t+1} - E_t r_{i,t+1}$ is the unexpected component of the log portfolio return.

We use the notation Var* and Cov* to denote the cross-sectional variance and covariance of observations at a point in time. Equation (10.28) implies a decomposition of the time-series average change in the cross-sectional variance of log wealth from one period to the next—the average change in wealth inequality—into three terms:

$$E[\text{Var}^*(w_{i,t+1}) - \text{Var}^*(w_{it})] = E[\text{Var}^*(E_t r_{i,t+1})] + E[\text{Var}^*(\tilde{r}_{i,t+1})]$$
$$+ 2E[\text{Cov}^*(w_{it}, E_t r_{i,t+1})]. \tag{10.29}$$

All the returns that appear on the right-hand side of equation (10.29) are log returns, not simple returns. Cross-sectional variation in expected log returns causes growing cross-sectional dispersion in wealth, consistent with the fact discussed in section 2.1.5 that in an economy without consumption, investors who maximize expected log returns and hold the growth-optimal portfolio control an ever-increasing share of wealth. This is important because uncompensated risk has no effect on expected simple returns but it lowers expected log returns at the portfolio level.[13] Hence, differences in diversification across investors can increase wealth inequality through this channel.

The first term on the right-hand side of (10.29) is the cross-sectional variance in expected log returns, and the third term is the cross-sectional covariance between log wealth and expected log returns. These terms result from differences across households in their diversification of uncompensated risk, their willingness to take compensated risk, or their investment skill. The second term is the cross-sectional variance in unexpected log returns, the result of either exposures to idiosyncratic risks or cross-sectionally varying exposures to common shocks. The third term is the covariance emphasized by Piketty (2014), although Piketty does not make the critical distinction between average return and average log return.

In any one period, the evolution of wealth inequality is also influenced by the cross-sectional covariance between log wealth and unexpected log returns and the cross-sectional covariance between expected and unexpected log returns. However, these covariances are driven by unexpected common shocks to assets favored by wealthy people or to assets with high expected returns, and thus they average to zero over time. The framework can be extended to include savings as an additional influence on the change in wealth inequality: this adds three new terms that reflect the cross-sectional variance

---

[13]Recall that when returns are conditionally lognormal, $E_t r_{i,t+1} = \log(E_t(1 + R_{i,t+1})) - (1/2)\text{Var}_t r_{i,t+1}$. Hence, an uncompensated increase in portfolio variance that leaves the average simple return unchanged lowers the average log return.

of savings rates, the cross-sectional covariances between wealth and savings, and between savings and expected investment returns.

Bach, Calvet, and Sodini (BCS 2016) study wealth inequality and implement this framework using Swedish administrative data over the period 2000–2008. They measure realized and expected returns on stocks held at the beginning of each year, assuming that no rebalancing occurs during the year and imposing a simple factor model and the assumption that alphas are zero on average in all wealth groups.

BCS report that the sum of the three terms in equation (10.29) is 0.059 per year, of which less than 1% comes from the cross-sectional variance of expected log returns, 25% comes from the cross-sectional variance of unexpected log returns, and 75% comes from the cross-sectional covariance between log wealth and expected log returns.[14] The cross-sectional variance of unexpected log returns is meaningful despite the relatively good diversification of risky portfolios documented by CCS, while the cross-sectional covariance between wealth and expected log returns is increased by the tendency for richer Swedish households to take more risk and to earn a higher Sharpe ratio through especially effective diversification. The cross-sectional standard deviation of expected log returns is small enough that when squared to form variance, it is relatively unimportant; it matters only through its association with log wealth, which is far more dispersed.

Evidence that average log returns vary cross-sectionally is not in itself evidence that households are choosing suboptimal investment strategies, since maximizing average log return is the investment objective only for an investor with log utility. However, it cannot be rational to take uncompensated idiosyncratic risk, and such uncompensated risk contributes to the evolution of wealth inequality in the Swedish data.

10.3.3 Asset Pricing Implications of Underdiversification

Undiversified investing has important implications for asset pricing, as emphasized by Merton (1987), Allen and Gale (1994), Duffie (2010), and other models in which certain assets or asset classes are understood and invested in by only a small subset of investors. While these models can become sophisticated and complex, the essential effect can be understood in a very simple example.

Consider a risky asset j that is held only by a group of homogeneous investors with wealth W_j. These investors hold only asset j and the riskless asset, and they have single-period power utility with risk aversion γ_j. Asset j has a terminal (next-period) payoff X_j that is lognormally distributed with $\mathrm{Var}(\log X_j) = \sigma_j^2$. Letting V_j denote the market value of the asset, $1 + R_j = X_j/V_j$, and the variance of its log return is also σ_j^2. Then the usual formula for portfolio choice with power utility is

$$\alpha_j = \frac{\overline{R}_j - R_f}{\gamma_j \sigma_j^2}. \tag{10.30}$$

[14]In the Swedish data the average annual change in the cross-sectional variance of log financial wealth is 0.037, almost 40% smaller than the sum of the three terms on the right-hand side of equation (10.29). Thus in Sweden unmodeled savings flows have reduced inequality in financial wealth over this period (possibly offset by increasing inequality in housing wealth in a period of rising house prices). These statistics and those in the text are reported in the Internet appendix to BCS (2016).

Equilibrium requires that the demand for the asset must equal its market value, which in turn must equal its expected payoff divided by its gross expected return:

$$\alpha_j W_j = V_j = \frac{\overline{X}_j}{1 + \overline{R}_j}. \tag{10.31}$$

Combining (10.30) and (10.31), the expected return on the asset must satisfy

$$(1 + \overline{R}_j)(\overline{R}_j - R_f) = \frac{\gamma_j \sigma_j^2 \overline{X}_j}{W_j}. \tag{10.32}$$

The left-hand side of equation (10.32) is a quadratic increasing function of $\overline{R}_j$. Hence, (10.32) tells us that the expected return on asset j is increasing in the risk aversion of its investors γ_j, the total variance of the asset's log return σ_j^2, the total expected payoff on the asset $\overline{X}_j$ (that determines the amount that must be held, or the "supply" of the asset), and the reciprocal of the wealth of the investor base W_j. The expected return increases less than linearly in these factors because as the expected return goes up, the desired portfolio share increases, and in addition the portfolio share that is required to equate demand and supply decreases because the value of the asset declines.[15]

Equation (10.32) treats the wealth of undiversified investors as exogenous. An alternative perspective in the context of a dynamic model is that these investors are already invested in asset j, so their wealth depends on the value of the asset. A particularly simple special case results from the assumption that undiversified investors are fully invested in the asset, so $\alpha_j = 1$ and $W_j = V_j$. In this case equation (10.30) can immediately be solved to yield

$$\overline{R}_j - R_f = \gamma_j \sigma_j^2. \tag{10.33}$$

This simple example demonstrates three important properties that also hold in more sophisticated models. First, because undiversified investors care about the total variance of an asset's return and not just its covariance with a broader index, idiosyncratic volatility is positively related to expected return. Merton (1987) shows that this is true even if investors can also hold a diversified index along with a subset of available risky assets. While this property seems to hold for asset classes such as mortgage-backed securities (Gabaix, Krishnamurthy, and Vigneron 2007), it does not seem to apply at the level of individual stocks. Ang et al. (2006) find that idiosyncratically volatile stocks tend to have anomalously low returns; this phenomenon may be related to disagreement and short-sales constraints as in the model of Harrison and Kreps (1978) discussed in section 11.4.2.

Second, the expected return on an asset depends on the supply of the asset in relation to the wealth and risk aversion of the investor base. When supply increases, asset prices fall and expected returns increase.[16] In other words, demand curves for assets and

---

[15]It is important in this analysis that the variance of the log return enters the portfolio choice formula (10.30). A decline in the value of the asset, with a fixed variance of terminal payoff, causes the variance of the simple return to increase but leaves the variance of the log return unchanged. This is what makes it possible to assume an exogenous variance σ_j^2.

[16]This could also be true in a diversified model to the extent that a supply increase for an individual asset alters the composition of the market portfolio and hence the covariance of the asset with the market portfolio. However, the price effect is much stronger in a model with undiversified investors, particularly if the wealth of the investor base increases with the price of the asset as in the special case of equation (10.33). We will return to this point when discussing liquidity spirals in section 12.3.4 of Chapter 12.

asset classes held by undiversified investors slope downward. This property has been verified by studying the responses of individual stocks to inclusion in indexes that are held by specialized investors such as index funds (Harris and Gurel 1986, Shleifer 1986). Krishnamurthy and Vissing-Jørgensen (2011, 2012) and Greenwood and Vayanos (2014) have recently argued that it also applies to the market for US Treasury bonds. Duffie (2010) builds a dynamic model of "slow-moving capital," in which short-term price responses to supply shocks are dampened by the anticipation of capital inflows, in other words, expected future increases in the wealth of specialized investors.

Third, an increase in portfolio diversification can lower expected returns and increase prices on all risky assets. Consider a model of the sort discussed in section 2.2.4, where a very large number of identical assets have equal variances σ^2 and equal correlations ρ with all other assets. Then a shift from undiversified investing to fully diversified investing reduces total risk at the portfolio level from σ^2 to $\rho\sigma^2$. In a model where all wealth is initially held in the set of risky assets, and where all investors have the same risk aversion γ, equation (10.33) implies that the expected returns on all assets decline by $(1-\rho)\gamma\sigma^2$. This drives up the value of risky assets as shown in equation (10.31). Such an effect may have contributed to a decline in the equity premium during the 20th century as index funds and other vehicles for low-cost diversified investing were introduced and popularized.

10.4 Responses to Changing Market Conditions

The behaviors we discussed in sections 10.2 and 10.3 are static and can be described using simple single-period models. However, the household finance literature has also identified many dynamic behaviors. We briefly summarize some of the more important ones in this section and draw implications for asset pricing.

Portfolio Inertia and Return Extrapolation

Portfolio inertia is the tendency to allow portfolio weights to drift with returns, without actively rebalancing toward a desired asset allocation. This appears to be particularly important in retirement savings accounts, where many participants accept a default allocation of contributions and rarely change it or rebalance their accumulated asset holdings (Madrian and Shea 2001, Agnew, Balduzzi, and Sunden 2003). Portfolio inertia allows realized returns on risky assets to influence asset allocation when the initial risky share is neither zero nor one. With a zero investment in risky assets, risky returns affect neither wealth nor the risky share; with full investment in risky assets, risky returns have a large effect on wealth but no effect on the risky share; with an initial risky share between zero and one, risky returns move the risky share in the same direction. Hence, in the presence of inertia the change in the risky share tends to be hump shaped in the initial risky share when risky returns exceed the riskless interest rate, and U-shaped otherwise.

A failure to rebalance need not indicate portfolio inertia if the desired risky share moves with the realized risky return. As a particularly important example, in general equilibrium with a representative agent and an exogenous endowment of risky assets, the risky share must always equal the market value of risky assets as a fraction of total wealth: prices always adjust to make the agent content to hold this risky share. To address this issue, Calvet, Campbell, and Sodini (CCS 2009) exploit the underdiversification of

Swedish investors discussed in the previous section. They show that investors who experience high idiosyncratic returns tend to sell risky assets to move their risky shares about halfway back to the initial level, while investors who experience low idiosyncratic returns do the opposite. They also show that financially sophisticated households, with greater wealth, income, and education, tend to rebalance more aggressively.

Failure to rebalance may also result from irrational extrapolation of past returns. It is rational to form return expectations using all the historical data that are available. However, it appears that in many cases, people rely on their own much more limited and specific experiences to form their beliefs. One type of evidence shows that people react to experiences shared within their cohort, for example, of stock returns and inflation (Malmendier and Nagel, 2011, 2016). Another type of evidence looks at idiosyncratic experiences that vary cross-sectionally within a cohort. For example, Choi et al. (2009) show that households save more in response to high idiosyncratic returns in their 401(k) accounts, consistent with the idea that they extrapolate these returns into the future, and Anagol, Balasubramaniam, and Ramadorai (2016) report that random allocations of newly issued Indian stocks positively affect the subsequent willingness of investors to hold the stocks, even among those who trade frequently. A related strand of the behavioral finance literature, for example, Barberis et al. (2015), argues that investors tend to extrapolate aggregate returns that have been realized over the recent past.

Inertia and return extrapolation can amplify the asset pricing effects of portfolio underdiversification discussed in the previous section. If undiversified investors have inertia or extrapolate returns, then an increase in the supply of a risky asset that lowers its price and increases its rationally expected return will induce less buying than would be the case with rational investors; hence, the effects of supply on price and expected return will be greater.

Mortgage Refinancing Inertia

Some financial instruments give households options that can add considerable value if properly exercised. The leading example is the standard US fixed-rate mortgage, which can be refinanced at relatively low cost, generating important savings when interest rates decline. Campbell (2006) observes that many US households fail to refinance even at interest savings that are far above both the optimal thresholds calculated by academics (Agarwal, Driscoll, and Laibson 2013) and the rules of thumb commonly used by financial advisers. In the US, some of this behavior could be explained by unmeasured constraints, but Andersen et al. (2015) show that the same is true in Denmark, where refinancing is always possible even for households with negative home equity or a poor credit score. Similarly, Johnson, Meier, and Toubia (2015) and Keys, Pope, and Pope (2016) document household failures to respond to prequalified refinancing offers.

This "refinancing inertia" has asset pricing implications because, in a competitive mortgage market, the extra payments made by households that fail to refinance are passed on to consumers in the form of lower up-front mortgage rates. This also implies that in equilibrium nonrefinancers subsidize refinancers, which is troubling to the extent that refinancers tend to be better educated and more sophisticated households.

Gabaix and Laibson (2006) have argued that cross-subsidization of this sort can block socially valuable financial innovation. To understand this possibility, consider a simple example: a market in which a fraction λ of the population is naive (denoted by N) and the remainder is sophisticated (S). An existing mortgage contract can be provided at an average cost per user of C_0, but sophisticated households pay a lower cost than naive households because there is a refinancing option that only sophisticated households exercise. In competitive equilibrium with full participation by both groups, their costs must be related by

$$\lambda C_{0N} + (1 - \lambda) C_{0S} = C_0. \tag{10.34}$$

Write x for the cross-subsidy from the naive to the sophisticated: $x = C_{0N} - C_{0S}$. Then

$$C_{0S} = C_0 - \lambda x. \tag{10.35}$$

The mortgage costs of sophisticated households fall with the fraction of naive households and the size of the cross-subsidy.

Now suppose that a new mortgage contract is invented that provides the same benefits at a lower cost $C_1 = C_0 - g$ that is the same for both types of households. The new contract might be, for example, an automatically refinancing mortgage that reduces the costs of refinancing or an inflation-indexed mortgage that reduces the need to refinance. Assume that the new contract is made available initially to a negligible fraction of the population, so that its introduction does not perturb the pricing of the existing contract. In the simplest setting only sophisticated households can understand the new product, but all households can be reached costlessly. Sophisticated households that opt for the new product gain directly from its lower cost but lose indirectly by giving up the cross-subsidy. They therefore switch to the new product only if it offers a social gain—a cost saving—larger than the per capita cross-subsidy from naive households using the existing product:

$$g > \lambda x. \tag{10.36}$$

New products with smaller social gains will not be adopted.

Gabaix and Laibson also argue that even if unsophisticated households can be educated about the benefits of a new product, it may not be worthwhile for competitive providers of the new product to pay even modest costs to provide such education. As an informal exercise, you are asked to lay out the reasoning behind this argument.

Intensive Trading and the Disposition Effect

By contrast with the evidence on portfolio inertia in retirement accounts, data from a US discount brokerage house show that individual investors who have brokerage accounts often trade intensively but have poor overall performance (Odean 1999, Barber and Odean 2000). Grinblatt and Keloharju (2000) and Barber et al. (2009) report similar results for individual investors in Finland and Taiwan. An interesting recent literature explores cross-sectional variation in both trading intensity and performance. Men trade more intensively than women, with negative effects on their performance (Barber and Odean 2001). Finnish investors with overconfident and sensation-seeking personalities tend to trade more intensively (Grinblatt and Keloharju 2009), while those with high IQ scores tend to perform better (Grinblatt, Keloharju, and Linnainmaa 2012). Seru, Shumway, and Stoffman (2010) and Linnainmaa (2011) find that good performance predicts subsequent trading intensity, a result that is consistent with several interpretations: that investors learn rationally about their trading skill, that they extrapolate their personal trading experience, or that they become overconfident after good performance.

Shefrin and Statman (1985) first described the "disposition effect," a tendency of investors to sell winning positions and hold losing positions. Odean (1998) uses administrative data on discount brokerage customers to show that the propensity to realize gains is substantially greater than the propensity to realize losses, except in December when tax-loss selling reverses the relationship. Selling winners can be a way to restore diversification to a portfolio that has become excessively concentrated, but the tendency to hold losers is hard to rationalize, both because it is tax inefficient and because it lowers pretax returns to the extent that stocks display momentum (Odean 1998, Grinblatt and Keloharju 2000).

Subsequent research has enriched our understanding of this effect. Ben-David and Hirshleifer (2012) find that the probability a stock is sold is asymmetrically V-shaped in the sale price relative to the purchase price, with the lowest probability for stocks trading at the original purchase price and even higher probability for large gains than for large losses. The disposition effect appears to be weaker among financially sophisticated investors (Dhar and Zhu 2006, CCS 2009) and those with higher IQ scores (Grinblatt, Keloharju, and Linnainmaa 2012). Importantly, there appears to be a reverse disposition effect for mutual funds (CCS 2009, Chang, Solomon, and Westerfield 2016), consistent with the view that investors judge fund managers on their performance and sell when fund results are poor.

A leading explanation of the disposition effect is that investors have the prospect-theory preferences of Kahneman and Tversky (1979), making them risk-averse in the domain of gains but risk-seeking in the domain of losses and that they frame gains and losses narrowly for each stock rather than at the portfolio level. Barberis and Xiong (2009) undertake a careful theoretical analysis of this explanation.

Grinblatt and Han (2005) and Frazzini (2006) argue that the disposition effect has implications for asset pricing. Specifically, good news about a stock causes the price to move upward, but this triggers sales that slow the upward price adjustment. Conversely, bad news causes a price decline that inhibits selling and slows downward price adjustment. Thus, if the disposition effect is sufficiently pervasive it can help to explain momentum in individual stock returns. Problem 10.2 asks you to explore the formalization of this idea presented by Grinblatt and Han.

10.5 Policy Responses

Many of the behaviors discussed in this chapter—nonparticipation, underdiversification, holding stocks that are highly correlated with labor income, portfolio and refinancing inertia, and the disposition effect—are hard to reconcile with rational optimizing models. This is true even after one takes into account realistic features of household financial problems such as labor income risk, borrowing constraints, and taxation. These behaviors also appear to be more common among less financially sophisticated and cognitively skilled investors. For both these reasons, the household finance literature has increasingly viewed them as mistakes (Campbell 2006) that may justify public policy responses.

The literature on consumer financial regulation is enormous and largely beyond the scope of this book. Recent reviews include Campbell et al. (2011) and Campbell (2016). The existence of investment mistakes provides a new set of justifications for intervention in markets, distinct from classic justifications such as the externalities discussed in Chapter 11. Policies may include financial education (Hastings, Madrian, and Skimmy-horn 2013, Lusardi and Mitchell 2014), disclosures, "nudges" that affect the decisions of behavioral agents while having negligible impact on rational agents (Thaler and Sunstein 2008), and regulation that imposes costs on financial products that are often mistakenly used, reducing mistakes by behavioral agents but imposing costs on rational agents. Problem 10.3 invites you to analyze a stylized model of this last type of financial regulation.

10.6 Solutions and Further Problems

As a first informal exercise, you were asked to relate the analysis of income and fixed commitments to the investment problem of Harvard University. During the late 1990s there was a large increase in the share of Harvard's budget supported by the endowment, as opposed to tuition or sponsored research funding, and in the mid-2000s the university made large fixed spending commitments. On a net basis, therefore, the university's nonendowment sources of income fell relative to its endowment income. Under the assumption that nonendowment income is safer than endowment income, this should have implied a more conservative investment strategy for the endowment. However, Harvard and other wealthy private universities did not make such an adjustment and were substantially exposed to investment risk during the market downturn of 2008–2009.

As a second informal exercise, you were asked to explain why, in the Gabaix and Laibson (2006) model of shrouded equilibrium, it might not be worthwhile for competitive providers of an innovative financial product to educate the unsophisticated consumers who would benefit from the product. The explanation is that once unsophisticated consumers are educated, they are likely to understand the cross-subsidy available in the existing product. Instead of buying the new product, they will simply reduce the cost of the existing product by managing it better. Education is effective in supporting a new product only if enough unsophisticated consumers can be educated to reduce the equilibrium cross-subsidy, and this requires a large educational effort relative to the size of the market.

Problem 10.1 The Risks of Adjustable-Rate and Fixed-Rate Mortgages

Consider a simplified model of mortgage choice with three dates, 0, 1, and 2. At date 0, a household buys a house of value M and finances it with a mortgage of equal value (so the loan-to-value ratio is 100%). At date 1, the household pays interest on the mortgage. At date 2, the household sells the house and repays the mortgage with interest. The household also receives a fixed income Y and chooses nonhousing consumption C at each date.

Mortgage contracts are specified in nominal terms, so the debt M is nominal. The house, however, is a real asset whose nominal value grows with inflation. The riskfree real interest rate is constant at r, but inflation can take one of two values, low or high, and uncertainty about inflation is resolved between dates 0 and 1. Thus, gross inflation between date 0 and date 1 is either $(1 + \pi_L)$ or $(1 + \pi_H)$, and cumulative gross inflation between dates 0 and 2 is either $(1+\pi_L)^2$ or $(1+\pi_H)^2$. This structure captures the historical tendency for inflation movements to be highly persistent.

The household can choose between two standard mortgage contracts. An adjustable-rate mortgage (ARM) requires nominal payments of $R_{AH}M$ at date 1 and $(1 + R_{AH})M$

at date 2 if inflation is high, and $R_{AL}M$ at date 1 and $(1 + R_{AL})M$ at date 2 if inflation is low. A fixed-rate mortgage (FRM) requires a nominal payment of $R_F M$ at date 1, and a nominal payment of $(1 + R_F)M$ at date 2. The fixed mortgage rate R_F is set at date 0, before inflation is observed.[17]

For simplicity we assume that there is no possibility of default and that lenders are risk-neutral so interest rates on both types of mortgages are set to equate the expected present value of real payments with the mortgage principal M.

(a) *ARM properties.*
  (i) Solve for the interest rates R_{AH} and R_{AL}.

  (ii) Write an expression for the required real payment on an ARM in period 1 as a function of M, r, and π_i. Show that this payment is increasing in the inflation rate π_i.

  (iii) Write an expression for the required real payment on an ARM in period 2 as a function of M, r, and π_i. Show that this payment is decreasing in the inflation rate.

  (iv) Show that the sum of these payments, discounted at the real interest rate r, does not depend on the inflation rate and always equals M.

(b) *FRM properties.*
  (i) Taking as given the FRM rate R_F, write an expression for the required real payment on an FRM in period 1 as a function of M, π_i, and R_F. Show that this payment is decreasing in the inflation rate π_i.

  (ii) Write an expression for the required real payment on an FRM in period 2 as a function of M, π_i, and R_F. Show that this payment is also decreasing in the inflation rate and therefore that the sum of all payments, discounted at the real interest rate r, is decreasing in the inflation rate.

(c) *Mortgage choice by unconstrained households.* Use your results from parts (a) and (b) to show that risk-averse households that are freely able to borrow and lend between periods 1 and 2 will always prefer ARMs unless the FRM rate is lower than the rate that equates the expected present value of mortgage payments across ARMs and FRMs. Explain the intuition for this result.

(d) *Mortgage choice by constrained households.* Now consider a risk-averse household that is borrowing-constrained in periods 1 and 2. In each of these periods, the household's consumption equals income less required mortgage payments.
  (i) Write expressions for consumption in periods 1 and 2 if the household has an ARM, and if the household has an FRM.

  (ii) Use a Taylor approximation around the average inflation rate to show that for small inflation volatility σ_π, the standard deviation of consumption in period 1 is, $M\sigma_\pi/(1 + \pi)^2$ for a household with an ARM, and only R_F times as large for a household with an FRM. Explain the intuition for this result.

---

[17]These mortgages do not correspond exactly to real-world mortgages, because they repay principal in one lump sum at maturity (like Treasury bonds), rather than amortizing the debt to produce level payments over the life of the mortgage. Level-payment mortgages, however, repay principal slowly at first and more rapidly later, and the assumptions of the model capture this pattern within a simplified two-period structure.

    (iii) Repeat this calculation for the standard deviation of consumption in period 2. Which type of mortgage implies greater consumption volatility in period 2? Explain.

    (iv) Using the above results, explain why a risk-averse borrowing-constrained household might prefer an FRM to an ARM.

(e) *Refinanceable FRMs.* FRMs in the US are refinanceable. We now consider the implications of allowing a household with an FRM in this model to repay the mortgage at nominal face value in period 1 and take out an ARM between periods 1 and 2.

    (i) Taking the refinanceable FRM rate R_{RF} as given, what are the required payments in periods 1 and 2 for a household with a refinanceable FRM, if inflation is low and if inflation is high?

    (ii) Show that if lenders are risk-neutral and equate the expected present value of all payments across mortgage types, then the refinanceable FRM has higher expected payments in period 1 than an ARM, and lower expected payments in period 2.

    (iii) Use the above results to argue that a risk-neutral household that is borrowing-constrained in period 1 will prefer an ARM, but a sufficiently risk-averse borrowing-constrained household will prefer an FRM.

(f) *Alternative mortgages.* Discuss alternative forms of mortgage contracts that would be preferable for risk-averse borrowers than either standard ARMs or FRMs.

Note: This problem is based on Campbell (2006).

Problem 10.2 The Disposition Effect and Momentum

In a market for an individual stock, a fraction μ of investors are subject to the disposition effect while the remaining investors are rational. The number of shares demanded by the rational investors takes the linear form

$$D_t^{RAT} = 1 + b(F_t - P_t), \tag{10.37}$$

where F_t is the stock's fundamental value and P_t is its price. The number of shares demanded by the disposition-effect investors is

$$D_t^{DISP} = 1 + b[(F_t - P_t) + \lambda(R_t - P_t)], \tag{10.38}$$

where R_t is a reference price and λ is positive. The disposition effect as formalized in (10.38) reduces demand for "winners" whose price is above the reference price and increases demand for "losers" whose price is below the reference price.

  (a) Assume that the supply of the stock is fixed at one unit. Equate supply and demand to show that the equilibrium price must satisfy

$$P_t = wF_t + (1 - w)R_t, \tag{10.39}$$

for a fixed parameter w. Show that w does not depend on b, and provide intuition for this result. Write a formula relating w to μ and λ, and again provide intuition.

(b) Now assume that fundamental value follows a random walk:

$$F_{t+1} = F_t + \varepsilon_{t+1},\qquad(10.40)$$

while the reference price adjusts gradually to the actual price:

$$R_{t+1} = vP_t + (1-v)R_t.\qquad(10.41)$$

How might the parameter v be related to the trading volume in the stock given that microeconomic studies show that an individual investor's purchase price appears to act as a reference price for the investor?

(c) Derive an expression relating the change in the stock price to current and lagged innovations in fundamental value ε_{t+1}. Show that lagged innovations have a positive effect on price changes whenever w is less than one. Discuss the effect of v on price dynamics. What testable implications does this model have relative to other possible explanations for momentum in stock returns?

Note: This problem is based on Grinblatt and Han (2005).

Problem 10.3 Consumer Financial Regulation

This question asks you to analyze a simple model that formalizes the case for consumer financial regulation. The model assumes that a fraction b of consumers are "behavioral" agents who make mistakes in using financial products, while the remaining consumers are rational. If a regulator cannot affect the choices of behavioral agents without distorting the choices of rational agents, regulation involves a tradeoff between benefits to behavioral agents and costs to rational agents.

Specifically, there are two financial products, A and B. Product A delivers utility normalized to zero for all consumers: $U_A = 0$. Product B is correctly preferred by some consumers but mistakenly chosen by others.

A continuum of agents, with mass normalized to one, believe that they receive nonnegative utility $U_B = u$ from product B.[18] u is uniformly distributed across agents from 0 to an upper bound h, and each agent knows her own value of u. At each level of u, a fraction b of the agents are behavioral agents who actually receive lower utility from the product, $U_B = u - 1$. The remaining fraction $(1 - b)$ of the agents are rational and receive utility u as they expect.

(a) *Regulatory charge.* Suppose that a paternalistic regulator imposes a charge c on product B, inducing all agents with $u \le c$ to switch to product A. The revenue from the charge is rebated to agents in a lump sum. The regulator maximizes the integral of true utility (not self-perceived utility) across all agents. You may assume that $c \le h$.

(i) Show that social welfare can be written as

$$W(c) = \left(1 - \frac{c}{h}\right)\left[\left(\frac{h+c}{2}\right) - b\right].$$

---

[18]There can also be agents who prefer product A in the absence of regulation, but these agents are unaffected by regulation and can be dropped from further consideration.

(ii) Use this to show that a zero charge is never optimal unless all agents are rational.

(iii) What is the optimal charge c and by what proportion does it shrink the market for product B? Explain intuitively how the optimal charge and the shrinkage of the market depend on the parameters b and h.

(b) *Regulatory charge with deadweight cost.* Now suppose that the regulatory charge imposes deadweight cost on the financial system. A fraction α of the regulatory charge cannot be rebated.

(i) Show that social welfare can be written as

$$W(c) = \left(1 - \frac{c}{h}\right)\left[\left(\frac{h+c}{2}\right) - b - \alpha c\right].$$

(ii) State conditions for the problem to be convex. (Hint: check the second derivative of the social welfare function.) Under these conditions, what is the optimal charge c? How does it depend on the parameters b, h, and α? For what parameter values is it larger or smaller than in part (a)? Explain.

(iii) Discuss optimal policy if the problem is not convex.

(c) *Regulatory charge with mistake mitigation.* Now assume that product B is not inherently unsuitable for behavioral consumers, and the regulatory charge can reduce the utility loss to these consumers from 1 to $1 - \theta c$ for $c \leq 1/\theta$.

(i) Show that the social welfare function takes the same form as in part (b) but replacing the parameter α with $\alpha^* = \alpha - b\theta$.

(ii) In this case, α^* can be negative. Show that if it is, then the effect of h on the optimal regulatory charge has the opposite sign from the one derived in part (b). Explain.

Note: This problem is based on Campbell (2016).

11

Risksharing and Speculation

EMPIRICAL TESTS OF perfect risksharing—the hypothesis that marginal utilities of different investors are perfectly correlated—unsurprisingly tend to reject it as discussed in section 4.1.6. While considerable risksharing does seem to occur, particularly with respect to smaller shocks and within smaller groups of people, risksharing is far from perfect. What then are the frictions that limit risksharing? And what are the implications for asset price behavior and for the welfare of agents in the economy?

We have already discussed several possible answers to these questions. Section 8.4.2 reviewed models in which trade between countries is costly, so the real exchange rate (the relative price of goods in one country versus another) adjusts in response to local fluctuations in the supply of goods. In such models, even if financial markets are complete the allocation of resources cannot eliminate local risks. Chapter 10 discussed the possibility that some people are exogenously excluded from asset market participation, choose not to participate, or do not optimally exploit the risksharing opportunities that they have. In this chapter we review several other limitations on risksharing that have stimulated important research in asset pricing.

A first possibility, discussed in section 11.1, is that markets are exogenously incomplete, so not all risks can be traded, but people take optimal and unrestricted positions in the assets that exist. The existence of untraded risks influences both the pricing of those assets that do exist and the welfare properties of the competitive market equilibrium. Section 11.1.1 discusses the asset pricing implications of untraded risks, following classic work of Grossman and Shiller (1982) and Constantinides and Duffie (1996). Next we discuss the welfare properties of equilibrium with incomplete markets. In a simple model with a single consumption good (section 11.1.2), competitive equilibrium is Pareto optimal conditional on the assets that exist, but different sets of traded assets imply different levels of social welfare (Athanasoulis and Shiller 2000). In a general model with incomplete markets and multiple goods (section 11.1.3), it is not necessarily the case that competitive equilibrium is Pareto optimal conditional on the assets that exist; recent research seeks to develop this point in a more concrete fashion.

A second limitation on risksharing arises when economic agents have private information about their skills or tastes, which limits the potential for insurance. This is the subject of the "new dynamic public finance" literature, and section 11.2 briefly discusses its asset pricing implications following Rogerson (1985), Golosov, Kocherlakota, and Tsyvinski (2003), and Kocherlakota and Pistaferri (2009).

A third reason for incomplete risksharing is that agents have the ability to default, and the punishments for doing so are insufficient to deter default if the incentives are large enough. To forestall default, people are prevented from issuing more than a certain quantity of contingent claims (Kehoe and Levine 1993, Alvarez and Jermann 2000, Chien and Lustig 2010). Section 11.3 reviews models where default is punished by exclusion from financial markets (section 11.3.1) or by seizure of collateral (section 11.3.2).

A fourth possibility, discussed in section 11.4, is that investors have heterogeneous beliefs and speculate against one another. Heterogeneous beliefs were discussed in Chapter 4 in the context of complete markets, but they have particularly interesting implications when not all assets are traded or when short positions and borrowing are restricted. Section 11.4.1 reviews models of trading between rational investors and noise traders with exogenous demands for risky assets, following Shiller (1984) and De Long et al. (1990a); section 11.4.2 discusses speculation with exogenous short-sales constraints following Harrison and Kreps (1978) and Scheinkman and Xiong (2003); and section 11.4.3 presents models with endogenous leverage constraints following Geanakoplos (2009) and Simsek (2013a).

11.1 Incomplete Markets

11.1.1 Asset Pricing with Uninsurable Income Risk

Grossman-Shiller: Uninsurable Risk Does Not Affect Risk Premia

A classic argument of Grossman and Shiller (1982) implies that uninsurable income risk should not affect risk premia, even if it causes idiosyncratic variation in investors' consumption. Grossman and Shiller approximate the first-order condition of an individual investor k, who compares two alternative assets with returns $R_{i,t+1}$ and $R_{j,t+1}$, as

$$
\begin{aligned}
0 &= E_t\left[(R_{i,t+1} - R_{j,t+1})\frac{u'(C_{k,t+1})}{u'(C_{kt})}\right] \\
&\approx E_t\left[(R_{i,t+1} - R_{j,t+1})\frac{u'(C_{k,t}) + (C_{k,t+1} - C_{kt})u''(C_{kt})}{u'(C_{kt})}\right] \\
&= E_t\left[(R_{i,t+1} - R_{j,t+1})(1 - A_{kt}\Delta C_{k,t+1}\right],
\end{aligned} \tag{11.1}
$$

where A_{kt} is investor k's absolute risk aversion, which can vary over time and with state variables such as the investor's wealth. This expression holds exactly when consumption and asset prices follow diffusion processes in continuous time.

Rearranging (11.1), we have

$$
\frac{1}{A_{kt}}E_t(R_{i,t+1} - R_{j,t+1}) = E_t\left[(R_{i,t+1} - R_{j,t+1})\Delta C_{k,t+1}\right]. \tag{11.2}
$$

Adding up across investors and rearranging terms,

$$
E_t(R_{i,t+1} - R_{j,t+1}) = \left(\sum_k \frac{1}{A_{kt}}\right)^{-1} E_t\left[(R_{i,t+1} - R_{j,t+1})\Delta C_{t+1}\right], \tag{11.3}
$$

where $\Delta C_{t+1} = \sum_k \Delta C_{k,t+1}$. This is an aggregate consumption-based asset pricing model, using the harmonic mean of individual investors' absolute risk aversion coefficients at time t. Only the covariance with aggregate consumption matters for asset pricing, just as would be the case if all investors were identical.

This result appears to leave no room for uninsurable income risk to affect the relative returns on different assets (although it does allow uninsurable risk to affect the level of all returns through the riskless interest rate).

Constantinides-Duffie: Yes It Does
Constantinides and Duffie (1996) present an alternative framework and reach a very different conclusion. They consider an economy in which individual investors k have different consumption levels C_{kt}. The cross-sectional distribution of individual consumption is lognormal, and the change from time t to time $t + 1$ in individual log consumption is cross-sectionally uncorrelated with the level of individual log consumption at time t. This implies that the economy has no steady-state cross-sectional distribution, because shocks continually increase the cross-sectional variance of log consumption. All investors have the same power utility function with time discount factor δ and coefficient of relative risk aversion γ.

In this economy each investor's own intertemporal marginal rate of substitution is a valid stochastic discount factor. Hence, the cross-sectional average of investors' intertemporal marginal rates of substitution is a valid stochastic discount factor. Write this as

$$M_{t+1}^* \equiv \delta \mathrm{E}_{t+1}^* \left[\left(\frac{C_{k,t+1}}{C_{kt}} \right)^{-\gamma} \right], \tag{11.4}$$

where E_t^* denotes a cross-sectional expectation: for any X_{kt},

$$\mathrm{E}_t^* X_{kt} = \lim_{K \to \infty} (1/K) \sum_{k=1}^K X_{kt}. \tag{11.5}$$

$\mathrm{E}_t^* X_{kt}$ can vary over time and need not be lognormally distributed conditional on past information.

Cross-sectional lognormality of consumption growth implies that the log SDF, $m_{t+1}^* \equiv \log(M_{t+1}^*)$, satisfies

$$m_{t+1}^* = \log(\delta) - \gamma \, \mathrm{E}_{t+1}^* \Delta c_{k,t+1} + \left(\frac{\gamma^2}{2} \right) \mathrm{Var}_{t+1}^* \Delta c_{k,t+1}, \tag{11.6}$$

where Var_t^* is defined by

$$\mathrm{Var}_t^* X_{kt} = \lim_{K \to \infty} (1/K) \sum_{k=1}^K (X_{kt} - \mathrm{E}_t^* X_{kt})^2. \tag{11.7}$$

An economist who knows the underlying preference parameters of investors, but does not understand the heterogeneity in this economy, might attempt to construct a representative-agent stochastic discount factor, M_{t+1}^{RA}, using aggregate consumption as in the models of Chapter 6:

$$M_{t+1}^{RA} \equiv \delta \left(\frac{\mathrm{E}_{t+1}^*[C_{k,t+1}]}{\mathrm{E}_t^*[C_{kt}]} \right)^{-\gamma}. \tag{11.8}$$

The log of this incorrectly specified or "false" SDF satisfies

$$m_{t+1}^{RA} = \log(\delta) - \gamma \, \mathrm{E}_{t+1}^* \Delta c_{k,t+1} - \left(\frac{\gamma}{2} \right) [\mathrm{Var}_{t+1}^* c_{k,t+1} - \mathrm{Var}_t^* c_{kt}]$$

$$= \log(\delta) - \gamma \, \mathrm{E}_{t+1}^* \Delta c_{k,t+1} - \left(\frac{\gamma}{2} \right) [\mathrm{Var}_{t+1}^* \Delta c_{k,t+1}], \tag{11.9}$$

where the second equality follows from $c_{k,t+1} = c_{kt} + \Delta c_{k,t+1}$ and the fact that $\Delta c_{k,t+1}$ is cross-sectionally uncorrelated with c_{kt}.

The difference between the true and false log SDF is

$$m_{t+1}^* - m_{t+1}^{RA} = \frac{\gamma \, (\gamma + 1)}{2} \mathrm{Var}_{t+1}^* \Delta c_{k,t+1}. \tag{11.10}$$

The time series of this difference can have a nonzero mean, helping to explain the riskfree rate puzzle, and a nonzero variance, helping to explain the equity premium puzzle. Specifically, if the cross-sectional variance of log consumption growth is negatively correlated with the level of aggregate consumption, so that idiosyncratic risk increases in economic downturns, then the true stochastic discount factor m_{t+1}^* will be more strongly countercyclical than the representative-agent stochastic discount factor constructed using the same preference parameters. This means that a representative-agent asset pricing model will underpredict the risk premia on procyclical assets like stocks, even if it correctly specifies the level of risk aversion. Problem 11.1 asks you to explore this effect in a simple example based on Mankiw (1986).

Does It Matter Empirically?
An important unresolved question is whether the heterogeneity we can measure has the characteristics that are needed to help resolve the asset pricing puzzles. In the Constantinides-Duffie model the heterogeneity must be large to have important effects on the stochastic discount factor; a cross-sectional standard deviation of log consumption growth of 20%, for example, is a cross-sectional variance of only 0.04, and it is variation in this number over time that is needed to explain the equity premium puzzle. Also, the effect of heterogeneity is strongly increasing in risk aversion since $\mathrm{Var}_{t+1}^* \Delta c_{k,t+1}$ is multiplied by $\gamma \, (\gamma + 1)/2$ in (11.10). This implies that heterogeneity is complementary to high risk aversion as an explanation for the equity premium puzzle.

Any model in which individual consumption moves gradually over time will tend to imply small effects of idiosyncratic risk. To understand this, recall the Grossman and Shiller (1982) result that uninsurable risk has no effect on risk premia in a continuous-time diffusion model. To reconcile Grossman-Shiller with Constantinides-Duffie, note that in a diffusion model (or in Grossman and Shiller's approximation) the cross-sectional variance of consumption is locally deterministic—heuristically, $\mathrm{Var}_{t+1}^* \Delta c_{k,t+1}$ in (11.10) is known at time t—and hence the false SDF M_{t+1}^{RA} correctly prices risk premia. In a discrete-time model like the one considered by Constantinides and Duffie, the cross-sectional variance of consumption can change randomly from one period to the next, but with gradual movements in individual consumption these changes are likely to be small. This limits the effects of uninsurable risk on risk premia.

To get around this problem, recent papers by Schmidt (2016) and Constantinides and Ghosh (2017) emphasize idiosyncratic rare disasters that make the distributions of individual income and consumption fat-tailed and negatively skewed and that are more likely to occur in bad states for the aggregate economy. These papers obtain larger effects of idiosyncratic risk than did earlier contributions by Heaton and Lucas (1996) and Lettau (2002).

The effects of heterogeneity can be increased if there are other frictions that limit borrowing or participation in risky asset markets. Heaton and Lucas (1996) and Krusell and Smith (1997) find that borrowing constraints or large costs of trading equities are needed to explain the equity premium. Constantinides, Donaldson, and Mehra (2002) focus on heterogeneity across generations. In their stylized overlapping generations model discussed in section 10.1.3, young agents have the strongest desire to hold equities because they have the largest ratio of labor income to financial wealth. If these agents are prevented from borrowing to buy equities, the equilibrium equity premium can be large. Failures of some agents to participate in risky asset markets, discussed in section 10.2, can also strengthen the effect of uninsurable idiosyncratic risk on risk premia as emphasized by Brav, Constantinides, and Geczy (2007).

11.1.2 Market Design with Incomplete Markets

Even if market incompleteness has no effect on the pricing of assets, it will affect social welfare. Athanasoulis and Shiller (AS 2000) consider the problem of designing a limited number of financial assets to maximize social welfare, subject to a constraint on the total number of assets that can be created. In their model, there is a single consumption good that allows them to ignore the failure of optimality of competitive equilibrium that can arise in a multiple-good model with incomplete markets (discussed in the next subsection 11.1.3).

The AS economy has J agents, each exogenously receiving a random endowment x_j, and $N \leq J$ financial assets in zero net supply. These assets take the form of futures contracts, with payments to the long side that can depend on the entire vector x of random endowments and a payment to the short side that is independent of the state. Without loss of generality, the payments to the long side are normalized to have mean zero and unit variance.

AS assume that agents have mean-variance utility with possibly heterogeneous absolute risk aversion γ_j. Each agent's optimal asset position has a speculative component, related to expected returns divided by risk and risk aversion, and a hedging component, related to the covariance of asset returns with the agent's endowment. The assumption of mean-variance utility implies that a version of the CAPM holds in this economy, so all assets can be priced by their covariance with the market portfolio or "world share" that pays the sum of all endowments. This is true whether or not the world share actually exists in the economy.

The novelty of the AS analysis is to write down social welfare, defined as the equally weighted sum of all agents' utilities, and to solve the social planner's problem of designing assets to maximize social welfare, subject to a constraint on the number of assets that can exist. The results reflect a tradeoff between two goals. On the one hand, if all agents have the same risk aversion, then the optimal assets enable agents to insure one another against idiosyncratic endowment fluctuations. In this case, the optimal assets have loadings on individual agents' endowments that are orthogonal to the loadings of the world share (which are all equal to one because the world share pays the sum of all endowments).[1] On the other hand, if agents have heterogeneous risk aversion, then assets whose loadings are correlated with the world share become a useful means for risk-tolerant agents to insure risk-averse agents against aggregate fluctuations. Problem 11.2 asks you to explore this tradeoff within the context of a simple example.

Athanasoulis and Shiller (2001) present an empirical implementation of these ideas. They argue that international risksharing can be improved by the use of GDP swaps, particularly among countries whose GDP has low correlation, such as Japan and the US.

AS assume that all agents have identical beliefs. Simsek (2013b) points out that if agents have different prior beliefs about asset payoffs, then they will use new markets to speculate as well as to hedge. If the speculative motive is stronger than the hedging motive, then introducing new markets can increase the cross-sectional volatility of consumption rather than reducing it. This is consistent with the finding discussed in section 10.1.3, that households often hold stocks of the industries they work for and thereby increase their overall risk exposure.

11.1.3 General Equilibrium with Imperfect Risksharing

General equilibrium can have unfamiliar properties when risksharing is imperfect. With two or more goods, competitive equilibrium may not be constrained Pareto optimal; that is, a social planner with sufficient information about agents' endowments and preferences can reallocate resources to make all agents better off even while respecting the missing markets, default constraints, or private information that limit risksharing.

Hart (1975) presented a simple example of this in a model with exogenous missing markets.[2] Geanakoplos and Polemarchakis (1986) showed that the failure of competitive equilibrium to be constrained Pareto optimal is generic in such a model, and Greenwald and Stiglitz (1986) presented similar results for a model with private information. The intuition is that the relative goods price in a spot market plays two roles. It clears the goods markets at a point in time, but it also determines the relative resources of agents at that point in time when the agents have different goods endowments. With complete financial markets, resources can be exchanged freely across dates and states so the second role is unimportant. However, in incomplete markets there may be a conflict between the two roles.

---

[1] This is a statement about the correlation of two vectors of loadings that define assets, not the time-series correlation of the returns on these assets. Depending on the variance-covariance structure of individual endowments, the optimal assets may have returns correlated with the return on the world share even if their loadings are uncorrelated with its loadings.

[2] Hart's example is an economy with two goods, traded in two periods, but with no intertemporal markets (no opportunities for borrowing or lending). The economy may have two competitive equilibria in each period, in which case there are four sets of equilibria across the two periods. If agents have different time preferences, these sets of equilibria may be Pareto ranked. For example, an equilibrium set that favors the impatient agent in the first period and the patient agent in the second period will be Pareto superior to an equilibrium set that does the reverse.

Another way to understand the result is to use the concept of a *pecuniary external-ity*. In any general equilibrium model, agents' demands for goods alter their prices and thus affect the welfare of other agents who are buying or selling those goods. In an unconstrained complete-markets equilibrium, pecuniary externalities have no effect at the margin because the marginal utilities of all agents are equated across dates and states (up to the single Lagrange multiplier for each agent), so the benefits of a marginal price increase to sellers are exactly offset by the costs of that price increase to buyers. (Larger changes in prices reduce welfare as shown by the standard welfare theorems.) However, pecuniary externalities fail to cancel at the margin in an incomplete-markets model and may imply that equilibria are constrained inefficient. That is, a planner can modify alloc-ations to induce price changes that improve the terms of trade for those agents with relatively high marginal utility in a given state.

A related phenomenon is that adding a market does not always improve welfare, unless enough markets are added to reach a complete-market optimum. If each compet-itive equilibrium were constrained Pareto optimal, then relaxing constraints by adding markets could only be Pareto improving.

In a model where financial constraints depend on the level of asset prices, as is some-times the case when constraints are motivated by the threat of default, another effect comes into play. Now an agent's demand for assets affects prices, which determine the value of collateral and thus the tightness of financial constraints that affect other agents. This is a second type of pecuniary externality (called a collateral externality by Dávila and Korinek (2017) to distinguish it from the distributive externality discussed earlier), which again implies that competitive equilibrium is generically not constrained Pareto optimal as shown by Kehoe and Levine (1993).

The recent macrofinance and public finance literature develops more concrete examples of this phenomenon. In order to guide public policy, one needs to have a clear sense of the direction of competitive market failure, but this requires tight restrictions on the environment because general results are not available. For example, Lorenzoni (2008) presents a model with two goods (capital and consumption goods) and two fin-ancially constrained agents (entrepreneurs and consumers). Entrepreneurs may have to sell capital goods in a "fire sale" in a bad state of the world. Competitive equilibrium has excessive borrowing because of the distributive pecuniary externality that entrepreneurs' borrowing lowers fire-sale prices and worsens financial constraints in the bad state, an effect that individual borrowers and lenders do not take into account. Farhi and Werning (2016) combine pecuniary externalities, of both the types discussed here, with aggregate demand externalities and present a series of relevant examples. Problem 11.3 asks you to analyze an example based on Lorenzoni (2015).

11.2 Private Information

The contrast between a constrained Pareto optimal allocation and competitive equilib-rium with incomplete markets also arises, and indeed is particularly striking, in a simple model with private information.

Consider an economy with one consumption good, additive separability between con-sumption and leisure (so that marginal utility of consumption does not depend on labor supply), and, to start, no aggregate uncertainty. Agents have privately observable skills, which evolve randomly over time, and publicly observable income. A social planner seeks to maximize a weighted sum of individual utilities, subject to the incentive-compatibility constraint that agents must be induced to reveal their skills truthfully. This constraint is a second reason why risksharing might be imperfect.

Golosov, Kocherlakota, and Tsyvinski (2003), building on Rogerson (1985), show that in a constrained Pareto optimum, an "inverse Euler equation" describes the consumption of each agent k:

$$\frac{1}{u'(C_{kt})} = \frac{1}{\beta(1 + R_{f,t+1})} E_t \frac{1}{u'(C_{k,t+1})}. \tag{11.11}$$

This is consistent with the ordinary Euler equation for optimal private investment only if the marginal utility of agent k is deterministic, which will only be the case if risksharing is complete.

To understand the inverse Euler equation, consider a perturbation of the consumption plan for agent k, in two successive periods t and $t + 1$:

$$C_{kt}^{new} = C_{kt} \qquad \frac{\varepsilon}{u'(C_{kt})}, \tag{11.12}$$

$$C_{k,t+1}^{new} = C_{k,t+1} + \frac{\varepsilon}{\beta u'(C_{k,t+1})} \tag{11.13}$$

in all possible states for agent k's period $t + 1$ consumption.

This perturbation does not change agent k's expected utility at time t, because

$$\Delta u_{kt} = -\frac{\varepsilon}{u'(C_{kt})} u'(C_{kt}) + \beta \frac{\varepsilon}{\beta u'(C_{k,t+1})} u'(C_{k,t+1}) = 0. \tag{11.14}$$

This has two important implications. First, if the original allocation was incentive compatible, the new one will be also. Second, the perturbation does not change the component of the social planner's objective function related to agent k.

These two implications tell us that if the perturbation alters the planner's resources, the planner can improve the welfare of some other agent without reducing the welfare of agent k, contrary to the assumption that the original consumption plan is a constrained Pareto optimum. It follows that the perturbation cannot change the planner's resources, so

$$\frac{\varepsilon}{u'(C_{kt})}(1 + R_{f,t+1}) = E_t \frac{\varepsilon}{\beta u'(C_{k,t+1})}, \tag{11.15}$$

which implies the inverse Euler equation.

Kocherlakota and Pistaferri (KP 2009) discuss the asset pricing implications of this approach. They allow for aggregate uncertainty, assume power utility, and assume that assets are traded by the social planner and not by individual agents (equivalently, that the social planner can tax capital income or make asset-contingent insurance payments to induce agents to hold asset positions that implement the social plan).

KP use the inverse Euler equation to show that in a private-information Pareto optimum (PIPO) the stochastic discount factor can be written as

$$M_{t+1}^{PIPO} = \beta \frac{E_t^*(C_{kt}^\gamma)}{E_{t+1}^*(C_{k,t+1}^\gamma)}, \tag{11.16}$$

where E^* denotes the cross-sectional mean as in section 10.1.1. Whenever risksharing is imperfect, this SDF differs from both the representative agent SDF,

$$M_{t+1}^{RA} = \beta \frac{\left(E_{t+1}^* C_{k,t+1}\right)^{-\gamma}}{(E_t^* C_{kt})^{-\gamma}}, \tag{11.17}$$

and an SDF that would be valid in an incomplete-markets model with unconstrained asset market trading,

$$M_{t+1}^{INC} = \beta \frac{E_{t+1}^* \left(C_{k,t+1}^{-\gamma}\right)}{E_t^* \left(C_{kt}^{-\gamma}\right)}. \tag{11.18}$$

(The SDF in (11.18) is slightly different from the one considered by Constantinides and Duffie, (11.4), but both are equally valid.)

KP construct empirical proxies for these SDF's using microdata from the Consumer Expenditure Survey and argue that the PIPO SDF does no worse than the others. The empirical comparison of these SDFs is challenging, particularly for high coefficients of risk aversion, since outlying high values of measured individual consumption have a large effect on the properties of (11.16), while outlying low values of measured individual consumption have a large effect on the properties of (11.18). It is a difficult problem to control for the effects of measurement error at the two extremes of the cross-sectional consumption distribution.

Another concern is that the PIPO SDF is inconsistent with unconstrained private trading in financial assets, and it does not seem that in reality the mechanisms exist that could enforce the private information Pareto optimum.

11.3 Default

A third limitation on risksharing is the possibility of default. Investors naturally limit their holdings of claims on other agents to those that they expect to be paid in equilibrium. The effect of this depends on the punishments that investors can inflict on defaulters. The stronger these punishments, the smaller the risk of default and the larger the asset positions that can be sustained in equilibrium. We discuss two alternative types of punishment: exclusion from financial markets in the future and seizure of collateral.

11.3.1 Punishment by Exclusion

Kehoe and Levine (1993) assume that the punishment for default is permanent exclusion from financial markets that forces defaulters into "autarky." This punishment makes some risksharing possible in a model with an infinite horizon, although risksharing would break down in a finite-horizon model since the punishment would be ineffective in the last period, and this would unravel risksharing in earlier periods as well.

Alvarez and Jermann (AJ 2000) present a canonical model with punishment by exclusion, combining the realism of limited risksharing with the tractability of complete-markets models. AJ consider the optimization problem of a social planner with complete markets and participation constraints that ensure that each agent in the economy weakly prefers financial market participation to autarky. They show that this is equivalent to a competitive equilibrium with solvency constraints that are as weak as possible while still preventing default.

Solvency constraints limit the contingent claims that agents can issue. They prevent agents from defaulting in good states in which their previously issued claims require them to make payments. Thus the default that is of concern here is quite different from real-world bankruptcy, which occurs in bad states and can be interpreted as a mechanism to convert fixed debt contracts into contingent claims.

Social Planner Problem

In the AJ model there are multiple agents $i = 1 \dots I$, and a single consumption good. A Markov process z_t describes the state of economy (all individual endowments, not just the aggregate endowment). The transition matrix of the process is Π.

We write z^t to denote the history $(z_0, z_1, \dots, z_t)$, $c_{i,t}$ and $e_{i,t}$ to denote individual consumption and endowment at time t, and c_i and e_i to denote the corresponding consumption and endowment processes. The utility of agent i in history z^t is

$$U(c_i)(z^t) = \sum_{s=t}^{\infty} \sum_{z^s} \beta^{s-t} u(c_{i,s}(z^s)) \pi(z^s | z^t). \tag{11.19}$$

The time discount factor here, β^{s-t}, can be generalized to a state-contingent form that allows for aggregate growth.

The constraints on the social planner are resource feasibility:

$$\sum_{i=1}^{I} c_{i,t}(z^t) = \sum_{i=1}^{I} e_{i,t}(z^t) \tag{11.20}$$

for all t and z^t, and participation constraints:

$$U(c_i(z^t)) \geq U(e_i(z^t)) \tag{11.21}$$

for all i, t, and z^t. Feasibility requires that both sets of constraints are satisfied.

Clearly we need an infinite horizon for this to make sense. Otherwise, there could be no risksharing in the final period, and risksharing would unravel in all previous periods as well. Thus transversality conditions are going to be important.

A "constrained efficient" allocation is feasible and not Pareto dominated by other feasible allocations. If autarky is constrained efficient, then as we discuss below it is the only constrained efficient allocation, but we are more interested in cases where autarky is not constrained efficient.

AJ show the following important result, which clarifies the effect of participation constraints on the marginal utilities of constrained agents.

Proposition. *Let* $\{c_i\}_{i=1\dots I}$ *be constrained efficient. Then if* $U(c_j)(z^t, z_{t+1}) > U(e_j)(z^t, z_{t+1})$ *(agent j is unconstrained in trading between time t and state z_{t+1}),*

$$\frac{u'(c_{j,t+1}(z^t, z_{t+1}))}{u'(c_{j,t}(z^t))} = \max_i \frac{u'(c_{i,t+1}(z^t, z_{t+1}))}{u'(c_{i,t}(z^t))}. \tag{11.22}$$

In words, the unconstrained agent has the highest intertemporal marginal rate of substitution (IMRS) between t and state z_{t+1} (and it must be the same for all unconstrained agents).

The proof of this proposition proceeds as follows. Suppose the contrary, that some agent $i \neq j$ has a higher IMRS. Then the social planner can increase current $c_{j,t}$ and decrease $c_{j,t+1}$ (feasible given the slack in agent j's participation constraint) in such a way that $U(c_j(z^t))$ is unchanged. The planner funds the operation by taking the resources from some other agent i at time t and giving them to the same agent i at $t+1$ so that $c_{i,t}$ falls and $c_{i,t+1}$ rises. This must be a Pareto improvement, since agent i has higher IMRS. But then the original allocation could not be constrained efficient.

The intuition is that constrained agents at $t+1$ have "too high" consumption at $t+1$, and it cannot be reduced without inducing them to prefer autarky. Hence, they have "too low" marginal utility at $t+1$.

Competitive Equilibrium
To analyze competitive equilibrium, AJ define the time t contingent claim price $q(z^t, z')$ for one unit of the consumption good to be delivered at $t+1$ in state z'. Agent i holds $a_{i,t+1}(z^t, z')$ of this security at time t and faces a "solvency constraint" that puts a lower limit on the agent's holdings of $B_{i,t+1}(z^t, z')$. The agent cannot issue so many claims for consumption goods to be delivered in state z' that the claims make the agent "insolvent" when the state arrives (where solvency is defined by the constraint).

Equilibrium is defined by a Bellman equation, budget constraint, and solvency constraints for each agent, together with market clearing (aggregate consumption equals aggregate endowment, and the sum of all contingent claim demands is zero since these claims are in zero net supply).

An equilibrium with solvency constraints that are "not too tight" has the continuation utility for each agent exactly equal to the utility of autarky when the constraints bind. Such constraints are the weakest ones that prevent default and imply

$$U(c_i)(z^t) \geq U(e_i)(z^t), \tag{11.23}$$

with equality if $a_{i,t}(z^t) = B_{i,t}(z^t)$. Of course, to construct such constraints requires complete information on the agent's preferences and endowment process.

For any solvency constraints, sufficient conditions for a maximum are the Euler equations,

$$-u'(c_{i,t}(z^t)) q_t(z^t, z') + \beta \pi(z'|z) u'(c_{i,t+1}(z^t, z')) \leq 0, \tag{11.24}$$

with equality if $a_{z'} > B_{i,t+1}(z^t, z')$, and the transversality conditions

$$\lim_{t \to \infty} \sum_{z^t} \beta^t u'(c_{i,t}(z^t)) [a_{i,t}(z^t) - B_{i,t}(z^t)] \pi(z^t|z_0) = 0. \tag{11.25}$$

Welfare Theorems
"High implied interest rates" (or low contingent claims prices) are a property of an allocation $\{c_i^*\}$, $i = 1 \ldots I$. Define

$$q_t^*(z^t, z') = \max_i \left\{ \beta \frac{u'(c_{i,t+1}^*(z^t, z'))}{u'(c_{i,t}^*(z^t))} \pi(z'|z^t) \right\} \tag{11.26}$$

as the highest contingent claim valuation of any agent. This valuation must be that of an unconstrained agent by the proposition above. Intuitively, the constraints limit the issuance of securities, not the purchase of securities, so they bind on agents with low security valuations, not high security valuations.

Over many periods we can define

$$Q_0^*(z^t|z_0) = q_0^*(z_0, z_1) q_1^*(z^1, z_2) \ldots q_{t-1}^*(z^{t-1}, z_t), \tag{11.27}$$

the corresponding date-0 value of one unit of consumption at date t in state z^t. Note Q_0^* is constructed from a series of one-period valuations of those agents who are unconstrained in each successive period and may not correspond to the valuation of any single agent.

High implied interest rates are defined by the property that

$$\sum_t \sum_{z^t} Q_0^*(z^t|z_0) (\sum_i c_{i,t}^*(z^t)) < \infty. \tag{11.28}$$

That is, the maximum contingent claims prices are low enough that the discounted present value of aggregate consumption, evaluated using the sequence of maximum contingent claims prices, is finite.

AJ use these ideas to show a version of the second welfare theorem of microeconomics: any constrained efficient allocation with high implied interest rates can be decentralized as a competitive equilibrium with solvency constraints that are not too tight.

A sketch of the proof is as follows. Given the allocation, define prices $q_t^*(z^t, z')$. Then go to individual budget constraints and find contingent claim holdings to make the allocation feasible. For the agents with highest intertemporal marginal rate of substitution, these will be optimal, since the q^* obey the first-order conditions of the highest IMRS agents. For other agents, set the solvency constraint equal to their security holdings. Finally, check the transversality condition. This will be satisfied if implied interest rates are high. (A technical wrinkle is the task of choosing solvency constraints for the highest-IMRS agents.)

Alvarez and Jermann also prove a version of the first welfare theorem: under technical conditions on consumption and utility, a competitive equilibrium with solvency constraints that are not too tight, and with high implied interest rates, is constrained efficient.

Characterizing Equilibrium
The AJ model has several interesting implications.

First, it provides a simple way to check whether any risksharing is possible. If the implied interest rates for autarky ($c_i = e_i$) are high, then autarky is constrained efficient, which implies that autarky is the only feasible allocation. In this case, no risksharing is possible.

To understand this result, set $a_{i,0} = 0$ and $B_{i,t} = 0$ for all z^t and all i. Then it is easy to see that autarky is a competitive equilibrium with solvency constraints that are not too tight. With high implied interest rates, the first welfare theorem applies so autarky is constrained efficient. But then no other equilibrium is feasible, since the participation constraints require a feasible allocation to Pareto dominate autarky.

AJ provide sufficient conditions for high implied interest rates in autarky as follows. Implied interest rates in autarky will be high if the time discount factor is small enough ($\beta \to 0$), that is, if agents are impatient enough. With extremely impatient agents, punishment for default is relatively ineffective because it is deferred. Implied interest rates in autarky will also be high if risk aversion is sufficiently small or if the idiosyncratic shocks that agents can insure themselves against by trading assets with one another have sufficiently low variance. In both these cases, punishment for default is relatively ineffective because the inability to trade contingent claims in the future is costly only in future states of the world with low idiosyncratic income and correspondingly high marginal utility. Finally, implied interest rates in autarky will be high if the transition matrix for income is sufficiently close to the identity matrix I, that is, if idiosyncratic income shocks are close to permanent. In this case positive income shocks are not offset by expectations of lower future income, increasing the incentive to default when such shocks occur.

Second, it follows from these conditions that in the AJ model, an increase in cross-sectional income risk can actually reduce cross-sectional consumption risk as agents react by sharing their risks more effectively.

Third, AJ show the intuitive result that in an equilibrium with high implied interest rates, $B_{i,t+1} < 0$, hence the constraints limit contingent borrowing.

Finally, given that solvency constraints limit the issue of contingent claims, we might presume that they increase contingent security prices and hence increase their sum and lower interest rates. AJ prove this in special cases with no aggregate risk, constant relative risk aversion, or quadratic utility. The fact that the result holds with quadratic utility shows that it does not depend on the precautionary savings motive.

Problem 11.4 asks you to work out a simplified AJ model with only two agents and quadratic utility.

11.3.2 Punishment by Seizure of Collateral

Chien and Lustig (2010) distinguish between collateralizable wealth and noncollateralizable claims to labor income. Chien and Lustig argue that a more realistic punishment for default is seizure of collateral, without subsequent exclusion from financial markets. In this case agents are prevented from issuing contingent claims that would require paying more than the value of their collateral. Rampini and Viswanathan (2010) develop the same idea in a corporate finance context.

The Chien and Lustig model has some advantages over models with punishment by exclusion. First, the constraints can be calculated knowing only agents' asset holdings, whereas the constraints under permanent exclusion require knowledge also of agents' preferences and endowment processes. Second, the value of collateral becomes an important state variable in the economy. When collateral is scarce, risksharing is less effective. This can alter asset prices in the manner described by Constantinides and Duffie (1996). For example, if idiosyncratic labor income is more volatile in bad states, then imperfect risksharing increases the equity premium so the equity premium should increase when the value of collateral falls.

Lustig and Van Nieuwerburgh (2005) suggest that the value of housing is a meaningful empirical proxy for the value of collateral. Long swings in the value of household real estate wealth relative to labor income do predict aggregate stock returns in the manner implied by the model. This is an intriguing observation, although the Lustig-Van Nieuwerburgh state variable appears to be highly correlated with the overall level of the stock market, which is already known to predict stock returns in 20th-century US data, so any mechanism that moves housing wealth with stock market wealth could account for the finding.

A fundamental difficulty with complete-markets models with default is that they imply counterfactual patterns of asset trading. In the Chien and Lustig model, households issue contingent claims that require large payments when their labor income is high. When a good state occurs that corresponds to a binding constraint, households exhaust their collateral. Thus the cross-sectional correlation between labor income and collateraliz-able wealth is negative, the opposite of the pattern that one sees in household-level data. To state the problem another way, default in this model occurs (or is narrowly preven-ted from occurring) in high-income states, not in low-income states. The theoretical concept of bankruptcy in the model is thus very different from empirically observed bankruptcy.

Related to this, the possibility of default unambiguously lowers welfare in complete-markets models, and an infinite punishment for default would restore the first-best equilibrium. Zame (1993) and Dubey, Geanakoplos, and Shubik (2005) show that in models with incomplete markets this is no longer true: the possibility of default allows for contingent payments that may not be contractible directly, and this may increase welfare.

11.4 Heterogeneous Beliefs

Another reason why risksharing may be imperfect is that market participants have differ-ent beliefs about the probabilities of different states of the economy. In this section we consider models of financial market equilibrium with heterogeneous beliefs. We assume that agents enter the market with different priors and do not believe that other agents have relevant information; thus they can "agree to disagree" without altering their beliefs in response to the beliefs of others. We defer until Chapter 12 the consideration of models in which agents have private information and learn from one another.

In a complete-markets model, belief heterogeneity breaks the equality of marginal utility ratios across states and dates shown in equation (4.19) of Chapter 4, but equality can be restored by taking account of the different state probabilities used by different agents, as in equation (4.32) of Chapter 4. Belief heterogeneity has more interesting effects once we allow for restrictions on the assets that can be traded. In this section we first consider models of noise traders due to Shiller (1984) and De Long et al. (1990a); then the model of Harrison and Kreps (1978), which restricts short sales; and finally the models of Geanakoplos (2009) and Simsek (2013a) which restrict state-contingent borrowing.

11.4.1 Noise Traders

Shiller (1984) initiated a large literature on financial market equilibrium when some mar-ket participants have exogenously shifting demands due to irrational beliefs, and other agents speculate against them. In Shiller's model, there is an exogenous supply, normal-ized to one, of a single risky asset with price P_t. This asset is naturally interpreted as the aggregate stock market. Rational agents have a linear demand function, which can be derived from constant absolute risk averse utility with an infinite horizon, as in Campbell and Kyle (1993). We write this as

$$Q_t = \frac{\mathrm{E}_t R_{t+1} - \rho}{\phi}, \qquad (11.29)$$

where Q_t is the number of shares demanded, ρ is the expected rate of return that induces zero demand, and ϕ governs the responsiveness of demand to expected returns. When $E_t R_{t+1} = \rho + \phi$, rational agents are content to hold the entire supply of risky assets, and thus we can interpret $\rho + \phi$ as the appropriate discount rate for stock dividends in a fully rational market.

In Shiller's model there are also "noise traders" who demand shares with value Y_t, which follows an exogenous process. In equilibrium, the total demand for shares from both rational agents and noise traders must sum to the unit supply:

$$Q_t + \frac{Y_t}{P_t} = 1. \tag{11.30}$$

Substituting (11.29) into (11.30), using $R_{t+1} = (P_{t+1} + D_{t+1})/P_t$ and solving forward, the stock price is given by

$$P_t = E_t \sum_{k=0}^{\infty} \frac{D_{t+1+k} + \phi Y_{t+k}}{(1 + \rho + \phi)^{k+1}}. \tag{11.31}$$

As the coefficient ϕ shrinks to zero, rational agents trade more aggressively against noise traders, so noise traders' demands Y_{t+k} have a smaller impact on equilibrium prices. Conversely, as the coefficient ϕ increases, current demands of noise traders have a larger influence on the stock price, which approaches Y_t as ϕ becomes large.

It is always possible to understand stock prices from the point of view of rational agents. From their perspective, periods with low-noise trader demand Y_t are periods where they increase their risk exposure and hence demand a higher expected return, while periods with high-noise trader demand induce rational investors to reduce their risk exposure in line with a lower expected return. The usual first-order conditions for rational portfolio choice describe the behavior of rational agents, but with a time-varying portfolio that reflects the residual supply not absorbed by noise traders, rather than the constant total supply of the asset.

De Long et al. (1990a) point out that rational agents are less willing to speculate against noise traders if they have short horizons. In the Shiller model, there must be some fundamental risk to explain why ϕ is nonzero. In a model with overlapping generations of two-period agents, however, a risky asset in fixed supply cannot be held indefinitely but must be sold to the next generation. If some members of this generation have volatile irrational expectations, the sales proceeds are risky even if the asset pays a deterministic dividend. Hence, noise trading can create risk that limits arbitrage and allows noise traders' demands to influence prices. The model of De Long et al. provides a theoretical foundation for the limits to arbitrage discussed in section 4.5 of Chapter 4.

An important question is whether noise traders tend to lose wealth over time, in which case they may have a diminishing influence over asset prices in the long run. This is sometimes called the "market selection hypothesis." De Long et al. (1990a) point out that if noise traders are bullish on average, they take more risk on average than rational investors. If rational investors have higher than unit risk aversion so that their portfolios are more conservative than the growth-optimal portfolio, then the higher average risk premium that irrational investors receive helps offset the drag on their performance caused by their tendency to buy at high prices and sell at lower prices. The ability of investors with irrational beliefs to remain relevant for price determination in the long run is a subtle issue that has been explored in subsequent work by De Long et al. (1991), Kogan et al. (2006), and Yan (2008) among others. Of course, it is possible to finesse this issue if investors randomly exit the market over time and are replaced by new investors with exogenous preferences and beliefs. Problem 11.5 asks you to examine the market selection hypothesis in a simple partial-equilibrium context.

More recent work has tried to open the black box of "noise trading" by modeling the dynamic evolution of investors' beliefs in response to market conditions. For example, if investors have extrapolative beliefs, becoming more optimistic in response to past increases in dividends or stock prices, then they may create short-run momentum and longer-run reversal in stock returns (De Long et al. 1990b, Barberis, Shleifer, and Vishny 1998, Barberis et al. 2015). Evidence from household finance, discussed in section 10.4, suggests that investor beliefs are likely heterogeneous since they may depend on personally experienced returns rather than the complete history of returns.

11.4.2 The Harrison-Kreps Model

Restrictions on short sales and heterogeneous beliefs interact in a way that increases asset prices above the level that would prevail if only one of these conditions were present. The basic mechanism is that emphasized by Miller (1977): if short sales are prohibited, pessimistic investors sell to optimistic investors but cannot supply additional assets to optimists by selling short. Hence, in equilibrium the most optimistic investors hold assets and prices equal the valuation of the marginal optimistic buyer.

When beliefs change over time so that different investors are most optimistic at different times, an additional effect comes into play that can increase asset prices above the fundamental value perceived by any individual investor. Harrison and Kreps (HK 1978) present an example that illustrates this possibility. In their example, the economy follows a discrete-state Markov process. A risky asset pays a dividend d_t of 0 in state 0, and 1 in state 1. There are two agents, indexed by a, who differ in their beliefs about the transition probabilities of the states.

We use the notation $q^a(d, d') = \mathrm{Pr}^a(d_{t+1} = d' \mid d_t = d)$ to denote the probability perceived by agent a that state d' will occur tomorrow given that the current state is d. These probabilities are stacked into a transition matrix Q^a:

$$Q^a = \begin{bmatrix} q^a(0,0) & q^a(0,1) \\ q^a(1,0) & q^a(1,1) \end{bmatrix}. \tag{11.32}$$

Both agents in the HK model are risk-neutral with a common time discount factor δ, implying that they estimate fundamental value of the asset by discounting expected future dividends. Given the Markov structure of the model, agent a calculates the expected dividend i periods ahead as

$$E_t d_{t+i} = (Q^a)^i \begin{bmatrix} 0 \\ 1 \end{bmatrix} \tag{11.33}$$

and fundamental value as

$$F_t^a = E_t^a \sum_{i=1}^{\infty} \delta^i d_{t+i} = \delta Q^a [I - \delta Q^a]^{-1} \begin{bmatrix} 0 \\ 1 \end{bmatrix}. \tag{11.34}$$

To understand Harrison and Kreps' point as simply as possible, we consider a symmetric example where the agents agree that the states have equal unconditional probabilities but differ on the persistence of the states. This leads the agents to disagree about the interpretation of public information (the current dividend) because they use different models of the economy as in Harris and Raviv (1993) and Kandel and Pearson (1995).

Specifically, assume that agent 1's beliefs are given by

$$Q^1 = \begin{bmatrix} \phi & 1-\phi \\ 1-\phi & \phi \end{bmatrix}, \tag{11.35}$$

while agent 2's beliefs are given by

$$Q^2 = \begin{bmatrix} 1-\phi & \phi \\ \phi & 1-\phi \end{bmatrix}. \tag{11.36}$$

Without loss of generality, we assume that $1/2 \le \phi < 1$, so agent 1 believes that good and bad states are persistent while agent 2 believes that good and bad states tend to alternate.

In this example, fundamental value as perceived by agent 1 is

$$F_t^1 = \frac{\delta}{(1-\delta)(1+\delta-2\delta\phi)} \begin{bmatrix} 1-\phi \\ \phi+\delta-2\delta\phi \end{bmatrix}. \tag{11.37}$$

Given $\phi \ge 1/2$, $\phi + \delta - 2\delta\phi = \delta(1-\phi) + \phi(1-\delta) \ge 1-\phi$. Therefore agent 1's perceived fundamental value for the asset is greater in state 1 than in state 0, because agent 1 believes that a high dividend today predicts a high dividend next period as well. The reverse, of course, is true for agent 2, who believes that a high dividend today predicts a low dividend tomorrow, and who therefore perceives a lower fundamental value in state 1 than in state 0.

Since agent 1 is more optimistic in state 1, while agent 2 is more optimistic in state 0, in equilibrium with short-sales constraints agent 1 will hold the risky asset in state 1 and agent 2 will hold it in state 0. The equilibrium price of the asset must satisfy

$$p(d_t) = \delta \max_{a=1,2}\{E^a[d_{t+1} + p(d_{t+1}) \mid d_t]\}. \tag{11.38}$$

This defines two equations for the prices $p(0)$ and $p(1)$:

$$p(0) = \delta \max\{\phi p(0) + (1-\phi)(1+p(1)), (1-\phi)p(0) + \phi(1+p(1))\}, \tag{11.39}$$

and

$$p(1) = \delta \max\{(1-\phi)p(0) + \phi(1+p(1)), \phi p(0) + (1-\phi)(1+p(1))\}. \tag{11.40}$$

The symmetry of the agents' expectations implies that these two equations have the same solution p. That is, the equilibrium market price does not vary across the two states. Substituting in a common price p and using the fact that $\phi \ge 1/2$, we have

$$p = \max\{\delta(1-\phi) + \delta p, \delta\phi + \delta p\} = \delta\phi + \delta p = \frac{\delta\phi}{1-\delta}. \tag{11.41}$$

If we now take the ratio of the fundamental value, as perceived by agent 1, to the equilibrium price, we find that the ratio is

$$\frac{F_t^1}{p} = \frac{1}{\phi(1 + \delta - 2\delta\phi)} \left[\frac{1 - \phi}{\phi + \delta - 2\delta\phi} \right]. \tag{11.42}$$

This ratio equals one when $\phi = 1/2$, the case where the agents have homogeneous beliefs. It declines with ϕ and approaches zero as ϕ approaches one. When the agents disagree, price is always above fundamental value.

It may not be surprising that the price exceeds agent 1's perception of fundamental value in state 0, where this agent is more pessimistic than agent 2. What is striking is that the price also exceeds agent 1's perceived fundamental value in state 1, where agent 1 is the more optimistic agent and is holding the asset. This implies that the price is always above both agents' perceived fundamental values and that agents are willing to hold the asset despite the fact that they perceive overvaluation. The explanation is that each agent believes he benefits from the existence of the other agent who he believes to have incorrect beliefs. The option to resell the asset to a counterparty with different beliefs, in a state where that counterparty is more optimistic, is valuable and increases the price at which each agent is willing to hold the asset.

To understand this, we can calculate the expected return on the asset, again from the point of view of agent 1. The expected return is

$$\frac{E_t^1 d_{t+1} + p}{p} = \frac{1}{\delta} \left(1 - \left[\begin{matrix} (2\phi - 1)(1 - \delta)/\phi \\ 0 \end{matrix} \right] \right), \tag{11.43}$$

which equals the required rate of return in state 1, where the agent holds the asset, and is lower in state 0. Since agent 1 is unable to short the asset in state 0, this expected return is consistent with equilibrium. Agent 2 has symmetrical expectations and expects the asset to deliver the required rate of return in state 0, but less in state 1. Both agents agree that the unconditional expected return on the asset is less than the riskless interest rate, but both believe that they can successfully avoid holding the asset in those periods that account for its poor average performance.

Warren Buffett, in a famous letter to shareholders included in the 1987 Berkshire Hathaway annual report (Buffett 1988), expressed the logic of the HK model as follows:

> Ben Graham, my friend and teacher, long ago described the mental attitude toward market fluctuations that I believe to be most conducive to investment success. He said that you should imagine market quotations as coming from a remarkably accommod-ating fellow named Mr. Market who is your partner in a private business. Without fail, Mr. Market appears daily and names a price at which he will either buy your interest or sell you his.
>
> Even though the business that the two of you own may have economic character-istics that are stable, Mr. Market's quotations will be anything but. For, sad to say, the poor fellow has incurable emotional problems. At times he feels euphoric and can see only the favorable factors affecting the business. When in that mood, he names a very high buy-sell price because he fears that you will snap up his interest and rob him of imminent gains. At other times he is depressed and can see nothing but trouble ahead for both the business and the world. On these occasions he will name a very low price, since he is terrified that you will unload your interest on him.

Mr. Market has another endearing characteristic: He doesn't mind being ignored. If his quotation is uninteresting to you today, he will be back with a new one tomorrow. Transactions are strictly at your option. Under these conditions, the more manic-depressive his behavior, the better for you.

While Warren Buffett emphasizes the effect of Mr. Market on the welfare of an asset owner, the HK model takes the next step to conclude that the equilibrium price will be higher if all investors believe they are partners with Mr. Market.

An interesting implication of the HK model is that asset holders are willing to pay higher prices relative to their perceived fundamentals when interest rates are low. Equation (11.42) shows that the derivative of agent 1's fundamental value-price ratio with respect to the time discount factor δ is negative in state 1, when agent 1 is the asset holder. The intuition is that resale of the asset occurs in the future, so low interest rates increase the present value of the option to resell. Rational bubbles, by contrast, grow at the interest rate so they grow more slowly when interest rates are low (although low interest rates may make it easier for rational bubbles to exist as discussed in section 5.2.3).

More recent research has developed the HK model into a quantitative empirical model that can be used to generate testable predictions. Scheinkman and Xiong (2003), for example, derive disagreement from overconfidence about the precision of private signals and show that overvaluation is positively correlated with market prices, volatility, and trading volume, and negatively correlated with free float (the available quantity of shares), because short-sales constraints are more binding when free float is low. As an informal exercise, you are asked to relate their results to the literature on asset pricing with underdiversification discussed in section 10.3.3 of Chapter 10.

11.4.3 Endogenou Margin Requirements

The literature on limits of arbitrage, discussed in section 4.5, initially assumed that arbitrageurs borrow to invest and face a constant margin requirement. When mispricing worsens, arbitrageurs lose capital and must reduce their positions (Shleifer and Vishny 1997).

A natural question to ask is what determines the level of the margin requirement. If lenders had the same perspective as arbitrageurs perceiving a riskless profit opportunity, they should be willing to reduce their margin requirement to zero, offering 100% financing. In that case the level of arbitrageur capital would become irrelevant. More realistically, with positive but variable margin requirements, an increase in the margin requirement has a similar effect to a loss of arbitrageur capital, so it becomes important to understand in what circumstances margin requirements increase. The empirical relevance of this topic was brought home by dramatic increases in margin requirements during the global financial crisis of the late 2000s.

Geanakoplos (2009) presents a simple model of the determination of margins (equivalently, leverage) in equilibrium. The model rules out short selling and allows only noncontingent nonrecourse collateralized borrowing. These asset market restrictions are central, as the Geanakoplos model is a decentralization of the Arrow-Debreu model when asset markets are complete.

Geanakoplos assumes a continuum of risk-neutral investors with a zero pure rate of time preference and different beliefs indexed by $h \in (0, 1)$. These beliefs concern the probabilities of two future states, good ("up") and bad ("down"). Agent h thinks the probability of the good state $\pi_U^h = h$, and the probability of the bad state $\pi_D^h = 1 - h$. There is a risky asset Y that pays one unit of consumption in the good state and $d < 1$ units of consumption in the bad state. All agents initially hold one unit of asset Y and one unit of the consumption good (endowment) at time zero.

In this model the more optimistic agents buy the asset from the more pessimistic agents, and the asset price adjusts to clear the market. In general optimists may also borrow from pessimists, but we first consider what happens if borrowing is precluded. The model without borrowing is a formalization of the verbal model in Miller (1977).

No Borrowing
Since investors are risk-neutral and have a zero rate of time preference, the asset price must equal the expected payoff perceived by the marginal buyer. If the marginal buyer is b (believing that the good state has probability b), the asset price must be

$$p = b + (1 - b)d. \tag{11.44}$$

This condition defines an upward-sloping relationship between the optimism of the marginal buyer and the price of the asset illustrated in Figure 11.1 below.

Investors who are more optimistic than the marginal buyer spend all their resources on shares, while more pessimistic investors sell their shares. Equating demand (the number of shares that the buyers can afford if they offer all their consumption good) and supply (the number of shares being sold), $(1 - b)/p = b$, so

$$p = (1 - b)/b. \tag{11.45}$$

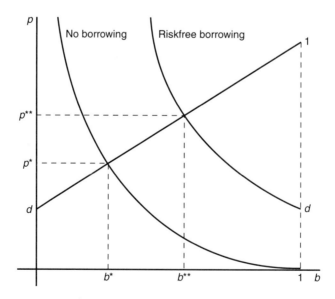

Figure 11.1. *Equilibrium in the Geanakoplos (2009) Model*

This condition defines a downward-sloping relationship between the optimism of the marginal buyer and the price of the asset as shown in Figure 11.1.

Equations (11.44) and (11.45) can be solved for the equilibrium price and the identities of the buyers and sellers. For example, if $d = 0.2$ and using stars to denote equilibrium values, we have $b^* = 0.6$ and $p^* = 0.68$.

Riskfree Borrowing
Now consider what happens if we allow borrowing, restricted to be noncontingent and nonrecourse. A loan is defined by the amount that it promises to pay and by the collateral that backs that promise. Without loss of generality, we normalize the collateral to one share of the risky asset and write ϕ for the amount promised in each state. In the event of default, the lender can seize the collateral, that is, the state-dependent payoff of the asset but has no other recourse against the borrower. The payment that the loan actually makes is then $\min(\phi, 1)$ in state U and $\min(\phi, d)$ in state D.

To begin, we assume an exogenous constraint $\phi \leq d$, which makes the debt riskfree since $\min(\phi, 1) = \min(\phi, d) = \phi$, the promised payment. In this case the debt has a zero interest rate because the pure rate of time preference is zero. The amount that can be borrowed today by promising ϕ in the future is equal to ϕ.

In equilibrium optimists hold all the shares and use them to borrow as much as they can. Since the aggregate supply of shares is normalized to one, the most that optimists can borrow is d, and this borrowing increases the resources they devote to buying shares by d. The new demand curve is $(1 - b + d)/p = b$, or

$$p = (1 - b + d)/b, \tag{11.46}$$

which is shifted up as illustrated in Figure 11.1.

The equilibrium with borrowing has fewer and more optimistic investors holding shares and paying a higher price for them. In the numerical example with $d = 0.2$, and using double stars to denote the new equilibrium values, we find $b^{**} = 0.69$ and $p^{**} = 0.75$, both higher than the values in the equilibrium without borrowing.

The margin requirement for investors in the risky asset is $(p-d)/p$, and their leverage is $p/(p - d)$. In the numerical example the margin requirement is 0.73, and leverage is 1.36.

The Possibility of Risky Borrowing
We now consider the possibility of risky borrowing, that is, a promised payment $\phi > d$. The amount that can be borrowed depends on the amount promised and can be written $\pi(\phi)$. The stated yield for risky borrowing is

$$1 + r(\phi) = \frac{\phi}{\pi(\phi)}. \tag{11.47}$$

For $\phi > d$, $r(\phi) > 0$ to compensate lenders for the payments that are lost when default occurs.

Geanakoplos shows that in equilibrium, only riskless borrowing occurs even though optimists can increase their leverage by using risky borrowing. This implies that risky loans are priced by the same marginal buyer b as in the case with only riskless borrowing. This marginal borrower's beliefs are used to price risky debt; thus

$$\pi(\phi) = b\phi + (1 - b)d. \tag{11.48}$$

In the numerical example where $b^{**} = 0.69$, $\pi(0.3) = 0.69 \times 0.3 + 0.31 \times 0.2 = 0.269$, and $r(0.3) = 0.3/0.269 - 1 = 12\%$. A risky promise of 0.3, collateralized by one share, has an interest rate of 12% rather than the zero riskless interest rate.

Why do optimists not take out risky loans, with lower collateral, to increase their leverage? The answer is that risky loans shift payments toward the good state and away from the bad state. The borrowers think the good state is more likely to occur than the lenders do, so they do not feel that this shift in payments is attractively priced. In equilibrium, only riskless borrowing occurs. This result depends, however, on several special features of the model: having two states at each node of the event tree and risk-neutral agents with a common discount rate and distinct beliefs.

Generating a Crash

The Geanakoplos model can generate interesting price patterns over time and in relation to investors' beliefs. In particular, it can generate a drop in asset price that exceeds the decline in any individual investor's perception of fundamental value. To see this, consider a two-period event tree with up and down realizations in each period. The risky asset pays 1 in states UU, UD, and DU. Two down moves are needed to get a payoff of 0.2 in state DD. Solving this two-period model, the equilibrium price is 0.95 at the initial date, 1 at the end of the first period in state U, and 0.69 at the end of the first period in state D. The price decline from 0.95 to 0.69 exceeds the decline in perceived fundamental value for any subjective probability h that the bad state will occur.

The reason for this effect is that two mechanisms amplify the effect of bad news in the first period of the Geanakoplos model. First, the price decline transfers wealth from leveraged optimistic buyers to pessimistic lenders. A new wealth distribution must be used to calculate asset prices in the second period, just as would be the case in a dynamic model with differences of risk aversion such as Chan and Kogan (2002). Second, equilibrium leverage falls from $0.95/(0.95-0.69) = 3.6$ in the first period to $0.69/(0.69-0.2) = 1.4$ in the second period. In this example the arrival of bad news in the first period increases uncertainty and thus the disagreement between optimists (borrowers) and pessimists (their creditors).

Simsek Model

Simsek (2013a) extends the Geanakoplos approach by considering a model with only two types of investors (pessimists P and optimists O) and a larger number (in general, a continuum) of states. He points out that once there are more than two states, risky borrowing can occur, and the nature of disagreement becomes important. To build intuition, consider a case with three states, good, neutral, and bad. If optimists and pessimists disagree about the probability of the bad state (with optimists feeling it is less likely), then pessimists set high interest rates for risky loans that optimists find unattractive. In this case optimists will be reluctant to increase their leverage by taking out risky loans. On the other hand, if optimists and pessimists agree about the probability of the bad state but disagree about the probability of the good state (with optimists feeling it is more likely), then the interest rates for risky loans seem fair to optimists, and they will borrow aggressively using risky debt. In the former case the price of the risky asset will be closer to the valuation of pessimists, while in the latter case it will be closer to the valuation of optimists. The key factor that allows risky borrowing is that optimists and pessimists may agree about the probability of states in which default occurs but disagree about the relative probabilities of states in which default does not occur.

The implications of Simsek's model for asset price valuation can be summarized by the following equation. If $\bar{v}$ is the threshold level of the asset's future value such that risky loans default for any $v < \bar{v}$ (in other words, if loans collateralized by one unit of risky asset promise to pay $\bar{v}$ in equilibrium), then the price of the risky asset today is given by

$$\text{Price} = \{\pi_P[v < \bar{v}]E_P[v \mid v < \bar{v}] + \pi_P[v \geq \bar{v}]E_O[v \mid v \geq \bar{v}]\}, \tag{11.49}$$

where $\pi_P[v < \bar{v}]$ is the probability of default perceived by pessimists, $E_P[v \mid v < \bar{v}]$ is pessimists' expected value of the asset conditional upon default, $\pi_P[v \geq \bar{v}] = 1 - \pi_P[v < \bar{v}]$ is the probability perceived by pessimists that loans will not default but will repay in full, and $E_O[v \mid v \geq \bar{v}]$ is optimists' expected value of the asset conditional upon full loan repayment. Optimists' beliefs only enter the last term of this equation, indicating that optimistic beliefs about good states have a greater effect upon asset prices than optimistic beliefs about bad states. Of course, the threshold $\bar{v}$ is endogenous, so the above equation is only a partial description of asset price determination in Simsek's model.

11.5 Solution and Further Problems

As an informal exercise, you were asked to relate the Harrison and Kreps (1978) model, as extended by Scheinkman and Xiong (2003), to the empirical literature on asset pricing with underdiversification discussed in section 10.3.3 of Chapter 10. That literature has found that volatile individual stocks have surprisingly low average returns (Ang et al., 2006). The Harrison and Kreps model can explain this fact if investors disagree about fundamentals and trade with one another subject to short-sales constraints. In that case, high volatility is a signal of high disagreement, which in turn corresponds to greater overpricing as shown by Scheinkman and Xiong (2003).

Problem 11.1 Idiosyncratic Income Risk and the Equity Premium

Consider an economy with two dates $t = 1, 2$ and a continuum of consumers. Each consumer receives a random endowment at date 2 and consumes only then. At date 1, securities are traded but no resources change hands until the second period. All consumers have log utility over terminal consumption.

(a) Suppose that all consumers' endowments are the same. They are m with probability $1/2$, and $(1 - a)m$ with probability $1/2$, where $0 < a < 1$. Suppose that a claim to the date-2 aggregate endowment is traded and that it costs p in either state, payable at date 2. Compute the equilibrium price p and the expected return on the claim.

(b) Now suppose that at date 2, with probability $1/2$, all consumers receive m; with probability $1/2$, a fraction $(1 - b)$ of consumers receive m and a fraction b receive $(1 - a/b)m$, where $b > a$. At date 1, all consumers face the same probability of being in the latter group, but no insurance markets exist through which they can hedge this risk. Compute the expected return on the claim defined in part (a). Is it higher or lower than before? How does it depend on a, b, and m?

(c) Which assumptions in the model are critical for the result in part (b) and to what extent might the result hold more generally?

Note: This problem is based on Mankiw (1986) and a problem in Campbell, Lo, and MacKinlay (1997).

Problem 11.2 Market Design and Risksharing

Consider a model with two dates $t = 1, 2$ and two agents. Agents receive income and consume only at date 2. Agent 1 has income $x_1 = c + v + \varepsilon$, while agent 2 has income $x_2 = c + v - \varepsilon$. The term c is deterministic, while v and ε are independent, normally distributed shocks with mean zero. The variance of the common income shock v is 1, while the variance of the relative income shock ε is a. Agent 1 has constant absolute risk aversion coefficient γ_1, while agent 2 has constant absolute risk aversion coefficient γ_2.

A single futures contract exists in this economy. The payoff on the contract is $\theta_1 v + \theta_2 \varepsilon$, and it costs p payable at date 2. Normalize the variance of the payoff to 1. (Note: this imposes restrictions on θ_1 and θ_2.) The contract is in zero net supply.

(a) Given the price p, solve for the quantities of the futures contract q_1 and q_2 that each agent wishes to hold.

(b) Solve for the price p that must hold in equilibrium given that the futures contract is in zero net supply.

(c) Write down an expression for the maximized utility of each agent. Add the maximized utility of agent 1 to the maximized utility of agent 2 to get an expression for social welfare.

(d) Now assume that $\gamma_1 = \gamma_2$. Show that a futures contract designer who wishes to maximize social welfare will set $\theta_1 = 0$. Interpret this result.

(e) Now assume that $\gamma_1 = 0$ while $\gamma_2 > 0$. Show that the welfare-maximizing contract designer will set $\theta_2 = -\theta_1$. Interpret this result.

(f) Now assume that $\gamma_2 = 0$ while $\gamma_1 > 0$. Show that the welfare-maximizing contract designer will set $\theta_2 = \theta_1$. Interpret this result.

(g) What assumptions would be needed for the welfare-maximizing contract to have $\theta_2 = 0$? Explain.

Note: This problem is based on Athanasoulis and Shiller (2000).

Problem 11.3 Distributive Pecuniary Externalities and Sudden Stops

In this exercise we will explore the welfare implications of the distributive pecuniary externalities discussed in section 11.1.3 in an international setting where countries are subject to "sudden stops" in their access to international financial markets.

Consider a model of three dates, $t = 0, 1, 2$ and two countries, Home and Foreign, each populated by a continuum of unit mass of identical agents. The two countries trade frictionlessly with each other. At every date, Home (Foreign) agents receive a constant endowment of Y (Y^*) units of the Home (Foreign) good.

Agents in Home have log intertemporal preferences, and Home's consumption bundle is a Cobb-Douglas aggregate of the two goods:

$$\max \mathrm{E}_0 \sum_{t=0}^{2} \beta^t \log C_t, \text{ where } C_t = \zeta C_{ht}^{\alpha} C_{ft}^{1-\alpha} \tag{11.50}$$

with $\zeta \equiv \alpha^{-\alpha}(1-\alpha)^{-(1-\alpha)}$. Agents in Foreign have linear intertemporal preferences, and Foreign's consumption bundle is quasilinear in the Foreign good:

$$\max \mathrm{E}_0 \sum_{t=0}^{2} \beta^t C_t^*, \text{ where } C_t^* = \xi \log C_{ht}^* + C_{ft}^*. \tag{11.51}$$

We assume throughout that we have an interior equilibrium, that is, C_{ht}, C_{ft}, C_{ht}^*, C_{ft}^*, are strictly positive in all dates. By market clearing, $Y = C_{ht} + C_{ht}^*$ and $Y^* = C_{ft} + C_{ft}^*$ for all t. Normalize the price of the foreign good in foreign currency to one, $p_{ft}^* \equiv 1$. Then the terms of trade, generally defined as the ratio of export to import prices, are equal to the price of the home good in foreign currency, $p_{ht}^* = p_{ht}/\varepsilon_t$, where ε_t denotes the nominal exchange rate (the price of foreign currency in units of domestic currency). Let p_t denote the consumption price index (CPI) of Home (in domestic currency), defined through $p_t C_t = p_{ht} C_{ht} + \varepsilon_t C_{ft}$.

There exists a single asset, a one-period nominal bond in zero net supply paying in units of foreign currency with a nominal interest rate of $1 + i_{t+1}^*$. Home enters date 0 with a stock of debt $D_0 > 0$[3] maturing at date 0 and optimally chooses the level of its debt maturing at date 1, D_1. Given the finite-horizon setting, Home and Foreign are also subject to the terminal condition $D_3 = 0$.

Home and Foreign are subject to the respective budget constraints (both expressed in units of foreign currency)

$$\frac{p_t}{\varepsilon_t} C_t = p_{ht}^* Y - TB_t \tag{11.52}$$

and

$$p_{ht}^* C_{ht}^* + C_{ft}^* = Y^* + TB_t. \tag{11.53}$$

where $TB_t = D_t - D_{t+1}/(1 + i_{t+1}^*)$ is Home's trade balance.

Agents know that at date 1 a sudden stop will occur with some probability π, $0 < \pi \leq 1$: foreign investors may, for unmodeled reasons, become concerned with the ability or willingness of Home agents to repay all of their debt at date 2 and are willing to only finance a maximum stock of debt $\bar{D}$ at date 1.[4] That is, Home must choose $D_2 \leq \bar{D}$ and thus sharply increase its trade balance at date 1 to $D_1 - \bar{D}/(1 + i_2^*)$ in order to finance the debt reduction. We assume throughout that Home's borrowing constraint during the sudden stop, $D_2 \leq \bar{D}$, is binding.

---

[3]That is, Home's net foreign asset (NFA) position at date 0 is $-D_0$ and Foreign's NFA is D_0, given that the bond is in zero net supply.

[4]We do not allow for default in this model but offer this explanation only as an informal motivation for the capital flight.

(a) Derive the following intratemporal relationships expressing equilibrium quantities as functions of the terms of trade, p_{ht}^*, and C_t that will be useful in the analysis to follow: $p_t/\varepsilon_t = p_{ht}^{*\,\alpha}$, $C_{ht} = \alpha p_{ht}^{*\,-(1-\alpha)} C_t$, $C_{ft} = (1-\alpha) p_{ht}^{*\,\alpha} C_t$, $C_{ht}^* = \xi p_{ht}^{*\,-1}$, and $C_{ft}^* = Y^* - (1-\alpha) p_{ht}^{*\,\alpha} C_t$.

(b) We assume that the financing constraint during the sudden stop only applies to Home agents. Therefore, the Euler equation of Foreign agents must hold at all dates and states. Show that $1 + i_{t+1}^* = 1/\beta$ for $t = 1, 2$.

(c) Consider the case $\pi = 1$. We solve for the full equilibrium backward.

    (i) Explain how a fall in the relative price of Home goods affects Home's date-1 consumption, C_1, all else equal. Calculate the equilibrium terms of trade at date 1, p_{h1}^*, as a function of D_1 and the parameters of the model. Show that

$$\frac{dp_{h1}^*}{dD_1} = -\frac{\alpha}{(1-\alpha)Y} < 0. \tag{11.54}$$

Explain why the relative price of the Home good is decreasing in D_1.

    (ii) Let $V_1(D_1, p_{h1}^*)$ and $V_1^*(D_1, p_{h1}^*)$ denote the date-1 continuation value functions of Home and Foreign, respectively. Explain why the private (internalized) marginal cost for Home agents of higher debt maturing in the sudden-stop state is (the absolute value of) $\partial V_1/\partial D_1$, while the social marginal cost for Home agents of higher debt is (the absolute value of) $dV_1/dD_1 \equiv \partial V_1/\partial D_1 + (\partial V_1/\partial p_{h1}^*)(dp_{h1}^*/dD_1)$.

    Show that

$$\frac{\partial V_1}{\partial p_{h1}^*} = -\frac{\partial V_1}{\partial D_1} C_{h1}^* \tag{11.55}$$

$$\frac{\partial V_1^*}{\partial p_{h1}^*} = -\frac{\partial V_1^*}{\partial D_1} C_{h1}^* = -C_{h1}^*.$$

Why is the welfare impact of a change in the terms of trade proportional to C_{h1}^*?

    (iii) We now move to date 0. Let $V_0(D_0)$ and $V_0^*(D_0)$ denote the ex-ante (date-0) value functions of Home and Foreign, respectively. Show that, at the competitive equilibrium,

$$\left|\frac{dV_0}{dD_1}\right| = \frac{dV_0^*}{dD_1} C_0^{-1} \frac{\varepsilon_0}{p_0}. \tag{11.56}$$

Use this result to argue that pecuniary externalities in this setting with $\pi = 1$ "net out" and the competitive equilibrium is constrained Pareto efficient.[5]

(d) We now consider the case $\pi < 1$, so that the sudden stop may or may not occur. If the sudden stop does not occur, Home is free to choose any level of D_2.[6]

---

[5] That is, a social planner who is constrained in the same way as private agents (unable to circumvent the financial friction at date 1) but can coordinate a reduction in D_1 along with a compensating transfer from Home to Foreign at date 0 (to leave Foreigners indifferent between the new and old equilibrium) will not be able to increase the welfare of Home agents.

[6] Recall that we assume that $\bar{D}$ is small enough that the financing constraint is strictly binding in the sudden-stop state. That is, we take as given that Home will choose a level of $D_2(ns) > \bar{D} = D_2(s)$. It can be easily verified that this is true for small enough $\bar{D}$, for example, for $\bar{D} = 0$.

Denote the sudden-stop state (no-sudden-stop state) by $s(ns)$. Once again, we solve backward.

  (i) Consider Home's intertemporal consumption choice between dates 1 and 2 in the no-sudden-stop state. Show that $D_2(ns) = D_1/(1+\beta)$, $p_{h1}^*(ns) = p_{h2}^*(ns)$, and $C_1(ns) = C_2(ns)$. Explain.

  (ii) Show that $dp_{h1}^*(s)/dD_1 = (1+\beta)\,dp_{h1}^*(ns)/dD_1$, $p_{h1}^*(s) < p_{h1}^*(ns)$, and $C_1(s) < C_1(ns)$. Explain.

  (iii) Show that the condition

$$\left|\frac{dV_0}{dD_1}\right| > \frac{dV_0^*}{dD_1} C_0^{-1} \frac{\varepsilon_0}{p_0} \tag{11.57}$$

is equivalent to the condition

$$\mathrm{Cov}\left(IMRS_{0,1},\, C_{h,1}^* \left|\frac{dp_{h1}^*}{dD_1}\right|\right) > \mathrm{Cov}\left(IMRS_{0,1}^*,\, C_{h,1}^* \left|\frac{dp_{h1}^*}{dD_1}\right|\right), \tag{11.58}$$

where $IMRS_{0,1}$ and $IMRS_{0,1}^*$ denote the intertemporal marginal rates of substitution between dates 0 and 1 of Home and Foreign agents, respectively, both in foreign currency units.

    Argue that this inequality holds in the competitive equilibrium of the model, and hence the competitive equilibrium is constrained Pareto inefficient.

(e) Explain the intuition behind the different conclusions in parts (c) and (d). How would the results be different in the $\pi < 1$ case if there was a second asset in addition to the foreign real bond?

Note: This problem draws on Lorenzoni (2015).

Problem 11.4 Solvency Constraints and Limits to Risksharing

Consider the risksharing problem of two infinitely lived agents, who receive random shares of a fixed endowment e. Each period there are two states of the economy. In state 1, agent 1 receives $e/2 + k$ and agent 2 receives $e/2 - k$, while in state 2 agent 1 receives $e/2 - k$ and agent 2 receives $e/2 + k$. The conditional probabilities of the two states are constant and equal. Each agent maximizes a discounted sum of expected period utilities, with time discount factor δ. Period utility is quadratic,

$$u(c) = \tilde{c} - \theta \tilde{c}^2, \tag{11.59}$$

where $\tilde{c} \equiv c - e/2$ and c is the level of consumption during the period.

    Following Alvarez and Jermann (2000), assume that the only punishment for default is permanent exclusion from the financial market.

  (a) Calculate an agent's expected utility under perfect risksharing.

  (b) Calculate an agent's expected utility under autarky, if the state is initially bad and if the state is initially good.

(c) Derive a condition under which no risksharing is possible.

(d) Show that this condition is equivalent to "high implied interest rates" in autarky as defined by Alvarez and Jermann.

(e) Characterize the conditions under which partial risksharing, but not full risksharing, is possible.

Problem 11.5 The Market Selection Hypothesis

A large literature, briefly discussed in section 11.4.1, examines the conditions under which agents with incorrect beliefs about fundamentals will be driven out of the market by rational agents in the long run. In this exercise we explore in a partial-equilibrium setting some forces that influence the long-run survival of agents with incorrect beliefs.

Consider two agents A and B with wealth levels W_t^A and W_t^B, respectively, who invest in two assets in perfectly elastic supply, a risky asset with log return r_{t+1} and a riskless asset with riskfree rate $r_{f,t+1}$. The returns to the two assets are iid over time, $r_{t+1} \sim \mathcal{N}(\mu, \sigma^2)$ and $r_{f,t+1} = r_f$ for all t. The two investors have heterogeneous beliefs about the mean of log returns; in particular, they perceive $r_{t+1} \sim^i \mathcal{N}(\mu^i, \sigma^2)$, where μ^i may be different from the true mean μ. The agents have common Epstein-Zin preferences given by equation (6.34) and no outside income.

Investor A is said to become extinct (relative to investor B) if $\lim_{t\to\infty} W_t^A / W_t^B \to 0$ with probability 1 and is said to survive in the long run otherwise (and similarly for investor B). Long-run survival depends on the logarithmic growth rates of agents' wealth, consistent with the discussions of sections 2.1.5 and 10.3.2; in particular, in this iid setting it can be shown that investor A survives if and only if $\mathrm{E}[\log(W_{t+1}^A / W_t^A)] \geq \mathrm{E}[\log(W_{t+1}^B / W_t^B)]$.

(a) Argue that the geometric average growth rate of investor i's wealth, $i = \{A, B\}$, is given by

$$\mathrm{E}[w_{t+1}^i - w_t^i] = \mathrm{E}[r_{p,t+1}^i] + \log(1 - cw^i), \tag{11.60}$$

where $w_{t+1}^i = \log W_{t+1}^i$, $r_{p,t+1}^i$ is the log return to investor i's financial portfolio, and cw^i is his consumption-wealth ratio.

(b) Using the portfolio approximation (2.24), show that

$$\mathrm{E}[r_{p,t+1}^i] = r_f + \frac{RP^i RP}{\gamma \sigma^2} - \frac{(RP^i)^2}{2\gamma^2 \sigma^2}, \tag{11.61}$$

where $RP = \mu - r_f + \sigma^2/2$ and $RP^i = \mu^i - r_f + \sigma^2/2$. Explain the intuition behind the second and third terms in this expression.

Suppose that B is rational ($\mu^B = \mu$) but A is not. Under what conditions will A choose a portfolio with higher mean log return than B?

(c) Show that agent i's consumption-wealth ratio satisfies

$$\log(1 - cw^i) = -\rho\psi + (\psi - 1)\left[r_f + \frac{(RP^i)^2}{2\gamma\sigma^2}\right]. \tag{11.62}$$

How do subjective beliefs influence the agent's saving rate?

Hint: To derive the expression, use the envelope theorem and equation (6.34) under the conjecture $U_t = vW_t$, for some constant v.

(d) Prove that agent i will survive if and only if he has the (weakly) lower survival index I^i, given by

$$I^i = (RP^i - RP)^2 - \left(\psi - \frac{1}{\gamma}\right)(RP^i)^2. \qquad (11.63)$$

Conclude that under common power utility preferences an irrational agent cannot survive in the presence of a rational agent. Explain why this conclusion can be overturned for general Epstein-Zin preferences.

(e) How would these conclusions change if we allowed for arbitrary heterogeneity in preferences? Based on the preceding analysis, assess the theoretical robustness of the market selection hypothesis, according to which irrational investors will eventually be driven out of financial markets by the rational ones.

12

Asymmetric Information and Liquidity

IN THIS FINAL chapter of the book, we explore models of asymmetric information, in which some investors lack information about payoffs that other investors possess, and try to learn that information by observing asset prices. We also discuss models of trading costs that seek to explain why buying an asset and then selling it again is costly on average—a fact that has been ignored in all earlier chapters of this book. Asymmetric information is one important explanation for trading costs, so these topics are closely related.

The word "liquid" is often used to describe a market in which trading costs are low, but it is also used to describe a market in which assets can be purchased on margin. The final part of this chapter relates liquidity, in both these senses, to the prices at which assets trade.

Section 12.1 discusses the important concept of a rational expectations equilibrium, in which asymmetrically informed investors learn rationally from market prices and trade optimally given their private information and their inferences about the information of others.[1] We distinguish a fully revealing equilibrium, in which all private information is revealed by observing market prices, from a partially revealing equilibrium, in which private information has some value even though prices are also informative. We also consider models in which investors choose whether to pay to acquire information.

This section introduces the concept of "higher-order expectations" or expectations about the expectations of others. When investors are asymmetrically informed, the cross-sectional average of their heterogeneous expectations need not obey the law of iterated expectations. This can have consequences for asset pricing in models of short-term speculation, where each investor plans to sell to other investors in the future and therefore must forecast the average expectation in the marketplace at the time of sale.

Section 12.2 presents simple models of trading costs taken from the extensive literature on market microstructure. These models help explain the economic determinants of the bid-ask spread (the difference between the price at which a small number of shares can be bought, and the price at which they can be sold), as well as market impact (the effect of increasing trade size on the price of an asset). This section also briefly discusses models of active asset management that draw upon similar ideas.

---

[1]This usage of the term rational expectations is standard in finance and information economics. It differs from the usage in macroeconomics, where rational expectations is used to mean that agents in a model have expectations consistent with that model, without any implication that the agents have private information.

Section 12.3 explores how trading costs affect asset prices, how the ability to buy assets on margin affects asset prices, and finally how trading costs and margins interact with one another.

12.1 Rational Expectations Equilibrium

In models of financial markets with asymmetric information, investors condition their asset demands on their beliefs, which they form by observing prices as well as their own private signals. The classical literature assumes that agents form their beliefs rationally, although more recent research has considered behavioral biases in belief formation. Variation across investors in beliefs and asset demands adds complexity to price determination, so these models are tractable only in simple cases. The literature focuses almost exclusively on a setting where investors have constant absolute risk aversion (CARA) utility and where risks are normally distributed. In this setting asset demands are linear, do not depend on the wealth distribution, and can often be aggregated to derive closed-form solutions for asset prices.

The discussion here will make these standard assumptions, and will abstract from all nonessential differences across investors. That is, investors will be modeled symmetrically as having equal risk aversion coefficients, private signals of equal quality, and so forth.

12.1.1 Fully Revealing Equilibrium

To set the stage, we first follow Grossman (1976) and show how important prices can be in conveying information to investors. To do this, we contrast an equilibrium in which investors ignore the information in prices with one in which they extract from prices all the relevant information possessed by the group of market participants. We consider a model with two dates and n different investors, indexed by i, who choose their portfolios in the first period to maximize expected CARA utility of wealth at the second date. All investors have identical absolute risk aversion A.

There is a riskfree asset in elastic supply with gross return $1+R_f$ and a single risky asset with fixed supply Z. The initial price of the asset is P per share, and the random payoff (terminal price) is v per share. The unconditional distribution of v is normal with mean μ_0 and variance σ_0^2. The zero subscripts on these moments denote an initial condition in which investors have no special information derived from observing private signals or market prices. These unconditional moments are known to all investors, implying that all investors have identical prior beliefs before observing private signals.

At the beginning of the first period, investor i observes a signal s_i that equals the terminal payoff plus noise:

$$s_i = v + \varepsilon_i, \tag{12.1}$$

where ε_i is normally distributed with mean zero and variance σ_s^2 and is independent of v.

Let X_i be the demand for shares by the i'th investor. Let I_i refer to the information available to this investor at the start of the period. The investor's maximization problem is equivalent to

$$\max \left\{ X_i(\mathrm{E}[v \mid I_i] - (1 + R_f)P) - \frac{1}{2}AX_i^2\mathrm{Var}(v \mid I_i) \right\}, \tag{12.2}$$

and the solution is

$$X_i = \frac{\mathrm{E}[v \mid I_i] - (1 + R_f)P}{A\mathrm{Var}(v \mid I_i)}. \tag{12.3}$$

This is the familiar result for CARA utility, equation (2.17) from Chapter 2.

Competitive Equilibrium
In a traditional "competitive equilibrium," where investors ignore the information in prices, each investor's information set is his own private signal (together with the known parameters of the model), so $I_i = \{s_i\}$. Then, using formulas (9.65) and (9.66) with prior precision $\tau_0 = 1/\sigma_0^2$ and signal s_i precision $\tau_s = 1/\sigma_s^2$, we get after rearranging terms

$$\mathrm{E}[v \mid I_i] = \mu_0 + \beta(s_i - \mu_0), \tag{12.4}$$

and

$$\mathrm{Var}(v \mid I_i) = \sigma_0^2(1 - \beta), \tag{12.5}$$

where

$$\beta = \frac{\sigma_0^2}{\sigma_0^2 + \sigma_s^2} = \frac{\tau_s}{\tau_0 + \tau_s} \tag{12.6}$$

is the regression coefficient of v on s_i. Note that β approaches zero as the signal variance increases, and approaches one as the signal variance decreases to zero or equivalently as the signal precision increases.

Substituting (12.4) and (12.5) into the demand function for risky shares, we get

$$X_i = \frac{\mu_0 + \beta(s_i - \mu_0) - (1 + R_f)P}{A\sigma_0^2(1 - \beta)}. \tag{12.7}$$

The investor's risky asset demand responds to her private signal with slope β, and for a given price level it is higher on average when risk aversion A is lower, fundamental risk σ_0^2 is lower, and the signal is more precise (β is closer to one).

Aggregating across all investors and equating demand and supply for shares, we have

$$Z = \sum_{i=1}^{n} X_i = \sum_{i=1}^{n} \frac{\mu_0 + \beta(s_i - \mu_0) - (1 + R_f)P}{A\sigma_0^2(1 - \beta)}, \tag{12.8}$$

which implies that

$$P = \left(\frac{1}{1 + R_f}\right)\left[\mu_0 + \beta(\bar{s} - \mu_0) - \left(\frac{A}{n}\right)\sigma_0^2(1 - \beta)Z\right], \tag{12.9}$$

where

$$\bar{s} = \left(\frac{1}{n}\right)\sum_{i=1}^{n} s_i \tag{12.10}$$

is the average signal.

In this equilibrium the price is increasing in the average signal, which has a greater effect on the price when investors receive relatively precise signals (β is close to one). The price is decreasing in the aggregate supply, which has a greater effect on the price when aggregate risk-bearing capacity in the economy is low (A is high or the number of investors n is small) and when the signals are relatively imprecise (β is close to zero).

The difficulty with the competitive equilibrium is that the only random shocks in the model are the signals received by the investors, hence the price in equation (12.9) reveals the sum of all these signals. Such information is useful for predicting the terminal payoff v, yet in the competitive equilibrium each investor is assumed to ignore it.

Rational Expectations Equilibrium
As an alternative, Grossman proposes a rational expectations equilibrium in which $I_i = \{s_i, P^*(s)\}$, where s is the vector of all signals $s_1 \ldots s_n$ and P^* is the rational expectations price function. In this case

$$P^*(s) = \left(\frac{1}{1+R_f}\right)\left[\mu_0 + \beta^*(\bar{s} - \mu_0) - \left(\frac{A}{n}\right)v_0^2(1-\beta^*)Z\right], \tag{12.11}$$

where

$$\beta^* = \frac{\sigma_0^2}{\sigma_0^2 + (\sigma_s^2/n)}. \tag{12.12}$$

The coefficient β^* is the regression coefficient of v on the average signal $\bar{s}$. We have $\beta^* > \beta$ because the average signal is more precise than any individual signal. As the number of investors n increases, the average signal becomes an almost perfect indicator of the terminal payoff, and β^* approaches one. Relative to the competitive equilibrium price, the rational expectations price is higher on average (because there is less risk after information has been shared among investors) and more sensitive to the average signal.

To understand the pricing equation (12.11), note that once again the equilibrium price reveals the average signal $\bar{s}$ because all other parameters in the price function are known. Because we have assumed that the signals are independent and have equal variance, the average signal is a sufficient statistic for the information contained in all the signals. The average signal has variance σ_s^2/n around the true payoff, so the optimal demand of investor i given this information is

$$X_i = \frac{\mu_0 + \beta^*(\bar{s} - \mu_0) - (1+R_f)P}{A\sigma_0^2(1-\beta^*)}, \tag{12.13}$$

which does not vary across investors. Aggregating these equal demands and equating demand and supply, the equilibrium price is $P^*(s)$ as given above.

Equation (12.13) shows that all investors have the same asset demand, and hence they trade with one another only if they have different initial endowments of the asset. There is no trade resulting purely from differences in information, because any such trade would reveal that the buyer and seller have different posterior beliefs arising from their signals; and such commonly known differences in posteriors cannot be rational given the assumption that investors have identical prior beliefs before signals are received. This is the "no-trade" theorem of Milgrom and Stokey (1982). It builds on Aumann's (1976) result that agents with identical priors must have identical posteriors if their posteriors are common knowledge; in other words, they cannot "agree to disagree."[2]

The rational expectations price in equation (12.11) is *fully revealing*. The price of the asset would be unchanged if all investors received a common signal equal to the average signal, or if they shared their information before trading. In the terminology of section 5.1 of Chapter 5, the market is strong-form efficient. The fully revealing nature of the equilibrium creates two problems for this model. First, it is unclear what mechanism reveals investors' information to the market, because investors' asset demands do not respond to their own private signals.[3] Second, investors do not benefit from their private information so any cost of obtaining it, no matter how small, will deter investors from gathering information and will cause the equilibrium to break down.

12.1.2 Partially Revealing Equilibrium

To resolve these problems, we need an additional source of uncertainty or "noise" in the model so that the price is only partially revealing. Following Hellwig (1980) and Diamond and Verrecchia (DV 1981), asset pricing models with asymmetric information almost always include such noise, described either as shocks to asset supply or as exogenous shocks to asset demand by noise traders or liquidity traders (agents trading because they have an unmodeled demand for cash). These shocks break the no-trade theorem, because it is no longer the case that a trade necessarily reveals the presence in the market of two traders with commonly known differences in posteriors.

In this section we present the DV model, which has interpretable closed-form solutions. The model has the same basic structure as the one in the previous section. There is a single risky asset with price P and random payoff v, normally distributed with mean μ_0 and precision $\tau_0 = 1/\sigma_0^2$. Investors receive noisy signals of this payoff, with precision $\tau_s = 1/\sigma_s^2$, as in equation (12.1). In addition, investors are endowed with random quantities of the asset and this creates randomness in the aggregate supply, about which investors have dispersed information since they know their own endowment but not the endowments of others. Investor i receives an endowment z_i with mean zero and variance σ_z^2, and aggregate supply is

$$Z = \sum_{i=1}^{n} z_i, \tag{12.14}$$

which has mean zero and variance $n\sigma_z^2$. We write $\bar{z} = Z/n$ for the average endowment of an individual investor.

To simplify notation and focus on the key properties of the model, DV assume that the coefficient of absolute risk aversion is one and that the net riskless interest rate is zero, so the gross riskless interest rate is one.

---

[2]"Two people, 1 and 2, are said to have common knowledge of an event E if both know it, 1 knows that 2 knows it, 2 knows that 1 knows it, 1 knows that 2 knows that 1 knows it, and so on" (Aumann 1976).

[3]As a symptom of this problem, one can show that if investors differ in their risk aversion, then in a competitive equilibrium signals received by more risk-tolerant investors have a greater effect on the price, because these investors trade more aggressively on their information. However, this is not the case in the fully revealing rational expectations equilibrium, implying that the mechanism for information revelation somehow operates independently of preferences.

Solving the Model

The solution of the DV model, like that of other asymmetric information models, proceeds in five steps. First, we conjecture that the asset price is linear in sufficient statistics. Second, given this price function and private signals, we form each investor's beliefs. Third, given investors' beliefs we solve for their asset demands. Fourth, we impose market clearing. Finally, we solve for the coefficients in the price function and verify the assumed linear form of the price function.

For the DV model, the conjectured price function in the first step takes the form

$$P = p_0\mu_0 + p_s\bar{s} - p_z\bar{z}, \tag{12.15}$$

where p_0, p_s, and p_z are coefficients that must be solved for by imposing the restrictions of the model. The symmetry of the model ensures that prices depend only on the cross-sectional averages of signals and supply shocks.

At the second step, the conditional mean and variance of the asset payoff v given each investor's information can be written as $\mu_i(s_i, \tau_i, P)$ and $\sigma_i^2(s_i, \tau_i, P)$. The conditional variance is equal across agents, and we write its reciprocal, the precision of each agent's information, as $\tau = 1/\sigma_i^2$.

At the third step, the assumptions of unit absolute risk aversion, normally distributed randomness, and a unit gross riskless interest rate imply that each investor's asset demand is

$$X_i = \frac{\mu_i - P}{\sigma_i^2} = \tau(\mu_i - P). \tag{12.16}$$

At the fourth step, market-clearing requires that aggregate asset demand equals aggregate asset supply, so

$$\bar{z} = \left(\frac{1}{n}\right)\sum_{i=1}^{n} X_i = \tau(\bar{\mu} - P), \tag{12.17}$$

where $\bar{\mu} = \sum_{i=1}^{n}\mu_i/n$. Solving for the equilibrium asset price, we have

$$P = \bar{\mu} - \frac{\bar{z}}{\tau}. \tag{12.18}$$

At the fifth step, DV solve for the precision of agents' information as

$$\tau = \tau_0 + \frac{\tau_s(n\tau_s + \sigma_z^2)}{\tau_s + \sigma_z^2}. \tag{12.19}$$

The limiting behavior of this expression delivers insights. As the variance of supply noise σ_z^2 increases, τ approaches $\tau_0 + \tau_s$, which is the precision available from observing one private signal. In other words, enough supply noise makes the price uninformative so that investors can learn nothing from it and must rely entirely on their own private signals. At the opposite extreme, as the variance of supply noise σ_z^2 approaches zero, τ approaches $\tau_0 + n\tau_s$, which is the precision available from observing the average of all private signals.

Thus the perfectly revealing Grossman (1976) equilibrium is a limiting case of the DV model. Globally, τ is a decreasing convex function of σ_z^2.[4]

The fifth step of the analysis also delivers closed-form expressions for the coefficients p_s and p_z in equation (12.15). We have

$$p_z = \frac{n\tau_s + \sigma_z^2}{\tau\left(\tau_s + \sigma_z^2\right)}, \tag{12.20}$$

and

$$p_s = \tau_s p_z. \tag{12.21}$$

Considering the same limiting cases as before, as the variance of supply noise σ_z^2 increases, p_z approaches $1/\tau = 1/(\tau_0 + \tau_s)$ and p_s approaches $\tau_s/(\tau_0 + \tau_s)$. These are the coefficients that would obtain in a traditional competitive equilibrium where investors learn nothing from prices. At the opposite extreme, as the variance of supply noise σ_z^2 approaches zero, p_z approaches $n/\tau = n/(\tau_0 + n\tau_s)$ and p_s approaches $n\tau_s/(\tau_0 + n\tau_s)$. The value of p_z becomes irrelevant in the limit where is no supply noise, but the limiting value of p_s is the effect that the average signal has on the asset price in a perfectly revealing equilibrium. The coefficient p_z is greater in the second limiting case with very little supply noise, because investors who are learning from prices misinterpret supply shocks as partly reflecting information, and shift their asset demands and the equilibrium price accordingly. We develop this theme further in section 12.2.

Finally, we can solve for μ_i, the expected value of the asset's payoff conditional on each investor's information. We have

$$\mu_i = \mu_0 + \frac{\tau_s(z_i + \sigma_z^2(s_i - \mu_0))}{\tau\left(\tau_s + \sigma_z^2\right)} + \frac{n\tau_s}{n\tau_s + \sigma_z^2}(P - \mu_0). \tag{12.22}$$

The first term on the right-hand side of (12.22) is the unconditional mean of the payoff, the second term gives the response of the conditional expectation to the investor's two sources of private information (endowment and signal), and the third term gives the response of the conditional expectation to the information conveyed by the market price of the asset. In the two limiting cases, as the variance of supply noise σ_z^2 increases, μ_i approaches $\mu_0 + (\tau_s/(\tau_0 + \tau_s))(s_i - \mu_0)$, which would be the value in a competitive equilibrium where investors learn nothing from prices. As the variance of supply noise decreases to zero, μ_i approaches P; that is, we approach a fully revealing equilibrium in which investors gain no benefit from their private information.

In summary, the DV model shows how a financial market can partially but not fully aggregate private information, allowing investors to benefit from private information and transmit it to the market through their trades. The market can come arbitrarily close to full revelation of information without encountering the paradoxes of the fully revealing equilibrium.[5]

---

[4]We can also consider what happens as the number of agents n increases. In this case, τ increases without limit, because the signals collectively available to investors eliminate all fundamental risk. For the same reason, τ increases without limit as τ_s, the precision of each individual signal, increases. Conversely, τ approaches the unconditional precision τ_0 as τ_s decreases, that is, as individual signals become uninformative.

[5]Similar points about information aggregation have been made in the context of auctions (Wilson 1977, Kremer 2002, Cripps and Swinkels 2005, Reny and Perry 2006).

12.1.3 News, Trading Volume, and Returns

Rational expectations models with partial revelation of information allow trade to occur on the basis of private information as well as to accommodate supply shocks (coming either from a separate class of investors or, as in the DV model, from the same investors who receive private signals). However, as discussed above, the supply shocks are essential for information-based trade to occur. This limits the fraction of trading volume that can be attributed to information and makes it hard for these models to generate trading volume comparable to what is empirically observed without assuming highly volatile supply shocks that are exogenous and unexplained.

This class of models can also generate some return predictability resulting from the interaction between the risk-bearing capacity of investors and shocks to the supply of assets they must hold, as in behavioral models of noise trading discussed in section 11.4.1. When supply increases, prices fall and expected returns increase; if supply shocks are transitory, this generates short-run negative autocorrelation in stock returns. Campbell, Grossman, and Wang (1993) present a model with both supply shocks, coming from a separate class of investors, and public signals about fundamentals. They argue that supply shocks create trading volume whereas public signals do not, hence if supply shocks are transitory stock returns should tend to reverse more when volume is high than when it is low.[6] They find some evidence in support of this prediction in aggregate US data. However, the implied return predictability is quite modest and should not affect the idiosyncratic components of individual stock returns whose risks can be diversified away.

These limitations of rational expectations models have stimulated interest in models where investors have private information but do not process it in a fully rational manner. Daniel, Hirshleifer, and Subrahmanyam (DHS 1998), for example, present a model in which investors are overconfident about the precision of their private information but correctly judge the precision of public information. This leads investors to overreact to private signals, trading more aggressively on them than a rational investor would do, while underreacting to public signals. Overreaction to private signals increases trading volume and generates negative autocorrelation in stock returns as the overreaction is gradually corrected.[7]

In order to generate positive short- to medium-term autocorrelation, DHS augment the model with a dynamic process for overconfidence itself. They assume that overconfidence increases when a confirming public signal is received after a private signal but does not decrease when an opposing public signal is received. This "biased self-attribution" implies that after a positive private signal arrives, a subsequent positive public signal increases the weight on the private signal and drives up stock prices substantially, whereas a subsequent negative public signal leaves the weight on the private signal unchanged and hence has a smaller negative effect on stock prices. The reverse occurs after the arrival of a negative private signal, implying shorter-term positive autocorrelation. Negative autocorrelation is still present in the longer run.

---

[6]Trading volume does in fact increase around public information releases such as earnings announcements. Harris and Raviv (1993) and Kandel and Pearson (1995) attribute this to investors' use of heterogeneous models to interpret public information.

[7]When all investors are overconfident as in DHS (1998), idiosyncratic stock returns can be predictable; a subsequent paper (DHS 2001) shows how return predictability in groups of correlated stocks can survive in a model that also includes risk-averse uninformed arbitrageurs. See also Kruger (2015).

An alternative type of irrational information processing has been proposed by Eyster, Rabin, and Vayanos (ERV 2015). ERV argue that investors fail to fully infer the information possessed by other investors and revealed in market prices. They call this failure "cursedness," after the winner's curse in auction theory. Cursed investors and overconfident investors behave similarly in many contexts, since both overweight their own private information relative to the information of others. However, cursedness has a more powerful effect in settings where others possess a large amount of information and becomes irrelevant in a context where a single investor is the only possessor of a private signal, as in the Kyle (1985) model discussed in section 12.2.2.

Revelation of Pent-Up Information
Stock prices sometimes move dramatically in the absence of any obvious public information announcement that might explain the move. A notorious example is the 20% decline in the US stock market on October 19, 1987. A model with private information can straightforwardly explain such a move if investors receive extreme private signals on the day the move occurs, but even after the fact observers are hard pressed to identify signals of the necessary magnitude. An interesting literature extends private information models to allow for the revelation on a single day of "pent-up" information received earlier and previously hidden. This reduces the magnitude of the signals that are needed to trigger a large market move.

Romer (1993) builds a model where all investors in an asset market are rational but where there is an additional level of uncertainty. In all states of the world, a first group of investors receives common private signals of medium precision, but a second group of investors receives highly precise common signals in some states and relatively imprecise signals in other states. Investors know the precision of their own signals but not the precision of others' signals. They must infer not only the information that other investors possess but also the precision of that information. In this model, a supply shock that is known to all investors reveals the slope of the aggregate demand curve for the asset and hence the precision of information. If, for example, the first investor group had negative information, while the second investor group had imprecise positive information, the market price will fall when the first investor group realizes the imprecision of the information that was previously thought to justify the price.[8] In this manner a large price decline can occur in response to a small supply shock that reveals pent-up information.

The Romer model is symmetrical and does not predict that large crashes should be more common than large upward moves in prices (as appears to be the case, at least over short periods of time and for aggregate stock indexes). Hong and Stein (2003) develop a model in which informed agents are overconfident and short sales constrained. Rational, but uninformed, risk-neutral arbitrageurs interact with these agents and try to infer their information. If information is received sequentially and the first informed agent receives a negative signal, this agent will sell stock to zero and the exact magnitude of his negative information will be hidden. If the second informed agent subsequently receives a negative signal, the price will fall as this agent sells, and the reaction of the first agent (either reentering the market to support the price or continuing to sit on the sidelines) may reveal to the arbitrageurs something about the first signal as well as the second signal. Importantly, this mechanism generates crashes from configurations

---

[8]This might be called an "emperor's new clothes" crash after Hans Christian Andersen's 1837 fable.

of negative signals but not upward jumps from comparable configurations of positive signals, because short-sales constraints only bind on the downside.

12.1.4 Equilibrium with Costly Information

In the models discussed so far, investors are endowed with information and do not pay anything to obtain it. In a setting where information is costly, we need to understand how investors who pay to obtain information are rewarded. Grossman and Stiglitz (GS 1980) present the classic model of rational expectations equilibrium with costly information. They assume the same structure as before with CARA utility, common risk aversion, and normally distributed risks; but instead of each investor receiving an idiosyncratic signal for free, there is a common signal that any investor can pay to observe. The risky asset has payoff per share

$$v = s + \varepsilon, \tag{12.23}$$

where s is observable at cost c, and ε is unobservable. The variables s and ε are independent of one another and have means zero and variances σ_s^2 and σ_ε^2, respectively.[9]

The supply of the risky asset is Z, and this must be random to prevent perfect inference by uninformed investors. Informed investors can infer Z from the equilibrium asset price because they know s, but uninformed investors cannot tell whether the asset price is high because s is high or because Z is low.

The price of the risky asset is P. The demand of an informed investor is

$$X_I(P, s) = \frac{s - (1 + R_f)P}{A\sigma_\varepsilon^2}. \tag{12.24}$$

The demand of an uninformed investor is

$$X_U(P) = \frac{\mathrm{E}[v \mid P] - (1 + R_f)P}{A\mathrm{Var}(v \mid P)}. \tag{12.25}$$

A fraction ϕ of investors decide to become informed. In equilibrium, we must have

$$\phi X_I + (1 - \phi) X_U = Z. \tag{12.26}$$

This defines a pricing function $P(\phi; s, Z)$ that clears the market for given ϕ. The pricing function can be characterized as follows. Define

$$w(\phi; s, Z) = s - \frac{A\sigma_\varepsilon^2}{\phi}(Z - \mathrm{E}Z). \tag{12.27}$$

$w(\phi; s, Z)$ is a weighted combination of s and Z. As the fraction of informed investors ϕ increases, the weight on the signal s increases relative to the weight on the asset supply Z. It can be shown that

$$P(\phi; s, Z) = \alpha_1(\phi) + \alpha_2(\phi) w(\phi; s, Z), \tag{12.28}$$

[9]The assumption that the payoff is signal plus noise is different from the assumption made earlier in this chapter that investors receive a signal that equals payoff plus noise. However, the difference is merely a renormalization of the model. Investors who receive a noisy signal of the sort assumed in sections 12.1.1 and 12.1.2 can calculate the conditional expectation of the payoff given the signal. The variable s in equation (12.23) is this conditional expectation.

where the notation $\alpha_1(\phi)$ and $\alpha_2(\phi)$ denotes that these coefficients may depend on ϕ, and $\alpha_2(\phi) > 0$ for all ϕ. Equation (12.28) shows that the price reveals $w(\phi; s, Z)$ but not s and Z individually.

The next step is to determine the fraction of investors that become informed. Under the assumption that an interior solution exists with $0 < \phi < 1$, the ex ante expected utility of informed and uninformed investors, before they observe s or P, must be equal at the equilibrium value of ϕ.

To understand the determinants of expected utility, note that the terminal wealth of an informed investor with initial wealth W_0 is

$$W_I(\phi; s, Z, \varepsilon) = (1 + R_f)(W_0 - c) + (v - (1 + R_f)P) X_I(P, s), \qquad (12.29)$$

while the terminal wealth of an uninformed investor with the same initial wealth is

$$W_U(\phi; s, Z, \varepsilon) = (1 + R_f) W_0 + (v - (1 + R_f)P) X_U(P). \qquad (12.30)$$

These wealth levels depend on ϕ because the pricing function P depends on ϕ. The expected difference between the terminal wealth of informed and uninformed investors is

$$\begin{aligned}
E[W_I - W_U] &= -c(1 + R_f) + E[(v - (1 + R_f)P)(X_I(P, s) - X_U(P))] \\
&= -c(1 + R_f) + E[(v - (1 + R_f)P)]E(X_I(P, s) - X_U(P))] \\
&\quad + \mathrm{Cov}((v - (1 + R_f)P), (X_I(P, s) - X_U(P)). \qquad (12.31)
\end{aligned}$$

Informed investors have lower expected terminal wealth because of the cost they must pay to become informed, but higher expected terminal wealth because their holdings of the risky asset are higher on average (since they perceive the asset to have less risk) and covary positively with the risky payoff.

Expected utility depends not only on expected wealth but also on the variance of wealth. GS define the utility ratio of the expected utility of the informed to the expected utility of the uninformed as

$$UR(\phi) = \frac{EU(W_I(\phi; s, Z, \varepsilon))}{EU(W_U(\phi; s, Z, \varepsilon))}.$$

Since exponential utility is negative, the informed investors are better off when $UR(\phi) < 1$, uninformed investors are better off when $UR(\phi) > 1$, and the two groups of investors are equally well off when $UR(\phi) = 1$. GS show that

$$UR(\phi) = \exp(Ac) \frac{\sigma_\varepsilon}{\sigma(v \mid w(\phi; s, Z))}. \qquad (12.32)$$

A low cost of information, low risk aversion, and high precision of non-public information reduce $UR(\phi)$ and hence increase the relative utility of informed investors for given ϕ. The ratio $UR(\phi)$ is monotonically increasing in ϕ, since a higher ϕ reduces the influence of the supply shock and makes the stock price more informative, reducing $\sigma(v \mid w(\phi; s, Z))$ and increasing $UR(\phi)$. Thus there is a unique ϕ that satisfies the condition for an interior solution, $UR(\phi) = 1$.

The informativeness of the price system can be measured by the squared correlation coefficient between the equilibrium price $P(\phi; s, Z)$ and the signal s. GS show that in an interior equilibrium,

$$[\text{Corr}(P(\phi; s, Z), s)]^2 = 1 - \frac{\exp(2Ac) - 1}{(\sigma_s^2/\sigma_\varepsilon^2)}. \tag{12.33}$$

Thus the price system becomes more informative when the cost of acquiring information c falls, when risk aversion A falls, and when the value of non-public information $(\sigma_s^2/\sigma_\varepsilon^2)$ rises. Nothing else affects the informativeness of the price system. In particular, the variance of supply shocks σ_Z^2 does not, because an increase in σ_Z^2 induces an increase in ϕ that offsets its direct negative effect on informativeness. In the next section we will see that the Kyle (1985) model of strategic trading by a single informed trader has the same property.

Finally, GS show that equilibrium cannot exist with perfect revelation of information and positive information cost c. Such an equilibrium would not reward investors for the cost of acquiring information. Investors who acquired information in the absence of noise would not be able to profit from it, for they would not be able to find counter-parties willing to trade with them (Milgrom and Stokey 1982). This nonexistence result is sometimes called the *Grossman-Stiglitz paradox*.

Extensions of the Grossman-Stiglitz Model

In the GS model, all investors have the same cost of gathering and processing information. It is natural to consider heterogeneity in such costs. In a heterogeneous-cost model, the marginal investor must be indifferent between becoming informed and remaining uninformed, but all investors with lower costs than the marginal investor strictly prefer to be informed and earn rents from their skill at processing information. This is one way to understand the profits earned by successful active investors.

The GS model has a single asset but can be extended to a setting with many assets where investors have a choice of which assets to learn about (Hirshleifer, Subrahmanyam, and Titman 1994). Van Nieuwerburgh and Veldkamp (2009) use a model of this sort and argue that if investors have a small initial informational advantage with regard to local stocks, they will optimally acquire more local information in order to receive signals that are as different as possible from the signals other investors receive. In this way investors may become particularly well informed about local stocks. Because informed investors perceive less risk they hold larger positions on average, so this model can help explain local bias, the tendency to overweight local stocks. A challenge for this type of model is that information also tends to increase the volatility of investors' positions as they trade in response to their signals, and it is unclear that locally biased portfolios are active enough to be consistent with an information-based explanation. Problem 12.1 asks you to analyze an informational model of local bias based on O'Hara (2003).

The GS model assumes rational investors, but behavioral phenomena such as over-confidence can readily be incorporated into this framework. Investors who overestimate the precision of private information are more inclined to invest in such information, other things equal, so overconfidence acts like a reduction in the cost of information and makes prices more informative, a point emphasized by Rubinstein (2001).

12.1.5 Higher-Order Expectations

In models where investors have heterogeneous information, each investor may wish to forecast the beliefs of other investors. This is particularly true when investors plan to sell assets to other investors before uncertainty is resolved. Beliefs about the beliefs of others are sometimes called higher-order beliefs or expectations. Keynes (1936, p. 156) famously described the importance of higher-order expectations in asset pricing:

> Professional investment may be likened to those newspaper competitions in which the competitors have to pick out the six prettiest faces from a hundred photographs, the prize being awarded to the competitor whose choice most nearly corresponds to the average preferences of the competitors as a whole; so that each competitor has to pick, not those faces which he himself finds prettiest, but those which he thinks likeliest to catch the fancy of the other competitors, all of whom are looking at the problem from the same point of view. It is not a case of choosing those which, to the best of one's judgement, are really the prettiest, nor even those which average opinion genuinely thinks the prettiest. We have reached the third degree where we devote our intelligences to anticipating what average opinion expects the average opinion to be. And there are some, I believe, who practise the fourth, fifth and higher degrees.

Allen, Morris, and Shin (AMS 2006) observe that such cross-sectional averages of expectations, unlike individual or public expectations, fail to satisfy the law of iterated expectations. This has interesting implications for asset pricing when traders have finite horizons that force them to sell to other investors before uncertainty is resolved.

For a random variable v (which might be the terminal payoff on a risky asset, as elsewhere in this section), let $E_{it}[v]$ be investor i's expectation of v at time t; write $\overline{E}_t(v)$ for the cross-sectional average expectation across investors i at time t; and write $E_t^*[v]$ for the time t expectation of v based only on publicly available information. It is well known that:

$$E_{it}[E_{i,t+1}[v]] = E_{it}[v] \tag{12.34}$$

and

$$E_t^*[E_{t+1}^*[v]] = E_t^*[v], \tag{12.35}$$

that is, the law of iterated expectations holds for both individual expectations and expectations conditional on only public information.

However, the law of iterated expectations does not generally describe the cross-sectional average of individual expectations:

$$\overline{E}_t[\overline{E}_{t+1}[v]] \neq \overline{E}_t[v]. \tag{12.36}$$

The average expectation today of the average expectation tomorrow need not equal the average expectation today.

For a concrete example, suppose that v is distributed normally with mean μ_0 and precision τ_0 and that each agent in a continuum receives a single private signal s_i with mean v and precision τ_s. Then:

$$E_i[v] = \frac{\tau_0 \mu_0 + \tau_s s_i}{\tau_0 + \tau_s} = (1 - \beta)\mu_0 + \beta s_i, \tag{12.37}$$

where $\beta = \tau_s / (\tau_0 + \tau_s)$ as in equation (12.6), and

$$\overline{\mathrm{E}}[v] = (1 - \beta)\mu_0 + \beta v, \tag{12.38}$$

because there is a continuum of agents so that the average signal is exactly v.

Taking investor i's expectation of this average expectation we have:

$$\begin{aligned}\mathrm{E}_i[\overline{\mathrm{E}}[v]] &= (1 - \beta)\mu_0 + \beta\mathrm{E}_i[v] \\ &= (1 - \beta^2)\mu_0 + \beta^2 s_i, \end{aligned} \tag{12.39}$$

where the second line follows by substituting in (12.37) and simplifying. Therefore the average expectation of the average expectation is:

$$\overline{\mathrm{E}}[\overline{\mathrm{E}}[v]] = \overline{\mathrm{E}}^2[v] = (1 - \beta^2)\mu_0 + \beta^2 v. \tag{12.40}$$

Repeating this calculation, we have

$$\overline{\mathrm{E}}^h[v] = (1 - \beta^k)\mu_0 + \beta^k v. \tag{12.41}$$

Notice that higher-order expectations are biased toward the public information μ_0 (indeed, as $k \to \infty$, $\overline{\mathrm{E}}^k(v) \to \mu_0$). So if there were an asset with time T terminal value of v priced according to Keynes' story in successive periods so that $p_t = \overline{\mathrm{E}}_t(p_{t+1})$, then its price would be biased toward the public signal and away from fundamentals.

AMS present a model that generates Keynesian pricing. A single risky asset is liquidated at time $T+1$ but is traded at dates 1 to T by overlapping generations of traders, each of which enters the market to buy the asset and then must sell it again the next period. Because traders cannot hold to the liquidation date, they form their demands by forecasting short-term price movements or, equivalently, the average beliefs of future traders. The asset price path in the AMS model deviates from the path of the average expected liquidation value—specifically, it is biased toward public information—and prices react sluggishly to changes in fundamentals.

12.2 Market Microstructure

The field of market microstructure studies the mechanisms that are used to trade financial assets and the costs of accomplishing transactions. The details of trading arrangements have been ignored in the asset pricing models discussed earlier in this book, and trading costs have been treated as negligible.

Conceptually, one can define the cost of trading an asset as the dollars lost in a round-trip transaction that buys the asset and then sells it again. This cost can be expressed in proportional terms by dividing by the purchase or sales price of the asset. Trading costs typically vary both with the size of a transaction and with the length of time it takes to accomplish. An asset is said to be *liquid* if it can be traded at a low cost.

Measuring transactions costs is not straightforward because they may be paid in several different forms, whose importance varies across markets. For heterogeneous, illiquid assets such as residential real estate, brokers match buyers and sellers and help them agree on a price in exchange for a commission. Commissions are easy to measure but become relatively unimportant in more liquid markets.

When assets are sufficiently homogeneous and traded sufficiently often, dealer markets emerge. In these markets, specialized dealers or marketmakers stand ready to trade with outside investors and typically take one side of each transaction. Marketmakers post offers to buy and sell (quotes), and investors can trade without delay if they are willing to buy high at the marketmaker's ask price and sell low at the marketmaker's bid price. The difference between these two prices is the *bid-ask spread*, a second form of transactions costs that can be measured by observing marketmakers' quotes.

In many modern financial markets, outside investors can compete with marketmakers by posting limit orders: offers to buy at or below a maximum price, or to sell at or above a minimum price. In such markets, the effective bid-ask spread is defined as the difference between the lowest price specified in an outstanding limit order to sell and the highest price specified in a limit order to buy.

Posted offers apply only for modest trade sizes. Larger trades move prices against them as marketmakers adjust their quotes, or increasingly less favorable limit orders are executed. This *market impact* increases trading costs at larger trade sizes and is particularly hard to measure, since it may depend on the dynamic reactions of marketmakers and limit orders to the arrival of a trade or a sequence of trades.

Recent developments in US equity markets have made transactions costs in these markets even harder to measure. Equity trades occur in many different venues with different trading mechanisms that are electronically connected to one another. Some of these venues pay fees to brokers who submit market orders (liquidity takers) or limit orders (liquidity makers). Such maker-taker fees may or may not be passed back to investors in the form of lower commissions. New order types have been created, beyond simple market orders and limit orders, that allow various complex contingencies. Quotes can be posted and withdrawn at extremely high frequency, creating the appearance of liquidity that may not actually be present when trades occur.

The academic literature on market microstructure extends well beyond the scope of this book. However, the basic theoretical models of market microstructure are important for asset pricing and are closely linked to the asymmetric information theory discussed earlier in this chapter. These models ask what determines the magnitude of trading costs, with particular attention to the bid-ask spread and market impact. The goal is to explain variation in trading costs across different types of assets and (in some models) across types of traders.

12.2.1 Information and the Bid-Ask Spread

Roll (1984) offers a simple explanation for the existence of a bid-ask spread that does not rely on any information asymmetry. In Roll's model, the spread compensates marketmakers for their fixed costs of doing business and for the costs of holding an inventory of assets to buffer the asynchronous arrival of buy and sell orders. In other words, the spread is akin to a markup of retail price over wholesale price in a grocery store. This theory explains why spreads tend to be higher on assets with lower trading volume, just as markups tend to be higher in small convenience stores than in large supermarkets. In both cases, fixed costs must be covered with a lower volume of transactions, requiring a higher profit per transaction. Roll's model also predicts that spreads should be higher for volatile assets if marketmakers are undiversified and reluctant to take risk in their inventories.

In Roll's model, ask and bid prices are set symmetrically around a midpoint that represents the hypothetical price that would prevail in a frictionless asset market. The

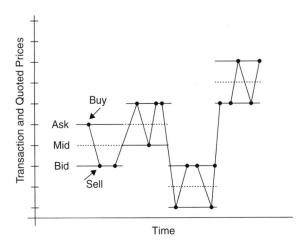

Figure 12.1.   Transaction and Quoted Prices in the Roll (1984) Model

midpoint itself follows a random walk whose innovations are driven by the arrival of public information. Changes in the midpoint are therefore serially uncorrelated, but price changes around the midpoint must be negatively serially correlated, since an increase from the bid price to the ask price (representing the arrival of a buy order following a sell order) can only be followed by a second transaction at an unchanged price if another buy order arrives, or a decline to the bid price if a sell order arrives, but cannot be followed by a second price increase. This price behavior is sometimes called *bid-ask bounce*. An illustrative price sequence in Roll's model is shown in Figure 12.1.

Roll points out that if the midpoint is constant, then a random sequence of equally likely buys and sells creates a negative autocovariance in price changes of $-(SPR/2)^2$, where SPR is the bid-ask spread in dollars. The variance of price changes is $SPR^2/2$. In the presence of unpredictable midpoint variation, the variance of price changes increases but the autocovariance remains the same. Hence, Roll proposes short-run autocovariance as an empirical measure of the effective bid-ask spread. Roll's measure is useful when quotes are not available or when the effective bid-ask spread is smaller than the quoted bid-ask spread because outside investors compete with marketmakers using limit orders.

Working with returns rather than dollar changes in prices to express the spread as a proportion of the price, Roll's measure of the proportional spread *spr* is

$$spr = 2\sqrt{-\mathrm{Cov}(R_t, R_{t-1})}, \tag{12.42}$$

where t indexes transactions rather than calendar time. While this measure encounters empirical difficulties when stocks have positive short-run autocovariances, the basic concept has been widely used. Pástor and Stambaugh (2003) and Nagel (2012), for example, use the negative daily autocovariances of individual stock returns, averaged across stocks, to measure the profits to marketmaking and the overall illiquidity of the equity market.

Bid-ask bounce increases the volatility of high-frequency returns, measured from transaction prices, relative to the true underlying volatility of the frictionless asset return. As the return horizon increases, the difference diminishes. This also affects measures of average returns. The geometric average return on an asset over a given sample period depends only on the cumulative return over the period, which is negligibly affected by bid-ask bounce. However, the arithmetic average return is approximately the geometric average return plus one-half the variance, so bid-ask bounce increases the arithmetic average of returns measured over short time intervals. This effect, on the order of $spr^2/4$, can be important for illiquid stocks, as pointed out by Blume and Stambaugh (1983).

The Glosten-Milgrom Model of an Information-Based Spread

Glosten and Milgrom (1985) offer a different explanation for the existence of a bid-ask spread. They consider the interaction between uninformed marketmakers and outside investors, some of whom have private information about asset values. They assume that outside orders arrive at random times and have an order size fixed at one that will be executed either at the ask or the bid price posted by the marketmakers. Marketmakers are risk-neutral and have no fixed costs.

Under these assumptions, marketmakers set bid and ask prices equal to their expectation of fundamental value conditional on their current information plus the event that the next investor wants to buy a unit (ask) or sell a unit (bid). If buy orders and sell orders arrive with equal probability, then the midpoint of the quotes is the expectation of fundamental value, so it follows a random walk. That is, at any time t, the midpoint is

$$\text{Mid}_t = \text{E}[V_t \mid I_t], \tag{12.43}$$

where V_t is the fundamental value of the asset (the expected present value of future dividends, discounted using the SDF) and I_t is the marketmaker's information set. The ask price is

$$\text{Ask}_t = \text{E}[V_t \mid I_t \text{ and buy order}], \tag{12.44}$$

while the bid price is

$$\text{Bid}_t = \text{E}[V_t \mid I_t \text{ and sell order}]. \tag{12.45}$$

If investors placing orders have private information about fundamentals, then a buy order implies a higher expected fundamental value than a sell order, so the ask price exceeds the bid and the bid-ask spread is positive.

When a buy (sell) order arrives, it is fulfilled at the ask (bid), which then becomes the midpoint of the new quotes. Since all trades occur at midpoints, which themselves are rational expectations of fundamentals, changes in traded prices are serially uncorrelated. Thus, there is no bid-ask bounce in the Glosten-Milgrom model, and the autocovariance of changes in transaction prices can no longer be used to measure the bid-ask spread. Instead, the spread must be measured from the impact of trades on subsequent quotes (Hasbrouck 1991). Price dynamics in the Glosten-Milgrom model are illustrated in Figure 12.2.

The idea that asymmetric information reduces liquidity is an important one. It can be used to explain variation in transactions costs both across assets and over time. Assets such as foreign currency and Treasury bonds are extremely cheap to trade, and there is

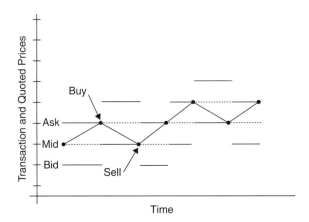

Figure 12.2.   *Transaction and Quoted Prices in the Glosten and Milgrom (1985) Model*

probably little asymmetric information about the payoffs on these assets. Within the stock market, small stocks are more expensive to trade than large ones, and informed trading is probably more prevalent relative to uninformed trading in small stocks. Spreads tend to widen in periods where asymmetric information is likely a concern, such as the days before earnings announcements. Finally, this idea can be used to understand why certain assets are particularly vulnerable to decreases in liquidity. Dang, Gorton, and Holmström (2012) have argued that in normal times, debt instruments are liquid because the chance of default is small, so debtholders have little incentive to obtain private information. In bad times, information about borrowers' repayment capacity becomes valuable, debtholders gather it, potential buyers of debt anticipate this, and the liquidity of the market dries up.

Easley et al. (EKOP 1996) elaborate on the Glosten-Milgrom model by assuming that buy and sell arrivals are persistent within the trading day when information events occur. With probability α, an information event occurs and is negative with probability δ, positive with probability $1 - \delta$. If it is negative, sells arrive at rate $\varepsilon + \mu$, while buys arrive at rate ε. If it is positive, the arrival rates of buys and sells are reversed. With probability $1 - \alpha$, no information event occurs and buys and sells occur at equal rates ε. EKOP estimate these parameters using the distributions of the total numbers of buys and sells across days. Stocks with higher α and μ relative to ε have fatter-tailed distributions across days. The probability that a particular trade is informed is $\alpha\mu/(\alpha\mu + 2\varepsilon)$ in this model, and stocks with high values of this probability should have higher average spreads. EKOP find that smaller stocks, which typically have higher spreads, also have higher estimated values of the probability of informed trading.

A final implication of the Glosten-Milgrom model is that if a trader can demonstrate that she has no private information, she will pay a lower spread. There is less empirical evidence in favor of this, although privatizations of state-owned companies are typically accomplished at modest transactions costs, and index funds often do manage to trade cheaply. Duffie, Gârleanu, and Pedersen (2005) use a search model to argue that marketmakers have some monopoly power over investors with search costs. Sophisticated investors pay lower spreads because they have lower search costs and are therefore less vulnerable to exploitation by marketmakers. Since sophisticated investors are also likely to have more private information, this offsets the Glosten-Milgrom effect.

12.2.2 Information and Market Impact

In the Glosten-Milgrom model, buy and sell orders have a fixed trade size. In reality, trade sizes vary and larger trades are more expensive to execute because they have market impact, moving prices unfavorably. We now discuss the Kyle (1985) model, which captures this effect and explains its magnitude.

The competitive rational expectations equilibrium models discussed in section 12.1 assume perfect competition and use risk aversion to limit the aggressiveness of traders trying to exploit their information. Risk aversion will have only a weak effect in the context of any single stock's idiosyncratic risk, so Kyle (1985) and many other market microstructure papers assume for simplicity that investors are risk-neutral. The aggressiveness of trading is limited not by risk aversion but by a single informed investor's understanding that his trades have market impact. The investor is no longer a price-taker but instead trades strategically. The investor interacts with risk-neutral uninformed marketmakers and with noise traders who prevent full revelation and permit profitable trading on information. Kyle also assumes that the informed investor submits a market order rather than a schedule of limit orders.

In the Kyle model an asset has an ex post value v, which is distributed normally with mean μ_0 and variance σ_0^2. Noise traders have demand z, which is distributed normally with mean zero and variance σ_z^2. A single insider observes v and chooses an asset demand x as a function of v:

$$x = X(v). \tag{12.46}$$

Risk-neutral, competitive marketmakers observe $x + z$ and set a price at which they are willing to buy or sell this amount,

$$p = P(x + z) = \mathrm{E}[v \mid x + z]. \tag{12.47}$$

The informed investor makes a profit

$$\pi = (v - p)x. \tag{12.48}$$

The investor chooses his demand x to maximize expected profit given the inside information, $\mathrm{E}[\pi \mid v]$.

Kyle shows that there exists a linear equilibrium in which both the informed investor and the marketmakers follow linear strategies. The informed investor trades with aggressiveness β:

$$X(v) = \beta(v - \mu_0). \tag{12.49}$$

The marketmakers set the price as a linear function of order flow, with intercept μ and slope coefficient λ:

$$P(x + z) = \mu + \lambda(x + z). \tag{12.50}$$

In equilibrium the intercept μ equals the unconditional mean payoff μ_0, and the slope coefficients in (12.49) and (12.50) are given by

$$\beta = \frac{\sigma_z}{\sigma_0} \tag{12.51}$$

and

$$\lambda = \frac{1}{2}\frac{\sigma_0}{\sigma_z}. \tag{12.52}$$

Thus $\beta = 1/2\lambda$.

To derive these results, take the linear pricing rule as given and solve the informed investor's problem:

$$\max \mathrm{E}[\pi \mid v] = \mathrm{E}[(v - \mu - \lambda(x + z))x] = (v - \mu - \lambda x)x. \tag{12.53}$$

The solution to this quadratic optimization problem is

$$x = \alpha + \beta v, \tag{12.54}$$

where $\alpha = -\mu/2\lambda$ and $\beta = 1/2\lambda$.

Now consider the marketmaker's problem. With normally distributed shocks and a linear strategy of the informed investor, the marketmaker chooses a pricing function to minimize the variance of the pricing error:

$$\min \mathrm{E}[(v - P(x+z))^2] = \mathrm{E}[(v - \mu - \lambda(x+z))^2]$$
$$= \mathrm{E}[(v - \mu - \lambda(\alpha + \beta v + z))^2]. \tag{12.55}$$

The solution to this problem sets

$$\lambda = \frac{\beta \sigma_0^2}{\beta^2 \sigma_0^2 + \sigma_z^2}. \tag{12.56}$$

Substituting in $\beta = 1/2\lambda$, we get the desired solution.

This equilibrium has some interesting properties. The solution for β shows that greater volatility of noise trading increases the aggressiveness of the insider (just as it increased the fraction of investors who chose to become informed in the Grossman-Stiglitz model). If we substitute the insider's trading out of the equilibrium price function, we find that

$$p = \mu + \lambda(x+z) = \mu + \lambda(\alpha + \beta v + z) = \frac{1}{2}(\mu_0 + v) + \lambda z. \tag{12.57}$$

Thus one-half of the insider's information gets into the price. The informativeness of the price in this model is independent of the volatility of noise trading, just as in the Grossman-Stiglitz model.

The expected profit of the insider, conditional on knowing v, is

$$\mathrm{E}[\pi \mid v] = \frac{\beta}{2}(v - \mu_0)^2 = \frac{1}{2}\left(\frac{\sigma_z}{\sigma_0}\right)(v - \mu_0)^2, \tag{12.58}$$

which is increasing in the distance of the information v from its unconditional mean. Unconditionally, the insider's expected profit is

$$\mathrm{E}[\pi] = \frac{1}{2}\left(\frac{\sigma_z}{\sigma_0}\right)\sigma_0^2 = \frac{1}{2}\sigma_z\sigma_0, \qquad (12.59)$$

which is proportional to the standard deviations of noise trading and inside information. The insider's expected profit is also the total expected loss of the noise traders, since the marketmakers set prices to avoid losing money on average.

The reciprocal of λ can be interpreted as the market "depth," the order flow needed to raise the market price by one dollar. We have

$$\frac{1}{\lambda} = 2\frac{\sigma_z}{\sigma_0}, \qquad (12.60)$$

so the market is deep when there is more noise trading and less inside information.

As an informal exercise, you are asked to consider whether noise traders benefit from trading when other noise traders do, in other words, at times when the standard deviation of noise trading σ_z is high, in light of the formulas given above. The answer is given at the end of the chapter.

Kyle (1985) also presents a continuous-time version of this model and shows that λ remains constant over time, while β increases and becomes infinite as the public revelation of the information approaches. Thus all private information enters the price eventually, and private trading is more aggressive when a shorter time is available to exploit an informational advantage.

Koudijs (2015) has recently presented evidence in support of this implication, using historical data from trading of English securities in Amsterdam during the 18th century. In this period, information about fundamentals and security prices in London reached Amsterdam by official mail packet boats that carried both public signals (newspapers) and private signals (private letters) and that sailed twice a week. Koudijs shows that after a boat arrived in Amsterdam, Amsterdam prices moved in the same direction as London prices did following the departure of that boat, even though no new contemporaneous information could reach both cities by other means. Koudijs explains this as the result of informed trading by business partners in London and Amsterdam who communicated by private letters transmitted by boat from London to Amsterdam. Strikingly, the initial comovement appears to have been stronger at times when weather conditions suggested that a subsequent boat, likely carrying newspapers reporting on the private information that had by then become public in London, would soon arrive and eliminate the informational advantage. Problem 12.2 asks you to analyze a version of Koudijs' model.

Although the Kyle (1985) model assumes a single informed trader who is risk-neutral, concerns about market impact can also affect optimal trading strategies when multiple traders are informed and all traders are risk-averse. Kyle (1989) develops a more general model of imperfectly competitive rational expectations equilibrium with informed and uninformed trading.

There is a debate in the literature about the functional form of price impact. Price impact is linear in Kyle (1985), but Hasbrouck and Seppi (2001), Gabaix et al. (2006), and Chacko, Jurek, and Stafford (2008) argue that price impact is concave in trade size and is well approximated by a square root rather than a linear function. However, definitive empirical results are hard to obtain in the absence of controlled experiments placing random buy and sell orders.

12.2.3 Diminishing Returns in Active Asset Management

The Kyle model distinguishes between informed investors who profit from their trading, marketmakers who break even, and noise traders who transact at a loss. This distinction has parallels in other parts of the finance literature. For example, Berk and Green (2004) model professional asset management. Their model has skilled (informed) fund managers, mutual fund investors who break even, and other active stock traders who lose to the fund managers. Fund managers charge a fee to their investors that is a fixed fraction of assets under management. Mutual fund investors judge managers' skill by past performance and update their beliefs rationally. Successful funds attract inflows, but inflows reduce the performance that results from any degree of skill because there are diminishing returns to scale (perhaps because of market impact). In equilibrium, fund investors rationally chase performance, but because they equate the expected after-fee returns on all funds, past performance does not predict future performance. Fund managers are rewarded for their skill at the expense of other active stock traders, while mutual fund investors break even after paying managers' fees. Stambaugh (2014) considers a variant of this model in which fund investors must be compensated for the active risk they take when they deviate from the passive market index.

The enormous literature on professional asset management is largely beyond the scope of this book. However, several empirical findings are broadly consistent with these ideas. First, there is evidence that mutual funds hold stocks that outperform benchmarks with comparable characteristics, before fees are charged (Daniel et al. 1997, Wermers 2000). Second, substantial asset management fees (French 2008) reduce the benefit of active asset management, particularly to retail investors. Del Guercio and Reuter (2014) argue that retail investors who buy directly sold mutual funds roughly break even after fees, while those who buy broker-sold funds underperform (possibly because fees are implicitly being charged for financial advice as well as for investment performance). Third, past performance predicts inflows to mutual funds and hedge funds, and this weakens the relationship between past performance and future performance while strengthening the relationship between past performance and future fund size and aggregate fees (Chevalier and Ellison 1997, Fung et al. 2008, Berk and van Binsbergen 2015). There are many outstanding questions in this literature, including the rewards to professional skill in different asset classes, the distribution of rewards between managers and their clients (which may be different for institutional clients than for retail clients), the extent to which diminishing returns apply to managers or to the active asset management industry as a whole, and the effects of alternative fee structures.

12.3 Liquidity and Asset Pricing

In this final section of the chapter, we review the literature on liquidity and asset prices. There are two main concepts of liquidity: first, low trading costs, which are the focus of the market microstructure literature; and second, the ability to borrow against an asset (use it as collateral for a loan) as emphasized by Holmström and Tirole (2001) among others. Brunnermeier and Pedersen (2009) call the first concept "market liquidity" and the second "funding liquidity." The recent literature has explored how each of these types of liquidity may affect asset prices, and how they are determined in equilibrium from deeper fundamental forces. Vayanos and Wang (2013) provide a comprehensive recent survey.

We begin by asking how trading costs affect asset prices. We use the Amihud and Mendelson (1986) model for the case of constant trading costs, and models by Acharya and Pedersen (2005) and Pástor and Stambaugh (2003) for the case of randomly time-varying trading costs.

Next, we ask how the ability to borrow against an asset affects its price. We discuss the margin-based asset pricing model of Gârleanu, and Pedersen (2011). We take margins as exogenous here, although Chapter 11 has already discussed how differences in investors' beliefs may influence the determination of margins in equilibrium.

Finally, we ask how these two concepts of liquidity are related. We summarize the work of Brunnermeier and Pedersen (2009) on the interaction between market liquidity and funding liquidity.

12.3.1 Constant Trading Costs and Asset Prices

Following the exposition in Amihud, Mendelson, and Pedersen (2005), we consider an overlapping generations model (a device to force trading) with risk-neutral agents who live two periods. The riskless interest rate is R_f, and riskless borrowing and lending incur no transactions costs. There are also risky assets $i = 1 \dots I$ that pay a dividend D_{it}, have price P_{it}, and can be traded at cost C_i paid by the seller. We assume that dividends are iid over time with mean $\overline{D}_i$ and look for a stationary equilibrium with constant prices P_i.

Given risk-neutrality and no portfolio constraints, we must have:

$$P_i = \frac{\overline{D}_i + P_i - C^i}{1 + R_f} = \frac{\overline{D}_i - C^i}{R_f}, \tag{12.61}$$

or equivalently

$$\mathrm{E}[R_i] = R_f + \frac{C_i}{P_i}. \tag{12.62}$$

This says that the expected gross return on each asset is the riskfree interest rate plus the proportional transactions cost that is paid each period. In other words, the expected return net of the transactions cost equals the riskfree interest rate.

It is easy to handle the case where agents have longer holding periods. We assume that with a constant probability $\theta \leq 1$, the investor exits the market each period and is forced to sell risky assets. The exit event can be reinterpreted as a sudden need for cash that forces an asset sale, although to sustain this interpretation one must must rule out the possibility that the exiting investor could borrow from other agents still in the market. Then the equilibrium conditions become

$$P_i = \frac{\overline{D}_i + \theta(P_i - C_i)}{R_f + \theta} = \frac{\overline{D}_i - \theta C_i}{R_f}, \tag{12.63}$$

and

$$\mathrm{E}[R_i] = R_f + \theta \frac{C_i}{P_i}. \tag{12.64}$$

Trading costs now have smaller effects on asset prices and required gross returns, because they are paid less often (every $1/\theta$ periods on average).

Amihud and Mendelson (AM 1986) consider what happens when the market has heterogeneous agents indexed by j, some with a short horizon (high θ_j) and others with a long horizon (low θ_j). We rule out the possibility of borrowing in order to get a risk-neutral equilibrium with wealth constraints. In equilibrium, the high-θ_j agents hold the most liquid securities; the low-θ_j agents hold the illiquid securities. We order the agents so that θ_j declines with j, and order assets so that $C_i/\overline{D}_i$ increases with i. Then the low-j agents hold low-i assets in equilibrium.

If type j agents are the marginal investors for security i, then AM show that

$$E[R_i] = R_j^* + \theta_j \frac{C_i}{P_i}, \tag{12.65}$$

where R_j^* is the rate of return on the most illiquid asset that the type $j-1$ agents hold, adjusted for type j's trading cost of that asset. The difference between R_j^* and R_f can be interpreted as a rent that agents with lower turnover earn for their willingness to hold more illiquid assets.

The return on any asset can also be written as

$$E[R_i] = \min_j \left(R_j^* + \theta_j \frac{C_i}{P_i} \right). \tag{12.66}$$

This is increasing and concave in trading costs, implying that gross returns increase with trading costs at a declining rate, because the investors holding more illiquid assets have longer holding periods and thus care less about trading costs.

Figure 12.3 illustrates the AM equilibrium for an example with three classes of investors. The slope of each line in the figure is the exit probability for a class of investor: highest for the first class that holds the most liquid assets, lower for the second class, and lower again for the third class. Observed expected returns are given by the piecewise linear function that is the lower envelope of the three lines. Extending the lines for the

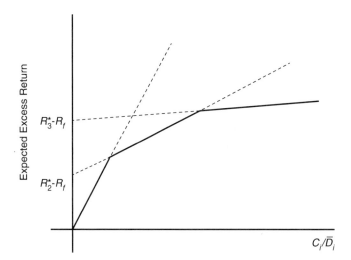

Figure 12.3.   *Expected Returns and Trading Costs in the Amihud and Mendelson (1986) Model*

second and third investor class to the vertical axis gives the rents $(R_2^* - R_f)$ and $(R_3^* - R_f)$ earned by the second and third investor class that have lower exit probabilities and longer average holding periods. The first investor class, with the highest exit probability, earns no rent in equilibrium.

There is evidence in support of the AM model's empirical prediction that expected returns increase with trading costs more rapidly for liquid assets than for illiquid assets. Small differences in trading costs have relatively large effects on the prices of liquid securities such as Treasury bonds and much smaller effects on the prices of relatively illiquid securities such as small stocks or corporate bonds. A difficulty with the framework is that it assumes an exogenous motivation for trade, and it is hard to rationalize a high trading frequency (short holding period) within standard economic models of portfolio choice.

12.3.2 Random Trading Costs and Asset Prices

Acharya and Pedersen (2005) consider what happens when trading costs are not constant but random. They derive a liquidity-adjusted CAPM that takes account of the risk that the market for an asset will become illiquid in the future. They set up a static model with CARA utility and normally distributed fundamentals. Trading costs are also normally distributed and may vary persistently over time.

We define the proportional trading cost of an asset as

$$c_{it} = \frac{C_{it}}{P_{it}}. \tag{12.67}$$

This can be aggregated to the market level to create a measure of market-wide trading costs or illiquidity:

$$c_{Mt} = \frac{\sum S_{it} C_{it}}{\sum S_{it} P_{it}}, \tag{12.68}$$

where S_{it} denotes the supply of security i at time t.

The liquidity-adjusted CAPM says that

$$E_t[R_{i,t+1} - c_{i,t+1}] = R_f + \lambda_t \frac{\text{Cov}_t(R_{i,t+1} - c_{i,t+1}, R_{M,t+1} - c_{M,t+1})}{\text{Var}_t(R_{M,t+1} - c_{M,t+1})}, \tag{12.69}$$

where $\lambda_t = E_t[R_{M,t+1} - c_{M,t+1} - R_f]$ is the expected return on the market, adjusted for transactions costs.

Equation (12.69) implies that one can write the risk premium on any asset in terms of four betas: the beta of the asset's return with the market return (the traditional CAPM beta), the beta of the asset's return with market-wide illiquidity (which has a negative price), the beta of the asset's illiquidity with the market return (which again has a negative price), and finally the beta of the asset's illiquidity with market-wide illiquidity.

For the liquidity adjustment to the traditional CAPM to be important, trading costs must be large. Pástor and Stambaugh (2003) argue that the beta of a stock's return with market-wide illiquidity is important. They measure each stock's illiquidity using price reversal in response to trading volume (bid-ask bounce). Market-wide illiquidity is the innovation in the average of stock-level illiquidity across stocks. Cross-sectionally, betas of stock returns with market-wide illiquidity correlate with average returns, but Pástor and

Stambaugh do not control for a stock's illiquidity level, which may well be cross-sectionally correlated with the stock's beta with market-wide illiquidity.

Even if the level of illiquidity is more important than random fluctuations in illiquidity in the stock market, this may not be the case in other asset classes that experience extreme changes in illiquidity, for example, mortgage-backed securities during the global financial crisis.

12.3.3 Margins and Asset Prices

Gârleanu and Pedersen (GP 2011) present a model of the effects of margins on asset prices, taking margins as exogenous. The model is set in continuous time, and we state its key results here without derivation.

GP consider a market with securities, indexed by i, that have exogenous margins m_{it}. Different securities can have the same cash flows but different margins. Investors maximize their utility by choosing the shares of their wealth to invest in security positions θ_i and uncollateralized lending/borrowing η_u, with the remaining fraction of wealth $1 - \sum_i \theta_i - \eta_u$ invested in the market for collateralized riskfree lending (repurchase agreements or repo). These choices are subject to a margin constraint:

$$\sum_i m_{it}|\theta_i| + \eta_u \leq 1. \tag{12.70}$$

The absolute value of θ_i appears in equation (12.70) because both long and short positions in risky securities require putting up margin; a short position does not generate margin just because a long position requires it. This formulation is key for realism and to derive the results of the paper, but it has sometimes been ignored in earlier work. On the other hand, uncollateralized lending η_u appears in (12.70) in levels, because while uncollateralized lending consumes capital, uncollateralized borrowing adds to capital and relaxes the margin constraint. Collateralized borrowing does not appear in the margin constraint, so the difference between the collateralized and uncollateralized interest rates is a natural proxy for the Lagrange multiplier on this constraint.

GP develop an example with two agents who have power utility, one conservative with relative risk aversion above one, and the other more aggressive with risk aversion equal to one. Both agents have margin constraints, which are more likely to bind for the aggressive agent. The conservative agent may also be constrained from trading derivative securities.

In the special case where the margin constraint does not bind for the conservative agent, the equilibrium condition for asset pricing can be written as:

$$E[R_i - R_f] = \gamma_t \beta_{C,it} + \lambda_t m_{it}. \tag{12.71}$$

The first term on the right-hand side of (12.71) is the standard prediction of a consumption-based asset pricing model. $\beta_{C,it}$ is the asset's instantaneous covariance with aggregate consumption growth, and γ_t (the "covariance risk premium") is a weighted harmonic mean of risk aversion of the two agents, where the weights are the agents' consumption shares. The second term on the right-hand side of (12.71) captures the importance of margin constraints. The coefficient λ_t (the "margin premium") is given by

$$\lambda_t = x_t \psi_t y_{it}, \tag{12.72}$$

where x_t is the fraction of the economy's risk-bearing capacity provided by the aggressive agent, ψ_t is the Lagrange multiplier on the aggressive agent's margin constraint, and y_{it} is a dummy variable that is +1 if the aggressive agent is long, −1 if he is short, and takes any intermediate value if he has no position. Equations (12.71) and (12.72) imply that when margin constraints are binding, risky assets have higher expected returns if margin-constrained arbitrageurs would like to take long positions but are deterred by high asset-specific margins.

The GP model is designed to deliver theoretical insight rather than empirical realism, but its predictions can be evaluated using the interest rate spread between collateralized and uncollateralized borrowing as a proxy for the Lagrange multiplier ψ_t. It is also possible to rewrite the equilibruim condition in CAPM form using covariance with a consumption-mimicking portfolio instead of covariance with aggregate consumption.

This model can also explain deviations from the law of one price (apparent arbitrage opportunities) when two assets have identical cash flows but different margins. An interesting example is the CDS-corporate bond basis, the price deviation between a corporate bond and a Treasury bond combined with a short CDS position that has the same risk. CDS have historically traded with lower margins than corporate bonds, so the GP model has the potential to explain the existence of and time variation in the basis. In the model this requires that both agents face binding constraints, most plausibly the margin constraint for the aggressive agent and a derivative trading constraint for the conservative agent.

Suppose the aggressive agent has a long position both in security i and in a related derivative k that has identical cash flows but a lower margin. Then

$$E[R_i - R_k] = \psi_t(m_{it} - m_{kt}) + (\beta_{Ait} - \beta_{Akt}), \qquad (12.73)$$

where β_A denotes an asset's covariance with the aggressive agent's consumption. It is an interesting possibility that different consumption covariances due to different equilibrium risk characteristics of the low- and high-margin securities can amplify the basis and imply a nonzero basis even in states of the world where the margin constraints are not currently binding.

12.3.4 Margins and Trading Costs

Brunnermeier and Pedersen (BP 2009) develop themes in Shleifer and Vishny (1997) to link the literatures on trading costs and margins. Margins affect trading costs if margin-constrained agents are marketmakers. Trading costs affect margins if capital providers set margins in relation to the short-run volatility of prices (as opposed to the long-run volatility of fundamentals or the deviation of current price from fundamentals). Together, these effects create the possibility of "liquidity spirals," in which funding problems for arbitrageurs disrupt markets and increase trading costs, allowing larger deviations of prices from fundamentals and in turn worsening funding conditions. Figure 12.4, a reproduction of BP Figure 2, illustrates this possibility.

To illustrate the BP mechanism, we consider a model with dates $t = 0, 1, 2$, a single risky asset in zero net supply whose payoff at time 2 is v_2, and a market for collateralized lending and borrowing (repo market) with the interest rate normalized to zero. $\Lambda_1 \equiv v_1 - p_1$ is the deviation of the price from the fundamental value $v_1 \equiv E_1[v_2]$ at date 1. The absolute value of Λ_1 is BP's measure of market illiquidity.

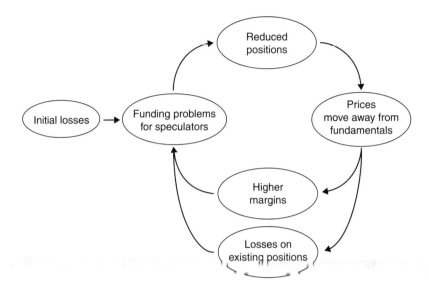

Figure 12.4. *Schematic Illustration of Liquidity Spirals* (Brunnermeier, Markus K., and Lasse Heje Pedersen, 2009, "Market Liquidity and Funding Liquidity," *Review of Financial Studies* 22, 2201–2238; reprinted by permission of Oxford University Press.)

There are two agents in the model: speculators (liquidity providers) and customers (noise traders). Speculators are risk-neutral and choose asset holdings x_t to maximize wealth at date 2 subject to the budget constraint

$$W_t = W_{t-1} + (p_t - p_{t-1})x_{t-1} + \eta_t, \tag{12.74}$$

where η_t is a wealth shock and W_0, x_0 are given. Speculators also face a margin constraint

$$m_t p_t |x_t| \leq W_t. \tag{12.75}$$

We use the notation $\widetilde{m}_t \equiv m_t p_t$ to denote the margin requirement per unit of the asset.

Customers' demand for the risky asset is given by $D_t(\Lambda_t, Z_t)$, where Z_t is a demand shock and D_t is increasing in both arguments. Market clearing implies

$$x_t + D_t = 0. \tag{12.76}$$

We focus on an equilibrium where speculators are capital-constrained at time 1 and, in particular, they have long positions in the asset, $p_1 < v_1$. Combining the margin constraint (12.75) and market clearing (12.76), we get

$$-\widetilde{m}_1 D(v_1 - p_1, Z_1) = b_0 + p_1 x_0 + \eta_1, \tag{12.77}$$

where the left-hand side is the margin that speculators must put up to hold the assets supplied by customers, and the right-hand side is the wealth of speculators. Here b_0 is the time-0 position of speculators in the repo market.

We can differentiate this expression to get the price sensitivity to a wealth shock:

$$\frac{\partial p_1}{\partial \eta_1} = \frac{1}{\widetilde{m}_1 \frac{\partial D_1}{\partial \Lambda_1} - \left[x_0 - \frac{\partial \widetilde{m}_1}{\partial p_1} x_1 \right]}. \tag{12.78}$$

Equation (12.78) nicely captures the intuition behind the loss and margin spirals of Figure 12.4. First consider the impact of a negative wealth shock of \$1 assuming a zero preexisting position in the asset, $x_0 = 0$, and a constant margin requirement, $\partial \widetilde{m}_1 / p_1 = 0$. Given the binding margin constraint, the speculators must reduce their position by \$$1/\widetilde{m}_1$, which causes the price to fall in equilibrium by \$$1/k$, $k \equiv \widetilde{m}_1 (\partial D_1 / \partial \Lambda_1)$, in order to incentivize the customers to increase their position and clear the market. This effect corresponds to the two upper arrows of Figure 12.4.

If speculators have a positive preexisting position in the asset, $x_0 > 0$, their wealth is further hit by the endogenous drop in the price. Similarly, if the price drop causes an increase in the margin requirement, $\partial \widetilde{m}_1 / p_1 < 0$ (margins are "destabilizing"), this further tightens the margin constraint. These two effects, which were first emphasized by Shleifer and Vishny (1997), cause an additional capital shortage of \$$l \equiv x_0 - (\partial \widetilde{m}_1 / \partial p_1) x_1$ per dollar of initial price drop, illustrated in the lower arrows of the loop of Figure 12.4. The overall price drop as a result of the initial wealth shock, after an infinite number of loops, equals \$$1/k + l/k^2 + l^2/k^3 + \ldots = \$1/(k-l)$ (assuming $|l| < k$), which is precisely the price sensitivity formula derived above. The formula also shows that the joint amplification effect of the two liquidity spirals is greater than the sum of the effects of each spiral operating separately, since $l_1/(k-l_1) + l_2/(k-l_2) < l/(k-l)$, where $l_1 = x_0$, $l_2 = -\partial \widetilde{m}_1 / p_1 x_1$.

In interpreting these results, it is important to keep in mind that the market liquidity captured by the BP model is lower frequency than the liquidity measures developed in the market microstructure literature. Speculators in the BP model set the price away from fundamentals to compensate for low-frequency exogenous movements in asset demand, like rational investors in the noise trader models discussed in Chapter 11, rather than bridging very short time intervals between the arrival of buy and sell orders in a liquid market.

Problem 12.3 asks you to develop this analysis further in a setting with multiple risky assets.

Margin Risk

When the margin constraint in the BP model varies unpredictably over time, it makes risk-neutral speculators behave as if they were risk-averse. Adrian, Etula, and Muir (AEM 2014) emphasize this point. In the BP model, risk-neutral speculators at time t maximize $E_t[\varphi_{t+1} W_{t+1}]$, where φ_{t+1} denotes the speculators' shadow cost of capital, which is increasing in the Lagrange multiplier on the margin constraint at time $t + 1$. Thus φ_{t+1} acts like marginal utility in a standard model of concave utility maximization. Problem 12.3 illustrates the link between φ_{t+1} and the stochastic discount factor.

AEM suggest that a natural empirical model for the shadow cost of capital is

$$\varphi_{t+1} = a - b \log(\text{leverage}_{t+1}), \tag{12.79}$$

where leverage (the reciprocal of margin) varies negatively with the tightness of margin constraints. AEM measure leverage as the ratio of the total financial assets held by security broker-dealers to the book net worth of these intermediaries, as reported in the US Flow of Funds accounts. As predicted by the theory, covariances with the broker-dealer leverage factor line up well with average returns on a cross-section of equity and bond portfolios.

In focusing on the first-order conditions of a particular class of investors, the AEM empirical model is similar to other models explored in the last part of this book, which recognize investor heterogeneity and seek to understand market prices from the point of view of certain specific investors. This approach is increasingly common and is one reason for the emphasis that this book has placed on portfolio choice theory as a complement to financial market equilibrium theory. However, it is important to keep in mind that ultimately we want to understand not only the pricing of assets' covariances with risk factors, but also the determinants of these covariances themselves. In the context of AEM's empirical analysis specifically, a full account of margin risk should explain why some assets covary more strongly than others with the leverage of security broker-dealers.

12.4 Solution and Further Problems

As an informal exercise you were asked to consider whether noise traders in the Kyle (1985) model benefit from the presence of other noise traders, that is, a high standard deviation of noise trading σ_z. The answer is that if noise traders can choose when to trade, as in the model of Admati and Pfleiderer (1988), they would like to trade when other noise traders do, because they benefit from market depth, which increases with σ_z as shown in equation (12.60). Even though the total losses of noise traders increase with the volume of noise trading, the loss per noise trader decreases. One might make an analogy with predators and prey. Herds of zebra form because any individual zebra is safer in a herd, even though most predation takes place from herds.

Problem 12.1 Asymmetric Information and Home Bias

Consider a static model in which a continuum of agents of unit mass with exponential (CARA) utility and coefficient of absolute risk aversion A invest their wealth in two risky assets (stocks) and a riskless asset. Stocks 1 and 2 have uncorrelated terminal payoffs v_j with common unconditional (prior) distribution $\mathcal{N}(\mu_0, 1/\tau_0)$. The quantities of these stocks supplied $Z_j, j = 1, 2$, at the initial date are also random (observed imperfectly) and uncorrelated, with common distribution $\mathcal{N}(\mu_Z, 1/\tau_Z)$. The riskless asset, with return R_f, is in perfectly elastic supply.

All agents observe a signal $s_1 \sim \mathcal{N}(v_1, 1/\tau_s)$ for the payoff of stock 1, corresponding to public information. Only a fraction ϕ of agents observe a signal $s_2 \sim \mathcal{N}(v_2, 1/\tau_s)$ for the payoff of stock 2, corresponding to private information. Signals are distributed independently from quantities supplied.

(a) Show that an agent's quantity demanded of each stock $X_j, j = 1, 2$, does not depend on the conditional distribution of the other stock's payoff.

(b) We first solve for the equilibrium price and returns in the market for stock 1.

   (i) What is the agents' conditional payoff distribution and demand $X_1(P_1, s_1)$ for stock 1?

   (ii) Compute the equilibrium price $P_1(s_1, Z_1)$ and unconditional expected excess return $E[v_1 - (1 + R_f)P_1]$.

(c) We now solve for the equilibrium in the market for stock 2, following the five steps for solving asymmetric information models discussed in section 12.1.2. Conjecture the pricing rule

$$P_2(s_2, Z_2) = p_0\mu_0 + p_s s_2 - p_z(Z_2 - \mu_Z).$$

   (i) Derive the informed agents' conditional payoff distribution and demand $X_2^I(P_2, s_2)$ for stock 2.

   (ii) Derive the uninformed agents' conditional payoff distribution and demand $X_2^U(P_2)$ for stock 2. How does their conditional variance for v_2 depend on τ_s, τ_Z, ϕ, and A? Explain.

   (iii) Impose market clearing to compute the equilibrium price $P_2(s_2, Z_2)$ and the unconditional expected excess return $E[v_2 - (1 + R_f)P_2]$.

(d) Which stock commands a higher risk premium $E[v_j - (1 + R_f)P_j]$? How does the risk premium for stock 2 depend on the fraction ϕ of informed traders? Explain.

(e) Do the informed or uninformed hold more of stock 2 on average? Explain.

(f) Offer an explanation for home bias in portfolio choice based on this model. How might you test the model's predictions using data on domestic and foreign investors' portfolio composition and on equity premia across different countries?

Note: This problem is based on O'Hara (2003).

Problem 12.2 Market Impact Over Time

Consider an extension of the Kyle (1985) model with two periods of trading. The fundamental value of an asset is v, which is distributed normally with prior mean μ_0 and variance σ_0^2 known to all agents. Noise traders have demand z, which is distributed normally in each period with mean zero and variance σ_z^2. A single risk-neutral insider observes v and chooses an asset demand x in each period as a function of v to maximize expected two-period profit. For simplicity, profits are not discounted.

With probability π, trading occurs in both periods. With probability $1 - \pi$, trading occurs only in the first period, after which fundamental value is revealed.

In trading at period 1, risk-neutral, competitive marketmakers set the price based on their observation of $x_1 + z_1$ as

$$p_1 = E[v \mid x_1 + z_1; \mu_0, \sigma_0^2]. \tag{12.80}$$

Similarly, in trading at period 2, the marketmakers set the price as

$$p_2 = E[v \mid x_2 + z_2; \mu_1, \sigma_1^2], \tag{12.81}$$

where μ_1 and σ_1^2 are the posterior mean and variance of v after observation of first-period order flow.

Conjecture a linear equilibrium in which the insider follows the trading rule

$$x_t = \beta_t(v - \mu_{t-1}), \tag{12.82}$$

and the marketmakers follow the pricing rule

$$p_t = \mu_{t-1} + \lambda_t(x_t + z_t) \tag{12.83}$$

for $t = 1, 2$.

(a) Derive an expression relating the pricing rule parameter λ_t to the variances σ_{t-1}^2 and σ_z^2 and the insider's trading parameter β_t, for arbitrary (not necessarily optimal) β_t.

(b) Show that $\mu_1 = p_1$. Explain.

(c) Derive an expression relating the variance σ_1^2 to the variances σ_0^2 and σ_z^2 and the insider's first-period trading parameter β_1.

(d) In the second period of trading, the equilibrium is described by the single-period Kyle model, conditional on μ_1 and σ_1^2. Show that the market is deeper in the second period (λ_2 is lower) if the insider traded more aggressively in the first period. Explain this fact intuitively.

(e) If in the first period of trading the insider believes that $\pi = 0$, the single-period Kyle model describes trading in that period too. For this case, derive the ratio of market depth in the second period to market depth in the first period, λ_1/λ_2. Show that market depth is greater in the second period. Why?

(f) Now consider what happens when the insider understands that $\pi > 0$. Show that the insider trades less aggressively in the first period, and explain why this is so. Discuss intuitively how this affects the relative depth of the market in the two periods.

Note: This problem is based on Koudijs (2015).

Problem 12.3 Funding Liquidity and the SDF

Consider the setting of section 12.3.4 but now allow for multiple risky assets $j = 1, \ldots, J$. The speculators' budget constraint and margin constraint are now given by $W_t = W_{t-1} + \sum_{j=1}^{J}(p_t^j - p_{t-1}^j)x_{t-1}^j + \eta_t$ and $\sum_{j=1}^{J} \tilde{m}_t^j|x_t^j| \leq W_t$, respectively. Customers' quantity demanded of asset j at date 1 is $D_1^j(\Lambda_1^j, Z_1^j)$, where $\Lambda_1^j \equiv v_1^j - p_1^j$. The speculators' date-1 wealth shock η_1 has zero mean and is uncorrelated with the demand shocks Z_1^j.

Assume $p_1^j \neq v_1^j$ for at least some j, so that speculators are capital-constrained at date 1 (with $W_1 > 0$).

(a) Derive speculators' demand x_1^j for each asset. Hint: Explain why speculators only trade assets with the highest $|\Lambda_1^j|/\tilde{m}_1^j$.

(b) Denote speculators' date-1 value function by $J_1(W_1) = E_1[W_2]$. Their date-1 shadow cost of capital φ_1, a measure of funding illiquidity, is defined through $\varphi_1 W_1 = J_1(W_1)$. Express φ_1 in terms of Λ_1^j and $\tilde{m}_1^j$, $j = 1, \ldots, J$.

(c) Express each asset's market illiquidity, $|\Lambda_1^j|$, in terms of φ_1, $\tilde{m}_1^j$, and parameters of the model.

(d) Now consider an additional initial period $t = 0$ with a margin constraint on speculators $\sum_{j=1}^{J} \tilde{m}_0^j |x_0^j| \leq W_0$. Assume that speculators have unlimited liability, and in particular $J_1(W_1) = \varphi_1 W_1$ for all values of W_1 (including negative ones), with φ_1 from part (b). This assumption raises the possibility that speculators do not trade to their constraint at date 0 if their wealth is high enough.

Assuming that speculators are unconstrained at $t = 0$, show that $\varphi_1 / E_0[\varphi_1]$ functions as an SDF in the economy. Explain intuitively why speculators choose to not trade to their constraint even though they are risk-neutral. Show that their date-0 cost of capital φ_0, defined through $\varphi_0 W_0 = J_0(W_0) = E_0[W_2]$, equals $E_0[\varphi_1]$.

(e) Now suppose that speculators' wealth W_0 is low enough that speculators are constrained at $t = 0$. Derive their date-0 cost of capital, φ_0.

Note: This problem is based on Brunnermeier and Pedersen (2009).

References

Abel, Andrew B., 1990, "Asset Pricing under Habit Formation and Catching Up with the Joneses," *American Economic Review Papers and Proceedings* 80, 38–42.

———, 1999, "Risk Premia and Term Premia in General Equilibrium," *Journal of Monetary Economics* 43, 3–33.

Abel, Andrew B., and Janice Eberly, 1994, "A Unified Model of Investment under Uncertainty," *American Economic Review* 84, 1369–1384.

Abel, Andrew B., N. Gregory Mankiw, Lawrence H. Summers, and Richard J. Zeckhauser, 1989, "Assessing Dynamic Efficiency: Theory and Evidence," *Review of Economic Studies* 56, 1–19.

Acharya, Viral V., and Lasse Heje Pedersen, 2005, "Asset Pricing with Liquidity Risk," *Journal of Financial Economics* 77, 375–410.

Admati, Anat R., and Paul Pfleiderer, 1988, "A Theory of Intraday Patterns: Volume and Price Variability," *Review of Financial Studies* 1, 3–40.

Adrian, Tobias, Richard K. Crump, and Emanuel Moench, 2015, "Regression-Based Estimation of Dynamic Asset Pricing Models," *Journal of Financial Economics* 118, 211–244.

Adrian, Tobias, Erkko Etula, and Tyler Muir, 2014, "Financial Intermediaries and the Cross-Section of Asset Returns," *Journal of Finance* 69, 2557–2596.

Agarwal, Sumit, John Driscoll, Xavier Gabaix, and David Laibson, 2009, "The Age of Reason: Financial Decisions over the Life Cycle and Implications for Regulation," *Brookings Papers on Economic Activity* 2, 51–117.

Agarwal, Sumit, John Driscoll, and David Laibson, 2013, "Optimal Mortgage Refinancing: A Closed-Form Solution," *Journal of Money, Credit and Banking* 45, 591–622.

Agnew, Julie, Pierluigi Balduzzi, and Annika Sunden, 2003, "Portfolio Choice and Trading in a Large 401(k) Plan," *American Economic Review* 93, 193–215.

Aït-Sahalia, Yacine, and Michael W. Brandt, 2001, "Variable Selection for Portfolio Choice," *Journal of Finance* 56, 1297–1351.

Allais, Maurice, 1953, "Le comportement de l'homme rationnel devant le risque: Critique des postulats et axiomes de l'école Américaine," *Econometrica* 21, 503–546.

Allen, Franklin, and Douglas Gale, 1994, "Limited Market Participation and Volatility of Asset Prices," *American Economic Review* 84, 933–955.

Allen, Franklin, Stephen Morris, and Hyun Song Shin, 2006, "Beauty Contests, Bubbles, and Iterated Expectations in Financial Markets," *Review of Financial Studies* 19, 719–752.

Alvarez, Fernando, and Urban Jermann, 2000, "Efficiency, Equilibrium, and Asset Pricing with Risk of Default," *Econometrica* 68, 775–797.

————, 2005, "Using Asset Prices to Measure the Persistence of the Marginal Utility of Wealth," *Econometrica* 73, 1977–2016.

Ameriks, John, and Stephen Zeldes, 2004, "How Do Household Portfolio Shares Vary with Age?," unpublished paper, Columbia University.

Amihud, Yakov, and Haim Mendelson, 1986, "Asset Pricing and the Bid–Ask Spread," *Journal of Financial Economics* 17, 223–249.

Amihud, Yakov, Haim Mendelson, and Lasse Heje Pedersen, 2005, "Liquidity and Asset Prices," *Foundations and Trends in Finance* 1, 269–364.

Anagol, Santosh, Vimal Balasubramaniam, and Tarun Ramadorai, 2016, "Endowment Effects in the Field: Evidence from India's IPO Lotteries," unpublished paper.

Andersen, Steffen, John Y. Campbell, Kasper Meisner Nielsen, and Tarun Ramadorai, 2015, "Inattention and Inertia in Household Finance: Evidence from the Danish Mortgage Market," NBER Working Paper No. 21386.

Andrews, Donald W. K., 1999, "Consistent Moment Selection Procedures for Generalized Method of Moments Estimation," *Econometrica* 67, 543–563.

Ang, Andrew, Geert Bekaert, and Min Wei, 2007, "Do Macro Variables, Asset Markets, or Surveys Forecast Inflation Better?," *Journal of Monetary Economics* 54, 1163–1212.

Ang, Andrew, Robert Hodrick, Yuhang Xing, and Xiaoyan Zhang, 2006, "The Cross-Section of Volatility and Expected Returns," *Journal of Finance* 61, 259–299.

Ang, Andrew, Jun Liu, and Krista Schwarz, 2016, "Using Stocks or Portfolios in Tests of Factor Models," unpublished paper.

Ang, Andrew, and Allan Timmermann, 2012, "Regime Changes and Financial Markets," *Annual Review of Financial Economics* 4, 313–337.

Angeletos, George-Marios, David Laibson, Andrea Repetto, Jeremy Tobacman, and Stephen Weinberg, 2001, "The Hyperbolic Consumption Model: Calibration, Simulation, and Empirical Evaluation," *Journal of Economic Perspectives* 15(3), 47–68.

Arrow, Kenneth J., 1971, "The Theory of Risk Aversion," in *Essays in the Theory of Risk Bearing*, Markham, Chicago, IL, 90–120.

Asness, Clifford S., 2003, "Fight the Fed Model: The Relationship between Future Returns and Stock and Bond Market Yields," *Journal of Portfolio Management* 30(1), 11–24.

Asness, Clifford S., Andrea Frazzini, and Lasse Heje Pedersen, 2013, "Quality Minus Junk," unpublished paper.

Athanasoulis, Stefano G., and Robert J. Shiller, 2000, "The Significance of the Market Portfolio," *Review of Financial Studies* 13, 301–329.

————, 2001, "World Income Components: Measuring and Exploiting Risk-Sharing Opportunities," *American Economic Review* 91, 1031–1054.

Aumann, Robert J., 1976, "Agreeing to Disagree," *Annals of Statistics* 4, 1236–1239.

Aumann, Robert J., and Roberto Serrano, 2008, "An Economic Index of Riskiness," *Journal of Political Economy* 116, 810–836.

Avdis, Efstathios, and Jessica A. Wachter, 2017, "Maximum Likelihood Estimation of the Equity Premium," forthcoming *Journal of Financial Economics*.

Bach, Laurent, Laurent Calvet, and Paolo Sodini, 2016, "Rich Pickings? Risk and Return in the Financial Portfolios of the Wealthy," unpublished paper.

Back, Kerry, 2010, *Asset Pricing and Portfolio Choice Theory*, Oxford University Press, New York.

Backus, David K., Mikhail Chernov, and Ian Martin, 2011, "Disasters Implied by Equity Index Options," *Journal of Finance* 66, 1969–2012.

Backus, David K., Silverio Foresi, and Chris I. Telmer, 2001, "Affine Term Structure Models and the Forward Premium Anomaly," *Journal of Finance* 56, 279–304.

Backus, David K., Bryan R. Routledge, and Stanley E. Zin, 2004, "Exotic Preferences for Macroeconomists," *NBER Macroeconomics Annual* 19, 319–390.

Baker, Malcolm, and Jeffrey Wurgler, 2000, "The Equity Share in New Issues and Aggregate Stock Returns," *Journal of Finance* 55, 2219–2257.

Bali, Turan G., Robert F. Engle, and Scott Murray, 2016, *Empirical Asset Pricing: The Cross Section of Stock Returns*, Wiley, Hoboken, NJ.

Ball, R., and P. Brown, 1968, "An Empirical Evaluation of Accounting Income Numbers," *Journal of Accounting Research* 6, 159–178.

Bandarchuk, Pavel, and Jens Hilscher, 2013, "Sources of Momentum Profits: Evidence on the Irrelevance of Characteristics," *Review of Finance* 17, 809–845.

Bansal, Ravi, Robert Dittmar, and Dana Kiku, 2009, "Co-integration and Consumption Risks in Asset Returns," *Review of Financial Studies* 22, 1343–1375.

Bansal, Ravi, Dana Kiku, Ivan Shaliastovich, and Amir Yaron, 2014, "Volatility, the Macroeconomy, and Asset Prices," *Journal of Finance* 69, 2471–2511.

Bansal, Ravi, Dana Kiku, and Amir Yaron, 2012, "An Empirical Evaluation of the Long-Run Risks Model for Asset Prices," *Critical Finance Review* 1, 183–221.

Bansal, Ravi, and Bruce N. Lehmann, 1997, "Growth-Optimal Portfolio Restrictions on Asset Pricing Models," *Macroeconomic Dynamics* 1, 333–354.

Bansal, Ravi, and Amir Yaron, 2004, "Risks for the Long Run: A Potential Resolution of Asset Pricing Puzzles," *Journal of Finance* 59, 1481–1509.

Banz, Rolf, 1981, "The Relationship between Return and Market Value of Common Stocks," *Journal of Financial Economics* 9, 3–18.

Barber, Brad M., Yi-Tsung Lee, Yu-Jane Liu, and Terrance Odean, 2009, "Just How Much Do Individual Investors Lose by Trading?," *Review of Financial Studies* 22, 609–632.

Barber, Brad M., and Terrance Odean, 2000, "Trading Is Hazardous to Your Wealth: The Common Stock Investment Performance of Individual Investors," *Journal of Finance* 55, 773–806.

———, 2001, "Boys Will Be Boys: Gender, Overconfidence, and Common Stock Investment," *Quarterly Journal of Economics* 116, 261–292.

Barberis, Nicholas, 2000, "Investing for the Long Run when Returns Are Predictable," *Journal of Finance* 55, 225–264.

Barberis, Nicholas, Robin Greenwood, Lawrence Jin, and Andrei Shleifer, 2015, "X-CAPM: An Extrapolative Capital Asset Pricing Model," *Journal of Financial Economics* 115, 1–24.

Barberis, Nicholas, Ming Huang, and Tano Santos, 2001, "Prospect Theory and Asset Prices," *Quarterly Journal of Economics* 116, 1–53.

Barberis, Nicholas, Ming Huang, and Richard H. Thaler, 2006, "Individual Preferences, Monetary Gambles, and Stock Market Participation: A Case for Narrow Framing," *American Economic Review* 96, 1069–1090.

Barberis, Nicholas, Andrei Shleifer, and Robert Vishny, 1998, "A Model of Investor Sentiment," *Journal of Financial Economics* 49, 307–343.

Barberis, Nicholas, and Wei Xiong, 2009, "What Drives the Disposition Effect? An Analysis of a Long-Standing Preference-Based Explanation," *Journal of Finance* 64, 751–784.

Barro, Robert, 2006, "Rare Disasters and Asset Markets in the Twentieth Century," *Quarterly Journal of Economics* 121, 823–866.

————, 2009, "Rare Disasters, Asset Prices, and Welfare Costs," *American Economic Review* 99, 243–264.

Barro, Robert, and Jose Ursua, 2008, "Macroeconomic Crises since 1870," *Brookings Papers on Economic Activity* 1, 255–350.

Basu, Sanjoy, 1977, "Investment Performance of Common Stocks in Relation to their Price-Earnings Ratios: A Test of the Efficient Market Hypothesis," *Journal of Finance* 32, 663–682.

————, 1983, "The Relation between Earnings Yield, Market Value, and Return for NYSE Common Stocks: Further Evidence," *Journal of Financial Economics* 12, 129–156.

Bauer, Michael D., and James D. Hamilton, 2016, "Robust Bond Risk Premia," unpublished paper, Federal Reserve Bank of San Francisco and UC San Diego.

Bazdresch, Santiago, Frederico Belo, and Xiaoji Lin, 2013, "Labor Hiring, Investment, and Stock Return Predictability in the Cross Section," *Journal of Political Economy* 122, 129–177.

Beaudry, Paul, and Franck Portier, 2006, "News, Stock Prices, and Economic Fluctuations," *American Economic Review* 96, 1293–1307.

Beeler, Jason, and John Y. Campbell, 2012, "The Long Run Risks Model and Aggregate Asset Prices: An Empirical Assessment," *Critical Finance Review* 1, 141–182.

Bekaert, Geert, Eric Engstrom, and Steven R. Grenadier, 2010, "Stock and Bond Returns with Moody Investors," *Journal of Empirical Finance* 17, 867–894.

Bekaert, Geert, Robert J. Hodrick, and David A. Marshall, 1997, "On Biases in Tests of the Expectations Hypothesis of the Term Structure of Interest Rates," *Journal of Financial Economics* 44, 309–348.

Bekaert, Geert, Kenton Hoyem, Wei-Yin Hu, and Enrichetta Ravina, 2015, "Who Is Internationally Diversified? Evidence from 296 401(k)," NBER Working Paper No. 21236.

Belo, Frederico, 2010, "Production-Based Measures of Risk for Asset Pricing," *Journal of Monetary Economics* 57, 146–163.

Belo, Frederico, Pierre Collin-Dufresne, and Robert S. Goldstein, 2015, "Dividend Dynamics and the Term Structure of Dividend Strips," *Journal of Finance* 70, 1115–1160.

Benartzi, Shlomo, 2001, "Excessive Extrapolation and the Allocation of 401(k) Accounts to Company Stock," *Journal of Finance* 56, 1747–1764.

Ben-David, Itzhak, and David Hirshleifer, 2012, "Are Investors Really Reluctant to Realize Their Losses? Trading Responses to Past Returns and the Disposition Effect," *Review of Financial Studies* 25, 2485–2532.

Berk, Jonathan, and Richard Green, 2004, "Mutual Fund Flows and Performance in Rational Markets," *Journal of Political Economy* 112, 1269–1295.

Berk, Jonathan B., and Jules H. van Binsbergen, 2015, "Measuring Skill in the Mutual Fund Industry," *Journal of Financial Economics* 118, 1–20.

Bernard, Victor L., and Jacob K. Thomas, 1989, "Post-Earnings-Announcement Drift: Delayed Price Response or Risk Premium?," *Journal of Accounting Research* 27, 1–36.

Bernstein, Peter, 1991, *Capital Ideas*, Wiley, New York.

Betermier, Sebastien, Laurent E. Calvet, and Paolo Sodini, 2017, "Who Are the Value and Growth Investors?," *Journal of Finance* 72, 5–46.

Bidder, Rhys, and Ian Dew-Becker, 2016, "Long-Run Risk Is the Worst-Case Scenario," *American Economic Review* 106, 2494–2527.

Binsbergen, Jules van, Michael Brandt, and Ralph Koijen, 2012, "On the Timing and Pricing of Dividends," *American Economic Review* 102, 1596–1618.

Binsbergen, Jules van, Wouter Hueskes, Ralph Koijen, and Evert Vrugt, 2013, "Equity Yields," *Journal of Financial Economics* 110, 503–519.

Binsbergen, Jules van, and Ralph Koijen, 2017, "The Term Structure of Returns: Facts and Theory," *Journal of Financial Economics* 124, 1–21.

Black, Fischer, 1972, "Capital Market Equilibrium with Restricted Borrowing," *Journal of Business* 45, 444–454.

Black, Fischer, Michael Jensen, and Myron Scholes, 1972, "The Capital Asset Pricing Model: Some Empirical Tests," in Michael Jensen ed. *Studies in the Theory of Capital Markets*, Praeger, New York, 79–121.

Black, Fischer, and Robert Litterman, 1992, "Global Portfolio Optimization," *Financial Analysts Journal* 48, 28–43.

Blanchard, Olivier, and Mark Watson, 1982, "Bubbles, Rational Expectations, and Financial Markets," in Paul Wachtel ed. *Crises in the Economic and Financial Structure*, Lexington, Lexington, MA, 295–315.

Blume, Marshall E., and Irwin Friend, 1975, "The Asset Structure of Individual Portfolios and Some Implications for Utility Functions," *Journal of Finance* 30, 585–603.

Blume, Marshall E., and Robert F. Stambaugh, 1983, "Biases in Computed Returns: An Application to the Size Effect," *Journal of Financial Economics* 12, 387–404.

Bodie, Zvi, Robert C. Merton, and William F. Samuelson, 1992, "Labor Supply Flexibility and Portfolio Choice in a Life Cycle Model," *Journal of Economic Dynamics and Control* 16, 427–449.

Boguth, Oliver, Murray Carlson, Adlai Fisher, and Mikhail Simutin, 2011, "Conditional Risk and Performance Evaluation: Volatility Timing, Overconditioning, and New Estimates of Momentum Alphas," *Journal of Financial Economics* 102, 363–389.

Boldrin, Michele, Lawrence J. Christiano, and Jonas D. M. Fisher, 2001, "Habit Persistence, Asset Returns, and the Business Cycle," *American Economic Review* 91, 149–166.

Bollerslev, Tim, George Tauchen, and Hao Zhou, 2009, "Expected Stock Returns and Variance Risk Premia," *Review of Financial Studies* 22, 4463–4492.

Borovička, Jaroslav, Lars Peter Hansen, and José A. Scheinkman, 2016, "Misspecified Recovery," *Journal of Finance* 71, 2493–2544.

Boudoukh, Jacob, Roni Michaely, Matthew Richardson, and Michael Roberts, 2007, "On the Importance of Measuring Payout Yield: Implications for Empirical Asset Pricing," *Journal of Finance* 62, 877–916.

Box, G., and D. Pierce, 1970, "Distribution of Residual Autocorrelations in Autoregressive-Integrated Moving Average Time Series Models," *Journal of the American Statistical Association* 65, 1509–1526.

Brandt, Michael W., 1999, "Estimating Portfolio and Consumption Choice: A Conditional Euler Equations Approach," *Journal of Finance* 54, 1609–1645.

Brandt, Michael W., John H. Cochrane, and Pedro Santa-Clara, 2006, "International Risk Sharing Is Better Than You Think, or Exchange Rates Are Too Smooth," *Journal of Monetary Economics* 53, 671–698.

Brav, Alon, George M. Constantinides, and Christopher C. Geczy, 2007, "Asset Pricing with Hetero-geneous Consumers and Limited Participation: Empirical Evidence," *Journal of Political Economy* 110, 793–824.

Breeden, Douglas T., Michael R. Gibbons, and Robert H. Litzenberger, 1989, "Empirical Tests of the Consumption-Oriented CAPM," *Journal of Finance* 44, 231–262.

Breeden, Douglas T., and Robert H. Litzenberger, 1978, "Prices of State-Contingent Claims Implicit in Option Prices," *Journal of Business* 51, 621–651.

Brennan, Michael J., Tarun Chordia, and Avanidhar Subrahmanyam, 1998, "Alternative Factor Specifications, Security Characteristics, and the Cross-Section of Expected Stock Returns," *Journal of Financial Economics* 49, 345–373.

Brennan, Michael J., Ashley W. Wang, and Yihong Xia, 2004, "Estimation and Test of a Simple Model of Intertemporal Asset Pricing," *Journal of Finance* 59, 1743–1775.

Brunnermeier, Markus K., and Lasse Heje Pedersen, 2009, "Market Liquidity and Funding Liquidity," *Review of Financial Studies* 22, 2201–2238.

Buffett, Warren E., 1988. Letter to the shareholders of Berkshire Hathaway Inc., February 29. http://www.berkshirehathaway.com/letters/1987.html.

Cagetti, Marco, Lars Peter Hansen, Thomas J. Sargent, and Noah Williams, 2002, "Robustness and Pricing with Uncertain Growth," *Review of Financial Studies* 15, 363–404.

Calvet, Laurent, John Y. Campbell, and Paolo Sodini, 2007, "Down or Out: Assessing the Welfare Costs of Household Investment Mistakes," *Journal of Political Economy* 115, 707–747.

———, 2009, "Fight or Flight? Portfolio Rebalancing by Individual Investors," *Quarterly Journal of Economics* 124, 301–348.

Campbell, John Y., 1986, "Bond and Stock Returns in a Simple Exchange Model," *Quarterly Journal of Economics* 101, 785–804.

———, 1987, "Stock Returns and the Term Structure," *Journal of Financial Economics* 18, 373–399.

———, 1991, "A Variance Decomposition for Stock Returns," *Economic Journal* 101, 157–179.

———, 1993, "Intertemporal Asset Pricing without Consumption Data," *American Economic Review* 83, 487–512.

———, 1994, "Inspecting the Mechanism: An Analytical Approach to the Stochastic Growth Model," *Journal of Monetary Economics* 33, 463–506.

———, 1996, "Understanding Risk and Return," *Journal of Political Economy* 104, 298–345.

———, 2000, "Asset Pricing at the Millennium," *Journal of Finance* 55, 1515–1567.

———, 2003, "Consumption-Based Asset Pricing," in George Constantinides, Milton Harris, and Rene Stulz eds. *Handbook of the Economics of Finance Vol. IB*, North-Holland, Amsterdam, 803–887.

———, 2006, "Household Finance," Presidential Address, *Journal of Finance* 61, 1553–1604.

———, 2008, "Estimating the Equity Premium," *Canadian Journal of Economics* 41, 1–21.

———, 2014, "Empirical Asset Pricing: Eugene Fama, Lars Peter Hansen, and Robert Shiller," *Scandinavian Journal of Economics* 116, 593–634.

———, 2016, "Restoring Rational Choice: The Challenge of Consumer Financial Regulation," Ely Lecture, *American Economic Review: Papers and Proceedings* 106, 1–30.

Campbell, John Y., Y. Lewis Chan, and Luis M. Viceira, 2003, "A Multivariate Model of Strategic Asset Allocation," *Journal of Financial Economics* 67, 41–80.

Campbell, John Y., and João F. Cocco, 2003, "Household Risk Management and Optimal Mortgage Choice," *Quarterly Journal of Economics* 118, 1449–1494.

Campbell, John Y., and John H. Cochrane, 1995, "By Force of Habit: A Consumption-Based Explanation of Aggregate Stock Market Behavior," NBER Working Paper No. 4995.

———, 1999, "By Force of Habit: A Consumption-Based Explanation of Aggregate Stock Market Behavior," *Journal of Political Economy* 107, 205–251.

———, 2015, "The Fragile Benefits of Endowment Destruction," *Journal of Political Economy* 123, 1214–1226.

Campbell, John Y., Stefano Giglio, Christopher Polk, and Robert Turley, 2017, "An Intertemporal CAPM with Stochastic Volatility," forthcoming *Journal of Financial Economics.*

Campbell, John Y., Sanford J. Grossman, and Jiang Wang, 1993, "Trading Volume and Serial Correlation in Stock Returns," *Quarterly Journal of Economics* 108, 905–939.

Campbell, John Y., Jens Hilscher, and Jan Szilagyi, 2008, "In Search of Distress Risk," *Journal of Finance* 63, 2899–2939.

Campbell, John Y., Howell Jackson, Brigitte Madrian, and Peter Tufano, 2011, "Consumer Financial Protection," *Journal of Economic Perspectives* 25(1), 91–114.

Campbell, John Y., and Albert S. Kyle, 1993, "Smart Money, Noise Trading and Stock Price Behaviour," *Review of Economic Studies* 60, 1–34.

Campbell, John Y., Martin Lettau, Burton Malkiel, and Yexiao Xu, 2001, "Have Individual Stocks Become More Volatile? An Empirical Exploration of Idiosyncratic Risk," *Journal of Finance* 56, 1–43.

Campbell, John Y., Andrew W. Lo, and A. Craig MacKinlay, 1997, *The Econometrics of Financial Markets*, Princeton University Press, Princeton, NJ.

Campbell, John Y., and N. Gregory Mankiw, 1989, "Consumption, Income, and Interest Rates: Reinterpreting the Time Series Evidence," *NBER Macroeconomics Annual* 4, 185–216.

Campbell, John Y., Christopher Polk, and Tuomo Vuolteenaho, 2010, "Growth or Glamour? Fundamentals and Systematic Risk in Stock Returns," *Review of Financial Studies* 23, 305–344.

Campbell, John Y., Karine Serfaty-de Medeiros, and Luis M. Viceira, 2010, "Global Currency Hedging," *Journal of Finance* 65, 87–121.

Campbell, John Y., and Robert J. Shiller, 1987, "Cointegration and Tests of Present Value Models," *Journal of Political Economy* 95, 1062–1088.

———, 1988a, "The Dividend-Price Ratio and Expectations of Future Dividends and Discount Factors," *Review of Financial Studies* 1, 195–228.

———, 1988b, "Stock Prices, Earnings, and Expected Dividends," *Journal of Finance* 43, 661–676.

———, 1991, "Yield Spreads and Interest Rate Movements: A Bird's Eye View," *Review of Economic Studies* 58, 495–514.

———, 2005, "Valuation Ratios and the Long-Run Stock Market Outlook: An Update," in Richard H. Thaler ed. *Advances in Behavioral Finance Vol. II*, Princeton University Press, Princeton, NJ, 173–201.

Campbell, John Y., Robert J. Shiller, and Luis M. Viceira, 2009, "Understanding Inflation-Indexed Bond Markets," *Brookings Papers on Economic Activity* 1, 79–120.

Campbell, John Y., Adi Sunderam, and Luis M. Viceira, 2017, "Inflation Bets or Deflation Hedges? Understanding the Risks of Nominal Bonds," forthcoming *Critical Finance Review.*

Campbell, John Y., and Samuel B. Thompson, 2008, "Predicting Excess Stock Returns Out of Sample: Can Anything Beat the Historical Average?," *Review of Financial Studies* 21, 1509–1531.

Campbell, John Y., and Argyris Tsiaras, 2017, *Financial Decisions and Markets: Problems and Solutions*, forthcoming Princeton University Press.

Campbell, John Y., and Luis M. Viceira, 1999, "Consumption and Portfolio Decisions When Expected Returns Are Time Varying," *Quarterly Journal of Economics* 114, 433–495.

———, 2001, "Who Should Buy Long-Term Bonds?," *American Economic Review* 91, 99–127.

———, 2002, *Strategic Asset Allocation: Portfolio Choice for Long-Term Investors*, Oxford University Press, New York.

Campbell, John Y., and Tuomo Vuolteenaho, 2004, "Bad Beta, Good Beta," *American Economic Review* 94, 1249–1275.

Campbell, John Y., and Motohiro Yogo, 2006, "Efficient Tests of Stock Return Predictability," *Journal of Financial Economics* 81, 27–60.

Canner, Niko, N. Gregory Mankiw, and David N. Weil, 1997, "An Asset Allocation Puzzle," *American Economic Review* 87, 181–191.

Carhart, Mark M., 1997, "On Persistence in Mutual Fund Performance," *Journal of Finance* 52, 57–82.

Carroll, Christopher D., 1997, "Buffer-Stock Saving and the Life Cycle/Permanent Income Hypothesis," *Quarterly Journal of Economics* 112, 1–55.

———, 2002, "Portfolios of the Rich," in Luigi Guiso, Michael Haliassos, and Tullio Jappelli eds. *Household Portfolios*, MIT Press, Cambridge, MA, 389–430.

Carroll, Christopher D., and Miles Kimball, 1996, "On the Concavity of the Consumption Function," *Econometrica* 64, 981–992.

Carter, R. B., F. H. Dark, and A. K. Singh, 1998, "Underwriter Reputation, Initial Returns, and the Long-Run Performance of IPO Stocks," *Journal of Finance* 53, 285–311.

Cavanagh, Christopher L., Graham Elliott, and James H. Stock, 1995, "Inference in Models with Nearly Integrated Regressors," *Econometric Theory* 11, 1131–1147.

Cederburg, Scott, and Michael S. O'Doherty, 2016, "Does It Pay to Bet Against Beta? On the Conditional Performance of the Beta Anomaly," *Journal of Finance* 71, 737–774.

Chacko, George C., Jakub W. Jurek, and Erik Stafford, 2008, "The Price of Immediacy," *Journal of Finance* 63, 1253–1290.

Chacko, George, and Luis M. Viceira, 2005, "Dynamic Consumption and Portfolio Choice with Stochastic Volatility in Incomplete Markets," *Review of Financial Studies* 18, 1369–1402.

Chan, Yeung Lewis, and Leonid Kogan, 2002, "Catching Up with the Joneses: Heterogeneous Preferences and the Dynamics of Asset Prices," *Journal of Political Economy* 110, 1255–1285.

Chang, Tom Y., David H. Solomon, and Mark M. Westerfield, 2016, "Looking for Someone to Blame: Delegation, Cognitive Dissonance, and the Disposition Effect," *Journal of Finance* 71, 267–302.

Chen, Long and Xinlei Zhao, 2009, "Return Decomposition," *Review of Financial Studies* 22, 5213–5249.

Chen, Nai-Fu, Richard Roll, and Stephen A. Ross, 1986, "Economic Forces and the Stock Market," *Journal of Business* 59, 383–403.

Cheng, Peng, and Olivier Scaillet, 2007, "Linear-Quadratic Jump-Diffusion Modeling," *Mathematical Finance* 17, 575–598.

Chetty, Raj, and Adam Szeidl, 2007, "Consumption Commitments and Risk Preferences," *Quarterly Journal of Economics* 122, 831–877.

Chevalier, Judith, and Glenn Ellison, 1997, "Risk Taking by Mutual Funds as a Response to Incentives," *Journal of Political Economy* 105, 1167–1200.

Chew, Soo Hong, 1983, "A Generalization of the Quasilinear Mean with Applications to the Measurement of Income Inequality and Decision Theory Resolving the Allais Paradox," *Econometrica* 51, 1065–1092.

Chien, YiLi, and Hanno Lustig, 2010, "The Market Price of Aggregate Risk and the Wealth Distribution," *Review of Financial Studies* 23, 1596–1650.

Chirinko, Robert S., 1993, "Business Fixed Investment Spending: Modeling Strategies, Empirical Results, and Policy Implications," *Journal of Economic Literature* 31, 1875–1911.

Choi, James J., David Laibson, Brigitte C. Madrian, and Andrew Metrick, 2009, "Reinforcement Learning and Savings Behavior," *Journal of Finance* 64, 2515–2534.

Christensen, Jens H. E., Francis X. Diebold, and Glenn D. Rudebusch, 2011, "The Affine Arbitrage-Free Class of Nelson-Siegel Term Structure Models," *Journal of Econometrics* 164, 4–20.

Christiano, Lawrence J., Roberto Motto, and Massimo Rostagno, 2014, "Risk Shocks," *American Economic Review* 104, 27–65.

Cocco, João F., Francisco J. Gomes, and Pascal J. Maenhout, 2005, "Consumption and Portfolio Choice over the Life Cycle," *Review of Financial Studies* 18, 491–533.

Cochrane, John H., 1988a, "How Big Is the Random Walk in GNP?," *Journal of Political Economy* 96, 893–920.

———, 1988b, "Production-Based Asset Pricing," NBER Working Paper No. 2776.

———, 1991a, "A Simple Test of Consumption Insurance," *Journal of Political Economy* 99, 957–976.

———, 1991b, "Production-Based Asset Pricing and the Link between Stock Returns and Economic Fluctuations," *Journal of Finance* 46, 209–237.

———, 1994, "Permanent and Transitory Components of GNP and Stock Prices," *Quarterly Journal of Economics* 109, 241–265.

———, 1996, "A Cross-Sectional Test of an Investment-Based Asset Pricing Model," *Journal of Political Economy* 104, 572–621.

———, 2005, *Asset Pricing*, revised ed., Princeton University Press, Princeton, NJ.

———, 2008, "The Dog That Did Not Bark: A Defense of Return Predictability," *Review of Financial Studies* 21, 1533–1575.

———, 2011, "Presidential Address: Discount Rates," *Journal of Finance* 66, 1047–1108.

———, 2014, "A Mean-Variance Benchmark for Intertemporal Portfolio Theory," *Journal of Finance* 69, 1–49.

Cochrane, John H., and Monika Piazzesi, 2005, "Bond Risk Premia," *American Economic Review* 95, 138–160.

Cochrane, John H., and Jesús Saá-Requejo, 2000, "Beyond Arbitrage: Good-Deal Asset Price Bounds in Incomplete Markets," *Journal of Political Economy* 108, 79–119.

Cohen, Lauren, Christopher Malloy, and Lukasz Pomorski, 2012, "Decoding Inside Information," *Journal of Finance* 57, 1009–1043.

Cohen, Randolph B., Paul A. Gompers, and Tuomo Vuolteenaho, 2002, "Who Underreacts to Cash-Flow News? Evidence from Trading between Individuals and Institutions," *Journal of Financial Economics* 66, 409–462.

Cohen, Randolph B., Christopher Polk, and Tuomo Vuolteenaho, 2005, "Money Illusion in the Stock Market: The Modigliani-Cohn Hypothesis," *Quarterly Journal of Economics* 120, 639–668.

———, 2009, "The Price Is (Almost) Right," *Journal of Finance* 64, 2739–2782.

Colacito, Riccardo, and Mariano M. Croce, 2011, "Risks for the Long Run and the Real Exchange Rate," *Journal of Political Economy* 119, 153–182.

Collin-Dufresne, Pierre, Michael Johannes, and Lars A. Lochstoer, 2016, "Parameter Learning in General Equilibrium: The Asset Pricing Implications," *American Economic Review* 106, 664–698.

Constantinides, George, 1982, "Intertemporal Asset Pricing with Heterogeneous Consumers and without Demand Aggregation," *Journal of Business* 55, 253–267.

———, 1990, "Habit Formation: A Resolution of the Equity Premium Puzzle," *Journal of Political Economy* 98, 519–543.

Constantinides, George M., John B. Donaldson, and Rajnish Mehra, 2002, "Junior Can't Borrow: A New Perspective on the Equity Premium Puzzle," *Quarterly Journal of Economics* 117, 269–296.

Constantinides, George M., and Darrell Duffie, 1996, "Asset Pricing with Heterogeneous Consumers," *Journal of Political Economy* 104, 219–240.

Constantinides, George M., and Anisha Ghosh, 2017, "Asset Pricing with Countercyclical Household Consumption Risk," *Journal of Finance* 72, 415–459.

Cooper, Michael, Huseyin Gulen, and Michael Schill, 2008, "Asset Growth and the Cross-Section of Stock Returns," *Journal of Finance* 63, 1609–1651.

Cox, John C., and Chi-fu Huang, 1989, "Optimal Consumption and Portfolio Policies When Asset Prices Follow a Diffusion Process," *Journal of Economic Theory* 49, 33–83.

Cox, John C., Jonathan E. Ingersoll, and Stephen A. Ross, 1985, "An Intertemporal General Equilibrium Model of Asset Prices," *Econometrica* 53, 363–384.

Cripps, Martin W., and Jeroen M. Swinkels, 2005, "Efficiency of Large Double Auctions," *Econometrica* 74, 47–92.

Cusatis, P., J. Miles, and J. Woolridge, 1993, "Restructuring Through Spinoffs," *Journal of Financial Economics* 33, 293–311.

Dai, Qiang. and Kenneth J. Singleton, 2000, "Specification Analysis of Affine Term Structure Models," *Journal of Finance* 55, 1943–1978.

Dang, Tri Vi, Gary Gorton, and Bengt Holmström, 2012, "Ignorance, Debt, and Financial Crises," unpublished paper.

Daniel, Kent D., Mark Grinblatt, Sheridan Titman, and Russ Wermers, 1997, "Measuring Mutual Fund Performance with Characteristic-Based Benchmarks," *Journal of Finance* 52, 1035–1058.

Daniel, Kent D., David Hirshleifer, and Avanidhar Subrahmanyam, 1998, "Investor Psychology and Security Market Under- and Overreactions," *Journal of Finance* 53, 1839–1886.

———, 2001, "Overconfidence, Arbitrage, and Equilibrium Asset Pricing," *Journal of Finance* 56, 921–965.

Daniel, Kent D., and David Marshall, 1997, "Equity-Premium and Risk-free-Rate Puzzles at Long Horizons," *Macroeconomic Dynamics* 1, 452–484.

Daniel, Kent D., and Sheridan Titman, 2006, "Market Reactions to Tangible and Intangible Information," *Journal of Finance* 61, 1609–1651.

Daniel, Kent D., and Sheridan Titman, 2012, "Testing Factor-Model Explanations of Market Anomalies," *Critical Finance Review* 1, 103–139.

Dávila, Eduardo, and Anton Korinek, 2017, "Pecuniary Externalities in Economies with Financial Frictions," forthcoming *Review of Economic Studies*.

Davis, Morris A., Andreas Lehnert, and Robert F. Martin, 2008, "The Rent-Price Ratio for the Aggregate Stock of Owner-Occupied Housing," *Review of Income and Wealth* 54, 279–284.

Deaton, Angus, 1991, "Saving and Liquidity Constraints," *Econometrica* 59, 1221–1248.

Deaton, Angus, and John Muellbauer, 1980, "An Almost Ideal Demand System," *American Economic Review* 70, 312–326.

DeBondt, Werner, and Richard Thaler, 1985, "Does the Stock Market Overreact?," *Journal of Finance* 40, 793–808.

Dechow, P., R. Sloan, and A. Sweeney, 1995, "Detecting Earnings Management," *Accounting Review* 70, 3–42.

Dekel, Eddie, 1986, "An Axiomatic Characterization of Preferences under Uncertainty: Weakening the Independence Axiom," *Journal of Economic Theory* 40, 304–318.

Del Guercio, Diane, and Jonathan Reuter, 2014, "Mutual Fund Performance and the Incentive to Generate Alpha," *Journal of Finance* 69, 1673–1704.

De Long, J. Bradford, Andrei Shleifer, Lawrence H. Summers, and Robert J. Waldmann, 1990a, "Noise Trader Risk in Financial Markets," *Journal of Political Economy* 98, 703–738.

———, 1990b, "Positive Feedback Investment Strategies and Destabilizing Rational Speculation," *Journal of Finance* 45, 379–395.

———, 1991, "The Survival of Noise Traders in Financial Markets," *Journal of Business* 64, 1–19.

DeMiguel, Victor, Lorenzo Garlappi, and Raman Uppal, 2009, "Optimal versus Naive Diversification: How Inefficient Is the 1/N Portfolio Strategy?," *Review of Financial Studies* 22, 1915–1953.

Desai, H., and P. Jain, 1997, "Long-Run Common Stock Returns Following Splits and Reverse Splits," *Journal of Business* 70, 409–433.

DeMarzo, Peter M., Ron Kaniel, and Ilan Kremer, 2004, "Diversification as a Public Good: Community Effects in Portfolio Choice," *Journal of Finance* 59, 1677–1716.

Dew-Becker, Ian, 2012, "A Model of Time-Varying Risk Premia with Habits and Production," unpublished paper, Federal Reserve Bank of San Francisco.

Dhar, Ravi, and Ning Zhu, 2006, "Up Close and Personal: Investor Sophistication and the Disposition Effect," *Management Science* 52, 726–740.

Dhume, Deepa, 2010, "Using Durable Consumption Risk to Explain Commodities Returns," unpublished paper, Harvard University.

Diamond, Douglas W., and Robert E. Verrecchia, 1981, "Information Aggregation in a Noisy Rational Expectations Economy," *Journal of Financial Economics* 9, 221–235.

Diba, Behzad T., and Herschel I. Grossman, 1987, "On the Inception of Rational Bubbles," *Quarterly Journal of Economics* 102, 697–700.

———, 1988, "Explosive Rational Bubbles in Stock Prices?," *American Economic Review* 78, 520–530.

Diebold, Francis X., Canlin Li, and Vivian Z. Yue, 2008, "Global Yield Curve Dynamics and Interactions: A Dynamic Nelson-Siegel Approach," *Journal of Econometrics* 146, 351–363.

Diether, Karl B., Christopher J. Malloy, and Anna Scherbina, 2002, "Differences of Opinion and the Cross Section of Stock Returns," *Journal of Finance* 57, 2113–2141.

Dimson, Elroy, Paul Marsh, and Mike Staunton, 2002, *Triumph of the Optimists: 101 Years of Global Investment Returns*, Princeton University Press, Princeton, NJ.

Døskeland, Trond M., and Hans K. Hvide, 2011, "Do Individual Investors Have Asymmetric Information Based on Work Experience?," *Journal of Finance* 66, 1011–1041.

Drechsler, Itamar, and Amir Yaron, 2011, "What's Vol Got to Do with It," *Review of Financial Studies* 24, 1–45.

Du, Wenxin, Alexander Tepper, and Adrien Verdelhan, 2016, "Deviations from Covered Interest Parity," unpublished paper.

Dubey, Pradeep, John Geanakoplos, and Martin Shubik, 2005, "Default and Punishment in General Equilibrium," *Econometrica* 73, 1–37.

Duffee, Gregory R., 2002, "Term Premia and Interest Rate Forecasts in Affine Models," *Journal of Finance* 57, 405–443.

———, 2011, "Information in (and not in) the Term Structure," *Review of Financial Studies* 24, 2895–2934.

———, 2013, "Bond Pricing and the Macroeconomy," in George Constantinides, Milton Harris, and René Stulz eds. *Handbook of the Economics of Finance Vol. 2B*, North-Holland, Amsterdam, 907–968.

Duffie, Darrell, 2001, *Dynamic Asset Pricing Theory*, 3rd ed., Princeton University Press, Princeton, NJ.

———, 2010, "Presidential Address: Asset Price Dynamics with Slow-Moving Capital," *Journal of Finance* 65, 1237–1267.

Duffie, Darrell, Nicolae Gârleanu, and Lasse Pedersen, 2005, "Over-The-Counter Markets," *Econometrica* 73, 1815–1847.

Duffie, Darrell, and Rui Kan, 1996, "A Yield-Factor Model of Interest Rates," *Mathematical Finance* 6, 379–406.

Dunn, Kenneth B., and Kenneth J. Singleton, 1986, "Modeling the Term Structure of Interest Rates under Non-Separable Utility and Durability of Goods," *Journal of Financial Economics* 17, 27–55.

Dybvig, Philip H., Jonathan E. Ingersoll Jr., and Stephen A. Ross, 1996, "Long Forward and Zero-Coupon Rates Can Never Fall," *Journal of Business* 69, 1–25.

Easley, David, Nicholas M. Kiefer, Maureen O'Hara, and Joseph B. Paperman, 1996, "Liquidity, Information, and Infrequently Traded Stocks," *Journal of Finance* 51, 1405–1436.

Eichenbaum, Martin, and Lars Peter Hansen, 1990, "Estimating Models with Intertemporal Substitution Using Aggregate Time Series Data," *Journal of Business and Economic Statistics* 8, 53–69.

Eisfeldt, Andrea L., and Dimitris Papanikolaou, 2013, "Organization Capital and the Cross-Section of Expected Returns," *Journal of Finance* 68, 1365–1406.

Eleswarapu, Venkat R., and Marc R. Reinganum, 2004, "The Predictability of Aggregate Stock Market Returns: Evidence Based on Glamour Stocks," *Journal of Business* 77, 275–294.

Ellsberg, Daniel, 1961, "Risk, Ambiguity, and the Savage Axioms," *Quarterly Journal of Economics* 75, 643–669.

Engel, Charles, 2014, "Exchange Rates and Interest Parity," in Gita Gopinath, Elhanan Helpman, and Kenneth Rogoff eds. *Handbook of International Economics Vol. 4*, North-Holland, Amsterdam, 453–522.

Engle, Robert F., and Clive W. J. Granger, 1987, "Co-Integration and Error Correction: Representation, Estimation, and Testing," *Econometrica* 55, 251–276.

Engsted, Tom, Thomas Q. Pedersen, and Carsten Tanggaard, 2012, "Pitfalls in VAR Based Return Decompositions: A Clarification," *Journal of Banking and Finance* 36, 1255–1265.

Epstein, Larry G., Emmanuel Farhi, and Tomasz Strzalecki, 2014, "How Much Would You Pay to Resolve Long-Run Risk?," *American Economic Review* 104, 2680–2697.

Epstein, Larry G., and Martin Schneider, 2010, "Ambiguity and Asset Markets," *Annual Review of Financial Economics* 2, 315–346.

Epstein, Larry G., and Tan Wang, 1994, "Intertemporal Asset Pricing under Knightian Uncertainty," *Econometrica* 62, 283–322.

Epstein, Larry G., and Stanley E. Zin, 1989, "Substitution, Risk Aversion, and the Temporal Behavior of Consumption and Asset Returns: A Theoretical Framework," *Econometrica* 57, 937–969.

————, 1990, "'First-Order' Risk Aversion and the Equity Premium Puzzle," *Journal of Monetary Economics* 26, 387–407.

————, "Substitution, Risk Aversion, and the Temporal Behavior of Consumption and Asset Returns: An Empirical Analysis," *Journal of Political Economy* 99, 263–286.

Erickson, Timothy, and Toni M. Whited, 2000, "Measurement Error and the Relationship between Investment and q," *Journal of Political Economy* 108, 1027–1057.

Evans, George W., 1991, "Pitfalls in Testing for Explosive Bubbles in Asset Prices," *American Economic Review* 81, 922–930.

Eyster, Erik, Matthew Rabin, and Dimitri Vayanos, 2015, "Financial Markets Where Traders Neglect the Informational Content of Prices," NBER Working Paper No. 21224.

Fagereng, Andreas, Charles Gottlieb, and Luigi Guiso, 2017, "Asset Market Participation and Portfolio Choice over the Life-Cycle," *Journal of Finance* 72, 705–750.

Fama, Eugene F., 1970, "Efficient Capital Markets: A Review of Theory and Empirical Work," *Journal of Finance* 25, 383–417.

————, 1984, "Forward and Spot Exchange Rates," *Journal of Monetary Economics* 14, 319–338.

————, 1998, "Market Efficiency, Long-Term Returns, and Behavioral Finance," *Journal of Financial Economics* 49, 283–306.

Fama, Eugene F., and Robert R. Bliss, 1987, "The Information in Long-Maturity Forward Rates," *American Economic Review* 77, 680–692.

Fama, Eugene F., and Kenneth R. French, 1988a, "Dividend Yields and Expected Stock Returns," *Journal of Financial Economics* 22, 3–25.

————, 1988b, "Permanent and Temporary Components of Stock Prices," *Journal of Political Economy* 96, 246–273.

————, 1989, "Business Conditions and Expected Returns on Stocks and Bonds," *Journal of Financial Economics* 25, 23–50.

————, 1992, "The Cross-Section of Expected Stock Returns," *Journal of Finance* 47, 427–465.

————, 1993, "Common Risk Factors in the Returns on Stocks and Bonds," *Journal of Financial Economics* 33, 3–56.

————, 1996, "Multifactor Explanations of Asset Pricing Anomalies," *Journal of Finance* 51, 55–84.

————, 2002, "The Equity Premium," *Journal of Finance* 57, 637–659.

————, 2004, "The Capital Asset Pricing Model: Theory and Evidence," *Journal of Economic Perspectives* 18(3), 25–46.

————, 2015, "A Five-Factor Asset Pricing Model," *Journal of Financial Economics* 116, 1–22.

Fama, Eugene F., and James D. MacBeth, 1973, "Risk, Return, and Equilibrium: Empirical Tests," *Journal of Political Economy* 81, 607–636.

Fama, Eugene F., and G. William Schwert, 1977, "Asset Returns and Inflation," *Journal of Financial Economics* 5, 115–146.

Farhi, Emmanuel, and Xavier Gabaix, 2016, "Rare Disasters and Exchange Rates," *Quarterly Journal of Economics* 131, 1–52.

Farhi, Emmanuel, and Stavros Panageas, 2007, "Saving and Investing for Early Retirement: A Theoretical Analysis," *Journal of Financial Economics* 83, 87–121.

Farhi, Emmanuel, and Jean Tirole, 2012, "Bubbly Liquidity," *Review of Economic Studies* 79, 678–706.

Farhi, Emmanuel, and Iván Werning, 2016, "A Theory of Macroprudential Policies in the Presence of Nominal Rigidities," *Econometrica* 84, 1645–1704.

Fazzari, Steven M., R. Glenn Hubbard, and Bruce C. Petersen, 1988, "Financing Constraints and Corporate Investment," *Brookings Papers on Economic Activity* 1, 141–195.

Foster, Dean P., and Sergiu Hart, 2009, "An Operational Measure of Riskiness," *Journal of Political Economy* 117, 785–814.

Foster, George, Chris Olsen, and Terry Shevlin, 1984, "Earnings Releases, Anomalies, and the Behavior of Security Returns," *Accounting Review* 59, 574–603.

Frazzini, Andrea, 2006, "The Disposition Effect and Underreaction to News," *Journal of Finance* 61, 2017–2046.

Frazzini, Andrea, and Owen Lamont, 2006, "The Earnings Announcement Premium and Trading Volume," unpublished paper.

French, Kenneth R., 2008, "The Cost of Active Investing," Presidential Address, *Journal of Finance* 63, 1537–1573.

Friend, Irwin, and Marshall E. Blume, 1975, "The Demand for Risky Assets," *American Economic Review* 65, 900–922.

Froot, Kenneth A., and Emil M. Dabora, 1999, "How Are Stock Prices Affected by the Location of Trade?," *Journal of Financial Economics* 53, 189–216.

Froot, Kenneth A., and André F. Perold, 1995, "New Trading Practices and Short-Run Market Efficiency," *Journal of Futures Markets* 15, 731–765.

Fung, William, David A. Hsieh, Narayan Y. Naik, and Tarun Ramadorai, 2008, "Hedge Funds: Performance, Risk, and Capital Formation," *Journal of Finance* 63, 1777–1803.

Gabaix, Xavier, 2009, "Linearity-Generating Processes: A Modelling Tool Yielding Closed Forms for Asset Prices," unpublished paper, New York University.

———, 2012, "Variable Rare Disasters: An Exactly Solved Framework for Ten Puzzles in Macro-Finance," *Quarterly Journal of Economics* 127, 645–700.

Gabaix, Xavier, Parameswaran Gopikrishnan, Vasiliki Plerou, and H. Eugene Stanley, 2006, "Institutional Investors and Stock Market Volatility," *Quarterly Journal of Economics* 121, 461–504.

Gabaix, Xavier, Arvind Krishnamurthy, and Olivier Vigneron, 2007, "Limits of Arbitrage: Theory and Evidence from the Mortgage-Backed Securities Market," *Journal of Finance* 62, 557–595.

Gabaix, Xavier, and David Laibson, 2001, "The 6D Bias and the Equity-Premium Puzzle," *NBER Macroeconomics Annual* 16, 257–330.

———, 2006, "Shrouded Attributes, Consumer Myopia, and Information Suppression in Competitive Markets," *Quarterly Journal of Economics* 121, 505–540.

Garcia, Rene, Eric Renault, and A. Semenov, 2006, "Disentangling Risk Aversion and Intertemporal Substitution through a Reference Level," *Finance Research Letters* 3, 181–193.

Gârleanu, Nicolae, Leonid Kogan, and Stavros Panageas, 2012, "Displacement Risk and Asset Returns," *Journal of Financial Economics* 105, 491–510.

Gârleanu, Nicolae, and Lasse Heje Pedersen, 2011, "Margin-Based Asset Pricing and Deviations from the Law of One Price," *Review of Financial Studies* 24, 1980–2022.

Geanakoplos, John, 2009, "The Leverage Cycle," *NBER Macroeconomics Annual* 24, 1–66.

Geanakoplos, John, and Heraklis M. Polemarchakis, 1986, "Existence, Regularity and Constrained Suboptimality of Competitive Allocations When the Asset Market Is Incomplete," in Walter P. Heller, Ross M. Starr, and David A. Starrett eds. *Uncertainty, Information and Communication: Essays in Honor of K. J. Arrow Vol. 3*, Cambridge University Press, Cambridge, UK, 65–96.

Geerolf, François, 2013, "Reassessing Dynamic Efficiency," unpublished paper.

George, Thomas J., and Chuan-Yang Hwang, 2010, "A Resolution of the Distress Risk and Leverage Puzzles in the Cross-Section of Stock Returns," *Journal of Financial Economics* 96, 56–79.

Geske, Robert, and Richard Roll, 1983, "The Fiscal and Monetary Linkage between Stock Returns and Inflation," *Journal of Finance* 38, 1–33.

Gibbons, Michael, Stephen Ross, and Jay Shanken, 1989, "A Test of the Efficiency of a Given Portfolio," *Econometrica* 57, 1121–1152.

Giglio, Stefano, Matteo Maggiori, and Johannes Stroebel, 2015, "Very Long-Run Discount Rates," *Quarterly Journal of Economics* 130, 1–53.

———, 2016, "No-Bubble Condition: Model-Free Tests in Housing Markets," *Econometrica* 84, 1047–1091.

Gilboa, Itzhak, and David Schmeidler, 1989, "Maxmin Expected Utility with Non-Unique Prior," *Journal of Mathematical Economics* 18, 141–153.

Gleason, Cristi A., and Charles M. C. Lee, 2003, "Analyst Forecast Revisions and Market Price Discovery," *Accounting Review* 78, 193–225.

Glosten, Lawrence, and Paul Milgrom, 1985, "Bid, Ask, and Transaction Prices in a Specialist Market with Heterogeneously Informed Traders," *Journal of Financial Economics* 14, 71–100.

Goetzmann, William N., and Alok Kumar, 2008, "Equity Portfolio Diversification," *Review of Finance* 12, 433–463.

Gollier, Christian, 2001, *The Economics of Risk and Time*, MIT Press, Cambridge, MA.

Golosov, Mikhail, Narayana Kocherlakota, and Aleh Tsyvinski, 2003, "Optimal Indirect and Capital Taxation," *Review of Economic Studies* 70, 569–587.

Gomes, Francisco, and Alexander Michaelides, 2005, "Optimal Life-Cycle Asset Allocation: Understanding the Empirical Evidence," *Journal of Finance* 60, 869–904.

———, 2008, "Asset Pricing with Limited Risk Sharing and Heterogeneous Agents," *Review of Financial Studies* 21, 415–448.

Gomes, João F., Leonid Kogan, and Motohiro Yogo, 2009, "Durability of Output and Expected Stock Returns," *Journal of Political Economy* 117, 941–986.

Gordon, Myron J., and Eli Shapiro, 1956, "Capital Equipment Analysis: The Required Rate of Profit," *Management Science* 3, 102–110.

Gourinchas, Pierre-Olivier, and Jonathan Parker, 2002, "Consumption over the Life Cycle," *Econometrica* 70, 47–89.

Gourio, François, 2012, "Disaster Risk and Business Cycles," *American Economic Review* 102, 2734–2766.

Graham, Benjamin, David Le Fevre Dodd, and Sidney Cottle, 1934, *Security Analysis*, McGraw-Hill, New York.

Greenwald, Bruce C., and Joseph E. Stiglitz, 1986, "Externalities in Economies with Imperfect Information and Incomplete Markets," *Quarterly Journal of Economics* 101, 229–264.

Greenwood, Robin, and Dimitri Vayanos, 2014, "Bond Supply and Excess Bond Returns," *Review of Financial Studies* 27, 663–713.

Grinblatt, Mark, and Bing Han, 2005, "Prospect Theory, Mental Accounting, and Momentum," *Journal of Financial Economics* 78, 311–339.

Grinblatt, Mark, and Matti Keloharju, 2000, "The Investment Behavior and Performance of Various Investor Types: A Study of Finland's Unique Data Set," *Journal of Financial Economics* 55, 43–67.

———, 2001, "How Distance, Language, and Culture Influence Stockholdings and Trades," *Journal of Finance* 56, 1053–1073.

———, 2009, "Sensation Seeking, Overconfidence, and Trading Activity," *Journal of Finance* 64, 549–578.

Grinblatt, Mark, Matti Keloharju, and Juhani Linnainmaa, 2011, "IQ and Stock Market Participation," *Journal of Finance* 66, 2121–2164.

———, 2012, "IQ, Trading Behavior, and Performance," *Journal of Financial Economics* 104, 339–362.

Grossman, Sanford J., 1976, "On the Efficiency of Competitive Stock Markets Where Trades Have Diverse Information," *Journal of Finance* 31, 573–585.

Grossman, Sanford J., and Robert J. Shiller, 1982, "Consumption Correlatedness and Risk Measurement in Economies with Non-Traded Assets and Heterogeneous Information," *Journal of Financial Economics* 10, 195–210.

Grossman, Sanford J., and Joseph E. Stiglitz, 1980, "On the Impossibility of Informationally Efficient Markets," *American Economic Review* 70, 393–408.

Guiso, Luigi, Tullio Jappelli, and Daniele Terlizzese, 1996, "Income Risk, Borrowing Constraints, and Portfolio Choice," *American Economic Review* 86, 158–172.

Guiso, Luigi, Paola Sapienza, and Luigi Zingales, 2008, "Trusting the Stock Market," *Journal of Finance* 63, 2557–2600.

Guiso, Luigi, and Paolo Sodini, 2013, "Household Finance: An Emerging Field," in George M. Constantinides, Milton Harris, and Rene M. Stulz eds. *Handbook of the Economics of Finance Vol. 2B*, North-Holland, Amsterdam, 1397–1531.

Gul, Faruk, 1991, "A Theory of Disappointment Aversion," *Econometrica* 59, 667–686.

Gürkaynak, Refet S., and Jonathan H. Wright, 2012, "Macroeconomics and the Term Structure," *Journal of Economic Literature* 50, 331–367.

Guvenen, Fatih, 2009, "A Parsimonious Macroeconomic Model for Asset Pricing," *Econometrica* 77, 1711–1750.

———, 2011, "Macroeconomics with Heterogeneity: A Practical Guide," *Federal Reserve Bank of Richmond Economic Quarterly* 97, 255–326.

Haliassos, Michael, and Carol Bertaut, 1995, "Why Do So Few Hold Stocks?," *Economic Journal* 105, 1110–1129.

Hall, Alastair R., 2005, *Generalized Method of Moments*, Oxford University Press, New York.

Hall, Robert E., 1988, "Intertemporal Substitution in Consumption," *Journal of Political Economy* 96, 221–273.

Hansen, Lars Peter, 1982a, "Consumption, Asset Markets, and Macroeconomic Fluctuations: A Comment," *Carnegie-Rochester Conference Series on Public Policy* 17, 239–250.

———, 1982b, "Large Sample Properties of Generalized Method of Moments Estimators," *Econometrica* 50, 1029–1054.

———, 1987, "Calculating Asset Prices in Three Example Economies," in Truman F. Bewley ed. *Advances in Econometrics, Fifth World Congress*, Cambridge University Press, Cambridge, UK, 207–243.

Hansen, Lars Peter, John C. Heaton, J. Lee, and Nicholas Roussanov, 2007, "Intertemporal Substitution and Risk Aversion," in J. J. Heckman and E. E. Leamer eds. *Handbook of Econometrics Vol. 6A*, North-Holland, Amsterdam, 3967–4056.

Hansen, Lars Peter, John C. Heaton, and Nan Li, 2008, "Consumption Strikes Back? Measuring Long-Run Risk," *Journal of Political Economy* 116, 260–302.

Hansen, Lars Peter, John C. Heaton, and Amir Yaron, 1996, "Finite-Sample Properties of Some Alternative GMM Estimators," *Journal of Business and Economic Statistics* 14, 262–280.

Hansen, Lars Peter, and Ravi Jagannathan, 1991, "Implications of Security Market Data for Models of Dynamic Economies," *Journal of Political Economy* 99, 225–262.

———, 1997, "Assessing Specification Errors in Stochastic Discount Factor Models," *Journal of Finance* 52, 557–590.

Hansen, Lars Peter, and Scott F. Richard, 1987, "The Role of Conditioning Information in Deducing Testable Restrictions Implied by Dynamic Asset Pricing Models," *Econometrica* 55, 587–613.

Hansen, Lars Peter, and Thomas J. Sargent, 2008, "Risk Sensitivity, Model Uncertainty, and Asset Pricing," in *Robustness*, Princeton University Press, Princeton, NJ, 307–325.

Hansen, Lars Peter, and José A. Scheinkman, 2009, "Long-Term Risk: An Operator Approach," *Econometrica* 77, 177–234.

Hansen Lars Peter, and Kenneth J. Singleton, 1982, "Generalized Instrumental Variables Estimation of Nonlinear Rational Expectations Models," *Econometrica* 50, 1269–1286.

———, 1983, "Stochastic Consumption, Risk Aversion, and the Temporal Behavior of Asset Returns," *Journal of Political Economy* 91, 249–265.

Harris, Lawrence, and Eitan Gurel, 1986, "Price and Volume Effects Associated with Changes in the S&P 500 List: New Evidence for the Existence of Price Pressures," *Journal of Finance* 41, 815–829.

Harris, Milton, and Artur Raviv, 1993, "Differences of Opinion Make a Horse Race," *Review of Financial Studies* 6, 473–506.

Harrison, J. Michael, and David M. Kreps, 1978, "Speculative Investor Behavior in a Stock Market with Heterogeneous Expectations," *Quarterly Journal of Economics* 92, 323–336.

———, 1979, "Martingales and Arbitrage in Multiperiod Securities Markets," *Journal of Economic Theory* 20, 381–408.

Hart, Oliver D., 1975, "On the Optimality of Equilibrium When the Market Structure Is Incomplete," *Journal of Economic Theory* 11, 418–443.

Harvey, Campbell R., 1989, "Time-Varying Conditional Covariances in Tests of Asset Pricing Models," *Journal of Financial Economics* 24, 289–317.

Hasbrouck, Joel, 1991, "Measuring the Information Content of Stock Trades," *Journal of Finance* 46, 179–207.

Hasbrouck, Joel, and Duane J. Seppi, 2001, "Common Factors in Prices, Order Flows, and Liquidity," *Journal of Financial Economics* 59, 383–411.

Hassan, Tarek A., and Rui C. Mano, 2015, "Forward and Spot Exchange Rates in a Multi-currency World," unpublished paper, University of Chicago and International Monetary Fund.

Hastings, Justine S., Brigitte C. Madrian, and William L. Skimmyhorn, 2013, "Financial Literacy, Financial Education, and Economic Outcomes," *Annual Review of Economics* 5, 347–373.

Hayashi, Fumio, 1982, "Tobin's Marginal q and Average q: A Neoclassical Interpretation," *Econometrica* 50, 213–224.

Heaton, John, and Deborah Lucas, 1996, "Evaluating the Effects of Incomplete Markets on Risk Sharing and Asset Pricing," *Journal of Political Economy* 104, 668–712.

———, 2000, "Portfolio Choice and Asset Prices: The Importance of Entrepreneurial Risk," *Journal of Finance* 55, 1163–1198.

Hellwig, Martin F., 1980, "On the Aggregation of Information in Competitive Markets," *Journal of Economic Theory* 22, 477–498.

Heston, Steven L., 1993, "A Closed-Form Solution for Options with Stochastic Volatility with Applications to Bond and Currency Options," *Review of Financial Studies* 6, 327–343.

Heston, Steven L., and Ronnie Sadka, 2008, "Seasonality in the Cross-Section of Stock Returns," *Journal of Financial Economics* 87, 418–445.

Hirshleifer, David, 1988, "Residual Risk, Trading Costs, and Commodity Futures Risk Premia," *Review of Financial Studies* 1, 173–193.

Hirshleifer, David, Kewei Hou, and Siew Hong Teoh, 2009, "Accruals, Cash Flows, and Aggregate Stock Returns," *Journal of Financial Economics* 91, 389–406.

Hirshleifer, David, Kewei Hou, Siew Hong Teoh, and Yinglei Zhang, 2004, "Do Investors Overvalue Firms with Bloated Balance Sheets?," *Journal of Accounting and Economics* 38, 297–331.

Hirshleifer, David, Jun Li, and Jianfeng Yu, 2015, "Asset Pricing in Production Economies with Extrapolative Expectations," *Journal of Monetary Economics* 76, 87–106.

Hirshleifer, David, Avanidhar Subrahmanyam, and Sheridan Titman, 1994, "Security Analysis and Trading Patterns When Some Investors Receive Information Before Others," *Journal of Finance* 49, 1665–1698.

Hodrick, Robert J., 1992, "Dividend Yields and Expected Stock Returns: Alternative Procedures for Inference and Measurement," *Review of Financial Studies* 5, 257–286.

Holmström, Bengt, and Jean Tirole, 2001, "LAPM: A Liquidity-Based Asset Pricing Model," *Journal of Finance* 56, 1837–1867.

Hong, Harrison, Jeffrey D. Kubik, and Jeremy C. Stein, 2004, "Social Interaction and Stock-Market Participation," *Journal of Finance* 59, 137–163.

Hong, Harrison, and Jeremy C. Stein, 2003, "Differences of Opinion, Short-Sales Constraints, and Market Crashes," *Review of Financial Studies* 16, 487–525.

Hou, Kewei, Chen Xue, and Lu Zhang, 2015, "Digesting Anomalies: An Investment Approach," *Review of Financial Studies* 28, 650–705.

Huang, Chi-fu, and Robert H. Litzenberger, 1998, *Foundations for Financial Economics*, North-Holland, Amsterdam.

Huberman, Gur, 2001, "Familiarity Breeds Investment," *Review of Financial Studies* 14, 659–680.

Ikenberry, D., J. Lakonishok, and T. Vermaelen, 1995, "Market Underreaction to Open Market Share Repurchases," *Journal of Financial Economics* 39, 181–208.

Ikenberry, D., G. Rankine, and E. Stice, 1996, "What Do Stock Splits Really Signal?," *Journal of Financial and Quantitative Analysis* 31, 357–377.

Ilmanen, Antti, 2011, *Expected Returns: An Investor's Guide to Harvesting Market Rewards*, Wiley, Chichester, UK.

Ingersoll, Jonathan E., Jr., 1987, *Theory of Financial Decision Making*, Rowman and Littlefield, Totowa, NJ.

Ivković, Zoran, and Scott Weisbenner, 2005, "Local Does as Local Is: Information Content of the Geography of Individual Investors' Common Stock Investments," *Journal of Finance* 60, 267–306.

Jagannathan, Ravi, and Yong Wang, 2007, "Lazy Investors, Discretionary Consumption, and the Cross-Section of Stock Returns," *Journal of Finance* 62, 1623–1661.

Jansson, Michael, and Marcelo J. Moreira, 2006, "Optimal Inference in Regression Models with Nearly Integrated Regressors," *Econometrica* 74, 681–714.

Jegadeesh, Narasimhan, and Sheridan Titman, 1993, "Returns to Buying Winners and Selling Losers: Implications for Stock Market Efficiency," *Journal of Finance* 48, 65–92.

Jeng, Leslie, Andrew Metrick, and Richard Zeckhauser, 2003, "Estimating the Returns to Insider Trading: A Performance-Evaluation Perspective," *Review of Economics and Statistics* 85, 453–471.

Jensen, Michael C., 1978, "Some Anomalous Evidence Regarding Market Efficiency," *Journal of Financial Economics* 6, 95–101.

Jermann, Urban J., 1998, "Asset Pricing in Production Economies," *Journal of Monetary Economics* 41, 257–275.

Johnson, Eric, Stephan Meier, and Olivier Toubia, 2015, "Leaving Money on the Kitchen Table: Exploring Sluggish Mortgage Refinancing Using Administrative Data, Surveys, and Field Experiments," unpublished paper.

Johnson, Norman L., Samuel Kotz, and N. Balakrishnan, 1994, *Continuous Univariate Distributions Vol. 1*, 2nd ed., Wiley, New York.

Jorion, Philippe, 1986, "Bayes-Stein Estimation for Portfolio Analysis," *Journal of Financial and Quantitative Analysis* 21, 279–292.

Joslin, Scott, Marcel Priebsch, and Kenneth J. Singleton, 2014, "Risk Premiums in Dynamic Term Structure Models with Unspanned Macro Risks," *Journal of Finance* 69, 1197–1233.

Jung, Jeeman, and Robert J. Shiller, 2005, "Samuelson's Dictum and the Stock Market," *Economic Inquiry* 43, 221–228.

Justiniano, Alejandro, Giorgio E. Primiceri, and Andrea Tambalotti, 2010, "Investment Shocks and Business Cycles," *Journal of Monetary Economics* 57, 132–145.

Kahneman, Daniel, and Amos Tversky, 1979, "Prospect Theory: An Analysis of Decision under Risk," *Econometrica* 47, 263–291.

Kandel, Eugene, and Neil D. Pearson, 1995, "Differential Interpretation of Public Signals and Trade in Speculative Markets," *Journal of Political Economy* 103, 831–872.

Kandel, Shmuel, and Robert F. Stambaugh, 1987, "On Correlations and Inferences About Mean-Variance Efficiency," *Journal of Financial Economics* 18, 61–90.

————, 1991, "Asset Returns and Intertemporal Preferences," *Journal of Monetary Economics* 27, 39–71.

Kaltenbrunner, Georg, and Lars A. Lochstoer, 2010, "Long-Run Risk through Consumption Smoothing," *Review of Financial Studies* 23, 3190–3224.

Kang, Johnny, Tapio Pekkala, Christopher Polk, and Ruy Ribeiro, 2015, "Stock Prices under Pressure: How Tax and Interest Rates Drive Returns at the Turn of the Tax Year," unpublished paper, London School of Economics.

Kaplan, Greg, and Giovanni L. Violante, 2014, "A Model of the Consumption Response to Fiscal Stimulus Payments," *Econometrica* 82, 1199–1239.

Kehoe, Timothy J., and David K. Levine, 1993, "Debt-Constrained Asset Markets," *Review of Economic Studies* 60, 865–888.

Keim, Donald B., 1983, "Size-Related Anomalies and Stock Return Seasonality: Further Empirical Evidence," *Journal of Financial Economics* 12, 13–32.

Keim, Donald B., and Robert F. Stambaugh, 1986, "Predicting Returns in the Stock and Bond Markets," *Journal of Financial Economics* 17, 357–390.

Kelly, Bryan T., and Seth Pruitt, 2013, "Market Expectations in the Cross-Section of Present Values," *Journal of Finance* 68, 1721–1756.

Keloharju, Matti, Juhani T. Linnainmaa, and Peter Nyberg, 2016, "Return Seasonalities," *Journal of Finance* 71, 1557–1590.

Kendall, Maurice G., 1954, "Note on Bias in the Estimation of Autocorrelation," *Biometrika* 41, 403–404.

Keynes, John M., 1936, *The General Theory of Employment, Interest, and Money*, Harcourt Brace, New York.

Keys, Benjamin C., Devin G. Pope, and Jared C. Pope, 2016, "Failure to Refinance," *Journal of Financial Economics* 122, 482–499.

Kim, Tong Suk, and Edward Omberg, 1996, "Dynamic Nonmyopic Portfolio Behavior," *Review of Financial Studies* 9, 141–161.

Kimball, Miles, 1990, "Precautionary Saving in the Small and in the Large," *Econometrica* 58, 53–73.

King, Robert G., Charles I. Plosser, and Sergio T. Rebelo, 1987, "Production, Growth, and Business Cycles: Technical Appendix," unpublished paper.

Kirby, Chris, and Barbara Ostdiek, 2012, "It's All in the Timing: Simple Active Portfolio Strategies That Outperform Naive Diversification," *Journal of Financial and Quantitative Analysis* 47, 437–467.

Kleidon, Allan W., 1986, "Variance Bounds Tests and Stock Price Valuation Models," *Journal of Political Economy* 94, 953–1001.

Klibanoff, Peter, Massimo Marinacci, and Sujoy Mukerji, 2005, "A Smooth Model of Decision Making under Ambiguity," *Econometrica* 73, 1849–1892.

Knight, Frank H., 1921, *Risk, Uncertainty, and Profit*, Houghton Mifflin, Boston.

Kocherlakota, Narayana, and Luigi Pistaferri, 2009, "Asset Pricing Implications of Pareto Optimality with Private Information," *Journal of Political Economy* 117, 555–590.

Kogan, Leonid, and Dimitris Papanikolaou, 2012, "Economic Activity of Firms and Asset Prices," *Annual Review of Financial Economics* 4, 361–384.

———, 2014, "Growth Opportunities, Technology Shocks, and Asset Prices," *Journal of Finance* 69, 675–718.

Kogan, Leonid, Stephen A. Ross, Jiang Wang, and Mark M. Westerfield, 2006, "The Price Impact and Survival of Irrational Traders," *Journal of Finance* 61, 195–229.

Koijen, Ralph S. J., Hanno Lustig, and Stijn Van Niewerburgh, 2017, "The Cross-Section and Time-Series of Stock and Bond Returns," forthcoming *Journal of Monetary Economics*.

Kothari, S. P., and Jay Shanken, 1997, "Book-to-Market, Dividend Yield, and Expected Market Returns: A Time-Series Analysis," *Journal of Financial Economics* 44, 169–203.

Koudijs, Peter, 2015, "Those Who Know Most: Insider Trading in Eighteenth-Century Amsterdam," *Journal of Political Economy* 123, 1356–1409.

Kraus, Alan, and Robert H. Litzenberger, 1976, "Skewness Preference and the Valuation of Risk Assets," *Journal of Finance* 31, 1085–1100.

Kremer, Ilan, 2002, "Information Aggregation in Common Value Auctions," *Econometrica* 70, 1675–1682.

Kreps, David M., and Evan L. Porteus, 1978, "Temporal Resolution of Uncertainty and Dynamic Choice Theory," *Econometrica* 46, 185–200.

Krishnamurthy, Arvind, and Annette Vissing-Jørgensen, 2011, "The Effects of Quantitative Easing on Interest Rates: Channels and Implications for Policy," *Brookings Papers on Economic Activity* 2, 215–265.

———, 2012, "The Aggregate Demand for Treasury Debt," *Journal of Political Economy* 120, 233–267.

Kritzman, Mark, 2000, *Puzzles of Finance: Six Practical Problems and Their Remarkable Solutions*, Wiley, New York.

Kritzman, Mark, Sebastien Page, and David Turkington, 2010, "In Defense of Optimization: The Fallacy of $1/N$," *Financial Analysts Journal* 66(2), 31–39.

Kroencke, Tim A., 2017, "Asset Pricing without Garbage," *Journal of Finance* 72, 47–98.

Kruger, Samuel, 2015, "Disagreement and Liquidity," unpublished paper.

Krusell, Per, and Anthony A. Smith, 1997, "Income and Wealth Heterogeneity, Portfolio Selection, and Equilibrium Asset Returns," *Macroeconomic Dynamics* 1, 387–422.

Kyle, Albert S., 1985, "Continuous Auctions and Insider Trading," *Econometrica* 53, 1315–1335.

———, 1989, "Informed Speculation with Imperfect Competition," *Review of Economic Studies* 56, 317–355.

Lamont, Owen A., 2000, "Investment Plans and Stock Returns," *Journal of Finance* 55, 2719–2745.

Lamont, Owen A., and Richard H. Thaler, 2003, "Anomalies: The Law of One Price in Financial Markets," *Journal of Economic Perspectives* 17(4), 191–202.

Ledoit, Olivier, and Michael Wolf, 2003, "Improved Estimation of the Covariance Matrix of Stock Returns with an Application to Portfolio Selection," *Journal of Empirical Finance* 10, 603–621.

Lee, Charles M. C., and Bhaskaran Swaminathan, 2000, "Price Momentum and Trading Volume," *Journal of Finance* 55, 2017–2069.

LeRoy, Stephen F., and Richard D. Porter, 1981, "The Present-Value Relation: Tests Based on Implied Variance Bounds," *Econometrica* 49, 555–574.

Lettau, Martin, 2002, "Idiosyncratic Risk and Volatility Bounds, or, Can Models with Idiosyncratic Risk Solve the Equity Premium Puzzle?," *Review of Economics and Statistics* 84, 376–380.

Lettau, Martin, and Sydney C. Ludvigson, 2001a, "Consumption, Aggregate Wealth, and Expected Stock Returns," *Journal of Finance* 56, 815–849.

———, 2001b, "Resurrecting the (C)CAPM: A Cross-Sectional Test When Risk Premia Are Time-Varying," *Journal of Political Economy* 109, 1238–1287.

———, 2013, "Shocks and Crashes," *NBER Macroeconomics Annual* 28, 293–354.

Lettau, Martin, Sydney C. Ludvigson, and Jessica A. Wachter, 2008, "The Declining Equity Premium: What Role Does Macroeconomic Risk Play?," *Review of Financial Studies* 21, 1653–1687.

Lettau, Martin, and Harald Uhlig, 2000, "Can Habit Formation Be Reconciled with Business Cycle Facts?," *Review of Economic Dynamics* 3, 79–99.

Lettau, Martin, and Jessica A. Wachter, 2007, "Why Is Long-Horizon Equity Less Risky? A Duration-Based Explanation of the Value Premium," *Journal of Finance* 62, 55–92.

———, 2011, "The Term Structures of Equity and Interest Rates," *Journal of Financial Economics* 101, 90–113.

Lewellen, Jonathan, 2004, "Predicting Returns with Financial Ratios," *Journal of Financial Economics* 74, 209–235.

———, 2015, "The Cross Section of Expected Stock Returns," *Critical Finance Review* 4, 1–44.

Lewellen, Jonathan, and Stefan Nagel, 2006, "The Conditional CAPM Does Not Explain Asset-Pricing Anomalies," *Journal of Financial Economics* 82, 289–314.

Lewellen, Jonathan, Stefan Nagel, and Jay Shanken, 2010, "A Skeptical Appraisal of Asset Pricing Tests," *Journal of Financial Economics* 96, 175–194.

Lewis, Karen, 1999, "Trying to Explain Home Bias in Equities and Consumption," *Journal of Economic Literature* 37, 571–608.

Liang, J. Nellie, and Steven A. Sharpe, 1999, "Share Repurchases and Employee Stock Options and their Implications for S&P 500 Share Retirements and Expected Returns," Finance and Economics Discussion Series 1999-59, Board of Governors of the Federal Reserve System.

Liew, Jimmy, and Maria Vassalou, 2000, "Can Book-to-Market, Size and Momentum Be Risk Factors That Predict Economic Growth?," *Journal of Financial Economics* 57, 221–245.

Linnainmaa, Juhani, 2011, "Why Do (Some) Households Trade So Much?," *Review of Financial Studies* 24, 1630–1666.

Lintner, John, 1956, "Distribution of Incomes of Corporations Among Dividends, Retained Earnings, and Taxes," *American Economic Review Papers and Proceedings* 46, 97–113.

———, 1965, "The Valuation of Risk Assets and the Selection of Risky Investments in Stock Portfolios and Capital Budgets," *Review of Economics and Statistics* 47, 13–37.

Litzenberger, Robert, and Krishna Ramaswamy, 1982, "The Effects of Dividends on Common Stock Prices: Tax Effects or Information Effects?," *Journal of Finance* 37, 429–443.

Litzenberger, Robert, and Mark Rubinstein, 1976, "The Strong Case for the Generalized Log Utility Model as the Premier Model of Financial Markets," *Journal of Finance* 31, 551–571.

Liu, Laura Xiaolei, Toni M. Whited, and Lu Zhang, 2009, "Investment-Based Expected Stock Returns," *Journal of Political Economy* 117, 1105–1139.

Ljungqvist, Lars, and Harald Uhlig, 2015, "Comment on the Campbell-Cochrane Habit Model," *Journal of Political Economy* 123, 1201–1213.

Lo, Andrew W., and A. Craig MacKinlay, 1988, "Stock Market Prices Do Not Follow Random Walks: Evidence from a Simple Specification Test," *Review of Financial Studies* 1, 41–66.

———, 1990a, "Data-Snooping Biases in Tests of Financial Asset Pricing Models," *Review of Financial Studies* 3, 431–468.

———, 1990b, "When Are Contrarian Profits Due to Stock Market Overreaction?." *Review of Financial Studies* 3, 172–205.

Long, John B., Jr., 1990, "The Numeraire Portfolio," *Journal of Financial Economics* 26, 29–69.

Lorenzoni, Guido, 2008, "Inefficient Credit Booms," *Review of Economic Studies* 75, 809–833.

Lorenzoni, Guido, 2015, "International Financial Crises," in Kenneth Rogoff, Elhanan Helpman, and Gita Gopinath eds. *Handbook of International Economics Vol. 4*, North-Holland, Amsterdam, 689–740.

Lucas, Robert E., Jr., 1967, "Adjustment Costs and the Theory of Supply," *Journal of Political Economy* 75, 321–334.

Ludvigson, Sydney C., and Serena Ng, 2009, "Macro Factors in Bond Risk Premia," *Review of Financial Studies* 22, 5027–5067.

Lusardi, Annamaria, and Olivia S. Mitchell, 2014, "The Economic Importance of Financial Literacy: Theory and Evidence," *Journal of Economic Literature* 52, 5–44.

Lustig, Hanno, and Stijn Van Nieuwerburgh, 2005, "Housing Collateral, Consumption Insurance, and Risk Premia: An Empirical Perspective," *Journal of Finance* 60, 1167–1219.

Lustig, Hanno, Stijn Van Nieuwerburgh, and Adrien Verdelhan, 2013, "The Wealth-Consumption Ratio," *Review of Asset Pricing Studies* 3, 38–94.

Lustig, Hanno, Andreas Stathopoulos, and Adrien Verdelhan, 2016, "Nominal Exchange Rate Stationarity and Long-Term Bond Returns," unpublished paper.

Lustig, Hanno, and Adrien Verdelhan, 2007, "The Cross Section of Foreign Currency Risk Premia and Consumption Growth Risk," *American Economic Review* 97, 89–117.

Mace, Barbara J., 1991, "Full Insurance in the Presence of Aggregate Uncertainty," *Journal of Political Economy* 99, 928–956.

Machina, Mark J., 1982, "'Expected Utility' Analysis without the Independence Axiom," *Econometrica* 50, 277–323.

MacKinlay, A. Craig, 1995, "Multifactor Models Do Not Explain Deviations from the CAPM," *Journal of Financial Economics* 38, 3–28.

Madrian, Brigitte, and Dennis Shea, 2001, "The Power of Suggestion: Inertia in 401(k) Participation and Savings Behavior," *Quarterly Journal of Economics* 116, 1149–1188.

Maenhout, Pascal J., 2004, "Robust Portfolio Rules and Asset Pricing," *Review of Financial Studies* 17, 951–983.

Malkiel, Burton, 1989, "Efficient Market Hypothesis," in Peter Newman, Murray Milgate, and John Eatwell eds. *The New Palgrave: Finance*, Macmillan, London, 127–134.

Malmendier, Ulrike, and Stefan Nagel, 2011, "Depression Babies: Do Macroeconomic Experiences Affect Risk-Taking?," *Quarterly Journal of Economics* 126, 373–416.

———, 2016, "Learning from Inflation Experiences," *Quarterly Journal of Economics* 131, 53–87.

Mankiw, N. Gregory, 1986, "The Equity Premium and the Concentration of Aggregate Shocks," *Journal of Financial Economics* 17, 211–219.

Markowitz, Harry M., 1952, "Portfolio Selection," *Journal of Finance* 7, 77–91.

———, 1976, "Investment for the Long Run: New Evidence for an Old Rule," *Journal of Finance* 31, 1273–1286.

Marsh, Terry A., and Robert C. Merton, 1986, "Dividend Variability and Variance Bound Tests for the Rationality of Stock Market Prices," *American Economic Review* 76, 483–498.

Martin, Ian W. R., 2012, "On the Valuation of Long-Dated Assets," *Journal of Political Economy* 120, 346–358.

———, 2013, "Consumption-Based Asset Pricing with Higher Cumulants," *Review of Economic Studies* 80, 745–773.

———, 2017, "What Is the Expected Return on the Market?," *Quarterly Journal of Economics* 132, 367–433.

Mas-Colell, Andreu, Michael Whinston, and Jerry Green, 1995, *Microeconomic Theory*, Oxford University Press, New York.

Massa, Massimo, and Andrei Simonov, 2006, "Hedging, Familiarity, and Portfolio Choice," *Review of Financial Studies* 19, 633–685.

Mayers, David, 1972, "Nonmarketable Assets and Capital Market Equilibrium under Uncertainty," in Michael Jensen ed. *Studies in the Theory of Capital Markets*, Praeger, New York 223–248.

McGrattan, Ellen R., and Edward C. Prescott, 2003, "Average Debt and Equity Returns: Puzzling?," *American Economic Review Papers and Proceedings* 93, 392–397.

———, 2005, "Taxes, Regulations, and the Value of US and UK Corporations," *Review of Economic Studies* 72, 767–796.

McLean, R. David, and Jeffrey Pontiff, 2016, "Does Academic Research Destroy Stock Return Predictability?," *Journal of Finance* 71, 5–32.

McQuade, Timothy, 2013, "Stochastic Volatility and Asset Pricing Puzzles," unpublished paper, Stanford University.

Mehra, Rajnish, and Edward Prescott, 1985, "The Equity Premium: A Puzzle," *Journal of Monetary Economics* 15:145–161.

Melino, Angelo, and Alan X. Yang, 2003, "State-Dependent Preferences Can Explain the Equity Premium Puzzle," *Review of Economic Dynamics* 6, 806–830.

Menzly, Lior, Tano Santos, and Pietro Veronesi, 2004, "Understanding Predictability," *Journal of Political Economy* 112, 1–47.

Merton, Robert C., 1973, "An Intertemporal Capital Asset Pricing Model," *Econometrica* 41, 867–887.

——, 1980, "On Estimating the Expected Return on the Market: An Exploratory Investigation," *Journal of Financial Economics* 8, 323–361.

——, 1987, "A Simple Model of Capital Market Equilibrium with Incomplete Information," *Journal of Finance* 42, 483–510.

Merz, Monika, and Eran Yashiv, 2007, "Labor and the Market Value of the Firm," *American Economic Review* 97, 1419–1431.

Michaely, Roni, Richard H. Thaler, and Kent L. Womack, 1995, "Price Reactions to Dividend Initiations and Omissions: Overreaction or Drift?," *Journal of Finance* 50, 573–608.

Milgrom, Paul, and Nancy Stokey, 1982, "Information, Trade, and Common Knowledge," *Journal of Economic Theory* 26, 17–27.

Miller, Edward M., 1977, "Risk, Uncertainty, and Divergence of Opinion," *Journal of Finance* 32, 1151–1168.

Miller, Merton, and Myron Scholes, 1982, "Dividends and Taxes: Some Empirical Evidence," *Journal of Political Economy* 90, 1118–1141.

Mitchell, Mark, Todd Pulvino, and Erik Stafford, 2002, "Limited Arbitrage in Equity Markets," *Journal of Finance* 57, 551–584.

Mitchell, Olivia S., and Stephen P. Utkus, 2003, "The Role of Company Stock in Defined Contribution Plans," in Olivia S. Mitchell and Kent Smetters eds. *The Pension Challenge: Risk Transfers and Retirement Income Security*, Oxford University Press, Oxford, UK, 33–70.

Modigliani, Franco, and Richard A. Cohn, 1979, "Inflation, Rational Valuation and the Market," *Financial Analysts Journal* 35(2), 24–44.

Moreira, Alan, and Tyler Muir, 2017, "Volatility Managed Portfolios," forthcoming *Journal of Finance*.

Munk, Claus, 2013, *Financial Asset Pricing Theory*, Oxford University Press, Oxford, UK.

Mussa, Michael, 1986, "Nominal Exchange Rate Regimes and the Behavior of Real Exchange Rates: Evidence and Implications," *Carnegie-Rochester Conference Series on Public Policy* 25, 117–214.

Nagel, Stefan, 2012, "Evaporating Liquidity," *Review of Financial Studies* 25, 2005–2039.

Nakamura, Emi, Jón Steinsson, Robert Barro, and José Ursúa, 2013, "Crises and Recoveries in an Empirical Model of Consumption Disasters," *American Economic Journal: Macroeconomics* 5, 35–74.

Nelson, Charles R., and Andrew F. Siegel, 1987, "Parsimonious Modeling of Yield Curves," *Journal of Business* 60, 473–489.

Newey, Whitney K., and Richard J. Smith, 2004, "Higher-Order Properties of GMM and Generalized Empirical Likelihood Estimators," *Econometrica* 72, 219–255.

Newey, Whitney K., and Kenneth D. West, 1987, "A Simple, Positive Semi-definite, Heteroskedasticity and Autocorrelation Consistent Covariance Matrix," *Econometrica* 55, 703–708.

Novy-Marx, Robert, 2013, "The Other Side of Value: The Gross Profitability Premium," *Journal of Financial Economics* 108, 1–28.

Odean, Terrance, 1998, "Are Investors Reluctant to Realize Their Losses?," *Journal of Finance* 53, 1775–1798.

——, 1999, "Do Investors Trade Too Much?," *American Economic Review* 89, 1279–1298.

Ogaki, Masao, and Qiang Zhang, 2001, "Decreasing Relative Risk Aversion and Tests of Risk Sharing," *Econometrica* 69, 515–526.

O'Hara, Maureen, 2003, "Presidential Address: Liquidity and Price Discovery," *Journal of Finance* 58, 1335–1354.

Papanikolaou, Dimitris, 2011, "Investment Shocks and Asset Prices," *Journal of Political Economy* 119, 639–685.

Parker, Jonathan, and Christian Julliard, 2005, "Consumption Risk and Cross-Sectional Returns," *Journal of Political Economy* 113, 185–222.

Pástor, Luboš, and Robert F. Stambaugh, 2003, "Liquidity Risk and Expected Stock Returns," *Journal of Political Economy* 111, 642–685.

———, 2009, "Predictive Systems: Living with Imperfect Predictors," *Journal of Finance* 64, 1583–1628.

———, 2012, "Are Stocks Really Less Volatile in the Long Run?," *Journal of Finance* 67, 431–478.

Pástor, Luboš, and Pietro Veronesi, 2003, "Stock Valuation and Learning About Profitability," *Journal of Finance* 58, 1749–1789.

———, 2006, "Was There a Nasdaq Bubble in the Late 1990s?," *Journal of Financial Economics* 81, 61–100.

Pennacchi, George, 2007, *Theory of Asset Pricing*, Pearson, Boston, MA.

Pflueger, Carolin E., and Luis M. Viceira, 2011, "Inflation-Indexed Bonds and the Expectations Hypothesis," *Annual Review of Financial Economics* 3, 139–158.

Phillips, Peter C. B., Yangru Wu, and Jun Yu, 2011, "Explosive Behavior in the 1990s Nasdaq: When Did Exuberance Escalate Asset Values?," *International Economic Review* 52, 201–226.

Piazzesi, Monika, 2010, "Affine Term Structure Models," in Yacine Aït-Sahalia and Lars Peter Hansen eds. *Handbook of Financial Econometrics Vol. 1*, North-Holland, Amsterdam, 699–766.

Piazzesi, Monika, and Martin Schneider, 2006, "Equilibrium Yield Curves," *NBER Macroeconomics Annual* 21, 389–472.

Piketty, Thomas, 2014, *Capital in the Twenty-First Century*. Harvard University Press, Cambridge, MA.

Polk, Christopher, Samuel Thompson, and Tuomo Vuolteenaho, 2006, "Cross-Sectional Forecasts of the Equity Premium," *Journal of Financial Economics* 81, 101–141.

Pontiff, Jeffrey, and Lawrence D. Schall, 1998, "Book-to-Market Ratios as Predictors of Market Returns," *Journal of Financial Economics* 49, 141–160.

Poterba, James M., and Lawrence H. Summers, 1988, "Mean Reversion in Stock Prices: Evidence and Implications," *Journal of Financial Economics* 22, 27–59.

Powers, Thomas Y., 2015, "The Commodity Currency Puzzle," unpublished paper, Harvard University.

Pratt, John W., 1964, "Risk Aversion in the Small and in the Large," *Econometrica* 32, 122–136.

Priestley, Maurice B., 1981, *Spectral Analysis and Time Series*, Academic Press, New York.

Rabin, Matthew, 2000, "Risk Aversion and Expected-Utility Theory: A Calibration Theorem," *Econometrica* 68, 1281–1292.

Rampini, Adriano A., and S. Viswanathan, 2010, "Collateral, Risk Management, and the Distribution of Debt Capacity," *Journal of Finance* 65, 2293–2322.

Ranish, Benjamin, 2013, "Why Do Households with Risky Labor Income Take Greater Financial Risks?," unpublished paper, Federal Reserve Board.

Ready, Robert C., Nikolai L. Roussanov, and Colin Ward, 2016, "Commodity Trade and the Carry Trade: A Tale of Two Countries," forthcoming *Journal of Finance*.

Reinganum, Marc R., 1983, "The Anomalous Stock Market Behavior of Small Firms in January: Empirical Tests for Tax-Loss Selling Effects," *Journal of Financial Economics* 12, 89–104.

Reny, Philip J., and Motty Perry, 2006, "Toward a Strategic Foundation for Rational Expectations Equilibrium," *Econometrica* 74, 1231–1269.

Restoy, Fernando, and Philippe Weil, 2011, "Approximate Equilibrium Asset Prices," *Review of Finance* 15, 1–28.

Richardson, Matthew, and James H. Stock, 1989, "Drawing Inferences from Statistics Based on Multiyear Asset Returns," *Journal of Financial Economics* 25, 323–348.

Rietz, Thomas, 1988, "The Equity Risk Premium: A Solution," *Journal of Monetary Economics* 22, 117–131.

Ritter, Jay R., and Ivo Welch, 2002, "A Review of IPO Activity, Pricing, and Allocations," *Journal of Finance* 57, 1795–1828.

Robertson, Donald, and Stephen Wright, 2006, "Dividends, Total Cash Flow to Shareholders, and Predictive Return Regressions," *Review of Economics and Statistics* 88, 91–99.

Rogerson, William P., 1985, "Repeated Moral Hazard," *Econometrica* 53, 69–76.

Roll, Richard, 1977, "A Critique of the Asset Pricing Theory's Tests: Part I," *Journal of Financial Economics* 4, 129–176.

———, 1984, "A Simple Implicit Measure of the Effective Bid-Ask Spread in an Efficient Market," *Journal of Finance* 39, 1127–1139.

Romer, David, 1993, "Rational Asset Price Movements without News," *American Economic Review* 83, 1112–1130.

Rosenberg, Barr, Kenneth Reid, and Ronald Lanstein, 1985, "Persuasive Evidence of Market Inefficiency," *Journal of Portfolio Management* 11, 9–17.

Ross, Stephen A., 1976, "The Arbitrage Theory of Capital Asset Pricing," *Journal of Economic Theory* 13, 341–360.

———, 1978, "A Simple Approach to the Valuation of Risky Streams," *Journal of Business* 51, 453–475.

———, 2015, "The Recovery Theorem," *Journal of Finance* 70, 615–648.

Rothschild, Michael, and Joseph E. Stiglitz, 1970, "Increasing Risk I: A Definition," *Journal of Economic Theory* 2, 225–243.

Rubinstein, Mark, 2001, "Rational Markets: Yes or No? The Affirmative Case," *Financial Analysts Journal* 57(3), 15–29.

Rudebusch, Glenn D., and Eric T. Swanson, 2008, "Examining the Bond Premium Puzzle with a DSGE Model," *Journal of Monetary Economics* 55, S111–S126.

Russett, Bruce, and Joel Slemrod, 1993, "Diminished Expectations of Nuclear War and Increased Personal Savings: Evidence from Individual Survey Data," *American Economic Review* 83, 1022–1033.

Samuelson, Paul A., 1969, "Lifetime Portfolio Selection by Dynamic Stochastic Programming," *Review of Economics and Statistics* 51, 239–246.

———, 1979, "Why We Should Not Make Mean Log of Wealth Big Though Years to Act Are Long," *Journal of Banking and Finance* 3, 305–307.

Savov, Alexi, 2011, "Asset Pricing with Garbage," *Journal of Finance* 66, 177–201.

Scheinkman, Jose, and Wei Xiong, 2003, "Overconfidence and Speculative Bubbles," *Journal of Political Economy* 111, 1183–1219.

Schmidt, Lawrence, 2016, "Climbing and Falling Off the Ladder: Asset Pricing Implications of Labor Market Event Risk," unpublished paper.

Segal, Uzi, and Avia Spivak, 1990, "First Order Versus Second Order Risk Aversion," *Journal of Economic Theory* 51, 111–125.

Seo, Sang Byung, and Jessica Wachter, 2016, "Option Prices in a Model with Stochastic Disaster Risk," unpublished paper.

Seru, Amit, Tyler Shumway, and Noah Stoffman, 2010, "Learning by Trading," *Review of Financial Studies* 23, 705–739.

Seyhun, H. Nejat, 1988, "The Information Content of Aggregate Insider Trading," *Journal of Business* 61, 1–24.

Shanken, Jay, 1987, "Multivariate Proxies and Asset Pricing Relations: Living with the Roll Critique," *Journal of Financial Economics* 18, 91–110.

Sharpe, William F., 1964, "Capital Asset Prices: A Theory of Market Equilibrium under Conditions of Risk," *Journal of Finance* 19, 425–442.

Shefrin, Hersh, and Meir Statman, 1985, "The Disposition to Sell Winners Too Early and Ride Losers Too Long: Theory and Evidence," *Journal of Finance* 40, 777–790.

Shiller, Robert J., 1979, "The Volatility of Long-Term Interest Rates and Expectations Models of the Term Structure," *Journal of Political Economy* 87, 1190–1219.

———, 1981, "Do Stock Prices Move Too Much to Be Justified by Subsequent Changes in Dividends?," *American Economic Review* 71, 421–436.

———, 1982, "Consumption, Asset Markets and Macroeconomic Fluctuations," *Carnegie-Rochester Conference Series on Public Policy* 17, 203–238.

———, 1984, "Stock Prices and Social Dynamics," *Brookings Papers on Economic Activity* 2, 457–510.

———, 2000, *Irrational Exuberance*, Princeton University Press, Princeton, NJ.

———, 2014, "Speculative Asset Prices," *American Economic Review* 104, 1486–1517.

Shiller, Robert J., John Y. Campbell, and Kermit L. Schoenholtz, 1983, "Forward Rates and Future Policy: Interpreting the Term Structure of Interest Rates," *Brookings Papers on Economic Activity* 1, 173–217.

Shleifer, Andrei, 1986, "Do Demand Curves for Stocks Slope Down?," *Journal of Finance* 41, 579–590.

Shleifer, Andrei, and Robert Vishny, 1997, "The Limits of Arbitrage," *Journal of Finance* 52, 35–55.

Siegel, Jeremy J., 1972, "Risk, Interest Rates and the Forward Exchange," *Quarterly Journal of Economics* 86, 303–309.

———, 1994, *Stocks for the Long Run*, 1st ed., McGraw-Hill, New York.

———, 2007, *Stocks for the Long Run*, 4th ed., McGraw-Hill, New York.

Simsek, Alp, 2013a, "Belief Disagreements and Collateral Constraints," *Econometrica* 81, 1–53.

———, 2013b, "Speculation and Risk Sharing with New Financial Assets," *Quarterly Journal of Economics* 128, 1365–1396.

Singleton, Kenneth J., 2006, *Empirical Dynamic Asset Pricing: Model Specification and Econometric Assessment*, Princeton University Press, Princeton, NJ.

Skiadas, Costis, 2009, *Asset Pricing Theory*, Princeton University Press, Princeton, NJ.

Sloan, Richard G., 1996, "Do Stock Prices Fully Reflect Information in Accruals and Cash Flows About Future Earnings?," *Accounting Review* 71, 289–315.

Spiess, D. Katherine, and John Affleck-Graves, 1995, "Underperformance in Long-Run Stock Returns Following Seasoned Equity Offerings," *Journal of Financial Economics* 38, 243–267.

———, 1999, "The Long-Run Performance of Stock Returns Following Debt Offerings," *Journal of Financial Economics* 54, 45–73.

Staiger, Douglas, and James H. Stock, 1997, "Instrumental Variables Regression with Weak Instruments," *Econometrica* 65, 557–586.

Stambaugh, Robert F., 1982, "On the Exclusion of Assets from Tests of the Two Parameter Model," *Journal of Financial Economics* 10, 235–268.

———, 1999, "Predictive Regressions," *Journal of Financial Economics* 54, 375–421.

———, 2014, "Presidential Address: Investment Noise and Trends," *Journal of Finance* 69, 1415–1453.

Stattman, Dennis, 1980, "Book Values and Stock Returns," *The Chicago MBA: A Journal of Selected Papers* 4, 25–45.

Storesletten, Kjetil, Christopher I. Telmer, and Amir Yaron, 2004, "Cyclical Dynamics in Idiosyncratic Labor Income Risk," *Journal of Political Economy* 112, 695–717.

———, 2007, "Asset Pricing with Idiosyncratic Risk and Overlapping Generations," *Review of Economic Dynamics* 10, 519–548.

Strzalecki, Tomasz, 2011, "Axiomatic Foundations of Multiplier Preferences," *Econometrica* 79, 47–73.

Stutzer, Michael, 1995, "A Bayesian Approach to Diagnosis of Asset Pricing Models," *Journal of Econometrics* 68, 367–397.

Swanson, Eric T., 2012, "Risk Aversion and the Labor Margin in Dynamic Equilibrium Models," *American Economic Review* 102, 1663–1691.

Tallarini, Thomas, 2000, "Risk-Sensitive Real Business Cycles," *Journal of Monetary Economics* 45, 507–532.

Thaler, Richard H., and Eric J. Johnson, 1990, "Gambling with the House Money and Trying to Break Even: The Effects of Prior Outcomes on Risky Choice," *Management Science* 36, 643–660.

Thaler, Richard H., and Cass R. Sunstein, 2008, *Nudge: Improving Decisions About Health, Wealth, and Happiness*, Yale University Press, New Haven, CT.

Tirole, Jean, 1985, "Asset Bubbles and Overlapping Generations," *Econometrica* 53, 1499–1528.

Titman, Sheridan, K. C. John Wei, and Feixue Xie, 2004, "Capital Investments and Stock Returns," *Journal of Financial and Quantitative Analysis* 39, 677–700.

Tobin, James, 1958, "Liquidity Preference as Behavior Towards Risk," *Review of Economic Studies* 25, 65–86.

———, 1969, "A General Equilibrium Approach to Monetary Theory," *Journal of Money, Credit and Banking* 1, 15–29.

Townsend, Robert M., 1994, "Risk and Insurance in Village India," *Econometrica* 62, 539–591.

Treynor, Jack L., and Fischer Black, 1973, "How to Use Security Analysis to Improve Portfolio Selection," *Journal of Business* 46, 66–86.

Tsai, Jerry, and Jessica A. Wachter, 2015, "Disaster Risk and its Implications for Asset Pricing," *Annual Review of Financial Economics* 7, 219–252.

Uhlig, Harald, 1999, "A Toolkit for Analysing Nonlinear Dynamic Stochastic Models Easily," in Ramon Marimon and Andrew Scott eds. *Computational Methods for the Study of Dynamic Economies*, Oxford University Press, Oxford, UK, 30–61.

Van Nieuwerburgh, Stijn, and Laura Veldkamp, 2009, "Information Immobility and the Home Bias Puzzle," *Journal of Finance* 64, 1187–1215.

Vasicek, Oldrich, 1977, "An Equilibrium Characterization of the Term Structure," *Journal of Financial Economics* 5, 177–188.

Vayanos, Dimitri, and Jiang Wang, 2013, "Market Liquidity–Theory and Empirical Evidence," in George M. Constantinides, Milton Harris, and Rene M. Stulz eds. *Handbook of the Economics of Finance Vol. 2B*, North-Holland, Amsterdam, 1289–1361.

Venti, Steven F., and David A. Wise, 2001, "Choice, Chance, and Wealth Dispersion at Retirement," in Seiritsu Ogura, Toshiaki Tachibanaki, and David A. Wise eds. *Aging Issues in the United States and Japan*, University of Chicago Press, Chicago, IL, 25–64.

Verdelhan, Adrien, 2010, "A Habit-Based Explanation of the Exchange Rate Risk Premium," *Journal of Finance* 65, 123–146.

Viceira, Luis M., 1998, *Optimal Consumption and Portfolio Choice for Long-Horizon Investors*, PhD dissertation, Harvard University.

———, 2001, "Optimal Portfolio Choice for Long-Horizon Investors with Nontradable Labor Income," *Journal of Finance* 56, 433–470.

Vissing-Jørgensen, Annette, 2002, "Limited Asset Market Participation and the Elasticity of Intertemporal Substitution," *Journal of Political Economy* 110, 825–853.

———, 2003, "Perspectives on Behavioral Finance: Does 'Irrationality' Disappear with Wealth? Evidence from Expectations and Actions," *NBER Macroeconomics Annual* 18, 139–194.

Vuolteenaho, Tuomo, 2002, "What Drives Firm-Level Stock Returns?," *Journal of Finance* 57, 233–264.

Wachter, Jessica A., 2006, "A Consumption-Based Model of the Term Structure of Interest Rates," *Journal of Financial Economics* 79, 365–399.

Wachter, Jessica, 2013, "Can Time-Varying Risk of Rare Disasters Explain Aggregate Stock Market Volatility?," *Journal of Finance* 68, 987–1035.

Weil, Philippe, 1989, "The Equity Premium Puzzle and the Risk-free Rate Puzzle," *Journal of Monetary Economics* 24, 401–421.

Weitzman, Martin L., 2007, "Subjective Expectations and Asset-Return Puzzles," *American Economic Review* 97, 1102–1130.

Welch, Ivo, and Amit Goyal, 2008, "A Comprehensive Look at the Empirical Performance of Equity Premium Prediction," *Review of Financial Studies* 21, 1455–1508.

Wermers, Russ, 2000, "Mutual Fund Performance: An Empirical Decomposition into Stock-Picking Talent, Style, Transactions Costs, and Expenses," *Journal of Finance* 55, 1655–1695.

West, Kenneth D., 1988, "Dividend Innovations and Stock Price Volatility," *Econometrica* 56, 37–61.

Williams, John B., 1938, *The Theory of Investment Value*, Harvard University Press, Cambridge, MA.

Wilson, Robert, 1977, "A Bidding Model of Perfect Competition," *Review of Economic Studies* 44, 511–518.

Womack, Kent L., 1996, "Do Brokerage Analysts' Recommendations Have Investment Value?," *Journal of Finance* 51, 137–167.

Yan, Hongjun, 2008, "Natural Selection in Financial Markets: Does It Work?," *Management Science* 54, 1935–1950.

Yogo, Motohiro, 2006, "A Consumption-Based Explanation of Expected Stock Returns," *Journal of Finance* 61, 539–580.

Zame, William R., 1993, "Efficiency and the Role of Default When Security Markets Are Incomplete," *American Economic Review* 83,1142–1164.

Zeldes, Stephen P., 1989, "Optimal Consumption with Stochastic Income: Deviations from Certainty Equivalence," *Quarterly Journal of Economics* 104, 275–298.

Zhang, Lu, 2005, "The Value Premium," *Journal of Finance* 60, 67–103.

Index